CYMBALS AND DANCES

Published by The Poole Family

Every effort has been made to secure permission to quote the poems and musical examples in copyright, with grateful thanks to:

Tim Rutter, for all material quoted
by kind permission of the Royal School of Church Music;
George Pearce of Music Sales Group,
concerning material by Sydney Campbell and Gerald Knight;
Robert Weddle and Tim Hewitt-Jones, on behalf of his father Tony,
for their *Salutations, Versicles & Responses and Litany.*

Alan Brownjohn FRSL for his kind permission to include
'We are Going To See The Rabbit'
© Alan Brownjohn 1959, 1987, c/o Rosica Colin Limited, London'

Roger McGough CBE, FRSL
for his kind permission to include *'My Busconductor Told Me'*

Enitharmon Press www.enitharmon.co.uk,
publishers of Ruth Pitter's *Collected Poems.*
for kind permission to include *'Help, Good Shepherd'*

'*A Wish*' from *Silver Sand and Snow*
by Eleanor Farjeon (Michael Joseph Ltd),
reproduced by permission of David Higham Associates.

Back cover photo of Joseph Poole, 1959, by Richard Sadler
Front cover: *Tambourine* graphic courtesy of www.clker.com
Dancer graphic courtesy of clipground.com
Cymbals graphic courtesy of Florida Center for Instructional Technology
Cross of Nails graphic from artwork by Judith Poole

ISBN 978-1-3999-2230-2
Printed and bound by Lulu Publishing

Stephen Gadd & Trixie Gadd appreciation

Cymbals and Dances had been given new life, thanks to the true and loving generosity of Stephen Gadd and his sister Trixie Gadd. Through the auspices of their *Docuracy Ltd* they have undertaken the substantial task of re-typing the manual typewritten copy in modern media, as a tribute to JWP and the help and kindness he showed them when they were young people in the Coventry Cathedral community and choir. We thank them wholeheartedly for their superb gift, which is truly appreciated by us all.

G, K & Q

CYMBALS AND DANCES

A handbook of advice
for Ministers and musicians of all denominations
in cathedrals, parish churches, chapels,
schools, colleges, and universities
on the performance and the writing of
Christian liturgies

with examples from
COVENTRY CATHEDRAL

by
J. W. POOLE

Precentor of Canterbury 1937-49
Rector of Merstham 1949-58
Precentor of Coventry 1958-77
Fellow of the Royal School of Church Music
Member of the Order of St John

~

Praise him in the cymbals and dances:
praise him upon the loud cymbals.
Let everything that hath breath: praise the Lord.

Psalm 150. Laudate Dominum

Published by The Poole Family.
Initiated by Stephen and Trixie Gadd of Durocracy Ltd
and enabled by their expertise.

In gratitude
to my Father and Mother
who taught me to love God
and
to my Aunt and Godmother Edith Weston
who first taught me music

~

In greeting
to all my fellow-choristers living and departed
who have sung God's praises in
St George's Chapel, Windsor Castle
since its foundation in 1352 by
King Edward III

~

In love
to Judith, Damian, Giles, Gillian,
Katharine, and Quentin

CONTENTS

Page numbers are given on page 47

Part III - Examples

Foreword

CYMBALS AND DANCES

The consecration of a new Coventry Cathedral in 1962 aroused international interest and in Britain its rising phoenix-like from the ashes of its blitzed predecessor seemed to herald the end of postwar austerity and the beginning of a new, happier era.

The challenge to fill the building appropriately with acts of worship that were both exciting and edifying was in the hands of the Precentor, Canon Joseph Poole, a priest of considerable flair whose appointment to the task was inspired. He combined sound knowledge of liturgical tradition with a sense of theatre and used the new building as a stage on which to produce forms of worship to suit every occasion.

He believed that all the senses as well as the whole building should be involved and that appropriate gestures and carefully chosen musical instruments should be found a place. Beyond the round of daily worship, special services and commemorations, of which the cathedral attracted a great many, each had its own sensitively arranged liturgy. There was nothing off the peg.

Above all, every service was planned in meticulous detail, and usually painstakingly rehearsed. "Only the best is good enough for the worship of God" he often declared, so anything slapdash was not to be tolerated.

All of which is expounded in this book and illustrated by a large number of services which encapsulate Poole's life's work and provide a treasury of ideas and resources that, with sensitive adaptation would enrich the worship offered not only in cathedrals but also in parishes churches, and school and university chapels.

The Church of England urgently needs to take note of this, since the long years spent on liturgical revision were not accompanied by any attention to the presentation of the results. And it shows - often disastrously.

TREVOR BEESON
Dean Emeritus of Winchester

Foreword

Canon Joseph Poole was one of the most innovative liturgists of the twentieth century. He brought to his work at Coventry Cathedral a wide knowledge of text and tradition, as any Precentor should. What Joseph added to that essential knowledge was an extraordinary dramatic vision. He used this vision to produce acts of worship of a rare quality – never for their own sake, and certainly not to be trendy (a word, incidentally, he would have certainly despised) – rather, he saw the importance of interpreting liturgy in order to enable the people of God to speak to God and to listen to God.

Joseph said 'Christian liturgy is the total oblation of the redeemed community to the Father through the Son in the Holy Spirit' and he was committed to this understanding of liturgy.

Joseph was way ahead of his time. In so many ways, his extraordinary liturgical imagination prefigured much of the liturgical developments within the Church of England in recent years and for this, and for much else, we here in Coventry feel rightly proud, as well as deeply thankful.

ADRIAN DAFFERN
Precentor Coventry Cathedral
2003-2010

Foreword

CYMBALS AND DANCES

We took sweet counsel together:
and walked in the house of God as friends.
Psalm 55. Exaudi, Deus

PREFACE

For secretarial assistance in the preparation of this book I owe my thanks to the Leverhulme Trust Fund of London, whose Trustees awarded me a Research Grant in 1978.

I have written the book with the importunate encouragement of two friends and former colleagues: the Right Reverend C.K.N. Bardsley, CBE, DD, lately Bishop of Coventry, and the Very Reverend H.C.N. Williams, LLD, the reigning Provost of Coventry. It was Dr Bardsley who in 1958 invited me to join the staff of his Cathedral as Precentor and Master of Ceremonies; and I was happy to be congratulated by my friends on my appointment as 'Cuthbert's choreographer'.

The Statutes of Coventry Cathedral reserve to the Provost alone the ordering of its public worship. The Statutes also provide that 'Each Residentiary Canon shall undertake such general responsibilities as the Provost shall assign to him'. I was the lucky man to whom the Provost assigned the responsibility for the Cathedral's liturgy; and that responsibility was mine for nineteen years.

Let me confess that the Provost and the Precentor were sometimes at odds. Let me in the same breath confess my admiration of Provost Williams as one of the unquestionably great priests and churchmen of our century, and my own gratitude for his unfaltering trust in me: for indeed he afforded me enough rope to hang myself with, not once but many times over.

The Provost assigned to me, I have said, the responsibility for liturgy in Coventry Cathedral. But the responsibility was not mine alone; I was only the instrument for the realising of a vision, a vision shared by the Cathedral staff both clerical and lay and by the congregation. The vision was the vision of many minds, all determined to make public worship the expression of deeply held convictions about the nature of God, and of the world he has created and redeemed and wills to sanctify. Our first task was to look at the liturgy ordained by authority, that is to say the divine Office and the Eucharist; to scrutinise every detail of these ordinances; to ask why this feature was included, and what purpose that feature was to serve; and then to decide how best to present the liturgy, with fresh imagination, so that it would appeal to the men and women of our day, and make sense to them.

For example, in 1959, three years before the Cathedral was completed and consecrated, five of us spent many days on our knees, poring over a ground plan of the building spread out on the floor; here, we said, the Epistle should be read, and read by a lay man or lay woman; here the Deacon should read the Gospel, preceded by an organ fanfare; and at the Intercession the biddings to prayer should be announced by another lay person, man or woman; and the whole of the Ante-Communion would be presented not at the altar but at the chancel step, with the ministers clothed in plain white albs. Only at the Offertory hymn would the ministers retire to put on the eucharistic vestments and move to the altar.

This was the kind of exercise which we believed to be necessary if our common vision was to be realised. For my part, I was resolved that no single detail in the presentation of public worship was too small to be rehearsed; music, speech, movement, gesture, all must be cared for with a scrupulous attention. And this was my inflexible way, not only in the presentation of the Office and the Eucharist, but equally in the preparation and presentation of those services of occasion which are now part of the ministry of every cathedral.

In the summer of 1977 the Cathedral Organists' Association held its annual conference at Coventry Cathedral. I addressed the conference on the liturgy of the Cathedral; and the members ended the conference by attending choral Evensong. Afterwards one of them said to me, 'I had no idea that your liturgy would be like this. I had supposed it would be full of gimmickry.'

The truth is, liturgy at Coventry appears almost old-fashioned. That is because it preserves a strong sense of tradition, of that *stabilitas* which the Provost very rightly cherishes and insists upon. A visitor, after attending the principal Eucharist on a Sunday morning, will ask in bewilderment, 'Is this place Catholic, or is it Protestant? Is it high church, or is it low church?' These are terms which the Cathedral staff never use, from one year's end to another. The terms appear to them irrelevant; useless reminders of 'old unhappy far off things, and battles long ago'. It is right to insist, however, that the Cathedral's liturgical style is catholic, not in any ultramontane sense but simply in the sense that it appeals to the whole man with all his five senses, and therefore uses the whole building, exploiting all its possibilities of sound, of movement, of colour. The cathedral, any cathedral, is a catholic conception; cathedrals were built and worshipped in for a thousand years before the Protestant Reformation was ever thought of, and before the Puritans tried to turn them into preaching houses.

And lest the reader should say, 'That's all very well; but I am not the Dean or Provost or Precentor of a cathedral, I am only a humble parish priest', I reply: the old parish churches of England are every bit as catholic in conception as the cathedrals. If you are the incumbent of such a church (or a modern one either), the liturgical style which is practised in Coventry Cathedral can just as easily be yours; for its principles are universally valid. The liturgy of the Church is nothing new; it has been there for many centuries; and it is an inheritance into which we enter, all of us, wherever our ministry may be. We can, if we have the will, use it, use it with common sense, with imagination, with minds wide open to the world we live in; and above all, with obedience.

~

The vision of liturgy shared by all of us at Coventry Cathedral could never have been realised without the help of a supremely competent staff, both clerical and lay; nor indeed without the affectionate interest and advice of many friends at home and abroad, in Australia and America, in Canada, in France, in Germany, and elsewhere. If I may express my own thanks to only two out of many hundreds who have enabled me to discharge the ministry assigned to me by the Provost, let me mention first my secretary, Mrs Eve L'Estrange, always kind, courteous, attentive, and in the art of laying out an order of service with precision and elegance, *prima donna assoluta*.

Capitally I thank my wife, a member of the Cathedral staff in her own right and my close colleague and friend. With her rugged good sense she has encouraged me, cajoled me, and if need be rebuked me; but she has always cherished me, as she promised to do at our marriage, thirty-five years ago, in Canterbury Cathedral

~

My admired Sir Thomas Browne, in his immortal *Religio Medici*, has a sentence which I love to recall. 'Surely there are', he says, 'in every man's life certain rubs, doublings, and wrenches, which pass a while under the effects of chance, but at the last, well examined, prove the meer hand of God'.

Prove? No, there is no proof, there can be none; there can only be, in a Christian believer, the heart's assurance.

SOLI DEO
GLORIA

JOSEPH W. POOLE

Leamington Spa
1980

OF PUBLIC WORSHIP

Shallow.	Jesu, Jesu, the mad days that I have spent! And to see how many of my old acquaintance are dead!
Silence.	We shall all follow, cousin.
Shallow.	Certain, 'tis certain, very sure, very sure. Death, as the Psalmist saith, is certain to all, all shall die. How a good yoke of bullocks at Stamford fair?
Silence.	By my troth, I was not there.
Shallow.	Death is certain. Is old Double of your town living yet?
Silence.	Dead, sir.
Shallow.	Jesu, Jesu, dead! a' drew a good bow – and dead! a' shot a fine shoot: John a Gaunt loved him well, and betted much money on his head. Dead! How a score of ewes now?
Silence.	Thereafter as they be, a score of good ewes may be worth ten pounds.
Shallow.	And is old Double dead!

2 Henry IV 3.2

PART I – PRINCIPLES

LITURGICAL PERSPECTIVE

What is Liturgy?

Let us first define our terms. Liturgy is not something said: it is something done. Liturgy is the total oblation of the creature to the Creator. Christian liturgy is the total oblation of the redeemed community to the Father through the Son in the Holy Spirit.

Does liturgy today enable us to make this total oblation of ourselves to God? Does it enable us to offer to God 'ourselves, our souls and bodies, to be a reasonable, holy and living sacrifice' to him? In so far as it makes this possible, a liturgy can be praised: in so far as its character, or its presentation, hinders us from the offering of this total oblation of ourselves, it is defective.

Does the Eucharist (for example) of the Book of Common Prayer, as it is often presented, enable this oblation of the redeemed community to God, or does it not?

Some years ago I was present at the Communion at eight o'clock on a Sunday morning in one of our English cathedrals. It was celebrated at the high altar. Perhaps there were forty people (all of them I think over fifty years of age) in the seats in the choir. Between these people and the high altar there was an empty space of not less than thirty yards. Now the only effective aural link between celebrant and people placed so far apart would have been the chant – it would have been song of some kind. But there was no choir present, and the service was spoken – no, it was shouted by the celebrant without benefit of loudspeaker, and it was murmured and mumbled by the people. There were four canons in the sanctuary, but they took no part in the performance. The celebrant, except for the epistle and gospel, faced the altar. The people's part was almost inaudible. In effect, the rite was a solo by the celebrant. It was so badly presented as to deny and contradict everything which the Communion stands for. There was no sense whatever of community or of sharing.

There were on this occasion three simple mistakes of presentation. First, the space in which the rite was enacted was far too large for so small a company of people: it should have been celebrated in a chapel. Secondly, the two lessons were read by the celebrant, when there were other priests present, who could have read the lessons and should have read them. Thirdly, the celebrant had his back to the people almost throughout. He did not look them in the eye and they did not look him in the eye. The total oblation of the redeemed community was not on this occasion enabled.

Living Liturgy

The clue to a living liturgy is to be found, I believe, in a single sentence in one of the general rubrics at the end of the Order for the Communion in the Prayer Book of 1662.

Here is the rubric.

> *And to take away all occasion of dissension and superstition, which any person hath or might have concerning the Bread and Wine, it shall suffice that the Bread be such as is usual to be eaten: but the best and purest wheat bread that conveniently may be gotten.*

Only the best is worthy to be offered in the worship of God – that is what the final clause of the rubric is saying; and of course that idea is familiar. It is a commonplace. That is not the clause which I now wish to examine. The clause which holds the clue to a living liturgy is the previous clause – 'it shall suffice that the Bread be such as is usual to be eaten'. The matter of the Eucharist – the stuff out of which the principal liturgical act is to be made – is as far as may be from anything churchy. It is a piece of the natural order.

The stuff out of which the principal liturgical act is to be made is bread, a staple article of diet the world over, among all men of all faiths, or of no faith; and bread such as is usual to be eaten. Liturgy is not alive unless it is intimately related to the secular order. The action of the redeemed community is set within a secular culture.

Two Elements in our Culture

Consider two elements in the culture in which we are living: firstly, the time scale; secondly, the use of images.

In 1662, when the Prayer Book was published, the population of England was five million – half the present population of London the capital city. What does this mean? It means that everyone then lived in the country: and the time scale was the time scale of the countryman. Now the Bible is the book of a pastoral and an agricultural people; and the Prayer Book is full of the Bible. Not only were the scriptural images of the Prayer Book familiar to the people of the seventeenth century – light and dark, heat and cold, shepherd and sheep; not only that, but the pace of life was a rural pace. Men had time on their hands. They were not in a hurry. They were ready, when they went to church on Sunday morning, to spend time on public worship; they were ready to hear Matins, and the Litany, and at least the Ante- Communion. They were ready to listen to whole chapters of the Bible read in course. They were happy enough, when they crowded to St Paul's in London to hear the great Dean preach, they were happy enough to listen to those elaborate and exquisite sermons of John Donne, which absolutely require an hour, or two hours, for the accumulation of his images to make their effect. They did not grow restive (one may suppose) under the verbosity of the Exhortations with which the Book of Common Prayer is crammed. Everyone lived in the country; and the pace at which their lives moved was the pace of the countryside; a pace determined by the slow revolutions of the seasons, and by the simple fact that without the aid of machinery everything must be slowly done by hand.

With the Industrial Revolution the pace began to quicken; and as the rural economy gave way to an urban economy, the time scale was drastically altered, and it is still altering now. We live in an urban culture, where not only is everything done more rapidly, but also where there are many more interesting and exciting things to do. Men are simply not willing to spend a great deal of time on the public exercises of religion. They will not go twice to church on Sunday; and when they go to church, they look for an economy, a conciseness, in the reading and preaching of the Word, and in the celebration of the Sacraments. They expect that what is said and what is done shall make its point with a sharper impact than their forefathers ever looked for.

In the writing of liturgies for today, I believe this new time scale is something to be taken into account. It is unreasonable to hope that liturgy made four hundred years ago, and fitted to the pace of a rural culture, will suit our urban culture without some drastic pruning.

The second element in our culture to be noted is the arrival of television. Something has happened, all over the world, which has violently modified our habits. It is simply that we have recovered the use of our eyes: we look as well as listen. If liturgy is to be rooted in the secular order, we must absolutely take note of this revolution in the habits of ordinary men and women. By this I don't at all mean that we must busily set about televising the liturgy. No: when I say that we must take account of the revolution which has recovered for men and women the use of their eyes, I mean that in liturgy too we must recover the use of our eyes. Television has in a few short years made irrelevant the puritan suspicion of the use of colour and movement and expressive ceremonial actions. Television has compelled us to treasure again what the Roman Church has had the honour of preserving in an unbroken liturgical devotion: the profoundly Christian understanding of the Word made flesh. The puritan theory of worship is that worship is a purely mental activity; and that words alone express or stimulate the act of worship. This is not a Christian way of thinking. The Christian belief is that the Word was made flesh; the idea must be incarnate; it must be bodied forth, it must be given physical expression, and it must be apprehended not only by the ears but by the eyes, and indeed by all the five senses. It is curious to reflect that among Christians whose worship eschews all sensuous appeal and is expressed only in words – it is curious that among such people there are some favourite hymns containing images of the most violent kind which appeal to the eye of the imagination. For example, Isaac Watts' great eucharistic hymn 'When I survey the wondrous Cross' has a verse which is commonly omitted, perhaps because it is thought to be too brutal:

> His dying crimson, like a robe,
> Spreads o'er his body on the Tree;
> Then am I dead to all the globe,
> And all the globe is dead to me.

His dying crimson! Or a related image from Charles Wesley:

Love's redeeming work is done;
Fought the fight, the battle won:
Lo, our sun's eclipse is o'er!
Lo, he sets in blood no more!

If we really think what we are singing when we repeat that hymn (but most of us don't, of course, think what we are singing) – if we really reflect upon those words, we shall realise how violently they appeal to the eye of the imagination. But if such visual images are allowable, why may we not set up a cross or a crucifix, and look at that with our physical eyes? At all events, television has recovered for us the use of our eyes: the secular culture to which the liturgical action is inescapably related is forcing us to rediscover the catholic treasures of devotion.

Liturgical Forms Reconsidered

'It shall suffice that the Bread shall be such as is usual to be eaten.' The roots of a living liturgy are not in the Church, they are in the world. The liturgical act is set within a secular culture. With these things in mind, let us look now more closely at what we do in church.

The language of worship must on the whole be such as is usually spoken. That does not imply either slang or colloquial English; it only implies the use of the various kinds of English which come naturally to the lips of men today. Here is a passage of critical importance by the novelist Richard Hughes.

If the clergy consider the semantic problem at all, it is usually to assume that the sole difficulty inherent in Prayer Book language is its sometimes-antiquated vocabulary. But the real difficulty goes far deeper than occasional difficulties of vocabulary. It lies in the Prayer Book employment of a syntax entirely alien to modern English speech. Syntax is the crux. For syntax is the structural frame of thinking; and please remember that we laymen simply cannot think in a frame entirely alien to our habitual thinking, however familiar the vocabulary. Semantically the 1662 Book is far more remote from us than are the plays of Shakespeare. Those plays, after all, were composed in English. They were thought in English, by an Englishman. But so much of the Book of Common Prayer was not: it was thought in Latin. Moreover it was thought in Latin many centuries before 1662, and has been only half-translated into the English language. 'Half-translated', because the Latin sentence-structures have been so often retained.

But the thinking of the ordinary modern Englishman, however intelligent, is normally couched more in the sentence-structure of the Daily Mirror than of Cicero. How on earth is he to learn to think in the involved and elongated sentences of so much of the Book of Common Prayer? – where the rare full stop is more a concession to the limited capacities of even clerical lungs than a genuine pause in the argument.

Now make no mistake: I am not suggesting that a reformed liturgy should use the vocabulary of the Daily Mirror any more than that it should utter the thoughts of the Daily Mirror. What I do assert is that the modern Englishman normally thinks in short sentences almost bereft of subordinate clauses and parentheses. Again, he leaves the relation between these sentences to be implied by their mere juxtaposition without any of the explanatory conjunctions so beloved of the latinist (he leaves a spark gap for the meaning to leap, rather than a connecting wire to conduct it). He certainly does not think in those immense periods punctuated by rare full stops: it would be truer to say that he thinks in a series of full stops punctuated by rare words.

The use of a latinate syntax is (I am sure) an insuperable barrier to the understanding of wayfaring men and women. It must give way to an English syntax, if the redeemed community is to be helped to make its oblation to God through Office and Sacrament.

Special Services

The Office and the Communion: these are the liturgical acts of the redeemed community. But there are other forms of worship, what the French call para-liturgy, which must be considered. Living liturgy must be related to the culture in which it is enacted. One of the most potent influences upon our culture has been the invention of the internal combustion engine and of the motor car. The car has introduced a quite new element into the situation: it has made possible the easy and rapid transport of immense numbers of people from all over a diocese or a county to the cathedral church. The Soroptimists, the Loyal Order of Moose, the Animal Welfare Societies, the Women's Cooperative Guild, the Guild of Cordwainers and a score of other societies send their members in their hundreds and thousands to all our cathedrals. Who are these people? They are not, for the most part, committed Christians; they are not perhaps in the habit of public worship; they would hesitate to recite the Christian creed. What sort of a liturgy will they use? What order of service will enable them to make their oblation? Not the Office; not the Communion. Something else must be devised. The composing of such orders of service is one of the principal subjects to be discussed in this book.

But the book will not be concerned only with English cathedrals. It is offered for the guidance and encouragement of Ministers and musicians of the Anglican Church across the world, not only in cathedrals but also in parish churches, schools, and universities; and indeed it may be of use to other denominations too. Its purpose is to help all who find themselves called upon, from time to time, to devise forms of worship for occasions not provided for in their Prayer Books.

O THE POWER OF CHURCH MUSIC!

Liturgy at St George's Chapel, Windsor 1592

In August 1592 Count Mümpellgart (whose name appears in The Merry Wives of Windsor as 'cosen Garmombles' and who a year later became Frederick, Duke of Würtemberg) spent three days at Windsor. His private secretary Jacob Rathgeb, in an account of the visit published in 1602, records that the Count was present at divine service in St George's Chapel on Sunday morning, 20 August 1592, and was enraptured by the music. He writes:

> *The Castle stands upon a knoll or hill. In the outer court is a very beautiful and spacious church, with a low flat roof covered with lead, as is common with all churches in England. In this church his highness listened for more than an hour to the beautiful music, the usual ceremonies, and the English sermon. The music, and especially the organ, was exquisitely played, for at times you could hear the sound of cornets, flutes, then fifes and other instruments. And there was a little boy who sang so sweetly amongst it all, and lent such charm to the music with his little tongue, that it was really wonderful to listen to him.*[1]

Liturgy at St Paul's 1621-31

Dr John Donne, poet and priest, was Dean of St Paul's in London from 1621 till his death in 1631.

Isaak Walton in his Life of Donne recalls one of his poems:

An hymn to God the Father

Wilt thou forgive that sin where I begun,
Which was my sin, though it were done before?
Wilt thou forgive that sin, through which I run,
And do run still: though still I do deplore?
When thou hast done, thou hast not done,
For, I have more.

Wilt thou forgive that sin, which I have won
Others to sin? and, made my sin their door?
Wilt thou forgive that sin which I did shun
A year, or two: but wallowed in, a score?
When thou hast done, thou hast not done,
For I have more.

[1] Quoted by W.B. Rye, *England as Seen by Foreigners in the Days of Elizabeth and James the First* (London, 1865).

I have a sin of fear, that when I have spun
My last thread, I shall perish on the shore;
But swear by thy self, that at my death thy son
Shall shine as he shines now, and heretofore;
And, having done that, thou hast done,
I fear no more.

Walton goes on:

> *I have the rather mentioned this Hymn, for that he caused it to be set to a most grave and solemn tune, and to be often sung to the organ by the choristers of St Paul's Church, in his own hearing; especially at the Evening Service; at his return from his customary devotions in that place, did occasionally say to a friend, 'The words of this Hymn have restored to me the same thoughts of joy that possessed my soul in my sickness when I composed it. And, O the power of church music! that harmony added to this Hymn has raised the affections of my heart, and quickned my graces of zeal and gratitude; and I observe, that I always return from paying this public duty of prayer and praise to God, with an inexpressible tranquillity of mind, and a willingness to leave the world'.*

Liturgy at Salisbury Cathedral 1630-33

Mr George Herbert, poet and priest, was Rector of the little country parish of Bemerton near Salisbury from 1630 till his death in 1633.

Isaak Walton in his *Life* of Herbert says:

> *His chiefest recreation was music, in which heavenly art he was a most excellent master, and did himself compose many divine hymns and anthems, which he set and sung to his lute or viol; and, though he was a lover of retiredness, yet his love to music was such, that he went usually twice every week on certain appointed days to the Cathedral Church in Salisbury, and at his return would say that his time spent in prayer and cathedral music elevated his soul, and was his heaven upon earth. But before his return thence to Bemerton, he would usually sing and play his part at an appointed private music meeting; and, to justify this practice he would often say, 'Religion does not banish mirth, but only moderates, and sets rules to it'.*

Liturgy at Canterbury Cathedral 1636

From a sermon by J.W.P. at the Eucharist in Coventry Cathedral on 20 June 1976, for Elaine Kindler, a month before her marriage there.

Come and sit here at Michaelmas-tide, late on a Sunday afternoon, while the music of Evensong fills the air of autumn; come and sit here; and as dusk falls, watch the rays of the setting sun move in slanting procession round the white walls of the Lady Chapel beyond the high altar.

O Strength and Stay upholding all creation,
   Who ever dost thyself unmoved abide,
Yet day by day the light in due gradation
   From hour to hour through all its changes guide.

The words grow on you, as the years pass: they have the ring of truth about them. God made the world: he made it, and he holds it in the hollow of his hand: and he abides. But you and I are mortal.

Your most beautiful bride who with garlands is crowned
And kills with each glance as she treads on the ground,
Whose lightness and brightness doth shine in such splendour
      That none but the stars
      Are thought fit to attend her,
Though now she be pleasant and sweet to the sense,
Will be damnable mouldy a hundred years hence.

Thomas Jordan

Yes, we shall die: but God abides.

O Strength and Stay upholding all creation,
   Who ever dost thyself unmoved abide,
Yet day by day the light in due gradation
   From hour to hour through all its changes guide.

Public worship is the homage paid by dying men to the living God: and this homage is due from all Christian people. But they cannot all be always at prayer: the work of the world must go on, and Christians must take their share in it. Lest however the work of the world should so occupy men's minds that the worship of God should be neglected and the habit of prayer be lost, there have been some Christians in every age who have been called to make public prayer their particular business; and there have been certain buildings – the most splendid, the most noble creations of the human mind – set apart for this public worship. Among these buildings are the cathedrals and abbeys of England.

CYMBALS AND DANCES

When the monasteries were dissolved 400 years ago there remained, in England and Ireland and Wales, twenty- seven cathedrals; and the greatest care was taken that in these places the public worship of the Church should be maintained.

Consider, for example, Canterbury Cathedral. The Statutes of that cathedral, drawn up by Henry VIII, and confirmed by Charles I in 1636, charge and implore the Archbishop of Canterbury 'to provide diligently that the praise of God be celebrated constantly morning and evening in the cathedral'; and for that purpose a college or society is appointed, consisting of the following persons:

One dean
twelve canons
six preachers
six minor canons (singing priests)
six substitutes
one organist
twelve lay clerks (choir men)
one master of the choristers
ten choristers
two instructors of the boys in grammar
fifty boys to be educated
twelve bedesmen
two sackbutteers
two cornetteers
    (in our terms, two trumpets and two trombones: a resident brass quartet.
    There's a richness for you!)
two vergers
two subsacrists
four servants in the church to ring the bells and put all things in order
two porters who shall also act as barbers
one registrar or chapter clerk
and (if there be a common table in the public hall)
    one manciple
    two butlers
    one cook
    one under-cook
each of which said persons is diligently to officiate in the church,
every one in his order.

In that remarkable muster of men and boys there are 139 persons. To them was committed the duty of public worship; the duty of appearing before God, as spokesmen of society at large, to offer to him due honour; the duty of witnessing to the truth that men are finite, fallible, and mortal; the duty of reminding men that their true home is not here, but yonder.

Every cathedral, whether through its music or its architecture, or through the hospitable and courteous address of its ministers, must be, in George Herbert's words, 'a way to heaven's door'. But let us beware: the meanest, most ramshackle shanty of a church is not so scandalous to God as an impenitent congregation.

> Hear us, O hear us Lord; to thee
>   A sinner is more music, when he prays,
> Than spheres', or Angels' praises be,
>   In panegyric Alleluias.

John Donne: A Litany

Panegyric alleluias are all very well; but if they rise from the lips of impenitent sinners, they are not pleasing to God. Once upon a time (as you may remember) two men went to church together; one was well known for his punctilio in religion and for his generous benefactions: the other was an obscure civil servant, who cut no figure at all in anyone's eyes, least of all in his own. 'God, have mercy', he said, 'on a sinner like me'. This man (said Jesus) was pleasing to God, and not the other.

> *Thus says the high and holy One, who inhabits eternity, whose name is Holy: I dwell in the high and holy place, with him also that is of a contrite and humble spirit.*

Isaiah 57. 15

Liturgy at Coventry Cathedral 1962-77

Two quotations from Evensong in Coventry Cathedral, the order of service which is placed in the hands of every visitor who attends choral Evensong:

What is Evensong?

Evensong in Coventry Cathedral is a very tiny fragment of something else: it is a fragment of the worship which is offered to God by Christian people, every hour of the twenty-four, in every part of the world. When you come to Evensong here, it is as if you were dropping in on a conversation already in progress – a conversation between God and men which began long before you were born, and will go on long after you are dead. So do not be surprised, or disturbed, if there are some things in the conversation which you do not at once understand.

The Music

Worship without music does not easily soar; and wherever the Church has been concerned to make worship really expressive of truth, music has been used: simple music for the untrained worshipper, more elaborate music for a trained choir. The music of a cathedral choir is the counterpart of the architecture and the stained glass of the building: it is a finely wrought music, in which the musicians offer on behalf of the people what the people would wish to do themselves, if they had the ability.

The music which so moved Count Mümpellgart at Windsor, Donne at St Paul's, and Herbert at Salisbury, many centuries ago, is still today a living influence.
You may hear this music, from time to time, in the concert hall: but it is not at home there. Yet even in the concert hall it has the power not only to beguile an audience by its beauty, but to remind our bleakly secular age of a land of lost content. Some years ago Alfred Deller and his fellow musicians were singing in Australia: and the music (he said) which made the deepest impression upon an audience of 2,000 people in the concert hall in Sydney was the five-part Mass of William Byrd. It subdued them to a silence that could be felt. Why was this? Why, because this music is prayer: it is what George Herbert said that prayer is –

> *Church-bells beyond the stars heard, the soul's blood,*
> *The land of spices, something understood.*

This music is prayer: it is the utterance of a community dedicated to prayer. And it is at home, not in the concert hall but in the cathedrals and collegiate churches for whose choirs it was composed.

This music is prayer: it is the prayer of a community whose members are bound to the love of God and the love of one another, and to the service of men. Where there is no love and no service, there ought to be no music, there can be none; for hate does not sing, and there is no music in hell. But where there is love, there is joy; and where there is joy, there will be music. There will be church music, the music which George Herbert, priest as well as poet, loved and knew the value of.

> But if I travel in your company,

he said of this music,

> But if I travel in your company,
> You know the way to heaven's door.

'You know the way to heaven's door.' Everyone today is travelling, everyone is on the move, everyone is on the way to somewhere. Is it not the duty of our cathedrals and choral foundations to show their innumerable visitors, if they can, the way to heaven's door? The great music of the Church, the music of high art, is one way to that door: for it is but the rehearsal in time of that adoration which persists in eternity. If ever this music is silenced, either through neglect or contempt, the fault will lie with a Church which has lost its vision and its nerve, and which has so allied itself with the secular fashion of the age as not to see that its music can give men what they most desperately need: a sense of eternity amid the flux of time.

THE CATHEDRAL

Duties of religion, performed by whole Societies of men, ought to have in them, according to our power, a sensible Excellency, correspondent to the majesty of him whom we worship.

Richard Hooker: The Laws of Ecclesiastical Polity, V.

The public worship of the Christian Church is of two kinds; each is necessary, each is good; and each is served by its appropriate music.

Worship in the parish church (or in the Nonconformist one) is concerted worship - family prayer, in which the congregation audibly takes part. Worship in the cathedral is delegated worship - the prayer offered by a religious community on behalf of the whole Christian society, prayer at which the presence of a congregation is not essential.

In a parish church the offering of public worship is for the most part, in the true meaning of the word, amateur; it is done for love; and the style of this worship will be such as the ability of amateurs can afford. In a cathedral the offering of public worship is for the most part professional; and the style of this worship will be the best that professional skill can contrive.

The cathedral, the physical structure, is already an act of praise; it is a doxology. Its architecture is not useful but expressive. In even a small cathedral there is room to seat two or three thousand people, but the size of the building is not determined by any consideration of that kind. There are more convenient ways, and cheaper ways, of erecting four walls and a roof to protect a large concourse of people from the weather. The cathedral is built on the grand scale in order that it may both express and suggest to the beholder the divine majesty. The feeling of awe, almost of dread, is the fundamental religious impulse; and nothing so quickly serves to awaken this feeling as vast spaces, adroitly defined by walls and pillars. There is a good deal of space on Hampstead Heath; but it is not awe-ful, it is not mysterious, like the space under the dome of St Paul's. To create this sense of space, the skill of the architect must be invoked; and if he is to succeed in this particular, he must work on the grand scale. Sheer size is therefore an essential element in the idea of a cathedral, whose function is pre-eminently to express and to suggest the divine majesty.

It is hardly possible to think of worship in the cathedral apart from the music which is the principal means of its realisation. There are two reasons why music should be used. I believe it was Henry Purcell who said that music is the exaltation of poetry; and song is the natural means of expressing any mood intensely felt, whether of joy or grief. Inevitably therefore music is pressed into the service of religion, which is dealing with human experience at its most profound and most exalted levels. But there is another reason for the use of music - a physical reason, grounded in the behaviour of sound. To create the sense of religious awe (we said) the architect of the cathedral uses large spaces, defined by walls and pillars of stone.

Stone surfaces reflect the sound impinging upon them, and set up echoes; the building, in virtue of its size and of the material of which it is constructed, is very resonant. The speaking voice, in order to carry the length of the building, must be loud; and in order not to set up conflicting echoes, its range of inflexion must be narrow. You will easily find by experiment that if you read a passage of prose aloud in a large resonant building, your voice tends to settle to an unvaried monotone, only broken by a slight fall in pitch at the ends of clauses or sentences. This kind of utterance, refined by a feeling for style and by the growth of musical sensibility, becomes the simple plainsong inflection such as is used in singing versicles and responses. The speaking voice becomes the singing voice, reading gives way to incantation; and this happens as the solution to the physical problem set by the building in which worship is offered. Incantation is more formal than speech, and therefore more fitted to be the vehicle of cathedral worship; but also it is much less fatiguing to the voice, and much more agreeable to the ear. There is good sense behind the rubric at Matins in the first English Book of Common Prayer:

> *To the end the people may the better hear, in such places where they do sing, there shall the lessons be sung in a plain tune after the manner of distinct reading: and likewise the Epistle and Gospel.*

In the cathedrals and choral foundations of the Church of England the music used in public worship is entrusted to a precentor (assisted by other singing priests), an organist, and a professional choir. A normal establishment consists of twenty- eight or thirty singers – about twelve men and sixteen boys. It is a small company, welded by the daily performance of divine service into a skilful team; and the music which it makes is a kind of chamber music, intimate and sensitive. Only a small band of singers is needed, because the very resonance which impedes the speaking voice has been wonderfully exploited by the composers, who have written music which largely depends for its charm and beauty on the prolonging of musical sound by the echoes of the building. This is the 'linked sweetness long drawn out' which so moved John Milton, and dissolved him into ecstasies. The music may truly be described as scored for voices and architecture; the architecture is part of the instrument. For this reason, cathedral music performed in a broadcasting studio or in a concert hall fails of half its effect; and for the same reason, while it may be useful to relay the spoken voice from one part of a cathedral to another, it is ruinous to relay music; its charm at once evaporates.

The cathedrals of England are not parish churches. They never can be, because they are too large to allow of that intimacy which a parish congregation rightly expects to find in its public worship. The mere size of a cathedral and the reverberation set up by the sound of music or of speech impinging on large surfaces of stone and glass impose a formal style (which does not mean an unfriendly style). The casual throw-away utterance is simply not heard.

The building calls for large gestures, both in sound and in movement. Everything must be on the grand scale. For example: the sound of a well-produced solo voice accompanied by a lute or an acoustic guitar, echoing through vast spaces, is one of the most ravishing things

imaginable; but you cannot keep a thousand singers together, even with a whole brigade of guitars. For that purpose the organ is the only effective instrument.
Speech is not the mode of utterance which is congenial to these great buildings. Music is. One of the reasons for this is the difference in the time scale between speech and music. For example: Say the phrase 'And the house was filled with smoke'. Say it as loudly and emphatically as you can; it will take you three seconds. And try as you will, you will not evoke Isaiah's picture of the incense rising in a cloud and filling every corner of the temple. And if you shout the phrase twenty times in succession, you will only appear to be demented. Now listen to that phrase set to Dr Stainer's music in his anthem I saw the Lord, composed for St Paul's Cathedral when he was organist there. Music makes its point (as speech rarely does) by iteration; and Stainer has one voice after another of his eight-part choir hurling the words aloft on a fragment of music, till the tension is almost unbearable; and as you listen, you are in imagination engulfed in the incense. Where the spoken utterance took three seconds, the musical utterance takes nearer thirty seconds. It is the large gesture.

Furthermore, these buildings call not only for the large gesture but for the professional gesture, the gesture of professional competence. The buildings themselves are enormously professional pieces of architecture. Remember Wordsworth's lines on King's College Chapel, Cambridge:

> Tax not the royal Saint with vain expense,
> With ill-matched aims the Architect who planned
> Albeit labouring for a scanty band
> Of white-robed Scholars only – this immense
> And glorious Work of fine intelligence!

It is certain that an English cathedral or collegiate church can never deliver the religious experience for which it was built without the use of a professional choir of high competence. When the monasteries were suppressed here in 1538, and a vernacular liturgy in 1549 succeeded the Latin, there remained in England, Wales and Ireland twenty-seven cathedrals where careful provision was made for the continuing musical performance of the liturgy by professional choirs. And the music used for this liturgy in the Chapel Royal of Elizabeth I was recognised throughout Europe as of supreme excellence.

I SAW THE LORD

8
ff
and the house was fill - ed with
and the house was fill - ed with smoke, was
smoke, was fill - ed with smoke, was fill - - - led with
and the
and the house was fill - ed with smoke, the
and the house was fill - ed with smoke, was fill - ed with smoke, the
house was fill - ed with smoke, was fill - ed with smoke, was fill - - -
13
fff
and the house was fill - ed with smoke, the house was fill - ed with smoke.
smoke, was fill - ed with smoke, the house was fill - ed with smoke.
fill - ed with smoke, the house, the house was fill - ed with smoke.
smoke, the house, the house was fill - ed with smoke.
house was fill - ed with smoke, the house was fill - ed with smoke, was fill - ed with smoke.
house was fill - ed with smoke, the house was fill - ed with smoke.
house was fill - ed with smoke, the house was fill - ed with smoke.
ed with smoke, the house was fill - ed with smoke.

LITURGY: NEW INSIGHTS? A NEW STYLE?

In 1976 a minister of the Presbyterian Church in the United States of America visited Coventry Cathedral. In conversation about liturgy he said to me, 'In the States today a Presbyterian minister is expected by his congregation to devise a new form of liturgy for every Sunday. In consequence the minister is no longer a minister, but a showman.'

This itch for change, for novelty at any cost, is a mischievous thing; it is destructive of spiritual growth. Liturgy and life run in parallel; and if life is for much of the time ordinary and even humdrum (with an occasional treat), so must liturgy be ordinary and even humdrum (with a festival from time to time). Liturgy is not a kind of entertainment; it is – in the old accurate phrase – Divine Service; and a service is the function of a servant. Or consider the other old and accurate phrase for public worship outside of the Eucharist – the Divine Office. Office here means duty; something done which it is the Church's duty to do, whether or not the doing of it is agreeable or amusing or entertaining. If this duty is discharged conscientiously, and with all the resources of skill and imagination possible, its effect on the worshipper will be tonic: but this tonic effect is the by-product of what is done as a duty owed to God. Even the Liturgy strictly so called – the Eucharist – even this is not done for the gratification of the worshipper: this also is the public service discharged by the citizens of the new kingdom in grateful response to the redeeming work of the king.

New Insights?

But surely, in this 20th century, we must take account of all the new insights into public worship which have been granted to us?

New insights? There are no new insights into public worship. The Church has been at worship for a very long time: make any proposal you like for a new way of worship, and you will find that every new way is in fact an old way, thought of long ago by our forefathers, discarded for a while, only lying buried somewhere in the long memory of the Church, waiting to be re-discovered and used again.

Lucernarium

There is a telling example of such a re-discovery to be found in the new Book of Common Prayer of the Episcopal Church in America, in a rite called An Order of Worship for the Evening. It may be used (says the rubric) in place of Evening Prayer, or as the introduction to Evening Prayer or some other service, or as the prelude to an evening meal or other activity. It is appropriate also for use in private houses. The rite is sparing of words: its nub is an action – the lighting of candles in the darkened church, a symbol of Christ the light of the world: and this action is followed by the hymn well known in England in Keble's translation, 'Hail, gladdening light'. The hymn in its Greek original is one of the very earliest hymns of the Church: it was 'an ancient formula' to St Basil, writing in 370, used (he says) at the Lighting of the Lamps, at the service called Lucernarium. The hymn still forms part of the Evening Service of the Orthodox Church. The Lucernarium is in the Taizé Office: and now it has been re-discovered by the Episcopal Church in America.

The Middle Voluntary

To come nearer home: in Coventry Cathedral we have re-discovered a means of adding variety and freshness to the daily Office (and indeed to the Eucharist) with what our forefathers called the Middle Voluntary. In the English cathedrals, and in some parish churches, at least from about 1600 to 1850, it was the custom for a voluntary to be played on the organ after the psalms at Morning and Evening Prayer. The purpose of the voluntary was to check the flow of words, and to provide some moments of relaxation. In Coventry Cathedral we observe the principle – the use of music as a means of relaxation: but we have extended the use to include music for piano or harpsichord, or for strings, or for solo woodwind, or for voice and instrument, or for dance. At the Sunday Eucharist a Middle Voluntary is played while the children go skipping out, before the sermon, to their classes in the undercroft; and sometimes, if the organist is in the mood, the music he plays is an improvisation on nursery rhymes: but it is never at this moment an academic exercise in strict counterpoint. There is nothing gimmicky about this; and here is no trace of 'a new insight into public worship'. Here is only the re-discovery, and the imaginative use, of something practised by our forefathers.

Holy Week

Or consider the recitation of the Passion Gospel during Holy Week. The Book of Common Prayer of 1662 requires the Passion to be recited at the Eucharist on Palm Sunday, on the following Monday, Tuesday and Wednesday, on Maundy Thursday, and on Good Friday: six times. In Coventry Cathedral the Passion on Good Friday is sung to the traditional plainsong, on the other five days it is said. But it is not read by one voice only. The deacon reads the story; two other voices read the words of individuals; and the whole congregation shouts the words of the crowd. The use of three deacons and a choir to sing the Passion is ancient; the use of three deacons and the congregation to speak it is new (though Coventry Cathedral was not the first place to adopt the idea). Once more, worship is refreshed by the re-discovery, and the imaginative extension, of an old way.

A New Style?

In the first paragraph of an essay lately published in England occurs the following phrase:

> *The clothes, the songs, the house where we meet (that is to say the vestments, the hymns and the church) somehow seem unsatisfactory.*

I know what this means, though I don't myself find any difficulty in using the traditional vestments, hymns and buildings. If the Church is to be the Church, then there must be a norm, at any rate in eucharistic liturgy: there must be one rite which is promulgated by authority and which must be followed at the principal Eucharist on every Sunday. But alongside this, the Eucharist may be presented in many different ways: for a living liturgy is the expression of the worship of a community in terms which are natural to that community. But of course the trouble is there are so many communities, so many cultures. It was not the case when the English Prayer Book was first published in 1549; there was then one culture and one community, more or less; at any rate the liturgy was imposed on the assumption that the culture was one and the community was one. The situation is now of course quite different.

The essay in question goes on to speak of the 'stifling formality' of our liturgical practice. But formality is not necessarily and in itself stifling at all; it may be strong and gracious, and in any case is on some occasions absolutely necessary. There must be, in every department of human life, some discipline, some formality, some etiquette, some code of manners, for the simple reason that we are all barbarians, and the barbarian is only a very little way beneath our skins. Liturgy shares with the rest of life the need for controlling this barbarian who is so ready to break out in a destructive and violent manner. Some sort of curb is essential; and the traditional gestures and movements of the eucharistic liturgy are nothing more nor less than a form of etiquette, a code of good manners, which protects us all from the barbarian. While there may be, and should be, many ways of presenting the Eucharist informally, there yet remains an essential need for the formal, dignified, ceremonious presentation of the eucharistic rite, at least once on a Sunday in any major place of worship.

'Liturgy is not alive' (we said in the chapter on **Liturgical Perspective**, page 1) 'unless it is intimately related to the secular order. The action of the redeemed community is set within a secular culture.' A living liturgy is the expression of the worship of a community in terms which are natural to that community. For example: the austerity of the old Book of Common Prayer is not natural to young people whose lives are dominated by pop music; they inhabit a different world of sensibility.

The point has been well taken by the Episcopal Church in America. In its new Book of Common Prayer, that Church reaches out in compassion to these young people (and to others), by providing An Order for Celebrating the Holy Eucharist in which they can be themselves, in which they can express their worship in terms which come naturally to them. This Eucharistic Order is entirely free from 'stifling formality'. It is worth our careful consideration. Here it is.

AN ORDER FOR CELEBRATING THE HOLY EUCHARIST

from The Book of Common Prayer of the Episcopal Church in America, 1979

This rite requires careful preparation by the Priest and other participants.
It is not intended for use at the principal Sunday or weekly celebration of the Holy Eucharist.

The People and the Priest

Gather in the Lord's Name

Proclaim and Respond to the Word of God
The proclamation and response may include readings, song, talk, dance, instrumental music, other art forms, silence.
A reading from the Gospel is always included.

Pray for the World and the Church

Exchange the Peace
Either here or elsewhere in the service, all greet one another in the name of the Lord.

Prepare the Table
Some of those present prepare the table; the bread, the cup of wine, and other offerings, are placed upon it.

Make Eucharist
The Great Thanksgiving is said by the Priest in the name of the gathering, using one of the eucharistic prayers provided.

The people respond – Amen!

Break the Bread

Share the Gifts of God
The Body and Blood of the Lord are shared in a reverent manner;
after all have received, any of the Sacrament that remains is then consumed.

When a common meal or Agapé is a part of the celebration, it follows here.

TWO PLEASURES

1. Of Divine Service

It is rather misleading to speak of 'the Lord's own Service', or 'the Lord's Service', as if the phrase excluded Matins or Evensong; for the worship in which our Lord took part and at which he preached was the Divine Service of the Synagogue, an order of Psalms, Lessons, and Prayers which was the pattern upon which the Divine Service of the Christian Church was formed.

Our two Services contribute an invaluable part of the Christian life, a great safeguard against distorted ideas and weak-minded devotions, a great instrument of sobriety, peace, intelligence, and depth in religion. The Divine Service is a service of quiet and thoughtful worship, of meditation, of learning, remembering, and reflection. There is much rest in it, much time to ponder, and pray, and to relax in God from the strain of mundane life, spreading our souls out in the sunshine of heaven, strengthening our inner life by the fellowship of the Common Prayer, and lifting up tranquil hearts in piety, thankfulness, and resolution to the God of our fathers.

Percy Dearmer, The Story of the Prayer Book (Oxford, 1948)

2. Of Ritual

The Middle English word solempne means something different, but not quite different, from modern English solemn. Like solemn it implies the opposite of what is familiar, free and easy, or ordinary. But unlike solemn it does not suggest gloom, oppression, or austerity. The ball in the first act of Romeo and Juliet was a 'solemnity'. The feast at the beginning of Gawain and the Green Knight is very much of a solemnity. A great mass by Mozart or Beethoven is as much a solemnity in its hilarious gloria as in its poignant crucifixus est. Feasts are, in this sense, more solemn than fasts. Easter is solempne, Good Friday is not. The solempne is the festal which is also the stately and the ceremonial, the proper occasion for pomp – and the very fact that pompous is now used only in a bad sense measures the degree to which we have lost the old idea of 'solemnity'. To recover it you must think of a court ball, or a coronation, or a victory march, as these things appear to people who enjoy them; in an age when everyone puts on his oldest clothes to be happy in, you must re- awake the simpler state of mind in which people put on gold and scarlet to be happy in. Above all, you must be rid of the hideous idea, fruit of a widespread inferiority complex, that pomp, on the proper occasions, has any connection with vanity or self-conceit. A celebrant approaching the altar, a princess led out by a king to dance a minuet, a general officer on a ceremonial parade, a major-domo preceding the boar's head at a

Christmas feast – all these wear unusual clothes and move with calculated dignity. This does not mean that they are vain, but that they are obedient; they are obeying the hoc age which presides over every solemnity. The modern habit of doing ceremonial things unceremoniously is no proof of humility; rather it proves the offender's inability to forget himself in the rite, and his readiness to spoil for everyone else the proper pleasure of ritual.

C.S. Lewis, A Preface to Paradise Lost (London, 1942)

A man performing a rite is not trying to make you think that this is his natural way of walking, these the unpremeditated gestures of his own domestic life. If long usage has in fact made the ritual unconscious, he must labour to make it look deliberate, in order that we, the assistants, may feel the weight of the solemnity pressing on his shoulders as well as on our own. Anything casual or familiar in his manner is not 'sincerity' or 'spontaneity', but impertinence. Even if his robes were not heavy in fact, they ought to look heavy.

C.S. Lewis, A Preface to Paradise Lost (London, 1942)

THREE QUESTIONS

1 : What is Common Prayer?

The title of the first English Prayer Book of 1549 (and of its successive revisions up to the book of 1928) was THE BOOK OF COMMON PRAYER.

The compilers of these books were quite clear what they meant by the phrase Common Prayer: they meant an order of public worship in the vernacular, which everyone could understand; and they meant an order of worship in which different groups of people were assigned their own particular parts. Thus the book of 1549 distributed the rite among three groups, viz.

1. The minister or ministers
2. The people
3. The clerks, that is to say the choir

Similarly the book of 1662 recognises the presence of the choir, in the rubric following the Third Collect at Morning and Evening Prayer:

In Quires and Places where they sing here followeth the Anthem.

Common Prayer, as the Church of England understands the matter, means an order of service shared between at least three groups of people; and to each group is assigned its own liturgy, its own specific offering. Common Prayer does not mean an order of service in which everyone says or sings everything.

I recall an occasion when I was invited to celebrate the Eucharist at a parish church. The rite was The Communion: Series 3[2]. In that rite the Thanksgiving is ordered to be said or sung by the President alone except for (1) the Sanctus, (2) an Acclamation after the Words of Institution, and (3) the last two lines of the Thanksgiving: these three items are assigned to the choir and people. But on this occasion, to my surprise and dismay, after the Acclamation the whole congregation filched from the President the rest of the Thanksgiving; and I wondered why I was there at all.

The congregation were guilty (though, bless their hearts, unwittingly) on three counts:

(1) They were guilty of disobedience: the rubric was clear, but they disregarded it.

(2) They were guilty of uncharitableness towards the President, the consequence of not realising that the priest is one who is appointed by authority, at certain

[2] Published in 1973 by the Liturgical Commission of The Church of England

moments, to speak to God on behalf of the people. That is his own liturgy; that is one of his functions.

(3) They were guilty of a failure to recognise the devotional value of the sound of a single voice speaking in counterpoint with the voices of the people or the choir. No liturgy is satisfying if it is presented on only one level of sound. My impression on this occasion was of worship ruthlessly vociferous: there was no peace in it.

In the pre-Reformation books the Lord's Prayer and the Collect *Deus cui omne cor* – the Collect for Purity – were ordered to be said privately by the Celebrant in the vestry while he was putting on the eucharistic vestments. In the first English book these two prayers were transferred to the Mass itself, and became part of the rite; but they were still reserved to the Celebrant.

> *The Priest standing humbly afore the midst of the altar shall say the Lord's Prayer, with this Collect.*

Let me say again: *Common Prayer does not mean an order of service in which everyone says or sings everything.*

2 : Of the Word 'Correct'

The Church has been at worship for a very long time. In composing liturgies for today it will be prudent to consult our forefathers; very likely we shall find, in earlier rites and ceremonies of the Church, some form of words, some way of doing things, which will serve our present purposes.

It is well to remember, however, that precedents make good servants but bad masters. A rite or ceremony that was once useful may not be useful any longer; it may not be relevant to our situation. We had better beware of arguing that because a rite or ceremony was once customary it is therefore 'correct'.

Peter Abelard[3] in one of his Letters of Direction to Heloise, Abbess of The Paraclete, wrote sternly:

> *We absolutely forbid that custom should ever be set above reason: a practice must never be defended on grounds of custom but only of reason, not because it is usual but because it is good, and it should be more readily accepted the better it is shown to be.*

[3] *The Letters of Abelard and Heloise,* trans. Betty Radice (London, 1974).

The men who made the first English liturgy were not deterred, by notions of what was customary and therefore 'correct', from sweeping away whatever obstructed their purpose. Their primary purpose was to restore to the Divine Office the continuous reading of the Bible, 'without breaking one piece thereof from another'.

> *For this cause* [they said in The Preface to the Prayer Book of 1549] *be cut off Anthems* [Antiphons to the Psalms], *Responds, Invitatories, and such like things, as did break the continual course of the reading of the scripture.*

The word 'correct' was not in the vocabulary of the Reformers.

They were equally ruthless over ceremonial. They made their mind very clear in the essay 'Of Ceremonies: Why some be abolished and some retained'. They were ruthless: yes, but they were reasonable. Consider their argument.

Some ceremonies are necessary

> *Without some ceremonies it is not possible to keep any order or quiet discipline in the church.*

Old ceremonies are to be revered

> *Granting some ceremonies are convenient to be had, where they may be well used, they should be revered for their antiquity. Innovations and new-fangledness are always to be eschewed.*

But old ceremonies are not immutable

> *The ceremonies that remain are retained for a discipline and order, which (upon just causes) may be altered and changed.*

Ceremonies must be either useful or expressive

> *Christ's Gospel is a religion to serve God in the freedom of spirit, being content only with those ceremonies which do serve to a decent order and godly discipline, and such as be apt to stir up the dull mind of man, to the remembrance of his duty to God by some notable and special signification, whereby he might be edified.*

The Reformers were determined on a liturgy purged of superstition and relieved of complexity. Ceremonies, they said, must be either useful or expressive. Ceremonies which were neither useful nor expressive, but only 'dark and dumb', were abolished. The word 'correct' was not in the vocabulary of the Reformers. Is there any good reason why it should be in ours?

3 : 'You' or 'Thou'?

It has become the fashion, in addressing the Godhead, to abandon 'thee' and 'thou' in favour of 'you' (which in today's English may be either singular or plural). I do not believe that the new fashion need imply any loss of respect for the Godhead or any loss of dignity in language.

The language to be used in a liturgy must have dignity; it must also, if possible, have distinction. If you know how to write English prose of dignity and distinction, have no fear; set to work – and use 'you' in addressing the Godhead.

For an example: turn now to the **Litany in praise of the Blessed Trinity** (page 369 in the example Litanies) below, and read it through to yourself. Read it aloud, as if you were the Minister conducting worship in the presence of a congregation. I believe your ear will tell you that the language induces a mood of hushed devotion. The diction, though deliberately heightened now and again, is the diction of contemporary speech.

Before I started to compose the Litany I asked whether I was to use 'you' or 'thou'. I was told that 'you' would be preferred. I therefore *began thinking in language which would accommodate 'you' without strain.*

To discover how far I succeeded, I have here transcribed two paragraphs which include contemporary (and even colloquial) phrases into a style using 'thou' and the appropriate archaic verbal inflexions; and the two styles refuse to mix. Look (and, come to that, listen):

O Lord Christ,
Thou didst feel compassion for thy fellow-men,
the lost ones, the unshepherded;
but they had no compassion on thee,
and in the end they destroyed thee;
and thou, who art equal in glory with the Father,
stoopedst to thy Passion
upon the bitter Cross.

O Lord Christ,
men thought that thou wast dead and done for,
out of sight, out of mind;
but they were mistaken,
for thou camest back from the grave
never again to die,
and thou didst return to the Father
equal in glory with the Father
as thou always wast,
and always wilt be.

Clearly there are some things which we want to say that can be said in contemporary English but cannot be said at all in the archaic style; and contemporary English therefore gives us the advantage.

But the two styles will not mix; they differ in tone, and they suggest two different tempers of mind. For this reason I believe it is offensive to use the two different styles in any one order of service; it is offensive because it begets in the worshipper a doubt about the temper of mind in which, from one moment to the next, he is to approach the Omnipotence.

I believe you must make a rule for yourself: you must write (and therefore think) either in one style or the other, and stick to it.

John Donne, a towering master of the English language both in prose and verse, demonstrates in his Holy Sonnets how to use 'you' and 'thou' indifferently. Here are two of the Sonnets.

> Thou hast made me. And shall thy work decay?
> Repair me now, for now mine end doth haste,
> I run to death, and death meets me as fast,
> And all my pleasures are like yesterday;
> I dare not move my dim eyes any way,
> Despair behind, and death before doth cast
> Such terror, and my feeble flesh doth waste
> By sin in it, which it t'wards hell doth weigh;
> Only thou art above, and when towards thee
> By thy leave I can look, I rise again;
> But our old subtle foe so tempteth me,
> That not one hour my self I can sustain;
> Thy grace may wing me to prevent his art,
> And thou like adamant draw mine iron heart.

> Batter my heart, three-person'd God; for you
> As yet but knock, breathe, shine, and seek to mend;
> That I may rise, and stand, o'erthrow me, and bend
> Your force, to break, blow, burn and make me new.
> I, like an usurped town, to another due,
> Labour to admit you, but O, to no end.
> Reason, your viceroy in me, me should defend,
> But is captiv'd, and proves weak or untrue.
> Yet dearly I love you, and would be loved fain,

But am betroth'd unto your enemy:
Divorce me, untie, or break that knot again,
Take me to you, imprison me, for I
Except you enthrall me, never shall be free,
Nor ever chaste, except you ravish me.

Read these two Sonnets aloud; and then ask yourself whether Donne is any the less the humble sinner before the throne of grace, and any the less the master of dignified language, in the second poem than in the first. But he does not use 'you' and 'thou' in the same poem.

Today's English

If you would compare a liturgy in today's English, and if you would write English prose of dignity and distinction, you will first sit down and read Stella Brook, The Language of the Book of Common Prayer (London, 1965).

If the whole fascinating book is too much for you, you will at least read 'Chapter V: The Prayers and Orders of Service', and 'Chapter VIII: The Book of Common Prayer and Twentieth Century English'.

You and Thou in the Collect

Even if you do not read Stella Brook's book, before you begin to write a collect in today's English, or translate an old collect, we implore you to read, and lay to heart, the section of this current book entitled ***You and Thou in the Collect*** (page 90)

COMPOSING AN ORDER OF SERVICE

You must first ask, and answer, these three questions:

1. Who will attend the service, and in what numbers?
2. What is to be the theme of the service?
3. What resources are available to me?

The answer to the first two questions will become clear to you in discussion. The answer to the third question will come out of your own survey of the possibilities.

How many people are likely to attend the service? One hundred? or fifteen hundred? This is a vital matter: the answer will determine whether in the composition of the service you will work towards intimacy and a touch of informality (as you may with a congregation of 100) or whether you will aim at formality, at the grand gesture.

If the congregation is to consist of regular church-goers, you may use the Office 'with intention' – Matins or Evensong with appropriate psalms, lessons, hymns, intercessions. Or you may use the Communion in a similar fashion – 'votive mass' is the technical term for a Eucharist 'with intention'. In either case, the framework of the service is already given, and so are some of the elements – the ordinary of the Eucharist, for example, is fixed; but the propers will be chosen to express the particular intention. And since the framework, and some of the elements, of the Office or of the Eucharist are already given, half your work has been done for you.

But suppose the congregation is not to consist of regular church-goers; suppose you are planning a service for The Royal Order of Moose, or for the Transatlantic Brides' Association, or for the Centenary of the Amateur Swimming Association; then you must not only plan the service, you must actually compose it. You must write the play that is to be presented in your church.

I believe that plays are written not by actors but by playwrights; just as I believe that poems are written not by committees but by poets. And I believe that liturgies, though they must express the concerns of a congregation, are written not by congregations but by liturgists. You are, in this situation, the liturgist, the maker of a liturgy.

Of course you will listen to suggestions, invite proposals, court advice: but all the time you will reserve your judgement. For in the end, the liturgy must be yours: it must be finally shaped and ordered by one mind: your mind. I said you will court advice: you will not necessarily accept advice. And if you listen to too many voices, the service will be a mingle-mangle.

How do you begin? You begin by inviting a few representatives of the society for whom you are planning the service to meet you, to talk it over together. And you ask this deceptively simple question: Why do you want to come to church together? Ten to one, the people on the opposite side of your table haven't got the answer clear to themselves. So you put the question in a different form: What do you want to say to God? And what do you think God may want to say to you?

By degrees, the aim of the service will become clear: it will usually be at least two-fold – gratitude for the past work of the society, and a desire for the divine blessing on its future. But the aim must be brought out: the service must say, with conviction and clarity, one thing which is of concern to the society or group in question.

You must insist that the service shall deal with one theme, and only one. That one theme must saturate the service.

Be warned: the Provost of Coventry once accepted an invitation to preach, at the Eucharist in a parish church, about The Community of the Cross of Nails. This theme should have permeated the whole Eucharist. But the preacher found that four other themes were to be included, *viz.*

1. The dedication of an extension to the parish hall
2. The offering of money raised in the parish
3. The dedication on the altar of drawings made by the children of the parish during the past few weeks
4. The First Communion of those lately confirmed

Such a diffusion of interest can only bemuse a congregation.

No: you will be resolute; you will decide in consultation with the folk round your table that the service you are planning with them shall <u>say one thing</u>, and say it clearly and forcibly.

You may now proceed further; for example, you can discuss what hymns might be used. But be careful: you will say 'What hymns do you think might be suitable? What hymns would you like me to consider?' You will <u>not</u> say 'What hymns would you like to have?' Consult the folk round your table: invite suggestions, court advice – but <u>make no promises</u>. Reserve your judgement. It is for them to tell you <u>what</u> they want to say to God: but it is not their business to decide <u>how</u> that is to be said. That, in the end, is your business, and nobody else's.

You won't know, yet, how it's to be said. You thank the visitors for coming to see you, and for the help they have given you; and you say goodbye to them.

They have gone. Now you can begin to brood over the matter – perhaps for days, perhaps for weeks. Keeping in mind the theme of the service (which you arrived at in conference) you review your resources.

Before you begin to compose your service, read through the next two chapters:

8 Resources
9 Elements in an Order of Service

When you have done that, remember these simple rules. Five Simple Rules

1. Use one theme only. The theme must saturate the service.
2. The argument must proceed in one unbroken line.
3. Use headings for the different sections of the service, to make the argument clear to the worshippers.
4. The beginning of the service must be firm and clear; the middle must not sag; and the end must arrive when the argument is concluded.
5. A well-made liturgy need not have length, but it must have depth and pith.

The Congregation's Part

It is possible to conduct a simple and informal service if a typed skeleton order is in the hands only of the officiating Minister, the organist, and the readers of the lessons, while the congregation uses the Prayer Book and a hymn book. Such a simple and informal mode of worship is sometimes appropriate: but it must be recognised that in these circumstances the vocal participation of the congregation must be confined to the singing of hymns, the recitation of a psalm, and the muttering of an Amen. Furthermore, directions which in a printed order of service can be silently conveyed by rubrics must in this situation be conveyed verbally; and unless this is done tersely and sympathetically the sequence of the service will be interrupted. Besides, the congregation does not know from one moment to another what is coming next; and it will not be easy to establish the mood of recollection and tranquillity which is of supreme importance.

There can be no question but that if the service is to have depth and variety, and is to carry the people forward from one mood to another, a complete typed or printed order of service must be in the hands of every person present.

RESOURCES

The resources available to any composer of liturgies fall under six main heads:

Music
Speech
Silence
Movement
Colour
Darkness and light

That looks a little meagre: but take a pencil and paper, and jot down under each head the possibilities open to you. You will find they are larger than you supposed. So:

Music

The sources of musical sound

For a grand occasion, in a well-found church
organ, chamber organ, pianoforte, harpsichord,
harmonium, chamber orchestra, string orchestra
solo violin, solo viola, solo 'cello, solo guitar,
guitar group, recorder group, solo recorder, solo flute
solo oboe, solo clarinet, solo trumpet, fanfare trumpets,
brass ensemble, bugles, drums, handbells
cantor
choir
congregation

For a smaller church or chapel
organ, pianoforte, harmonium
solo violin, solo viola, solo 'cello, solo guitar, guitar group,
recorder group, solo recorder, solo flute, solo oboe, solo clarinet,
solo trumpet, bugles, drums, handbells, congregation

It is unlikely that any small church will have on its staff any players of these instruments, except for the organist. But all these instruments are taught in schools; I dare to say that there is not a church or chapel in England which cannot find within a circumference of twenty miles a girl or boy who is a competent performer on one instrument or another. Ask a flautist to play the melody of a hymn along with the people; ask him at the final verse to play the melody an octave higher. You will be surprised to discover how exciting this can be.

If Evensong is the core of your 'special service', invite a string player to play an unaccompanied solo, either as the Middle Voluntary (between the Psalms and the First Lesson), or as a meditation after the Intercessions, or after the Sermon. Nothing could better aid recollection.

Or suppose you are planning to hold after dark a Christmas Carol Service. Invite a team of handbell ringers to help you. Ask them to play for fifteen minutes before the service begins; and forego the organ voluntary, which can sound so drearily churchy and earth-bound and expected – for the atmosphere you wish to create is the atmosphere of fairyland, of an event altogether improbable and unexpected.

As your folk approach the church they see hanging in the porch the Advent wreath with its cluster of lighted candles gleaming against the darkness. Inside the church the electric lights are dimmed or extinguished; candles are burning on every altar and in the embrasure of every window; the Christmas tree exhales upon the warm air its resinous perfume. And when the worshippers are past the porch and inside the church, they become aware of the shimmering hum of the handbells; and they are half way already to fairyland.

But the ringers can intervene, with magical effect, in the actual course of the service. The story of the birth of Jesus in Bethlehem (Luke 2. 1-7) will be read, with its poignant close: 'because there was no room for them in the inn'. Let this story tell: let it be followed by a silence for thirty seconds, and then by a two minutes' shimmer of gentle sound from the handbells (somewhere out of sight). The story will continue (Luke 2. 8-16) with the vision granted to the shepherds 'abiding in the field, keeping watch over their flock by night'. 'And suddenly there was with the angel a multitude of the heavenly host praising God, and saying, Glory to God in the highest, and on earth peace, good will toward men'. No silence now, but instantly a vigorous happy peal from the bells, lasting one minute. Then the reader continues the story.

Among the sources of musical sound (listed above) available in a smaller church or chapel, there is no mention of a choir. If in composing your 'special service' you reflect that you have no choir, don't waste time wishing you had one. Think always not in terms of what you wish you had, but in terms of what, with a little imagination and resourcefulness, you can lay your hands on. Be assured that it is quite possible to compose a satisfactory service without a choir. You will find an example in the service for **Trafalgar Day** (page 317) in the chapter with Commentaries on Orders of Service.

The Musical Elements in a Service

Acclamations
Anthems
Antiphons
Canticles
Carols
Collects
Dance
Fanfares
Folk songs
Hymns
Invocations
Litanies
National Anthem,
Prayers
Psalms
Versicles and responses
Voluntaries

Not all of these musical elements will be used in any one service; but many of them can be used in even the smallest church. Within the diocese there will be Boy Scouts to play fanfares; a singer with a good voice to sing a folk song to his guitar; or a dance group.

There is really no lack of resources in Great Britain. What is lacking is the imagination to see how they can be used, and the resolution to go out and find them.

Speech

A welcome to the congregation

Lessons (a) from the Bible
(b) from secular literature
(c) read by one voice
(d) read by two or three voices

Poetry (a) read by one voice
(b) read by many voices

Acclamations

Collects

Prayers

Psalms

Litanies

The Sermon

Silence

Had you thought of that?

But you can almost always use silence; it can be a very positive thing. Only it must be planned, not fortuitous. A silence which happens by mistake (because someone is late on his cue, or because the next piece of music is not ready on the organist's desk) – that kind of silence is simply embarrassing and destructive. But the silence which is calculated, and prepared for, and noted in a rubric, can be the most searching and pregnant moment of the whole occasion.

Movement

A liturgical Procession (consult **Processions**, page 189).

The movement of the choir, in the course of the service, from one part of the church to another (consult **Christmas Eve**, page 291).

Dancing, by a solo dancer or by a team (consult **Dance**, page 113).

Colour

Balloons

You may sometimes decorate the church with clusters of coloured balloons, at any rate for a Sunday School festival, or for some other occasion when the congregation will consist largely of children. Coloured balloons say 'This is a party': and if you wish to create a party feeling even among grown-ups, perhaps the church's Patronal Festival will be an occasion to use them.

Banners

Banners are intended to be used in procession; they are not ornaments of the sanctuary. Banners are effective if they are:

- simple in design;
- bold in colour;
- worked in fabrics appropriate to the design, perhaps silver kid appliquéd on silk, or wool embroidered on linen;
- interesting to look at on the back, as well as on the front;
- varied, and used selectively and with purpose, in order to define the occasion on which they are used.

Banner poles add resonance if they are painted in strong colours – vermilion, emerald, black. For the design of the banner, and for the materials to be used, ask the advice of a local college of art; then make the banner yourself.

Flowers

Flowers lend colour to a church, and a sense of refreshment to worship. Their presence can give to the most austere building 'a human face', a welcome feeling of homeliness; and on high festivals a hint of glory.

What is more, the presence of fresh flowers in the building is a visible demonstration that the church is loved and cherished. A bowl of fresh flowers says clearly 'Somebody has been here today to arrange these flowers. Somebody loves and cherishes this house of prayer.'

Be bold in the choice of flowers and foliage; branches laden with cherry blossom in an English spring; the purple leaves of a cabbage; whole branches of golden oak leaves in autumn; and in America, all the glowing colours of the fall.

But beware of overloading the altar; rather than two brass vases of flowers standing primly to attention on the altar itself, go for a bowl of flowers as lavish as you like, with sprays and tendrils depending from it, placed on a stand to one side of the altar. The effect can be splendid, and the colour will draw the eye to the holy table.

Two bowls on stands near the west end of the church, or its principal door, will be a visible gesture of welcome. And for a christening, a bowl on a stand near the font will add lustre to the occasion. It is not certain, however, that to place flowers actually on the font cover at a high festival is appropriate; for it suggests that the font is not likely to be used for its proper purpose – to hold water for the sacrament of baptism.

In many churches the font lacks the honour due to it. Unless it is already distinguished by a handsome cover suspended on a chain and pulley above it, or by colour integral with its design, it should be graced by a bowl of flowers, perhaps at its base, at all times, and not only when baptism is to be administered at it.

The Passiontide Cross

In some of the old parish churches of England the chancel was divided from the nave by a wooden screen surmounted by a rood, that is to say the carved figure of Christ on the cross, with the figures of St John (the beloved disciple) and the Virgin Mary, one on either side.

In any cathedral or parish church where there is no screen or rood, a striking and effective equivalent of the rood can be used to mark Passiontide. In Coventry Cathedral, from the eve of Passion Sunday until the early morning of Easter Eve, there is hung from the roof above the chancel step a huge black cross, the arms of which are draped with a crimson cloth. The cross is seven feet high, the arms are five feet across. Throughout the two weeks of passiontide this emblem of the Passion is lit up by a spotlight, from early morning till ten o'clock at night; and after dark it is potently visible through the glass west wall to the passers-by. Indeed, even in daylight it draws the eye away from the figure of Christ in glory, in the tapestry beyond the high altar. It is somehow terrifying; and this is the consequence, partly of its dominating size and partly of the clanging contrast of its two colours, the black of the cross and the crimson of the draped cloth. Those who are familiar with Isaac Watts' hymn 'When I survey the wondrous cross' are reminded of the violent imagery of one of its stanzas:

> His dying crimson like a robe
> Spreads o'er his body on the Tree;
> Then am I dead to all the globe,
> And all the globe is dead to me.

The example of the Cathedral has been followed by several churches in the diocese of Coventry, in a similar or modified form. We dare to commend Coventry's example to those who are reflecting on Colour as one of the six resources of liturgy.

Vestments, and the Cope

The eucharistic vestments bring a welcome colour into worship, welcome at least to those who can agree with C.S. Lewis that 'in an age when every one puts on his oldest clothes to be happy in, you must re-awake the simpler state of mind in which people put on gold and scarlet to be happy in' (see page 25).

The Cope

The cope (which means simply a cloak) is not a eucharistic vestment; indeed it is not a sacerdotal garment at all, but only a dress for a party occasion, traditionally worn by lay people as much as by ordained Ministers.

This tradition is well attested. Consider the following evidence.

In pre-Reformation Salisbury Cathedral on Sundays and double feasts silk copes were worn by the men and boys of the choir, according to a rubric in the Sarum Processional.

The use of copes by the choir of the Chapel Royal continued long after the Reformation. The Diary of Henry Machyn records:

> *The xxiii day of April [1562] was St George's Day, and at Whitehall the Queen's grace went from her Chapel with twelve Knights of the Garter in robes with collars of gold with garters, twenty of her Chapel in copes of cloth of gold, to the offering, singing the English procession from the Chapel round about the Hall and back again to the Chapel singing.*

And in Scrinia Reserata (1692), J. Hacket has this account of the entertainment offered to the French ambassadors by John Williams, Dean of Westminster Abbey, in 1624; the Frenchmen were in London to negotiate the marriage of Henrietta Maria to Prince Charles. Before a banquet in the Jerusalem Chamber at Westminster Abbey, the visitors were taken into the Abbey itself 'that they might cast their eyes on the stateliness of the church'.

> *At their entrance, the organ was touched by the best finger of that age, Mr Orlando Gibbons. The Lords ambassadors and their great train took up all the stalls, where they continued half an hour while the choirmen, vested in their rich copes, with their choristers, sang three several anthems, with most exquisite voices before them.*

And sixty years later, at the Coronation in 1685 of James II in Westminster Abbey, when the choirs both of the Abbey and of the Chapel Royal were on duty, the 32 Gentlemen and the 12 Children of the Chapel Royal were all vested in copes.

No church today can afford to dress its choir in silk copes; but it is a pity to forego the colour which copes can infuse into a festal occasion on the mistaken assumption that the cope ought to be worn only by ordained Ministers; a pity that its use should be suspect as the badge of high sacerdotal doctrine, for it is nothing of the kind.

Darkness and Light

In modern cities 'there is everywhere an undertone of fear. It is as if people were constantly watching for some ferocity to leap out upon them from the swirling crowds or the speeding cars or the international crisis.' So said Professor A.C. McGill in *The Celebration of Flesh*, his book about the poetry of T.S. Eliot.

That is true. On the other hand, technology has in many ways insulated us from primitive and elemental terrors – for example, fear of the dark. We need no longer fear the dark, because we can banish it with a touch on the electric light switch. The beautiful closing collect in the Prayer Book Evening Office –

> *Lighten our darkness, we beseech thee, O Lord;*
> *and by thy great mercy defend us*
>
> *from all perils and dangers of this night*

– this prayer suddenly rings true for young choristers drinking their cocoa round the camp fire after prayers, late on a summer evening, before they turn in. Beyond the glow of the fire there is darkness; and who knows (they feel) what unseen perils and dangers may not be lurking there?

Yet in the Jewish and Christian tradition the night and its darkness are recognised for their real worth, as the merciful provision by the Creator of a time of rest and repose for his children. The night is seen, in this tradition, as a divinely ordered preparation for the coming day; and indeed, in Catholic liturgy Sunday begins on the previous Saturday evening, and every red-letter festival begins on its eve. The Prayer Book rubric is explicit:

> *Note, that the Collect appointed for every Sunday, or for any Holy-day*
> *that hath a Vigil or Eve, shall be said at the Evening Service next before.*

Those who would expunge this rubric from the evening Office are not only flouting a tradition of three thousand years of liturgical practice; they are severing worship from the pulse of nature. For the liturgical use of darkness is the recognition of the rhythm of the universe; it is a homage to the Creator's handiwork. If you can use darkness, and light which is its opposite, you will be working with the grain of the universe; and that will bring into worship a dimension of startling potency.

The first example that springs to mind is the Vigil of Easter Eve. The Vigil begins, late on Easter Eve, in darkness; the new fire is brought into the church, and from it is lit the paschal candle; and from that single glowing flame other candles are lit, till the whole building blazes with light, and the Easter Eucharist proclaims the Resurrection: 'Christ is risen!' To celebrate the Easter Vigil in broad daylight, during the morning or afternoon of Easter Eve, is a piece of wasteful folly.

Or consider the Three Hours devotion on Good Friday. 'There was darkness over all the land', says the Gospel story, 'from 12 noon till 3 o'clock'. In 1785 the Cathedral of Cadiz commissioned Haydn to compose music for The Seven Last Words. After each of the Seven Words (given by Haydn to a bass in recitative) the Bishop delivered his commentary and exhortation, and then while he prostrated himself at the altar, the appropriate 'Sonata' was played. In fact the music was a series of seven intermezzi in a sermon. But what is relevant to our discussion is this: during the whole Three Hours the Cathedral was in almost total darkness; for the windows were occluded with curtains of black velvet, and the only light was a single lamp hanging from the roof.

No cathedral or large church today could afford the expense of blacking out all the windows to exclude daylight; but in a small church this might be feasible, and the Three Hours would indeed take on a new dimension.

A third example of the liturgical use of darkness – natural darkness, freely available at no cost whatever – is a carol service on Christmas Eve, when the darkness is relieved only by the light of candles. If you would create a sense of mystery, of the mystery of the Incarnation, this is one way of doing it; for broad daylight banishes mystery. The device is carefully exploited in the carol service on Christmas Eve at Coventry Cathedral: you will find the complete text of the service with a commentary in **The Form of a Servant** (page 291).

Finally, consider the use of darkness in the observance of All Souls (consult **All Souls'-tide**, page 247).

It is not often, perhaps, that a service of occasion will be held in the evening after darkness has fallen; but when that does happen, it is worthwhile to exercise your imagination in planning a moment when for part of the time the light in the church is dimmed, if such a moment seems to be the natural thing to happen; but of course it must not appear forced or arbitrary or merely contrived.

PART II – DEFINITIONS

ELEMENTS IN AN ORDER OF SERVICE

Here is a list of thirty different liturgical forms. Some of them you will never have occasion to use. They will not all be used in any one service. Most of them should be tucked away in your mind, ready to be summoned for duty at a moment's notice.

1. Acclamations

What is an Acclamation? An Acclamation can be sung, or it can be said: but essentially it is a shout. If it is said, it must be shouted.

Here is an example of a psalm treated as an Acclamation.

~~~~~~

THE ACCLAMATION Psalm 93. Dominus regnavit

At the altar the Minister calls out, and everyone shouts in answer, with a swift unflagging impulse:

loud ℣ The Lord is King,
and hath put on glorious apparel:
℟ **the Lord hath put on his apparel,
and girded himself with strength.**

℣ He hath made the round world so sure:
℟ **that it cannot be moved.**

softer ℣ Ever since the world began hath thy seat been prepared:
℟ **thou art from everlasting.**

louder ℣ The floods are risen, O Lord,
the floods have lift up their voice:
℟ **the floods life up their waves.**

loud ℣ The waves of the sea are mighty, and rage horribly:
very loud ℟ **BUT YET THE LORD,
WHO DWELLETH ON HIGH, IS MIGHTIER**

Minister Almighty and everlasting God,
you govern all things in heaven and earth:
Mercifully hear the supplications of your people,
and grant us your peace
all the days of our life;
through Jesus Christ our Lord.

Everyone: **AMEN.**

This Hymn follows at once:

HYMN

Let all the world in every corner sing,
My God and King!
~~~~~~

That looks, perhaps, easy to bring off: but don't be deceived. It won't work unless the Minister with a firm energetic delivery of his lines stimulates, and indeed provokes, the replies of the people. The Acclamation begins forte and moves through a crescendo to fortissimo on the last three lines printed or typed in capitals (and make sure they are so printed and typed). The hymn that follows clinches the argument: and it must follow without a moment's delay, played over on the organ with plenty of power.

This kind of exercise can be used in a church with the slenderest resources, when (for example) no choir is available. But if there is a choir, it goes without saying that the choir must have rehearsed the Acclamation beforehand. And if you can so arrange matters that the Acclamation is used at a moment when the choir is standing among the people towards the end of a procession, then the people will be encouraged to let themselves go. If you have no choir, persuade a group of twenty people – sidesmen, or Scouts and Guides, or servers, or members of your youth club – to rehearse beforehand, and to sit together at the service somewhere in the middle of the congregation, just to lead the Acclamation. It will be trouble well spent.

Now for an Acclamation which follows the anthem at choral Evensong (replacing the usual intercessions) on the occasion of the Patronal Festival of Michaelmas at Coventry Cathedral.

~~~~~~

THE ACCLAMATION

At the end of the Anthem the people stand, and the Provost is conducted to the gate of the sanctuary. Flanked by two lights, he turns to the people and calls out:

The Provost: There was war in heaven: Michael and his angels fought against the dragon: and the dragon fought and his angels, and prevailed not. And I heard a loud voice saying in heaven, [Rev. 12. 7, 8, 10, 11]

The choir and people *shout aloud:*

Now is come salvation,
and strength,
and the kingdom of our God,
and the power of his Christ:
for the accuser of our brethren is cast down,
which accused them before our God day and night,

The Provost: And they overcame him by the blood of the Lamb,
and by the word of their testimony;

The choir and people:

And they loved not their lives unto the death.
~~~~~~

The Provost goes up to the altar, while the Precentor and the choir sing:

℣ O praise the Lord, ye angels of his, ye that excel in strength:
℟ **Ye that fulfil his commandments,**
and hearken unto the voice of his words.
℣ O praise the Lord, all ye his hosts:
℟ **Ye servants of his that do his pleasure.**

God, whom angels and archangels and all the company of heaven adore and obey: Grant that we who hear the story of St Michael triumphing over evil may be assured of the victory of thy truth, and may see every rebel will at last made captive to thy mercy: through Jesus Christ our Lord. Amen.

The Provost at the altar turns to the people and says:

I beheld, and I heard the voice of many angels round about the throne, and the beasts and the elders: and the number of them was ten thousand times ten thousand, and thousands of thousands, saying with a loud voice, [Rev. 5. 10-13]

The choir and people *shout aloud:*

Worthy is the Lamb that was slain
To receive power,
and riches,
and wisdom,
and strength,
and honour,
and glory,
and blessing.

The Provost: And every creature which is in heaven, and on the earth, and under the earth, and such as are in the sea, and all that are in them, heard I saying,

The choir and people:

Blessing and honour, and glory and power,
be unto him that sitteth upon the throne,
and unto the Lamb for ever and ever.

This Hymn follows at once:

HYMN

Stars of the morning, so gloriously bright

~~~~~~
~~~~~~

The shouted Acclamation above is in two parts, separated by the singing of versicles and responses and a collect, during which the Provost goes from the gate of the sanctuary up to the high altar. The eye reinforces the ear; the Provost is now standing at the highest point in the building, and his physical elevation lends added force to the shouting of the second part of the Acclamation.

The congregation needs no musical skill for this exercise: it needs only courage and resolution. But it needs the support of the choir, which should have rehearsed the Acclamation beforehand.

Many societies and associations in Great Britain are honoured by the patronage of the Sovereign, or of some other member of the royal family. It is not difficult to make an Acclamation out of the prayers for the royal patron; this is a more interesting and compelling way of intercession than a single prayer from the Minister with an Amen from the congregation. There is mounting excitement, with a final release of emotion in the singing of the National Anthem.

Like this:

~~~~~~

TO SERVE THE QUEEN

At the altar the Precentor turns to the people, and says:

Let us, as in duty bound, pray for our Sovereign Lady the Queen, and for the Commonwealth.

Eternal God, who rulest in the kingdoms of men: Grant, we most humbly beseech thee, honour and safety to our Sovereign Lady, Queen Elizabeth; peace throughout the Commonwealth of her peoples; promotion to true religion; encouragement to learning and godly living; a patient service to the concord of the world; and, by all these, glory to thy holy name; through Jesus Christ our Lord.

℟ **Amen.**

Raising his voice, the Precentor says:

Say Amen to these prayers.

The Precentor calls out, and the people shout in reply:

God bless Elizabeth the Queen Mother,
Charles Prince of Wales,
Philip Duke of Edinburgh,
and all the Royal Family.

℟ **Amen.**
~~~~~~

God bless the President of the Girl Guides Association,
Her Royal Highness the Princess Margaret.
℟ **God bless the Princess Margaret.**

God save and defend our most gracious Sovereign Lady,
Queen Elizabeth.
℟ **God keep our Sovereign Lady Queen Elizabeth.**

Louder God bless her Majesty.
Very loud ℟ **GOD SAVE THE QUEEN.**

Here the whole company sings:

GOD save our gracious Queen

[Coventry Cathedral: For Queen's Guides, 1975]

There follows a more elaborate Acclamation for a specifically royal occasion, the Queen's Jubilee 1977.

Again the Acclamation is in two parts. The mood of the first part is one of prayer for the Sovereign, and is ushered in by a fanfare marked grave, 'solemnly'. The prayer is divided between two voices; the speakers are or may be invisible. The mood of the second part is quite different; it is a kind of 'three cheers for the Queen', ushered in by a fanfare *goioso e brillante*, 'joyfully and brilliantly'; and the speaker, so far from being invisible, is at the visual centre of attention: he stands at the high altar, and is flanked by four lighted candles.

In this second part four verbs are used, viz. save, defend, keep, bless. Their sequence is not fortuitous; the ear judges which verb is to be used to the best advantage. The punch line, which leads directly into the singing of the National Anthem, must clearly be GOD SAVE THE QUEEN; and of the four verbs, therefore, the verb 'save' must come last.

THE ROYAL ACCLAMATION

FANFARE grave

Two voices in turn call out, and the people reply, loudly and firmly, AMEN.

1 The Lord bless and keep Her Majesty Queen ELIZABETH.
℟ **Amen.**

2 The Lord protect her in all her ways, and prosper all her handiwork.
℟ **Amen.**
1 The Lord give her faithful Parliaments and quiet Realms;
℟ **Amen.**
2 Sure defence against all her enemies;
℟ **Amen.**
1 Fruitful lands and a prosperous industry;
℟ **Amen.**
2 Wise counsellors and upright magistrates;
℟ **Amen.**
1 Leaders of integrity in learning and labour;
℟ **Amen.**
2 A devout, learnèd and useful clergy;
℟ **Amen.**
1 Honest, peaceable and dutiful citizens;
℟ **Amen.**

A brief silence

1 May Wisdom and Knowledge be the Stability of her Times,
2 and the Fear of the Lord her Treasure.
℟ **Amen.**
1 The Lord who has made her Queen over her Peoples give her increase of grace, honour, and happiness in this world.
2 And make her partaker of his eternal felicity in the world to come.
℟ **Amen.**

From the Order
for the Coronation of Her Majesty Queen Elizabeth II
in Westminster Abbey, 2 June 1953.

FANFARE *goioso e brillante*

The Precentor, flanked by lighted tapers, calls out, and the choir and people shout in answer, with growing fervour:

God save and defend Elizabeth the Queen Mother.
℟ **God keep her, God defend her.**
God save and defend Philip Duke of Edinburgh.
℟ **God keep him, God defend him.**
God save and defend Charles Prince of Wales.
℟ **God keep him, God defend him.**

God save and defend all the Royal Family.
℟ **God keep them, God defend them all.**

God save and defend our most gracious Sovereign Lady Queen Elizabeth.
℟ **God keep our Sovereign Lady Queen Elizabeth.**
God bless Her Majesty.
GOD SAVE THE QUEEN.

The whole company sings:
God save our gracious Queen

~~~~~~

The following Acclamation was used in Coventry Cathedral at an International Students' Festival on Saturday 15 February 1964. Its climax was a solo on drums and cymbals; a wordless offering of praise which those who heard it will never forget.

~~~~~~

THE ACCLAMATION

The Cross of Nails, escorted by four lights, moves swiftly to the chancel step, where the Cross is held aloft. The Ministers stand on either side of the Cross, facing the people; and the Precentor says:

Let us bring our prayers to a close by offering our praises to our Lord Jesus Christ risen, ascended, and glorified.

Raising his voice the Precentor calls out:
Lift up your heads, O ye gates,
And be ye lift up, ye everlasting doors;

At the top of their voices the people shout in reply:

And the King of glory shall come in.

℣ Who is this King of Glory?
℟ **The Lord of hosts, he is the King of glory.**
℣ Thou art the King of glory, O Christ;
℟ **Thou art the everlasting Son of the Father.**
℣ When thou hadst overcome the sharpness of death;
℟ **Thou didst open the kingdom of heaven to all believers.**

℣ Thou sittest at the right hand of God;
℟ **In the glory of the Father.**
℣ King of kings, And Lord of lords;
℟ **KING OF KINGS,**
AND LORD OF LORDS.
℣ Risen!
℟ **RISEN!**
℣ Ascended!
℟ **ASCENDED!**
℣ Glorified!
℟ **GLORIFIED!**

At once this Hymn is sung:

The head that once was crowned with thorns
Is crowned with glory now:
A royal diadem adorns
The mighty Victor's brow.

The highest place that heaven affords
Is his, is his by right,
The King of kings and Lord of lords,
And heaven's eternal Light;

The joy of all who dwell above,
The joy of all below,
To whom he manifests his love,
And grants his name to know.

People on the left
To them the Cross, with all its shame,
With all its grace is given;
Their name an everlasting name,
Their joy the joy of heaven.

People on the right
They suffer with their Lord below,
They reign with him above,
Their profit and their joy to know
The mystery of his love.

Everyone **The Cross he bore is life and health,
Though shame and death to him;
His people's hope, his people's wealth,
Their everlasting theme.**

St Magnus AMR 218

*The Acclamation is continued
on DRUMS AND CYMBALS played by TREVOR MORAIS.*

O praise God in his holiness: praise him in the firmament of his power.
Praise him in his noble acts: praise him according to his excellent greatness.
Praise him in the sound of the trumpet: praise him upon the lute and harp.
Praise him in the cymbals and
s: praise him upon the strings and pipe.
Praise him upon the well-tuned cymbals: praise him upon the loud cymbals.
Let every thing that hath breath: praise the Lord.

Psalm 150. Laudate Dominum

Interlude

TIME STOPS

The singers were as boring as all pop singers are – boring, because none of them can sing; they can only bawl or mewl into a microphone. But the drummer! Within two minutes he had haled my guts into my mouth with the frenzy and the subtlety of his rhythms. And the tears were in my eyes. But why? What was there to cry about? A young man of twenty, lithe as they come, in his jeans and his pansy jacket, with black frizzled hair and coffee complexion and brilliant brown eyes, beating it out on drums and cymbals as though he were making the first music that ever was made, and revelling in his powers – what was there in this to make an onlooker weep? The sheer style of it, for one thing: and for another, a sense that among all the millions of teenagers, across the five continents, who are lost and bewildered and aimless, here was one of them who had found himself; a child of God who had discovered what God made him for, and was intent on fulfilling his vocation with every fibre of his being.

I rang up the theatre manager. 'I've just seen your show. Can I speak to Mr Morais, your drummer? He's a virtuoso.' 'Oh! you mean Trevor. Yes, Trevor does work very hard for his living! I'll fix it for you. Come to the stage door at 7.15, before the next show.'

I called at the stage door, and was shown into the office, a room about five feet square with a desk and two telephones and a secretary. I sat down, and Trevor came in, chewing gum and smoking a cigarette. (Mint and tobacco on the palate together! I winced a little.) The telephones rang, actors in dressing-gowns and grease-paint flitted in and out, and the call-boy bellowed in the passage. In this pandemonium we began our conversation.

'Mr Morais, I saw your show last night. Your drumming was terrific. I am planning a service in the Cathedral to be attended by university students of many nations – young men and women of your age. Will you come and drum for us? Play what you played last night?' 'Yes, I'll come and play.'

'Good. I'm not asking for charity. We'll pay you a professional fee.'

'I don't care about the money. I'll always play for a cause.'

'Look here,' I said, 'are you a Christian?'

'I'm a Roman Catholic. My pals are all Non-conformists, and they told me they were right and I was wrong. So I went round to their churches to see. But there's no difference: we're all on the same road.'

'No need to defend yourself', I said. 'I'm not asking what Church you belong to. The point is just this: if I say to you that when you are drumming, and playing as if nothing else in the world matters to you, then you are singing a Te Deum, you are praising God – if I talk in those terms, do you understand what I'm driving at?'

'Yes, I know what you mean.'

At that instant of time the order of service which I was planning came together in my mind's ear, a whole and perfect thing, with its heights and depths, its moments of climax and of relaxation. I knew precisely where the drum solo was to be placed, how long it should last, and what effect it would produce. I had only to go home, sit down in my armchair, light a pipe, and write the thing down. To prepare the manuscript for the press would take some hours, but that was a mechanical process; the precedent act of imagination was already complete, there in the five square feet of the office by the stage door.

But for the sake of the pleasure I took in the vivid personality of this young musician, I pursued the conversation a little further, while the telephones rang and the call-boy bellowed and the clock ticked on towards curtain-up.

'When did you start drumming?'

'Three years ago, when I was 17. Till then I didn't know what I wanted to do. I tried sport; I was good at sport. Then I took to drumming. Taught myself. Now I don't want to do anything else.'

'Do you play pieces already composed, or do you ad-lib?'

'I always ad-lib. Sometimes I play for three minutes, sometimes for five. The other night I played for ten. Nobody got bored – I know, because I was watching them.'

'When you play in the Cathedral, I want you to play for four minutes. If you play longer, you will throw the whole thing out of proportion.'

Curtain up. We parted.

The drum solo would be so exciting that it could only be used as the climax of an act of praise. That is how it was. The Acclamation began with a shouted exchange, between priest and people, of words of scripture, in praise of the risen Christ. Then the hymn 'The head that once was crowned with thorns'. Then, said the rubric, 'The Acclamation is continued on drums and cymbals'. And beneath the rubric was printed Psalm 150:

> *Praise him in the cymbals and dances: praise him upon the loud cymbals.*
>
> *Let everything that hath breath: praise the Lord.*

Trevor was sitting with friends at the front of the nave. At the appointed moment he left his seat, looked up at the Christ in the tapestry above the altar, genuflected, crossed himself; then he crept to his drums. The echoes of the hymn died on the air; and Trevor began to play. He began at fifteen minutes after noon and played for exactly four minutes.

But that's nonsense. While Trevor played, time stopped. This young man from Liverpool, this talented child of God, lifted us out of time altogether. Praise of this quality cannot be measured by any chronometer.

For the record: the date was 15 February 1964.

2. Admission to Office

In any form of admission to office in a religious society (as for example in admission to Holy Orders) there are four elements, viz.

1. The presentation of the candidate to the person who has authority to admit him;
2. The scrutiny or public examination of the candidate, by question and answer;
3. The actual admission, betokened by a physical gesture accompanied by a spoken formula. The person who admits the candidate will lay hands on his head; or he will shake hands with him; or he will hang round the candidate's neck a ribbon with a badge of office;
4. Prayer for the candidate; perhaps only a single sentence, as for example 'N., the Lord prosper you; we wish you good luck in the name of the Lord' (Psalm 129. 8).

On more solemn occasions the candidate may also be invested; that is to say, clothed in some garment which declares his office – the episcopal habit, or a surplice, or a gown.

In the form of admission given below there is no investiture, but the four basic elements are there. Examine in turn the first two.

1. The presentation is a miniature example of the dialogue (discussed on page 139). The dialogue publishes, and so puts on record, two pieces of information: the candidate's name, and the name of the office which he is to hold.
2. The scrutiny is threefold. Three times the Provost (a) makes a statement, and (b) asks a question. The question each time is the same: Will you remember?

The candidate's answer is also, each time, the same: I will. This threefold repetition of a simple question and a simple answer is designed to set the candidate at his ease; for one thing, he will have no need to be encumbered by holding in his hand the form of admission.

The statements made by the Provost in the course of the scrutiny are in simple words: but they are not shallow. Each statement reminds the candidate (and the audience) that, whatever may be his office in the society, he is appointed to it for one overriding purpose: the service of Jesus Christ.

The statements suggest what the servant of Jesus may look forward to. 'Where I am', said Jesus, 'there shall also my servant be.' Will that be comfortable or consoling? But no: it may mean crucifixion. And it may mean an inconceivable splendour, the companionship of Love himself. 'Yet I am not alone', said Jesus as he went to his death, 'for the Father is with me.'

Further: 'If any man serve me, him will my Father honour.' Let the candidate be reminded of some other words of Jesus about faithful servants. 'Blessed are those servants whom the lord' – he means the master of the house, returning home late from a wedding party – 'shall find watching; verily I say unto you, that he shall gird himself, and make them to sit down to meat, and will come forth and serve them.'

Love bade me welcome; yet my soul drew back,
  Guilty of dust and sin.
But quick-eyed Love, observing me grow slack
  From my first entrance in,
Drew nearer to me, sweetly questioning
  If I lacked any thing.

A guest, I answered, worthy to be here.
  Love said, you shall be he.
I the unkind, ungrateful? Ah, my dear,
  I cannot look on thee.
Love took my hand, and smiling did reply,
  Who made the eyes but I?

Truth Lord, but I have marr'd them: let my shame
  Go where it doth deserve.
And know you not, says Love, who bore the blame?
  My dear, then I will serve.
You must sit down, says Love, and taste my meat.
  So I did sit and eat.

George Herbert

THE FORM OF ADMISSION TO OFFICE

The presenter conducts the candidate by the hand to stand before the Provost.
He addresses the Provost:

Mr Provost, I present to you N., To be admitted to the office of ....

The Provost addresses the candidate:

N., in the office to which I have appointed you, you are at all times to be the servant of Jesus Christ. Will you remember this?

Answer: I will.

Provost: Jesus said, If any man serve me, let him follow me: and where I am, there shall also my servant be.

Jesus said also, If any man serve me, him will my Father honour.

N., will you remember these words of Jesus, and lay them to heart?

Answer: I will.

Provost: If you would serve Jesus Christ, you must love and serve his people, here and elsewhere.

Will you remember this?

Answer: I will.

Provost: Then I will admit you to your office.

The Provost shakes hands with the candidate, and says:

N., by the authority committed to me
I admit you to the office of .....

Then the Provost makes the sign of the cross over the candidate, saying:

God keep you in his care; Christ win you and save you;
The Holy Spirit guide you in the ways of truth and love always. Amen.

The candidate bows to the Provost; and the presenter conducts the candidate back to his seat.

Coventry Cathedral 1977

~~~~~~

3. Antiphons

An antiphon is a brief phrase sung or said before a psalm or canticle, and repeated after the Gloria Patri. The phrase may be drawn from the psalm itself, or it may be borrowed from elsewhere. The antiphon serves to direct and enforce the meaning of the psalm or canticle.

In the pre-Reformation services, antiphons were always used with the psalms, which were sung in unison to plainsong tones. The Reformers abolished antiphons; but they left one antiphon (perhaps by mistake) in the English Litany, and William Byrd set it to music in four-part harmony. Byrd's setting is given on page 391 of Part IV – Examples of Music, with some other examples of harmonised antiphons for use with Anglican chants.
~~~~~~

A substantial and convincing prologue to an order of service can be contrived by having the Venite, preceded and followed by an antiphon, spoken. In the following example a single voice (the Provost's) is answered by two groups of voices, the voices of the choir (speaking, not singing) and the voices of the congregation. No matter if you have no choir: what you must have is simply two groups of voices speaking in counterpoint with each other. Instead of a choir, you could have Scouts, or Guides, or your branch of the Church of England Men's Society – any compact group who would be willing to rehearse with you beforehand (as indeed a choir must do), so as to be ready to speak loudly and rhythmically the words allotted to them, and in that way encourage the people to do the same in their turn. Indeed, the simplest way of all would be to allot verses in turn to the men and women of the congregation.

The example here given is taken from a service entitled **Consider the Lilies**, held in Coventry Cathedral in 1968 on the occasion of a Flower Festival. It is in the chapter with Commentaries on Orders of Service (page 255).

~~~~~~

ANTIPHON

The Provost: O Come, let us worship and fall down:
and kneel before the Lord our Maker.

Choir and People:
For he is the Lord our God:
and we are the people of his pasture,
and the sheep of his hand.

PSALM 95. Venite exultemus

Provost: O Come, let us sing unto the Lord:
let us heartily rejoice in the strength of our salvation.

Choir: Let us come before his presence with thanksgiving:
and show ourselves glad in him with psalms.

People: For the Lord is a great God:
and a great King above all gods.

Choir: In his hand are all the corners of the earth:
and the strength of the hills is his also.

People: The sea is his, and he made it:
and his hands prepared the dry land.
~~~~~~

Choir: O come, let us worship and fall down:
and kneel before the Lord our maker.

People: For he is the Lord our God:
and we are the people of his pasture, and the sheep of his hand.

Provost: Glory be to the Father, and to the Son: and to the Holy Ghost:

Everyone: As it was in the beginning, is now, and ever shall be:
world without end. Amen.

Provost: O come, let us worship and fall down:
and kneel before the Lord our Maker.

Choir and People:
For he is the Lord our God:
and we are the people of his pasture, and the sheep of his hand.

~~~~~~
~~~~~~

4. Antiphony

In the English cathedrals of the Old Foundation (i.e. those which were secular cathedrals before the Reformation) the precentor is a dignitary, and a member of the chapter, ranking second in seniority to the dean. The precentor sits opposite the dean, whence the name for the two sides of the choir, Decani (i.e. 'of the dean') and Cantoris (i.e. 'of the precentor'). In the cathedrals of the New Foundation (i.e. those which were monastic churches and were secularised by Henry VIII) the precentor is a minor canon and is not a member of the chapter; but he too sits on the side opposite the dean, though he does not occupy the stall of a canon.

In effect, the singers in cathedrals both of the Old and the New Foundations are divided into two choirs, the Decani and the Cantoris choir; each choir has its proper complement of voices: treble, alto, tenor, and bass. The composers often assign one passage of the music to the Decani choir and another to the Cantoris choir, so that one choir answers another. This effect is called antiphony. There may be antiphony not only between one choir and the other, but also between a cantor and the full choir (full means Decani and Cantoris choirs singing together), or between a semi-chorus and the full choir.

The Puritans disliked antiphonal singing. In 1572 a London clergyman named John Field even wrote 'An Admonition to the Parliament', criticising the Anglican Service where 'there is no edification, according to the Rule of the Apostle, but confusion; they toss the Psalms in most places like tennis-balls'. But the composers pursued their own way, and continued to use antiphony in the cathedrals; and indeed it is an obvious and easy way to secure variety and interest.

The same play between the voices can of course be used not only in cathedrals but in any parish church, or school or university chapel, furnished with a competent choir.

Antiphony can be used with magical effect if the opposing singers are separated by large spaces. Place your precentor at the west end of the nave, to be answered by the full choir in the chancel. Place a quartet of singers half-way down one aisle, to be answered again by the rest of the choir in the chancel. Place half the choir in one aisle, to be answered by the other half in the opposite aisle. You will find examples of all these procedures in the section of this book devoted to music (page 60).

But even if you have no choir, you can always use antiphony in the hymns. A long hymn sung by everyone, without any variety, is tedious: so give one verse to men's voices, another to women's voices; give one verse to the people on the right, another to those on the left; for a touch of surprise give one verse to fathers and sons, another to mothers and daughters, like this:

Fathers and sons

For the joy of human love,
Brother, sister, parent, child,
Friends on earth, and friends above,
Pleasures pure and undefiled,
Lord of all, to thee we raise
This our grateful hymn of praise.

Mothers and daughters

For each perfect gift of thine,
To our race so freely given,
Graces human and divine,
Flowers of earth and birds of heaven,
Lord of all, to thee we raise
This our grateful hymn of praise.

5. Beginnings and Endings

Beginnings and endings in a service of occasion need not be as dull as they often are. It is not difficult to contrive some variations.

Beginnings

1. To begin with a hymn is usual: it is also sensible, because such an action shared by everyone sets the worshippers at ease. But note: the music of this hymn must be massive, virile, and above all familiar; the text must be God-ward. The hymn is the first common utterance in the service; if this is hesitant, recovery from a bad start will not be easy.
2. For a change, set this first hymn in the context of an Invocation. You will find examples in **Invocations** (page 149).
3. Try beginning with Silence, followed by music for an unaccompanied solo instrument. For example:

Beginning with silence

The Ministers enter and go to their places.
Everyone sits down. There is silence.
Then follows:

MUSIC FOR SOLO FLUTE
Incantation no. 1
André Jolivet 1905-1974

THE ADDRESS
by Maurice Edelman, Esq.,
Member of Parliament for Coventry North-West

Coventry Cathedral 1974: Memorial Service
for Richard Crossman, MP for Coventry East 1945-74

4. Begin without music of any kind, except perhaps a fanfare: begin with Voices calling aloud from different points in the building. For example:

Beginning with Voices

At 7.00 the Ministers enter and go to their seats in the chancel,
and the people stand up.

FANFARE

First voice, from the north, loudly and urgently
Except the Lord build the house: their labour is but lost that build it.

Second voice, from the south
Except the Lord keep the city:
the watchman waketh but in vain.

Third voice, from the west
We build in vain unless the Lord build with us.
Can you keep the city that the Lord keeps not with you?
A thousand policemen directing the traffic
Cannot tell you why you come or where you go.

First voice
Except the Lord build the house: their labour is but lost that build it.

Second voice
Except the Lord keep the city:
the watchman waketh but in vain.

This **HYMN**, *immediately*
Wareham AMR 582

**Rejoice, O land, in God thy might;
His will obey, him serve aright;
For thee the saints uplift their voice:
Fear not, O land, in God rejoice.**

**Glad shalt thou be, with blessing crowned,
With joy and peace thou shalt abound;
Yea, love with thee shall make his home
Until thou see God's Kingdom come.**

**He shall forgive thy sins untold:
Remember thou his love of old;
Walk in his way, his word adore,
And keep his truth for evermore.**

Coventry Cathedral 1972: A Civic Service

5. Begin with a Dialogue between the Minister and the people, a conversation which by the use of question and answer compels the congregation to articulate the reasons why they have come to church together, and in so doing perhaps to become aware of those reasons for the first time. For example:

Beginning with a dialogue

At 3.00 the Ministers arrive at the west door.
A FANFARE is played, and the people stand and
turn towards the west door to greet the Ministers.

The Precentor *calls out:*
Friends and neighbours, welcome to you all.

The people *shout in answer:*
Welcome to you.

The Precentor Who are you?

The people: Members of the Soroptimist International Association.

The Precentor: Why are you here?

The people: To keep our Golden Jubilee, to praise God,
to confess our faults, to renew our obedience.

The Precentor: God prosper your Association,
God accept your praises,
God forgive your faults,
God uphold your obedience.
You are here to praise God. Then praise him now.

The people turn again towards the altar to sing the Hymn PRAISE TO THE LORD, THE ALMIGHTY, *and the procession moves through the nave to the chancel in this order:*

THE MACE OF CANADA
THE MICHAEL CROSS
TWO LIGHTS
THE MACE OF AUSTRALIA
THE PREACHER
THE CANONS
THE MACE OF COVENTRY
THE PRECENTOR

HYMN
Praxis Pietatis AMR 382

Praise to the Lord, the Almighty, the King of creation;
O my soul, praise him, for he is thy health and salvation:
All ye who hear, now to his temple draw near,
Joining in glad adoration.

Praise to the Lord, who o'er all things so wondrously reigneth,
Shieldeth thee gently from harm, or when fainting sustaineth:
Has thou not seen how thy heart's wishes have been
Granted in what he ordaineth?

Praise to the Lord, who doth prosper thy work
and defend thee;
Surely his goodness and mercy shall daily attend thee:
Ponder anew what the Almighty can do,
If to the end he befriend thee.

Praise to the Lord! O let all that is in me adore him!
All that hath life and breath, come now with praises before him!
Let the Amen sound from his people again:
Gladly for ay we adore him.

Coventry Cathedral 1971:
The Golden Jubilee of the Soroptimists

6. Include a Welcome to the people. This may be friendly and informal. But there are occasions when informality is out of place, and where the Welcome should be calculated to attune the atmosphere to the theme. There are some examples (and please think them worth your examination) in **The Welcome** (page 239).
In your imagination accustom yourself, in preparing an order of service, to begin the service anywhere but in the chancel. You may, for instance, often begin in the nave, at the west end of the building, without causing anyone to say 'How odd! What a strange way of doing things!'

7. In a cathedral or collegiate church, where the choir and nave are separated by a stone screen so that the people in these two spaces are invisible to each other, there is a particular advantage to be gained by beginning in the nave. You must bring the choir and Ministers down among the people in the nave, where they can see each other; thus you at once suggest that they are all in fact one body of folk assembled for worship.

Indeed, in any parish church also, even where no screen hides the choir from the people, you will encourage the same feeling of the union of the two groups, both engaged in a common purpose, if you begin with the choir and Ministers standing in the nave at the west end and singing something there. For example:

Beginning in the nave: Evensong

The choir and Ministers go to the west end of the church.
THE PEOPLE REMAIN SEATED.
At the west end the choir sings the First Anthem.

God liveth still; Trust, my soul, and fear no ill.
God is good; from his compassion
Earthly help and comfort flow;
Strong is his right hand to fashion
All things well for man below.
Trial oft the most distressing
In the end has prov'd a blessing:
Wherefore then, my soul, despair?
God still lives who heareth prayer.

God liveth still; Trust, my soul, and fear no ill:
He who gives the clouds their measure,
Stretching out the heavens above,
He who stores the earth with treasure,
Is not far from every one;
God in hour of need defendeth
Him whose heart in love ascendeth;
Wherefore then, my soul, despair?
God still lives who heareth prayer.

J.S. Bach

At the end of the Anthem the people stand.

The Minister and the choir sing:

℣ Jesus said, This is my commandment: love one another;
℟ As I have loved you.
℣ There is no greater lover than this;
℟ That a man should lay down his life for his friends.
℣ Only be faithful till death;
℟ And I will give you the crown of life.

℣ O Lord, open thou our lips;
℟ And our mouth shall shew forth thy praise.
℣ O God, make speed to save us;
℟ O Lord, make haste to help us.
℣ Glory be to the Father, and to the Son: and to the Holy Ghost;
℟ As it was in the beginning, is now, and ever shall be:
world without end. Amen.
℣ Praise ye the Lord;
℟ The Lord's name be praised.

The procession goes forward to the chancel, while the choir and people sing this Hymn.

HYMN

Old 100th AMR 166

**All people that on earth do dwell,
Sing to the Lord with cheerful voice;
Him serve with fear, his praise forth tell,
Come ye before him, and rejoice.**

**The Lord, ye know, is God indeed;
Without our aid he did us make;
We are his folk, he doth us feed,
And for his sheep he doth us take.**

**O enter then his gates with praise,
Approach with joy his courts unto;
Praise, laud, and bless his name always,
For it is seemly so to do.**

Choir

For why? the Lord our God is good,
His mercy is for ever sure:
His truth at all times firmly stood,
And shall from age to age endure.

Everyone

**To Father, Son and Holy Ghost,
The God whom heaven and earth adore,
From men and from the angel-host
Be praise and glory evermore.**

The hymn is in fact the Office hymn. When it is ended, the people sit down, and Evensong proceeds with the appointed psalm sung by the choir.

Coventry Cathedral 1971:
The Presentation to the Provost and Chapter of the Victoria Cross,
posthumously awarded to Petty Officer Alfred Edward Sephton,
killed in action in HMS Coventry, 18 May 1941

Beginning in the nave: The Reception of the Bishop at his Cathedral

THE RECEPTION OF THE BISHOP

At 10.25 the Cathedral procession leaves St Michael's Hall and goes by the north aisle of the nave to take up its position in the middle alley.
THE PEOPLE REMAIN SEATED.
At 10.30 the Bishop with his Chaplains is received by the Provost at the west door.
Then the choir standing in the nave sings this Anthem.

ANTHEM

He is the Way.
Follow him through the Land of Unlikeness;
You will see rare beasts and have unique adventures.

He is the Truth.
Seek him in the Kingdom of Anxiety.
You will come to a great city that has expected your return for years.

He is the Life.
Love him in the World of the Flesh;
And at your marriage all its occasions shall dance for joy.

Words by W.H.Auden 1907-73
Music by Alan Ridout, commissioned by
the Friends of Coventry Cathedral in 1973

FANFARE

The people stand, and turn towards the Bishop.
They exchange greetings. The Bishop calls out, and the people reply:

℣ Friends in Christ Jesus, welcome to you all.
℟ **Welcome to you, Father.**

FANFARE

The people greet the Bishop with applause.

The Bishop

I am your Bishop,
John, Bishop of Coventry.
I am your servant, for Jesus' sake. I ask for your prayers.
Pray with me now.

THE INVOCATION

Bishop and people

℣ Hear my prayer, O Lord, and consider my desire;
℟ Hearken unto me for thy truth and righteousness' sake.
℣ O let me hear thy loving-kindness betimes in the morning, for in thee is my trust;
℟ Shew thou me the way that I should walk in,
for I lift up my soul unto thee.
℣ Teach me to do the things that pleaseth thee, for thou art my God;
℟ Let thy loving Spirit lead me forth
into the land of righteousness.

Psalm 143. Domine, exaudi

The Bishop

Come, Holy Spirit, the free dispenser of all graces: Visit the hearts of thy faithful servants, and replenish them with thy sacred inspirations; illuminate our understandings, and inflame our affections, and sanctify all the faculties of our souls; that we may know, and love, and constantly do the things that belong to our peace, our everlasting peace; who with the Father and the Son reignest God, world without end. Amen.

The choir and people turn again towards the altar, to sing the Entrance Hymn, and the procession goes forward to the chancel.

Coventry Cathedral 1976:
The Communion at the Bishop's Enthronement

Beginning in the nave: The Reception of the Bishop at a Parish Church in his Diocese

THE RECEPTION OF THE LORD BISHOP

7.30 FANFARE
The people stand, and TURN TOWARDS THE ENTRANCE.
The Bishop and his Chaplain enter the church, and stand facing the altar.

The Vicar, *facing the Bishop, addresses him:*
My Lord Bishop,
we are glad to see you here. Welcome to Canley.

The people, *loudly and cheerfully:*
Right Reverend Father in God, we are glad to see you here.
Welcome to Canley.

The Bishop: Good evening to you all.
I am John, your Bishop.
I am John, your friend.
I am John, your servant
in the faith of Jesus Christ.
I am glad to be here with you.

The people greet the Bishop with loud applause.

Then a girl steps forward, carrying two nosegays. She curtseys to the Bishop.
Then she says:

Father, this is to welcome you,

and she presents a nosegay to the Bishop.

Then she stands before the Bishop's Chaplain.
She says:

And here's one for you, Sir,

and she present the other nosegay to the Chaplain.

This Hymn follows.
The people turn to the altar, while the Bishop's procession goes forward by the middle alley to the sanctuary.

St Stephen's Church, Canley 1978:
The Dedication of the Bell Tower

Beginning in the nave: An Invocation

An example is given in **Invocations** (page 149).

Beginning in the nave: The Arrival of the Bride at her Wedding

An example is given in **Dance** (page 113).

Endings

1. End with a hymn, by all means: but if the hymn is indeed the end of the service, make sure that it really is the end, the final utterance, the full stop. The hymn is a complete verbal and musical statement: the outgoing organ voluntary is also a complete musical statement. Don't blur the two by an organ improvisation linking the hymn and the voluntary. End the hymn; then a silence of 10 seconds; then begin the voluntary.

2. Be sparing of Blessings. A blessing is not a disguised form of dismissal; it is not a churchy way of saying 'That's all for today. You may go now.' No: it is a moment of solemn devotion; and the time for such a moment may have arrived at an earlier point. Among the Five Simple Rules for composing an order of service (page 78) was this: 'The end must arrive when the argument is concluded.' Before you add a blessing, therefore, ask yourself, 'Is the argument already concluded? Or is a blessing necessary to conclude the argument?'

   If a blessing is indeed needed to conclude the argument, then add a blessing. But if it is not needed, then don't have one.

3. You may end with Silence, just as you began with silence. This will bring any occasion to a close in utter relaxation. For example:

Ending with silence

The Bishop returns to his Throne. Everyone sits down.

Silence

MUSIC FOR SOLO FLUTE

Density 21.5 Edgard Varèse 1883-1965

Silence

After a while, music is played on the organ.

MUSIC FOR ORGAN

Prelude in C minor BWV 546 J.S. Bach

The Ministers go through the nave to the west door. When the Bishop has left the chancel, the choir withdraws by the north aisle to St Michael's Hall.

Coventry Cathedral 1976:
Memorial Service for Maurice Edelman,
MP for Coventry 1945-75

4. End with Voices calling aloud, if you began in that way. The voices at the end can repeat the phrases spoken at the beginning; an echo, recalling ideas which the worshippers will carry away in their memories. For example:

Ending with voices

First voice — A vision of the holy city, where the will of God prevails.
I saw a new heaven and a new earth:
for the first heaven and the first earth were passed away;
and there was no more sea.

Second voice — I saw the holy city, new Jerusalem,
coming down from God out of heaven,
prepared as a bride adorned for her husband.

Third voice — And the city had no need of sun or moon to shine upon it;
for the glory of God gave it light, and the Lamb is the light of it.

First voice — By its light shall the nations walk,
and the kings of the earth shall bring their glory and honour into it.

Second voice — And the gates of it shall not be shut at all by day: and there shall be no night there.

Third voice — And they shall bring the glory and honour of the nations unto it:
but nothing unclean shall enter,
nor anyone whose ways are false or foul:

Three together — but only those who are inscribed
in the Lamb's book of life.

Revelation 21: 1-2, 23-27

The Minister at the altar, urgently and loudly

Come, Lord, come;

Everyone with emphasis loudly

Stablish our faith, renew our hope, deepen our love;
refresh us again with the vision of the city
where your word is heard,
your will is done, your presence is adored,

declaim **NOW, TOMORROW, ALWAYS. AMEN.**

A voice, mezzo-forte but with conviction

Except the Lord build the house:
their labour is but lost that build it.

Another voice, slowly and emphatically

Except the Lord keep the city:
the watchman waketh but in vain.

A brief silence

The Royal School of Church Music:
Festival Service Book 8 THE CITY

5. One of the marks of the Church – especially of the Church of England, which by law has a pastoral responsibility for every citizen – is generosity. Its ministrations are available to men of good will who turn to it in their need, even though they do not subscribe to every article of its Creed.

Now suppose that you are a parish priest, and that you are asked to hold a Memorial Service for a devout and practising Jew. You cannot end with the specifically Christian farewell, Profiscere anima christiana, Go forth upon thy journey from this world, O Christian soul. No: but you can use an appropriate passage from the Old Testament. For example:

Ending a Memorial Service for a Devout and Practising Jew

THE AFFIRMATION

When the Hymn ends, the Bishop at the altar turns to the people and pronounces this Affirmation from the prophet Malachi (Malachi 3. 16, 17).

> Those who feared the Lord talked together; and the Lord paid heed and listened. And a book of remembrance was written before him of those who feared the Lord and kept his name in mind.
> And they shall be mine, says the Lord of hosts, in that day when I make up my jewels.

Everyone, with great conviction:

> **They shall be mine, says the Lord of hosts,**
> **in that day when I make up my jewels.**

Coventry Cathedral 1976:
Memorial Service for Maurice Edelman
MP for Coventry 1945-75

6. The ending of a Funeral Service is an opportunity for establishing a mood of Christian hope. In the example given below, as the body is carried through the building on its last journey there is music for the organ - music which is intrinsically gentle and consoling; but its message of hope is made quite explicit by the words of the hymn on which the music is a meditation; and the words are printed in the order of service for all to read (just as in the **Middle Voluntary** on page 199).

   The music for organ is followed by a hymn sung by the choir, unaccompanied, as the body is carried through the nave to the west door.

The Ending of a Funeral Service

*As the body is carried through the Quire,
the organ will play this Choral Prelude by J.S. Bach.*

Hark! A voice saith, all are mortal
O Jerusalem, how clearly
Dost thou shine, thou city fair!
Lo! I hear the tones more nearly,
Ever sweetly sounding there!
O what peace and joy hast thou!
Lo! the sun is rising now,
And the breaking day I see
That shall never end for me.

In the Nave the Choir sings:

My soul, there is a country
Far beyond the stars,
Where stands a wingèd sentry
All skilful in the wars:

There above noise, and danger,
Sweet peace sits crowned with smiles,
And one born in a manger
Commands the beauteous files.

He is thy gracious friend,
And – O my soul, awake! –
Did in pure love descend,
To die here for thy sake.

If thou canst get but thither,
There grows the flower of peace,
The Rose that cannot wither,
Thy fortress and thy ease.

Leave then thy foolish ranges,
For none can thee secure
But one, who never changes,
Thy God, thy life, thy cure.

Canterbury Cathedral 1944:
The Funeral of Archbishop William Temple

6. Biddings

The word bidding comes from the Old English verb bidden, to beg, entreat, pray.

Five centuries ago bidding meant praying; and the bidding of prayer meant the praying of prayer, or simply praying. A century later there is a shift in meaning; the bidding of prayer now means the directing or enjoining of prayer. The authorised form of doing this during divine service - the *Ordo precationem hortandi* - was set out in the Constitutions and Canons Ecclesiastical of the Church of England published in 1603 (we give here only an outline):

55. The form of a Prayer to be used by all Preachers before their Sermons

> *Before all Sermons, Lectures, and Homilies, the Preachers and Ministers shall move the people to join with them in prayer in this form:*
>
> *Ye shall pray for Christ's holy Catholic Church ...*
> *and for the King's most excellent Majesty ...*
> *Ye shall also pray for our gracious Queen ...*
> *Ye shall also pray for the Ministers of God's holy Word and Sacraments ...*
> *Ye shall also pray for the whole Commons of this realm ...*
> *Finally, let us praise God for all those which are departed*
> *out of this life in the faith of Christ ...*
> *always concluding with the Lord's Prayer.*

Notice the wording: 'the Preachers and Ministers shall move the people to join with them in prayer in this form'. But this is exhortation to prayer; it is not prayer. It is addressed to men, not to God. There is no prayer, there is no address to God, until the Lord's Prayer at the conclusion. The whole composition is now (mistakenly) called The Bidding Prayer.

A bidding to prayer still means today what it meant in 1603. It is exhortation, not prayer. Lay this rule to heart:

> Distinguish between a bidding and a prayer. A bidding is addressed to men; its purpose is to inform the worshippers what to pray for.
>
> A prayer is addressed to God, who is not in need of information: 'Your heavenly Father knows what you need before you ask him.'

The distinction between a bidding and a prayer is frequently and lamentably not understood, or not made. Let us try to make the distinction clear.

Let us suppose that your concern is for suicides. You can express this concern in a bidding addressed to the congregation:

> Remember in your prayers those who woke this morning in fear, and will lie down tonight in despair; and if they die by their own hand, pray God to forgive them, and to receive them into his kingdom of peace and light.
> ℣ Lord, in your mercy
> ℟ Hear our prayer.

Or you can express your concern in a prayer addressed to God:

> Remember, O God, those who woke this morning in fear, and will lie down tonight in despair; and if they die by their own hand, forgive them, and receive them into your kingdom of peace and light.
> ℣ Lord, in your mercy
> ℟ Hear our prayer.

But now consider this:

> *Remember in your prayers* those who woke this morning in fear, and will lie down tonight in despair; and if they die by their own hand, forgive them, and receive them into your kingdom of peace and light.

What has happened? The speaker begins with a bidding addressed to the congregation; but by the time he reaches the final clause, he has forgotten whom he is talking to; he slips into prayer, addressed to God, without realising it.

This is inexcusably slipshod. The attentive worshipper finds himself adrift on a sea of uncertainty. Is he being instructed by a fellow man? Or is he on his knees, humbly imploring the mercy of the most holy God?

Distinguish between a bidding and a prayer. A bidding is addressed to men; its purpose is to inform the worshippers what to pray for. A prayer is addressed to God, who is not in need of information: 'Your heavenly Father knows what you need before you ask him.'

The Intercession during the Communion at Coventry Cathedral

The Remembrancer (a lay man or lay woman) reads the biddings. He reads them from a typescript carefully prepared beforehand by the Precentor; and he is always rehearsed.

It is not his business to offer prayers: his business is to tell the congregation what to pray for.

After the bidding there is silence, during which the people may pray in their own fashion.

Then the Celebrant sums up the section by reading aloud the printed formula. Every formula is deliberately begun with an address to God, to make clear to everyone that bidding (i.e. information transmitted to the congregation) is over, and has given way to prayer.
The section of prayer read out by the Celebrant is followed by:

℣ Lord, in thy mercy
℟ **Hear our prayer**.

which is only an amplified Amen.

At a simple celebration in a chapel, the Celebrant can himself be the Remembrancer. But he must get clear in his own mind the distinction between the bidding and the following prayer. The people must be left in no doubt when he leaves off informing them, and turns to God in prayer.

During the Prayers of the Church the choir and the Ministers remain seated. The people may sit or kneel at their own discretion.

THE PRAYERS OF THE CHURCH

Standing at the chancel lectern with the two Deacons, the Celebrant (whether a priest, or the Bishop attended by his Chaplains) begins the Prayers.

Let us pray for the whole Church of God, and for all men
according to their needs.

The Remembrancer bids prayer or thanksgiving for the diocese and its Bishop; for the clergy and people; and for the Church at home and overseas.

SILENCE

The Celebrant: Grant, O Lord, that we and all who confess thy Name
may be united in thy truth, live together in thy love,
and show forth thy glory in the world.
Lord, in thy mercy
℟ **Hear our prayer.**

The Remembrancer bids prayer or thanksgiving for the Queen and the Realm; for the nations of the world; and for men in their various callings.

SILENCE

The Celebrant: Defend, O Lord, our Sovereign Lady Queen ELIZABETH; give us wise and upright rulers, incorruptible judges and magistrates, and peace at home and abroad.
Lord, in thy mercy
℟ **Hear our prayer.**

The Remembrancer bids prayer for the poor, for the sick, for the bereaved, and for others in trouble.

SILENCE

The Celebrant: Comfort and succour, O Lord, all those who in this transitory life are in trouble, sorrow, need, sickness, or any other adversity.
Lord, in thy mercy
℟ **Hear our prayer.**

The Remembrancer bids thanksgiving or prayer for the dead.

SILENCE

The Celebrant: Remember, O Lord, those who have died in thy faith and fear: remember also in thy compassion those who die without faith and without hope; and grant us all a share in thy eternal kingdom.
Lord, in thy mercy
℟ **Hear our prayer.**

Grant these our prayers, O merciful Father, for the sake of thy Son, our Saviour Jesus Christ.
℟ **Amen.**

Coventry Cathedral 1973

Here is a twentieth century Bidding Prayer of great beauty. It observes strictly the seventeenth century form; that is to say, it consists of a series of exhortations (addressed to the worshippers) and concludes with the Lord's Prayer (addressed to God).

We are met together to do honor to the Lord, to acknowledge with joy the reign of our Savior Christ, and to pray for the gifts of the Holy Spirit to be dispersed among us, that we may in spirit sing these praises, make these offerings, and receive the blessings of God.

In your prayers give gratitude to God for this company of singers and players; for this Guild, founded to promote God's praise; for all the friendships it has fostered, all the learning it has nourished, and all the visions it has opened to us.

Repent before God for the moments of failure, the missed opportunities and the false ambitions; and remember in his presence, that to him for whom a thousand years are as yesterday, no sin or failure of which his children truly repent is ever beyond recovery, and no mistaken journey ever beyond his power to recall.

Remember before God all those who having made music on this earth, now join in the praises of heaven: all composers, performers, and faithful worshippers who have assisted us to perfect the praise of God in his Church on earth; those who have been known all over the world, and those who have no memorial but the comfort they have brought to the people of God in their own place.

Remember with compassion all those in whose lives there is no praise; those upon whom the pressures of life, the unkindness of their fellows, or their own sin have borne heavily; those who at this time are turned away from joy by the oppression of anxiety or pain, and commend them all to the loving heart of the Father.

And finally, whatever things are honorable, excellent and worthy of celebration; whatever things are lovely and gracious and of good report - think on these, and thank God who is the creator of them all.

Praise the Lord. With all your talents and your love, praise him. In the company of angels and archangels and all the choir of heaven, praise him. Let us gather up our prayers and praises in the words which our Lord himself taught us:

Our Father

Composed by the Reverend Dr Erik Routley
(and reproduced with his permission)
for the National Biennial Convention
of The American Guild of Organists
held at Seattle, Washington, 1978

7. Collects and Prayers

The Collect

A 'regular' collect consists of five parts: (1) the address to God; expanded (2) by a relative clause indicating the special grounds on which we approach him; (3) the petition; (4) the purpose of our petition; (5) the ending; thus: (1) O God, (2) who hast prepared for them that love thee such good things as pass man's understanding: (3) Pour into our hearts such love toward thee, (4) that we, loving thee above all things, may obtain thy promises, which exceed all that we can desire; (5) through Jesus Christ our Lord.

This 'regular' form is capable of infinite variation, by the reduplication or omission of parts 2, 3 and 4, as may be seen at once by reference to the collects in the Prayer Book.

The collect, for all its complexity, is a single sentence without a full stop in it. In saying it, however, full weight must be given to its lesser stops.

The Prayer

The Prayer on the other hand is a series of parallel sentences, whether they be petitions or confessions or thanksgivings or all in turn; e.g. (in the Book of Common Prayer) the General Confession, the General Thanksgiving, the Prayer for all Sorts and Conditions of Men, and the Lord's Prayer itself.

Prayers are often too verbose. In a service of occasion, attended personally by many who are infrequently at church and who are not accustomed to formal prayer of any kind, a good prayer will make one point only. In a large and resonant building, a windy or garrulous prayer will defeat the attention of the worshipper: he cannot make his own any prayer whose outline is not clear-cut or whose meaning is not lucid. Every word, every phrase of the prayer must work: not a word must be idle. Consider this prayer. It has two sentences, and 84 words (without the conclusion).

> O merciful Father, who hast wonderfully fashioned man in thine image, and made his body to be a temple of the Holy Ghost: Sanctify, we pray thee, all those whom thou hast called to study and practise the arts of healing the sick, and the prevention of disease and pain. Strengthen them in body and soul, and bless their work, that they may themselves live as members and servants of Christ, and give comfort to those whom he lived and died to save; through...

The prayer will gain a sharper impact if it is reduced in length by one third (from 84 words to 55) and compressed into a single sentence so that it becomes a 'regular' collect, like this:

> O merciful Father, who hast fashioned man in thine image, and hast made his body a temple of thy Holy Spirit: Bless all who are engaged in the science and art of healing; that in the service of Jesus Christ they may learn to comfort and restore those whom he lived and died to save; through the same...

You and Thou in the Collect

If you propose to write a new collect in today's English, or if you transpose an old collect into modern terms,

BE WARNED!

Recall the remarks of the novelist Richard Hughes quoted in the opening chapter: The real difficulty of the Prayer Book language is not its sometimes antiquated vocabulary but its syntax, its structural frame of thinking (page 4). The Book of Common Prayer uses a syntax entirely alien to modern English speech. The Prayer Book was thought in Latin, and has been only half-translated into the English language. 'Half- translated', because the Latin syntax, the Latin sentence-structure, has been so often retained.

For an illustration of Hughes' argument, here is a secular collect, written (as near as makes no matter) in Prayer Book style:

> O John, who art the quickest runner in the class: Go thou, I beseech thee, to the house of the Headmaster, and say unto him that, our lesson being yet unfinished, we shall therefore come late to the school dinner.

In that parody of a collect there are three English archaisms and three latinisms.

English archaisms

'O John' ~ the interjection 'O' or 'Oh' is current in colloquial use to express pleasure, 'O John, what a lovely surprise!'; contempt, 'O you silly fool'; distress, 'O what a dreary winter we're having!'; affirmation, 'O yes, you did!'; denial, 'O no, she didn't!' But 'O' is no longer used in formal address to another person.

'Go thou' ~ the combination of imperative verb and personal pronoun was current in 1611, 'Follow thou me' (John 22.22), 'Go ye therefore' (Matthew 28.19). It was current in 1662, 'Drink ye all of this'. Modern English employs the verb alone, unless for special emphasis, 'Drink this, all of you'; or colloquially, 'Mark you', 'Mind you'.

'Say unto him' ~ 'unto' is now obsolete; current use requires 'to'.

Latinisms

'who art' ~ a relative clause, where today's English would use a main clause.
'our lesson being yet unfinished' ~ a dependent participial clause, where today's English would use a main clause.

'therefore' ~ a conjunction, redundant in today's English, which leaves unspoken the obvious relationship between 'our lesson being unfinished' and 'our being late' in consequence.

Remove the English archaisms and the latinisms and you have today's English:

> John, you're the quickest runner in the class,
> please go to the Headmaster and tell him our lesson isn't finished,
> we'll be late for dinner.

Translating Prayer Book Collects into today's English

Occasional Prayers 17. For Sunday Schools (1928)

> Almighty God, our heavenly Father, who hast committed to thy holy Church the care and nurture of thy children: Enlighten with thy wisdom those who teach and those who learn; that, rejoicing in the knowledge of thy truth, they may worship thee and serve thee all the days of their life.

With my own eyes and horrified incredulity, I have seen, in a serious and responsible publication, the following translation of the address in that collect:

> Almighty God, our heavenly Father, who has committed to your holy Church the care and nurture of your children

What is wrong? This: 'Almighty God, our heavenly Father' is in the vocative case, the case of address, for the speaker is addressing one person; and the verb must agree in person and number, it must be in the second person singular.

But 'has' is the third person singular. Could you, in conversation with your neighbour, say to him, 'Bill, you has left your gate open'? Would you not say, 'Bill, you have left your gate open'?

No: the collect must begin:

> Almighty God, our heavenly Father, who have committed

That is grammatically correct, but it is not idiomatic English. Try putting in the antecedent pronoun:

> Almighty God, our heavenly Father, you who have committed

That is better, but it is still clumsy. The remedy is simple: omit the relative pronoun 'who' and so turn the dependent clause into a main clause:

> Almighty God, our heavenly Father, you have committed to your holy Church the care and nurture of your children

That is easy, idiomatic English, today's English.

So much for the address; the petition follows – another main clause, without any conjunction to link it with the preceding clause:

> Enlighten with your wisdom both teachers and learners

and the reason for the petition; turn the dependent participial clause 'rejoicing in the knowledge of thy truth' into a main clause 'they may rejoice', followed by yet another main clause. The whole collect, then will run easily in twentieth century style:

> Almighty God, our heavenly Father, you have committed to your holy Church the care and nurture of your children: Enlighten with your wisdom both teachers and learners, so that they may rejoice in the knowledge of your truth, and may worship you and serve you all their life long.

The Collect of Epiphany II (1662)

> Almighty and everlasting God, who dost govern all things in heaven and earth: Mercifully hear the supplications of thy people, and grant us thy peace all the days of our life.

I have seen with my own eyes and with horrified incredulity, in a serious and responsible publication, a proposal to translate the address thus:

> Almighty and everlasting God,
> who governs all things in heaven and earth

What is wrong? This: 'Almighty and everlasting God' is in the vocative case, the case of address, for the speaker is addressing one person; and the verb must agree in person and number; it must be in the second person singular.

But 'governs' is the third person singular. Would you, in conversation with the President, say to him, 'You governs better than the last man'? Would you not say, 'You govern better than the last man'?

No: let us use today's English:

> Almighty and everlasting God, you govern everything in heaven and earth: Mercifully hear the supplications of your people, and grant us your peace as long as we live.

The Collect of Easter III (1662)

> Almighty God, who shewest to them that be in error the light of thy truth, to the intent that they may return into the way of righteousness: Grant unto all them that are admitted into the fellowship of Christ's Religion, that they may eschew those things that are contrary to their profession, and follow all such things as are agreeable to the same.

Error is the action of one who errs, who strays from the path and gets lost: 'We have erred and strayed from thy ways like lost sheep.' This is a rural metaphor: no townsman can feel on his pulses the force of it.

And if you have strayed from the path, what you need is the light of divine truth to show you the way back onto the road of righteousness. What a searching, lovely prayer this is! To translate it into today's English is not easy; but a modern version might run something like this:

> Almighty God, when we lose our way, your truth is the torch to light us back to the road of righteousness: Enable all those who are admitted into the fellowship of the Christian faith to eschew whatever contradicts their profession, and to follow whatever agrees with it.

In any case, the phrase 'them that' is inadmissible in today's English: it must always be translated 'those who'.

The Collect of St John the Evangelist's Day (1662)

> Merciful Lord, we beseech thee to cast thy bright beams of light upon thy Church, that it being enlightened by the doctrine of thy blessed Apostle and Evangelist St John may so walk in the light of thy truth, that it may at length attain unto the light of everlasting life.

The phrase 'it being enlightened' is a hanging participle; this is a Latin construction, not English. Replace this participial phrase by a main verb, thus:

> Merciful Lord, we beseech you to cast your bright beams of light upon your Church, that it may be enlightened by the doctrine of your blessed Apostle and Evangelist Saint John, and may so walk, etc.

Better still (because more idiomatic in English) change the passive voice 'be enlightened' into the active voice and the imperative mood 'enlighten'; you will then have a collect in easy modern English, like this:

> Merciful Lord, we beseech you to cast your bright beams of light upon your Church: Enlighten it by the doctrine of your blessed Apostle and Evangelist Saint John, so that it may walk in the light of your truth, and may at length attain to the light of everlasting life.

Punctuation in a Collect

A collect (we said at the beginning of this chapter) is a single sentence without a full stop in it.

This is an inflexible rule; if you break the rule, you are not writing a collect.

Refer back to our modern version of the Collect of Epiphany II:

> Almighty God, you govern everything in heaven and earth: Mercifully hear the supplications of your people, and grant us your peace as long as we live.

We dispensed with the original relative clause (a Latin usage) 'who dost govern', in favour of a main verb 'you govern' (the English way); and then came a second main verb in the imperative mood, 'Mercifully hear'. The sense, of course, is: Because you govern everything, therefore you can give us peace, and that is what we ask you to do. To make it clear that the second verb 'hear' is related to the first verb 'you govern', as effect is related to cause, the two parts of the prayer are divided not by a full stop but by a colon. The collect remains, as it should do, a single sentence.

Be assured that this is not pedantry: it is a matter of respect for the real nature of the collect. Bishop W.H. Frere, in the Truro Diocesan Gazette of May 1931, put the point forcefully:

> *A Collect proper, like an epigram, is content to say one thing shortly and sharply, and have done with it. A committee cannot make epigrams. They are essentially the reflections of an individual mind on the situation.*

There are (need I say?) other forms of prayer, what in French is called oraison and what in English used to be called orison, forms which are legitimate, useful, and beautiful, as for example the General Thanksgiving in the Book of Common Prayer. Such prayers are lengthy, exuberant, oratorical; and if they are badly composed, they are garrulous and diffuse.

But a collect is none of these things: it is on the contrary brief, terse, and epigrammatical.

You may write a prayer consisting of two sentences, or three, or more, and it may be a good prayer of its kind; but do not deceive yourself into thinking that you have written a collect.

The Close of the Collect

The officiant reaches the end of the collect, and the people reply with one word, Amen. There are times when this reply, because it is so brief, lacks conviction. You can secure a more hearty co-operation by the people if a rubric directs them to say together the whole of the closing doxology, like this:

Almighty God,
we beseech you graciously to behold this your family,
for which our Lord Jesus Christ
was contented to be betrayed,
and given up into the hands of wicked men,
and to suffer death upon the Cross;

Everyone **who now lives and reigns**
with you and the Holy Spirit,
one God, world without end. Amen.

If you are using several collects in sequence, the enthusiasm generated by the people's saying the ending together will be cumulative.

You are invited to look up the examples in **Dance for the Feast of the Epiphany** (page 115).

Themes in the Prayer Book Collects

When you are hard put to it to compose or discover a new prayer on a particular theme, try making use of a collect from the Prayer Book, preceded by a bidding carefully phrased so as to focus or refresh the attention. A wide range of themes can be compassed by the Prayer Book collects used in this way.

The following tables may be consulted: they are based on The Collects in our Prayers by John Northridge (SPCK).

The Collects in the Book of Common Prayer: Index of Themes

Bible, The	1	Love	14
Christlikeness	2	New Life for Old	15
Church, The	3	Peace	16
Daily Life	4	Pilgrimage	17
Discipleship	5	Prayer	18
Divine Action	6	Programme	19
Endurance	7	Recreation	20
Faith	8	Redemption	21
Forgiveness	9	Sex	22
Games	10	Spiritual Maturity	23
Guidance	11	Thoughts	24
Habits	12	Unity	25
Life Eternal	13	World, The	26

Themes of Prayer in the BCP Collects

1 Bible, The

that it may be made ours	Advent 2
on heeding the voice of God	St Andrew
on listening to the Lessons	Collect 3 after The Communion
the pulpit and the pew	St Peter, St Bartholomew

2 Christlikeness

for purity of motives and methods	Epiphany 6
for humility and patience	Palm Sunday
for grace to accept the standards of Christ, and to live by them	Easter 2

3 Church, The

for all who preach, teach and write	Advent 3
for every member	Good Friday
that the Church may practise what it preaches	Easter 3
for the opportunity of service in a world at peace	Trinity 5
for continual reformation	Trinity 16

4 Daily Life

for a right sense of values	Trinity 4
against waste of time	Trinity 13
for the best use of talents	St Barnabas
for the unseen aid of spiritual forces	St Michael

5 Discipleship

for faith in persecution	St Stephen
that the birth and death of Christ may beget faith in his resurrection	The Annunciation
that we may understand the truth and have grace to follow it	Whitsunday
for obedience	Trinity 1, Trinity 18

6 Divine Action

that God may work through us	Easter Day
that grace may precede and follow us	Trinity 17

7 Endurance

for God's assistance in the rough and tumble of life	Epiphany 3, Epiphany 4, Lent 3
for steadfastness	Easter 3

8 Faith

that our honest doubts may be resolved	St Thomas
that the unseen God is with us	Epiphany

9 Forgiveness

contrition, penitence, forgiveness	Ash Wednesday
exchanging a guilty conscience for peace and joy	Trinity 12

10 Games

see Recreation

11 Guidance

that through prayer we may plan wisely and act effectively	Epiphany 1
for a right judgement	Whitsunday
for wisdom and obedience	Trinity 9, Trinity 19
dependence on God	Collect 5 after The Communion

12 Habits

to be set free from bad habits	Trinity 24
to establish good habits	Easter Day

13 Life Eternal

the vision of God	Advent 1 Advent 2 St John the Evangelist Epiphany Palm Sunday Easter Eve Sunday after Ascension Day Trinity 4 Trinity 13 All Saints

14 Love

for generosity	Quinquagesima
for prayers to keep steadfastly the royal law	Trinity 1
that we may love to obey	Trinity 14
for the joyful secret of the saints	All Saints

15 New Life for Old

for daily renewal	Christmas Day
for grace	Easter Day, Trinity 17, Trinity 18

16 Peace

peace every day	Epiphany 2
peace of mind	Trinity 21

17 Pilgrimage

in the path of duty	Advent 4
through dangers and temptations	Epiphany 4
a fixed resolve	Easter 4
the goal	Trinity 4, Trinity 11, Trinity 13

18 Prayer

that prayer may fortify	Trinity 3
that we may not ask amiss	Trinity 10
that we may pray in faith	Trinity 23

19 Programme

concern for work planned	Collect 4 after The Communion

20 Recreation

to avoid self-indulgence	Collect 2 after The Communion

21 Redemption

Sons of God	Epiphany 6
partakers of the resurrection	Palm Sunday
grace to receive redemption and to follow the Redeemer	Easter 2

22 Sex

for the pure use of our natural instincts	Lent 2 Collect 2 after The Communion

23 Spiritual Maturity

for growth	Trinity 7
against marking time	Trinity 11

24 Thoughts

thinking and doing	Easter 5
a pure intention	Collect at the beginning of The Communion

25 Unity

the bond of brotherly care	Quinquagesima

26 World, The

for the whole family of mankind	Good Friday, Collect 1

The Lord's Prayer in the BCP Collects

Our Father	Easter 1 Trinity 4 Trinity 8
Thy kingdom come	Advent 1 Epiphany 6
Thy will be done	Trinity 9 Trinity 13 Trinity 19
Our daily bread bodily needs	 Lent 2 Lent 5
abstinences	Lent 1
Forgiveness	Ash Wednesday Trinity 12 Trinity 21 Trinity 24
Temptation	Epiphany 4 Trinity 18
Deliverance	Advent 4 Trinity 1 Trinity 8 Trinity 24

The Creed in the BCP Collects

I believe in –

GOD

The Father	Easter 1 Trinity 4 Trinity 8
The Son	Advent 1 Christmas Day Palm Sunday Good Friday Easter Eve Easter Day Ascension Day Sunday after Ascension Day
The Holy Spirit	Christmas Day Lent 1 Sunday after Ascension Day Whitsunday Trinity 19

THE CHURCH

The Bible	Advent 2 St Bartholomew
The Ministry	Advent 3 Good Friday Collect 2 St Matthias St Peter
The Sacrament of Baptism	Easter Eve
State of Health of the Church	Epiphany 3 Lent 5 Trinity 15 Trinity 16 Trinity 22 Trinity 23
Unity	St Simon & St Jude

THE FORGIVENESS OF SINS	Ash Wednesday Trinity 12 Trinity 21 Trinity 24
THE LIFE EVERLASTING	Advent 1 Epiphany Epiphany 6 Easter Eve Trinity 4 Trinity 13 All Saints

8. Commissioning

The Admission to an office is the public recognition of a status of dignity conferred upon the candidate; whereas his Commissioning gives him authority to undertake a specific task or course of action. The four elements in both, however, are the same. The elements are described in **Admission to Office** (page 86), which the reader is invited to consult.

Here is an example of a Commissioning.

The Cathedral community is to send a working party of men and women to Dresden to undertake a task of friendship and reconciliation with a former enemy. Some kind of ceremony is called for, when the party can be given authority to act and the good wishes of the community can be expressed.

The ceremony takes place in the course of the Communion on Sunday morning, when the community meets to re-affirm its vocation as the people of God. The members of the party are to be publicly presented to the head of the community; he will examine them, and then give them authority.

First, then, the presentation of the party to the Provost by the Youth Officer. In his address to the Provost the Youth Officer

1. makes two statements about those whom he is presenting;
2. defines the meaning of the phrase 'our representatives';
3. makes two requests to the Provost.

The party has been presented to the Provost; now the Provost presents the party to the congregation; he calls them to the platform, so to speak, in order that they may identify themselves by sight and sound.

The scrutiny follows; then the Commissioning in the name of the Trinity. The usual formula 'In the name of the father, and of the Son, and of the Holy Spirit' is expanded; each Person of the Trinity is characterised by a phrase based on Scripture. The Commissioning is followed by a blessing in trinitarian form; and then by silence.

Finally the good wishes of the community are expressed in shouted exclamations, and in a well-known prayer with a change of the pronoun 'my' to 'your'.

Commissioning

After the Creed the Provost asks the people to sit down. He gives out notices. Then he proceeds to the Commissioning. He says:

I am ready to commission the party. Let them come forward.

The members of the party come forward and stand in a semi- circle below the chancel step. The Cathedral Youth Officer advances, and presents them to the Provost:

Provost, these are our representatives who are to go to Germany to rebuild the Church Hospital in Dresden. In the name of all of us who are here today, and in the name of many well-wishers in this country and overseas, I ask you to commission them for their work, and to give them your blessing.

The Provost addresses the party:

We shall remember each of you by name in our prayers. Come to the microphone and tell us who you are, and what you do.

The members of the party, led by the Cathedral Youth Officer, move in single file to the chancel lectern, where one after another they announce their names and avocations; and then return to their places below the chancel step.

The Provost addresses them again:

Provost: Do you believe that peace among men and nations is the fruit of humility and of penitence?

Answer: We do.

Provost: Do you believe that loving and humble service to our enemies has power to heal the hurts and the sorrows of war?

Answer: We do.

Provost: Do you believe yourselves called to such a ministry of reconciliation in Dresden?

Answer: We do.

Provost: Will you so discipline yourselves there as to meet every circumstance with love and patience and good humour?

Answer: We will.

Provost: Will you remember that the reputation of Christ and his Church is in your hands?

Answer: We will.

Provost: Then I will commission you for your task.

They kneel down. The Provost extends his right arm over them, and says:

IN THE NAME OF GOD, WHO HAS CREATED ALL MEN
FOR FRIENDSHIP WITH HIMSELF;
IN THE NAME OF JESUS CHRIST, WHO BADE US
LOVE OUR ENEMIES;
IN THE NAME OF OUR LORD THE SPIRIT,
WHO RESCUES AND RESTORES US;
WE SEND YOU TO DRESDEN.

RECEIVE OUR COMMISSION
TO SERVE CHRIST THERE IN YOUR FELLOW MEN.

The Provost makes the sign of the Cross over them, and blesses them:

God keep you in his care; Christ win you and save you;
The Holy Spirit guide you in the ways of truth and love always.
Amen.

There is silence. After a while the Provost says:

Stand up, and receive our good wishes.

They stand, and the whole company stands with them. The choir turns toward them.

Raising his voice, the Provost says:

The Lord prosper you.
We wish you luck in the name of the Lord.

Psalm 129.8

The choir shouts:

Good luck in the name of the Lord.

The people shout:

Good luck in the name of the Lord.

Choir and people:

God be in your head,
and in your understanding;
God be in your eyes,
and in your looking;
God be in your mouth,
and in your speaking;
God be in your heart,
and in your thinking;
God be at your end,
and at your departing.

Sarum Primer, 1558

The party retires, and the Provost asks all except the children to sit down. He says a prayer for the children, who withdraw; and the service proceeds.

Coventry Cathedral:
The Commissioning of the Dresden Working Party 1965

9. Confession

In composing a form of confession for a service of occasion, bear in mind the following points.

1. No sins must be confessed which those confessing could not possibly have committed. The confession of other people's sins is strictly meaningless.
2. In our secular age the sense of sin is dim; and if your congregation consists of many who are not often at church they will have only a hazy notion of what sin is, as the Church understands it. It is therefore prudent to remind them, by an apt choice of word and phrase, of the divine law, and of our disobedience. Be as specific as you can.
3. One way to be specific is to use a litany of penitence. The Minister specifies the sins to be confessed, one by one, and the people ask forgiveness of each sin in the refrain which recurs throughout the litany. This is the method used in the first example below.

   A variant of this appears in the second example. Here the Minister begins the definition of a sin, and the people in their response complete the definition; and the request for forgiveness is deferred till the succeeding collect.
4. In either case, the pacing of the act of penitence is vitally important; and this rests entirely with the Minister. After each response by the people he must pause for some moments of silence to allow them time for unhurried reflection, time (if need be) to accuse themselves. This is the more necessary if the congregation is unfamiliar with the ways of public worship, and unused to the examination of conscience.
5. For such people the exhortation 'Let us confess our sins' is too brief and too abrupt. In an irreligious mind the unspoken riposte will be 'Why should we?' To introduce the confession, something more kindly and more persuasive from the Minister is called for; perhaps something on the lines of the examples below.
6. A confession is always an appeal to God's mercy for his absolution.

Deny it as they may, there is lodged in men's hearts the conviction that they ought to be virtuous, but are not virtuous: and the conflict set up by this moral failure is something which they cannot resolve for themselves.

Shakespeare's tragedy Macbeth illustrates the situation in unforgettably vivid terms. Lady Macbeth, after procuring the murder of Duncan, appears on the stage at night walking in her sleep, and rubbing her hands. 'It is an accustomed action with her', says her waiting-woman, 'to seem thus washing her hands: I have known her continue in this a quarter of an hour.' And Lady Macbeth: 'What, will these hands ne'er be clean? Here's the smell of the blood still: all the perfumes of Arabia will not sweeten this little hand. Oh! Oh! Oh!'

That is true. Lady Macbeth needs forgiveness: and she cannot forgive herself. Lady Macbeth is every one of us that ever was born or ever will be born. We need forgiveness: and we cannot forgive ourselves. The mischief is done; we have done it, one way or another; and we cannot atone for it.

That is why the formal confession of sin in public worship must always be followed by the formal declaration of the divine mercy and absolution.

A confession at a service for Girl Guides. The moral law is recalled in phrases from the Catechism in the Book of Common Prayer.

~~~~~~

Confession

The Precentor: What is your duty towards God?

The Guides, *without hurry:*

My duty towards God
Is to believe in him, to fear him, and to love him,
With all my heart, with all my mind,
With all my soul, and with all my strength;
To worship him, to give him thanks,
To put my whole trust in him, to call upon him,
To honour his holy name and his Word,
And to serve him truly all the days of my life.

The Precentor: What is your duty towards your neighbour?

The Guides, *without hurry:*

My duty towards my neighbour
Is to love him as myself, And to do to all men
As I wish they should do to me:
To hurt nobody by word nor deed:
To be true and just in all my dealing:
To bear no malice nor hatred in my heart:
To keep my hands from picking and stealing,
And my tongue from evil-speaking, lying, and slandering:
To keep my body in temperance, soberness, and chastity:
Not to covet nor desire other men's goods.

A brief silence
~~~~~~

The Precentor: Now we have reminded ourselves of our duty towards God, and of our duty towards our neighbour.

But how often we fail in our duty! And since never a day passes but we disobey God, one way or another, we must make our humble confession to him.

A brief silence

℣ Because we forget you,
℟ **Lord, forgive us.**
℣ Because we do not thank you,
℟ **Lord, forgive us.**
℣ Because we do not trust you,
℟ **Lord, forgive us.**

A brief silence

℣ Our unkindness to each other,
℟ **O Lord, forgive.**
℣ Our selfishness and self-will,
℟ **O Lord, forgive.**
℣ Our disloyalties,
℟ **O Lord, forgive.**
℣ Our dishonesties,
℟ **O Lord, forgive.**
℣ Our broken promises,
℟ **O Lord, forgive.**
℣ Our secret sins,
℟ **O Lord, forgive.**

A brief silence.
Then the Precentor continues:

Let us all say together this prayer:

O Lord God,
Forgive what we have been,
Sanctify what we are,
Direct what we shall be;
For Jesus Christ's sake. Amen.

The Bishop pronounces this Absolution:

THE Almighty and merciful Lord grant you pardon and remission of all your sins, time to do better, and the grace and comfort of his Holy Spirit.

℟ **Amen.**

Coventry Cathedral: For Queen's Guides 1975

~~~~~~

A confession at a service on a naval occasion. The full text of the service is given in **Trafalgar Day** (page 317).

~~~~~~

Confession

The Provost addresses the people:

God, who made the world, made us also, and set us here to serve him and obey him. In our heart of hearts we know that our service is fitful, and our obedience is imperfect.

Here in God's presence let us in silence recall our shortcomings, and our need of his forgiveness.

There is silence. Then the Provost says and the people reply:

℣ We know and confess, O God;
℟ **That our hearts are unworthy to receive thee.**
℣ Day by day we have enjoyed thy gifts;
℟ **But have forgotten that thou wast the giver of them.**
℣ Thou hast shown us what thou wouldst have us do;
℟ **But we have not followed thy way.**
℣ Thou hast spoken to us in thy Word;
℟ **But we have not listened.**

Silence is kept. Then all say together:

Grant, we beseech thee, merciful Lord, to thy faithful people pardon and peace,

that we may be cleansed from all our sins, and serve thee with a quiet mind: through Jesus Christ our Lord. Amen.

The Bishop: May the Almighty and merciful Lord grant you pardon and remission of all your sins, time for amendment of life, and the grace and comfort of the Holy Spirit.

℟ **Amen.**

HYMN

Father of heaven, whose love profound
A ransom for our souls hath found,
Before thy throne we sinners bend,
To us thy pardoning love extend.

Almighty Son, incarnate Word,
Our Prophet, Priest, Redeemer, Lord,
Before thy throne we sinners bend,
To us thy saving grace extend.

Eternal Spirit, by whose breath
The soul is raised from sin and death,
Before thy throne we sinners bend,
To us thy quickening power extend.

Thrice Holy! Father, Spirit, Son;
Mysterious Godhead, Three in One,
Before thy throne we sinners bend,
Grace, pardon, life to us extend.

RIVAULX AMR 164

10. Dance

Both in Great Britain and in the United States of America the members of Anglican congregations themselves are learning to use dance in the course of public worship: but I write here only about dance presented before the worshippers, or among them, by professional dancers or by trained amateurs.

Dance at the Divine Office

If you have a competent choir, the dancers may dance Magnificat and Nunc Dimittis at Evensong. The seraphic setting of these canticles in G major by C.V. Stanford has proved an ideal accompaniment to the dance.

Dance at the Eucharist

The Offertory procession can be danced. Let the dancers precede the Bread and the Wine as these gifts are carried from the west end of the nave or chancel to the altar. But the dance is a beauty in its own right: better therefore let the hymn be ended (if a hymn is sung here) before the dance begins, so that the people may enjoy watching the movement of the dancers. The dance may be accompanied by the organ, or by a piano; or (if you are lucky) by two harpsichords playing the Concerto in G major by Antonio Soler.

Morris dancing may find a place at the Eucharist. The dancers, wearing their traditional dress with little bells tinkling at their ankles, will be accompanied by drum and fife, or by a fiddle, or by an accordion. They will bring a sense of open air happiness into worship; and when the Eucharist is over, they can dance again outside. This is the way to celebrate a Great Festival, or a special occasion in the life of the parish.

~~~~~~

Dance at a Service of the Arts

by students of the Royal Ballet School directed by Ninette de Valois

King David expresses his homage to God by dancing in God's presence.

A voice:

> David went and brought up the ark of God from the house of Obed-edom into the city of David with gladness. And it was so, that when they that bore the ark of the Lord had gone six paces, he sacrificed oxen and fatlings. And David danced before the Lord with all his might. So David and all the house of Israel brought up the ark of the Lord with shouting, and with the sound of the trumpet.
~~~~~~

And as the ark of the Lord came into the city of David, Michal, Saul's daughter, looked through a window, and saw King David leaping and dancing before the Lord; and she despised him in her heart.

Then David returned to bless his household. And Michal, the daughter of Saul, came out to meet David, and said, How glorious was the king of Israel today, who uncovered himself today in the eyes of the handmaids of his servants, as one of the vain fellows shamelessly uncovereth himself! And David said unto Michal, It was before the Lord, which chose me before thy father, and before all his house, to appoint me ruler over the people of the Lord; therefore will I play before the Lord.

2 Samuel 6. 12, 16, 20, 21

DANCE OF THE MUSES

The Muses, the nine sisters who typify the arts,
dance a ballet in homage to God,
with whose praise the whole creation resounds.

A ballet is danced. The dancers retire.

Then a voice says:

I beheld, and I heard the voice of many angels round about the throne and the beasts and the elders: and the number of them was ten thousand times ten thousand, and thousands of thousands; saying with a loud voice, Worthy is the Lamb that was slain to receive power, and riches, and wisdom, and strength, and honour, and glory, and blessing. And every creature which is in heaven, and on the earth, and under the earth, and such as are in the sea, and all that are in them, heard I saying, Blessing, and honour, and glory, and power, be unto him that sitteth upon the throne, and unto the Lamb for ever and ever.

Revelation 5. 11-13

Coventry Cathedral: A Service of the Arts 1962

Dance for the Feast of the Epiphany

by professionally trained amateurs of several Anglican parishes

The Devotion of the Wise Men

The three strange gifts of the Wise Men are presented as dances.

Gold

ANTIPHON

by the choir

All they from Saba shall come, bringing gold and incense,
and shall show forth the praises of the Lord.
℣ Arise, and shine, O Jerusalem:
for the glory of the Lord is risen upon thee. Alleluia.
℣ We have seen his star in the east,
and are come with offerings to worship the Lord. Alleluia.

Gradual and Alleluia of the Mass of the Epiphany

The Dance of the Golden Crown

Music for organ:

For the Royal Fireworks

G.F. Handel 1685-1759

Incense

ANTIPHON

repeated at a higher pitch

The Dance of the Incense Offering

Anthem by the choir

LO! star-led chiefs Assyrian odours bring,
And bending Magi seek their infant King.
Marked ye, where, hovering o'er his radiant head,
The Dove's white wings celestial glory shed?

William Crotch 1775-1847

Myrrh

ANTIPHON

repeated at a higher pitch

The Dance of the Sacrificial Death

Music played by the dancers

Everyone stands.

The Prayer and Praise of God's People

PRAYERS

These three Prayers are offered by the dancers.

The King	O Christ the King of kings
You were invested with your royal dignity
by bitter humbling and a crown of thorns;
Teach us how to be faithful
in the fellowship of your sufferings,
that we may follow on to your glory:

Everyone	**who live and reign**
with the Father and the Spirit,
one God, now and for ever. Amen.

The Incarnate God
O Christ, Son of the living God,
through you the invisible and most high
became visible to mortal men:
Grant that by the grace and power of your immortal Spirit
we may live on earth
as those whose true house is in heaven;

Everyone	**where you live and reign**
with the Father and the same Spirit,
one God, now and for ever. Amen.

The Victim	Almighty God,
we beseech you graciously to behold this your family,
for which our Lord Jesus Christ was contented to be betrayed,
and given up into the hands of wicked men,
and to suffer death upon the cross;

Everyone **who now lives and reigns with you and the Holy Spirit, one God, now and for ever. Amen.**

Choir and people sit down.

A DANCE OF PRAYER

Silence

THE ACCLAMATION

ORGAN FANFARE. Everyone stands

The Precentor and the whole company shout aloud:

℣ Yours, O Lord, is the greatness, the power, the glory,
the splendour, and the majesty;
℟ **for everything in heaven and on earth is yours.**
℣ Yours, O Lord, is the sovereignty;
℟ **and you are exalted as head over all.**
℣ Wealth and honour come from you;
℟ **might and power are at your disposal.**
℣ We give you thanks, O God;
℟ **And praise your glorious name.**

Almighty God,
your Son has opened for us
a new and living way into your presence:
Give us pure hearts and steadfast wills
to worship you in spirit and in truth;

Everyone **through the same Jesus Christ our Lord. Amen.**

Silence

The Precentor with the other Ministers turns towards the altar.

He slowly raises his hands in a gesture of adoration.
The dancers, Ministers, and people do the same.
Then all except the dancers sit down.

A DANCE OF PRAISE

Music for organ: Scherzo

Alan Ridout

THE OFFERING

Music for organ: Basse et dessus de trompette

L.N. Clérambault 1676-1749

The Precentor is conducted to the altar.
The offerings of the people are collected, and are carried
by two servers to the altar, to be presented there.

Coventry Cathedral: Party at Bethlehem 1975

~~~~~~

Dance at a Marriage

by students of Pattison's Dance Academy in Coventry

The use of dance on this occasion was inspired by Edmund Spenser's poem Epithalamium written in honour of his marriage to Elizabeth Boyle in 1594. Some lines of the poem were printed in the order of service at the appropriate places. The dancers danced three times: at the entrance of the bride, at the Offertory in the Eucharist, and at the departure of the bride and bridegroom.

The First Dance: at the entrance of the bride

At 12.00 the bride arrives at the west door.

A FANFARE is played, and everyone stands, and turns towards the bride to welcome her.

The three ministers go to the chancel step.

The dancers dance before the bride as she is conducted through the nave to the chancel step, where the bridegroom joins her.

But most of all the damzels do delite,
When they their timbrels smite,
And thereunto do dance and carol sweet,
That all the senses they do ravish quite.
~~~~~~

The Second Dance: at the Offertory

The Offertory follows immediately.

The Celebrant, standing at the Lord's Table, begins the Offertory, saying this sentence:

I will offer in his dwelling an oblation with great gladness:
I will sing and speak praises unto the Lord.

The Deacons go down to the gate of the sanctuary.
The bride and bridegroom go to the chancel step to receive the Bread and Wine for the Communion.
They return through the chancel to offer the Bread and Wine to the Deacons, who carry the Elements to the Celebrant at the Holy Table.
The clerks bring water to the Celebrant to wash his hands.

Meanwhile choir and people sing this Hymn.

HYMN
Tallis AMR 231

O Holy Spirit, Lord of grace,
Eternal fount of love,
Inflame, we pray, our inmost hearts
With fire from heaven above.

As thou in bond of love dost join
The Father and the Son,
So fill us all with mutual love,
And knit our hearts in one.

All glory to the Father be,
All glory to the Son,
All glory, Holy Ghost, to thee,
While endless ages run.

At the end of the Hymn everyone sits down.

The dancers dance again.

When the dance ends, the choir and people stand, and the Celebrant sings:

Priest The Lord be with you:
Answer **The Lord bless you**.
Priest Lift up your hearts.
Answer **We lift them up unto the Lord.**

The Third Dance:
at the departure of the bride and bridegroom

Choir

Ye saints who toil below,
Adore your heavenly King.
And onward as ye go
Some joyful anthem sing;
Take what he gives
And praise him still,
Through good and ill,
Who ever lives.

Everyone

My soul, bear thou thy part,
Triumph in God above,
And with a well-tuned heart
Sing thou the songs of love.
Let all thy days
Till life shall end,
Whate'er he send,
Be filled with praise.

*

Now all is done; bring home the bride again,
Bring home the triumph of our victory,
Bring home with you the glory of her gain,
With joyance bring her & with jollity.
Crown ye God Bacchus with a coronal,
And Hymen also crown with wreaths of vine,
And let the Graces dance unto the rest;
For they can do it best.

THE WITHDRAWAL

When the Hymn is ended, the dancers dance before the bride and bridegroom as a verger conducts them through the nave to the west door, and so by St. Michael's Steps to the Chapter House door. The people turn to watch them go.

Coventry Cathedral 1971

~~~~~~
~~~~~~

11. Dedication

The Dedication of Persons

Here is a Dedication in the form of a Scrutiny.

The Scrutiny only has force in the context of the Prayers which precede it: it is therefore reproduced here in that context.

Note that the Prayer of St Francis *'O Eternal God, in whose will is our peace'*, is divided between the Minister and the people; partly because that is in itself a desirable thing, and partly because the phrase beginning 'May we seek not so much' proves in practice difficult for a congregation to say together without stumbling; it is therefore best assigned to a single voice.

~~~~~~

THE PRAYERS

The people remain standing.
At the chancel lectern the Minister begins the Prayers.

God, who has made all men in thy likeness
and lovest all whom thou hast made:
Reconcile us with one another and with thee;
and as thy Son our Saviour was born of a Hebrew mother,
but rejoiced in the faith of a Syrian woman
and of a Roman soldier,
welcomed the Greeks who sought him,
and suffered a man from Africa to carry his cross:
so teach us to look upon the members of all races
as fellow-heirs of the kingdom of Jesus Christ our Lord.

The people say: **Amen.**
~~~~~~

O eternal God, in whose will is our peace,
Make us instruments of thy peace.

The people **Where there is hatred, let us sow love;**
where there is injury, pardon;
where there is discord, union;
where there is doubt, faith;
where there is despair, hope;
where there is darkness, light;
where there is sadness, joy.

The Minister: May we seek not so much
to be consoled, as to console;
to be understood, as to understand;
to be loved, as to love.

The people: **For it is in giving that we receive;**
it is in pardoning that we are pardoned;
it is in dying that we are born to life eternal;
in thy blessed Son Jesus Christ our Lord. Amen.

The Minister: O Lord, we beseech thee mercifully to receive the prayers of thy people which call upon thee; and grant that they may both perceive and know what things they ought to do, and also may have grace and power faithfully to fulfil the same; through Jesus Christ our Lord.

℟ **Amen.**

There follows a silence for private prayer, concluded by:

℣ Lord, hear our prayer;
℟ **And let our cry come unto thee.**

THE DEDICATION

The Precentor: Members of the Association,
I call upon you to renew your obedience.

℣ Will you endeavour in your professional life to act honourably,
to serve willingly, and to promote the welfare of others
as much as your own?
℟ **We will.**
℣ Will you be ready to uphold and to advance
the status of women as best you may?
℟ **We will.**

℣ Will you be ready to banish rancour and to set forward peace and quietness, in your own families and among your colleagues?
℟ **We will.**
℣ Will you remember that the most holy God requires us
to cherish all the men and women whom he has created,
and to love the unlovely as he loves them?
℟ **We will.**

The Precentor says:

Members of the Association,
we stand in the presence of God.
To him all hearts are open;
to him all desires are known;
from him no secrets are hidden.

He pauses for some moments. Then he continues:

Let us lay our resolves before him, and ask him to accept them.

O Almighty God,
in whose presence we stand,
at whose judgement we falter,
in whose mercy we confide:
Accept the pledges we have given and the promises we have made;
and give us grace to keep our word by a willing service
and a steadfast obedience at all times and in all ways;
through Jesus Christ our Lord;

The people answer:

Amen.

Let us say together:

Our Father

The Dedication of Things

The general form of the Dedication is this:

1. A Prayer for God's acceptance of the gift
2. The Dedication
3. A Prayer or Prayers relating to:
   (a) the special function of the gift, or
   (b) the memorial purpose of the gift, or
   (c) some element of the Christian Faith suggested by the occasion.

There may also be a Dialogue, declaring, for the benefit of posterity as well as of the congregation, exactly what is being done – what is being given, why it is being given, who is giving it, and who is receiving it. But much of this information may be incorporated in the actual formula of Dedication.

The formula of Dedication will be on these lines:

> In the Faith of Jesus Christ
> and in memory of his servant N.
> we dedicate this ...
> to be ...;
> In the name of the Father,
> and of the Son, and of the Holy Spirit. Amen.

In addition to the items set out above in the general form of the Dedication, other items may be used to give greater richness and distinction to the occasion.

Here are examples, in alphabetical order:

1. An Altar
2. A Bell Tower and Bell
3. A Chapel
4. A Hostel for Students
5. An Organ
6. A Statue

1. The dedication of an Altar in the nave at the Eucharist on Ascension Day

At the Offertory

Accept, O Lord God, at our hands these gifts,
which we dedicate to your service:
this + platform, in memory of WALTER REGINALD TUGBY;
this + altar, in memory of DAPHNE GREEN;
and this + fair linen cloth;
and use our gifts, O Lord, to make known to us
the love declared in your Son,
Jesus Christ our Saviour and our Redeemer;
who is alive and reigns with you and the Holy Spirit,
one blessed and adorable Trinity,
world without end. Amen.

The Proper Preface (Thanksgiving)

And now we give you thanks, because in his risen body he appeared to his disciples and in their sight was taken into heaven,
to reign with you in glory;

through him we humbly pray you by the grace of your Holy and life-giving Spirit
[here the President makes the sign of the Cross over the four corners of the Holy Table and over the centre of it]

to BL+ESS,

HAL+LOW,

and CONSE+CRATE

this altar now made ready for the Mysteries, which the same your Son Jesus Christ ordained for a continual memorial of himself, and of his one oblation once offered upon the Cross; who being in the form of God made himself of no reputation, and took upon him the form of a servant, and was by you exalted to the right hand of the throne of your Majesty.

Therefore with angels, etc.

St James' Church, Styvechale, Coventry 1978

2. The Dedication of a Bell Tower and Bell

The Bishop and his Chaplain go to the altar, and there turn to the people.

A procession goes in silence from the back of the church to the sanctuary.

The Churchwardens
The Architect, bringing his plans of the tower
The Builders bringing a tally of the work
The Treasurer of the Parochial Church Council bringing
a list of subscribers to the work

The Bishop's Chaplain receives these records from the bearers,
and hands the records one at a time to the Bishop, who lays them upon the altar.

Then the Bishop makes the sign of the Cross over them, and says:

Accept, O Lord, these + tokens of the work of our minds, of our hands, and of our hearts, the gifts we bring to your service; and use our gifts to make known to us all the love declared in your Son, Jesus Christ our Lord.

Everyone, *heartily:*

AMEN.

The bearers retire.

The Bishop now goes to bless and dedicate the Tower and Bell.
The people turn towards the Tower as the Bishop passes them.

The Verger
The Cross
Two Lights
The Servers
The Visiting Priests
The Churchwardens
The Vicar
The Bishop's Chaplain
THE LORD BISHOP

Near the Tower the servers and the visiting priests form a semi-circle about the Bishop.
The Bishop and his Chaplain face the Tower.

The servers raise their tapers aloft.

The Bishop raises his right hand in blessing towards the Tower; and he says:

In the faith of Jesus Christ

we bless and hallow this + Tower,
to be a witness to the people of Canley
of the majesty and the mercy of God;
and this + Bell,
to summon them to worship God,
the Father, the Son, and the Holy Spirit,
who is blessèd for evermore.

Everyone, *heartily*:

AMEN.

The Vicar rings the Bell:

nine strokes, three strokes for each of the Three Persons of the Trinity.

FANFARE

Then LOUD APPLAUSE *by everyone, for joy at the completion of the church.*

This Doxology is then to be sung:

Old 100th AMR 166

Praise God, from whom all blessings flow,
Praise him, all creatures here below,
Praise him above, angelic host,
Praise Father, Son, and Holy Ghost.

St Stephen's Church, Canley, Coventry 1978

3. The Dedication of a Chapel

THE ALLOCUTION

The Provost speaks about Bishop Haigh.

Then the choir sings:

BEATI quorum via integra est: qui ambulant in lege domini.

C.V. Stanford

Blessed are those that are undefiled in the way:
and walk in the law of the Lord

THE DEDICATION

The Provost addresses the Bishop of Coventry:

Right Reverend Father in God,
Will you dedicate this Chapel of the Resurrection,
now restored and re-furnished
in memory of MERVYN GEORGE HAIGH?

The Bishop: I will.

O Holy, blessed and glorious Trinity, whom angels and archangels and all the company of the redeemed worship and adore: Accept at our hands this Chapel, now restored in memory of thy servant Mervyn George Haigh; and grant, that we who dedicate it may render to thee here a pure obedience, and hereafter, with him in whose memory it is dedicated, may enjoy an immortal felicity in the courts of heaven: through the merits of our Redeemer, Jesus Christ.
℟ **Amen.**

The Bishop turns towards the Chapel, and with his right hand uplifted he says:

IN THE FAITH OF JESUS CHRIST
WE DEDICATE THIS CHAPEL
IN MEMORY OF HIS SERVANT MERVYN,
IN THE NAME OF THE FATHER AND OF THE SON
AND OF THE HOLY SPIRIT. AMEN.

Then he says:

O Lord, the maker and redeemer of all believers: Grant to the faithful departed all the unsearchable benefits of thy Son's passion; that in the day of his appearing they may be manifested as thy true children; through the same Jesus Christ our Lord.
℟ **Amen.**

Provost R.T. Howard reads THE LESSON

Revelation 1. 10, 12-18

I was in the Spirit on the Lord's day, and heard behind me a great voice, as of a trumpet, and I turned to see the voice that spake with me. And being turned, I saw seven golden candlesticks; and in the midst of the seven candlesticks one like unto the Son of man, clothed with a garment down to the foot, and girt about the paps with a golden girdle. His head and his hairs were white like wool, as white as snow; and his eyes were as a flame of fire; and his voice as the sound of many waters.

And he had in his right hand seven stars: and out of his mouth went a sharp two-edged sword: and his countenance was as the sun shineth in his strength. And when I saw him, I fell at his feet as dead. And he laid his right hand upon me, saying unto me, Fear not; I am the first and the last: I am he that liveth, and was dead; and, behold, I am alive for evermore, Amen; and have the keys of hell and of death.

The choir sings:

At the round earth's imagin'd corners, blow
Your trumpets, Angels, and arise, arise
From death, you numberless infinities
Of souls, and to your scattered bodies go.
All whom the flood did, and fire shall o'erthrow.
All whom war, dearth, age, agues, tyrannies,
Despair, law, chance, hath slain, and you whose eyes
Shall behold God, and never taste death's woe.
But let them sleep, Lord, and me mourn a space:
For, if above all these, my sins abound,
'Tis late to ask abundance of thy grace.
When we are there; here on this lowly ground,
Teach me how to repent; for that's as good
As if thou hadst seal'd my pardon, with thy blood.

John Donne (1573-1631), Dean of St Paul's
Tony Hewitt-Jones (1926-1989)

Precentor and choir:

℣ Fear not; I am the first and the last.
℟ I am alive for evermore, Amen; and have the keys of hell and of death.

℣ Vouchsafe us, O God, in our mortal days, so fast a hold of thy truth and so rich a possession in thy love as death may not loose nor interrupt; but thy grace complete in life without end; through our Lord and Saviour Jesus Christ.
℟ Amen.

The Bishop says:

Bring us, O Lord God, at our last awakening into the house and gate of heaven, to enter into that gate and dwell in that house, where there shall be no darkness nor dazzling, but one equal light; no noise nor silence, but one equal music; no fears nor hopes, but one equal possession; no ends nor beginnings, but one equal eternity; in the habitations of thy glory and dominion, world without end.

℟ Amen.

Coventry Cathedral:
The Dedication of the Chapel of the Resurrection
(restored in memory of Bishop Haigh)
on Ascension Day 1965

4. The Dedication of a Hostel for Students

The Bishop dedicates the House in the form following:

The people stand, and the Bishop says:

Jesus said, 'I am the way, the truth, and the life; no one comes to the Father except by me. If you knew me you would know my Father too.' Philip said to him, 'Lord, show us the Father and we ask no more.' Jesus answered, 'Have I been all this time with you, Philip, and you still do not know me? Anyone who has seen me has seen the Father.'

John 14. 6-9

The Bishop turns towards the House, and with his right hand uplifted he says:

In the faith of Jesus Christ
and in memory of his servant John Fitzgerald Kennedy
we dedicate this House
to be a home of friendship for young people
where they may learn the truth
as it is in Jesus:
In the name of the Father, and of the Son,
and of the Holy Spirit. Amen.

The Bishop continues:

We beseech thee, O God, the God of truth,
that what we know not of things we ought to know,
thou wilt teach us;
That what we know of truth,
thou wilt keep us in it;
That what we are mistaken in, as men must be,
thou wilt correct;
That at whatsoever truths we stumble,
thou wilt yet establish us;
And from all that is false,
and from all knowledge that would hurt us,
thou wilt for ever deliver us;
through Jesus Christ our Lord.
Amen.

Peace be to this House
and to all who lodge in it,
from Christ,
who is our peace.
Amen.

Coventry Cathedral:
The Dedication of John F. Kennedy House 1965

5. The Dedication of an Organ during Evensong

*After the Third Collect the people stand,
and the Dedication follows, beginning with a brief Dialogue.*

Dr. Ringdal addresses the Provost:

MR PROVOST,
On behalf of the people of Norway we ask you to accept this organ,
and to dedicate it for use in Coventry Cathedral.

The Provost replies:

DR. RINGDAL,
On behalf of the Provost and Chapter of Coventry I accept your gift.
We thank you, and all whom you represent, for your generosity.

The Provost shakes hands with the donors and the builder of the organ.

The people remain standing, and the Provost proceeds to the Dedication of the organ.

He says:

Let us pray.
O holy, blessed and glorious Trinity, whom angels and archangels and all the company of the redeemed worship and adore:
Be pleased to receive at our hands this organ which we dedicate to thy service; and so bless us as we sing thy praises here upon earth, that hereafter we may sing the new song in the heavenly city, where thou reignest God, world without end.
Amen.

The Provost makes the sign of the Cross towards *the* organ, *with these words:*

IN THE FAITH OF JESUS CHRIST
WE DEDICATE THIS ORGAN
TO THE SERVICE OF GOD,
IN THE NAME OF THE FATHER AND OF THE SON
AND OF THE HOLY SPIRIT. AMEN.

Raising his voice the Provost says, and the people shout in reply:

℣ Thou art worthy, O Lord,
to receive glory and honour and power;
℟ **For thou hast created all things,**
and for thy pleasure they are, and were created.
℣ O sing praises, sing praises unto our God:
℟ **O sing praises, sing praises unto our King.**
℣ For God is the King of all the earth;
℟ **Sing ye praises with understanding.**

This Hymn follows, and the Provost and his companions retire.

O praise ye the Lord!
praise him in the height;
Rejoice in his word,
ye angels of light;
Ye heavens, adore him
by whom ye were made,
And worship before him,
in brightness array'd.

O praise ye the Lord!
praise him upon earth,
In tuneful accord,
ye sons of new birth:
Praise him who hath brought you
his grace from above,
Praise him who hath taught you
to sing of his love.

O praise ye the Lord,
all things that give sound;
Each jubilant chord,
re-echo around;
Loud organs, his glory
forth tell in deep tone,
And sweet harp, the story
of what he hath done.

O praise ye the Lord!
Thanksgiving and song
To him be outpour'd
all ages along:
For love in creation,
for heaven restored,
For grace of salvation,
O praise ye the Lord!

After the Hymn, the choir and people sit down,
and the Organist of Coventry Cathedral plays on the Norwegian organ:

Aria Sebaldina (theme and eight variations)
from Hexachordum Apollinis (1699) by Johann Pachelbel (1653-1706).

Then the Provost offers these Prayers, the choir and the people kneeling:

Let us pray.

Craftsmen

O holy and adorable Trinity, creating man in thine image to be a maker and craftsman, and in the joy of creation to be a mirror of thy triune Majesty: Remember for good the men who have imagined and made this organ now dedicated to thy service; and grant that none of these whose truth is in their craft may miss the true knowledge of thee, whose truth is in Jesus Christ our Maker and Redeemer. Amen.

The people of Norway

Remember, O lord, for good the whole people of Norway; send them fruitful lands and a prosperous industry; wise counsellors and upright magistrates; leaders of integrity in learning and labour; a devout, learned, and useful clergy; honest, peaceable, and dutiful citizens; and thy blessing at all times and in all ways: through Jesus Christ our Lord. Amen.

Eternal Life

Bring us, O Lord God, at our last awakening into the house and gate of heaven, to enter into that gate and dwell in that house, where there shall be no darkness nor dazzling, but one equal light; no noise nor silence, but one equal music; no fears nor hopes, but one equal possession; no ends nor beginnings, but one equal eternity; in the habitations of thy glory and dominion, world without end. Amen.

There follows a silence for private prayer, concluded by:

℣ Lord, hear our prayer;
℟ **And let our cry come unto thee.**

The Precentor and the choir rise to sing these Suffrages:

℣ Keep us, O Lord, so awake in the duties of our calling;
℟ **That we may sleep in thy peace, and wake in thy glory.**
℣ God grant to the living, grace;
to the departed, rest;
to the Church, the Queen, the Commonwealth,
and all mankind, peace and concord;
℟ **And to us and all his servants life everlasting.**
℣ Let us bless the Lord;
℟ **Thanks be to God.**

This Hymn follows:

Songs of praise the angels sang,
Heaven with Alleluias rang,
When creation was begun,
When God spake and it was done.

Songs of praise awoke the morn
When the Prince of Peace was born;
Songs of praise arose when he
Captive led captivity.

Choir Heaven and earth must pass away;
Songs of praise shall crown that day:
God will make new heavens and earth;
Songs of praise shall hail their birth.

Boys And will man alone be dumb
Till that glorious Kingdom come?
Men No, the Church delights to raise
Psalms and hymns and songs of praise.

Saints below, with heart and voice,
till in songs of praise rejoice;
Learning here, by faith and love,
Songs of praise to sing above.

Unison **Hymns of glory, songs of praise,**
Father, unto thee we raise,
Jesu, glory unto thee,
With the Spirit, ever be.

Coventry Cathedral:
The Dedication of the Norwegian Organ 1967

~~~~~~
~~~~~~

6. The Dedication of a Statue

The dedication of Sir Jacob Epstein's statue **ECCE HOMO**
on the Eve of Passion Sunday, Saturday 22 March 1969 at 2.30 p.m.

~~~~~~

THE ORDER OF SERVICE

The Provost speaks about the gift of the statue.

The Precentor reads the Lesson: St. John 19. 1-6, 14b, 15, 16.

Tunc ergo adprehendit Pilatus lesum, et flagellauit. Et milites plectentes coronam de spinis, inposuerunt capiti eius: et ueste purpurea circumdederunt eum. Et euniebant ad eum, et dicebant: Haue, rex Iudaeorum: et dabant ci alapas. Exiit iterum Pilatus foras, et dicit eis: Ecce adduco uobis eum foras, ut cognoscatis quia in eo nullam causam inuenio. Exiit ergo Iesus portans spineam coronam, et purpureum uestimentum: et dicit eis:

ECCE HOMO

Pilate now took Jesus and had him flogged; and the soldiers plaited a crown of thorns and placed it on his head, and robed him in a purple cloak. Then time after time they came up to him, crying, 'Hail, King of the Jews!', and struck him on the face.

Once more Pilate came out and said to the Jews, 'Here he is; I am bringing him out to let you know that I find no cause against him'; and Jesus came out, wearing the crown of thorns and the purple cloak. Pilate said,

'BEHOLD THE MAN!'

The chief priests and their henchmen saw him and shouted, 'Crucify! crucify!'

Pilate said to the Jews, 'Here is your king.' They shouted, 'Away with him! Away with him! Crucify him!' 'Crucify your king?' said Pilate. 'We have no king but Caesar', the Jews replied. Then at last, to satisfy them, he handed Jesus over to be crucified.

The Provost requests the Bishop of Coventry to dedicate the statue.

The Bishop proceeds to the dedication.
~~~~~~

Turning to the statue, and making the sign of the Cross towards it, he says:

In the Catholic faith
We dedicate this figure of

THE MAN

Jesus of Nazareth
Who spoke the truth
And was falsely done to death:
In the name of the Father, and of the Son,
And of the Holy Spirit. Amen.

The Bishop says:
O Saviour of the world,
who by thy cross and passion hast redeemed us;

The people reply:
Save us, and help us, we humbly beseech thee, O Lord.

The Bishop: O God, the Father of mankind, who didst suffer thine only Son to be set forth as a spectacle, despised, derided and scornfully arrayed, the more in his humiliation to reveal his majesty: Draw us daily, we beseech thee, both to behold the man and to worship the King, immortal, eternal, world without end.
℟ **Amen.**

The Bishop delivers an Address.

The Provost offers these Prayers:
O Lord, our Redeemer and King, doomed by the hoarse cry of thine own people, Crucify him, crucify: Deliver us from the impulses and lies of popular passion, and consecrate both our minds and voices to the ministry of truth; for thine honour and glory always.
℟ **Amen.**

Almighty God, we beseech thee graciously to behold this thy family, for which our Lord Jesus Christ was contented to be betrayed, and given up into the hands of wicked men, and to suffer death upon the cross; who now liveth and reigneth with thee and the Holy Spirit, ever one God, world without end.
℟ **Amen.**

OUR FATHER

This Hymn follows:

**When I survey the wondrous cross
On which the Prince of Glory died,
My richest gain I count but loss,
And pour contempt on all my pride.**

**Forbid it, Lord, that I should boast
Save in the Cross of Christ my God;
All the vain things that charm me most,
I sacrifice them to his Blood.**

**See from his head, his hands, his feet,
Sorrow and love flow mingling down;
Did e'er such love and sorrow meet,
Or thorns compose so rich a crown?**

**Were the whole realm of nature mine,
That were an offering far too small;
Love so amazing, so divine,
Demands my soul, my life, my all.**

Coventry Cathedral 1969

12. Dialogue

The dialogue is almost indispensable on such occasions as the offering and dedication of a gift to a church. It is a stylized conversation between the donor and the recipient. The purpose of such a dialogue is not simply an exchange of courtesies; it is to declare publicly, for the benefit of posterity as well as of the congregation, exactly what is being done - what is being given, why it is being given, who is giving it, and who is receiving it. It is a formal record of the occasion. The language used must be formal and precise, yet neither ponderous nor archaic.

Note the use of the dialogue in the form of a scrutiny or examination. Here the dialogue proceeds by question and answer. This is a very ancient and well-tried formula, used for example in the rites of Baptism, and Marriage, and Ordination. It is still capable of useful application. Brief examples may be seen in **Commissioning** (page 103) and **Scrutinies** (page 221).

13. Fanfares

Your purist dislikes fanfares in Christian worship. To him they smack of military parades. Let him take note that music for brass has for centuries been a feature of divine worship in the Chapel Royal of England, and not only in the Chapel Royal: the Laudian statutes of Canterbury Cathedral, for example, include in the list of members of the Foundation a resident brass quartet of two trumpets and two trombones. It is certain that in any large and resonant building music for brass can be one of the most exciting sounds imaginable; and no other sound so readily contributes a sense of occasion.

It will however be only rarely that brass players of professional ability are available. The fanfares now under discussion will usually be played on the organ; and if in a church or chapel of modest resources there is only a piano, fanfares can quite effectively be performed on that.

A fanfare will vary in length, and in its character, according to its function in the service. It may last only 10 seconds; it may last 20 seconds. It may be joyful; it may be solemn.

The functions of a fanfare may be classified in this way:

1. **To announce the arrival** at the church of a person of importance: the Bishop of the diocese, or the Mayor of the city or town, or a Minister of the Crown. The fanfare says 'He's here', or 'She's here'. The fanfare must be brief and heraldic.
2. **To summon the congregation to their feet** at the beginning of the service. The fanfare says simply 'Stand up now. It's time to begin.' It will be brief, even peremptory.
3. **To suggest a mood**. Turn, for example, to the **Royal Acclamation** on page 52. The first part of the Acclamation is introduced by a fanfare which is to be played *grave*, that is to say solemnly: the fanfare says 'This is a moment of solemn intercession for the Sovereign.' The second fanfare is to be played *goioso e brillante*, that is to say happily and brilliantly: the fanfare says 'Three cheers for the Queen and the Royal Family.'
4. **To indicate a moment of climax**.

Here are some examples.

Before the Gospel at the Eucharist

After the Gradual everyone stands up.
A FANFARE is played;
the First Deacon announces the Gospel; the choir and people sing

Glory be to thee, O Lord.

and the Deacon reads the Gospel.

Coventry Cathedral:
The Communion 1973

After the Prayer of Consecration at the Eucharist

I was once on holiday in Brittany when the villagers were celebrating a Pardon. At Mass in the parish church the Prayer of Consecration was followed immediately by a noisy razzamataz from the village band. To a staid English visitor this was both surprising and exhilarating.

I remembered that occasion when we came to prepare the Order for the Consecration of Coventry Cathedral in 1962. At the Eucharist the Prayer of Consecration was followed, not by Breton exuberance but by a Solemn Music for Brass. The music expressed awe, humility, devotion, before the Sacramental Presence. It was a moment of penetrating truth. It was a moment when the dictum was verified, 'Music begins where words leave off.'

At the RECOGNITION of the Bishop at his Enthronement

The Provost with the Bishop and his Chaplains ascends the dais.
A FANFARE sounds. The Provost calls out to the people:

We present to you the Right Reverend Father in God,
JOHN, Bishop of Coventry

A FANFARE sounds.
The people greet the Bishop with hearty applause.

Then the Bishop calls out:
The peace of the Lord be with you all.

The people reply: **Peace to you.**

Coventry Cathedral:
The Bishop's Enthronement 1976

At a service for Scouts or Guides

The reading aloud of the Scout/Guide Law is a moment of climax in such a service. The reading of the Law can be framed by two fanfares, one before the reading and another after it. The fanfares can be played on bugles and drums: a simple offering by the worshippers of their own skills.

The Scout/Guide Law may go for nothing if it is repeated casually, as it sometimes is. It will gain in impact through the observing of two simple tricks of the trade:

1. Arrange for the Law to be read by three voices in turn. The speakers may all speak at one lectern: but better still if each speaks from a different place; one at the centre, the second at the north side of the building, the third at the south.
2. Insist on a silence of about five seconds between the reading of each Law, to allow time for each phrase really to be heard and listened to. Ten seconds of silence would seem ponderous and oppressive; five seconds will give poise. Needless to say, the whole Law must be rehearsed by the speakers beforehand. So:

FANFARE

The Commissioner: Let the Guide Law be read.

THE GUIDE LAW
Three voices in turn read the Guide Law aloud.

1 A Guide's honour is to be trusted.
2 A Guide is loyal.
3 A Guide's duty is to be useful and to help others.
1 A Guide is a friend to all, and a sister to every other Guide.
2 A Guide is courteous.
3 A Guide is a friend to animals.
1 A Guide obeys orders.
2 A Guide smiles and sings under all difficulties.
3 A Guide is thrifty.
1 A Guide is pure in thought, word and deed.

FANFARE

14. Hymns

Their popularity

In the Book of Common Prayer no hymns are prescribed, except for the Veni Creator in the Ordering of Priests. This does not mean, however, that the use of hymns in the public worship of the Church of England lacks authority. Their use was authorised by Elizabeth's Injunctions in 1559:

> *In the beginning, or in the end of the common prayers, either at morning or evening, there may be sung a hymn, or such like song to the praise of Almighty God, in the best sort of melody and music that may be conveniently devised, having respect that the sentence* [meaning] *of the hymn may be understanded and perceived.*

This was begun immediately. Strype relates how, at St. Antholin's in the City, before 'the new Morning Prayer':

> *A Psalm was sung after the Geneva fashion, all the congregation, men, women, and boys, singing together ... which custom was about this time brought also into St. Paul's.*

A psalm 'after the Geneva fashion', that is to say a psalm in metre, was the only kind of hymn in the vernacular that was available at this date and indeed for another century and a half. Metrical psalms were nevertheless, as we have already suggested, very popular, for the good reason that they were technically within the competence of the man in the pew. The man in the pew has never lost his love of hymns; naturally, for they were invented for his special benefit. Hymns in the vernacular were not written for the professional choirs of the choral foundations; they were written for the use of congregations, whether in church or chapel.

What is a hymn?

In his preface to Olney Hymns, published in 1779, the Rev. John Newton wrote:

> *Hymns should be Hymns, not Odes, if designed for public worship and for the use of plain people. Perspicacity, simplicity, and ease should be chiefly attended to: and the image and colouring of poetry, if admitted at all, should be indulged sparingly and with great judgement. The late Dr. Watts might, as a poet, have a right to say that it cost him labour to restrain his fire and to accommodate himself to the capacity of common readers.*

And the poet Tennyson, in a conversation towards the end of his life with Dr Warren, President of Magdalen, is reported to have remarked:

> *A good hymn is the most difficult thing in the world to write. In a good hymn you have to be commonplace and practical. The moment you cease to be commonplace and put in any expression at all out of the common, it ceases to be a hymn.*

Now the congregation at a service of occasion will consist for the most part of plain people, who not only love to sing hymns but who expect that the hymns that they are to sing will be within their capacity. They will be disappointed of their expectations, and so put into an ill humour, if they are asked to sing a hymn whose text is recondite or fanciful or subtle. For example, Emily Bronte's lines 'No coward love is mine', are noble poetry, but they do not make a good hymn. John Donne's 'Wilt thou forgive that sin' is a solemn and deeply felt meditation, dear to its author, who (as Isaac Walton tells us) often had it sung by the choir of his cathedral when he was Dean of St. Paul's: but whatever the choir of St. Paul's made of it, the text is too subtle to commend itself for use as a hymn to be sung by plain people.

We urge, therefore, that hymns in a service of occasion should be genuine hymns, whose texts deal with the great themes of the Christian faith in a manner direct and unambiguous. They should be, as a rule, familiar texts, sung to familiar tunes. There is a place in public worship for new texts and for new tunes: but the place for new tunes, at any rate, is not the service of occasion.

A hymn at the beginning

In a service of occasion it is best to introduce a hymn at the beginning, or very near the beginning. Such a common action helps to beget a common mind among people probably unknown to each other and possibly unused to public worship: and without this common mind there can be no common prayer. But note: the music of this hymn must be well-known, massive and virile; the text must be God-ward. It is the first common utterance in the service; if this is hesitant, recovery from a bad start will be difficult.

Variety

Hymns may become tedious if there are too many of them, or if they are handled without imagination. Use variety; have some verses, for example, sung in unison with a varied organ accompaniment; one verse by all the treble voices of choir and people, another by all the men's voices; one verse by the people seated on one side of the building, and one by the people seated on the other side; and occasionally a verse sung by the choir alone, preferably without accompaniment. Especially in a procession is this antiphony between choir and congregation effective and desirable.

Office hymns

The choir Offices will often form the core of a service of occasion. We therefore make no apology for referring briefly to the subject of the Office hymn. There are two questions: (a) What is an Office hymn? and (b) At what point is it to be sung? The answer to the second question depends upon the answer to the first.

The Office hymn is a hymn whose use is prescribed in each of the canonical hours; it is an integral part of the rite, as much as the psalms and lessons. It is not an optional addition to the Office: neither its use, nor its text, nor its position in the Office, is at the discretion of the Minister. It has its own proper function, and its function determines its character. Its character is objective; it expounds the Christian verities: and its function is to lend to the Office a particular mood and intention, by reference to the verities which a given feast, or season, or hour of the day, proclaims.

In the Book of Common Prayer there is only one example of a hymn whose use and text and position in the rite are prescribed, namely the Veni Creator in the Ordinal. Any other hymns used in the course of the liturgy of the Church of England are optional additions. There is no Office hymn in Matins or Evensong.

The question now arises, If an Office hymn is to be intruded into the Prayer Book rites of Matins or Evensong, at what point in the Office is it to be placed? In view of its function as defining the mood or intention of the Office, the answer surely is: As early in the Office as possible.

It is worth recalling that when he came to compose a reformed liturgy for the Church of England, Cranmer made two Latin drafts of the choir Offices before embarking on the Prayer Book in English, and that in both drafts he provided for an Office hymn to be sung immediately after the opening preces and before the psalms. This seems the place appropriate to the function and character of the Office hymn, if it is to be used in our Prayer Book Offices.

Hymns of today

During recent years many good new hymns have been written and published. They scarcely appear in this book, not because the author has any prejudice against them, but for practical reasons, chiefly financial.

In a service of occasion the text of a new hymn may with the permission of the holder of the copyright be printed in the order of service; and if the text can be sung to a familiar tune, no difficulty arises.

The provision of a new book for regular use by choir and people is another matter. The congregation must have copies containing the text and the melody; the choir must have the full musical edition. In Coventry Cathedral there must be fifty copies of the full musical edition, kept in the chancel; there must also be another fifty copies kept on the desks in the practice room downstairs. The cost of one hundred copies of a full musical edition today (1980) will be £400 at least, and that sum is for the choir's use alone. Copies of the edition containing text and melody for use by a congregation of 1,800 will cost at least £2,500.

The expenditure of nearly £3,000 on a new hymn book must be weighed against the cost, not only of maintaining a choir of professional competence, but also of sustaining the whole ministry of the Cathedral. In that ministry music plays an indispensable rôle; but the ministry is wider than the music.

Nevertheless, today's worship must be refreshed by today's hymns; and those who are alive to that need will see to it that, in one way or another, the need is met.

15. Invocations

An Invocation is a plea to God to be present among his worshippers. It may be addressed to the Three Persons of the Trinity, as at the beginning of the Litany in the Book of Common Prayer; or to any one of the Persons. It may include versicles and responses, a collect, a hymn, an anthem. For example:

1. <u>An Invocation addressed to Christ</u>

In this example the first two rubrics direct the choir to enter (and go to their stalls in the chancel), but the Ministers to assemble at the west end. The third rubric explains why:

> *Standing near the west end of the church the Precentor sings, and the choir in the chancel replies.*

This is antiphony between soloist and chorus; but note that there is a spatial separation between the soloist and the chorus. The device is simple, the effect is telling: the effect is to wrap up in prayer the congregation placed between the soloist at the west end of the building and the chorus at the east end.

Here is a way to add a touch of distinction to the occasion; but of course the antiphony would still be effective if the Precentor and the choir were all in the chancel together.

The versicles and responses are a meditation on the holy city, and on Christ who is its light and its glory. The collect puts into prayer the subject of the meditation.

The versicles and responses could be sung to simple plainsong inflections, like the suffrages before the collects of Matins and Evensong in the Prayer Book; but a more elaborate and expressive setting is given among the music examples at the end of this book.

ORGAN VOLUNTARY

Master Tallis's Testament
Herbert Howells (1892-1983)

At 3.55 the choir enters.

At 4.00 the choir sings this Anthem, while the Ministers assemble at the west end.

ANTHEM

How lovely are thy dwellings fair, O Lord of hosts.
My soul ever longeth and fainteth sore for the blest courts of the Lord;
my heart and flesh do cry to God, cry to the living God.
O blest are they that in thy house are dwelling;
they ever praise thee, O Lord, praise thee for evermore.

I THE INVOCATION

FANFARE

The people stand.

Standing near the west end of the church the Precentor sings, and the choir in the chancel replies:

℣ Jesus said, I am the light of the world;
he that followeth me shall not walk in darkness;
℟ but shall have the light of life.
℣ God, who commanded the light to shine out of darkness,
hath shined in our hearts;
℟ to give the light of the knowledge of the glory of God
in the face of Jesus Christ.
℣ He showed me that great city, the Holy Jerusalem,
descending out of heaven from God, having the glory of God;
℟ and her light was like unto a stone more precious,
even like a jasper stone, clear as crystal.
℣ And the city had no need of the sun, neither of the moon,
to shine in it;
℟ for the glory of God did lighten it,
and the Lamb is the light thereof.

The Precentor:

O Lord Jesus Christ, the very Light of Light, whom men in the darkness of Gethsemane approached with lanterns and torches: Keep us from following the little lights of the world, that deepen our night; and lead us into that holy city where with the Father and the Holy Spirit thou livest and reignest, God, world without end.

℟ **Amen.**

The Ministers advance to the sanctuary during this Hymn.

HYMN

AMR 620 Tune: Westminster Abbey

Christ is made the sure Foundation,
Christ the Head and Corner-stone,
Chosen of the Lord, and precious,
Binding all the Church in one,
Holy Sion's help for ever,
And her confidence alone.

All that dedicated city,
Dearly loved of God on high,
In exultant jubilation
Pours perpetual melody,
God the One in Three adoring
In glad hymns eternally.

To this temple, where we call thee,
Come, O Lord of Hosts, to-day;
With thy wonted loving-kindness
Hear thy servants as they pray,
And thy fullest benediction
Shed within its walls away.

Choir only

Here vouchsafe to all thy servants
What they ask of thee to gain,
What they gain from thee for ever
With the blessed to retain,
And hereafter in thy glory
Evermore with thee to reign

Everyone

Laud and honour to the Father,
Laud and honour to the Son,
Laud and honour to the Spirit,
Ever Three, and ever One,
Consubstantial, co-eternal,
While unending ages run.

The University Church of Christ the King, London 1978:
An Order of Service to conclude the 13th Annual Conference
of The (American) Association of Anglican Musicians

2. An Invocation addressed to the Holy Spirit

The Bishop at the Throne calls out, and the people reply:

℣ The Spirit of the Lord fills the whole world.
℟ **Come, Holy Spirit.**
℣ If the Spirit is the source of our life,
let the Spirit also direct our course.
℟ **Come, Holy Spirit.**
℣ The harvest of the spirit is love.
℟ **Holy Spirit, come.**
℣ Joy,
℟ **Holy Spirit, come.**
℣ Peace,
℟ **Holy Spirit, come.**
℣ Patience,
℟ **Holy Spirit, come.**
℣ Kindness,
℟ **Holy Spirit, come.**
℣ Generosity,
℟ **Holy Spirit, come.**
℣ Fidelity,
℟ **Holy Spirit, come.**
℣ Gentleness,
℟ **Holy Spirit, come.**
℣ Self-control,
℟ **Holy Spirit, come.**

℣ We are not our own, but the temples of the Holy Spirit;
let us dedicate ourselves entirely to his service.
℟ **Come, Holy Spirit.**

The Bishop:

Come, Holy Spirit, the free dispenser of all graces: Visit the hearts of thy faithful servants, and replenish them with thy sacred inspirations; illuminate our understandings, and inflame our affections, and sanctify all the faculties of our souls; that we may know, and love, and constantly do the things that belong to our peace, our everlasting peace; who with the Father and the Son reignest God, world without end.
℟ **Amen.**

The people sit down, and the choir sings this Anthem:

Come, Holy Ghost the Maker, come:
Take in the souls of thine thy place;
Thou whom our hearts had being from,
O fill them with thy heav'nly grace.
Thou art that comfort from above
The Highest doth by gift impart;
Thou, spring of life, a fire of love
And the anointing Spirit art.

Coventry Cathedral 1967: A Vision of Europe

3. An Invocation addressed to the Holy Spirit

You will find another example under **Elements in an Order of Service 5: Beginnings and Endings; The Reception of the Bishop at his cathedral** (page 75).

16. The Laying Up of Colours

A congregation of 2,000 people assembles to witness a specific thing, the Laying Up of the Colours of a County regiment in the cathedral. This action is significant and moving: but it lasts only a few minutes. The action must be set within a context of Christian truth; it must be enveloped in prayer.

The first aim will be to establish the sense of the presence of God; and this is the purpose of the opening part of the service entitled The Preparation, which must be allowed to unfold itself at an unhurried, deliberate pace. It will last ten or twelve minutes at least. The Preparation is concerned with man as he is, always and everywhere - a sinner who needs forgiveness. Only after this situation has been recognised does the service proceed to the main business.

The Laying Up of Colours mingles military and ecclesiastical ceremonial. The Colours are carried through the congregation to the chancel step, where the Colour Party presents arms. They are then handed over to the care of the cathedral; and as they are borne through the chancel to the altar they are escorted by lights, two in front of them and two behind. The moving lights do honour to the Colours; and at the same time they draw the eyes of the people and focus the attention, even of those who are standing at some distance, on a significant moment. The action is brought to a close by the sounding of the Last Post.

The service proceeds by an easy transition to the Commemoration of the Fallen, which is given an unmistakeably Christian emphasis. The stress is laid not upon the death of the Fallen but upon the Christian hope of resurrection.

The Provost escorts the Bishop to his Throne,
and then goes to the chancel step, where he welcomes the people.

THE PREPARATION

This Hymn follows, during which the Standards of the Regimental Association
are carried from the west end of the church through the nave to the chancel step,
and from there into the north and south aisles.

O God, our help in ages past,
Our hope for years to come,
Our shelter from the stormy blast,
And our eternal home;

Beneath the shadow of thy throne
Thy saints have dwelt secure;
Sufficient is thine arm alone,
And our defence is sure.

Before the hills in order stood,
Or earth received her frame,
From everlasting thou are God,
To endless years the same.

People on the left

A thousand ages in thy sight
Are like an evening gone;
Short as the watch that ends the night
Before the rising sun.

People on the right

Time, like an ever-rolling stream,
Bears all its sons away;
They fly forgotten, as a dream
Dies at the opening day.

All the people **O God, our help in ages past,**
Our hope for years to come,
Be thou our guard while troubles last,
And our eternal home.

ST. ANNE AMR 165

The Precentor at the chancel step says:

Lord, who shall dwell in thy tabernacle:
or who shall rest upon thy holy hill?

The people answer:

Even he, that leadeth an uncorrupt life:
and doeth the thing which is right,
and speaketh the truth from his heart.

The Precentor:

My son, forget not my law; but let thine heart keep my commandments: for length of days, and years of life, and peace, shall they add to thee. Let not mercy and truth forsake thee: bind them about thy neck; write them upon the table of thine heart; so shalt thou find favour and good understanding in the sight of God and man. Trust in the Lord with all thine heart, and lean not upon thine own understanding: in all thy ways acknowledge him, and he shall direct thy paths.

Proverbs 3, 1-6

The Precentor says, and the people answer:

℣ We know and confess, O God:
℟ **That our hearts are unworthy to receive thee.**
℣ Day by day we have enjoyed thy gifts;
℟ **But have forgotten that thou wast the giver of them.**
℣ Thou hast shown us what thou wouldst have us do;
℟ **But we have not followed thy way.**
℣ Thou hast spoken to us in thy Word;
℟ **But we have not listened.**

Silence is kept. Then all say together:

Grant, we beseech thee, merciful Lord,
to thy faithful people pardon and peace,
that we may be cleansed from all our sins,
and serve thee with a quiet mind:
through Jesus Christ our Lord. Amen.

The Bishop:

May the Almighty and merciful Lord grant you pardon and remission of all your sins, time for amendment of life, and the grace and comfort of the Holy Spirit.
℟ **Amen.**

When the following Hymn begins Major-General R.C. Macdonald, D.S.O., O.B.E., Colonel of the Regiment, is conducted to the lectern to read the Lesson.

Father of heaven, whose love profound
A ransom for our souls hath found,
Before thy throne we sinners bend,
To us thy pardoning love extend.

Almighty Son, incarnate Word,
Our Prophet, Priest, Redeemer, Lord,
Before thy throne we sinners bend,
To us thy saving grace extend.

Eternal Spirit, by whose breath
The soul is raised from sin and death,
Before thy throne we sinners bend,
To us thy quickening power extend.

Thrice Holy! Father, Spirit, Son;
Mysterious Godhead, Three in One,
Before thy throne we sinners bend,
Grace, pardon, life to us extend.

RIVAULX AMR 164

MR VALIANT-FOR-TRUTH

THE LESSON: JOHN BUNYAN: The Pilgrim's Progress

After this, it was noised abroad that Mr. Valiant-for-truth was taken with a summons, and had this for a token that the summons was true, that his pitcher was broken at the fountain. When he understood it, he called for his friends, and told them of it. Then said he, I am going to my Father's, and though with great difficulty I am got hither, yet now I do not repent me of all the trouble I have been at to arrive where I am. My sword, I give to him that shall succeed me in my pilgrimage, and my courage and skill, to him that can get it. My marks and scars I carry with me, to be a witness for me, that I have fought his battles, who now will be my rewarder.

When the day that he must go hence, was come, many accompanied him to the river side, into which, as he went, he said, Death, where is thy sting? And as he went down deeper, he said, Grave where is thy victory?

So he passed over, and all the trumpets sounded for him on the other side.

The reader retires, and the people stand.

THE LAYING UP OF THE COLOURS

A Roll of Drums, during which the Colonel of the Regiment and the Honorary Colonel of the 7th Battalion are escorted by the Churchwardens to the chancel step, where they stand facing the people.

The Precentor and the Provost stand at the chancel step, flanked by four lights, facing the people.

A Fanfare is sounded.

To the Regimental Slow March the Colour Party advances from the west end of the church and halts before the Colonel of the Regiment and the Honorary Colonel of the 7th Battalion.

The Colonels take the Colours from the Officers carrying them.

The Colour Party presents arms.

The Colonels then turn about.

The Honorary Colonel hands the Regimental Colour to the Provost, who hands it to the Precentor. The Colonel of the Regiment then hands the Queen's Colour to the Provost, who retains it.

The Colonel of the Regiment addresses the Provost:

MR PROVOST,

These consecrated Colours, formerly carried in the service of our Sovereign and Empire, I now deliver into your hands for safe custody within these walls.

The Provost replies.

The Colour Party shoulders arms.

The Precentor and the Provost, bearing the Colours, move through the chancel to the Sanctuary; the Colonels, escorted by the Churchwardens, following.

THE PROVOST'S VERGER
TWO CANDLEBEARERS
THE PRECENTOR WITH THE REGIMENTAL COLOUR
THE PROVOST WITH THE QUEEN'S COLOUR
TWO CANDLEBEARERS
THE VICAR'S WARDEN
TWO WARDENS
THE COLONEL OF THE REGIMENT AND THE COLONEL OF THE 7TH BATTALION
TWO WARDENS

The Precentor and the Provost enter the Sanctuary and go up to the Altar; and the Provost lays the Colours upon the Altar.

When this has been done, the Regimental Call and the Last Post are sounded.

The Colour Party withdraws, and the Churchwardens escort the Colonels to their seats in the nave. The Precentor and the Provost return to their stalls.

THE COMMEMORATION OF THE FALLEN

The Very Reverend R.T. Howard, Provost Emeritus, is conducted to the chancel steps.

There he says:

Many of the Jews came to Martha and Mary, to comfort them concerning their brother. Then Martha, as soon as she heard that Jesus was coming, went and met him. Then said Martha unto Jesus, Lord, if thou hadst been here, my brother had not died. Jesus saith unto her, Thy brother shall rise again. Martha saith unto him, I know that he shall rise again in the resurrection at the last day. Jesus saith unto her, I am the resurrection, and the life: he that believeth in me, though he were dead, yet shall he live: and whosoever liveth and believeth in me shall never die.

John 11. 19-21, 23-26

Here in God's presence let us gratefully remember our brothers who gave their lives in war.

Silence falls. After a while the Minister continues:

Whither shall I go then from thy Spirit? or whither shall I go then from thy presence? If I climb up into heaven, thou art there: if I go down to hell, thou art there also. If I take the wings of the morning, and remain in the uttermost parts of the sea; even there also shall thy hand lead me, and thy right hand shall hold me.

Psalm 139. 6-9

The Minister says and the people answer:

℣ Jesus said, This is my commandment, that you love one another;
℟ **As I have loved you.**
℣ Greater love hath no man than this;
℟ **That a man lay down his life for his friends.**
℣ Be thou faithful unto death;
℟ **And I will give thee a crown of life.**

The Minister:

O God, the Creator and Father both of our mortal and immortal life: We give thee high praise and humble thanks for all thy sons who counted not their lives dear to themselves, but laid them down for their friends; beseeching thee that they may be numbered among those who by faithfulness unto death are given a crown of life, according to thy most sure promise; through Jesus Christ our Lord.
℟ **Amen.**

Coventry Cathedral: The Laying up of the Colours of the 7th Battalion The Royal Warwickshire Fusiliers 1964

17. Lessons

The choice of lessons

Remember that a lesson (like every other element in an order of service) has work to do; be sure you see clearly what purpose a given lesson is designed to serve. It must be apposite; it must illuminate the theme in hand; it must carry forward the thought of the worshipper from one point to the next, or establish in him the appropriate mood of penitence or hope, love or aspiration.

In choosing a lesson, do not hesitate to omit verses from the passage of Scripture under consideration; by the omission of what is not really relevant to your theme, the lesson will gain in impact. Aim to be concise. A lesson consisting of verses which are not contiguous in the chapter of the Bible from which they are culled will be the more easily read from the order of service in which they are printed out, than from the Bible itself: and to make sure that the reader reads what you intend him to read, you had better remove the Bible from the lectern or desk, replacing it with a copy of the order of service open at the lesson.

The number of lessons: lessons in sequence

In services freely composed there is nothing sacrosanct about the number of lessons. There may be only one; there may be two; there may be more than two. If more than two lessons are used, they may be in sequence; and they must not be long. A sequence of lessons may be instructive and moving, as it traces the development of some great theme through the pages of Scripture; and it will afford an opportunity for several persons to take a share in the reading of God's word.

In historic liturgy the dignity of a feast is marked by the number of lessons read in sequence. The well-known service of Nine Lessons and Carols is directly based on this ancient liturgical practice. At the last lesson of a sequence the people may stand, if a pretext can be found in the climactic sense of the lesson, or in the dignity of the reader, or in both conjoined. It is worth noting that in the Scandinavian churches the people sit for psalms and canticles, but stand for the lessons.

Sources of lessons

The temper of our Prayer Book is thoroughly scriptural. The compilers of the Prayer Book commended it because (they said) 'nothing is ordained to be read but the very pure word of God, the Holy Scriptures, or that which is agreeable to the same'. *Nevertheless in composing a service of occasion we may sometimes go for a lesson to

---

* *The Book of Common Prayer, 1549: The Preface*

other sources than the Bible. We must of course avoid 'planting in uncertain stories, and legends';† we must choose what is orthodox in matter and appropriate in manner. During the long centuries that have elapsed since the canon of Scripture was established the Holy Spirit has not ceased his life-giving work in the hearts of the people of God; and in the writings of saints, doctors and great preachers there are magnificent passages that may justly be called inspired, and that are well fitted to be read aloud in public worship. John Bunyan, for example, comes to mind as an author steeped in Scripture, who utters Christian truth in language very close to that of our own liturgy. For an example of a lesson chosen from Bunyan, see **The Laying up of Colours** (page 155). For other non-scriptural lessons consult A.C. Bouquet, *A Lectionary of Christian Prose* (Derby, 1965).

Announcing a lesson

Compose a single sentence or phrase which will sum up the import of the lesson and direct the attention of the worshippers towards it. Such a sentence had best be printed in the order of service, together with a reference to the source of the lesson. The reader need not announce this reference, but after reading the sentence he will at once begin the lesson. See the examples below, at the lessons from Ecclesiasticus and from Revelation.

A lesson read by more than one voice

To relieve the tedium of a long lesson, allot it to several voices.

For example, the story of the creation in the first chapter of Genesis may be divided between three voices like this:

First Reader	In the beginning God created the heaven and the earth. And the earth was without form, and void: etc.
Second Reader	And God said, Let the waters under the heaven be gathered together unto one place, etc.
Third Reader	And God said, Let the waters bring forth abundantly the moving creature that hath life, etc.
Three together	Thus the heavens and the earth were finished, and all the host of them. And on the seventh day God ended his work which he had made; and he rested on the seventh day from all his work which he had made.

Genesis 1. 1-27, 31-2.2

† *Ibid*

Here is a lesson divided between two voices:

First voice	The farm hand, the smith, the potter: types of the craftsman, whose labour is indispensable to the welfare of human society. The wisdom of the scribe cometh by opportunity of leisure: etc.
Second voice	So is the smith sitting by the anvil, And considering the unwrought iron; etc.
First voice	So is the potter sitting at his work, And turning the wheel about with his feet, etc.
Second voice	All these put their trust in their hands; And each becometh wise in his own work. etc.
Both together	But they will maintain the fabric of the world; And in the handywork of their craft is their prayer.

Ecclesiasticus 38. 24-26, 28-34

And another lesson divided between three voices:

First voice	A vision of the holy city, where the will of God prevails. I saw a new heaven and a new earth: for the first heaven and the first earth were passed away; and there was no more sea.
Second voice	I saw the holy city, new Jerusalem, coming down from God out of heaven, prepared as a bride adorned for her husband.
Third voice	And the city had no need of sun or moon to shine upon it; for the glory of God gave it light, and the Lamb is the light of it.
First voice	By its light shall the nations walk, and the kings of the earth shall bring their glory and honour into it.
Second voice	And the gates of it shall not be shut at all by day; and there shall be no night there.
Third voice	And they shall bring the glory and honour of the nations into it: but nothing unclean shall enter, nor anyone whose ways are false or foul:
Three together	but only those who are inscribed in the Lamb's book of life.

Revelation 21. 1-2, 23-27

In each of these three lessons the final paragraph, or sentence, or clause, clinches the argument; and its importance is made clear when the volume of sound is doubled or trebled, as the voices join together to read it. The effect is surprising and impressive.

The singing of lessons

The singing of lessons need not be confined to the lessons at the Communion. In the Prayer Book of 1549 and 1552 a rubric at Matins ordered that in choral foundations the lessons of the choir Office, as well as those of the Communion, should be sung:

> *And (to the end the people may the better hear) in such places where they do sing, there shall the lessons be sung in a plain tune after the manner of distinct reading: and likewise the epistle and gospel.*

In choral foundations today the singing of a lesson, especially in a procession, may sometimes be found appropriate and moving.

It is worth noting that in the old English uses the lessons of the choir Office were sung, and were followed at once by a responsory, also sung. Lesson and responsory are fused into a single act: the lesson propounds a theme, the responsory comments on it, expands it, exhibits one facet of its truth for the contemplation of the worshipper. Here is a form worth bringing again into use where there are competent singers and musicians. But the framing of a responsory needs care.

The printing of lessons

In a large building it is essential, and in a small building it is often desirable, that lessons should be printed out in full in the order of service, in case they should be badly read. If the lessons, not being printed out, are inaudibly read, there will be gaps in the sequence of thought or mood, and the service will languish.

The rehearsal of lessons

If a lesson is to be read by a layman who is not accustomed to read in public, he should be persuaded, if circumstances allow, to rehearse beforehand in the church. The resonance of a large building will prove unexpectedly baffling to one who lacks experience in dealing with it; and the novice should not be excused from rehearsal on the grounds of his eminence or ability in other fields. But such a man will usually be glad of the opportunity of getting on terms with what he is to read, and with the place in which he is to read it, at a private rehearsal.

18. Litanies

The word Litany is thus defined by the Shorter English Dictionary:

> *A form of public prayer, usually penitential, consisting of a series of petitions, in which the clergy lead and the people respond. A litany may be used either as part of a service or by itself, in the latter case often in procession.*

The Litany in the Book of Common Prayer was published, set to simple music, in 1544. It was the very first form of public prayer in English; and perhaps the finest. It was composed by Archbishop Cranmer, to be sung in procession before the Sunday Eucharist.

Dr Brightman has called it 'one of the magnificences of Christendom'. Dr Percy Dearmer in 1933 wrote of it:

> *The Prayer Book Litany, while it combines the two original objects of processions - prayer against evils and dangers and prayer for the fruits of the earth - greatly extends the realm of intercession, stretching out those touching and melodious phrases, which are now of the very marrow of the English language, to all human needs, dangers, sorrows, aspirations, and efforts towards perfection, and ending with the two beautiful supplications in which the people turn at length to pray for their own necessities. In contrast to the tedious iteration of the Latin Litanies and to the weak and selfish spirit of many popular modern devotions, we think proudly of the English Litany, and have a right to be proud of it. We are indeed brought to the centre of our worship through a noble gate, through the preparation of that generous, unselfish, and humble intercession for the human race which the Litany has given us.*

The Prayer Book Litany, however, will not always serve our purpose in a service of occasion. Other litanies can be written.

When should a litany be used? Use a litany to engage the interest and the active participation of the congregation. Use it to avoid the monotony of a succession of prayers read by the Minister. Use it to bring within the orbit of prayer a series of subjects, or several facets of a single subject, with brevity and economy.

Litanies need not be only penitential. They can deal with any of the moods of public prayer. Consult the Litanies section in the chapter on **Forms of Prayer** (page 362).

19. The Middle Voluntary

Its history

> *The insertion of an organ voluntary after the psalms both at the Morning and Evening Service was a custom that prevailed to the latter part of the nineteenth century. For a long time a definite composition was played, but latterly it became usual for the organist to extemporize at this place in the service. Samuel Sebastian Wesley, when organist at Winchester Cathedral (1849-65), was famous for his extempore playing after the psalms, before the anthem, and at the end of the service.*

E.H. Fellowes, English Cathedral Music (London, 1941)

James Clifford, minor canon of St Paul's, in his Divine Services and Anthems published in 1664, noted the exact procedure usually followed at the Sunday services not only in his own time but also in the years immediately before the Civil War. Clifford's purpose was to place on record the conditions, as he remembered them, before the churches had been closed, whereas he feared that many important details might otherwise have been forgotten and neglected. Clifford remarks:

> *The first service in the morning*
>
> *After the Psalms a Voluntary on the organ alone*
>
> *At Evening Service*
>
> *After the Psalms a Voluntary alone by the organ*

In the eighteenth century one writer was moved to 'lament that the idea of a voluntary on the organ is lost in those Capriccios on a single stop, which, as well in our parochial as cathedral service, follow the psalms', where previously there had been 'a slow solemn movement'. *

In 1736 the Dean of Salisbury wrote to the Minister and churchwardens of the parish church of Calne in Wiltshire:

> *that whereas the parishioners had been scandalized by some persons 'playing on the Organ light gay Tunes, highly improper and indecent to be play'd in the House of God, We do strictly enjoyn the said Minister, etc., for the future not to permit anyone to play on the Organ during Divine Service, but the Organist himself; and not to suffer him to play anything more than a grave voluntary after the Reading Psalms'.†*

---

* *Christopher Dearnley: English Church Music 1650-1750* (Oxford, 1972)
† *Ibid*

The Middle Voluntary today

The use of the Middle Voluntary today during the Office and the Eucharist is discussed in the earlier Chapter about today's perspective on liturgy (page 20).

In any order of service you may insert a Middle Voluntary:

1. to allow some moments of relaxation;
2. to allow time for reflection on a preceding lesson, or sermon, or intercession;
3. to establish a mood, whether of joy, or of peace, or of trust, or of some other mood called for at a particular moment.

And remember you need not use only the organ; use piano, or harpsichord, or harp, or guitar, or solo string, or solo woodwind.

Here are some examples of each of the three uses of the Middle Voluntary.

1. for relaxation

THE SECOND LESSON,
from the New Testament

THE MIDDLE VOLUNTARY

Music for Organ, or for some other instrument,
or for voice and instrument, or to accompany a dance

Coventry Cathedral: Morning Prayer 1977

2. for reflection

The music here is a choral prelude for the organ. The words of the hymn on which the prelude was composed are printed in the order of service.

At the end of the Lesson the reader retires.
The whole congregation sits in silence while there is played on the organ
J.S. Bach's choral prelude on the Hymn Liebster Jesu, wir sind hier.

THE MIDDLE VOLUNTARY

Blessed Jesu, at thy word
We are gather'd all to hear thee:
Let our hearts and souls be stirr'd
Now to seek and love and fear thee;
By thy teachings sweet and holy
Drawn from earth to love thee solely.

Coventry Cathedral:
The Girls' Friendly Society Centenary 1975

2. for reflection

The lesson here is full of grief; it is a lament. The music for oboe solo which follows the lesson not only allows time for reflection on the lesson, but also reinforces its mood, for Britten's music is itself a lament.

III THE AFFLICTIONS OF GOD'S PEOPLE

THE FIRST LESSON:

Lamentations 5 (New English Bible)

A prayer for remembrance and restoration

Remember, O Lord, what has befallen us;
look, and see how we are scorned.
Our patrimony is turned over to strangers
and our homes to foreigners.
We are like orphans, without a father; our mothers are like widows.
We must buy our own water to drink,
our own wood can only be had at a price.
The yoke is on our necks, we are overdriven;
we are weary and are given no rest.
We came to terms, now with the Egyptians,
now with the Assyrians, to provide us with food.
Our fathers sinned and are no more,
and we bear the burden of their guilt.
Slaves have become our rulers,
and there is no one to rescue us from them.
We must bring in our food from the wilderness,
risking our lives in the scorching heat.
Our skins are blackened as in a furnace by the ravages of starvation.

Women were raped in Zion, virgins raped in the cities of Judah.
Princes were hung up by their hands, and elders received no honour.
Young men toil to grind corn, and boys stumble under loads of wood.
Elders have left off their sessions in the gate,
and young men no longer pluck the strings.
Joy has fled from our hearts, and our dances are turned to mourning.
The garlands have fallen from our heads;
woe betide us, sinners that we are.
For this we are sick at heart, for all this our eyes grow dim:
because Mount Zion is desolate and over it the jackals run wild.

O Lord, thou art enthroned for ever,
thy throne endures from one generation to another.
Why wilt thou quite forget us and forsake us these many days?
O Lord, turn us back to thyself, and we will come back;
renew our days as in times long past.
For if thou hast utterly rejected us,
then great indeed has been thy anger against us.

A brief silence.

THE MIDDLE VOLUNTARY

Niobe, from Six Metamorphoses after Ovid, for oboe solo
Benjamin Britten (1913-77)

The Royal School of Church Music:
The American Association of Anglican Musicians 1978

3. to set a mood

The Middle Voluntary establishes a mood of festivity at the Jubilee of the Royal School of Church Music, celebrated at the Royal Albert Hall, London, in 1977. The Introduction to the order of service remarked that 'Boyce's Symphony, to be played tonight as the Middle Voluntary, is happy and carefree music of superb quality: it is there simply to be enjoyed by everyone'.

MIDDLE VOLUNTARY

SYMPHONY No 4 IN F by William Boyce (1710-79)
Allegro Vivace ma non troppo Gavot

The Royal School of Church Music: The Jubilee 1977

20. The National Anthem

On national and civic occasions, especially when the Armed Forces are present, the National Anthem is expected to be sung. It may be used – not very profitably – at the beginning of a service, when it serves as little more than a summons to attention.

But with a little care it is possible to introduce the National Anthem in such a way that it becomes what in fact it is – a prayer for the Sovereign. It may be set in a context of intercession (during which the congregation must of course be standing, not kneeling).

Consult **Elements in an Order of Service: 1: Acclamations** (page 48) and **16: Laying Up of Colours** (page 155); and **Orders of Service 6: Trafalgar Day** (page 317).

21. Poetry

Poetry is delight, ecstasy, grief, wit, wisdom, illumination, in a concentrated form. Poetry is also memorable.

Here, for example, is wonder, expressed in Hebrew poetry translated into an English prose which yet has the intensity, the memorable pith, of poetry:

> I will consider thy heavens, even the works of thy fingers:
> the moon and the stars, which thou hast ordained.
> What is man, that thou art mindful of him:
> and the son of man, that thou visitest him?

Psalm 8. Domine, Dominus noster

And here is wonder, expressed in a nursery rhyme which, if not poetry, is at any rate verse, and for that reason memorable – for if you learnt it in the nursery you will remember it always.

> Twinkle, twinkle, little star,
> How I wonder what you are!
> Up above the world so high,
> Like a diamond in the sky.

Taylor (1783-1824), Rhymes for the Nursery

A single poem, carefully placed in an order of service so that its relevance to the occasion is clear, will appeal to people who do not usually read poetry at all. There is an example in **A Memorial Service for a Righteous Unbeliever** on page 329 of this book. The same poem is used in **Elvis Presley: In Memoriam**, on page 339.

Similarly, one stanza of a poem may serve, in a sermon or elsewhere, to drive home an argument, especially if the poet surprises and shocks the reader with an unexpected turn of phrase in the last line, as in this stanza from verses by Thomas Jordan (1612-85):

> Your most beautiful bride who with garlands is crowned,
> And kills with each glance as she treads on the ground,
> Whose lightness and brightness doth shine in such splendour
> That none but the stars
> Are thought fit to attend her,
> Though now she be pleasant and sweet to the sense,
> Will be damnable mouldy a hundred years hence.

But there are other poems which require a certain sophistication among the worshippers. In the sequence of poems given below, the poem entitled **To See the Rabbit** would simply mystify an unlettered congregation: they would not get the drift of it. Those whose education equips them to appreciate it will find this poem both amusing and terrifying.

Here is one section of an order of service, a section in which poetry, prose, scripture, and music are mingled, to carry the argument forward.

The City marred by sin

Readers

What is sin?
Sin is men's failure to be themselves, their best selves,
themselves as God means them to be.
It is men's failure to trust one another.
And this is rebellion:
it is rebellion against the nature of the universe.

The City severed from the natural order.

TO SEE THE RABBIT

We are going to see the rabbit.
We are going to see the rabbit.
Which rabbit, people say?
Which rabbit, ask the children?
Which rabbit?
The only rabbit,
The only rabbit in England,
Sitting behind a barbed-wire fence
Under the floodlights, neon lights,
Sodium lights,
Nibbling grass
On the only patch of grass

In England, in England
(Except the grass by the hoardings
Which doesn't count.)
We are going to see the rabbit
And we must be there on time.

First we shall go by escalator,
Then we shall go by underground,
And then we shall go by motorway,
And then by helicopterway,
And the last ten yards we shall have to go
On foot.
And now we are going
All the way to see the rabbit,
We are nearly there,
We are longing to see it,
And so is the crowd
Which is here in thousands
With mounted policemen
And big loudspeakers
And bands and banners,
And everyone has come a long way.
But soon we shall see it
Sitting and nibbling
The blades of grass
On the only patch of grass
In – but something has gone wrong!
Why is everyone so angry,
Why is everyone jostling
And slanging and complaining?
The rabbit has gone,
Yes, the rabbit has gone.
He has actually burrowed down into the earth
And made himself a warren, under the earth,
Despite all these people,
And what shall we do?
What can we do?
It is all a pity, you must be disappointed,
Go home and do something else for today,
Go home again, go home for today.
For you cannot hear the rabbit, under the earth,
Remarking rather sadly to himself, by himself,
As he rests in his warren, under the earth:
'It won't be long, they are bound to come,
They are bound to come and find me, even here.'

Alan Brownjohn

The City a place of loneliness

In This City

In this city, perhaps a street.
In this street, perhaps a house.
In this house, perhaps a room
And in this room a woman sitting,
Sitting in the darkness, sitting and crying
For someone who has just gone through the door
And who has just switched off the light
Forgetting she was there.

Alan Brownjohn

The City a place of fear

Unreal City

Under the brown fog of a winter dawn,
A crowd flowed over London Bridge, so many,
I had not thought death had undone so many.
Sighs, short and infrequent, were exhaled,
And each man fixed his eyes before his feet.
Flowed up the hill and down King William Street,
To where Saint Mary Woolnoth kept the hours
With a dead sound on the final stroke of nine.
There I saw one I knew, and stopped him, crying: 'Stetson!
'You who were with me in the ships at Mylae!
'That corpse you planted last year in your garden,
'Has it begun to sprout? Will it bloom this year?
'Or has the sudden frost disturbed its bed?
'Oh keep the Dog far hence, that's friend to men,
'Or with his nails he'll dig it up again!
'You! hypocrite lecteur! – non semblable, - mon frère!'

T.S. Eliot: The Waste Land

Notes on T.S. Eliot's poem The Waste Land

What enters the poem in the final section is active evil. The world in its immediate impact is not just empty of life, but is full of the positive power of death. It has become a demonic realm. The forces that rule it and that are always secretly working behind its normal façade are forces of sheer destruction.

This way of experiencing the world pervades the consciousness and language of all people in modern cities. There is everywhere an undertone of fear, which keeps rising to the surface of voices and then subsiding. It is as if people were constantly watching for some ferocity to break out upon them from the swirling crowds or the speeding cars or the international crisis.

The language in which the Christian community speaks of its Lord does not have to be always assured, always exalted. Alongside its proclamation of the good news, it can also echo within itself the agonies of city life.

The Waste Land is a kind of poetry that the Christian community must constantly read. To hear, not exalted visions, but the actual tones of living speech, to explore the dull sufferings that reign there without revulsion or evasion - this is an essential part of its life in Christ and its service to the world.

A.C. McGill, Associate Professor of Religion
in Princeton University: The Celebration of Flesh

As Jesus looked at the crowds he was moved with compassion for them, for they were as bewildered and miserable as a flock of sheep with no shepherd.

Matthew 9. 36

Jesus said, I am the good shepherd; the good shepherd lays down his life for the sheep.

John 10. 11

HELP, GOOD SHEPHERD

Turn not aside, Shepherd,
to see How bright the constellations are,
Hanging in heaven, or on the tree;
The skyborn or terrestrial star

Brood not upon; the waters fleet,
Willows, or thy crown-destined thorn,
Full of her rubies, as is meet,
Or whitening in the eye of morn,

Pause not beside: shepherds' delight,
The pipe and tabor in the vale,
And mirthful watchfires of a night,
And herdsman's rest in wattled pale,

Forsake, though dearly earned: and still
Sound with thy crook the darkling flood,
Still range the sides of shelvy hill
And call about in underwood:

For on the hill are many strayed,
Some held in thickets plunge and cry,
And the deep waters make us afraid.
Come then and help us, or we die.

Ruth Pitter

Choir

Salvator mundi, salva nos, qui per crucem et sanguinem redemisti nos: auxiliare nobis, te deprecamur, Deus noster.

Thomas Tallis (1505-85)

O saviour of the world, who by thy cross and precious blood hast redeemed us: save us, and help us, we humbly beseech thee, O Lord.

The people stand to sing this Hymn.

HYMN
Repton AMR 184

Dear Lord and Father of mankind,
Forgive our foolish ways!
Re-clothe us in our rightful mind,
In purer lives thy service find,
In deeper reverence praise.

In simple trust like theirs who heard,
Beside the Syrian sea,
The gracious calling of the Lord,
Let us, like them, without a word
Rise up and follow thee.

Drop thy still dews of quietness,
Till all our strivings cease;
Take from our souls the strain and stress,
And let our ordered lives confess
The beauty of thy peace.

A poem, like a lesson, may be read by more than one voice. The poem above, entitled To See the Rabbit, was indeed read by three voices, as follows:

TO SEE THE RABBIT

pointed for 3 voices

1 We are going to see the rabbit.
All We are going to see the rabbit.
2 Which rabbit, people say?
3 Which rabbit, ask the children?
1 Which rabbit?
All The only rabbit.
1 The only rabbit in England,
Sitting behind a barbed-wire fence
Under the floodlights, neon lights,
Sodium lights,
Nibbling grass
On the only patch of grass
In England, All in England
2 (Except the grass by the hoardings
Which doesn't count.)
All We are going to see the rabbit
And we must be there on time.

3 First we shall go by escalator,
2 Then we shall go by underground,
3 And then we shall go by motorway,
2 And then by helicopterway,
1 And the last ten yards we shall have to go
On foot.

3 And now we are going
All the way to see the rabbit,
We are nearly there,
We are longing to see it,
And so is the crowd
Which is here in thousands
With mounted policemen
And big loudspeakers
And bands and banners,
All And everyone has come a long way.

1 But soon we shall see it
Sitting and nibbling
The blades of grass
On the only patch of grass
In – but something has gone wrong!
Why is everyone so angry,
Why is everyone jostling
And slanging and complaining?

2 The rabbit has gone,
All Yes, the rabbit has gone.
3 He has actually burrowed down into the earth
And made himself a warren, under the earth,
Despite all these people,
And what shall we do?
All What CAN we do?
2 It is all a pity, you must be disappointed,
Go home and do something else for today,
Go home again, go home for today.
3 For you cannot hear the rabbit under the earth,
Remarking rather sadly to himself, by himself,
As he rests in his warren, under the earth:
1 'It won't be long, they are bound to come,
They are bound to come and find me, even here.'

NOTE on the qualities of the voices: Voice 1 a youthful man's voice; Voice 2 an older, dark, man's voice; Voice 3 a light, woman's voice

A sequence of poems from **This Airy Day**: A divertimento for the spring-time of the year, composed by James Walker in celebration of the Stratford-upon-Avon Choral Society's 150th year, first performed in the Collegiate Church of the Holy Trinity at Stratford in April 1978.

I

Let's away with study

RANT

For Baritone Solo, Chorus and Orchestra

Obmittamus studia, from the Carmina Burana (13th century)
translated by HELEN WADDELL

Rant = a merrymaking, a spree

Let's away with study,
Folly's sweet.
Treasure all the pleasure
Of our youth:
Time enough for age
To think on Truth.
So short a day,
And life so quickly hasting,
And in study wasting
Youth that would be gay!

'Tis our spring that's
slipping,
Winter draweth near,
Life itself we're losing,
And this sorry cheer
Dries the blood and chills
the heart,
Shrivels all delight.
Age and all its crowd of ills
Terrifies our sight.
So short a day,
And life so quickly hasting,
And in study wasting
Youth that would be gay!

Let us as the gods do,
'Tis the wiser part:
Leisure and love's pleasure
Seek the young in heart.
Follow the old fashion,
Down into the street!
Down among the maidens,
And the dancing feet!
So short a day,
And life so quickly hasting,
And in study wasting
Youth that would be gay!

There for the seeing
Is all loveliness,
White limbs moving
Light in wantonness.
Gay go the dancers,
I stand and see,
Gaze, till their glances
Steal myself from me.
So short a day,
And life so quickly hasting,
And in study wasting
Youth that would be gay!

II

My Busconductor

REVERIE

Intimations of Mortality For Chorus and Orchestra

ROGER MCGOUGH

My busconductor tells me
he only has one kidney
and that may soon go on strike
through overwork.
Each busticket
takes on now a different shape
and texture.
He holds a ninepenny single
as if it were a rose
and puts the shilling in his bag
as a child into a gasmeter.
His thin lips
have no quips
for fat factorygirls
and he ignores
the drunk who snores
and the oldman who talks to himself
and gets off at the wrong stop.
He goes gently to the bedroom
of the bus
to collect
and watch familiar shops and pubs passby
(perhaps for the last time?)
The sameold streets look different now
more distinct
as through new glasses.
And the sky
was it ever so blue?
And all the time
deepdown in the deserted busshelter of his mind
he thinks about his journey nearly done.
One day he'll clock on and never clock off
or clock off and never clock on.

III

With rue my heart is laden

LAMENT

For Chorus and Orchestra

A.E. HOUSMAN

With rue my heart is laden
For golden friends I had
For many a rose-lipt maiden
And many a lightfoot lad.

By brooks too broad for leaping
The lightfoot boys are laid;
The rose-lipt girls are sleeping
In fields where roses fade.

IV

This airy day

RÉJOUISSANCE

For Baritone Solo, Chorus and Orchestra

W.R. RODGERS

In the end of the Sabbath, as it began to dawn toward the first day of the week, came Mary Magdalene.

The tomb, the tomb, that
was her core and care, her one sore.
The light had hardly scarleted the dark
Or the first bird sung when Mary came in sight
With eager feet. Grief, like last night's frost,
Whitened her face and tightened all her tears.
It was there, then, there at the blinding turn
Of the bare future that she met her past.
She only heard his Angel tell her how
The holding stone broke open and gave birth
To her dear Lord, and how his shadow ran
To meet him like a dog.

And as the sun
Burns through the simmering muslins of the mist
Slowly his darkened voice, that seemed like doubt,
Morninged into noon; the summering bees
Mounted and boiled over in the bell-flowers.
'Come out of your jail, Mary', he said, 'the doors are open
and joy has its ears cocked for your coming.
Earth now is no place to mope in. So throw away
Your doubt, cast every clout of care,
Hang all your hallelujahs out
This airy day.'

V

My beloved spake

EPITHALAMION

For Chorus and Orchestra

The Song of Songs
in the Authorised Version of The Bible

My beloved spake, and said unto me, Rise up, my love, my fair one, and come away. For, lo, the winter is past, the rain is over and gone; the flowers appear on the earth; the time of the singing of birds is come, and the voice of the turtle is heard in our land: the fig tree putteth forth her green figs, and the vines with the tender grape give a good smell. Arise, my love, my fair one, and come away.

VI

A Young Man's Song

PASTOURELLE

For Baritone Solo and Orchestra

WILLIAM BELL

Pastourelle = 1. Shepherdess; 2. A country dance

Maidens who this burning May
through the woods in quaint distress
wander till you find your way,
attend to what I have to say,
but ask me nothing,
ask me nothing,
ask me nothing you can guess.

Here I learned a year ago
this burden from a shepherdess:
'Love is wakefulness and woe,
'where it hurts you ought to know,
'so ask me nothing,
'ask me nothing,
'ask me nothing you can guess.'

Said I 'when such as you complain
'you cry to courtesy for redress:
'then may not I avenge your pain?'
but still she sang the same refrain,
'Ask me nothing,
'ask me nothing,
'ask me nothing you can guess.'

In the thicket where we hid
we found a primrose-bank to press,
and there I served her as she bid.
Let me shew you what we did!
but ask me nothing,
ask me nothing,
ask me nothing you can guess.

VII

The Trumpet

REVALLY

For Chorus and Orchestra

EDWARD THOMAS

Rise up, rise up,
And, as the trumpet blowing
Chases the dreams of men,
As the dawn glowing
The stars that left unlit
The land and water,
Rise up and scatter
The dew that covers
The print of last night's lovers –
Scatter it, scatter it!

While you are listening
To the clear horn,
Forget, men, everything
On this earth new-born,
Except that it is lovelier
Than any mysteries.
Open your eyes to the air
That has washed the eyes of the stars
Through all the dewy night:
Up with the light,
To the old wars;
Arise, arise!

22. Processions

A procession is an act of worship, not a mere perambulation. It is worship expressed as much by movement and colour as by the voice. 'A Perambulation alone is not a Procession: a Procession means going somewhere to do something. It is not necessary to say or do anything while going; but the priest and clerks must have somewhere to go and something to do when they get there.'[1]

There are in England, quite apart from the cathedrals, many large parish churches whose spacious aisles and transepts are daunting in their emptiness. These great spaces cease to be daunting as soon as they are used for expressive ceremonial actions such as a Procession. Especially in these large churches (but certainly also in smaller churches) the Procession affords an opportunity of offering prayer in many parts of the building, particularly at places – the altar of a saint, a tomb, a window – consecrated to the memory of persons and events notable in the life and tradition of the Christian Church. In this way the whole building, not merely the sanctuary, may in course of time become instinct with worship for those who frequent it.

The structure of a Procession

A Procession must have a clearly articulated structure; otherwise it will be desultory and tedious. In the course of it there will be at least one halt (called a 'station') for the offering of prayer, or the reading of a lection (not necessarily taken from the Bible), or for music.

Stations will be made at places in the church which are or may become the focus of devotion – the font, or an altar, or the picture of a saint in a window. The Procession of Thanksgiving on a festival should not lack its stations; one may be made at the entrance into the chancel (for this is a place of devotional significance, whether or not there is a rood there); and a station at the high altar will bring the Procession to its conclusion.

Beginning a Procession

The beginning of a Procession should be clear-cut. When the Litany of 1662 is sung in procession, there is no difficulty: for the Invocations the Ministers stand before the altar facing it; at 'Remember not' they all turn together and begin to move.

In other Processions, if a hymn is sung at the beginning, let the Ministers stand fast, facing the altar, while the hymn is played over on the organ; and let them turn together and begin to move as the first line of the hymn is sung. Nothing need usually be sung

[1] T.A. Lacey, The Liturgical Use of the Litany (London, 1883).

by way of preface to the hymn; but if any preface seems desirable, something more pregnant can be devised than the customary versicle and response –

℣ Let us proceed in peace;
℟ **In the name of the Lord. Amen.**

This is too brief; and it says nothing worth the saying. Far better would be a series of several versicles and responses, expressing the theme or purpose of the Procession which is to follow.

Hymns in a Procession

Where there is a choir, let one hymn in the Procession be diversified by having a verse, or two verses, sung by the choir alone. Perhaps only the Ministers are walking in the Procession and the choir are remaining in their stalls; no matter, the antiphony between choir and congregation will bring interest and relief. If the choir is walking in the Procession, the interest will be so much the greater; in this case the choir's verses may be unaccompanied, indeed must be so if the building is large and the choir is at a distance from the organ. The temporary silence of the organ will rest the sated ear; and when the organ resumes, its authority will be so much the greater.

A hymn must be of the right length to cover the movement of the Procession between one station and the next. The only way to make sure of this is to go over the route beforehand, walking at the pace to be adopted in the Procession, singing the hymn at the pace appropriate to the music, to the size of the building, and to the expected size of the congregation. (But you need not court unwelcome publicity by singing aloud; *chant intérieur* will suffice.)

The deportment of the choir

The members of the choir going in procession must not seem to be dawdling or sauntering: they must cultivate a bodily recollectedness, trunk steady, head erect, eyes front. The two ranks may either walk shoulder to shoulder (as they do at King's College, Cambridge), or else they may walk as far apart as will allow a choirmaster room to walk between the two leaders at the head of the choir. Turning a corner, each pair must execute a true right or left wheel, the inner man halting and pivoting through 90 degrees, the outer man walking along the circumference of one quarter of a circle, then both moving forward together.

Not many choirs walk well in procession. It is a thing which calls for calculated care and discipline – and rehearsal. If the route of the Procession is unfamiliar, the choir must not only be instructed where to go, it must actually be rehearsed in going there. Unrehearsed Processions have a randomness about them which is not edifying; a want of purposefulness, which is neatly mocked in a Latin couplet attributed to Canon

Henry Balmforth (but he is thinking of the clergy, who in this matter are known to be recalcitrant):

> *Hinc illinc pia turba virum proficiscitur ardens,*
>
> *Quid tamen efficiat dicere nemo potest.*
>
> *A mob of clerics assembles, and gets off to an eager start;*
>
> *but what the aim of it all may be is anybody's guess.*

The dress of the choir

Finally, a Procession will fail of its full effect if the choir is robed in the brief wisps of cotton which too commonly do duty for surplices. The traditional English surplice (such as you may see in the Cathedrals of Canterbury, Coventry, St Paul's, and Southwark) is very long, reaching nearly to the hem of the cassock beneath it, and cut very full, so that it ripples and undulates with the motion of the body. A line of such surplices in motion will charm the eye with an effect which Herrick, writing *Upon Julia's Clothes*, has happily described:

> *When as in silks my Julia goes,*
> *Then, then, methinks, how sweetly flows*
> *The liquefaction of her clothes!*

Here follow three Processions used in Coventry Cathedral:

1 Of Ascensiontide
2 For the Centenary of the Girls' Friendly Society
3 At a Memorial Service

In each of these Processions there are stations at the Tablets of the Word. These Tablets are slabs of concrete 15 feet long, affixed to the walls of the nave, four on the north wall and four on the south. On the Tablets are incised biblical texts describing the Person and the Work of Jesus Christ: and in the course of a Procession the texts are as it were lifted from the walls and made into matter for reflection, for instruction, and for prayer. At a station, the text of the Tablet is printed in the order of service; the text is followed by a lesson from which the text is drawn, and then (if the choir is present) by an anthem or carol; and the station ends with a repetition of the text thrown into versicles and responses, and a collect on the theme of the text.

There is also a station in the nave; this means that the Ministers (and the choir) are standing in the middle of the congregation; they are physically and obviously all one company of worshippers, who can join, for example, in a spoken Acclamation – something which calls for no musical skill but only for courage and enthusiasm.

Of Ascensiontide

Evensong is sung as far as the Third Collect and the Anthem. The Procession follows at once.

The Procession

The Procession goes from the chancel eastwards by the south choir aisle and the Lady Chapel to the Eighth Tablet of the Word in the north choir aisle.

HYMN

Come, ye faithful, raise the anthem,
Cleave the skies with shouts of praise;
Sing to him who found the ransom,
Ancient of eternal Days,
God of God, the Word incarnate,
Whom the heaven of heaven obeys.

Ere he raised the lofty mountains,
Formed the seas, or built the sky,
Love eternal, free, and boundless,
Moved the Lord of Life to die,
Fore-ordained the Prince of Princes
For the throne of Calvary.

People **There, for us and our redemption,**
See him all his life-blood pour!
There he wins our full salvation,
Dies that we may die no more;
Then, arising, lives for ever,
Reigning where he was before.

Choir High on yon celestial mountains
Stands his sapphire throne, all bright,
Midst unending Alleluias
Bursting from the sons of light;
Sion's people tell his praises,
Victor after hard-won fight.

People **Bring your harps, and bring your incense,**
Sweep the string and pour the lay;
Let the earth proclaim his wonders,
King of that celestial day;
He the Lamb once slain is worthy,
Who was dead, and lives for ay.

Laud and honour to the Father,
Laud and honour to the Son,
Laud and honour to the Spirit,
Ever Three and ever One,
Consubstantial, co-eternal,
While unending ages run.

UNSER HERRSCHER AMR 222

At the Eighth Tablet of the Word

FEAR NOT; I AM THE FIRST AND THE LAST.
I AM ALIVE FOR EVERMORE, AMEN;
AND HAVE THE KEYS OF HELL AND OF DEATH.

The people sit down.

The Provost reads THE LESSON: Revelation 1. 10, 12-18

I was in the Spirit on the Lord's day, and heard behind me a great voice, as of a trumpet, and I turned to see the voice that spake with me. And being turned, I saw seven golden candlesticks; and in the midst of the seven candlesticks one like unto the Son of man, clothed with a garment down to the foot, and girt about the paps with a golden girdle. His head and his hairs were white like wool, as white as snow; and his eyes were as a flame of fire; and his feet like unto fine brass, as if they burned in a furnace; and his voice as the sound of many waters. And he had in his right hand seven stars; and out of his mouth went a sharp two-edged sword; and his countenance was as the sun shineth in his strength. And when I saw him, I fell at his feet as dead. And he laid his right hand upon me, saying unto me, Fear not; I am the first and the last; I am he that liveth, and was dead; and, behold, I am alive for evermore, Amen; and have the keys of hell and of death.

The choir sings:

Ascendit Deus in jubilatione, et Dominus in voce tubae. Alleluia.
Dominus in coelo paravit sedem suam. Alleluia.

Peter Philips (d. 1628)

God is gone up with a merry noise; and the Lord with the sound of the trump. Alleluia. The Lord hath prepared his seat in heaven. Alleluia.

The people stand. The Precentor and the choir sing:

℣ Fear not; I am the first and the last.
℟ **I am alive for evermore, Amen;**
and have the keys of hell and of death.

O God the King of glory, who hast exalted thine only Son Jesus Christ with great triumph unto thy kingdom in heaven: We beseech thee, leave us not comfortless; but send to us thine Holy Ghost to comfort us, and exalt us unto the same place whither our Saviour Christ is gone before; who liveth and reigneth with thee and the same Holy Spirit, one God, world without end.
℟ **Amen.**

The procession moves westwards down the north aisle of choir and nave, and eastwards up the middle of the nave.

HYMN

People

Crown him with many crowns,
The Lamb upon his throne;
Hark! how the heavenly anthem drowns
All music but its own:
Awake, my soul, and sing
Of him who died for thee,
And hail him as thy matchless King
Through all eternity.

Choir and people

Crown him the Virgin's Son,
The God incarnate born,
Whose arm those crimson trophies won
Which now his brow adorn:
Fruit of the mystic Rose,
As of that Rose the Stem;
The Root whence mercy ever flows,
The Babe of Bethlehem.

Choir

Crown him the Lord of love;
Behold his hands and side,
Those wounds yet visible above
In beauty glorified:
No angel in the sky
Can fully bear that sight,
But downward bends his burning eye
At mysteries so bright.

People

Crown him the Lord of peace,
Whose power a sceptre sways
From pole to pole, that wars may cease,
And all be prayer and praise:
His reign shall know no end,
And round his piercèd feet
Fair flowers of Paradise extend
Their fragrance ever sweet.

Choir and people

Crown him the Lord of years,
The Potentate of time,
Creator of the rolling spheres,
Ineffably sublime:
All hail, Redeemer, hail!
For thou hast died for me;
Thy praise shall never, never fail
Throughout eternity

DIADEMATA AMR 224

In the Nave

THE ACCLAMATION

The Precentor calls out:

Lift up your heads, O ye gates,
And be ye lift up, ye everlasting doors;

Choir and people shout in answer:

And the King of glory shall come in.

℣ Who is the King of glory?
℟ **The Lord of hosts, he is the King of glory.**
℣ Thou art the King of glory, O Christ;
℟ **Thou art the everlasting Son of the Father.**
℣ When thou hadst overcome the sharpness of death;
℟ **Thou didst open the kingdom of heaven to all believers.**
℣ Thou sittest at the right hand of God;
℟ **In the glory of the Father.**
℣ King of kings, And Lord of lords;
℟ **KING OF KINGS, AND LORD OF LORDS.**
℣ Risen!
℟ **RISEN!**
℣ Ascended!
℟ **ASCENDED!**
℣ Glorified!
℟ **GLORIFIED!**

At once there follows this Hymn; the procession moves towards the chancel:

**All hail the power of Jesus' name!
Let angels prostrate fall;
Bring forth the royal diadem
And crown him Lord of all.**

**Crown him ye morning stars of light,
Who fixed this floating ball;
Now hail the Strength of Israel's might,
And crown him Lord of all.**

Crown him, ye martyrs of your God,
Who from his altar call;
Extol the Stem-of-Jesse's Rod,
And crown him Lord of all.

Ye seed of Israel's chosen race,
Ye ransomed of the fall,
Hail him who saves you by his grace,
And crown him Lord of all.

Sinners, whose love can ne'er forget
The wormwood and the gall,
Go spread your trophies at his feet,
And crown him Lord of all.

Let every tribe and every tongue
Before him prostrate fall,
And shout in universal song
The crownèd Lord of all.

MILES LANE AMR 217

The Precentor goes to the gate of the Sanctuary; the choir to their stalls; the clergy to the Sanctuary; the Bishop with his Chaplains to the High Altar.

At the High Altar

Precentor and choir:

℣ Fear not; I am the first and the last.
℟ **I am alive for evermore, Amen;**
and have the keys of hell and of death.

Deliver us, O Lord Christ, from fear and from despair and from the bitter pains of death; and in thy presence assure us of a happiness that nothing can ever assail; because with the Father and the Spirit thou reignest God, world without end.
℟ **Amen.**

The choir, the ministers and the people kneel.

The Bishop turns to them and blesses them:

May the eternal Father,
who dwells in light unapproachable, shine into your hearts.

May the eternal Son,
who is the light of the world, illuminate all your ways.

May the eternal Spirit
bring you out of darkness and error
into the clear light and true knowledge of the triune God.

May the same God in the plenitude of his love
pour upon you the torrents of his grace,
bless you and keep you in his holy fear,
prepare you for a happy eternity,
and receive you at last into immortal glory.

The choir sings:

Amen.

~~~~~~

4. For the Centenary of the Girls' Friendly Society 1975

The Procession is a meditation on Christian discipleship. It begins not with a hymn but with a lesson (one of the most powerful passages in the Old Testament) read from the Sanctuary.

In the first hymn of the Procession, 'Bright the vision', which picks up the imagery of the lesson, the last line of the second verse suggests antiphony between two groups of singers, repeating 'Each to each the alternate hymn'. Accordingly, the third verse is allotted to the people on the left, and the following verse to the people on the right.

The Procession

When the Hymn is ended and the alms have been presented,
the Bishop and his Chaplains turn to the people.
The Precentor is conducted to the Sanctuary, where he also turns to the people.
The Cross and lights take up their places in readiness for the procession.
~~~~~~

THE CLEANSING FIRE

The Precentor reads THE LESSON: Isaiah 6. 1-8

> I saw the Lord sitting upon a throne, high and lifted up, and his train filled the temple. Above it stood the seraphims: each one had six wings; with twain he covered his face, and with twain he covered his feet, and with twain he did fly. And one cried unto another, and said, Holy, holy, holy, is the Lord of hosts: the whole earth is full of his glory. And the posts of the door moved at the voice of him that cried, and the house was filled with smoke. Then said I, Woe is me! for I am undone; because I am a man of unclean lips, and I dwell in the midst of a people of unclean lips: for mine eyes have seen the King, the Lord of hosts. Then flew one of the seraphims unto me, having a live coal in his hand, which he had taken with the tongs from off the altar: and he laid it upon my mouth, and said, Lo, this hath touched thy lips; and thine iniquity is taken away, and thy sin purged. Also I heard the voice of the Lord, saying, Whom shall I send, and who will go for us? Then said I, Here am I; send me.

In a loud voice the Bishop calls out, and the people shout in reply:

PSALM 103. Benedic, anima mea

℣ Praise the Lord, O my soul:
℟ **And all that is within me praise his holy name.**
℣ Praise the Lord, O my soul:
℟ **And forget not all his benefits.**
℣ Who forgiveth all thy sin:
℟ **And healeth all thine infirmities.**

The Bishop:

Lord God Almighty, who has given to us the vision of thy holiness, and therewith of our unworthiness to be thy witnesses: Touch, we pray thee, our lips with thy cleansing fire; that so cleansed and hallowed, we may go forth among men as those whom thou hast sent; through Jesus Christ our Lord.
℟ **Amen.**

The procession goes from the Sanctuary
to the Fifth Tablet of the Word in the south aisle, during this Hymn:

Laus Deo AMR 161

Bright the vision that delighted
Once the sight of Judah's seer;
Sweet the countless tongues united
To entrance the prophet's ear.

Round the Lord in glory seated
Cherubim and seraphim
Filled his temple, and repeated
Each to each the alternate hymn:

People on the left

'Lord, thy glory fills the heaven;
Earth is with its fulness stored;
Unto thee be glory given
Holy, Holy, Holy, Lord.'

People on the right

Heaven is still with glory ringing,
Earth takes up the angels' cry,
'Holy, Holy, Holy,' singing,
'Lord of Hosts, the Lord most high.'

Everyone **With his seraph train before him,**
With his holy Church below,
Thus unite we to adore him,
Bid we thus our anthem flow:

'Lord, thy glory fills the heaven;
Earth is with its fulness stored;
Unto thee be glory given,
Holy, Holy, Holy, Lord.'

THE VINE AND THE BRANCHES

At the Fifth Tablet of the Word

I AM THE VINE, YE ARE THE BRANCHES.
HE THAT ABIDETH IN ME, AND I IN HIM,
THE SAME BEARETH MUCH FRUIT;
FOR APART FROM ME YE CAN DO NOTHING.

A Chaplain reads THE LESSON: John 15. 4-7

Jesus said, 'Just as the branch cannot bear any fruit unless it shares the life of the vine, so you can produce nothing unless you go on growing in me. I am the vine itself, you are the branches. It is the man who shares my life and whose life I share who proves fruitful. For the plain fact is that apart from me you can do nothing at all. The man who does not share my life is like a branch that is broken off and withers away. He becomes just like the dry sticks that men pick up and use for firewood. But if you live your life in me, and my words live in your hearts, you can ask for whatever you like and it will come true for you.'

The Bishop:

Lord, who hast warned us that without thee we can do nothing: So take and possess us, that our weakness may be transformed by thy power; that we be no longer our own, but thine; who now reignest with the Father and the Holy Spirit, God for ever.
℟ **Amen.**

The procession moves to the Sixth Tablet of the Word in the north aisle, while a voluntary is played on the organ.

YE ALSO SHALL BEAR WITNESS

At the Sixth Tablet of the Word

WHEN THE COMFORTER IS COME,
WHOM I WILL SEND UNTO YOU FROM THE FATHER,
EVEN THE SPIRIT OF TRUTH, WHICH PROCEEDETH FROM THE FATHER,
HE SHALL TESTIFY OF ME:
AND YE ALSO SHALL BEAR WITNESS.

Another Chaplain reads THE LESSON: St John 15. 16, 20, 26, 27

Jesus said: 'It is not that you have chosen me; but it is I who have chosen you. I have appointed you to go and bear fruit that will be lasting; so that whatever you ask the Father in my name, he will give it you.

Do you remember what I said to you, "The servant is not greater than his master"? If they have persecuted me, they will persecute you as well, but if they have followed my teaching, they will also follow yours.

But when the helper comes, that is, the Spirit of truth, who comes from the Father and whom I myself will send to you from the Father, he will speak plainly about me. And you yourselves will also speak plainly about me, because you have been with me.'

Bishop and people:

℣ When the Comforter is come,
whom I will send unto you from the Father;
℟ **Even the Spirit of truth, which proceedeth from the Father;**
℣ He shall testify of me:
℟ **And ye also shall bear witness.**

The Bishop:

Bless, O Lord, all who bear witness in thy name, by teaching, by healing, by leadership, in the far outposts of the world; and set our hearts on fire to serve thee, and to spread thy kingdom; for Jesus Christ's sake.
℟ **Amen.**

The procession moves westwards down the north aisle of the nave, and eastwards up the middle of the nave, during this Hymn:

WINCHESTER OLD AMR 154

When God of old came down from heaven,
In power and wrath he came;
Before his feet the clouds were riven,
Half darkness and half flame:

But, when he came the second time,
He came in power and love;
Softer than gale at morning prime
Hovered his holy Dove.

The fires, that rushed on Sinai down
In sudden torrents dread,
Now gently light, a glorious crown,
On every sainted head.

And as on Israel's awestruck ear
The voice exceeding loud,
The trump that angels quake to hear,
Thrilled from the deep, dark cloud;

People on the left

So, when the Spirit of our God
Came down his flock to find,
A voice from heaven was heard abroad,
A rushing, mighty wind.

People on the right

It fills the Church of God; it fills
The sinful world around:
Only in stubborn hearts and wills
No place for it is found.

Everyone **Come, Lord, come Wisdom, Love, and Power,**
Open our ears to hear;
Let us not miss the accepted hour:
Save, Lord, by love or fear.

PREPARING THE WAY

In the Nave

The Bishop reads THE LESSON: Matthew 11. 2-10

John the Baptist was in prison when he heard what Christ was doing, and he sent a message through his own disciples asking the question, 'Are you the one who was to come or are we to look for somebody else?'

Jesus gave them this reply, 'Go and tell John what you see and hear – that blind men are recovering their sight, cripples are walking, lepers being healed, the deaf hearing, the dead being brought to life and the good news is being given to those in need. And happy is the man who never loses his faith in me.'

As John's disciples were going away Jesus began talking to the crowd about John:

'What did you go out into the desert to look at? A reed waving in the breeze? No? Then what was it you went out to see? – a man dressed in fine clothes? But the men who wear fine clothes live in the courts of kings! But what did you really go to see – a prophet? Yes, I tell you, a prophet and far more than a prophet! This is the man of whom the scripture says –

Behold, I send my messenger before thy face, Who shall prepare thy way before thee.'

The Bishop continues:

Friends in Jesus Christ,
Do you believe in God who made you?
℟ **We believe.**
Do you believe in Christ who redeemed you?
℟ **We believe.**
Do you believe in the Holy Spirit who makes you holy?
℟ **We believe.**

Will you thank the Father for his love?
℟ **We will thank the Father.**
Will you trust the Son who forgives you and saves you?
℟ **We will trust the Son.**
Will you obey our Lord the Spirit at all times and in all ways?
℟ **We will obey our Lord the Spirit.**

Glory be to the Father, and to the Son, and to the Holy Spirit:
℟ **As it was in the beginning, is now, and ever shall be: world without end. Amen.**

The Bishop:

O God, who hast sent thy servants to prepare thy way: Fill our hearts with love, and strengthen our hands to work, that we may make ready the way of our King; for Jesus Christ's sake.
℟ **Amen.**

The procession moves through the nave and the chancel to the Sanctuary during this Hymn:

Laudate Dominum AMR 376

Ye servants of God, your Master proclaim,
And publish abroad his wonderful name;
The name all-victorious of Jesus extol:
His Kingdom is glorious, and rules over all.

God ruleth on high, almighty to save;
And still he is nigh: his presence we have.
The great congregation his triumph shall sing,
Ascribing salvation to Jesus our King.

Salvation to God who sits on the throne!
Let all cry aloud, and honour the Son.
The praises of Jesus the angels proclaim,
Fall down on their faces, and worship the Lamb.

Then let us adore, and give him his right;
All glory and power, all wisdom and might,
And honour and blessing, with angels above,
And thanks never-ceasing, and infinite love.

The Precentor goes to the gate of the Sanctuary;
the Diocesan Chaplains to the Sanctuary;
the Bishop to the High Altar, where he turns to the people.

At the High Altar
Bishop and people:

℣ When the Comforter is come,
whom I will send unto you from the Father;
℟ **Even the Spirit of truth, which proceedeth from the Father;**
℣ He shall testify of me;
℟ **And ye also shall bear witness.**

Bring us, O Holy Spirit, into the way that leadeth to all virtues, beauties, adorations and graces, to all praises, triumphs and thanksgivings, to holiness and communion with thee, and to blessedness here and hereafter; through Jesus Christ our Lord.
℟ **Amen.**

The ministers and the people kneel. The Bishop blesses them:

Unto God's gracious mercy and protection we commit you.
The Lord bless you and keep you.
The Lord make his face to shine upon you,
and be gracious unto you.
The Lord lift up the light of his countenance upon you,
and give you peace,
now and always.
℟ **Amen.**

5. At a Memorial Service for Stella Marchioness of Reading 1971

Lady Reading gave to Coventry Cathedral in 1953 the processional cross, called the Michael Cross, bearing on its face the figure of St Michael, the Cathedral's patron saint. The Michael Cross heads the Eucharistic company at the Eucharist on every Sunday of the year except in Lent, when the processional Cross of Nails is used instead.

At this Memorial Service for Lady Reading the Michael Cross carried at the head of the liturgical Procession powerfully recalled the donor's person and work.

A PAEAN is played.

Then the people stand to sing this Hymn,
and the Ministers assemble at the chancel step in readiness for the Procession.
The Michael Cross is escorted by members of the Women's Royal Voluntary Service.

HYMN

Victory AMR 135

Alleluia! Alleluia! Alleluia!
The strife is o'er, the battle done;
Now is the Victor's triumph won;
O let the song of praise be sung:
Alleluia!

Death's mightiest powers have done their worst,
And Jesus hath his foes dispersed;
Let shouts of praise and joy outburst:
Alleluia!

On the third morn he rose again
Glorious in majesty to reign:
O let us swell the joyful strain:
Alleluia!

Lord, by the stripes which wounded thee
From death's dread sting thy servant free,
That we may live, and sing to thee
Alleluia!

THE PROCESSION

At the chancel step

I THE VICTORY OF LOVE

FANFARE

The Vice-Provost:

There was a war in heaven: Michael and his angels fought against the dragon: and the dragon fought and his angels, and prevailed not.

And I heard a loud voice saying in heaven,

The people shout aloud:

Now is come salvation, and strength,
and the kingdom of our God, and the power of his Christ:
for the accuser of our brethren is cast down,
which accused them before our God day and night.

The Vice-Provost:

And they overcame him by the blood of the Lamb,
and by the word of their testimony;

The people:

And they loved not their lives unto the death.

FANFARE

℣ O praise the Lord, ye angels of his, ye that excel in strength:
℟ **Ye that fulfil his commandments,**
and hearken unto the voice of his words.
℣ O praise the Lord, all ye his hosts:
℟ **Ye servants of his that do his pleasure.**

The Vice-Provost:

God, whom angels and archangels and all the company of heaven adore and obey: Grant that we who hear the story of St Michael triumphing over evil may be assured of the victory of thy truth, and may see every rebel will at last made captive to thy mercy; through Jesus Christ our Lord.

Answer: **Amen.**

This Hymn follows at once,
and the procession moves westwards by the middle alley of the nave
and eastwards by the south aisle
to the Fourth Tablet of the Word in the north aisle.

HYMN

Crucis milites AMR 305

Soldiers of the Cross arise!
Gird you with your armour bright:
Mighty are your enemies,
Hard the battle ye must fight.

O'er a faithless fallen world
Raise your banner in the sky;
Let it float there wide unfurled;
Bear it onwards, lift it high.

'Mid the homes of want and woe,
Strangers to the living word,
Let the Saviour's herald go,
Let the voice of hope be heard.

Where the shadows deepest lie,
Carry truth's unsullied ray;
Where are crimes of blackest dye,
There the saving sign display.

People on the left

To the weary and the worn
Tell of realms where sorrows cease;
To the outcast and forlorn
Speak of mercy and of peace.

People on the right

Guard the helpless, seek the strayed;
Comfort troubles, banish grief;
In the might of God arrayed,
Scatter sin and unbelief.

Everyone **Be the banner still unfurled,**
Still unsheathed the Spirit's sword,
Till the kingdoms of the world
Are the Kingdom of the Lord.

The people sit down.

II THE EXAMPLE OF LOVE

At the Fourth Tablet of the Word

A NEW COMMANDMENT I GIVE UNTO YOU,
THAT YE LOVE ONE ANOTHER,
AS I HAVE LOVED YOU.

THE LESSON: John 13. 3-5, 12-15, 34, 35

During supper, Jesus, well aware that the Father had entrusted everything to him, and that he had come from God and was going back to God, rose from table, laid aside his garments, and taking a towel, tied it round him. Then he poured water into a basin, and began to wash his disciples' feet and to wipe them with the towel.

After washing their feet and taking his garments again, he sat down. 'Do you understand what I have done for you?' he asked. 'You call me "Master" and "Lord", and rightly so, for that is what I am. Then if I, your Lord and Master, have washed your feet, you also ought to wash one another's feet. I have set you an example: you are to do as I have done for you.

I give you a new commandment: love one another; as I have loved you, so you are to love one another. If there is this love among you, then all will know that you are my disciples.'

The people stand.

The Vice-Provost and the people:

℣ If I, your Lord and Master, have washed your feet;
℟ **You also ought to wash one another's feet.**
℣ If there is this love among you;
℟ **Then all will know that you are my disciples.**

The Vice-Provost:

Lord Jesus Christ, who hast taught us the greatest of all is the servant of all: Cast out from us all false ambitions, and make us to reign by serving our brothers; for thy name's sake.

Answer: **Amen.**

The procession moves westwards by the north aisle
and eastwards by the middle alley to the sanctuary during this Hymn:

HYMN

Darwall's 148th AMR 371

Ye holy angels bright,
Who wait at God's right hand,
Or through the realms of light
Fly at your Lord's command,
Assist our song,
For else the theme
Too high doth seem
For mortal tongue.

Ye blessed souls at rest,
Who ran this earthly race,
And now, from sin released,
Behold the Saviour's face,
His praises sound,
As in his light
With sweet delight
Ye do abound.

Ye saints, who toil below,
Adore your heavenly King,
And onward as ye go
Some joyful anthem sing;
Take what he gives
And praise him still,
Through good and ill,
Who ever lives.

My soul, bear thou thy part,
Triumph in God above,
And with a well-tuned heart
Sing thou the songs of love.
Let all thy days
Till life shall end,
Whate'er he send,
Be filled with praise.

A TRUMPET TUNE is played.

The clergy stand within the sanctuary.
The Vice-Provost goes up to the altar, and turns to the people.

III THE ASSURANCE OF LOVE

At the high altar

The Vice-Provost:

Who shall separate us from the love of Christ? I am persuaded, that neither death, nor life, nor angels, nor principalities, nor powers, nor things present, nor things to come, nor height, nor depth, nor any other creature, shall be able to separate us from the love of God, which is in Christ Jesus our Lord.

Romans 8

O Almighty God, who hast knit together thine elect in one communion and fellowship, in the mystical body of thy Son Christ our Lord: Grant us grace so to follow thy blessed Saints in all virtuous and godly living, that we may come to those unspeakable joys, which thou hast prepared for them that unfeignedly love thee; through the same Jesus Christ our Lord.

Answer: **Amen.**

Unto God's gracious mercy and protection we commit you.
The Lord bless you, and keep you.
The Lord make his face to shine upon you,
and be gracious unto you.
The Lord lift up the light of his countenance upon you,
and give you peace.

Answer: **Amen.**

THE WITHDRAWAL

The Michael Cross is escorted through the nave to the west door,
where the clergy say goodbye to the people as they leave.

23. Psalms and Canticles

The Psalter has always found a place in Christian worship. In a service of occasion of which the core is a choir Office, a psalm or psalms will certainly be included: in a service freely composed, there may or may not be a psalm.

The prose version of the English psalter has been sung continuously in our cathedrals: it has only within the last hundred years been sung by the congregations in parish churches, and by them it has not been sung well. It must be remembered that the singing of a prose text, with its infinitely various rhythms and its verses of irregular length, is beyond the capacity of most congregations. It can only be effectively done by a choir (whether professional or amateur) well disciplined and thoroughly rehearsed. There is a further difficulty: it is that at a service of occasion the congregation is likely to include churchmen accustomed to widely various methods of pointing the psalms, as well as many who do not go regularly to church and who are quite unfamiliar with the psalter.

If the prose version of the psalter is to be used in a service of occasion, there are three ways of dealing with the difficulties of its performance:

1 The psalm may be reserved to the choir. A psalm sung by the choir alone, whether to a plainsong tone or an Anglican chant, is particularly effective when sung in procession.

2 The psalm may be sung by the congregation. If the congregation is numerous, the choir will be powerless to lead the people through the complexities of prose rhythms; if any cohesion is attained, it will be imposed by a loud and brutal organ accompaniment, which can only be an embarrassment to persons of any sensibility. The subtle beauties of the text will go for nothing.

3 The psalm may be said. There can be antiphony either between priest and people, or between one half of the congregation and the other: a rubric will direct precisely what is to be done. At first sight, this may appear a dull and uninteresting way of treating a psalm: in practice it has proved very effective.

The truth of the matter is that prose rhythms are not suited to congregational song. This was perceived as soon as the Church of England adopted a vernacular liturgy. No sooner had the Book of Common Prayer been published than attempts were made to translate the psalter into verse; for it was realised that verse, with its regular beat and fixed length of line, is the appropriate vehicle of popular song. When the psalms were sung in parish churches, they were sung in metre. The metrical psalters of Sternhold and Hopkins (published in 1562) and of Tate and Brady (published in 1696) were immensely popular and went through more than 700 editions. For two hundred years they held the field, until Isaac Watts, with the publication in 1707 or his Hymns and Spiritual Songs, laid the foundations of English hymnody.

The psalms as presented in the old metrical psalters were sorry stuff: John Wesley, who had the fastidious ear of a scholar, dismissed them for 'scandalous doggerel'. It is not surprising that the metrical psalms which have survived the judgement of time and are still found acceptable among present-day congregations can be counted on the fingers of one hand. But if the achievement of their authors is disputable, the principle on which they worked is still valid. It is simply that verse is easy for a congregation to sing, and that prose is very difficult. It is a principle which needs to be borne in mind in framing an order of service for popular use.

It is worth noting that many hymn books now in common use include a score of hymns based on psalms, which may be used on those occasions when it seems unwise to ask a congregation to sing a psalm in prose. Among these hymns are Watts' metrical version of Psalm 90; two versions (Kethe's and Watts') of Psalm 100; and of Psalm 23, the graceful version by Herbert, the more 'artificial' but equally beautiful version by Addison, and the version by Sir H.W. Baker with its exquisite eucharistic inflexion of the fifth verse.

Psalm Praise

In our own day, a group of priests and lay people of the Church of England, acting upon the principle that verse is easy for a congregation to sing and that prose is difficult, has made a fresh attempt at a metrical psalter. Their book is called Psalm Praise (London, 1973), and is intended for use not only in church services but also in informal gatherings. It contains verse translations in today's English of most of the Psalter, and of all the canticles of the Prayer Book Offices, as well as new metrical psalms based on passages of Scripture relevant to the seasons of the Church's year. The book also includes psalms and canticles in the prose of the Book of Common Prayer, and in the pointing of The Parish Psalter, set to Anglican chants both old and newly composed.

Among the new chants are many examples of what the compilers call 'People's Chants', chants created for use with The Parish Psalter by the Rev. N.L. Warren with the aim of making chanting easy for the congregation while giving scope to choir and organ. Here the people have the same simple melody (over a varied accompaniment) in the second and fourth quarters of the chant; the choir or soloist have different and more difficult parts in the first and third quarters.

All the Anglican chants have sobriety and dignity. For many of the metrical psalms a guitar accompaniment is provided – a happy and welcome innovation. The music to which the metrical psalms and canticles are set is sometimes commonplace, and will not please professional musicians. Let them credit the compilers with that pastoral good sense which every liturgical situation requires; and let them recall an affirmation in the earlier Chapter on liturgical relevance for today (page 21): 'A living liturgy is the expression of the worship of a community in terms which are natural to that community.'

24. Rubrics

Rubrics have the power of suggesting one of two things: either that the church is a museum, or that it is a company of living, breathing men and women. How do men naturally talk today? Do they say 'Here endeth the lesson', or do they say 'That is the lesson'? Do they say 'Silence shall be kept for a space', or simply 'Silence falls'? The plain fact is that rubrics are simply stage directions. In writing rubrics, therefore, use short sentences; avoid subordinate clauses, and parentheses, and conjunctions. Above all, avoid the mandatory future tense – 'Then shall the priest say'.

Let us try our hand at translating an old rubric into modern terms. Here is a rubric, majestic and picturesque, but unmistakeably latinate in structure, from the English Coronation Rite. It uses only three sentences to define ten different actions.

> *Then the Queen still sitting in King Edward's Chair, the Archbishop, assisted with other Bishops, shall come from the Altar: the Dean of Westminster shall bring the Crown, and the Archbishop taking it off him shall reverently put it upon the Queen's head. At the sight whereof the people, with loud and repeated shouts, shall cry:*
>
> GOD SAVE THE QUEEN
>
> *The Princes and Princesses, the Peers and Peeresses shall put on their coronets and caps, and the Kings of Arms their Crowns; and the trumpets shall sound, and by a signal given, the great guns at the Tower shall be shot off.*

Here is the rubric translated. It uses not three but seven sentences to define the same ten actions.

> *The Queen remains seated in King Edward's Chair. The Archbishop, assisted by other Bishops, comes from the Altar. The Dean of Westminster brings the Crown. The Archbishop takes it from him and reverently puts it on the Queen's head. At the sight of this the people shout again and again:*
>
> GOD SAVE THE QUEEN
>
> *The Princes and Princesses, the Peers and Peeresses, put on their Coronets and caps, and the Kings of Arms their Crowns. There is a fanfare of trumpets, and a volley from the guns at the Tower.*

For one more exercise in translation, take a passage from a twentieth-century play and re-write the stage directions in the style of the rubrics of the Prayer Book. Here is a celebrated passage from Shaw's Pygmalion. Note the stage directions:

HIGGINS *[rising and looking at his watch]* Ahem!

LIZA *[looking at him; taking the hint; and rising]* Well: I must go.

[They all rise. Freddy goes to the door.]

LIZA So pleased to have met you. Goodbye.
[She shakes hands with Mrs Higgins.]

MRS HIGGINS Goodbye.

LIZA Goodbye, Colonel Pickering.

PICKERING Goodbye, Miss Doolittle.

[They shake hands.]

LIZA *[nodding to the others]* Goodbye, all.

FREDDY *[opening the door for her]* Are you walking across the Park, Miss Doolittle? If so –

LIZA Walk! Not bloody likely. *[Sensation]* I am going in a taxi.

[She goes out. Pickering gasps and sits down.]

There are fifty-nine words in those stage directions. Turn them into rubrics and you will need 131 words to say the same thing – and you will not be talking English.

Higgins shall rise; and looking at his watch, he shall say:
Ahem!
Liza shall look round at him; and having taken the hint, she shall rise, saying:
Well: I must go.
Thereupon they shall all rise; and Freddy going to the door, Liza shall continue, saying:
So pleased to have met you. Good bye.
She shall give the right hand of fellowship to Mrs Higgins, who shall say:
Goodbye.
Then Liza shall address Colonel Pickering, saying:
Goodbye, Colonel Pickering.
And Pickering shall answer, saying:
Goodbye, Miss Doolittle.

Meanwhile Pickering and Liza shall give the right hand of fellowship each to the other. Which done, Liza shall nod the head to those present, saying:

Goodbye, all.

Thereupon Freddy shall open the door for her, saying:

Are you walking across the Park, Miss Doolittle? If so –

Liza shall answer, saying:

Walk! Not bloody likely.

Those present being moved with surprise and indignation, Liza shall continue, saying:

I am going in a taxi.

This said, Liza shall go out; and Pickering having gasped shall sit down.

Rules for the writing of rubrics

1 Rubrics are to be written in the language of today.

2 Rubrics must be ample; they must tell everyone – including the congregation – what is happening and what is to be done.

3 Rubrics must be economical; they must say all that needs to be said without a single superfluous phrase or word.

4 Rubrics must be precise; an imprecise rubric, a rubric which raises a question instead of answering a question, is worthless.

5 Rubrics must be obeyed. Experience proves that there is no room for second thoughts: once the service is begun, the prescribed order must be followed, even though a better or at least a different way of doing things may occur, during the course of the service, to some of those engaged in it. Improvisation is dangerous: it always creates a muddle. Improvisation will in any case be unnecessary if the compiler has provided rubrics of the right quality.

6 You cannot write effective rubrics unless you have in your mind a complete picture of the sequence of events from beginning to end of the service.

7 In an elaborate service, rubrics which are of concern, or of interest, to the congregation are to be printed in the course of the text; rubrics which do not concern the congregation, but only the persons responsible for making the occasion run smoothly, are to be printed in the margin alongside the text to which the rubrics are related. For examples of this please turn to the chapter with Commentaries on Orders of Service: **A Fanfare for Europe** (page 269.) and **The Form of a Servant** (page 291).

8 Rubrics prescribe what is to be done, not what is to be thought.

Here, for example, is a rubric from the order of service for the consecration of Liverpool Cathedral in 1924, which steps outside the proper function of a rubric (the offending phrase is underlined here):

Taking the keys in his right hand, and the crozier in his left hand, the Bishop, alone and unattended, and bearing in mind the flock committed to his charge, shall measure the length of the fold of the Temple of God, passing up through the Choir to the Holy Table.

If your rubrics are as good as they should be, there will be no need to make any kind of announcement, or to shout any directions, during the course of the service.

9 Once the rite has reached its end, a rubric must make clear how the company is to disperse. The rubric must deliver this information in such a way that its instructions are instantly, and at one glance, obvious.

Does the following rubric fulfil those requirements?

THE LORD BISHOP OF COVENTRY
preceded by a verger, the banners of the See of Coventry, the Cross of Nails, two candlebearers, and a clerk, attended by two Chaplains, and supported by the Registrar of the Diocese of Coventry and by the Chancellor of the Diocese of Coventry, follows the Provost of Coventry, who is preceded by the Provost's Verger.

If you unravel this bundle of words, the information concealed within it will appear like this:

The Provost's Verger
The Provost of Coventry
A Verger
Banners of the See of Coventry
The Cross of Nails
Two Candlebearers
A Clerk
A Chaplain
THE LORD BISHOP OF COVENTRY
A Chaplain
The Registrar of the Diocese of Coventry
The Chancellor of the Diocese of Coventry

25. Salutations

The traditional salutation is:

℣ The Lord be with you;
℟ **And with thy spirit.**

If you meet a friend in the street, and you call out to him 'Good morning!', what will his answer be? He may answer 'Hallo!' or 'How are you?' or 'Hi!' or 'Glad to see you!' He may equally well answer simply 'Good morning!' He throws your words back to you. Very well then; why not this?

℣ The Lord be with you;
℟ **The Lord be with you.**

But if you prefer to be biblical, turn to Ruth 2.4:

> And behold, Boaz came from Bethlehem, and said unto the reapers,
> The Lord be with you. And they answered him, The Lord bless thee.

So:

℣ The Lord be with you;
℟ **The Lord bless you.**

At the Eucharist:

℣ The peace of the Lord be always with you;
℟ **Peace to you.**

'Peace to you' comes naturally and easily. And if the peace is enacted as well as said, and you are to shake hands with our neighbour who is a friend of yours, you can as you do so address him by name:

Peace to you, John.

A Salutation can emerge easily out of the preceding text, as it does here out of the versicles and responses* sung at the Christmas Crib:

* For the music, see p. 407 in Part IV – Examples of Music

The Versicles and Responses

℣ The Word became flesh;
he came to dwell among us, and we saw his glory;
℟ **such glory as befits the Father's only Son,**
full of grace and truth.
℣ No one has ever seen God;
℟ **but God's only Son,**
he who is nearest to the Father's heart,
he has made him known.

The Salutation

℣ Grace and truth be with you;
℟ **Peace to you.**

When a notable visitor is to be received at the principal doors of the church, a salutation may be exchanged in the formal language of Scripture; for example:

The Bishop of Coventry welcomes the visitors with these words:

Friends in Christ Jesus,
In the name of this Cathedral Church of St Michael
I greet you, and I bid you welcome.
Grace and peace to you
from God our Father and the Lord Jesus Christ.
Peace to you all who belong to Christ.

Romans 1.7,1; Peter 5.14

The Apostolic Delegate replies:

All who are with me send you greetings.
My greetings to those who are our friends in the faith.
Grace be with you all.

Titus 3.15

26. Scrutinies

A Scrutiny is a careful and searching examination of things or persons. In liturgy it is the examination of persons by question and answer, 'openly in the church'. So the first rubric after the Catechism in the Book of Common Prayer:

> *The Curate of every Parish shall diligently upon Sundays and Holy-days, after the Second Lesson at Evening Prayer openly in the church instruct and examine so many children of his Parish sent unto him, as he shall think convenient, in some part of this Catechism.*

The scrutiny is more frequently used in liturgy than one might suppose. In the Prayer Book it is an essential feature of the rites of Baptism, Confirmation, Matrimony, and (capitally) Ordination. These are rites of admission into a society, or into a status within the society; and the society must ask if the candidates for admission are in earnest, and if they understand the responsibilities they are undertaking.

The scrutiny finds a natural place in the following orders, which you may consult **Admission to Office** (page 61); **Commissioning** (page 103); **The Dedication of Persons** (page 121).

The scrutiny may develop into something more genial, something which has less the nature of an inquisition than of a meditation. In the following example the congregation are not candidates for admission into any society or status, for they already have the status of husbands and wives and parents. The scrutiny is simply a means of enabling them to reflect upon the Lesson from the Bible which they have just heard, and in the light of it to examine their own conduct.

A scrutiny of this kind might be included in a service for the Mothers' Union, or for husbands and wives who come to church to renew their marriage vows. In reading such a scrutiny the Minister will speak with an unhurried deliberation, and will allow some moments of silence to elapse after each question has been answered.

From a service attended by the Transatlantic Brides and Parents Association in Coventry Cathedral, 1964

The Harvest of the Spirit

THE SECOND LESSON: Galatians 5. 19-22, 24, 25

Anyone can see the kind of behaviour that belongs to the lower nature: fornication, impurity, and indecency; idolatry and sorcery; quarrels, a contentious temper, envy, fits of rage, selfish ambitions, dissensions, party intrigues, and jealousies; drinking bouts, orgies, and the like. I warn you, as I warned you before, that those who behave in such ways will never inherit the kingdom of God.

But the harvest of the Spirit is love, joy, peace, patience, kindness, goodness, gentleness, and self-control. And those who belong to Christ Jesus have crucified the lower nature with its passions and desires. If the Spirit is the source of our life, let the Spirit also direct our course.

After the Lesson the people rise,
and the Precentor at the chancel step addresses them:

LOVE

Will you love and serve your wives, your husbands,
and your children?

Will you serve and love, in Christ's name,
the unlovely and the unloved among your neighbours?

℟ **We will.**

JOY

Will you be grateful for God's mercies to you,
till joy leaves no room in your hearts for moroseness and self-pity?

℟ **We will.**

PEACE

Will you learn to rest in God, so that you live in his peace,
and enfold in his peace your families and households?

℟ **We will.**

PATIENCE

Will you cherish patience,
subduing every impulse of anger and irritation?

℟ **We will.**

KINDNESS

Will you be kind to your children?
Will you be kind to those who serve you or your families?
Will you be kind to those who are unkind to you?

℟ **We will.**

GOODNESS

Will you trust always in the power of goodness,
against all odds, to subdue evil and overcome it?

℟ **We will.**

FIDELITY

Will you practise fidelity to your wives and husbands,
to your children, to your friends, and to your Church?

℟ **We will.**

GENTLENESS

Will you prefer gentleness and courtesy to fretfulness and wrangling?

℟ **We will.**

SELF-CONTROL

Will you so learn self-control
that you may be master of yourself, and the servant of Christ?

℟ **We will.**

Almighty God, who has given you the will to do all these things:
Grant you strength and power to perform them;
through Jesus Christ our Lord.
℟ **Amen.**

For the use of this scrutiny in the form of a litany see **Of the Nine Gifts of the Spirit** (page 372) in the section with example prayers.

27. Sermons

A Sermon is not always necessary.

At a service attended by a group of people – a group of twenty, a group of two hundred, a group of two thousand – if they are well-instructed Christians who have had some practice in recollection – at such a service there need be no sermon, provided that the service has the qualities of good liturgy; that is to say, provided that the theme is clear and clearly set out, that the argument proceeds in one unbroken line, and that the whole order has depth and pith.

The sermon and the service

Let us suppose, however, that your service of occasion is to include a sermon. The sermon must be knit firmly into the order of service; and there are two ways of bringing this about.

1 The sermon determines the theme

You invite your man, weeks or months in advance, to preach, and you will tell him what the occasion is to be. You will ask him what subject he will choose to preach about, and whether he cares to propose a passage of Scripture, related to his subject, to be read as one of the lessons. When you have his answers, you can then compose your service around the sermon; and you will find many ways to illuminate the subject of the sermon.

The sermon determines the theme.

2 The theme determines the sermon

But if, in planning your service, you have consulted its sponsors, and have already decided with them what the theme is to be, then your invitation to the preacher will be phrased differently. You will tell him what the occasion is to be; you will also tell him what the theme of the service is to be; and you will invite him to preach a sermon on that theme.

The theme determines the sermon.

Informing the Preacher

The second of these two ways of knitting the sermon firmly into the order of service is probably the safer way. But in either case, you should give the preacher all the help you can. He will need information. Make sure he knows:

1 the likely number of his audiences;

2 their age; are they young, or middle-aged, or old, or a mixed bag?

3 their quality; are they upper class, middle class, working class? are they artisans, or are the tradespeople, or are they professional people?
4 their culture; are they urban, or rural; are they well-read, or not so well-read?
5 are they regular churchgoers, or are they not?

Your preacher will also need to know:

Is the building large or small?
Is the building very resonant, or not?
Is a public address system in use?

The building determines the style

A visiting preacher, if he is unfamiliar with your church, should always be invited to arrive in good time before the service and to spend a few minutes actually speaking in the building, 'getting the feel of it'; and if the building is resonant and difficult to speak in, he should be warned of this before he writes his sermon. For the building will determine the style he adopts: a large and resonant building will call for a slow delivery, and will not be patient of a casual or informal style (but a formal style does not mean an unfriendly style). In such a building, chatty off-the-cuff remarks will simply not be heard.

The length of the sermon

The length of the sermon must be in proportion to the length of the service.

No service of occasion (unless it be an Ordination, or a bishop's Enthronement) need last longer than one hour; and a sermon occupying fifteen minutes of that hour will be long enough. Anything longer will be liable to bore the congregation; they will grow restive; and the skill you have bestowed on composing your service will go for nothing.

A sermon badly made, or badly delivered, or lasting twice too long, will destroy any service, however cunningly constructed the service may be.

When you invite the preacher, you must use what tact you can in telling him how long you hope his sermon will last.

28. The Unveiling of a Memorial

To unveil a memorial inscription, somebody must tug at a string which draws aside a curtain, revealing the inscription on the wall behind it.

Very well then; here is the man (or woman) waiting to do it. He tugs at the string, the curtain moves, perhaps unsteadily, to one side; and there is the inscription, uncovered for all to read. The whole action has lasted five seconds. The job is done, and we can all go home.

Ridiculous? But of course! The simple action of drawing aside a curtain on a wall must be enveloped in prayer, in reflection upon the Christian faith, in an ambience of devotion. A sense of occasion must be created.

The Unveiling of an Inscription in memory of SIR BASIL SPENCE,
the Architect of Coventry Cathedral,
during the Communion on Sunday 10 December 1978

The ceremony takes place during the principal Eucharist on a Sunday morning in Advent. The liturgical colour proper to Advent is blue*: but the unveiling of the memorial to the architect of the Cathedral is an occasion of gratitude, of joy, of Christian hope; the Ministers therefore wear copes of gold for the procession to the site of the memorial.

The Memorial Inscription is on a wall of the Porch outside the building. If the congregation in the nave were to continue to face the altar during the ceremony they would feel excluded from it: a rubric therefore directs them to turn towards the Porch as the procession passes them. This may appear trivial; but recall the **Rules for the writing of Rubrics** on page 215 above:

6 You cannot write effective rubrics unless you have in your mind a complete picture of the sequence of events from beginning to end of the service.

The procession has arrived in the Porch, though the choir has halted at the west end of the nave; at the site of the Memorial there follows a brief dialogue between the Provost and Lady Spence, who is to unveil the Inscription. Their voices will be relayed to the people inside. The people will naturally wish to know what the Inscription says; and they will not know unless someone tells them. The Provost does tell them. This is a simple and subtle way of assuring them that they are not excluded from the ceremony, though they cannot all see it.

---

* *Editor's note: The liturgical colour for Advent is purple in many churches; it can also be royal or deep blue.*

The Provost invites Lady Spence to unveil the Inscription; and Lady Spence makes a brief reply. This is not simply a matter of courtesy; her reply gives the congregation a chance to hear her voice, and so to become aware of her, and in some small degree to imagine what sort of person she may be.

Lady Spence unveils the Inscription; and then, to provide an ambience of prayer, the Provost begins The Thanksgiving, with a particular mention of the man whose memory is being honoured. The Thanksgiving ends with a prayer for the divine blessing on the Cathedral which the architect, with many other distinguished artists and craftsmen, had conceived and brought into being.

The Memorial Inscription has been unveiled; prayer has been offered; but the occasion is not yet over. The procession re-enters the Cathedral, where Lady Spence and her family sit down at the west end. The choir (we remember) is also at the west end; and there the choir, in heart-easing music, sings of that 'blessed hope of everlasting life' which the Book of Common Prayer never allows us to lose sight of. The same theme informs the passage of Scripture which the Provost then reads (the last three lines are echoed by the congregation); and the majestic collect by John Donne drives the argument home. The procession returns through the nave while Handel's *La Réjouissance* is played on the organ; and this blazing affirmation of joy brings the ceremony to its conclusion.

The Ministers lay aside their gold copes and put on blue vestments; and the Advent Eucharist proceeds.

THE SERMON

by the Provost

THE UNVEILING

After the sermon a march is played on the organ,
and a procession is made through the nave to St Michael's Porch.
As the procession passes, the people turn towards the Porch.

Lady Spence and her family will be led by two churchwardens after the Ministers.

At the west end the choir turns aside, and stands facing the high altar.
The rest of the procession passes into the Porch.

Standing near the Memorial Inscription, the Provost addresses Lady Spence:

Lady Spence,
Here upon the wall of St Michael's Porch, where all who pass by may see them, we have inscribed these words:

REMEMBER WITH GRATITUDE SIR BASIL SPENCE, O.M., K.B.E.
ARCHITECT OF THIS CATHEDRAL

I now invite you to unveil this Inscription in memory of your husband.

Lady Spence replies:

Mr Provost,
Thank you for your invitation. I have pleasure in accepting it.

Lady Spence unveils the Inscription.

THE THANKSGIVING

The Provost says:

The glory of this latter house shall be greater than of the former, says the Lord of Hosts:
and in this place will I give peace, says the Lord of Hosts.
Let us thank God for his blessings.

For the restoration of this Cathedral, by the folly of men defaced and ruined, by the love of men refashioned to a greater glory, we praise God,
℟ **We thank him.**

For the skill of the administrators, artists and craftsmen who built and furnished the Cathedral, we praise God,
℟ **We thank him.**

For the artists in every age, who by obedience to the truth as they see it, have uncovered the springs of joy, for the delight and recreation of their fellow men, we praise God,
℟ **We thank him.**

For BASIL SPENCE, the Architect of this Cathedral, we praise God.
℟ **We thank him.**

O God, who by the prayers and hands of thy servants
hast built again this Cathedral church
to be a continuing witness to thy majesty and thy mercy:
Bless those who serve this building,
bless those who visit it,
bless those who worship in it;
and accept the offering of our time, our skill, and our obedience,
in the service of thy Son, Jesus Christ our Lord.
℟ **Amen.**

The people in the nave sit down.
The Ministers with Lady Spence and her family re-enter the Cathedral, and sit down in the seats reserved for them at the west end.

Then the choir sings this anthem, by Sir Hubert Parry:

My soul, there is a country
Far beyond the stars,
Where stands a wingèd sentry
All skilful in the wars.

There above noise, and danger,
Sweet peace sits crowned with smiles,
And one born in a manger
Commands the beauteous files.

He is thy gracious Friend,
And – O my soul, awake! –
Did in pure love descend,
To die here for thy sake.

If thou canst get but thither,
There grows the flower of peace,
The Rose that cannot wither,
Thy fortress and thy ease.

Leave then thy foolish ranges,
For none can thee secure
But one who never changes,
Thy God, thy life, thy cure.

After the anthem everyone stands.

The Provost at the west end says:

Those who feared the Lord talked together; and the Lord paid heed and listened. And a book of remembrance was written before him of those who feared the Lord and kept his name in mind.

And they shall be mine, says the Lord of Hosts, in that day when I make up my jewels.

Malachi 3. 16-17

Everyone, with great conviction:

**They shall be mine, says the Lord of Hosts,
in that day when I make up my jewels.**

The Provost:

Bring us, O Lord God, at our last awakening into the house and gate of heaven, to enter into that gate and dwell in that house, where there shall be no darkness nor dazzling, but one equal light; no noise nor silence, but one equal music; no fears nor hopes, but one equal possession; no ends nor beginnings, but one equal eternity, in the habitation of thy glory and dominion, world without end.
℟ **Amen.**

A RÉJOUISSANCE by G.F. Handel is played on the organ, while the procession, walking in the same order as before, returns to the chancel.

The Offertory Hymn follows.

The Ministers take off their gold copes and put on the blue vestments proper to Advent†.

† *Editor's note: The liturgical colour for Advent is purple in many churches; it can also be royal or deep blue.*

29. Versicles and Responses

In the course of a discussion how to make worship vital and real to men today, a colleague of mine remarked, 'I should like to hear from you a defence of the use of versicles and responses'. He implied, I think, that this was not a natural mode of speech, not the way men talk in the free and easy discourse of the home. Well no, of course it is not: for liturgy is not a spontaneous undisciplined affair, it is essentially the imposing of order upon our random emotions and utterances.

Nevertheless, I am inclined to believe that the use of versicle and response is something nearer than we might suppose to speech between any two individuals, or between an individual and a group, when seized by a common excitement or sharing an intensely felt experience.

There comes to my mind the memory of Christmas Day at Canterbury Cathedral in 1942. Two boys of the choir were invited to luncheon at the Old Palace with the Archbishop and Mrs William Temple. They had never before sat down to a meal with an Archbishop of Canterbury, and they were naturally excited about it. On their return from the Old Palace for Evensong, I asked them how they had fared.

Now these two boys were twins, and they were so intimate that a single train of thought seemed to run simultaneously through the minds of both. When they came to express themselves, one would begin a sentence, the other would take over and finish it. On this occasion the excitement which they both felt generated an explosion of versicles and responses:

1 ℣ Did you enjoy yourselves?
2 ℟ Yes, Sir,
3 ℣ Very much, Sir,
2 ℟ It was wonderful, Sir,
3 ℣ There were lots of crackers
2 ℟ With paper caps for everyone.
3 ℣ He wore one, Sir,
2 ℟ And so did Mrs Temple, Sir.
1 ℣ And did you have turkey to eat?
2 ℟ Yes, Sir, and a plum pudding –
3 ℣ It was enormous, Sir, as big as a –
2 ℟ As big as a football, Sir,
3 ℣ With flames all round it, Sir,
2 ℟ And holly on top,
3 ℣ And do you know
2 ℟ She calls him Bill, Sir!

Now consider the versicles and responses which begin the eucharistic consecration:

℣ The Lord be with you;
℟ **And with thy spirit.**
℣ Lift up your hearts;
℟ **We lift them up unto the Lord.**
℣ Let us give thanks unto our Lord God;
℟ **It is meet and right so to do.**

These words were in use at the Eucharist before the Peace of the Church, at a time when Christians met in private houses for worship, often in fear of persecution by the government. In such a situation it is easy to imagine the intense emotion which the members of a little congregation would share. It is easy to believe that beneath the formal exchange of words with which we are familiar lies an exchange less formal, more spontaneous, generated by a deeply felt common experience.

Pare the phrases to the bone, and you have this:

℣ God be with you.
℟ **And with you.**
℣ Hearts up!
℟ **So they are.**
℣ Let's thank God.
℟ **So we should.**

This is excited conversation, no more: perhaps a scrap of conversation once actually heard in one of those early Christian assemblies, recalled to memory by the unknown liturgist who set the phrases down in the form, only slightly expanded, which has survived on the lips of the Church from that day to this.

Experience at any rate proves that versicle and response can still be used to express and to release a common excitement.

In short, versicle and response are stylised conversation. The subjects of conversation among Christian people are drawn often from the Bible; so it is natural to turn to the Bible for phrases which fall easily into versicle and response. And as conversation gives way to prayer, so versicle and response are followed by a collect.

If the conversation consists of a series of requests, then you have what are called suffrages: as for example the suffrages after the Creed at Matins and Evensong in the Prayer Book; and the proper suffrages appointed for use in the same place in the Accession Service.

The conversation can tell a story:

AT THE CRIB

Precentor	It came to pass, as the angels were gone away from them into heaven, the shepherds said one to another:
Choir 1	Let us now go even unto Bethlehem, and see this thing which is come to pass, which the Lord hath made known unto us,
Choir 2	Which the Lord hath made known unto us.
Precentor	And they came with haste, and found Mary, and Joseph;
Choir 1	And the babe lying in a manger,
Choir 2	Lying in a manger.
Precentor	The Lord be with you;
Choir 1	And with thy spirit.
Choir 2	And with thy spirit.
Precentor	Lord Jesus, Child of Bethlehem, for love of men made man: Create in us love so pure and perfect that whatsoever our heart loveth may be after thy will, in thy name, and for thy sake. **Amen.**

A musical setting is to be found in Part IV – Examples of Music (page **Error! Bookmark not defined.**).

The conversation can be a meditation:

℣ Jesus said, I am the light of the world:
he that followeth me shall not walk in darkness;
℟ **But shall have the light of life.**
℣ God, who commanded the light to shine out of darkness,
hath shined in our hearts;
℟ **To give the light of the knowledge**
of the glory of God in the face of Jesus Christ.
℣ He showed me that great city, the Holy Jerusalem,
descending out of heaven from God, having the glory of God;
℟ **And her light was like unto a stone most precious,**
even like a jasper stone, clear as crystal.
℣ And the city had no need of the sun,
neither of the moon, to shine in it;
℟ **For the glory of God did lighten it,**
and the Lamb is the light thereof.

O Lord Jesus Christ, the very Light of Light, whom men in the darkness of Gethsemane approached with lanterns and torches: Keep us from following the little lights of the world, that deepen our night; and lead us into that holy city where the true light shineth and never goeth down; and thou with the Father and the Holy Spirit livest and reignest, God, world without end.
Amen.

A musical setting is to be found in Part IV – Examples of Music (page 403).

Versicles and Responses at the end of a Choir Office

In cathedrals and collegiate churches where the Office is sung by a professional choir, the Intercessions after the Anthem are sometimes spoken not sung. This may appear friendly and humane; but in fact there is a danger that the Amens may be mumbled half-heartedly (unless the choir is very well disciplined) and the Office crumble away in a desultory fashion.

It is easy to guard against this dispiriting conclusion by having brief suffrages sung by the choir after the spoken prayers. The effect can be exhilarating; and the true nature of the Choir Office – the offering of song – will not have been denied.

In the example given here the first versicle and response are from a sermon by John Donne. A musical setting of the suffrages is to be found in on page **Error! Bookmark not defined.** of Part IV – Examples of Music..

THE INTERCESSIONS

The choir and the people kneel.
One of the Ministers offers three prayers,
to each of which the choir and the people reply:
Amen.

There follows a silence for private prayer, concluded by:

℣ Lord, hear our prayer;
℟ And let our cry come unto thee.

The Precentor and the choir stand to sing these Suffrages:

℣ Keep us, O Lord, so awake in the duties of our calling;
℟ That we may sleep in thy peace, and wake in thy glory.

℣ God grant to the living, grace; to the departed, rest;
to the Church, the Queen, the Commonwealth, and all mankind,
peace and concord;
℟ And to us and all his servants life everlasting.
℣ Let us bless the Lord;
℟ Thanks be to God.

Coventry Cathedral: Evensong

NOTE. Quite apart from 'Quires, and places where they sing', these Suffrages may be sung or said in any church or chapel, and at any service of occasion, as a firm conclusion to Prayers of Thanksgiving or of Intercession.

30. The Welcome

On any special occasion a Welcome from the presiding Minister is useful and fitting: it is a simple expression of that hospitality which is the mark of a Christian community. If the occasion is formal, a friendly welcome will relax the tension, and will put the congregation at their ease.

At what point in the service will the Welcome be placed? At Matins or Evensong it may sometimes fit comfortably immediately before the First Lesson: but it will usually come earlier. If the service begins with a hymn, the Welcome can follow the hymn; for the hymn has the effect of shutting the door upon the everyday hustle of the world, and of bringing the worshippers into a receptive frame of mind.

But be careful: with the opening hymn, worship has begun; and if the Welcome is prolonged, the rhythm of worship will be broken. The Welcome must be friendly: it must also be brief, terse, and to the point.

The parish priest who is practised in public speaking may choose to deliver an informal and impromptu Welcome: but the tyro had better write out the Welcome beforehand, especially if the occasion is formal. He will wish not to be garrulous or diffuse; and he will aim not only to set the company at their ease, but also, with as light a touch as possible, to persuade them to enter happily and seriously into prayer.

There are some formal occasions when the Welcome should not only be written out beforehand for the guidance of the speaker but actually be printed in the order of service, to enable the worshippers, as they read the Welcome while it is delivered, to compose their random and wandering thoughts and to sharpen their attention. For example:

A welcome to soldiers before a hazardous enterprise

The Dean standing before the Altar will say,

> We are proud to welcome you to our Cathedral Church today. You come at a critical moment in the history of our country, when you are on the point of engaging in a combat that will be decisive, as it will certainly be hard. Here in this place, where prayer is daily offered for all His Majesty's Forces, you are gathered in the presence of God, whom Christ has taught us to call our Father. As you join with us in worship, lay aside your immediate cares, and enter with a quiet mind into the Father's presence. He is waiting to give to us his children, as we call on him with humble trust, the assurance of his power and strength for the duties that lie before us.

The congregation will sit down, and the Choir will sing this Anthem.

After this, it was noised abroad that Mr. Valiant-for-truth was taken with a summons, and had this for a token that the summons was true, That his pitcher was broken at the fountain. When he understood it, he called for his friends, and told them of it. Then said he, I am going to my Father's, and though with great difficultly I am got hither, yet now I do not repent me of all the trouble I have been at to arrive where I am. My Sword, I give to him that shall succeed me in my pilgrimage, and my Courage and Skill, to him that can get it. My Marks and Scars I carry with me, to be a witness for me, that I have fought his battles who now will be my rewarder. When the day that he must go hence, was come, many accompanied him to the river side, into which, as he went, he said, Death, where is thy sting? And as he went down deeper, he said, Grave, where is thy victory? So he passed over, and all the trumpets sounded for him on the other side.

Canterbury Cathedral: A Service before Battle,
a week before the Allied Invasion of Europe
on 6 June 1944

A Welcome commenting upon the place of blindness in the divine providence

We are here to celebrate a birthday – the twenty-first birthday of THE ROYAL COMMONWEALTH SOCIETY FOR THE BLIND.

The Society is one of the most remarkable organisations of our time, and one of the most beneficent. The success of the Society in the cure of blindness, and still more in the prevention of blindness, is indeed a cause for celebration; and we have come to express before God our gratitude and our joy over what has been so nobly accomplished.

When the Bishop of Coventry consecrated his Cathedral in 1962 he traced with his staff, on the floor between the Font and the Chapel of Unity, the first letters of the word CHRIST, to show that this building belongs to Jesus Christ. What does that mean for us today?

We affirm, with the Church in every age, that Jesus Christ is the express image of God. In him we discover the will of God for his children. As we listen to the Gospels we shall become aware that it is not the will of the Father that any of his children should be blind. We shall realise that those who use their love, and their skill of mind and hand, to cure blindness or to prevent it, are working with the grain of the universe, and not against the grain. Let them take courage; and let them believe that in this battle they are on the winning side.

The people sit down.

THE FIRST LESSON: Luke 4. 14-21

Then Jesus, armed with the power of the Spirit, returned to Galilee; and reports about him spread through the whole country-side. He taught in their synagogues and all men sang his praises. So he came to Nazareth, where he had been brought up, and went to synagogue on the Sabbath day as he regularly did. He stood up to read the lesson and was handed the scroll of the prophet Isaiah. He opened the scroll and found the passage which says, 'The spirit of the Lord is upon me because he has anointed me; he has sent me to announce good news to the poor, to proclaim release for prisoners and recovery of sight for the blind; to let the broken victims go free, to proclaim the year of the Lord's favour.' He rolled up the scroll, gave it back to the attendant, and sat down; and all eyes in the synagogue were fixed on him. He began to speak: 'Today', he said, 'in your very hearing this text has come true.'

THE SECOND LESSON: Mark 10. 46-52

They came to Jericho; and as he was leaving the town, with his disciples and a large crowd, Bartimaeus son of Timaeus, a blind beggar, was seated at the roadside. Hearing that it was Jesus of Nazareth, he began to shout, 'Son of David, Jesus, have pity on me!' Many of the people told him to hold his tongue; but he shouted all the more, 'Son of David, have pity on me.' Jesus stopped and said, 'Call him'; so they called the blind man and said, 'Take heart; stand up; he is calling you.' At that he threw off his cloak, sprang up, and came to Jesus. Jesus said to him, 'What do you want me to do for you?' 'Master,' the blind man answered, 'I want my sight back.' Jesus said to him, 'Go; your faith has cured you.' And at once he recovered his sight and followed him on the road.

Coventry Cathedral:
The Royal Commonwealth Society for the Blind 1971

A Welcome at a Memorial Service

We have come to remember before God, with pride and gratitude, one of the greatest women of our time, and one of the best loved, STELLA, MARCHIONESS OF READING.

The Women's Royal Voluntary Service, which she created and inspired, is her splendid and public memorial: but there are many thousands of people all over the world who cherish their private and personal memories of her genius, of her force of character, and of her kindness. You who are here today represent a multitude of men and women who wish to pay tribute to her, and to thank God for her.

So we acclaim her now; with sorrow because we shall not see her again in this world; and with exaltation, because she proved, and persuaded others to believe, that where there is imagination, and courage, and patience, and love, there is no task that cannot be accomplished, and no evil that cannot be faced and overcome.

The people sit down.

A voice: Servants of God! or sons
Shall I not call you? because
Not as servants ye knew
Your Father's innermost mind,
His, who unwillingly sees
One of his little ones lost –
Yours is the praise, if mankind
Hath not as yet in its march
Fainted, and fallen, and died!

Matthew Arnold

Another voice: Solemn the drums thrill: Death august and royal
Sings sorrow up into immortal spheres.
There is music in the midst of desolation
And a glory that shines upon our tears.

Laurence Binyon

A FUNERAL MARCH is played.

Coventry Cathedral:
In Memory of Stella,
Dowager Marchioness of Reading 1971

PART III – EXAMPLE LITURGIES

ORDERS OF SERVICE with commentaries

1. All Souls'-Tide

All Souls'-Tide at Coventry Cathedral

On All Souls' Day the names of the members of the Cathedral community who have died during the past year, together with the names of others for whose souls prayer is desired, are remembered at the Eucharist.

Some other way, however, of observing an occasion which is more important than one might suppose to many people who are not church-goers, seems to be required.

Accordingly, the Requiem of Gabriel Fauré is performed in the evening, on the Sunday within the octave of All Souls' Day, by the Cathedral choir, accompanied by the organ in a version transcribed from the orchestral full score. The event is included in the Cathedral's music brochure, among the year's concerts and recitals; but no charge is made for admission. Fauré's Requiem is not presented as a concert, but as a solemn devotion, in the following manner.

> The time is 7 o'clock in the evening, and darkness has fallen. The Cathedral is dimly lit. There is no music of any kind before the devotion begins. The choir wear no white surplices, only their rose-red cassocks; the Ministers wear cassocks and gowns. The choir and Ministers assemble at the west end, and move in silence through the seated congregation into the chancel.
>
> A Minister reads the brief Introduction set out at the head of the programme. The lights in the nave are then extinguished, and the congregation is in darkness: but round the high altar is a radiance of eight great candles, points of gold among the shadows.
>
> A voice now reads the immortal passage (in the Authorised Version) from Wisdom 5. 1-16, about the contrasting fates of the unrighteous and the righteous. The purpose of this is two-fold: (1) to set ringing in our ears some of the most exalted language ever written about the dead; and (2) to quieten us all down, to shut the door upon the hurrying world of every day, and to prepare us to receive what the music has to give us.
>
> Then at last the Requiem begins. After each section there is a silence, lasting a minute, or two minutes.
>
> When the music of the *In Paradisum* has died on the air, nobody stirs; the people remain seated in the darkened nave; and the Minister reads the following prayers, very quietly, very leisurely, but with an added intensity in the Antiphon of Many Confessors.

PRAYERS

God be in my head,
And in my understanding;
God be in my eyes,
And in my looking;
God be in my mouth,
And in my speaking;
God be in my heart,
And in my thinking;
God be at my end,
And at my departing.

For Suicides

Remember, O Lord, in thy compassion those whose courage fails them in the moment of despair; when they begin to lose heart, renew their hope; when they are beaten to the ground, raise them up again; if they die by their own hand forgive them, and forgive us all; and assure them, both of thy love and of their own worth; through our Redeemer Jesus Christ. Amen.

The Collect of All Souls

O Lord, the maker and redeemer of all believers: Grant to the faithful departed all the unsearchable benefits of thy Son's passion; that in the day of his appearing they may be manifested as thy true children; through the same thy Son Jesus Christ our Lord. Amen.

The Antiphon of Many Confessors

Holy is the true light, and passing wonderful, lending radiance to them that endured in the heat of the conflict: from Christ they inherit a home of unfading splendour, wherein they rejoice with gladness evermore.

The lights in the nave are not put on again: the choir and Ministers withdraw in silence through the midst of the people to the west end, and disappear by the stairs into the undercroft.

A note on the Collect for Suicides

The original version of this collect was composed for a service In Praise of Courage held in Coventry Cathedral in 1967 to celebrate Sir Francis Chichester's solo voyage round the world in his yacht. That version lacked the words 'and forgive us all'.

When I came to choose prayers to follow this Requiem for All Souls'-tide I remembered the collect for Suicides. And I remembered something else. I remembered as an undergraduate at Cambridge hearing a remark casually dropped by Dr Nairne (then Lady Margaret Professor of Divinity) into a discussion about capital punishment. 'Whenever a man is hanged,' he said, 'we should all go down on our knees and cry Lord, have mercy – have mercy, not on the hanged criminal but on ourselves; for every criminal is infected by the corruption of the society in which he lives.' That casual utterance, heard half a century ago and long forgotten, now reverberated in my memory with unexpected power; for surely (I thought) the suicide is in the same class as the criminal. So I have emended the original version of the collect for Suicides, which was

> *if they die by their own hand*
> *forgive them,*

and the collect now runs

> *if they die by their own hand*
> *forgive them,*
> *and forgive us all.*

2. The Centenary of the Coventry and District Association of Building Trades Employers 1876-1976: 'to be released from their bondage to time'

Coventry Cathedral, July 1976

Every liturgical situation is a pastoral situation; that is to say, those who prepare and present a service must have a keen sense, a pastoral sense, of the needs of the congregation. They must be like Jesus the good shepherd: 'When he saw the multitudes, he was moved with compassion, because they were like sheep without a shepherd.'

People today, when there is no consensus behind Christianity, are lost and bewildered, wondering what to believe and what to do. When they come to church (as they still do) as members of a Society or Corporation, the Church must have compassion on them, must try to meet them at their point of need; so that they go away feeling that someone has understood them, and has recognised in them an interior desolation which they can hardly articulate even to themselves.

The sermon is not the only means, or always the best means, of saying something to the point. Any cathedral, any great church, any school or college chapel, has other means – architectural beauty, music, eloquent prose or poetry, silence.

A pastoral concern for an Association of Building Trade Employers suggested that their one need, when they came to their cathedral, was simply an opportunity to be still, to be quiet, to be released from their bondage to time. The service given in outline below was built on that assumption. Each element was brief; the whole service was over in forty minutes. It began with gentle music for harpsichord – the Sarabande from Bach's French Suite in G – undemanding music which predisposes the listener to relax. More music for harpsichord followed the address. The nub of the service was one of Michel Quoist's prayers, which we print here in full: 'Lord, I have time'. This was spoken by three male voices; voice No. 1 was the Minister's, who stood, visible to everyone, at the altar of the Lady Chapel where the congregation was seated. The other two speakers were behind the people, one to the right of the chapel, the other to the left. The prayer was followed by silence (indicated in a rubric).

Welcome
Music for Harpsichord
Litany of thanksgiving
Hymn: All people that on earth do dwell
Litany of penitence
Lesson
Address
Music for harpsichord

Lord, I have time

from **Prayers of Life** by Michel Quoist, read by three voices:

1 I went out, Lord.
Men were coming out.
They were coming and going.
Walking and running.
Everything was rushing, cars, lorries, the street, the whole town.
Men were rushing not to waste time.
They were rushing after time.
To catch up with time.
To gain time.

3 Goodbye sir, excuse me, I haven't time.

2 I'll come back, I can't wait, I haven't time.

3 I must end this letter – I haven't time.

2 I'd love to help you, but I haven't time.

3 I can't accept, having no time.

2 I can't think, I can't read, I'm swamped, I haven't time.

3 I'd like to pray, but I haven't time.

1 You understand, Lord, they simply haven't the time.

2 The child is playing, he hasn't time right now ... Later on ....

3 The schoolboy has his homework to do, he hasn't time ...
Later on ...

2 The student has his courses, and so much work, he hasn't time ...
Later on ...

3 The young man is at his sports, he hasn't time ... Later on ...

2 The young married man has his new house, he has to fix it up, he hasn't time ... Later on ...

3 The grandparents have their grandchildren, they haven't time ...
Later on ...

2 They are ill, they have their treatments, they haven't time ...
Later on ...

3 They are dying, they have no ...

2 Too late! ... They have no more time!

1 And so all men run after time, Lord.
They pass through life running – hurried, jostled, overburdened, frantic, and they never get there.
They haven't time.

In spite of all their efforts they're still short of time, of a great deal of time.

2 Lord, you must have made a mistake in your calculations.
There is a big mistake somewhere.
The hours are too short,
The days are too short,
Our lives are too short.

1 You who are beyond time, Lord, you smile to see us fighting it.
And you know what you are doing.
You make no mistakes in your distribution of time to men.
You give each one time to do what you want him to do.

3 But we must not lose time,
waste time,
kill time,
For time is a gift that you give us,
But a perishable gift,
A gift that does not keep.

1 Lord, I have time,
I have plenty of time,
All the time that you give me,

3 The years of my life,

2 The days of my years,

3 The hours of my days,

1 They are all mine.

3 Mine to fill, quietly, calmly,
But to fill completely, up to the brim,
To offer them to you, that of their insipid water
You may make a rich wine such as you made once in Cana of Galilee.

1 I am not asking you today, Lord, for time to do this and then that,
But your grace to do conscientiously, in the time that you give me, what you want me to do.

Silence

Hymn: Forth in thy name

Blessing

to store up in them before they're full [illegible] a great deal of pain.

Lord, you must have made a mistake [illegible]
There is [illegible] somewhere [illegible]
[illegible] hearts are constant,
[illegible] are too [illegible],
[illegible]

[illegible]
[illegible]
[illegible]
[illegible]
[illegible]

3. Consider the Lilies

For a Festival of Flowers

In an order of service composed for any special occasion the theme must saturate the service. If you will read through this order attentively you will find that the theme is present on almost every page.

The order consists of a brief Office and a Procession. The Prologue begins the Office, which includes the reading of the Venite preceded and followed by its Antiphon, spoken by a solo voice (the Provost) and two groups of voices (the choir and the congregation). The Office continues with an Old Testament lesson and the Sermon.

There follows a meditation – **Consider the lilies** – poetry and prose spoken by several voices; and by way of climax, speech blossoms into music with the anthem 'My beloved spake'.

The Procession has three stations.

1 **The first station**: at the design of flowers representing Reconciliation.

A passage of prose is read, from one of Bacon's essays.

A carol is sung by the choir.

A versicle and response – made out of the text on which the whole service is based – and a collect, are sung by priest and choir.

In the section on **Processions** (page 189) the rule was laid down:

A perambulation alone is not a Procession: a Procession means going somewhere to do something. It is not necessary to say or do anything while going; but the priest and clerks must have somewhere to go and something to do when they get there.

In obedience to that rule, the priest and clerks have nothing to sing as they now move to the second station; but if they moved in silence the effect would be depressing. As they move, a voluntary is played on the organ: and this provides an opportunity for the proper liturgical use of the organ. The voluntary is a musical event in its own right: it is an expression of praise in purely instrumental terms.

2 **The second station:** in the nave

No music is used. The Bishop of the diocese is present; and it is the Bishop who now leads the Thanksgiving. This serves two purposes: *(1)* the Bishop's office and dignity are given proper respect, and *(2)* the congregation has the pleasure of hearing the Bishop as well as seeing him.

The Thanksgiving is in two parts:
(1) verses from the Te Deum, divided between Bishop and people, and
(2) a Litany of Thanksgiving.

3 **The third station**: at the High Altar

Music is used again: the same versicle and response – the theme of the service – as at the first station, and another collect.

The two collects sung during the Procession were written for the occasion. They are given in contemporary form – 'your' instead of 'thy' or 'thine' – in the Chapter giving **Examples of Prayer** (page 356).

~~~~~~

Consider the Lilies

A THANKSGIVING
ON THE OCCASION OF A
DESIGN WITH FLOWERS
FOR THE JUBILEE OF THE DIOCESE

MICHAELMAS DAY

Sunday 29 September 1968
at 5.30 p.m.

The people are to remain seated until a fanfare announces the arrival of the Bishop at the west door.

THE RECEPTION OF THE BISHOP OF COVENTRY

At 5.27 the members of the Foundation leave St Michael's Hall. The choir go to their stalls in the chancel. The ministers go by the north aisle of the choir and nave to the west door to receive the Lord Bishop.

At 5.30 the Bishop arrives at the west door and is received by the Provost. A FANFARE is played, and the choir and people stand.

The choir at once begins the Anthem I WAS GLAD, and the procession moves through the nave to the chancel in this order:
~~~~~~

A VERGER
TWO LIGHTS
THE CROSS OF ST MICHAEL
TWO LIGHTS
THE PRECENTOR
A VERGER
THE CATHEDRAL CHAPLAINS
THE CHAPTER
THE PROVOST'S VERGER
THE PROVOST
A VERGER
BANNERS OF THE SEE OF COVENTRY
A CHAPLAIN **THE LORD BISHOP** A CHAPLAIN

I was glad when they said unto me, We will go into the house of the Lord. Our feet shall stand in thy gates, O Jerusalem. Jerusalem is builded as a city that is at unity in itself. O pray for the peace of Jerusalem: they shall prosper that love thee. Peace be within thy walls, and plenteousness within thy palaces.

Hubert Parry (1848-1918)

The Provost escorts the Bishop to his Throne, and then goes to his stall.

PROLOGUE

As soon as the Anthem is ended, the choir and people sing this Hymn.

HYMN
Regent Square AMR 573

Christ is made the sure Foundation,
Christ the Head and Corner-stone,
Chosen of the Lord, and precious,
Binding all the Church in one,
Holy Sion's help for ever,
And her confidence alone.

To this temple, where we call thee,
Come O Lord of Hosts, to-day;
With thy wonted loving-kindness
Hear thy servants as they pray,
And thy fullest benediction
Shed within its walls alway.

Choir Here vouchsafe to all thy servants
What they ask of thee to gain,
What they gain from thee for ever
With the blessed to retain,
And hereafter in thy glory
Evermore with thee to reign.

Everyone **Laud and honour to the Father,**
Laud and honour to the Son,
Laud and honour to the Spirit,
Ever Three, and ever One,
Consubstantial, co-eternal,
While unending ages run.

Then the Provost at the chancel step welcomes the people.

Then he continues:

O come, let us worship and fall down:
and kneel before the Lord our Maker.

Choir and people

For he is the Lord our God:
and we are the people of his pasture,
and the sheep of his hand.

PSALM 95. Venite exultemus

Provost O COME, let us sing unto the Lord:
let us heartily rejoice in the strength of our salvation.

Choir Let us come before his presence with thanksgiving:
and show ourselves glad in him with psalms.

People **For the Lord is a great God:**
and a great King above all gods.

Choir In his hand are all the corners of the earth:
and the strength of the hills is his also.

People **The sea is his, and he made it:**
and his hands prepared the dry land.

Choir O come, let us worship and fall down:
and kneel before the Lord our maker.

People **For he is the Lord our God:**
and we are the people of his pasture,
and the sheep of his hand.

Provost Glory be to the Father, and to the Son:
and to the Holy Ghost;

Everyone **As it was in the beginning,**
is now, and ever shall be:
world without end. Amen.

Provost O come, let us worship and fall down:
and kneel before the Lord our Maker.

Choir and people

For he is the Lord our God:
and we are the people of his pasture,
and the sheep of his hand.

The people sit down, and the choir sings:

How lovely are thy dwellings fair, O Lord of hosts. My soul ever longeth and fainteth sore for the blest courts of the Lord; my heart and flesh do cry to God, cry to the living God. O blest are they that in thy house are dwelling; they ever praise thee, O Lord, praise thee for evermore.

Johannes Brahms (1833-97)

THE WORD OF GOD

THE LESSON

read by Mrs V.M. GIBBS,
Chairman of the National Association of Flower Arrangement Societies

Man is given dominion over the created order, and is answerable to God for the use he makes of it.

And God said, Let us make man in our image, after our likeness: and let them have dominion over the fish of the sea, and over the fowl of the air, and over the cattle, and over all the earth, and over every creeping thing that creepeth upon the earth. So God created man in his own image, in the image of God created he him; male and female created he them. And God blessed them, and God said unto them, Be fruitful, and multiply, and replenish the earth, and subdue it: and have dominion over the fish of the sea, and over the fowl of the air, and over every living thing that moveth upon the earth. And God said, Behold I have given you every herb bearing seed, which is upon the face of all the earth, and every tree, in the which is the fruit of a tree yielding seed; to you it shall be for meat. And to every beast of the earth, and to every fowl of the air, and to everything that creepeth upon the earth, wherein there is life, I have given every green herb for meat: and it was so. And God saw every thing that he had made, and, behold, it was very good.

Genesis 1. 26-31a

THE ADDRESS

by the Very Reverend H.C.N. Williams, LL.D., Provost of Coventry

Choir and people stand to sing this Hymn.

HYMN
Warrington AMR 153

Give to our God immortal praise,
Mercy and truth are all his ways;
Wonders of grace to God belong,
Repeat his mercies in your song.

Give to the Lord of lords renown;
The King of kings with glory crown:
His mercies ever shall endure,
When lords and kings are known no more.

He fills the sun with morning light,
He bids the moon direct the night:
His mercies ever shall endure,
When suns and moons shall shine no more.

Choir and people sit down.

CONSIDER THE LILIES

Readers

Jesus said: Consider the lilies of the field, how they grow; they toil not, neither do they spin; and yet I say unto you, that even Solomon in all his glory was not arrayed like one of these.

Matthew 6. 28b, 29

WILD FLOWERS

This much of gardens; but I tell
Also of native flowers in wood and dell;
Of campion and the little pimpernel;
Of kexen parsley and the varied vetch;
Of the living mesh, cats-cradle in a ditch;
Of gorse and broom and whins;
Of hops and buckwheat and the wild woodbine
That with their stems must twine
Like the way of the sun to left from right;
Of berried bindweeds, twisting widdershins;
Of all the tangle of the hedgerow, laced
With thorny dog-rose and the deadly dwale;
Throughout the seasons do I count their tale,
But orderly, that those who walk abroad
In lane and wood
May find them in their season as they grow.

V. Sackville-West: *The Land*

TREES

Loveliest of trees, the cherry now
Is hung with bloom along the bough,
And stands about the woodland ride
Wearing white for Eastertide.

Now, of my threescore years and ten,
Twenty will not come again,
And take from seventy springs a score,
It only leaves me fifty more.

And since to look at things in bloom
Fifty springs are little room,
About the woodlands I will go
To see the cherry hung with snow.

A.E. Housman: A Shropshire Lad

FRUITS

The best sorts of Apples serve at the last course for the table, in most mens houses of account, where, if there grow any rare or excellent kind of fruit, it is then set forth to be seene and tasted. Divers other sorts serve to bake, either for the Masters table, or the meynes sustenance, eyther in pyes or pans, or else stewed dishes with Rose water and sugar, and Cinnamon or Ginger cast upon. Some kindes are fittest to roaste in the winter time, to warme a cup of wine, ale or beere; or to be eaten alone, for the nature of some fruit is never so good, or worth the eating, as when they are roasted. Some sorts are best to make cider of, as in the West Country of England. It is usually seene that those fruits that are neither fit to eate raw, roasted nor baked, are fittest for cider and make the best.

John Parkinson (1629)

SPICES

How lovely thy caressing, my sister, my spouse,
Sweeter than wine are thy endearments,
Beyond all odorous spices the fragrance of thy balm.
Thy lips, my spouse, are like the dropping honeycomb,
Honey and milk beneath thy tongue
And the odour of thy garments is like Lebanon.
My sister, my spouse, is a garden enclosed,
A spring fenced round, a fountain sealed,
A pleasance planted with pomegranates
And every orchard fruit.
Henna with spikenard,
Spikenard and saffron,
Sugar cane and cinnamon, each Lebanonian tree.
Myrrh and aloes with every spice excellent:
A fountain in a garden,
A well of living waters
Streaming down from Lebanon!
O North wind waken
And O South wind come
Blow through my garden
And set its spice aflow.

The Song of Songs

Choir

THE SPRING

My beloved spake, and said unto me, Rise up, my love, my fair one, and come away. For lo, the winter is past, the rain is over and gone; the flowers appear on the earth; and the time of the singing of birds is come, and the voice of the turtle is heard in our land; the fig-tree putteth forth her green figs, and the vine with her tender grapes gives a good smell. Arise, my love, my fair one, and come away.

The Song of Songs. Music by Patrick Hadley (1899-1973)

THE PROCESSION

The Procession goes from the chancel by the south aisle to the design with flowers representing Reconciliation.

HYMN
Easter Song AMR 172

All creatures of our God and King,
Lift up your voice and with us sing
Alleluia, alleluia!
Thou burning sun with golden beam,
Thou silver moon with softer gleam,
O praise him, O praise him,
Alleluia, alleluia, alleluia!

Dear mother earth, who day by day
Unfoldest blessings on our way,
O praise him, alleluia!
The flowers and fruits that in thee grow,
Let them his glory also show;
O praise him, O praise him,
Alleluia, alleluia, alleluia!

Let all things their Creator bless,
And worship him in humbleness;
O praise him, alleluia!
Praise, praise the Father, praise the Son,
And praise the Spirit, Three in One;
O praise him, O praise him, Alleluia, alleluia, alleluia!

The people sit down.

At the design representing Reconciliation

GARDENS

And because the breath of flowers is far sweeter in the air (where it comes and goes, like the warbling of music) than in the hand, therefore nothing is more fit for that delight, than to know what be the flowers and plants that do best perfume the air. Roses, damask and red, are fast flowers of their smells; so that you may walk by a whole row of them, and find nothing of their sweetness, yea, though it be in a morning's dew. That which, above all others, yields the sweetest smell in the air is the violet; especially the white double violet, which comes twice a year – about the middle of April, and about Bartholomew-tide. But those which perfume the air most delightfully, not passed by as the rest, but being trodden upon and crushed, are three, that is, burnet, wild thyme, and water-mints; therefore, you are to set whole alleys of them, to have the pleasure when you walk or tread.

Francis Bacon: *Of Gardens*

Choir

King Jesus hath a garden, full of divers flowers,
Where I go culling posies gay, all times and hours.
There naught is heard but Paradise bird,
Harp, dulcimer, lute,
With cymbal, trump and tymbal,
And the tender soothing flute.

The Lily, white in blossom there, is Chastity:
The Violet, with sweet perfume, Humility.

The bonny Damask-rose is known as Patience:
The blithe and thrifty Marygold, Obedience.

The Crown Imperial bloometh too in yonder place,
'Tis Charity, of stock divine, the flower of grace.

Yet, 'mid the brave, the bravest prize of all may claim
The Star of Bethlehem – Jesus – blessèd be his Name!

Ah! Jesu Lord, my heal and weal, my bliss complete,
Make thou my heart thy garden-plot, fair, trim and neat.
That I may hear this musick clear:
Harp, dulcimer, lute,
With cymbal, trump and tymbal,
And the tender, soothing flute.

17thC Dutch carol

The people stand

Precentor and choir

℣ Consider the lilies of the field, how they grow;

℟ Even Solomon in all his glory was not arrayed like one of these.

℣ Refresh us, O Lord God, as we consider the glories of thy creation, with these tokens of thy love towards us; and send us on our way with humility towards thee and a patient charity towards each other, till we reach home at last, to be refreshed with the unfading glories of the courts of heaven; through Jesus Christ our Lord.

℟ Amen.

The Procession moves westwards down the south aisle, and eastwards up the middle of the nave, while a voluntary is played on the organ.

In the nave

THE THANKSGIVING

Bishop and people, with a loud voice

℣ Yours is the praise, O God,
You are our sovereign Lord.
℟ **To you, eternal Father,**
The wide world pays its homage.
℣ From all the angels in their bright array,
From heaven and all the Powers.
℟ **To you goes up the cry, the unremitting cry,**
℣ Holy, holy, holy is the Lord,
Sovereign Commander of the hosts of heaven.
℟ **There is no corner of the earth or sky**
But rings with your renown.

Let us thank God for all his mercies.

For the order and constancy of nature,
For the beauty and the bounty of the world,
For day and night, summer and winter, seedtime and harvest,
For the diverse gifts of loveliness and use which each season brings,
We praise God,
℟ **We thank him.**

For the artist's eye and the artist's hand
At work upon God's creation
And out of its beauties fashioning fresh glories,
We praise God,
℟ **We thank him.**

For our homes and the joys of home,
For our friends, and for all occasions of fellowship,
For all the gracious ministries of human affection,
We praise God,
℟ **We thank him.**

For communion with God, who created us and holds us ever within the embrace of his love,
For the life, death, and resurrection of Jesus Christ, who shows us who God is, sets us free, and makes us one,
For the Holy Spirit, who touches our hearts to love and obedience,
We praise God,
℟ **We thank him.**

Glory be to the Father, and to the Son: and to the Holy Spirit;
℟ **As it was in the beginning,**
Is now, and ever shall be;
World without end. Amen.

The Procession moves towards the chancel.

HYMN
Dix AMR 171

For the beauty of the earth.
For the beauty of the skies,
For the love which from our birth
Over and around us lies,
Lord of all, to thee we raise
This our grateful hymn of praise.

For the beauty of each hour
Of the day and of the night,
Hill and vale, and tree and flower,
Sun and moon and stars of light,
Lord of all, to thee we raise
This our grateful hymn of praise.

People **For the joys of human love,**
Brother, sister, parent, child,
Friends on earth, and friends above,
Pleasures pure and undefiled,
Lord of all, to thee we raise
This our grateful hymn of praise.

Choir For each perfect gift of thine,
To our race so freely given,
Graces human and divine,
Flowers of earth and buds of heaven,
Lord of all, to thee we raise
This our grateful hymn of praise.

Everyone **For thy Church which evermore**
Lifteth holy hands above,
Offering up on every shore
Her pure sacrifice of love,
Lord of all, to thee we raise
This our grateful hymn of praise.

The Precentor goes to the gate of the sanctuary; the choir to their stalls; the clergy to the sanctuary; the Bishop and his Chaplains to the high altar.

At the High Altar

Precentor and choir

℣ Consider the lilies of the field, how they grow;
℟ Even Solomon in all his glory was not arrayed like one of these.

℣ O Almighty God, creator of heaven and earth: Make us grateful for thy glory here, and make us worthy of thy glory hereafter; through Jesus Christ our Lord.
℟ Amen.

During the following Hymn the offerings of the people are collected and are brought to two servers at the chancel step, to be carried by them to the altar to be presented by the Bishop.

HYMN
Laudate Dominum AMR 376

**O praise ye the Lord! praise him in the height;
Rejoice in his word, ye angels of light;
Ye heavens adore him by whom ye were made,
And worship before him, in brightness arrayed.**

**O praise ye the Lord! praise him upon earth,
In tuneful accord, ye sons of new birth;
Praise him who hath brought you his grace from above,
Praise him who hath taught you to sing of his love.**

**O praise ye the Lord, all things that give sound;
Each jubilant chord re-echo around;
Loud organs, his glory forth tell in deep tone,
And, sweet harp, the story of what he hath done.**

**O praise ye the Lord! thanksgiving and song
To him be outpoured all ages along:
For love in creation, for heaven restored,
For grace of salvation, O praise ye the Lord! Amen.**

THE BLESSING

After the Hymn the people kneel, and the Bishop says:

Unto God's gracious mercy and protection we commit you.

The Lord bless you, and keep you,
The Lord make his face to shine upon you,
And be gracious unto you.
The Lord lift up the light of his countenance upon you,
and give you peace,
now and always.

The choir sings: Amen.

THE WITHDRAWAL

The Bishop and his clergy withdraw from the chancel through the nave to the west door, to say goodbye to the people as they leave.

When the Bishop has left the chancel, the choir withdraws by the Swedish Steps to St Michael's Hall.

4. Fanfare for Europe: A Votive Eucharist

Coventry Cathedral, 7 January 1973

The congregation numbered 1,600, including nationals of the nine countries of the EEC.

The theme: a celebration of the entry of Great Britain into the European Economic Community.

Resources: the cathedral choir, the organ, and brass of the Royal Military School of Music.

The rite is a conflation of the two Eucharistic orders which were legally authorised in the Church of England in 1970, i.e. the rite of 1662/1928 and The Communion Series 2. The rite follows the sequence of Series 2; but the language is that of 1662/1928, or language modelled on that. The composite rite was authorised by the Bishop of Coventry for use in his Cathedral.

The rubrics which concern the congregation are printed in the course of the text. Rubrics which concern the musicians and other persons responsible for presenting the service efficiently are printed in the margin alongside the text to which the rubrics are related.

The text was printed in Times New Roman 10 point on a 12 point body. Details of the words and music of each hymn are printed immediately below the hymn in 8 point, not leaded. Every item in the service is set in capitals, to make the sequence of events immediately clear.

Information about the music, the musicians, and the ministers both clerical and lay, is given on the final page.

~~~~~~

The entry of the choir and Ministers

The procession goes westwards by the north aisle of the nave to the west end, where it turns eastwards to take up its position in the middle alley. A rubric directs the people to remain seated.

The purpose of this mode of entry is two-fold:

1 The choir and Ministers stand among the congregation at the very outset, to make it clear that they are all one company of worshippers assembled to do the Eucharist together. The distinction between 'them' in the chancel and 'us' in the nave is visibly denied. This is a simple trick of the trade, but very important.
~~~~~~

2 When the entrance hymn begins, the choir, standing among the congregation and singing the hymn in unison (that is to say, all singing the melody) supports and encourages the people.

The Anthem

On this occasion, as is done in Coventry Cathedral before the entrance hymn on all the Principal Feasts and on other days of special note, the choir standing in the nave sings an anthem. This makes an agreeable change from the usual organ voluntary; and visitors who arrive late find themselves at once engulfed in the sound of praise.

The Fanfare

The beginning of the actual service is announced by a fanfare, which calls the people to their feet. The entrance hymn follows. One verse is allotted to the choir, who by this time will be in their stalls in the chancel; they sing this verse in harmony, unaccompanied.

The Intrada

The nine flags of the EEC now advance from the west end through the nave, during the Intrada for brass and organ. The people's attention is not divided between the attempt to sing a hymn and their natural desire to watch the procession of flags: and here is a simple example of the plea made in the first chapter of this book, to allow the worshippers to use their eyes when they come to church.

The Sermon comes now, early in the service (as happens at an Ordination), in order that the theme of the service may be expounded before it is seen and heard unfolding as the rite proceeds.

The Collect is preceded by the form of salutation always used at the Eucharist in Coventry Cathedral:

℣ The Lord be with you;
℟ **The Lord bless you.**

This was a Eucharist of great splendour. No ordinary collect would have been adequate, so it seemed worthwhile to compose something in the nature of a set piece at a display of fireworks.

If you examine the prayer closely, you will realise that:

1 It is addressed to the Blessed Trinity.
2 It is a true collect, for
   (a) it is a single sentence, with no full stop in the course of it;

(b) it has all the five parts of a regular collect, *viz.*
   1 The address to God
   2 The attributes of God in virtue of which the petition is made
   3 The petition
   4 The reason for the petition
   5 The close

The collect is intricate, and rich in direction. In the fourth section there are two quotations; one line is from Milton, another line is from Dante.

The Epistle at any Eucharist is taken from one of the New Testament letters, which were in origin messages exchanged between one Christian congregation and another, scattered about the Roman world. At this Fanfare for Europe the New Testament custom was followed; instead of a passage from the Bible, messages from Christians of Europe to the Church in Coventry were read aloud.

The Gospel is preceded by a fanfare, as is the custom at every Sunday Eucharist at Coventry Cathedral. It is usually, of course, played on the organ: but on this occasion it was played by the trumpeters of the Royal Military School of Music; and for good measure they played another fanfare after the Gospel.

The Middle Voluntary played on the organ affords some moments of quiet, and also covers the movement of the Celebrant from the Bishop's throne to the chancel lectern where he is to conduct the Intercession.

The Intercession

The method of conducting the Intercession is fully discussed in **Biddings** (page 83). Please refer to that section.

At the normal Sunday Eucharist the Intercession is followed by the Preparation of the People, viz. the Invitation, the Confession, the Absolution, and the Prayer of Humble Access, all in the form and language of 1662. The Preparation of the People is sometimes omitted, as it is here, to allow the rite to proceed with greater expedition. The note of penitence has already been sounded in the 9-fold kyrie at the beginning of the Eucharist.

The Offertory

In accordance with the custom of the Cathedral, the altar at the Ante-Communion is bare, and there are no candles lit on it or near it; for the Ante-Communion is conducted at the chancel lectern, and the Ministers there are robed only in alb and stole.

When the offertory hymn begins, the Celebrant and the two deacons withdraw to the south choir aisle to put on chasuble and dalmatics, and then go up through the chancel to the east side of the altar, where they face the people. Meanwhile the servers with disciplined alacrity spread upon the altar the fair linen cloth (which is 27 feet long and 5 feet deep); and a verger lights the two candles on the altar, and the six huge candles standing three to the left of it and three to the right.

Then the alms of the people are carried in procession through the nave to the sanctuary, followed by two delegates from the congregation bringing the bread and wine for the Communion.

The Consecration

Everyone stands throughout the Prayer of Consecration. The people kneel at the Fraction, after the Peace.

The Consecration begins with the same salutation as used before the collect.

After the Words of Institution there is **Solemn Music for Brass**. This is only rarely done. It is very impressive and moving. You will find a note about it in **Fanfares** (page 142).

The Lord's Prayer is sung by choir and congregation, loudly, firmly, rather quickly, to the ancient traditional plainsong melody.

'The cup of blessing which we bless' is said by the Celebrant and the people, in the indicative mood, not in the form of a question – 'Is it not a sharing?'

The Peace is both spoken and enacted. Note the form of words:

℣ The peace of the Lord be always with you;
℟ **Peace to you.**

The Withdrawal

Note the way in which this is set out. The order in which the company is to disperse, and the route to be taken by each group of people, is obvious at a single glance. You will find a note about this in **Rubrics** (page 218).

THE ORDER OF SERVICE

The flags of the nine countries of EEC are grouped at the west end of the nave. At 10.17 the Cathedral procession leaves St Michael's Hall and goes as usual by the north aisle of the nave to take up its position in the middle alley.

The people remain seated.

The trumpeters take up their position before the high altar.

The choir standing in the middle alley of the nave sings this Salute to Jesus Christ.

ANTHEM

Hosanna to the Son of David.
Blessed be the king that cometh in the name of the Lord. Hosanna.
Thou that sittest in the highest heavens.
Hosanna in excelsis Deo.

Thomas Weelkes 1574-1623

The Ante-Communion will be broadcast in colour by Associated Television

THE ANTE-COMMUNION

At 10.30 **FANFARE**
The people stand.

HYMN

Trumpets

The procession goes forward to the chancel

**All people that on earth do dwell,
Sing to the Lord with cheerful voice;
Him serve with fear, his praise forth tell,
Come ye before him, and rejoice.**

**The Lord, ye know, is God indeed;
Without our aid he did us make;
We are his folk, he doth us feed,
And for his sheep he doth us take.**

Trumpets

**O enter then his gates with praise,
Approach with joy his courts unto;
Praise, laud, and bless his name always,
For it is seemly so to do.**

Choir

For why? the Lord our God is good;
His mercy is for ever sure;
His truth at all times firmly stood,
And shall from age to age endure.

Everyone. Trumpets

To Father, Son, and Holy Ghost,
The God whom heaven and earth adore,
From men and from the angel-host
Be praise and glory evermore.

Old 100th from Day's Psalter 1561.
Tune from the French Genevan Psalter 1551.
AMR 166.

At the chancel lectern the Provost briefly welcomes the congregation, and sends greetings to viewers. He then invites the national flags to come forward.

INTRADA for brass and organ

The flags are carried in procession from the west end, to be set down below the great lectern and the pulpit.

The trumpeters withdraw to the south choir aisle.

THE SERMON
By the Very Reverend H.C.N. Williams, LL.D.,
Provost of Coventry

After the Sermon the people remain seated.

There are some moments of silence.
Then the choir sings:

THE KYRIE
Kyrie, eleison. *Lord have mercy.*
Christe, eleison. *Christ have mercy.*
Kyrie, eleison. *Lord have mercy.*

The people stand.

The Celebrant at the Throne says:
The Lord be with you.
℟ **The Lord bless you.**

THE COLLECT

Come, Father and Lord, creator of this beautiful
and hospitable world,
Come, Lord Jesus Christ, the light which the darkness has
never mastered, and never will,
Come, Holy Spirit, Lord and Life-giver,
Come, Lord, come:

Accept the tribute which we pay
of gratitude for the graces and beauties of Europe,
of sorrow for the follies and crimes of Europe,
of reverence for the sanctities of Europe:

Come, puissant Lord,
refresh us with the riches of thy creation,
Come, benign Redeemer,
rescue us from the misuse of thy creation,
Come, Holy Spirit, the only Ruler of our unruly appetites and
affections,
dispose us to share the resources of thy creation,
Come, Lord, come:

Create among the nations of Europe
justice
and comity,
and joy,
for now all things sigh to be renewed,
and only in thy will is our peace;
who reignest God today,
tomorrow,
always.

℟ **Amen**.

Everyone sits down.

MESSAGES from Christians of Europe
to the Church in Coventry

A representative of one country stands in the Provost's stall, and the representative of another country in the Precentor's stall. The Second Deacon stands at the chancel lectern.

The Second Deacon announces:

A message from a Christian from [ ]
to the Church in Coventry

The message is read aloud by the representative in English.

Then everyone stands to sing this Hymn.

HYMN

The trumpeters return

Now thank we all our God,
With heart and hands and voices,
Who wondrous things hath done,
In whom his world rejoices;
Who from our mother's arms
Hath blessed us on our way
With countless gifts of love,
And still is ours today.

O may this bounteous God
Through all our life be near us,
With ever joyful hearts
And blessed peace to cheer us;
And keep us in his grace,
And guide us when perplexed,
And free us from all ills
In this world and the next.

All praise and thanks to God
The Father now be given,
The Son, and him who reigns
With them in highest heaven,
The one eternal God,
Whom earth and heaven adore,
For thus it was, is now,
And shall be evermore.

Words by R. Rinkart 1586-1649,
tr. Catherine Winkworth in her
Lyra Germanica 1858. The tune
Nun danket alle Gott is from
Praxis Pietatis Melica 1647. AMR 379

FANFARE

At the chancel lectern the First Deacon announces the Gospel. Everyone sings:

Glory be to thee, O Lord.

THE GOSPEL: Matthew 2.1-11

The tribute of the nations to Jesus Christ

Jesus was born at Bethlehem in Judaea during the reign of Herod. After his birth astrologers from the east arrived in Jerusalem, asking, 'Where is the child who is born to be king of the Jews? We observed the rising of his star, and we have come to pay him homage.' King Herod was greatly perturbed when he heard this; and so was the whole of Jerusalem. He called a meeting of the chief priests and lawyers of the Jewish people, and put before them the question: 'Where is it that the Messiah is to be born?' 'At Bethlehem in Judaea', they replied; and they referred him to the prophecy which reads: 'Bethlehem in the land of Judah, you are far from least in the eyes of the rulers of Judah; for out of you shall come a leader to be the shepherd of my people Israel.' Herod next called the astrologers to meet him in private, and ascertained from them the time when the star had appeared. He then sent them on to Bethlehem, and said, 'Go and make a careful inquiry for the child. When you have found him, report to me, so that I may go myself and pay him homage.' They set out at the king's bidding; and the star which they had seen at its rising went ahead of them until it stopped above the place where the child lay. At the sight of the star they were overjoyed. Entering the house, they saw the child with Mary his mother, and bowed to the ground in homage to him; then they opened their treasures and offered him gifts: gold, frankincense, and myrrh.

Everyone sings:

Praise to thee, O Christ.

FANFARE

The trumpeters withdraw to the south choir aisle.

THE CONFESSION OF FAITH

The Celebrant at the Throne begins:

I believe in one God

The choir and people take it up:
The Father Almighty,
Maker of heaven and earth,
And of all things visible and invisible;
And in one Lord Jesus Christ,
The only-begotten Son of God,
Begotten of his Father before all worlds,
God of God,
Light of Light,
Very God of Very God,
Begotten, not made,
Being of one substance with the Father,
By whom all things were made:
Who for us men and for our salvation
came down from heaven,
And was incarnate by the Holy Ghost of the Virgin Mary,
And was made man,
And was crucified also for us under Pontius Pilate.
He suffered and was buried,
And the third day he rose again
according to the Scriptures,
And ascended into heaven,
And sitteth on the right hand of the Father.
And he shall come again with glory
to judge both the quick and the dead:
Whose kingdom shall have no end.

And I believe in the Holy Ghost,
The Lord and giver of Life,
Who proceedeth from the Father and the Son,
Who with the Father and the Son together
is worshipped and glorified,
Who spoke by the Prophets.

And I believe one holy catholic and apostolic Church.
I acknowledge one Baptism for the remission of sins.
And I look for the Resurrection of the dead,
And the life of the world to come. Amen.

Everyone sits down. The Remembrancer goes to the Precentor's stall; the Celebrant to the chancel lectern.

THE MIDDLE VOLUNTARY
Kyrie from Fiori Musicali 1635

Girolamo Frescobaldi 1583-1643

THE INTERCESSION

The choir and the Ministers remain seated.
The people may sit or kneel at their own discretion.

Standing at the chancel lectern with his Chaplains and the two Deacons

The Celebrant:
Let us pray for the whole Church of God, and for all men according to their needs.

The Remembrancer bids prayer or thanksgiving for the diocese and its Bishop; for the clergy and people; and for the Church at home and overseas.

Silence

The Celebrant:
Grant, O Lord, that we and all who confess thy Name may be united in thy truth, live together in thy love, and show forth thy glory in the world.

Lord in thy mercy
℟ **Hear our prayer.**

The Remembrancer bids prayer or thanksgiving for the Queen and the Realm; for the nations of the world; and for men in their various callings

Silence

The Celebrant:
Defend, O Lord, our Sovereign Lady Queen ELIZABETH; give us wise and upright rulers, incorruptible judges and magistrates, and peace at home and abroad.

Lord in thy mercy
℟ **Hear our prayer.**

The Remembrancer bids prayer for the poor, for the sick, for the bereaved, and for others in trouble

Silence

The Celebrant:
Comfort and succour, O Lord, all those who in this transitory life are in trouble, sorrow, need, sickness, or any other adversity.

Lord in thy mercy
℟ **Hear our prayer.**

The Remembrancer bids prayer or thanksgiving for the dead

Silence

The Celebrant:
Remember, O Lord, those who have died in thy faith and fear; remember also in thy compassion those who die without faith and without hope; and grant us all a share in thy eternal kingdom.

Lord in thy mercy
℟ **Hear our prayer.**

Grant these our prayers, O merciful Father, for the sake of thy Son, our Saviour Jesus Christ.

℟ **Amen**.

The Celebrant with his Chaplains goes up through the chancel to the Throne.

At a signal from the Deacon everyone stands.

The Offertory Hymn follows at once.

THE COMMUNION

OFFERTORY HYMN

The cloth is laid upon the altar. The offerings of the people are collected, and are carried, with the bread and wine for the Communion, from the nave to the altar.

Trumpets

**Of the Father's love begotten
Ere the worlds began to be,
He is Alpha and Omega,
He the source, the ending he,
Of the things that are, that have been,
And that future years shall see,
Evermore and evermore.**

**At his word they were created;
He commanded; it was done:
Heaven and earth and depths of ocean
In their threefold order one;
All that grows beneath the shining
Of the light of moon and sun,
Evermore and evermore.**

Choir

O that birth for ever blessed!
When the Virgin, full of grace,
By the Holy Ghost conceiving,
Bare the Saviour of our race,
And the Babe, the world's Redeemer,
First revealed his sacred face,
Evermore and evermore.

Everyone

**This is he whom seers and sages
Sang of old with one accord;
Whom the writings of the Prophets
Promised in their faithful word;
Now he shines, the long-expected:
Let creation praise its Lord,
Evermore and evermore.**

Trumpets

**Now let old and young men's voices
Join with boys' thy name to sing,
Matrons, virgins, little maidens
In glad chorus answering;
Let their guileless songs re-echo,
And the heart its praises bring,
Evermore and evermore.**

Trumpets

**Christ, to thee, with God the Father,
And, O Holy Ghost, to thee,
Hymn and chant and high thanksgiving
And unwearied praises be,
Honour, glory, and dominion,
And eternal victory,
Evermore and evermore.**

The broadcast ends here.

Words from the Latin of the Spaniard
Prudentius 348-413. The tune
Divinum Mysterium is from
Piae Cantiones 1582, but is in fact
many centuries older. AMR 591

THE CONSECRATION

In order to celebrate the triumph of Christ's Passion, now to be visibly re-presented at the Altar in Bread and Wine, everyone stands together from this moment until the end of the Peace.

The Celebrant sings:
℣ The Lord be with you;
℟ **The Lord bless you.**
℣ Lift up your hearts;
℟ **We lift them up unto the Lord.**
℣ Let us give thanks unto our Lord God;
℟ **It is meet and right so to do.**

It is very meet, right, and our bounden duty, that we should at all times, and in all places, give thanks unto thee, O Lord, Holy Father, Almighty, Everlasting God:

Therefore with angels and archangels, and with all the company of heaven, we laud and magnify thy glorious name; evermore praising thee, and saying,

The choir sings:
Holy, holy, holy, Lord God of hosts, heaven and earth are full of thy glory. Glory be to thee, O Lord most High. Amen. Blessed is he that cometh in the name of the Lord: hosanna in the highest.

The Celebrant continues without note:
Hear us, O merciful Father, we most humbly beseech thee; and grant that we receiving these thy creatures of bread and wine, according to thy Son our Saviour Jesus Christ's holy institution, in remembrance of his death and passion, may be partakers of his most blessed Body and Blood: who, in the same night that he was betrayed, [*Here the Bishop is to take the Paten into his hands:*] took Bread; and, when he had given thanks to thee, [*And here to break the Bread*] he broke it, and gave it to his disciples, saying, Take, eat; [*And here to lay his hand upon the Bread*] this is my Body which is given for you: Do this in remembrance of me. [*Here the Celebrant and all within the Sanctuary bow profoundly.*]

Likewise after supper [*Here he is to take the Cup into his hand:*] he took the Cup; and, when he had given thanks to thee, he gave it to them, saying, Drink this, all of you; for this [*And here to lay his hand upon the Cup.*] is my Blood of the New Covenant, which is shed for you and for many for the remission of sins: Do this, as often as you drink it, in remembrance of me. [*Here the Celebrant and all within the Sanctuary bow again.*]

SOLEMN MUSIC for brass

The Celebrant:
Wherefore, O Lord, with this bread and this cup we make the memorial of his saving passion, his resurrection from the dead, and his glorious ascension into heaven, while we look for the coming of his kingdom. We pray thee to accept this our duty and service, and grant that we may so eat and drink these holy things in the presence of thy divine majesty, that we may be filled with thy grace and heavenly blessing; Through the same Christ our Lord, to whom with thee, O Father, and thee, O Holy Spirit, with the whole company of the redeemed, we offer praise for ever.
℟ **Amen.**

The Celebrant sings:

As our Saviour Christ hath commanded and taught us, we are bold to say:

The choir and people:

**Our Father, which art in heaven,
Hallowed be thy name;
Thy kingdom come; Thy will be done,
In earth as it is in heaven.
Give us this day our daily bread.
And forgive us our trespasses,
As we forgive them that trespass against us.
And lead us not into temptation;
But deliver us from evil:
For thine is the kingdom,
The power, and the glory,
For ever and ever. Amen.**

The Celebrant says:

The cup of blessing which we bless

Everyone joins with him:

**is a sharing of the blood of Christ.
The bread which we break
is a sharing of the Body of Christ.
We being many are one bread, one Body, for we all partake of the one bread.**

THE PEACE

*A profound SILENCE follows.
After a while the Celebrant greets the people:*

The peace of the Lord be always with you;

The people reply: **Peace to you.**

The Celebrant greets successively the two Deacons, clasping their right hands in both of his; and they in turn pass the Peace to all who are within the Sanctuary. The Crossbearer carries the Peace to those (the choir excepted) who are in the chancel, while two servers go to the chancel step to give the Peace to two representatives of the congregation.

The people may exchange the Peace with one another.

THE FRACTION

The people kneel; the choir, and all within the Sanctuary, remain standing. While the Bread is broken, the choir sings:

O LAMB OF GOD,
that takest away the sins of the world:
have mercy upon us. *(x2)*

O LAMB OF GOD,
that takest away the sins of the world:
grant us thy peace.

The Celebrant communicates first himself, then the Deacons. He then administers the Bread, and the First Deacon the Cup, to those within the Sanctuary; who thereupon (unless they are vested) withdraw by the choir aisles to their places in the nave.

THE COMMUNION

The Celebrant says:

Draw near with faith: receive the Body of our Lord Jesus Christ, which was given for you, and his Blood, which was shed for you; and feed on him in your heart by faith with thanksgiving.

All who are communicant members in good standing of their own Churches, are invited to receive the Communion.

At the delivery of the Bread the Minister says:
THE BODY OF CHRIST GIVEN FOR YOU
and the communicant replies:
Amen.

At the delivery of the Cup the Minister says:
THE BLOOD OF CHRIST SHED FOR YOU
and the communicant replies:
Amen.

During the Communion of the people the choir sings:

HYMN

Bread of the world in mercy broken,
Wine of the soul in mercy shed,
By whom the words of life were spoken,
And in whose Death our sins are dead;

Look on the heart by sorrow broken,
Look on the tears by sinners shed;
And be thy feast to us the token,
That by thy grace our souls are fed.

Tune by Louis Bourgeois in the
Genevan Psalter 1543.
AMR 409.

ANTHEM

Ave verum corpus, natum
De Maria Virgine,
Vere passum, immolatum
In cruce pro homine,
Cujus latus perforatum
Unda fluxit sanguine;
Esto nobis praegustatum,
In mortis examine.

Music by W.A. Mozart 1756-91

Jesu, Word of God incarnate,
Of the Virgin Mary born,
On the cross thy sacred body
For us men with nails was torn.
Cleanse us by the blood and water
Streaming from thy piercèd side;
Feed us with thy body broken
Now, and in death's agony.

When all have received the Communion the Celebrant and the two Deacons stand at the west side of the Altar, and the Celebrant says:

Let us pray.
Almighty and everlasting God, we thank thee that thou dost feed us in these holy mysteries with the Body and Blood of thy Son our Saviour Jesus Christ, and that thou dost keep us thereby in the Body of thy Son, which is the blessed company of all faithful

people; and we pray thee that we may continue as living members of that holy fellowship, and do all such works as thou hast prepared for us to walk in; through the same thy Son Jesus Christ our Lord, who liveth and reigneth with thee in the unity of the Holy Spirit, one God, world without end.
℟ **Amen.**

THE BENEDICTION

The Celebrant blesses the people:

The peace of God, which passes all understanding, keep your hearts and minds in the knowledge and love of God, and of his Son Jesus Christ our Lord: and the blessing of God Almighty, the Father, the Son, and the Holy Ghost, be amongst you and remain with you always.

The choir sings: Amen.

HYMN

Trumpets

The Lord will come and not be slow,
His footsteps cannot err;
Before him righteousness shall go,
His royal harbinger.

Truth from the earth, like to a flower,
Shall bud and blossom then;
And justice, from her heavenly bower,
Look down on mortal men.

Voices in unison. Trumpets.

Rise, God, judge thou the earth in might,
This wicked earth redress;
For thou art he who shalt by right
The nations all possess.

Choir

The nations all whom thou hast made
Shall come, and all shall frame
To bow them low before thee, Lord,
And glorify thy name.

Everyone. Trumpets

For great thou art, and wonders great
By thy strong hand are done:
Thou in thy everlasting seat
Remainest God alone.

Words by John Milton, 1608-74. A cento from
Milton's translation of the psalms:
Nine of the Psalms done into Metre,
headed 'April 1648. J.M.'
The tune St. Stephen is by the Rev. W Jones,
vicar of Nayland. It is found at the end of his work
Ten Church Pieces for the Organ 1789. AMR 52.

SOLI DEO GLORIA

THE WITHDRAWAL

I *To the west door*
THE CATHEDRAL PROCESSION
THE NATIONAL FLAGS
THE LORD MAYOR'S COMPANY
THE PRINCIPAL GUESTS

II *By the north choir aisle to St Michael's Hall*
THE CHOIR

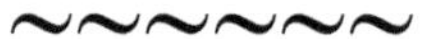

THE MUSIC

The music of the Communion is by Edmund Rubbra: *Mass of St. Dominic,* Op. 66.

The music for brass has been composed for this service by John Hotchkis, and is played by members of the Royal Military School of Music under the Director of Music Lieutenant-Colonel Rodney Bashford, M.B.E.

THE MINISTERS

Celebrant: The Right Reverend C.K.N. Bardsley, C.B.E., D.D., Lord Bishop of Coventry

First Deacon: The Provost *Second Deacon:* The Precentor

Remembrancer: Mr. J.A. Gillespie

Delegates: The Warden and Assistant Warden of John F. Kennedy House

The Delegates carry the Bread and Wine for the Communion to the altar in the offertory procession. John F. Kennedy House, named after the President of the United States of America, is a residential hostel standing in the Cathedral grounds. It was opened in 1965 by Herr Willy Brandt, then Governing Mayor of West Berlin, and has been since that time the centre of the international ministry of Coventry Cathedral. The present Warden is an American; his wife the Assistant Warden is Norwegian.

5. The Form of a Servant

CHRISTMAS EVE: The Festival of Nine Lessons and Carols: its origin and history

The diocese of Truro in Cornwall was established in 1877; and its first bishop was Edward White Benson (1829-96), who in 1883 became Archbishop of Canterbury. He was the last Archbishop to reside at Addington Palace, now the headquarters of the Royal School of Church Music.

At the time when the diocese of Truro was created there was no Cathedral. Until the new Truro Cathedral was opened and consecrated in 1910 worship was carried on in a temporary wooden building, which has now completely disappeared.

Bishop Benson (writes his son A.C. Benson) 'arranged from ancient sources a little service for Christmas Eve – nine carols and nine tiny lessons, which were read by various officers of the church, beginning with a chorister, and ending, through the different grades, with the Bishop'.

It was in the little wooden Cathedral of Truro that this service was first performed at 10 p.m. on Christmas Eve in 1880. Though nobody knew it at the time, this was the beginning of the Festival of Nine Lessons and Carols.

In 1918 the Reverend Dr E.A. Milner-White tried out the devotion in the Chapel of King's College, Cambridge, of which he was then Dean. He was not satisfied with the service in its new setting, and in 1919 he re-ordered it into the form which it has retained ever since; and he himself composed for the occasion the beautiful Bidding Prayer, which is now widely known and loved.

The service attracted vast crowds to Cambridge; and even before the BBC first broadcast it in 1928 and made it a world institution, it had spread throughout England (including non-Anglican churches and chapels) and to all the Dominions. Now, one hundred years after its humble origin in the wooden Cathedral of Truro, the King's College Festival of Nine Lessons and Carols, performed and broadcast every year on Christmas Eve, is heard with a rapturous interest in every corner of the globe.

Their sound is gone out into all lands:

and their words into the ends of the world.

Whenever the Festival is spoken of, two men are to be remembered and honoured: Edward Benson, Bishop of Truro, and Eric Milner-White, Dean of King's; and the Festival is, without question, one of the precious gifts bestowed upon humanity by the Church of England.

The Festival of Nine Lessons and Carols: its universal appeal

If we ask what is the secret of the universal appeal of the King's College service, we may answer:

First, it tells a story, the story as the Bible unfolds it of man's redemption by Jesus Christ; and this is its liturgical strength. The carols are not chosen at haphazard; they are chosen to illustrate and comment upon the story.

Secondly, there is a charm in hearing the story unfolded, in lesson after lesson, as different members of the Christian community take it in turn to read; there is a sense of true comity. This is a feature introduced at the very beginning by Bishop Benson at Truro, and maintained ever since.

Thirdly, and perhaps capitally, the service breathes a sense of joy and of adoration. Its universal popularity suggests that it meets a profound need of human nature; the need, which our secular age professes to have outgrown, of pure worship. For the service does not preach at us, it does not adjure us, it does not scold us: it simply invites us to attend, for a brief hour, to heavenly things, and to be refreshed at the deepest level of our being.

Another way of keeping Christmas Eve

When Coventry Cathedral had been consecrated on 25 May 1962 the staff sat down together to consider how best to celebrate Christmas Eve. There was no point in trying to emulate King's College, Cambridge; perhaps there was another way, more immediately suited to the City of Coventry. Here was a bustling, thrusting community, supporting no fewer than 400 different industries: what was the real need of such a community? And what had the Cathedral, by virtue of its history, to say to the community?

By virtue of its history the Cathedral had to speak of reconciliation: reconciliation of man with God, and of man with man. Where men are not reconciled with God and with one another, it is because they are sinners. The first requirement, therefore, in a service celebrating the birth of the Redeemer, must be penitence; there must be a touch of astringency about it.

And what was the deep need of the City, the bustling, thrusting City of Coventry? It was, we believed, simply peace, tranquillity, a quiet mind; a chance to be still.

Out of such considerations as these came our carol service for Christmas Eve; and we called it **The Form of a Servant**. For we recalled the Redeemer's vocation; we recalled what must also be the vocation of his followers. 'I am among you,' he said, 'as one that serves'. And on the eve of his Passion he said to his friends, 'Know ye what I have done unto you? Ye call me Master and Lord: and ye say well; for so I am. If I then, your Lord and Master, have washed your feet; ye also ought to wash one another's feet. For I have given you an example, that ye should do as I have done to you.'

THE FORM OF A SERVANT

a carol service sung annually on Christmas Eve
at Coventry Cathedral

The service begins with penitence; it continues with the Advent hymn 'Hail to the Lord's Anointed', and then with an outburst of joy at the birth of Jesus. The emotional temperature rises as the service proceeds. There is a blaze of light everywhere until Part V THE MYSTERY; now the electric lights are turned off, and the building is in darkness except for the dim lights at the eight Tablets of the Word and the hundreds of twinkling lights upon the giant Christmas tree near the west end. In this dim light, and in the silence which the rubric requires, a voice is heard reading the lesson which tells of Jesus who 'took upon him the form of a servant'.

Now three streams of flickering gold lights move from the east end to the west: down the middle of the nave go four lights escorting the Lady Banner and the Cross of Nails, and simultaneously the two choirs carrying lighted tapers go by the north and south aisles to the west end, where they meet, and take their places at the Christmas tree.

At the tree the choir sings a carol; and then, to the silvery tones of the harpsichord, the choir, still carrying lighted tapers, withdraws eastward by the middle alley of the nave to the chancel, where the two sides of the choir divide to move through the Lady Chapel, and so disappear.

By this time the whole building is wrapped in a profound peace; the quiet, the tranquillity, the chance to be still, has been brought about.

When the choir has vanished, it is some time before anyone stirs; and only the electric lights over the doors at the west end are turned on, to show people the way out. The mystery lingers.

If you would visualize the service, pay careful attention to all the rubrics. The rubrics which concern the congregation are printed in the course of the text. Rubrics which concern the Ministers and choir and other persons responsible for presenting the service efficiently are printed in the margin alongside the text to which the rubrics are related.

Notice particularly the rubrics at the crib. There are two choirs here. Choir 2, at the crib, is a semi-chorus: four boys (two trebles and two altos) and two men (a tenor and a bass). The rest of the choir is Choir 1, in the chancel. The two choirs are spatially separated by a distance of 50 yards; and it is the antiphony between these widely separated groups which lends a magic, an unforgettable magic, to this Christmas Eve.

The music sung by the two choirs is to be found in the final chapter of this book.

COVENTRY CATHEDRAL

THE FORM OF A SERVANT
A Service for Christmas Eve
24 December 1975 at 7.30 p.m.

~~~~~~~~~~~~~~~~~~~~~~~~

THE ORDER OF SERVICE
At 7.25 the choir and Ministers take up their positions at the west end.

At 7.30 F A N F A R E
The people stand.

HYMN AMR 49

The refrain at the end of every verse is to be sung by everyone, loudly and cheerfully.

O come, O come, Emmanuel,
And ransom captive Israel,
That mourns in lonely exile here,
Until the Son of God appear.
Rejoice! Rejoice! Emmanuel
Shall come to thee, O Israel.

Boys of the choir
O come, thou Rod of Jesse, free
Thine own from Satan's tyranny;
From depths of hell thy people save,
And give them victory o'er the grave.

Everyone
O come, thou Dayspring, come and cheer
Our spirits by thine advent here;
Disperse the gloomy clouds of night,
And death's dark shadows put to flight.

Boys of the choir
O come, thou Key of David, come,
And open wide our heavenly home;
Make safe the way that leads on high,
And close the path to misery.

Everyone
O come, O come, thou Lord of Might,
Who to thy tribes, on Sinai's height,
In ancient times didst give the law
In cloud and majesty and awe.
The Ministers and people sit down.
~~~~~~~~~~~~~~~~~~~~~~~~

The Precentor at the chancel lectern

We have come once again to celebrate the Birth of Jesus Christ.

This carol service is in five parts: Penitence, Joy, Adoration, Offering, The Mystery.

Penitence first: we remember that every one of us is in some way at fault; and so we must say we are sorry, and ask God's forgiveness.

Penitence gives way to Joy, with the news of the birth of Jesus.

Joy leads on to Adoration; and Adoration is then expressed in the Offering, both of our money and of our obedience.

The service reaches its climax as we recall the Mystery of the Incarnation, and are reminded of the God who came to visit us in the form of a servant. The conclusion is a moment of absolute stillness and peace. We hope that you will find here, this evening, a quiet mind; and that you will go home at peace, and be happy, this Christmas Eve.

I PENITENCE

CAROL CC23 *The choir at the west end*

The Coventry Carol, sung in the Coventry Pageant of the Shearmen and Tailors (1591) by the women of Bethlehem, just as soldiers come in to massacre their children. It is sung tonight as a lament for suffering children everywhere.

Lully, lully, thou little tiny child,
By by, lully, lullay,
Thou little tiny child,
By by, lully, lullay.

O sisters too,
How may we do
For to preserve this day
This poor youngling,
For whom we do sing
By, by, lully lullay?

Herod, the king,
In his raging,
Chargèd he hath this day
His men of might,
In his own sight,
All young children to slay.

That woe is me,
Poor child for thee:
And ever morn and day,
For thy parting
Neither say nor sing
By, by, lully, lullay!

The Provost at the chancel lectern

All over the world, at this moment, men are longing for peace. But peace cannot be had for the asking. Peace must be won.

The Christian believes that peace among men and nations is the fruit of humility and of penitence.

The Christian believes that loving and humble service to those who have hurt us, or whom we have hurt, has power to heal our sorrows.

A voice

There were two others with Jesus, criminals who were being led away to execution; and when they reached the place called The Skull they crucified him there, and the criminals with him, one on his right and the other on his left. Jesus said, 'Father, forgive them; they do not know what they are doing'.

Luke 23. 32-34

THE LITANY OF RECONCILIATION

The Provost Remember St. Paul's words:

All have sinned, and come short of the glory of God.

The Letter to Rome

The HATRED which divides nation from nation,
race from race, class from class,

Father, forgive.

The COVETOUS desires of men and nations
to possess what is not their own,

Father, forgive.

The GREED which exploits the labours of men,
and lays waste the earth,

Father, forgive.

Our ENVY of the welfare and happiness of others.

Father, forgive.

Our INDIFFERENCE to the plight of the homeless
and the refugee,

Father, forgive.

The LUST which uses for ignoble ends
the bodies of men and women,

Father, forgive.

The PRIDE which leads us to trust in ourselves, and not in God,

Father, forgive.

Remember St Paul's words:

Be kind one to another, tender-hearted, forgiving one another,
as God in Christ forgave you.

The Letter to Ephesus

INTERCESSION

That it may please thee to succour, help, and comfort all that are in danger, necessity, and tribulation;

We beseech thee to hear us, good Lord.

That it may please thee to preserve all that travel by air, land, water, all women labouring of child, all sick persons, and young children; and to shew thy pity upon all prisoners and captives;

We beseech thee to hear us, good Lord.

That it may please thee to defend, and provide for, the fatherless children, and widows, and all that are desolate and oppressed;

We beseech thee to hear us, good Lord.

That it may please thee to have mercy upon all men;

We beseech thee to hear us, good Lord.

Lord Jesus Christ, who hast taught us that the greatest of all is the servant of all: Cast out from us all false ambitions, and make us to reign by serving our brothers; for thy name's sake. Amen.

Silence

ANTHEM

Agnus dei, qui tollis peccata mundi, miserere nostri.
Thomas Morley 1557-1602

O Lamb of God, that takest away the sins of the world, have mercy upon us.

HYMN
AMR 219

during which the offerings of the people, in aid of the ministry of Coventry Cathedral, are collected and taken to the west end.

The procession moves through the nave to the chancel. The Provost escorts the Bishop to the throne, and then goes to his stall.

**Hail to the Lord's Anointed,
Great David's greater Son!
Hail, in the time appointed,
His reign on earth begun!
He comes to break oppression,
To set the captive free,
To take away transgression,
And rule in equity.**

**He comes with succour speedy
To those who suffer wrong;
To help the poor and needy,
And bid the weak be strong;
To give them songs for sighing,
Their darkness turn to light,
Whose souls, condemned and dying,
Were precious in his sight.**

People

**He shall come down like showers,
Upon the fruitful earth,
And love, joy, hope, like flowers,
Spring in his path to birth:
Before him on the mountains
Shall peace, the herald, go;
And righteousness in fountains
From hill to valley flow.**

Choir

Kings shall bow down before him,
And gold and incense bring;
All nations shall adore him,
His praise all people sing:
To him shall prayer unceasing
And daily vows ascend;
His kingdom still increasing,
A kingdom without end.

Everyone, *triumphantly*

**O'er every foe victorious,
He on his throne shall rest;
From age to age more glorious,
All-blessing and all-blest:
The tide of time shall never
His covenant remove;
His name shall stand for ever,
His changeless name of Love.**

The Ministers and the people sit down.

II JOY POEM *The Precentor at the chancel lectern*

The Wish

A glad New Year to all!
Since many a tear,
Do what we can, must fall,
The greater need to wish a glad New Year.

Since lovely youth is brief,
O girl and boy,
And no one can escape a share of grief,
I wish you joy.

Since hate is with us still,
I wish men love;
I wish, since hovering hawks still strike to kill,
The coming of the dove;

And since the ghouls of terror and despair
Are still abroad,
I wish the world once more within the care
Of those who have seen God.

Eleanor Farjeon

THREE SONGS OF HAPPINESS

CAROL A Merry Christmas CC19

The choir at the chancel steps

We wish you a merry Christmas
And a happy New Year.

Good tidings I bring
To you and your kin.

Now bring us some figgy pudding,
Now bring some out here.

For we all like figgy pudding,
So bring some out here.

West Country traditional,
arranged by Arthur Warrel

CAROL The Twelve Days of Christmas CC2.30

The Twelve Days of Christmas: Christmas Day till The Epiphany (6 January)

On the first day of Christmas my true love sent to me
A partridge in a pear tree.

On the second day of Christmas my true love sent to me
Two turtle doves and a partridge in a pear tree.

On the third day of Christmas my true love sent to me
Three French hens, two turtle doves and
a partridge in a pear tree.

On the fourth day of Christmas my true love sent to me
Four calling birds, etc.

On the fifth day of Christmas my true love sent to me
Five gold rings, etc.

On the sixth day of Christmas my true love sent to me
Six geese a-laying, etc.

On the seventh day of Christmas my true love sent to me
Seven swans a-swimming, etc.

On the eighth day of Christmas my true love sent to me
Eight maids a-milking, etc.

On the ninth day of Christmas my true love sent to me
Nine ladies dancing, etc.

On the tenth day of Christmas my true love sent to me
Ten lords a-leaping, etc.

On the eleventh day of Christmas my true love sent to me
'leven pipers piping, etc.

On the twelfth day of Christmas my true love sent to me
Twelve drummers drumming, etc.

English traditional,
arranged by John Rutter

Everyone stands. The choir go to their stalls.

HYMN CC14

Everyone

Hark! The herald-angels sing
Glory to the new-born King,
Peace on earth, and mercy mild,
God and sinners reconciled.
Joyful, all ye nations, rise,
Join the triumph of the skies;
With the angelic host proclaim,
'Christ is born in Bethlehem'.

Hark! the herald-angels sing
Glory to the new-born King.
Christ, by highest heaven adored,
Christ, the everlasting Lord,
Late in time behold him come,
Offspring of the Virgin's womb.
Veiled in flesh the Godhead see!
Hail, the incarnate Deity!
Pleased as Man with man to dwell,
Jesus, our Emmanuel.

Descant

Hail, the heaven-born Prince of Peace!
Hail, the Sun of Righteousness!
Light and life to all he brings,
Risen with healing in his wings.
Mild he lays his glory by,
Born that man no more may die,
Born to raise the sons of earth,
Born to give them second birth.

Everyone sits down.

LESSON

A reader in the great lectern

In those days a decree was issued by the Emperor Augustus for a registration to be made throughout the Roman world. This was the first registration of its kind; it took place when Quirinius was governor of Syria. For this purpose everyone made his way to his own town; and so Joseph went up to Judaea from the town of Nazareth in Galilee, to register at the city of David, called Bethlehem, because he was of the house of David by descent; and with him went Mary who was betrothed to him. She was expecting a child, and while they were there the time came for her baby to be born, and she gave birth to a son, her first-born. She wrapped him in his swaddling clothes, and laid him in a manger, because there was no room for them to lodge in the house.

Luke 2. 1-7

Everyone stands.

III. ADORATION

THE PROCESSION TO THE CRIB

HYMN CC1

A great and mighty wonder,
A full and holy cure!
The Virgin bears the Infant
With virgin-honour pure:

Repeat the hymn again!
'To God on high be glory,
And peace on earth to men.'

The Word becomes incarnate,
And yet remains on high;
And cherubim sing anthems
To shepherds from the sky:

Repeat the hymn again!

While thus they sing your Monarch,
Those bright angelic bands,
Rejoice, ye vales and mountains,
Ye oceans, clap your hands:

Repeat the hymn again!

Since all he comes to ransom,
By all be he adored,
The infant born in Bethlem,
The Saviour and the Lord:

Repeat the hymn again!

Everyone sits down.

AT THE CRIB

Choir 1 in the chancel
Choir 2 and Precentor at the crib

Precentor When all things began, the Word already was;
Choir 1 and through him all things came to be,
Choir 2 all things came to be.
Precentor The Word became flesh;
he came to dwell among us,
and we saw his glory;
Choir 1 such glory as befits the Father's only Son,
full of grace and truth,
Choir 2 full of grace and truth.
Precentor No one has ever seen God;
Choir 1 but God's only Son,
he who is nearest to the Father's heart
he has made him known,
Choir 2 he has made him known.
Precentor Grace and truth be with you;
Choir 1 peace to you,
Choir 2 peace to you.

Precentor O everlasting God, who has declared thy love to men by the birth of the Holy Child at Bethlehem: Help us at his coming to welcome him with gladness, and to make room for him in our common days; who with thee and the Holy Spirit reigneth God, world without end.

Choir 1 Amen, Amen, Amen,
Choir 2 Amen.

CAROL CC3
Choir 1 A boy was born in Bethlehem;
Rejoice for that, Jerusalem!
Alleluia, alleluia, alleluia.

Choir 2 He let himself a servant be,
That all mankind he might set free:

Choir 1 Alleluia.
Choir 2 Alleluia.
Choir 1 Alleluia.

Choir 1 Then praise the Word of God who came
To dwell within a human frame:
Alleluia, alleluia.

Choir 2 Alleluia, alleluia.

Choir 1 Alleluia.

Benjamin Britten

Everyone stands.

IV OFFERING

HYMN CC2.31

The procession moves westwards by the north aisle and eastwards by the Christmas tree into the middle of the nave, and so to the chancel.

The Bishop with his Chaplains goes to a seat before the sanctuary, and sits down in it; the Banners of his See standing on either side. Then two lights go to the chancel step, where the Provost joins them.

Choir 2, unaccompanied

Once in royal David's city
Stood a lowly cattle shed,
Where a mother laid her baby
In a manger for his bed:
Mary was that Mother mild,
Jesus Christ her little Child.

Everyone

He came down to earth from heaven
Who is God and Lord of all,
And his shelter was a stable,
and his cradle was a stall;
With the poor and mean and lowly
Lived on earth our Saviour holy.

And through all his wondrous childhood
He would honour and obey,
Love and watch that lowly Maiden,
In whose gentle arms he lay:
Christian children all must be
Mild, obedient, good as he.

Choir

For his is our childhood's pattern,
Day by day like us he grew,
He was little, weak, and helpless,
Tears and smiles like us he knew;
And he feeleth for our sadness,
And he shareth in our gladness.

People

At the fifth verse of the Hymn the bearers of the offerings, walking two by two and preceded by a verger, carry the offerings from the west end to the chancel step, and from there, preceded by the Provost, to the Bishop.

And our eyes at last shall see him,
Through his own redeeming love,
For that Child so dear and gentle
Is our Lord in heaven above;
And he leads his children on
To the place where he is gone.

Everyone

Not in that poor lowly stable,
With the oxen standing by,
We shall see him, but in heaven,
Set at God's right hand on high;
Where like stars his children crowned
All in white shall wait around.

The Provost stands before the Bishop; and when the Hymn ends he says:

Right Reverent Father in God,
We bring you our offerings in aid of the ministry of this Cathedral. I ask you to receive the gifts and to offer them to God in token of our will to promote peace and good will among men.

A Verger
Two Lights
The Provost's Verger
The Provost
The Bearers

The bearers advance and hand the offerings to the Bishop; and then return to their places, one file going to the left by the north aisle of choir and nave, the other going to the right by the south aisle.

When all are again in their places, the Bishop rises and goes up to the altar, attended by his Chaplains, who carry the offerings to the altar and lay them down on it.

The Bishop gives his staff and mitre to his Chaplains; and then, making the Sign of the Cross over the offerings, he says:

Accept, O Lord, at our hands these offerings, the tokens of our will to serve thee and our fellows: and use both these gifts, and our obedience, to make known to thy children thy compassion and thy mercy declared in thy Son, Jesus Christ our Lord.

All the people answer firmly and clearly:
Amen.

The Bishop returns to his Throne, and the Ministers and people sit down. Then the choir sings this carol:

CAROL The Kings CC40

Three Kings from Persian lands afar
To Jordan follow the pointing star:
And this the quest of the travellers three;
Where the newborn King of the Jews may be.
Full royal gifts they bear for the King;
Gold, incense, myrrh are their offering.

The star shines out with a steadfast ray;
The Kings to Bethlehem make their way,
And there in worship they bend the knee,
As Mary's child in her lap they see;
Their royal gifts they show to the King,
Gold, incense, myrrh are their offering.

Thou child of man – lo, to Bethlehem
The kings are travelling – travel with them!
The star of mercy, the star of grace,
Shall lead thy heart to its resting place.
Gold, incense, myrrh thou canst not bring;
Offer thy heart to the infant King,
Offer thy heart!

Everyone stands.

V THE MYSTERY

The two sides of the choir move severally into the north and south choir aisles.

HYMN AMR 591

Of the Father's love begotten
Ere the worlds began to be,
He is Alpha and Omega,
He the source, the ending he,
Of the things that are, that have been,
And that future years shall see,
Evermore and evermore.

O that birth for ever blessed!
When the Virgin, full of grace,
By the Holy Ghost conceiving,
Bare the Saviour of our race,
And the Babe, the world's Redeemer,
First revealed his sacred face,
Evermore and evermore.

**O ye heights of heaven, adore him;
Angel-hosts, his praises sing;
Powers, dominions, bow before him,
And extol our God and King:
Let no tongue on earth be silent,
Every voice in concert ring,
Evermore and evermore.**

**This is he whom seers and sages
Sang of old with one accord;
Whom the writings of the Prophets
Promised in their faithful word;
Now he shines, the long-expected:
Let creation praise its Lord,
Evermore and evermore.**

Men and boys	Now let old and young men's voices Join with boys' thy name to sing,
Women and girls	Matrons, virgins, little maidens In glad chorus answering;
Everyone	**Let their guileless songs re-echo, And the heart its praises bring, Evermore and evermore.**

**Christ, to thee, with God the Father,
And, O Holy Ghost, to thee,
Hymn and chant and high thanksgiving
And unwearied praises be,
Honour, glory, and dominion, And eternal victory,
Evermore and evermore.**

Ministers and people sit down.

The people are asked to remain seated, in perfect silence, till the end of the music for harpsichord at the end of the service.

When the people have sat down, the lights on the Tapestry, in the Lady Chapel, the chancel roof, and the nave are extinguished.

CAROL CC2.36 *to be sung antiphonally*

Shepherds left their flocks astraying,
God's command with joy obeying,
When they heard the angel saying:
'Christ is born in Bethlehem.'

Wise men came from far, and saw him:
Knelt in homage to adore him;
Precious gifts they laid before him:
Gold and frankincense and myrrh.

Let us now in ev'ry nation
Sing his praise with exultation.
All the world shall find salvation
In the birth of Mary's Son.

German 14th century,
arranged by John Rutter

LESSON

A voice

Let this mind be in you, which was also in Christ Jesus: who, being in the form of God, thought it not a thing to be snatched at to be equal with God; but made himself of no reputation, and took upon him the form of a servant, and was made in the likeness of men: and being found in fashion as a man, he humbled himself, and became obedient unto death, even the death of the cross.

Wherefore God also hath highly exalted him, and given him a name which is above every name: that at the name of Jesus every knee should bow, of things in heaven, and things in earth, and things under the earth; and that every tongue should confess that Jesus Christ is Lord, to the glory of God the Father.

Philippians 2. 5-11

After the Lesson, lighted tapers are distributed to the choirs.

When the organ music begins, the Ministers preceded by the Lady Banner and the Cross of Nails and four lights go from the chancel through the nave to the west door.

MUSIC FOR ORGAN

In dulci jubilo: J.S. Bach 1685-1750

At the same time the two choirs carrying lighted tapers go by the north and south aisles to the west end, where they meet, and take their places at the Christmas tree.

CAROL OBC109 *at the Christmas Tree*

O little one sweet, O little one mild,
Thy Father's purpose thou hast fulfilled;
Thou cam'st from heav'n to mortal ken,
Equal to be with us poor men,
O little one sweet, O little one mild.

O little one sweet, O little one mild,
With joy thou hast the whole world filled;
Thou camest here from heav'n's domain,
To bring men comfort in their pain,
O little one sweet, O little one mild.

O little one sweet, O little one mild,
In thee Love's beauties are all distilled;
Then light in us thy love's bright flame,
That we may give thee back the same,
O little one sweet, O little one mild.

O little one sweet, O little one mild,
Help us to do as thou hast willed.
Lo, all we have belongs to thee!
Ah, keep us in our fealty!
O little one sweet, O little one mild.

German 17th century

The choir, still carrying lights, withdraws by the middle alley of the nave, the chancel, and the Lady Chapel, to St Michael's Hall.

MUSIC FOR HARPSICHORD
Saraband

from the *Partita in B flat major*: J.S. Bach

The church is to remain darkened till the choir is quite out of sight, and the music ceases.

The Bishop and his clergy remain standing at the west end, to greet the people as they leave.

~~~~~~
~~~~~~

VARIANTS

The structure of **The Form of a Servant** has been constant at least since 1968: but within that structure the details have varied. Here are some of the variants.

1. Instead of II JOY, the following:

THE BIRTH OF JESUS

The Precentor at the chancel step

This is the Month, and this the happy morn
Wherein the Son of Heav'ns eternal King,
Of wedded Maid, and Virgin Mother born,
Our great redemption from above did bring;
For so holy sages once did sing,
That he our deadly forfeit should release,
And with his Father work us a perpetual peace.

That glorious Form, that Light unsufferable,
And that far-beaming blaze of Majesty,
Wherewith he wont at Heav'n's high Council-Table,
To sit the midst of Trinal Unity,
He laid aside; and here with us to be,
Forsook the Courts of everlasting Day,
And chose with us a darksome House of Mortal Clay.

John Milton, *On the morning of Christ's Nativity*

2 Instead of III ADORATION, the following:

THE PROCESSION TO THE CRIB

HYMN

The procession goes from the chancel to the Crib in the north aisle.

While shepherds watched their flocks by night
All seated on the ground,
The angel of the Lord came down,
And glory shone around.

'Fear not', said he (for might dread
Had seized their troubled mind);
'Glad tidings of great joy I bring
To you and all mankind.

'To you in David's town this day
Is born of David's line
A Saviour, who is Christ the Lord;
And this shall be the sign:

'The heavenly Babe you there shall find
To human view displayed,
All meanly wrapped in swathing bands,
And in a manger laid'.

First choir only Thus spake the seraph; and forthwith
Appeared a shining throng
Of angels praising God, who thus
Addressed their joyful song:

Everyone **'All glory be to God on high,**
And to the earth be peace;
Good will henceforth from heaven to men
Begin and never cease'.

Luke 2. 8-14

At the Crib

Precentor It came to pass, as the angels were gone away from them into heaven, the shepherds said to one another:

Choir 1 Let us now go even unto Bethlehem, and see this thing which is come to pass, which the Lord hath made known unto us.

Choir 2 Which the Lord hath made known unto us.

Precentor And they came with haste, and found Mary, and Joseph;

Choir 1 And the babe lying in a manger

Luke 2. 15, 16

Choir 2 Lying in a manger.

Precentor The Lord be with you;

Choir 1 And with thy spirit.

Choir 2 And with thy spirit.

Precentor Almighty God, who hast given us thy only- begotten Son to take our nature upon him, and as at this time to be born of a pure Virgin: Grant that we being regenerate, and made thy children by adoption and grace, may daily be renewed by thy Holy Spirit; through the same our Lord Jesus Christ, who liveth and reigneth with thee and the same Spirit, ever one God, world without end.

Choir 1 Amen, Amen, Amen.

Choir 2 Amen.

The Ministers sit down on the pilgrim bench by the Crib.

The people sit down.

CAROL

SONG OF THE NUNS OF CHESTER

Four boys at the Crib sing the first verse; the boys in the chancel sing the second verse; and so on to the end.

Qui creavit coelum Lully, lully, lu, Nascitur in stabulo, By, by, by, by, by, Rex qui regit saeculum, Lully, lully, lu.	The creator of the sky, Lully, lully, lu, Is born in a stable, By, by, by, by, by, The King who rules the world, Lully, lully, lu.
Joseph emit panniculum, Mater involvit puerum, Et ponit in praesepio.	Joseph has bought a shawl; The mother wraps the boy in it, And lays him in the manger.
Inter animalia Jacent mundi gaudia Dulcis super omnia.	Among the animals Lies the darling of the world, Sweeter than all things.
Lactat mater domini, Osculatur parvulum, Et adorat dominum.	God is at his mother's breast; She kisses her baby And adores the Lord.
Roga mater filium Ut det nobis gaudium In perenni gloria.	Mother, pray thy Son To give us joy In glory without end.
In sempiterna saecula, In eternum et ultra, Det nobis sua gaudia.	For ever and ever, For eternity and beyond May he give us his joy.

3 In IV THE OFFERING, after the offering of the alms at the altar, instead of the carol called The Kings, the following carol:

The Bishop returns to the Throne, and the Ministers and people sit down. Then the choir sing this carol.

CAROL

Personent Hodie Voces puerulae, Laudantes jocunde Qui nobis est natus, Summo Deo datus. Et de vir, vir, vir Et de vir, vir, vir Et de virgineo Ventre procreatus.	Let's have a song then from the boys, A merry song to welcome The baby; he's our Christmas Present, straight from heaven. And who laid, Who laid, Who laid his lady mother? Nobody laid her.
In mundo nascitur, Pannis involvitur, Praesepi ponitur Stabulo brutorum Rector supernorum. Perdidit, dit, dit, Perdidit, dit, dit, Perdidit spolia Princeps infernorum.	He's one of us now, Wrapped in old rags, Dossed down in a manger Where the cattle stand – The Master Mind himself. He's done for, He's done for, He's done for, Is Old Nick.
Magi tres venerunt, Parvulum inquirunt, Bethlehem aderunt, Stellulam sequendo, Ipsum adorando. Aurum, thus, thus, thus, Aurum, thus, thus, thus, Aurum, thus, et myrrham Ei offerendo.	Three wise men have come Looking for a little boy, Looking everywhere; and a star Twinkled in front of them. Down they fall now, with their Incense and gold, Incense and gold, Gold, incense, and myrrh – His Christmas present.

Omnes clericuli,	Sing up, men, all of you!
Pariter pueri,	Sing up, boys! There's a song,
Cantent ut angeli:	A song in the air; where's yours?
Advenisti mundo,	Jesus, you've come to stay,
Laudes tibi fundo.	And I'm wild with joy.
Ideo, o, o,	And that's why,
Ideo, o, o,	That's why,
Ideo Gloria	That's why our songs
In excelsis Deo.	Must hit the sky, the sky.

German melody of 1360 arranged by Gustav Holst.
Words from *Piae Cantiones* (1582) translated by J.W.P.

6. A Service for Trafalgar Day

THE DEDICATION OF A STANDARD

For the Coventry Branch of The Royal Naval Association 1962

An example of a service composed for an occasion when no choir was available.

Trafalgar Day

They that go down to the sea in ships:
and occupy their business in great waters;

These men see the works of the Lord: and his wonders in the deep.

The words come naturally to mind as one begins to gather material for a service for a naval occasion. But how are they to be used?

In the Psalter the words introduce a vivid description of a storm at sea, from which the crew pray to be delivered; and the stilling of the storm is seen by the psalmist as the evidence of God's mercy. The whole passage, then, can here be recited as a celebration of the majesty and the mercy of God. The verses are said by priest and people alternately, and they are laid out on the page in such a way as to make their public recitation easy – one line to a breath. The last two verses are an exhortation to praise; and the opening verses of Te Deum then follow naturally.

The appropriate sequel to praise is penitence; and a paragraph of three brief sentences spoken by the Provost effects the transition from one mood to the other.

Praise, confession, and absolution prepare the people to listen to the Word of God. The passage of Scripture chosen is one of the cardinal passages of the New Testament on the subject of service; and when the lesson has been read, a few sentences spoken by the Provost make clear its relevance to the ceremony of the Dedication of a Standard which now follows.

The Standard is carried in procession from the west end of the church to the chancel step. The ensuing dialogue between the Provost and the people defines exactly the meaning of the action in which they are engaged. The language is terse and precise; above all, it is the language of everyday speech. The Provost does not address the congregation as 'Dearly beloved brethren', or even as 'Good people'; he says simply 'Men of the Royal Naval Association'. He reminds them what they have come to do; they have come (1) to renew their pledge of service, and (2) to dedicate their

Standard. He reminds them further what the Standard is for; it is, he says, 'to represent to you your duty to your Queen and your country'.

The purpose of the meeting has now been precisely stated; it is then with equal precision carried into effect. The men renew their pledge of service, and the Provost, in the moment of hallowing the Standard, again formally defines its significance; it is 'to be a sign of our duty towards our Queen and our country in the sight of God'.

The Dedication of the Standard leads naturally to prayer; first to a prayer for grace to fulfil the pledges just renewed, and then to intercession for the Queen. This intercession takes two forms: (1) the prayer composed by Dr Eric Milner-White for use at the time of the coronation of Queen Elizabeth II, and (2) the National Anthem. There follows the sonorous prayer for the Royal Navy from the Book of Common Prayer, laid out on the page, one line to a breath, for recitation by the whole congregation; a prayer for faithfulness, the Lord's Prayer, and the Grace; and finally the hymn 'Eternal Father, strong to save'. This is a hymn whose inclusion can hardly be avoided in a naval service; and there is no reason why it should not be used, provided it can be placed as to do the work it is clearly fitted to do. It is not a hymn of praise or of thanksgiving or of penitence; it is a prayer of intercession. Fervently sung by a crowd of men, it firmly clinches the argument. While it is sung, the newly dedicated Standard is carried forward through the chancel to be laid upon the altar.

The service continued with the Bishop's sermon, another hymn of praise, and the Bishop's Blessing. Finally the Standard was removed from the altar and returned to the Standard bearer, to be escorted at the head of the procession through the nave to the west door.

THE ORDER OF SERVICE

The Reception of the Lord Bishop of Coventry

At 2.55 p.m. the members of the Foundation leave St Michael's Hall and go through the chancel and the nave to the west door to receive the Lord Bishop of Coventry; and the people rise.

At 3.00 p.m. the Bishop enters the Cathedral; and at once the whole company sings this Hymn:

All people that on earth do dwell,
Sing to the Lord with cheerful voice;
Him serve with fear, his praise forth tell,
Come ye before him, and rejoice.

**The Lord, ye know, is God indeed;
Without our aid he did us make;
We are his folk, he doth us feed,
And for his sheep he doth us take.**

**O enter then his gates with praise,
Approach with joy his courts unto;
Praise, laud, and bless his name always,
For it is seemly so to do.**

**For why? the Lord our God is good;
His mercy is for ever sure;
His truth at all times firmly stood,
And shall from age to age endure.**

**To Father, Son, and Holy Ghost,
The God whom heaven and earth adore,
From men and from the angel-host
Be praise and glory evermore.**

Old 100th AMR 166

The procession moves through the nave to the chancel, in this order:

A VERGER
THE GREAT CROSS
TWO CANDLEBEARERS
A VERGER
THE CHAPTER
THE PROVOST'S VERGER
THE PROVOST
A VERGER
BANNERS OF THE SEE OF COVENTRY
A CHAPLAIN THE LORD BISHOP OF COVENTRY A CHAPLAIN

*The Provost escorts the Bishop to his Throne,
and then goes to the chancel step, where he welcomes the people.*

PRAISE

Then the Provost says:

Let us remind ourselves of the majesty and the mercy of God,
in words which a poet wrote, long ago, about the sea.

CYMBALS AND DANCES

The Provost and the people read this Psalm, verse by verse alternately, in a loud firm voice:

PSALM 107. 23-32

℣ They that go down to the sea in ships:
and occupy their business in great waters;
℟ **These men see the works of the Lord:**
and his wonders in the deep.
℣ For at his word the stormy wind ariseth:
which lifteth up the waves thereof.
℟ **They are carried up to the heaven, and down again to the deep: their soul melteth away because of the trouble.**
℣ They reel to and fro, and stagger like a drunken man:
and are at their wits' end.
℟ **So when they cry unto the Lord in their trouble: he delivereth them out of their distress.**
℣ For he maketh the storm to cease:
so that the waves thereof are still.
℟ **Then are they glad, because they are at rest: and so he bringeth them unto the haven where they would be.**
℣ O that men would therefore praise the Lord for his goodness:
and declare the wonders that he doeth for the children of men!
℟ **That they would exalt him also in the congregation of the people: and praise him in the seat of the elders!**

The Provost continues alone:

We praise thee, O God: we acknowledge thee to be the Lord.
All the earth doth worship thee: the Father everlasting.
To thee all angels cry aloud: the Heavens, and all the Powers therein.
To thee Cherubin, and Seraphin: continually do cry,
Holy, Holy, Holy,
Lord God of Sabaoth;

The people join in:

Heaven and earth are full of the Majesty of thy glory.

CONFESSION

The Provost addresses the people:

God, who made the world, made us also, and set us here to serve him and obey him. In our heart of hearts we know that our service is fitful, and our obedience is imperfect.

Here in God's presence let us in silence recall our shortcomings, and our need of his forgiveness.

There is silence. Then the Provost says and the people reply:

℣ We know and confess, O God;
℟ **That our hearts are unworthy to receive thee.**
℣ Day by day we have enjoyed thy gifts;
℟ **But have forgotten that thou wast the giver of them.**
℣ Thou hast shown us what thou wouldst have us do;
℟ **But we have not followed thy way.**
℣ Thou hast spoken to us in thy Word;
℟ **But we have not listened.**

Silence is kept. Then all say together:

Grant, we beseech thee, merciful Lord,
to thy faithful people pardon and peace,
that we may be cleansed from all our sins,
and serve thee with a quiet mind:
through Jesus Christ our Lord. Amen.

The Bishop:

May the Almighty and merciful Lord
grant you pardon and remission of all your sins,
time for amendment of life,
and the grace and comfort of the Holy Spirit.
℟ **Amen.**

This Hymn follows, during which the Provost goes to his stall,
and Rear Admiral H.C. Martell is conducted to the lectern to read the Lesson.

Father of heaven, whose love profound
A ransom for our souls hath found,
Before thy throne we sinners bend,
To us thy pardoning love extend.

Almighty Son, incarnate Word,
Our Prophet, Priest, Redeemer, Lord,
Before thy throne we sinners bend,
To us thy saving grace extend.

Eternal Spirit, by whose breath
The soul is raised from sin and death,
Before thy throne we sinners bend,
To us thy quickening power extend.

Thrice Holy! Father, Spirit, Son;
Mysterious Godhead, Three in One,
Before thy throne we sinners bend,
Grace, pardon, life to us extend.

RIVAULX AMR 164

The Hymn ended, the people sit down.

THE WORD OF GOD

THE LESSON: Matthew 20. 20-28

The mother of Zebedee's sons then came before him, with her sons. She bowed low and begged a favour. 'What is it you wish?' asked Jesus. 'I want you', she said, 'to give orders that in your kingdom my two sons here may sit next to you, one at your right, and the other at your left.' Jesus turned to the brothers and said, 'You do not understand what you are asking. Can you drink the cup that I am to drink?' 'We can,' they replied. Then he said to them, 'You shall indeed share my cup; but to sit at my right or left is not for me to grant; it is for those to whom it has already been assigned by my Father.'

When the other ten heard this, they were indignant with the two brothers. So Jesus called them to him and said, 'You know that in the world, rulers lord it over their subjects, and their great men make them feel the weight of authority; but it shall not be so with you. Among you, whoever wants to be great must be your servant, and whoever would be first must be the willing slave of all – like the Son of Man; he did not come to be served, but to serve, and to surrender his life as a ransom for many.'

At the end of the Lesson the reader stands fast,
and there follow some moments of silence.

After a while the Provost rises and goes again to the chancel step.
There he says:

You have heard what Jesus said to his friends. 'Among you,' he said, 'whoever wants to be great must be your servant, and whoever would be first must be the willing slave of all.' He calls us to serve one another. The Standard of the Royal Naval Association which we are now to dedicate is a symbol of such willing service.

THE DEDICATION OF A STANDARD

The people rise, and Rear Admiral H.C. Martell is conducted from the lectern to his seat.

Music is played while the Standard to be dedicated is carried through the nave from the west end of the church to the chancel step.

A VERGER
THE CHAIRMAN OF THE COVENTRY BRANCH OF THE ROYAL NAVAL ASSOCIATION
AN ESCORT THE STANDARD AN ESCORT

At the chancel step
the Chairman of the Coventry Branch of the Royal Naval Association
addresses the Provost:

MR. PROVOST,
On behalf of the Coventry Branch of the Royal Naval Association
I ask you to bid God's blessing on this Standard.

The Provost replies:

I am glad to do so.

He continues:

Men of the Royal Naval Association in Coventry, you have come to renew your pledge of service, and to ask the blessing of God on your Standard, which is to represent to you your duty to your Queen and your country.

Are you ready to renew your pledge?

The men of the Royal Naval Association in Coventry reply, firmly and resolutely:

We are ready.

The Provost:

Will you honour the Standard now to be committed to you?

Answer:

We will honour the Standard.

The Provost:

May God prosper your Association, accept your service,
and keep you steadfast in your obedience to his will.

The Provost proceeds to the Dedication of the Standard:

To the service of God and of our fellows;
Answer: **We pledge ourselves.**

Provost: To the love of our Queen and our country,
and to the welfare of mankind;
Answer: **We pledge ourselves.**

Provost: To the maintenance of honour,
and the sanctity of man's plighted word;
Answer: **We pledge ourselves.**

Provost: In continual remembrance of our pledge,
and in token of our resolve faithfully to keep it;
Answer: **We dedicate our Standard.**

Then the Provost lays his hand upon the Standard, saying:

IN THE FAITH OF JESUS CHRIST
WE DEDICATE AND SET APART THIS STANDARD,
TO BE A SIGN OF OUR DUTY
TOWARDS OUR QUEEN AND OUR COUNTRY
IN THE SIGHT OF GOD:
IN THE NAME OF THE FATHER, AND OF THE SON,
AND OF THE HOLY SPIRIT. AMEN.

The Provost:

Remember, O Lord, what thou hast wrought in us, and not what we deserve; and as thou hast called us to thy service, make us worthy of our calling; through Jesus Christ our Lord.

All the people reply: **Amen.**

O God, bless our Queen:
Crown her with all thy gifts:
Crown her with grace to love her people
and to rule them well:
Crown with happiness her home and family,
Prince Philip, her consort,
and Charles, Anne, and Andrew, their children.
Make her reign glorious
by the peace of her people,
and their trust and love everywhere;
through Jesus Christ our Lord.
℟ **Amen**.

There follows the NATIONAL ANTHEM:

God save our gracious Queen,
Long live our noble Queen,
God save the Queen!
Send her victorious
Happy and glorious
Long to reign over us;
God save the Queen!

Thy choicest gifts in store
On her be pleased to pour,
Long may she reign;
May she defend our laws,
And ever give us cause
To sing with heart and voice
God save the Queen!

The Provost continues:

O eternal Lord God,
who alone spreadest out the heavens,
and rulest the raging of the sea;
who hast compassed the waters with bounds
until day and night come to an end:

The people join in:

Be pleased to receive into thy almighty
and most gracious protection
the men of the Royal Navy,
and the Fleet in which they serve;

preserve them from the dangers of the sea,
and from the violence of the enemy,
that they may be a safeguard
to our most gracious Sovereign Lady, Queen Elizabeth,
and a security for such as pass on the seas
upon their lawful occasions;
that the inhabitants of our island
may in peace and quietness serve thee our God;
and that they may return in safety
to enjoy the blessings of the land,
with the fruits of their labours,
and with a thankful remembrance of thy mercies
to praise and glorify thy holy name;
through Jesus Christ our Lord. Amen.

The Provost:

Give us, O Lord, a steadfast heart,
which no unworthy thought can drag downwards;
an unconquered heart, which no tribulation can wear out;
an upright heart, which no unworthy purpose may tempt aside;
Give us understanding to know thee,
diligence to seek thee,
wisdom to find thee,
and a faithfulness that may finally embrace thee;
through Jesus Christ our Lord.
℟ **Amen.**

All say together:

Our Father, which art in heaven, hallowed be thy name;
Thy kingdom come; Thy will be done; in earth as it is in heaven.
Give us this day our daily bread.
And forgive us our trespasses,
as we forgive them that trespass against us.
And lead us not into temptation; But deliver us from evil;
For thine is the kingdom, The power, and the glory,
For ever and ever. Amen.

℣ The grace of our Lord Jesus Christ;
℟ **Be with us all.**
℣ The love of God;
℟ **Be with us all.**
℣ The fellowship of the Holy Spirit;
℟ **Be with us all. Amen.**

Now follows the Hymn ETERNAL FATHER. When the Hymn begins, the Provost, preceded by the Provost's Verger, goes up to the Altar.

The Standard is carried through the chancel to the gate of the Sanctuary, where it is received by a clerk, who takes it up to the Provost to be laid by him upon the Altar. The Provost goes to his seat in the Sanctuary; and the Standard bearer and his escorts withdraw by the south choir aisle to seats at the east end of the nave.

Eternal Father, strong to save,
Whose arm hath bound the restless wave,
Who bidd'st the mighty ocean deep
Its own appointed limits keep:
O hear us when we cry to thee
For those in peril on the sea.

O Christ, whose voice the waters heard
And hushed their raging at thy word,
Who walkedst on the foaming deep,
And calm amid the storm didst sleep:
O hear us when we cry to thee
For those in peril on the sea.

O Holy Spirit, who didst brood
Upon the waters dark and rude,
And bid their angry tumult cease,
And give, for wild confusion, peace:
O hear us when we cry to thee
For those in peril on the sea.

O Trinity of love and power,
Our brethren shield in danger's hour;
From rock and tempest, fire and foe,
Protect them wheresoe'er they go:
Thus evermore shall rise to thee
Glad hymns of praise from land and sea.

MELITA AMR 487

7. A Memorial Service for a Righteous Unbeliever

A MEMORIAL SERVICE FOR A RIGHTEOUS UNBELIEVER

RICHARD CROSSMAN, MP for Coventry East 1945-74
COVENTRY CATHEDRAL
Saturday 27 April 1974 at 12 o'clock

The service begins with silence; unusual, but effective. The silence is broken by the sound of an unaccompanied solo flute. The player is out of sight, in the Lady Chapel eastward of the high altar.

The first section of the service is entitled **The Man**. The congregation must be given a clear picture of the person whom they are to commemorate; and this picture is provided, at the outset of the service, by the Address.

But the congregation wish not only to remember the dead man; they wish also to grieve for him, they need an opportunity to express the grief which is the first, and the natural, emotion felt at the death of any man, Christian or agnostic.

Their grief is expressed for them in Housman's poem *'The rain, it streams on stone and hillock'*. The poem is in fact an elegy spoken at the grave of a dead friend. In the first four stanzas the poet assumes an off-hand casual tone which belies the sorrow he feels; in these stanzas he pretends that he need not grieve over the loss of one friend, because he will find other friends, 'friends no worse than you'. The nub of the poem is in the fifth and final stanzas:

> But oh, my man, the house is fallen
> That none can build again.

He will find other friends; yes, but this particular friend is dead, this one person of unique and irreplaceable value has vanished.

What is the purpose of placing this poem written by an avowed atheist* within a Christian memorial service? It is here because it expresses <u>in secular terms</u>, to which an unbeliever can give assent, something which the Church affirms: the unique value of every human being.

---

* *Housman wrote to an enquirer: 'I was brought up in the Church of England and in the High Church party, which is much the best religion I have ever come across. But Lemprière's Classical Dictionary, which fell into my hands when I was eight, attached my affection to paganism. I became a deist at thirteen and an atheist at twenty- one.'*

But the poem by itself is too brief to allow the emotions of the mourners to be fully expressed; and words alone do not discharge emotion as adequately as music does; for music begins where words leave off. Some kind of song seems called for; not necessarily vocal song, but instrumental song, the sort of song suggested by Laurence Binyon's words in his poem for the Fallen:

> Solemn the drums thrill: Death august and royal
> Sings sorrow up into immortal spheres.
> There is music in the midst of desolation,
> And a glory that shines upon our tears.

The 'music in the midst of desolation' is provided by Chopin's *Funeral March*, played on the piano. This music might have been played on the organ; but it was composed for the piano; and in a large and resonant building the piano can sing sublimely.

The first section of the service has been concerned with man; both with one particular man whose death is mourned, and with man the creature of God, created for eternal life but nevertheless doomed to die in his mortal body.

The second section, headed **The Eternal God**, deliberately points the contrast between the creature and the Creator. The Minister and the people read aloud Psalm 139. Domine, probasti, a meditation on the providence of the Creator, who holds all his creatures in his care. And once more, since music begins where words leave off, poetry is succeeded by music, by the hymn 'O God, our help', which again expresses the care of the Creator for his creatures.

The third section, headed **The Service of the Commonwealth**, is a meditation on the work of men prominent in public affairs, who by their disinterested service to their fellows do in fact discharge their obedience to God even while they do not avow their allegiance to him. St Matthew's Parable of Judgment, 'When the Son of man comes in his glory', is a New Testament lesson, which might have been read by a single voice; but it gains in impact if it is distributed between a single voice and the whole congregation. The next passage from St Matthew is read by a single voice, read with great deliberation; it expresses with economy and cogency the obedience of the man who appears to refuse the call of God but does nevertheless do God's will.

The **Prayers** now narrow our attention upon one particular man; not a man in a parable, but a man whom we knew, whose services to his city and his country we recall with gratitude, and whom we commend by name – 'thy servant Richard' – to the divine mercy.

The final Hymn 'O God of truth' is appropriate to one who used his intellect in the service of his fellows; but it reminds us that to fight for truth is not enough to justify us in the eyes of God. We must be 'true within', for (in the august words of the Epistle to the Hebrews) 'everything lies naked and exposed to the eyes of the One with whom we have to reckon'.

The service ends, as it began, with music for unaccompanied solo flute, fading into silence. The sound comes from behind the people, for the player is now at the west end of the building.

THE ORDER OF SERVICE

The Ministers enter and go to their places.
Everyone sits down. There is silence.
Then follows:

MUSIC FOR SOLO FLUTE

Incantation no. 1 André Jolivet 1905-74

THE MAN

THE ADDRESS
by Maurice Edelman, Esq.,
Member of Parliament for Coventry North-West

A voice

The rain, it streams on stone and hillock.
The boot clings to the clay.
Since all is done that's due and right
Let's home; and now, my lad, good-night,
For I must turn away.

Good-night, my lad, for nought's eternal;
No league of ours, for sure.
To-morrow I shall miss you less,
And ache of heart and heaviness
Are things that time should cure.

Over the hill the highway marches
And what's beyond is wide:
Oh soon enough will pine to nought
Remembrance and the faithful thought
That sits the grave beside.

The skies, they are not always raining
Nor grey the twelvemonth through;
And I shall meet good days and mirth,
And range the lovely lands of earth
With friends no worse than you.

But oh, my man, the house is fallen
That none can build again;
My man, how full of joy and woe
Your mother bore you years ago
To-night to lie in the rain.

A.E. Housman: *Last Poems*

MUSIC FOR PIANO

Funeral March Fredéric Chopin 1810-49

THE ETERNAL GOD

Everyone stands.
The Precentor and the people read aloud this Psalm, verse by verse alternately.

PSALM 139. Domine, probasti

O Lord, thou hast searched me out, and known me:
thou knowest my down-sitting, and mine up-rising,
thou understandest my thoughts long before.

Thou art about my path, and about my bed:
and spiest out all my ways.

For lo, there is not a word in my tongue:
but thou, O Lord, knowest it altogether.

Thou hast fashioned me behind and before:
and laid thine hand upon me.

Such knowledge is too wonderful and excellent for me:
I cannot attain unto it.

Whither shall I go then from thy Spirit:
or whither shall I go then from thy presence?

If I climb up into heaven, thou art there:
if I go down to hell, thou art there also.

If I take the wings of the morning:
and remain in the uttermost parts of the sea;

Even there also shall thy hand lead me:
and thy right hand shall hold me.

If I say, Peradventure the darkness shall cover me:
then shall my night be turned to day.

Yea, the darkness is no darkness with thee, but the night is as clear
as the day: the darkness and light to thee are both alike.

For my reins are thine:
thou hast covered me in my mother's womb.

I will give thanks unto thee, for I am fearfully and wonderfully made:
marvellous are thy works,
and that my soul knoweth right well.

My bones are not hid from thee: though I be made secretly,
and fashioned beneath in the earth.

Thine eyes did see my substance, yet being imperfect:
and in thy book all my members written;

Which day by day were fashioned:
when as yet there was none of them.

This Hymn follows.

HYMN

St Anne AMR 165

O God, our help in ages past
Our hope for years to come,
Our shelter from the stormy blast,
And our eternal home.

Beneath the shadow of thy throne
Thy saints have dwelt secure;
Sufficient is thine arm alone,
And our defence is sure.

Before the hills in order stood,
Or earth received her frame,
From everlasting thou art God,
To endless years the same.

A thousand ages in thy sight
Are like an evening gone;
Short as the watch that ends the night
Before the rising sun.

O God, our help in ages past,
Our hope for years to come,
Be thou our guard while troubles last,
And our eternal home.

Everyone sits down.

THE SERVICE OF THE COMMONWEALTH

A voice

It is therefore our business carefully to cultivate in our minds, to rear to the most perfect vigour and maturity, every sort of generous and honest feeling that belongs to our nature. To bring the dispositions that are lovely in private life into the service and conduct of the commonwealth; so to be patriots as not to forget we are gentlemen. To cultivate friendships, and to incur enmities. To have both strong, but both selected: in the one, to be placable; in the other, immovable. To model our principles to our duties and our situation. To be fully persuaded that all virtue which is impracticable is spurious; and rather to run the risk of falling into faults in a course which leads us to act with effect and energy, than to loiter out our days without blame, and without use. Public life is a situation of power and energy; he trespasses against his duty who sleeps upon his watch, as well as he that goes over to the enemy.

Edmund Burke:
Thought on the Cause of the Present Discontents, 1770

A voice

When the Son of Man comes in his glory with all his angels with him, then he will take his seat on his glorious throne. All the nations will be assembled before him, and he will separate men from each other like a shepherd separating sheep from goats. He will place the sheep on his right hand and the goats on his left.

Then the King will say to those on his right: 'Come, you who have won my Father's blessing! Take your inheritance – the Kingdom reserved for you since the foundation of the world.

'For I was hungry and you gave me food.
I was thirsty and you gave me drink.
I was lonely and you made me welcome. I was naked and you clothed me.
I was ill and you came and looked after me.
I was in prison and you came to see me there.'

The people

Lord, when did we see you hungry, and give you food?
When did we see you thirsty, and give you drink?
When did we see you lonely, and make you welcome?
Or see you naked, and clothe you?
Or see you ill or in prison, and go to see you?

The voice

I tell you this:
Whatever you did for the humblest of these my brothers, you did for me.

Matthew 25. 31-40

A voice

Jesus said, 'But what do you think about this? A man had two sons. He went to the first, and said, "My boy, go and work today in the vineyard". "I will, sir," the boy replied; but he never went. The father came to the second and said the same. "I will not," he replied, but afterwards he changed his mind and went. Which of these two did as his father wished?' 'The second,' they said.

Matthew 21. 28-31

The people stand.

THE PRAYERS

The Vice-Provost

O give thanks unto the Lord, for he is gracious:
because his mercy endureth for ever.
Let Israel now confess that he is gracious:
and that his mercy endureth for ever.

Let us thank God for the life and work of DICK CROSSMAN.

Sure he that made us with such large discourse
Looking before and after, gave us not
That capability and godlike reason
To fust in us unused.

Hamlet IV. 4

For Dick's intellectual power, exercised with unflinching vigour as a Member of Parliament, as a writer, and as a journalist, we praise God,
℟ **We thank him.**

For the man's uncompromising honesty,
and for his defence of the truth as he saw it, we praise God,
℟ **We thank him.**

For his abilities as a teacher, beloved by many disciples,
we praise God,
℟ **We thank him.**

For his humanity and his compassion,
and his concern for the welfare of his fellows, we praise God,
℟ **We thank him.**

For his untiring service of the public good, and especially for his devotion to the interests of the City of Coventry, we praise God,
℟ **We thank him.**

For his friendship with the people of Israel; and with the people of Germany, once the enemies of his country, we praise God,
℟ **We thank him.**

Incline thine ear, O Lord, to our prayers wherewith we beseech thy mercy for the soul of thy servant RICHARD, whom thou hast bidden to leave this world; command him a place in the kingdom of peace and light, and grant him the company of thy saints; through Jesus Christ our Lord.
℟ **Amen.**

O God our Father, who hast raised up for us many benefactors, known and unknown, remembered and forgotten, whose harvest we today are reaping: Make us also faithful in this our day, that we may sow a generous harvest, which others shall reap hereafter; through Jesus Christ our Lord.
℟ **Amen.**

This Hymn follows.

HYMN

Richmond AMR 373

O God of truth, whose living word
Upholds whate'er hath breath,
Look down on thy creation, Lord,
Enslaved by sin and death.

Set up thy standard, Lord, that we
Who claim a heavenly birth
May march with thee to smite the lies
That vex thy ransomed earth.

Ah, would we join that blest array,
And follow in the might
Of him, the Faithful and the True,
In raiment clean and white

People on the left

We fight for truth? we fight for God?
Poor slaves of lies and sin!
He who would fight for thee on earth
Must first be true within.

People on the right

Then, God of truth, for whom we long,
Thou who wilt hear our prayer,
Do thine own battle in our hearts,
And slay the falsehood there.

Everyone

Yea, come! Then, tried as in the fire,
From every lie set free,
Thy perfect truth shall dwell in us,
And we shall live in thee.

The people sit down.

MUSIC FOR SOLO FLUTE

Density 21.5 Edgard Varèse 1885-1965

Silence

After a while, music is played on the organ, and the clergy go to the west door. The Vice-Provost escorts the principal visitors to the door, where he says goodbye to them.

~~~~~~

Organ and piano Richard Lowry
Flute James Dower
~~~~~~

8. Elvis Presley In Memoriam

ELVIS PRESLEY: In Memoriam

At the Climax Inn, Coventry 19 August 1977

Every liturgical situation is a pastoral situation; that is to say, those who prepare and present a service must have a keen sense, a pastoral sense, of the needs of the congregation. They must be like Jesus the good shepherd: 'When he saw the multitudes, he was moved with compassion, because they were like sheep without a shepherd.'

The story which follows illustrates two things:
1. an attempt to be aware of a pastoral situation, and to meet the needs of the congregation; and
2. the sheer authority, the powerful authority, of the language of the Book of Common Prayer, when that language is heard by people who are moved by a spiritual desolation, though they may never have heard it before in all their lives, since it is alien to their habits of thought and feeling.

~~~~~~

At 12 noon on 19 August 1977 I was sitting in my office in Coventry Cathedral when the telephone rang. I picked up the receiver: 'Who's there?', I said. 'This is the chairman of the Elvis Presley Fan Club in Coventry. I'm a bus driver, that's my trade; but I'm speaking for the Elvis Presley fans. You know he died the other day. We want to have a service in his memory tonight, and I'm asking if the Cathedral can help us.'

Two thoughts flashed simultaneously through my mind. 'What an honour for the Cathedral to be invited by these people to help them'; and 'Of course we must help them if we can.'

'Where is this service to be held?', I asked. 'In the Climax Inn – you know where that is, it's in the Arcade in the City centre.'

'And at what time is the service to be?' 'At about 9.15 tonight.'

'Of course we will help you. See you at the Climax tonight at about 9.15.'

I rang off. Then I rang up the Cathedral's Youth Officer. 'Pam, the Elvis Presley fans in Coventry are holding a memorial service for Elvis at the Climax Inn tonight. You must come with me, please; and bring some of the Youth Club members with you. Meet me at the Cathedral at 9 o'clock.'

So we met at the Cathedral at 9 o'clock; for I was determined to go properly dressed as a priest, wearing my grey Coventry Cathedral cassock, and white bands, and my big
~~~~~~

black cloak, and my black hat, and my walking stick. We called on the verger, entered the Cathedral, and made our way to the vestry, where I put on my clerical gear.

Then we set out, Pam and I and a few youngsters, in a drizzling rain, for the Climax Inn. When we reached the Climax we found three or four teenagers standing round the door, with mugs of beer in their hands. 'Lucky men', I thought to myself. We climbed the stairs, and found ourselves in 'a large upper room', crowded with folk in their late teens and early twenties. The room was dark, and music came belting at us from the loudspeakers, music so loud that you could feel it going right through you. It was, in short, a disco.

'How on earth, Pam', I said, 'are we to find the chairman in all this crowd? There must be a bar somewhere; perhaps we shall find him there. But where's the bar?'

We made our way through the crowd to the far end of the room; and there, sure enough, was the bar, and the chairman (who else could it be?) standing behind the counter, pulling the beer handles. We presented ourselves to the chairman.

I was not introduced to the fans; but a microphone was thrust into my hand, and I heard myself shouting into it 'ONE, TWO, THREE, FOUR, testing, testing, testing'.

The chairman rapped sharply on the bar counter: 'Silence, please, we're going to 'ave a service.'

Instantly, there was silence. The atmosphere was not hysterical; but the silence was tense with grief; and now and then a girl sobbed quietly. Into this silence I began to speak: the silence was absolute.

~~~~~~

> My name is Joseph – Father Joseph Poole, from the Cathedral. And here at my side is my friend and colleague Mrs Pam Robinson, the Cathedral's Youth Officer; and with her are some members of the Cathedral youth club.
>
> A Christian priest, as he looks out upon the world, finds it full of interest: things are interesting, people are interesting. And as he grows older with the passing of the years, he finds himself not simply interested in people; he feels a deeper and deeper compassion for them.
>
> He comes to realise that some people are living in hell all the time; and that most people are living in hell some of the time.
>
> This, hell, I believe, is (very often) loneliness. This unbearable loneliness lies heavy upon many young people; and it was this loneliness which afflicted young people twenty years ago when Elvis Presley first appeared, first came within their sights.
>
> Elvis banished this loneliness. Their admiration of him, and their affection for him, bound them together, millions of them all over the world, into a
~~~~~~

company of people who no longer felt alone. They were united with Elvis, and with one another. Here was a man of their own age, of their own generation, who thought their thoughts, spoke their language, sang their music. He became their friend.

For this gift of friendship which Elvis bestowed on so many millions of people, we must all be grateful.

But Elvis had other gifts and graces to share with us. He had a graceful appearance: he was softly spoken. Looking at the BBC television broadcast, shown in his honour a few nights ago, I was struck by his speaking voice – a sweet, soft voice it was, very attractive, very easy to listen to.

And he was completely professional. In that same television broadcast Elvis appeared in a clip from an old film. He was singing a song – I forget its name – into the mike; and as he sang, with the mike in one hand, he bent down to kiss the girls in the audience, one after another. One lady seized the opportunity to kiss and hug him for a long long time. Elvis was not put out; every kiss was perfectly adjusted to the beat of the song. The timing was masterly. It was a totally professional performance.

To watch anybody, in any trade or profession, putting up a professional performance – this is always a pleasure: and this was one of the pleasures which Elvis gave us all.

This was the man, this was the friend, whose voice is now stilled.

I should like, as my own tribute to Elvis tonight, to read you a poem. The poet describes the funeral of his friend, a funeral held on a wet day, with the rain falling just as it is falling here this evening. The poet says that, after all, life is still before him; and he will find, in the days to come, other friends. Yes, but this one friend lies dead.

The rain, it streams on stone and hillock,
The boot clings to the clay.
Since all is done that's due and right
Let's home; and now, my lad, good-night,
For I must turn away.

Good-night, my lad, for nought's eternal;
No league of ours, for sure.
To-morrow I shall miss you less,
And ache of heart and heaviness
Are things that time should cure.

Over the hill the highway marches
And what's beyond is wide:
Oh soon enough will pine to nought
Remembrance and the faithful thought
That sits the grave beside.

The skies, they are not always raining
Nor grey the twelvemonth through;
And I shall meet good days and mirth,
And range the lovely lands of earth
With friends no worse than you.

But oh, my man, the house is fallen
That none can build again;
My man, how full of joy and woe
Your mother bore you years ago
To-night to lie in the rain.

A.E. Housman: *Last Poems*

Now I am going to read you a Psalm, a Psalm whose words have been on people's lips for many hundreds of years as they mourn the death of one they loved.

PSALM 130. *De profundis*

Out of the deep have I called unto thee, O Lord: Lord, hear my voice.

O let thine ears consider well: the voice of my complaint.

If thou, O Lord, wilt be extreme to mark what is done amiss: O Lord, who may abide it?

For there is mercy with thee: therefore shalt thou be feared.

I look for the Lord; my soul doth wait for him: in his word is my trust.

My soul fleeth unto the Lord: before the morning watch, I say, before the morning watch.

O Israel, trust in the Lord, for with the Lord there is mercy: and with him is plenteous redemption.

And he shall redeem Israel: from all his sins.

Rest eternal grant unto him, O Lord;
And let light perpetual shine upon him.

And here is a prayer for Elvis, a prayer commending his soul to God.

> Grant, O Lord God, that the soul of thy servant ELVIS who at thy bidding has left this world, may rest in thy peace and protection, and reign in thy kingdom in heaven; through Jesus Christ our Lord. Amen.

And to end with, here is a blessing for all of you.

> Unto God's gracious mercy and protection we commit you.
> The Lord bless you, and keep you.
> The Lord make his face to shine upon you, and be gracious unto you.
> The Lord lift up the light of his countenance upon you,
> and give you peace,
> now and always.
> Amen.

~~~~~~

When I had finished speaking, there was silence still, a silence which lasted for some time. Then a very strange thing happened. There was a sharp outburst of clapping, as sharp as rifle-fire. Never before, in all my life, had I heard Divine Service applauded.

Someone said to me, 'Have a drink?' 'I will', I said; and a mug of beer was handed to me. It was the nicest half-pint I have ever tasted. And as I sipped my beer, sitting on a stool before the bar in my grey cassock and black cloak, ten or a dozen men came up and shook hands with me. They said nothing, for their hearts were too full of sorrow; but they wanted to thank me.

At last I finished the beer. 'Come on, Pam, it's time we went home.' So we picked ourselves up, and began to thread our way through the crowd, in the dim light and the deafening music of an Elvis song. As we passed towards the door two young men (unknown to me) one after the other threw their arms round my neck, and kissed me. They said not a word; and indeed no words could have been as eloquent as their embrace. They wished only to thank a man who had tried to stand with them, and to understand them.
~~~~~~

MURDER: SEVEN WAYS TO KILL A SERVICE STONE DEAD

1. Here is an organist who has no sense of occasion.

It is Christmas Eve, and a large congregation is assembled for carols. The service is to begin (very reasonably) with the Advent hymn 'O come, O come, Emmanuel', to the well-loved tune VENI EMMANUEL.

The organist has agreed to play the tune in the version best fitted to congregational use, that is to say in regular rhythm, four crotchets to a bar. But the time-signature is not 4:4 but 2:2 there are only two pulses in each bar.

This is a hymn of urgent appeal to the Incarnate Lord, and of eager joy in the certainty of his coming. The hymn must therefore move swiftly. However numerous the congregation and however resonant the building, the pace must not be slower than minim = 72 (crotchet = 144).

The organist misjudges the mood of the hymn; he plays the tune at a plodding 4 crotchets in the bar, at crotchet = 108, and for five stanzas of six lines each.

The service is strangled at birth.

2. Here is an organist who has no pastoral sense.

The congregation consists of 1,600 old age pensioners. They love 'a good sing', they look forward to their old favourites among the hymns; but at their time of life they are a trifle scant of breath; they like to take time over things, they like to be eased gently over the ends of lines.

These obvious facts mean nothing to the organist; he plays every hymn at a spanking pace, the pace at which a professional choir would be happy enough to sing it. But the old people in the pews are left behind.

The service dies several times over. It dies at every hymn.

3. Here is an organist who loves his choir, but hates the congregation.

He thinks (quite mistakenly) that the inclusion of a couple of hymns in choral Matins or Evensong is a threat to the integrity of the choral tradition of which, as a cathedral organist, he is the guardian.

He hates the congregation; and so he does his best, by his handling of the organ, to destroy the congregation's pleasure in singing the hymns. He does this by playing the hymns too quickly for their comfort, or too slowly; or by an unsympathetic accompaniment, whether by an overwhelming use of his chorus reeds or (at the opposite extreme) by 'footling on the flutes' (an immortal phrase coined by Christopher Hillyard, some time Sacrist of Westminster Abbey).

Our organist is a murderer, *tout court.*

4. Here is a preacher who oversteps the time allotted to his sermon.

There was a day when the Croydon Youth Fellowship came to a service, carefully devised for them, in Canterbury Cathedral. The visiting preacher began by telling his young hearers that he proposed only to say a few words to them. He forgot that, soon enough; he preached three sermons on end, and he preached, without a pause, for 45 minutes. Long before he stopped talking, his audience had stopped listening.

'They think that they shall be heard for their much speaking'. It is not so. The service died of a surfeit of words from the pulpit.

5. Here is a preacher who has disdained the kind invitation of the Precentor to rehearse the use of the public address system before he preaches.

'No thanks, my dear man, I can manage without a rehearsal. After all, I am used to speaking in public.'

So he preaches for twenty minutes, without having discovered the acoustic difficulties of the building, or the way to overcome them. Nobody but the people in the first five rows hear one word of the sermon.

Murder by disdain!

6. Here is a preacher who is to address 1,600 children, seated in a cathedral nave.

The children at the back of the nave are 75 yards distant from the pulpit. The preacher, primed with the prevailing fad for using visual aids when speaking to children, takes with him into the pulpit an orange. And he begins, in what he hopes is an irresistibly alluring tone of voice, by saying, 'Children, look! I have something to show you. This is an orange. I hope you can all see it'; and he holds up the orange. The orange is just visible to the children immediately below the pulpit, but to nobody else.

The children pay no further attention.

Murder through sheer silliness!

7. At a civic service the authorities have paid the Mayor the compliment of asking him to read the lesson.

But the authorities have made the mistake of printing in the order of service only the reference to the book of the Bible from which the lesson is chosen, instead of printing out the text in full. Nor have they invited the Mayor to come to the church some days beforehand to rehearse the reading of the lesson.

The Mayor is an estimable First Citizen; but he is not remarkable for his skill in reading the Bible aloud. His lesson is heard by few, and understood by none.

The service dies of inanition: but it is not the fault of the Mayor.

FORMS OF PRAYER
COMPOSED OR COMPILED BY THE AUTHOR

Affirmations and Aspirations

Since 1552 the Prayer Book Offices of Morning and Evening Prayer have begun with Sentences of Scripture read out by the Minister.

At Morning Prayer in Coventry Cathedral that precedent is followed, but with a difference; the Sentences are read as versicles and responses by the Minister and the people; and Sentences of Scripture, treated in the same fashion, are read also at the close of the Office.

The opening Sentences are called The Affirmation; The Affirmation is a statement. The closing Sentences are called The Aspiration; the Aspiration is a prayer.

The Affirmation and The Aspiration share the same theme. Themes are provided for the Proper of Time and the Proper of Saints, and for other occasions also.
Here are some examples.

~~~~~~

EPIPHANY

Affirmation

In the name of the Father, the Son, and the Holy Spirit.
℣ They saw the young child with Mary his mother;
℟ **and they fell down and worshipped him.**
℣ When they had opened their treasures, they offered him gifts;
℟ **gold and frankincense and myrrh.**
℣ Blessèd be Christ.
℟ **Amen.**
~~~~~~

Aspiration
℣ May the Holy Spirit enable us to offer to Christ our Lord our love and our obedience;
℟ **at all times and in all ways.**
℣ Blessèd be Christ.
℟ **Amen.**

ASH WEDNESDAY AND LENT

Affirmation
In the name of the Father, the Son, and the Holy Spirit.
℣ The Lord is full of compassion and mercy:
℟ **long-suffering, and of great goodness.**
℣ He will not always be chiding:
℟ **neither keepeth he his anger for ever.**
℣ Yea, like as a father pitieth his own children:
℟ **even so is the Lord merciful unto them that fear him.**
℣ For he knoweth whereof we are made:
℟ **he remembereth that we are but dust.**
℣ Blessèd be Christ.
℟ **Amen.**

Aspiration
℣ My son, be mindful of the Lord our God all thy days,
℟ **and let not thy will be set to sin,**
or to transgress his commandments.
℣ Do uprightly all thy life long,
℟ **and follow not the ways of unrighteousness.**
℣ Let us hear the conclusion of the whole matter:
Fear God, and keep his commandments;
℟ **For this is the whole duty of men.**
℣ Blessèd be Christ.
℟ **Amen.**

TRANSFIGURATION

Affirmation
In the name of the Father, the Son, and the Holy Spirit.
℣ The divine glory of the Incarnate Word shone forth
upon the Holy Mount before the chosen witnesses of his majesty;
℟ **And a voice from heaven proclaimed,**
This is my beloved Son; listen to him.
℣ Blessèd be Christ.
℟ **Amen.**

Aspiration

℣ May God give us grace, in our mortal days,
to listen to Jesus his beloved Son;

℟ **And grant us, all the days of eternity, to see his glory.**

℣ Blessèd be Christ.

℟ **Amen.**

WINTER

Affirmation

In the name of the Father, the Son, and the Holy Spirit.

℣ He casteth forth his ice like morsels;

℟ **Who is able to abide his frost?**

℣ Blessèd be Christ.

℟ **Amen.**

Aspiration

℣ O ye frost and cold, bless ye the Lord;

℟ **Praise him, and magnify him for ever.**

℣ O ye ice and snow, bless ye the Lord;

℟ **Praise him, and magnify him for ever.**

℣ Blessèd be Christ.

℟ **Amen.**

FAIR WEATHER

Affirmation

In the name of the Father, the Son, and the Holy Spirit.

℣ O Lord my God, thou art become exceeding glorious;

℟ **thou art clothed with majesty and honour.**

℣ Thou deckest thyself with light as it were with a garment;

℟ **and spreadest out the heavens like a curtain.**

℣ Blessèd be Christ.

℟ **Amen.**

Aspiration

℣ O speak good of the Lord, all ye works of his,
in all places of his dominion;

℟ **praise thou the Lord, O my soul; praise the Lord.**

℣ Blessèd be Christ.

℟ **Amen.**

WORK

Affirmation

In the name of the Father, the Son, and the Holy Spirit.

℣ As the door turns upon its hinges,

℟ **so does the slothful upon his bed.**

℣ Yet a little sleep, a little slumber,
a little folding of the hands to sleep,

℟ **and poverty will come upon you like a robber,
want like a ruffian.**

℣ Blessèd be Christ.

℟ **Amen.**

Aspiration

℣ O Lord, thou knowest how busy I must be this day;

℟ **If I forget thee, do not thou forget me.**

℣ Blessèd be Christ.

℟ **Amen.**

AGAINST TALE-BEARING

Affirmation

In the name of the Father, the Son, and the Holy Spirit.

℣ A scoundrel, a mischievous man,
is he who prowls about with crooked talk –

℟ **a wink of the eye,
a touch with the foot,
a sign with the fingers.**

℣ Subversion is the evil that he is plotting,

℟ **he stirs up quarrels all the time.**

℣ Blessèd be Christ.

℟ **Amen.**

Aspiration

℣ Hear the voice of my humble petitions,
when I cry unto thee:

℟ **when I hold up my hands towards
the mercy-seat of thy holy temple.**

℣ O pluck me not away,
neither destroy me with the ungodly and wicked doers:

℟ **which speak friendly to their neighbours,
but imagine mischief in their hearts.**

℣ Blessèd be Christ.

℟ **Amen.**

Blessings

May the eternal Father, who dwells in light unapproachable,
shine into your hearts.
May the eternal Son, who is the light of the world,
illuminate all your ways.
May the eternal Spirit bring you out of darkness and error
into the clear light and true knowledge of the triune God.
May the same God in the plenitude of his love pour upon you the torrents of his grace, bless you and keep you in his holy fear, prepare you for a happy eternity[i], and receive you at last into immortal glory.

Coventry Cathedral: written by J.W.P.
for the Blessing of the Undercroft on 31 December 1958.
The phrase 'the torrents of his grace' was used
by the Bishop of Coventry, Dr Cuthbert Bardsley,
in the course of his sermon at the
Installation of Dr H.C.N. Williams as Provost
in the Old Cathedral on 27 September 1958.

God keep you in his care;
Christ win you and save you;
The Holy Spirit guide you
in the ways of truth and love always.

Coventry Cathedral

Collects

1. For Artists

O God, your Son Jesus Christ found recreation and ease of mind in the company of his friends: Accept the ministry of artists [musicians, or players], and enable all who serve their art to use their talents responsibly for the honest recreation of their fellow men, to bring them pleasure and to lighten their cares; through the same Jesus Christ our Lord.

Coventry Cathedral: A Service of the Arts 1962

[i] *'God keep us in his holy fear and prepare us for a happy eternity'*: Thomas Ken, Bishop of Bath and Wells, in a letter to the Bishop of Norwich, 20 March 1703-4.

2. Of Ascension-tide

Deliver us, O Lord Christ, from fear and from despair and from the bitter pains of death; and in your presence assure us of a happiness that nothing can ever assail; because with the Father and the Spirit you are alive and reign God, world without end.

Coventry Cathedral: Procession of Ascension-tide[i]

3. For the Blind

Remember, O Lord, in your compassion those who were born blind, those whose eyes have never seen the sun, or looked into the eyes of friends or lovers.
℣ Lord, in your mercy
℟ **Hear our prayer.**

Remember, O Lord, in your compassion those whose blinded eyes ache with the memory of beauties which once they saw and will not see again; and sustain them along the way, until, on another shore and in a greater light, with new eyes they see your face, and are surprised by all the felicities of heaven.
℣ Lord, in your mercy
℟ **Hear our prayer.**

Coventry Cathedral:
The Royal Commonwealth Society for the Blind 1971

4. For Craftsmen

God, you created man in your image to be a maker and craftsman, and in the joy of creation to be a mirror of your triune Majesty: Remember for good the craftsmen whose work we have laid upon this altar [or offered to you], and with them remember their fellow-craftsmen everywhere; and grant, that none of these, whose truth is in their craft, may miss the true knowledge of yourself, whose truth is in your Son Jesus Christ our Lord.

Coventry Cathedral:
In Praise of Craftsmen 1963

---

[i] In this Procession a station is made at the Eighth Tablet of the Word, on which are incised these words from The Revelation 1. 17, 18: *'Fear not; I am the first and the last. I am alive for evermore, Amen; and have the keys of hell and of death.'*

5. At the Christmas Crib

O God, you have clothed with bodily senses the immortal spirits of us your children, so that in earthly masques and shadows we may discern the bright ways of your glory: Grant that as we behold this picture of your Son's incarnation we may in heart and mind ascend into the light of your presence; through the same your Son Jesus Christ our Lord.

Canterbury Cathedral 1938:
based on a poem by Henry Vaughan

6. Of Dedication

O almighty God
in whose presence we stand,
at whose judgment we falter,
in whose mercy we confide:
Accept the pledges we have given
and the promises we have made;
and give us grace to keep our word
by a willing service
and a steadfast obedience
at all times
and in all ways;
through Jesus Christ our Lord.

Coventry Cathedral:
The Golden Jubilee of the
Soroptimist International Association 1971

7. For Europe

Come, Father and Lord,
creator of this beautiful and hospitable world,
Come, Lord Jesus Christ,
the light which the darkness has never mastered, and never will,
Come, Holy Spirit,
Lord and Life-giver,
Come, Lord, come.

Accept the tribute which we pay
of gratitude for the graces and beauties of Europe,
of sorrow for the follies and crimes of Europe,
of reverence for the sanctities of Europe:

Come, puissant Lord,
refresh us with the riches of thy creation,
Come, benign Redeemer,
rescue us from the misuse of thy creation,
Come, Holy Spirit,
the only Ruler of our unruly appetites and affections,
dispose us to share the resources of thy creation,
Come, Lord, come:

Create among the nations of Europe
justice,
and comity,
and joy;
for now all things sigh to be renewed,
and only in thy will is our peace;
who reignest God today,
tomorrow, always.
℟ **Amen.**

Coventry Cathedral:
Fanfare for Europe 1973

8. For a Flower Festival

Refresh us, O Lord, as we consider the glories of your creation, with these tokens of your love towards us; and send us on our way with humility towards yourself and a patient charity towards each other, till we reach home at last, to be refreshed with the unfading glories of the courts of heaven; through Jesus Christ our Lord.

O almighty God, creator of heaven and earth: Make us grateful for your glory here, and make us worthy of your glory hereafter; through Jesus Christ our Lord.

Coventry Cathedral:
Consider the Lilies 1968

9. For the Funeral of a Child

Receive, O Lord Jesus Christ, into the arms of thy mercy thy child GUY; and keep him so close to thy presence that he may never be assailed by any evil, and may grow up into that perfection which is thy will for him; who with the Father and the Holy Spirit reignest, God for ever.

Coventry Cathedral: Farewell to
Guy Nicholas Williamson,
Choral Scholar 1966

10. Of Michaelmas

God, whom angels and archangels and all the company of heaven adore and obey: Grant that we who hear the story of St Michael triumphing over evil may be assured of the victory of your truth, and may see every rebel will at last made captive to your mercy;[i] through Jesus Christ our Lord.

Coventry Cathedral: Evensong of Michaelmas

11. Old Age

Come, Lord, come;
stablish our faith,
renew our hope,
deepen our love;
refresh us again
with the vision of the holy city
where your word is heard,
your will is done,
your presence is adored,
the city we have longed for;
and at our journey's end
welcome us home,
to live with you in your kingdom
among the unfading glories
of the courts of heaven.
Amen.

For the Retired Clergy Association, 1979

12. For Past Worshippers

O God, who by the prayers and hands of thy servants hast built and preserved this [Cathedral] church to be a continuing witness to thy divine Majesty: Remember for good all who have worked and worshipped here; and so fortify us by their examples, that we may willingly offer our time, our skill, and our love, in the service of their Master and ours, Jesus Christ our Lord.

Canterbury Cathedral: Office of the Women's Guild 1949

---

[i] The phrase *'made captive to your mercy'* deliberately echoes the Collect of Trinity XI in the Prayer Book of 1662: *"O God, who declarest thy almighty power most chiefly in showing mercy and pity."*

O God, by the prayers and hands of your servants you have built and preserved this church to be a continuing witness to your divine Majesty: Remember for good all who have worshipped here; and so fortify us by their examples, that we may willingly offer our time, our skill, and our love, in the service of their Master and ours, Jesus Christ our Lord.

13. For the Queen and the Realm

O God, bless our Queen, bless the people of this Realm, bless our children, bless our homes; hold us fast upon the way of truth, till we come at last to possess the immortal happiness we desire but can never deserve, the gift of your Son, Jesus Christ our Lord.

The Consecration of Coventry Cathedral 1962

14. Of the Feast of the Reconciliation

Teach us, O God, through the Passion of thy Christ, how to forgive and be forgiven; so that we may be at ease with one another and at ease with thee, and may walk unafraid in the way of obedience to thy Son Jesus Christ our Lord.

The Communion of the Feast, or Solemnity, of the Reconciliation is celebrated annually in Coventry Cathedral on the Sunday nearest November 14, the date of the destruction of the Old Cathedral by hostile aircraft in 1940. The same Sunday is observed in Great Britain as Remembrance Sunday, when the nation honours the memory of the men and women who fell in the First and Second World Wars.

The Collect of the Feast is given above. The rest of the Propers are:

The Proclamation at the beginning of the Communion

℣ God was in Christ, reconciling the world to himself;
℟ **He has entrusted us with the message of reconciliation.**
℣ When anyone is united to Christ, there is a new world;
℟ **The old order has gone; a new order has already begun.**
℣ We come as Christ's ambassadors;
in Christ's name, we implore you, be reconciled to God;
℟ **He has entrusted us with the message of reconciliation.**
℣ The old order has gone;
℟ **A new order has already begun.**

2 Corinthians 5. 19, 17, 20, 19, 17

The Epistle: Ephesians 2. 11-18 (J.B. Phillips)

The Gospel: Luke 23. 13-26, 32-34 (NEB)

The Preface

Because thou hast reconciled us to thyself by Jesus Christ,
and hast given to us the ministry of reconciliation.

Therefore with angels, etc.

The Anthem at the Communion

O Saviour of the world, who by thy Cross and precious blood hast redeemed us: Save us, and help us, we humbly beseech thee, O Lord.

The colour of the Feast is Passiontide red.

15. For Relations and Friends

We remember, O God, before thy [your] throne of grace,
those whom we love;
those who love us;
those for whom we are bound to pray:
beseeching thee [you] to hold them so close to thy [your] presence
that they may be unscathed by any evil,
and may grow into that perfection
which is thy [your] will for them, here and hereafter; through…

For St Katherine's Church,
Keith, South Australia, 1979[i]

16. Of the Stewardship of Creation

O Everlasting God, you have made us the masters of your creation and the stewards of its resources: Teach us to practise so wise a husbandry of land and water as will turn penury into plenty, to nourish our bodies with food and to ravish our senses with delight; through Jesus Christ our Lord.

Coventry Cathedral:
Tennessee Valley Authority 1971

---

[i] This prayer uses some phrases from For the Funeral of a Child (page 391), which was written earlier.

17. For Suicides

Remember, O Lord, in your compassion
those whose courage fails them in the moment of despair;
when they begin to lose heart, renew their hope;
when they are beaten to the ground, raise them up again;
if they die by their own hand, forgive them, and forgive us all;
and assure them, both of your love and of their own worth;
through our Redeemer Jesus Christ.

Coventry Cathedral: All Souls'-tide

18. Work

Accept, O Lord God,
accept the work we do,
the work which is a ministry to others,
the work which serves the welfare of others,
promotes their happiness, relieves their distresses;
this work, O Lord God, be pleased to accept,
and bless us as we do it:
but that work which is done to others' harm,
that work which corrupts others, degrades others,
and robs them of their human dignity,
that work, O Lord God, repudiate and disown;
do not prosper the doers of it,[i]
but refine them in the fire of contrition,
and refashion them in the fire of thy [your] Holy Spirit,
after the pattern of holiness
declared to us in the obedience of thy [your] Son Jesus of Nazareth;
who with thee [you] and the same Holy Spirit, etc.

For St Katherine's Church,
Keith, South Australia, 1979

[i] Some work is inherently dishonourable, and we cannot invoke the divine blessing upon it: the work of the promoters of pornography, the promoters of sex shops, the keepers of brothels, the pedlars of drugs. We cannot ask the blessing of God on this work: no, but those who engage in it and make a living by it must not be excluded from our compassion and our prayers.

19. Work: The night shift

Almighty and everlasting God, we commend to thy [your] unfailing providence the men and women who through the hours of darkness watch over our lives and our homes, or pursue the unresting commerce of the world by land and sea and air; beseeching thee [you] to make us grateful for their services, who must be at work while we are asleep; through…

For St Katherine's Church,
Keith, South Australia, 1979

Litanies

1. Of the Church

This Litany was composed for the Consecration of Coventry Cathedral on 25 May 1962, and was sung in procession as the members of the Foundation moved from the chancel to the west door to receive Her Majesty Queen Elizabeth II.

It has since been used at Ordinations in Coventry Cathedral, with the petition for those who are 'to be admitted to the Order of Deacons or of Priests'. With the omission of this clause the Litany can be used at any time as a prayer for the Church.

In the Prayer Book Litany the words 'miserable sinners' in the opening Invocations are liable to be misunderstood. The word 'miserable', which formerly meant 'deserving of pity', now suggests 'mean', 'squalid', 'joyless'. In this Ordination Litany the words 'miserable sinners' are avoided, and new Invocations are provided, drawn from the Prayer Book Catechism. These Invocations can be sung comfortably to the musical settings of the Prayer Book Litany by Byrd, Cranmer, Day, Loosemore, Tallis, and Wanless.

A contemporary musical setting of this Litany of the Church will be found on page **Error! Bookmark not defined.** of **Part IV – Examples of Music**.

O God the Father, who has made us and all the world;
    Hear us, and have mercy.
O God the Son, who hast redeemed us and all mankind;
    Hear us, and have mercy.
O God the Holy Spirit, who sanctifiest us
    and all elect people of God;
    Hear us, and have mercy.
O holy, blessed, and adorable Trinity,
    Creator, Redeemer, and Sanctifier;
    Hear us, and have mercy.

Let us pray for the peace of the whole world, and for the welfare and unity of the Church of God;
    We beseech thee to hear us, good Lord.
Let us pray for all kings, rulers, and governors,
    and especially for our Sovereign Lady, Queen ELIZABETH;
    We beseech thee to hear us, good Lord.
Let us pray for the whole Clergy,
    especially for N. Archbishop of this Province,
    for N. Bishop of this Diocese,
    and for all who are called to a ministry in the household of God.
    We beseech thee to hear us, good Lord.

Let us pray for the servants of God at this time to be admitted
to the Order of Deacons or of Priests,
that by his grace
they may be faithful ministers and stewards of his mysteries;
We beseech thee to hear us, good Lord.
Let us pray for one another, and for all whose hearts are with us,
who desire to be remembered in our prayers,
and remember us in their own;
We beseech thee to hear us, good Lord.
That we may follow the way that leads to truth,
and follow the truth that leads to life;
We beseech thee to hear us, good Lord.
That we may follow the steps of our Redeemer Jesus Christ,
who alone is the way, the truth, and the life;
We beseech thee to hear us, good Lord.
That finishing here the work of our salvation,
we may rest hereafter in thy holy peace;
We beseech thee to hear us, good Lord.
Son of God: we beseech thee to hear us.
Son of God: we beseech thee to hear us.
O Lamb of God; that takest away the sins of the world:
Grant us thy peace.
O Lamb of God; that takest away the sins of the world:
Have mercy upon us.
O Christ, hear us.
O Christ, hear us.

Lord, have mercy upon us.
Lord, have mercy upon us.
Christ, have mercy upon us.
Christ have mercy upon us.
Lord, have mercy upon us.
Lord, have mercy upon us.

2. Of Intercession

For Wounded Minds

Remember, O Lord, in your compassion
those whose minds are scarred by memories of battle.
℣ Lord, in your mercy
℟ **Hear our prayer.**

Remember, O Lord, in your compassion
those whose wounded minds are darkened
by the shadows of old sorrows and forgotten joys.
℣ Lord, in your mercy
℟ **Hear our prayer.**

Remember, O Lord, in your compassion
those whose minds are so impaired
that they do not know who they once were,
or who they now are, or why they live.
℣ Lord, in your mercy
℟ **Hear our prayer.**

Remember, O Lord, in your compassion
those whose courage fails them in the moment of despair;
when they begin to lose heart, renew their hope;
when they are beaten to the ground, raise them up again;
if they die by their own hand forgive them, and forgive us all;
and assure them, both of your love and of their own worth;
through our Redeemer Jesus Christ.

Coventry Cathedral:
For Wounded Minds 1969

3. Penitence

A Litany of Reconciliation

This Litany of Reconciliation is based on the seven capital sins. It was written in 1959, and since that year it has been recited every Friday at 12 noon before the Altar of Reconciliation in the sanctuary of the Old Cathedral at Coventry.

Versions of the Litany are also available in French and in German.

FATHER, FORGIVE

All have sinned, and come short of the glory of God.

St Paul's Letter to the Romans

℣ The HATRED which divides nation from nation,
race from race, class from class,
℟ **Father, forgive.**
℣ The COVETOUS desires of men and nations
to possess what is not their own,
℟ **Father forgive**.
℣ The GREED which exploits the labours of men,
and lays waste the earth,
℟ **Father forgive**.
℣ Our ENVY of the welfare and happiness of others,
℟ **Father forgive.**
℣ Our INDIFFERENCE to the plight of the homeless
and the refugee,
℟ **Father forgive.**
℣ The LUST which uses for ignoble ends
the bodies of men and women,
℟ **Father forgive**.
℣ The PRIDE which leads us to trust in ourselves, and not in God,
℟ **Father forgive**.

Be kind to one another, tenderhearted,
forgiving one another, as God in Christ forgave you.

St Paul's Letter to the Ephesians

4. Of Praise

A Litany in praise of The Blessed Trinity

I THE PRAISE OF GOD THE FATHER

Lord, you are God;
yesterday,
today,
tomorrow,
always,
you are God.
℣ We praise you;
℟ **We worship you.**

Lord, you are God;
before the mountains were brought forth,
or ever the earth and the world were made,
you are God, without beginning or end.
To your eyes a thousand years
are like yesterday, come and gone,
no more than a watch in the night.
Lord, you are God.
℣ We praise you;
℟ **We worship you.**

Lord, you were there;
in the beginning,
when darkness lay upon the face of the deep,
your life-giving Spirit moved upon the waters of chaos,
and at your word there was light.
Lord, you were there.
℣ We praise you;
℟ **We worship you**.

Lord, you are here;
You hold heaven and earth in the embrace of your love;
without you nothing is strong, nothing is holy;
you keep mercy for your people
who walk before the presence of your glory.
Lord, you are here.
℣ We praise you;
℟ **We worship you**.

II THE PRAISE OF GOD THE SON

O Lord Christ,
Word of the Father,
always with the Father,
equal in glory with the Father,
℣ We praise you;
℟ **We worship you.**

O Lord Christ,
in the fullness of time
you who are always with the Father
were made man,
made one of us.
℣ We praise you;
℟ **We worship you.**

O Lord Christ,
no one has ever seen God;
but you who are nearest to the Father's heart,
you who have made him known;
and he who has seen you
has seen the Father.
℣ We praise you;
℟ **We worship you.**

O Lord Christ,
your mother bore you in Bethlehem,
cherished you at Nazareth,
watched you die on Calvary;
and you loved her, as you died,
and gave her into the care of John, your dear friend.
℣ We praise you;
℟ **We worship you.**

O Lord Christ,
you felt compassion for your fellow-men,
the lost ones, the unshepherded;
but they had no compassion on you,
and in the end they destroyed you;
and you, who are equal in glory with the Father,
stooped to your Passion upon the bitter cross.
℣ We praise you;
℟ **We worship you.**

O Lord Christ,
men thought you were dead and done for;
out of sight, out of mind;
but they were mistaken,
for you came back from the grave
never again to die,
and you returned to the Father
equal in glory with the Father
as you always were
and always will be.
℣ We praise you;
℟ **We worship you.**

III THE PRAISE OF GOD THE HOLY SPIRIT

O Holy Spirit,
Lord and Life-giver,
reflecting like a mirror the glory of the Father
and the work of the Son,
℣ We praise you;
℟ **We worship you**.

O Holy Spirit,
Through your glorious power
the joy of the everlasting gospel
has gone out all over the world.
℣ We praise you;
℟ **We worship you.**

O Holy Spirit,
through your energy
we have been brought out of darkness and error
into the clear light and true knowledge
of God who created us,
and of God who redeems us.
℣ We praise you;
℟ **We worship you.**

O Holy Spirit,
you fill our hearts with sacred inspirations;
you illuminate our understandings;
you sanctify all the faculties of our souls;
you set our faltering steps once more
upon the highway of faith.
℣ We praise you;
℟ **We worship you.**

℣ Glory be to the Father, and to the Son, and to the Holy Spirit:
℟ **As it was in the beginning, is now, and ever shall be:
world without end. Amen.**

IV THE PRAISE OF THE BLESSED TRINITY [i]

The Godhead of the Father, of the Son, and of the Holy Spirit, is all one: the glory equal, the majesty co-eternal.
Therefore we praise and worship the Blessed Trinity.

O Blessed Majesty of God,
filling, containing, and ordering the whole world,
℣ We praise you;
℟ **We worship you.**

O Holy King of saints,
builder, upholder, and defender of the Catholic Church,
℣ We praise you;
℟ **We worship you.**

O Blessed hand of God,
sanctifying, blessing, and replenishing all things,
℣ We praise you;
℟ **We worship you.**

O Blessed and Holy Trinity,
the source of all purity, probity, and beauty,
℣ We praise you;
℟ **We worship you.** [ii]

---

[i] In Section IV the Invocations are from the Order for the Consecration of Coventry Cathedral 1962.
[ii] Compiled by J.W.P. for St Mark's Church, Bilton, Rugby, at the request of the Rector, the Rev. D.K. Collard, and televised by the BBC on Trinity Sunday 1977

5. Of the Holy Spirit

A Litany of the Holy Spirit 1

This Litany of the Holy Spirit was written for A Service of International Reconciliation held in Coventry Cathedral on Wednesday 6 June 1962. The opening prayer 'Come, Holy Spirit' is the Antiphon upon Benedictus in the office of Lauds for the Holy Ghost, in the Devotions of John Austin (1613-69).

Come, Holy Spirit, the free dispenser of all graces:
Visit the hearts of thy faithful servants, and replenish them with thy sacred inspirations; illuminate our understandings, and inflame our affections, and sanctify all the faculties of our souls; that we may know, and love, and constantly do the things that belong to our peace, our everlasting peace; who with the Father and the Son reignest God, world without end.
Amen.

Teach us, O Holy Spirit,
To have done with anger and suspicion and envy,
which are the seeds of discord,
and in all our dealings to look for the best in one another,
and not for the worst.
℣ Holy Spirit, hear us;
℟ **Holy Spirit, help us.**

Teach us, O Holy Spirit,
To use the discoveries of science not for our ruin and destruction,
but for the wellbeing of ourselves and of our children,
and of generations yet unborn.
℣ Holy Spirit, hear us;
℟ **Holy Spirit, help us.**

Teach us, O Holy Spirit,
To share with one another for our common good
the resources of trade, industry, and commerce.
℣ Holy Spirit, hear us;
℟ **Holy Spirit, help us.**

Teach us, O Holy Spirit,
To use men's labour justly;
and to practise so wise a husbandry of the earth and the seas
as may banish want and hunger from the world.
℣ Holy Spirit, hear us;
℟ **Holy Spirit, help us.**

Teach us, O Holy Spirit,
To rejoice in the just and honourable achievements
of other men and other nations,
and to desire their happiness as much as our own.
℣ Holy Spirit, hear us;
℟ **Holy Spirit, help us.**

Teach us, O Holy Spirit,
To be quick to aid and succour
those who have neither food nor shelter,
livelihood nor home.
℣ Holy Spirit, hear us;
℟ **Holy Spirit, help us.**

Teach us, O Holy Spirit,
To honour the vows of marriage;
to cherish our homes and families;
to rule our children wisely, and to serve them courteously.
℣ Holy Spirit, hear us;
℟ **Holy Spirit, help us.**

Teach us, O Holy Spirit,
To believe that we may be mistaken;
teach us how to repent;
teach us how to forgive and be forgiven;
teach us obedience to the sovereign will of God.
℣ Holy Spirit, hear us;
℟ **Holy Spirit, help us.**

O God, forasmuch as without thee we are not able to please thee: Mercifully grant, that thy Holy Spirit may in all things direct and rule our hearts, through Jesus Christ our Lord.

6. Of the Holy Spirit

A Litany of the Holy Spirit 2

This Litany is the Scrutiny on the Harvest of the Spirit **(Scrutinies,** page 221**)** turned into litany form.

The Litany is divided into three sections, each of which deals with three of the Nine Gifts of the Spirit. Each section ends with a collect on one of the three Gifts. The collect may be followed by an appropriate hymn.

~~~~~~

A LITANY
of the Nine Gifts of the Spirit

THE LESSON

> Anyone can see the kind of behaviour that belongs to the lower nature: fornication, impurity, and indecency; idolatry and sorcery; quarrels, a contentious temper, envy, fits of rage, selfish ambitions, dissensions, party intrigues, and jealousies; drinking bouts, orgies, and the like. I warn you, as I warned you before, that those who behave in such ways will never inherit the kingdom of God.
>
> But the fruits of the Spirit are love, joy, peace, patience, kindness, goodness, fidelity, gentleness, and self-control. And those who belong to Christ Jesus have crucified the lower nature with its passions and desires. If the Spirit is the source of our life, let the Spirit also direct our course.

Galatians 5. 19-22, 24, 25
~~~~~~

THE LITANY

1 The First Three: Love, Joy, Peace

Minister

Peace to you all from our Lord the Spirit;
℟ **Peace to you.**

Let us pray.
Teach us, O Holy Spirit,
to cherish our homes and families;
teach us to rule our children wisely;
teach us to serve them courteously;
teach us to serve and love,
in Christ's name,
the unlovely and the unloved among our neighbours.
℣ Holy Spirit, hear us.
℟ **Holy Spirit, help us.**

Teach us, O Holy Spirit,
to be grateful for your mercies to us,
till joy leaves no room in our hearts for moroseness and self-pity.
℣ Holy Spirit, hear us.
℟ **Holy Spirit, help us.**

Teach us, O Holy Spirit,
to rest in your peace;
to live in your peace;
to enfold in your peace
our families and households.
℣ Holy Spirit, hear us.
℟ **Holy Spirit, help us.**

Almighty and everlasting God,
you govern all things in heaven and earth:
Mercifully hear the supplications of your people,
and grant us your peace
every day of our life;
through Jesus Christ our Lord.
℟ **Amen.**

2 The Second Three: Patience, Kindness, Goodness

Minister

Peace to you all from our Lord the Spirit;
℟ **Peace to you.**

Let us pray.
Teach us, O Holy Spirit,
to practise patience,
subduing every impulse of anger
and irritation.
℣ Holy Spirit, hear us.
℟ **Holy Spirit, help us.**

Teach us, O Holy Spirit,
to be kind to one another,
tender-hearted,
forgiving one another;
teach us to be kind to our children;
teach us to be kind to those who serve us;
teach us to be kind
to those who are unkind to us.
℣ Holy Spirit, hear us.
℟ **Holy Spirit, help us.**

Teach us, O Holy Spirit,
to trust always in the power of goodness,
against all odds,
to subdue evil and overcome it.
℣ Holy Spirit, hear us.
℟ **Holy Spirit, help us.**

Almighty and everlasting God,
by whose Spirit the whole body of the Church
is governed and sanctified:
Receive our supplications and prayers
which we offer before you
for all estates of men in your holy Church;
that every member of it,
in his vocation and ministry,
may serve you and be true to you
as he should;
through Jesus Christ our Lord.
℟ **Amen.**

3 The Third Three: Fidelity, Gentleness, Self-Control

Minister

Peace to you all from our Lord the Spirit.
℟ **Peace to you.**

Let us pray.
Teach us, O Holy Spirit,
to practise fidelity
to our wives and husbands,
to our children,
to our friends,
and to our Church.
℣ Holy Spirit, hear us.
℟ **Holy Spirit, help us.**

Teach us, O Holy Spirit,
to prefer gentleness and courtesy
to fretfulness and wrangling.
℣ Holy Spirit, hear us.
℟ **Holy Spirit, help us.**

Teach us, O Holy Spirit,
so to learn self-control
that we may be the masters of ourselves,
and the servants of Christ.
℣ Holy Spirit, hear us.
℟ **Holy Spirit, help us.**

Enable us, O Lord God,
to walk in your way
with integrity and cheerfulness,
faithfully believing your Word
and faithfully doing your commandments,
faithfully worshipping you
and faithfully serving our neighbour;
through Jesus Christ our Lord.
℟ **Amen.**

7. Of Thanksgiving

For the Benedictine Order

Let us thank God for his mercies.

For the gospel of our Lord and Saviour Jesus Christ, committed to his Church for the reconciliation of the world to God,
℟ **Thanks be to God.**

For our forefathers in the faith, whose obedience through succeeding generations has conveyed the gospel in safety to our own day.
℟ **Thanks be to God.**

For SAINT BENEDICT, Abbot of Monte Cassino, Patron of Europe,
℟ **Thanks be to God.**

For the puissance and the renown of the Rule of Saint Benedict,
℟ **Thanks be to God.**

For the services of the Order of Saint Benedict to the sanctifying and the perfecting of men and women,
℟ **Thanks be to God.**

For the contribution of the Order to art and culture and the graces of civilisation,
℟ **Thanks be to God.**

For Leofric and Godiva, founders of the Benedictine Abbey of Coventry,
℟ **Thanks be to God.**

For this Cathedral Church of Saint Michael,
by the folly of men destroyed, by the love of men
restored to a greater glory and a wider usefulness,
℟ **Thanks be to God.**

There are some moments of silence. Then the reader continues:

For the gift of his Spirit,
℟ **Blessed be Christ.**

For the Catholic Church,
℟ **Blessed be Christ.**

For the means of grace,
℟ **Blessed be Christ.**

For the hope of glory,
℟ **Blessed be Christ.**

For the triumphs of his gospel,
℟ **Blessed be Christ.**

For the lives of his saints,
℟ **Blessed be Christ.**

Now and to the end of the ages,
℟ **Blessed be Christ.**

And all declaim together:

**Blessing and honour and thanksgiving and praise,
More than we can utter,
More than we can conceive,
Be to thee, O holy and glorious Trinity,
Father, Son, and Holy Spirit,
By all angels,
All men,
All creatures,
To the end of time. Amen.**

Coventry Cathedral:
A Vision of Europe 1967

Thanksgiving for the City

For the vigour and renown of our City, and for its Mayoralty,
preserved and faithfully discharged during six hundred years,
℣ Let us bless the Lord;
℟ **Thanks be to God.**

For councillors, and other officers of government,
who by their conduct of public affairs have deserved well of the City,
℣ Let us bless the Lord;
℟ **Thanks be to God.**

For men and women who have exercised civic authority
as a vocation and ministry, to serve God and their fellows,
℣ Let us bless the Lord;
℟ **Thanks be to God.**

For all citizens who by prudence, by enterprise, by vision,
by generosity, by compassion, and by fair dealing,
have enriched and ennobled the corporate life,
℣ Let us bless the Lord;
℟ **Thanks be to God.**

For these and all his mercies let us thank God, and say:

Almighty God,
Father of all mercies:

Here the people join in:

We thine[i] unworthy servants
do give thee most humble and hearty thanks
for all thy goodness and loving-kindness
to us and to all men;
We bless thee for our creation, preservation,
and all the blessings of this life;
but above all, for thine inestimable love
in the redemption of the world by our Lord Jesus Christ,
for the means of grace,
and for the hope of glory.

And, we beseech thee,
give us that due sense of all thy mercies,
that our hearts may be unfeignedly thankful,
and that we shew forth thy praise,
not only with our lips, but in our lives;
by giving up ourselves to thy service,
and by walking before thee
in holiness and righteousness all our days;
through Jesus Christ our Lord,
to whom with thee and the Holy Ghost
be all honour and glory,
world without end. Amen.

O God our Father, who hast [you have] raised up for us many benefactors, known and unknown, remembered and forgotten, whose harvest we today are reaping: Make us also faithful in this our day, that we may sow a generous harvest, which others shall reap hereafter; through Jesus Christ our Lord. Amen.

Coventry Cathedral:
A Civic Service 1972

[i] *'You'* and *'your'* may be substituted for *'thee'* and *'thy'* or *'thine'*.

Thanksgiving for the Harvest

For the order and constancy of nature,
For the beauty and the bounty of the world,
For day and night, summer and winter, seedtime and harvest,
For the diverse gifts of loveliness and use which each season brings,
we praise God,
℟ **We thank him.**

For the artist's eye and the artist's hand
At work upon God's creation,
And out of its beauties fashioning fresh glories,
we praise God,
℟ **We thank him.**

For our homes and the joys of home,
For our friends, and for all occasions of fellowship,
For all the gracious ministries of human affection,
we praise God
℟ **We thank him.**

For communion with God,
who created us and holds us ever within the embrace of his love,
For the life, death, and resurrection of Jesus Christ,
who shows us who God is, sets us free, and makes us one,
For the Holy Spirit, who touches our hearts to love and obedience,
we praise God,
℟ **We thank him.**

Glory be to the Father, and to the Son: and to the Holy Spirit;
℟ **As it was in the beginning,**
Is now, and ever shall be:
World without end. Amen.

O Almighty God, creator of heaven and earth:
Make us grateful for thy [your] glory here,
and make us worthy of thy [your] glory hereafter;
through Jesus Christ our Lord.
℟ **Amen.**

Coventry Cathedral:
Consider the Lilies 1968

Thanksgiving for the Mothers' Union

For the Church of England, at home and overseas,
which has been the nursery of men and women of learning,
of sanctity, and of singular genius in many professions,
we praise God,
℟ **We thank him.**

For GEORGE SUMNER, Rector of Old Alresford,
and husband of Mary Sumner,
we praise God,
℟ **We thank him.**

For MARY SUMNER, the lady of the rectory,
the wife, the mother, the visionary,
who founded the Mothers' Union in 1876,
we praise God,
℟ **We thank him.**

For the Patrons, the friends, and the benefactors
who have sustained and encouraged the Mothers' Union
during one hundred years,
we praise God,
℟ **We thank him.**

For the members of the Mothers' Union
who have been faithful in their obedience to Jesus Christ,
and steadfast in upholding the standards of Christian marriage,
we praise God,
℟ **We thank him.**

For the work of the Mothers' Union
in the Christian education of children,
and in the publication of Christian literature,
we praise God,
℟ **We thank him.**

For the compassion which the Mothers' Union bestows
on those who need a friend to talk to, a shoulder to cry on,
or a good holiday, we praise God,
℟ **We thank him.**

Coventry Cathedral:
The Centenary of the Mothers' Union 1976

TE DEUM LAUDAMUS

℣ Yours is the praise, O God,
You are our sovereign Lord.
℟ **To you, eternal Father,**
The wide world pays its homage.
℣ From all the angels in their bright array,
From heaven and all the Powers
℟ **To you goes up the cry, the unremitting cry,**
℣ Holy, holy, holy is the Lord,
Sovereign Commander of the hosts of heaven.
℟ **There is no corner of the earth or sky**
But rings with your renown.
℣ The renownèd company of the Apostles sing your praises,
℟ **The illustrious fellowship of the Prophets sing your praises,**
℣ The bright-robed army of Martyrs sing your praises,
℟ **The holy Church in every continent confesses you**
℣ The Father, of a majesty that none can measure,
℟ **Your very Son, your only Son, whom all must worship,**
And the Holy Spirit, the Advocate.
℣ O Christ, renownèd King,
The Father's everlasting Son,
℟ **When you would stoop to set men free**
You deigned to be Our Lady's child.
℣ Death probed you to the quick,
But could not master you,
℟ **And to your loyal followers**
You opened wide the royal domains of heaven.
℣ You sit at God's right hand,
And share the Father's glory.
℟ **We are your servants,**
And with your life you paid our ransom.
℣ Come then, come to judge us as you will,
But come to help us too,
℟ **And number us among your saints**
In everlasting glory.

J.W.P. 1966

WHY DO CHORISTERS WEAR CASSOCKS AND SURPLICES?

A Letter to a Choirmaster

My dear Choirmaster,

Thank you for your letter in which you ask me:
1 Why do choristers wear cassocks and surplices?
2 How old is this tradition?
3 What do these garments represent?

You add 'I wish to maintain the tradition but at the same time wish to know why'. Here is the information you ask for.

~

Ecclesiastical garments were not, in the first place, invented: they merely happened. The first Christians wore the same clothes in public worship as they wore at any other time. They wore the garments usually worn in the first century A.D. by Roman citizens.

~

The indoor garment of a Roman citizen was a white tunic with sleeves, caught at the waist with a girdle. The tunic of a soldier, or of a labourer, was short, reaching to the knees. Persons of distinction, for example a magistrate or a bishop, wore the tunic very long, reaching down to the ankles.

The Latin name for the long tunic was tunica talaris, the ankle-length tunic. The Latin name for the white tunic was tunica alba.

Religious custom is conservative. Civilian fashions change; but in church the tunica alba was retained, and was recognised as an ecclesiastical garment. From the first century A.D. till today the long tunica alba has always been worn in church, not only by the clergy but also by their assistants, the acolytes or servers.

The tunica alba is what we call the alb. The adjective alba (white) is kept; the noun tunica is omitted for the sake of brevity. So today we say 'At the cricket match boys will wear their whites' – which is short for 'white flannel trousers and white shirts'. Or at football 'Shorts will be worn', meaning 'short trousers'.

~

In northern climates (in England, for example) churches in winter were very cold: so the ministers wore a fur-lined undergarment called pellicium (in English pelisse). You can't wear a narrow-sleeved alb over the pellicium; so in the 12th century they made the alb much fuller, left off the girdle, and enlarged the sleeves. The garment was then called superpellicium, the thing you put on over the fur-lined pellicium: and superpellicium, if you speak rapidly and slur the syllables together, becomes SURPLICE.

The surplice represents the triumph of good sense over tradition. It was worn at all services except the Eucharist, for which the alb was retained, as it still is. The celebrant at the Eucharist does not need to keep warm by wearing a fur-lined undergarment, because over the alb he wears another garment, the chasuble, which was originally a warm woollen overcoat in the form of a circle, with a hole in the middle to put your head through.

If you wish to be fashionable today you buy a poncho: this is a chasuble.

If you want to go bicycling in the rain, and you go to Halford's bicycle shop to buy a waterproof cape, what you will get is a chasuble – not of wool but of rubber or plastic. Good sense persuaded our forefathers to invent the surplice, which could be worn (instead of the alb) over a fur- lined undergarment in cold churches. Their good sense became obvious to me in the following way, when I was Precentor of Canterbury Cathedral.

On the evening of Trinity Sunday 1942 the German air force launched an attack on Canterbury. The Cathedral was not hit, but all the windows were blown out by the blast of the bombs. This was in early summer. When the winter came, it was of course useless to light the stoves to heat the Cathedral; and the building was perishing cold.

What did we do? We kept our overcoats on, and wore the surplice on top of the overcoat.

The surplice, then, is a modified form of the alb, which was the indoor dress of a Roman citizen in the time of Christ, worn both at worship and at other times. The surplice was invented for use in church; the alb was not. But the surplice was derived from the alb. If you dress your choristers in surplices, they are within a tradition which goes back in unbroken continuity to the very first days of the Christian Church. You are making a statement about the Christian Faith; you are saying that it is founded on something that actually happened in the Roman Empire in the early years of the first century A.D., just as you say in the Creed that Jesus 'suffered under Pontius Pilate'.

But remember: the alb was ankle-length; it reached down to the feet. The surplice derives from the alb; and a properly made surplice is nearly as long as the alb; it ends six inches above the hem of the cassock. The sleeves of the surplice are large and full, usually terminating in a point. The points of the sleeve must reach to the bottom hem of the surplice. No garment less ample than this is fit to be called a surplice, or fit to be used in church.

When full-bottomed wigs were in fashion, the surplice could not be put on over the wig; so it was made open in front, and only secured by a button at the neck. In this form (though the wig has disappeared) the surplice is still worn in the chapels of the colleges of Oxford and Cambridge. It is still full and long; and by lay people it is worn over their civilian clothes, not over a cassock.

~

The cassock is an undergarment, the common out-of-door dress of Ministers and lay people at least until the 14th century. It is still the dress worn by the boys of one of our English public schools, Christ's Hospital; they wear a cassock of dark blue and so are commonly called Blue-coat boys.

The cassock is also the official out-of-door dress of the clergy; but they wear it in church too, putting on over it the garments used for worship.

When the alb was worn (as it once was) for all services, it reached down to the ankles; and the cassock underneath was hidden, and was therefore of no special importance. When the surplice was introduced, it was at first as long as the alb, and it concealed the cassock; but in course of time the surplice grew shorter (more's the pity) and then the cassock became visible; and the next step, naturally enough, was to introduce cassocks of different colours.

Red cassocks are a royal prerogative, forbidden to be worn by commoners. There is one other dress worn by choristers which is also a royal prerogative.

At St James' Palace in London the choristers of the Chapel Royal do not wear the traditional ecclesiastical garments at all. As members of the royal household and servants of the Sovereign they wear in chapel a livery. The livery consists of a scarlet and gold coat, with ruffs at the wrist and linen bands at the neck, over scarlet knee-breeches and black stockings.

PART IV – EXAMPLES OF MUSIC

EXAMPLES OF MUSIC

Page

Antiphons

Invocations

Salutations

Versicles and Responses

A Litany of the Church

Antiphons

In the Litany: Antiphon to Psalm 44, *Deus, auribus*, the plainsong canto fermo is in the tenor.

William Byrd (1543-1623)

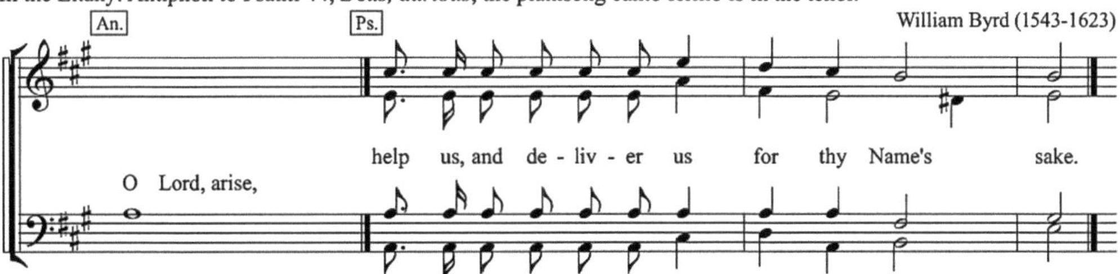

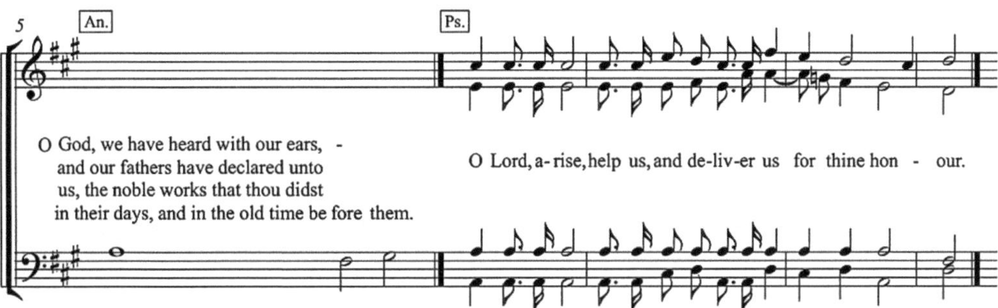

ANTIPHON at the entrance of the consecrating Bishop

J.W.P.

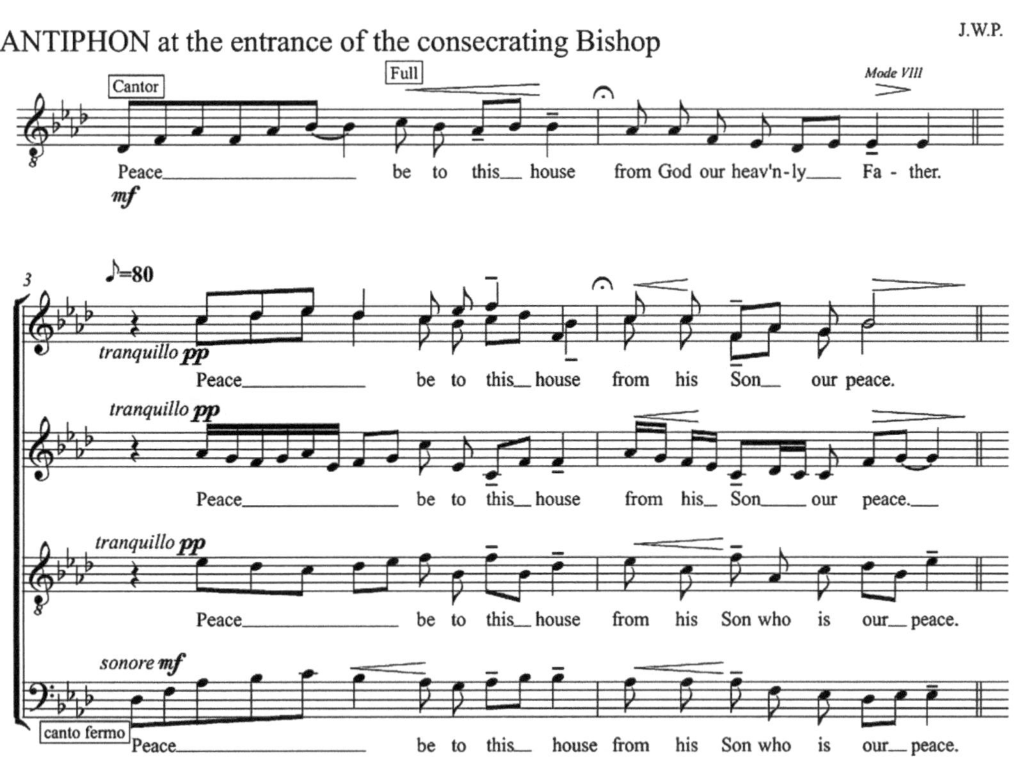

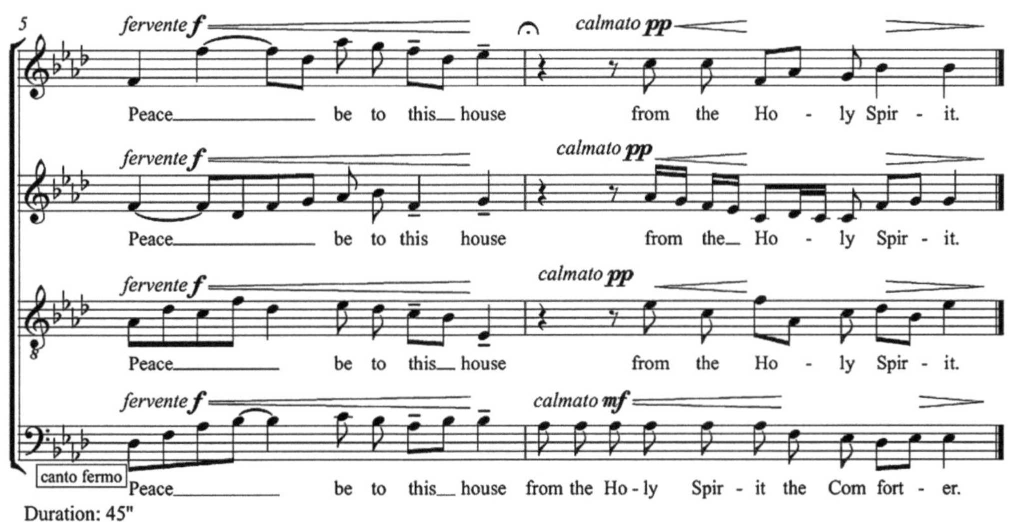

THE ANTIPHON *Lift up your heads* follows at once

ANTIPHON to Psalm 24, *Domini est terra*
in procession before the consecrating Bishop

2
31
6. This is the portion of them that seek him: even of them that seek the God of Ja - cob.
33
f
A. c.f.
S
7. Lift up your heads, O ye gates, and be ye lift up ye ever - last - ing doors.
36
mf
f
and the King of glo - ry shall come in.
8. Who is the King of glo - ry?
40
Tenors
f
Basses
It is the Lord strong and mighty, e - ven the Lord might - y in bat - tle.
43
f
A. c.f.
S
9. Lift up your heads, O ye gates, and be ye lift up ye ever - last - ing doors.
46
mf
f
and the King of glo - ry shall come in.
10.Who is the King of glo - ry?
50
Tenors
f
Basses
Even the Lord of hosts, He is the King of glo - ry.

REPEAT THE ANTIPHON *Lift up your heads*
Duration: Antiphon 20", Psalm 2', Total 2'40"
Composed for the Consecration of Coventry Cathedral on 25 May 1962

CYMBALS AND DANCES

ANTIPHON to Psalm 95, *Venite, exultemus*
Bernard Rose (b.1916)
Composed for the Royal School of Church Music
Festive Service Book 9, *Voice and Verse*
♩=72
O come let us wor - ship, and fall down: and
♩=72
4
kneel be - fore the Lord
our ma - ker.
our ma - ker.

Psalm 95 G.J. Elvey (1816-1893)

O come let us ' sing unto • the Lord;
let us heartily rejoice in the ' strength of ' our sal'vation.

2 Let us come before his ' presence • with ' thanksgiving;
and show ourselves ' glad in ' him with ' psalms.

3 For the Lord is a ' great God;
and a great ' King a•bove ' all ' gods.

4 In his hand are all the ' corners • of the ' earth;
and the strength of the ' hills is ' his ' also.

2nd Part 5 The sea is his, and ' he ' made it;
and his hands prepared the dry land.

6 O come, let us worship and ' fall ' down,
and kneel before the ' Lord our ' Maker.

7 For he is the ' Lord our ' God;
and we are the people of his pasture, and the ' sheep of ' his ' hand.

Glory be to the Father, and ' to the ' Son:
and ' to the ' Holy ' Ghost;

As it was in the beginning, is now and ' ever ' shall be;
world without ' end. ' A- ' men.

our ma - ker.
and we are the
For he is the Lord our God:
and we
our ma - ker.
and we are the
and we
mf
13
peo - ple of his pas - ture, and the sheep
f
are the peo - ple of his pas - ture, and the sheep
peo - ple of his pas - ture, and the sheep
are the peo - ple of his pas - ture, and the sheep
f
17
of his hand.
of his hand.
of his hand.
of his hand.

ANTIPHON before Psalm 122, *Laetatus sum*
Henry G. Ley (1887-1962)
Composed for the Founders' Commemoration day
at King's College, Cambridge, September 1938
Unaccompanied
Organ
f
And the Lord said unto the King;
f
I have hal-lowed this house which thou hast
built, to put my Name there for
e - - - - - - - - - ver.

Psalm 122
Richard Woodward

ANTIPHON after Psalm 122

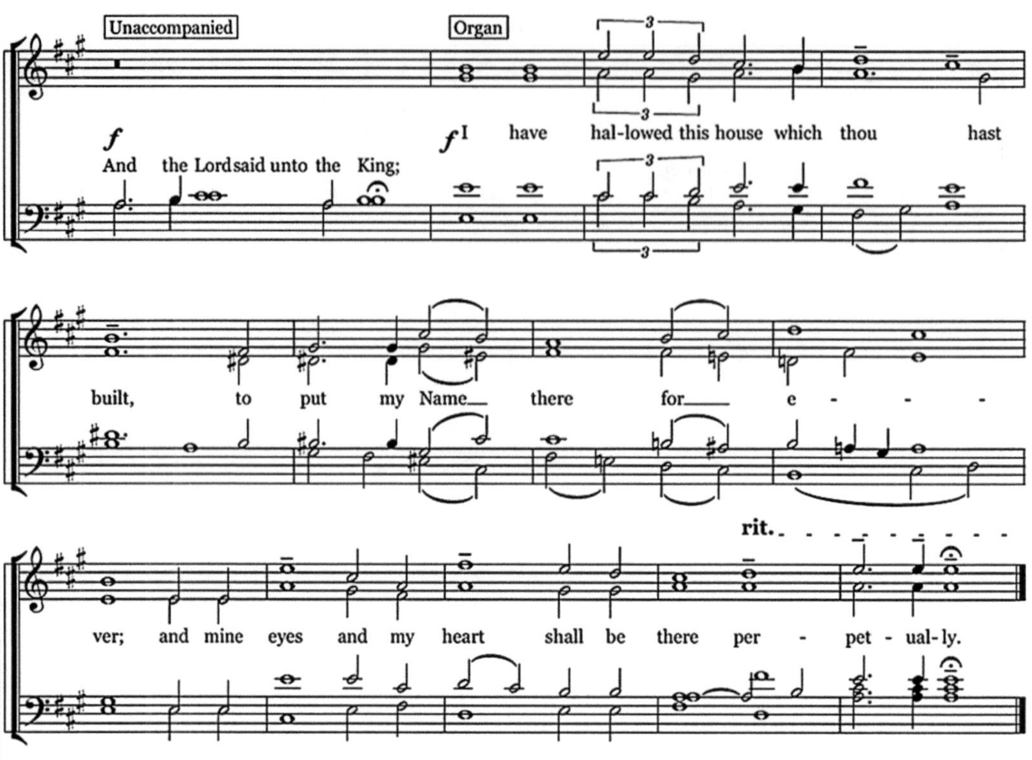

INVOCATIONS

Sidney S. Campbell (1909-)

Precentor

Jesus said, I am the light of the world: he that followeth me shall not walk in dark- ness;

Choir ♩=60

f

But shall have the light___ of life.

Precentor

God, who commanded the light to shine out of dark - ness: hath shi - ned in our hearts;

Choir ♩=60

f

To give the light of the know-ledge of the glo - ry of God in the face of Je - sus Christ.

Precentor

He showed me that great city, the ho - ly Je - ru - sa - lem:

descending out of heaven from God, having the glo - ry of God;

Choir
♩=60
f
And her light was like un - to a stone most pre - cious:
♩=♩
sost.....
e - ven like a jas - per stone, clear as cry - stal.
Precentor
And the city had no need of the sun: neither of the moon to shine in it;
Choir
♩=60
f
ff
For the glo - ry of God did light-en it: and the Lamb is the light there - of.
Precentor
O Lord Jesus Christ, ... with - - out end.
Choir
A - men.

SALUTATIONS
Robert G. Weddle (b.1941)
Versicles and Responses at the Crib
Cantor (at the crib) When all things began, the Word al - rea - dy was;
Choir I (in choir stalls)
Choir II (at the crib)
mf and through Him all things came to be, all things came to be.
Cantor The Word be - came flesh, He came to dwell among us and we saw his glo - ry;
Choir I
Such glo - ry, such glo - ry as be-fits the Fa-ther's on-ly Son, Full of grace and truth,
Choir II
Full of grace and truth.
Cantor
Noone has ever seen God:
Choir I
But God's on-ly son, he who is near-est to the
Fa - ther's heart, He has made Him known,
Choir II
He has made Him known.
The Salutation
Choir I
Choir II
pp Peace to you, Peace to you.
Cantor
Grace and truth be with you;
COLLECT
Choir I
Choir II
Cantor
A- men, A- men, A - men, pp A - men.
O everlasting ...with-out end.

VERSICLES & RESPONSES

At the Crib

Sidney S. Campbell

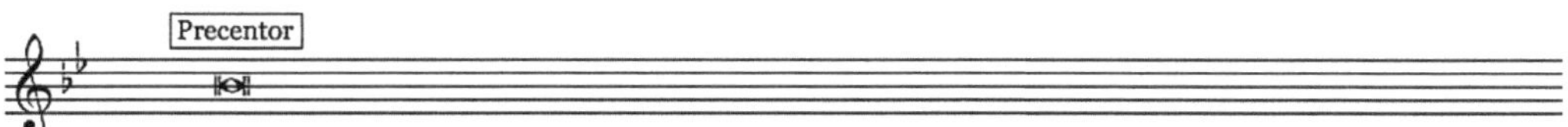
Precentor
Lord Jesus, Child of Bethlehem, for Love of men made man: Create in us Love so pure and perfect that

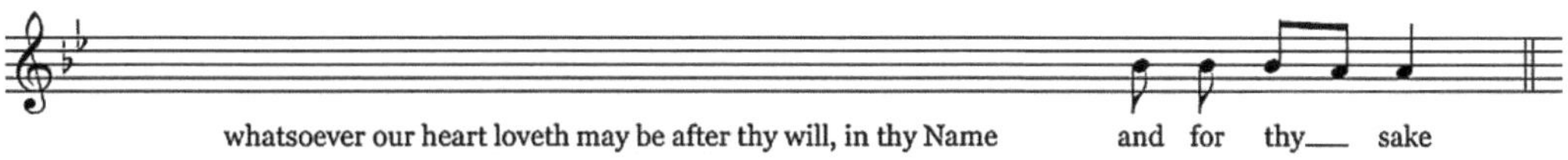
whatsoever our heart loveth may be after thy will, in thy Name and for thy sake

Choir 1
A men, A men, A

Choir 2
f
rit.
p
men. A men.

VERSICLES & RESPONSES

At the end of Evensong

Gerald Knight
(1908-79)

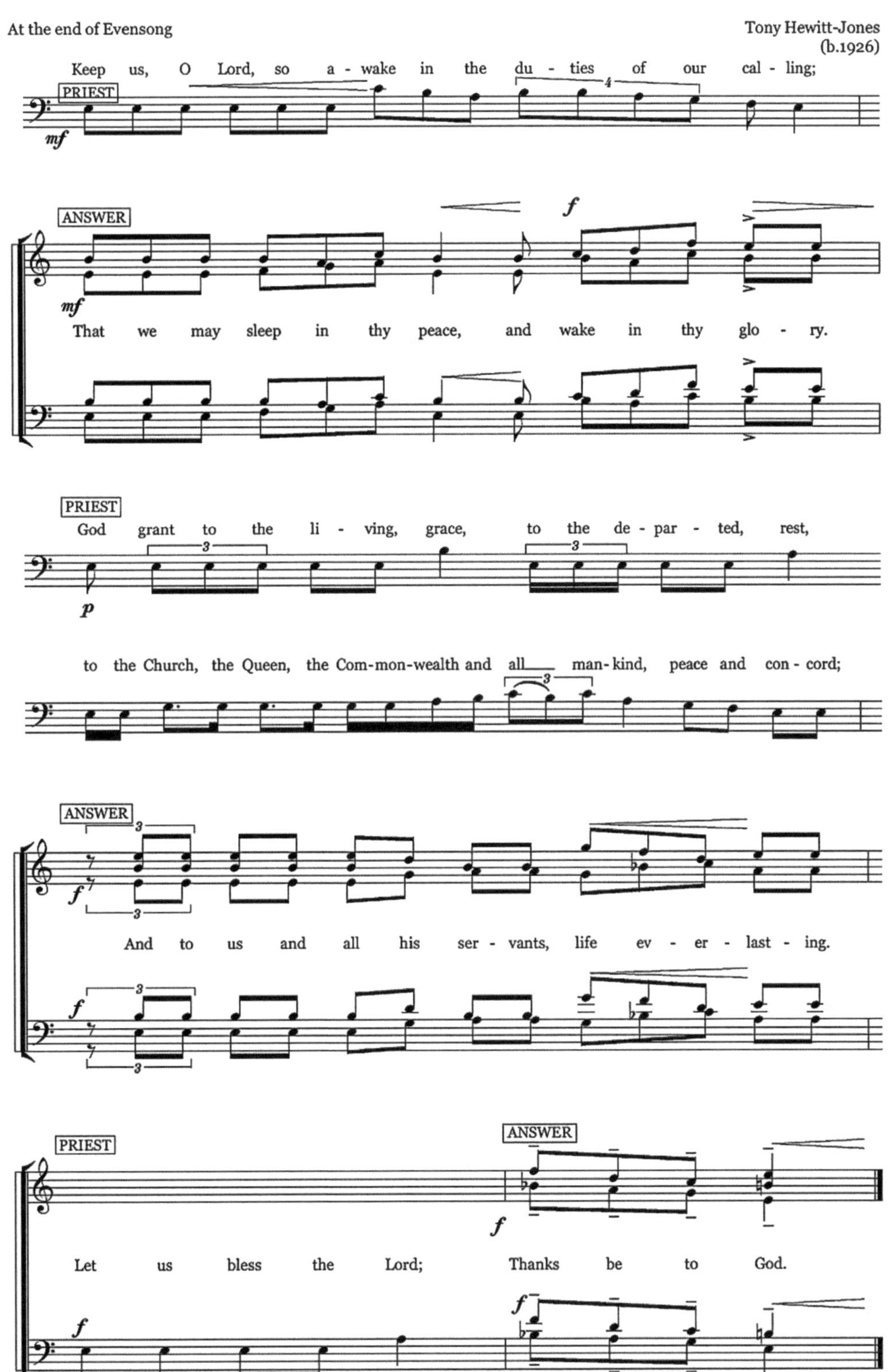
At the end of Evensong
Tony Hewitt-Jones
(b.1926)
PRIEST
Keep us, O Lord, so a - wake in the du - ties of our cal - ling;
ANSWER
That we may sleep in thy peace, and wake in thy glo - ry.
PRIEST
God grant to the li - ving, grace, to the de - par - ted, rest,
to the Church, the Queen, the Com-mon-wealth and all man-kind, peace and con - cord;
ANSWER
And to us and all his ser - vants, life ev - er - last - ing.
PRIEST
ANSWER
Let us bless the Lord; Thanks be to God.

CYMBALS AND DANCES

A Litany of the Church

Tony Hewitt-Jones

Let us pray for the whole Clergy, especially for [N.] Archbishop of this Province, for [N.] Bishop of this Diocese, and for all who are called to a min-is-try in the house-hold of God;
The Bishop
Let us pray for the servants of God at this time to be admitted to the Order of Deacons or Priests, that by his grace they may be faithful ministers and stew-ards of his mys-ter- ies;
Precentor
Let us pray for one another and for all whose hearts are with us,
who de - sire to be re - mem-bered in our prayers and re - mem-ber us in their own;
That we may follow the way that leads to truth, and fol - low the truth that leads to life;
That we may follow the steps of our Redeemer Je - sus Christ, who a-lone is the Way, the Truth and the life;
That finishing here the work of our sal - va-tion we may rest here-af - ter in thy ho - ly peace;
S.A.
Son of God: we be seech thee to hear us; Son of God: we be - seech thee to hear us;
T.B.

Precentor
O Lamb of God: that tak-est a-way the sins of the world;
S.A.
grant us thy peace.
T.B.
Precentor
O Lamb of God: that tak-est a-way the sins of the world;
S.A.
have mer-cy up-on us.
T.B.
Precentor
O Christ, hear us:
S.A.
O Christ, hear us.
T.B.
O Christ, hear us.
Precentor
Lord have mer - cy up - on us;
S.A.
Lord have mer - cy up - on us.
T.B.
Lord have mer - cy up - on us.
S
Christ have mer - cy up - on us.
A
Christ have mer - cy up - on us.
T
Christ have mer - cy up - on us.
Precentor
Christ have mer - cy up - on us;
B
Christ have mer - cy up - on us.
Lord have mer - cy up - on us.
Lord have mer - cy up - on us.
Lord have mer - cy up - on us.
Precentor

APPENDICES

APPENDIX A

For further reading

Books about music in worship

Matthew Britt, D.S.B. (ed.), revised edition, *The Hymns of the Breviary and Missal* (New York, 1952).

Latin texts and English translations of the hymns under four heads:
1 Hymns of the Psalter 2 Proper of the Season
3 Proper of the Saints 4 Common of the Saints
This is an American Roman Catholic book of scholarly distinction and practical utility.

Maurice Frost (ed.), *Historical Companion to Hymns Ancient and Modern* (London, 1962).

This is a revision of Bishop Frere's Historical Edition of Hymns Ancient and Modern, 1909. It is a scholarly book of immense range and accuracy.

Percy A. Scholes, The Oxford Companion to Music, 10th edition (Oxford, 1978).

This is a miracle of scholarship and industry: an incomparable book. With sympathy and inflexible accuracy the author writes of every aspect of music in worship among all branches of the Church.

Charles S. Phillips, *Hymnody Past and Present* (London, 1937).

Edmund H. Fellowes, *English Cathedral Music* (London, 1941).
(Revised edition by J.A. Westrup, 1969.)

Charles H. Phillips, *The Singing Church* (London, 1945).
Erik Routley, *Hymns and Human Life* (London, 1952).
Erik Routley, *Hymns and the Faith* (London, 1955).
Erik Routley, *The Music of Christian Hymnody* (London, 1957).
Erik Routley, *The English Carol* (London, 1958).
Denis Stevens, *Tudor Church Music* (London, 1961).
Erik Routley, *Twentieth Century Church Music,* revised edition (London, 1966).
Peter Le Huray, *Music and the Reformation in England 1549-1660* (London, 1967).
Arthur Hutchings, *Church Music in the Nineteenth Century* (London, 1967).
Bernarr Rainbow, *The Choral Revival in the Anglican Church* (London, 1970).
Christopher Dearnley, *English Church Music 1650-1750* (London, 1970).

Carols

The Oxford Book of Carols (Oxford, 1928, re-set 1964).
Sir Richard R. Terry (ed.), *Two Hundred Folk Carols* (London, 1933).
Reginald Jacques and David Willcocks (eds), *Carols for Choirs 1: Fifty Christmas Carols* (Oxford, 1961).
David Willcocks and John Rutter (eds), *Carols for Choirs 2: Fifty Carols for Christmas and Advent* (Oxford, 1970).
David Willcocks and John Rutter (eds), *Carols for Choirs 3* (Oxford, 1978).
Louis Halsey and Basil Ramsey (eds), *Sing Nowell: 51 Carols new and arranged* (London, 1963).
Carols of Today: 17 original settings for mixed voices (Oxford, 1965).
Elizabeth Poston (ed.), *The Penguin Book of Christmas Carols* (London, 1965).
Elizabeth Poston (ed.), *The Second Penguin Book of Christmas Carols: Carols from USA* (London, 1970).

Hymn Books: British

David Mowbray, *Kingdom Come: Fifty hymns for parish services* (London, 1940).
David Holbrook and Elizabeth Poston (eds), *The Cambridge Hymnal* (Cambridge, 1967).
100 Hymns for Today: A supplement to Hymns Ancient & Modern (London, 1969).
More Hymns for Today (Norwich, 1980).
Hymns and Songs (London, 1969). A supplement to the 1933 Methodist Hymn Book.
The New Catholic Hymnal (London, 1971).
Praise the Lord (London, 1972).
The Church Hymnary, third edition (London, 1973).
New Church Praise (Edinburgh, 1975).
A supplemental collection for the use of the United Reformed Church (1972)
English Praise (Oxford, 1976).
A supplement to the English Hymnal (1906, 1933)
A Song in Season (London, 1976).

Hymn Books: English-Speaking Overseas

The Mennonite Hymnal (Scottdale, PA, 1969).
The Worshipbook (Philadelphia, 1972). [Presbyterian]
Worship II (Chicago, 1975). [Roman Catholic]
More Hymns and Spiritual Songs, second edition (New York, 1977).
A supplement to the (Episcopalian) Hymnal 1940.

The Lutheran Book of Worship (Minneapolis and St Louis, 1978).

The Hymn Book (Toronto, 1971).

The authorized hymnal of the United Church of Canada and the Episcopal Church in Canada

The Australian Hymn Book (Mulgrave, Victoria, 1977).

The hymnal of the Uniting Churches in Australia

With One Voice (London, 1979).

This is the Australian Hymn Book under a fresh title for sale in Great Britain and America.

The Psalter

Words only

The Psalms (London, 1966).

A new translation from the Hebrew arranged for singing to the psalmody of Joseph Gelineau. Music for selected psalms from The Grail, 58 Sloane Street, London, SW1.

Sing a New Song (London, 1972).

The psalms in Today's English Version, first published by the American Bible Society under the title The Psalms for Modern Man.

The Psalms (London, 1977).

A New Translation for Worship printed for singing to Anglican Chant

Words and Music

Psalm Praise (London, 1973).

This collection is something entirely new and fresh, apt for services at a popular level. Every writer of liturgies for today will be wise to consult it. It is discussed in **Psalms and Canticles** (page 213).

APPENDIX B

Associations for the Promotion of Music in Worship *

American Associations for the promotion of music in worship

(where the Association publishes a journal its title is mentioned)

The American Guild of Organists: 630 Fifth Avenue, Suite 2010, New York, NY 10020. *The Diapason.*

The Association of Anglican Musicians: c/o the Standing Commission on Worship, 815 Second Avenue, New York, NY10017

The Fellowship of Baptist Musicians: *Newsletter.*

The National Association of Pastoral Musicians (Roman Catholic): 1029 Vermont Avenue NW, Washington, DC 20005. *Pastoral Music.*

Choristers' Guild: PO Box 38188, Dallas, TX 75238. *Choristers' Guild Letter.*

The Fellowship of United Methodist Musicians: c/o/ Abingdon Press, 210 Eighth Avenue South, Nashville, TN 37202. *Music Ministry.*

The Presbyterian Association of Musicians: 1000 East Morehead Street, Charlotte, NC 28204. *Reformed Liturgy and Music.*

The Hymn Society of America: Wittenberg University, Springfield, OH 45501. *The Hymn.*

Other journals devoted to this subject:

Church Music (Lutheran Church, Missouri Synod), Concordia Publishing House, 3558 South Jefferson Street, St Louis, MI 63118

Journal of Church Music (Lutheran Church in America and American Lutheran Church), Fortress Press, 2900 Queen Lane, Philadelphia, PA 19129

The Church Musician, Southern Baptist Convention, 127 Ninth Avenue North, Nashville, TN 37234

* EDITOR'S NOTE:
The list of organisations and contacts in this section are as collated by the author in the late 1970s. Details may not now be correct and some organisations may no longer be extant.

British Associations for the promotion of music in worship.

(where the Association publishes a journal the title is mentioned)

The Royal School of Church Music: Addington Palace, Croydon CR9 5AD. Founded in 1927 by Dr Sydney Nicholson (then Organist of Westminster Abbey) for the Church of England, but now used also by other Churches including the Roman Catholic Church. There are 8,000 affiliated choirs (6,300 in Great Britain, 1,700 overseas). Church Music issued quarterly free of charge to affiliated choirs and individual members. *English Church Music*, a collection of essays published annually in June.

The Gregorian Association: *The Gregorian.*

The Plainsong and Mediaeval Music Society.

The Baptist Music Society.

The Free Church Choir Union

The Methodist Church Music Society: *Bulletin.*

The Society of Saint Gregory (Roman Catholic): c/o 9-11 Henry Road, London N4 2LH. *Music and Liturgy.*

The United Reformed Church Guild of Organists and Choirmasters: *Guild Review.*

The Hymn Society of Great Britain and Ireland: *Bulletin.*

Index

L - #0106 - 100522 - C0 - 246/189/25 - PB - DID3310931

MODI @ 20

MODI @ 20

DREAMS MEET DELIVERY

EDITED AND COMPILED BY

BLUEKRAFT DIGITAL FOUNDATION

RUPA

First published by
Rupa Publications India Pvt. Ltd 2022
7/16, Ansari Road, Daryaganj
New Delhi 110002

Sales Centres:

Allahabad Bengaluru Chennai
Hyderabad Jaipur Kathmandu
Kolkata Mumbai

We are thankful to narendramodi.in for being a repository of many rare pictures.

ISBN: 978-93-5520-363-2

Fifth impression 2022

10 9 8 7 6 5

Printed in India

CONTENTS

Section Three
Jan Dhan: An Economy for Everyone

Section Four
A New Paradigm in Governance

Section Five
Vasudhaiva Kutumbakam: India and the World

FOREWORD

Lata Mangeshkar

Bharat Ratna awardee

I consider myself blessed to be born in a nation that is as timeless and glorious as ours. A nation that has given so much to the world and has always worked for the larger global good. The virtues of kindness and compassion are ingrained in our people. Yes, we have faced periodic challenges, but eventually we as a people have always prevailed.

The leader of our nation at this moment in history, occupying the Prime Minister's chair, is our beloved Narendra bhai. I have known him since many years and followed with great interest the exceptional work he has done for the people of India.

On 7 October 2021, Narendra bhai completed twenty continuous years as the head of a democratically-elected government.

By temperament, Narendra bhai is not what we conventionally imagine of a politician. From my various conversations with him, I sense that his pursuits are different. He has no attachment to power.

His goal is larger; to be able to do something for the people of India. His passion lies in the fact that he wants the growth story to be meaningful for every person in our country. In India's history, the name of Mahatma Gandhi is etched in golden letters because he turned the entire freedom struggle into a mass movement. He motivated every citizen to think that any action they do would strengthen India's resolve for freedom. In the same spirit, Narendra bhai is turning India's development journey into a mass movement. He is connecting every citizen of India to this goal.

We all know that before becoming Prime Minister, Narendra bhai had an impressive track record as a Chief Minister, which also enabled him to understand the nuances of governance. As Chief Minister, Narendra bhai put Gujarat on the map of development. He addressed all the development needs of the state, be it in agriculture or industry. My friends in Gujarat tell me that one of his lasting impacts has been the streamlining of the power sector. Distant tribal areas, where development had not reached for years, got the fruits of development.

In 2014, the people of India gave Narendra bhai a mandate that was unseen in decades. I vividly remember the fervour among the people to see him as their Prime Minister. No Indian will forget the emotional sight of Narendra bhai bowing to the Parliament and the Constitution of India. His first address from the ramparts of Red Fort captured the imagination of the nation when he talked about toilets and when he asked parents to question their sons instead of their daughters when it came to women's safety.

In the past seven years, he has brought in several unique initiatives aimed at removing poverty and suffering. Due to his efforts, the poor have got bank accounts, social security, homes, electricity and water. It is a testimony to his hard work that he was given yet another sweeping mandate by the people in 2019. I can say with confidence that the world is talking about his governance.

Narendra bhai stands out because people trust him. People know that, however hard the challenge is, he will work with the best intent and resolve it. Such trust, in intent and action, differentiates a leader from the rest. I have no hesitation in saying that in every part of the country, people think of him as a family member who talks about issues that are relatable.

I am delighted to see a book being penned on Narendra Modi ji, celebrating his twenty years in the political arena.

I am sure this book will be engraved as an inspiring and remarkable narrative for all of us.

I would like to mention a very special moment that culminated in my association with Narendra bhai. In 2013, when he was the Chief Minister of Gujarat, Narendra bhai, on our invitation, very graciously took time out of his busy schedule and inaugurated our Deenanath Mangeshkar Super Speciality hospital in Pune.

Very spontaneously, a genuine brother-sister bond evolved, and it reflects in every moment of our relationship.

I cherish our bond and will continue to do so.

As a proud Indian, I always wish to see my country remain an inspiring and evolving embodiment of our rich heritage and reach the heights for which our freedom fighters fought.

My heartiest wishes to our Prime Minister Narendra bhai, and I hope and pray he continues to lead our nation on a path of glory with his dynamism, passion and courage.

INTRODUCTION

All democracies by their very nature are argumentative and competitive. Liberal democracies, with constitutionally guaranteed free speech, a free press, an independent judiciary and a vibrant civil society are even more competitive for everyone is afforded the same opportunity to fearlessly pitch their ideas. A nation like India, with millennia old history and rich traditions of parallel debates and multiple discussions, is at the apogee of such contests. Add to it a billion plus scale—comprising a young population and a fascinating diversity of languages, cultures and geography—and one can visualize the complexity and the near-impossibility of any single idea or thought holding centrestage in India for a sustained period of time. And yet, one such thought—the 'idea of Modi'—has held sway for over two decades. From the perspective of nation-building, however, it is actually the 'ideas by Modi' that have refashioned and redefined India in the 21st century.

Narendra Modi first assumed an elected office on 7 October 2001 when he was sworn in as Chief Minister of the western Indian state of Gujarat. In 2021, he completed uninterrupted 20 years as head of a democratically elected government—twelve and a half years as Chief Minister and over seven and a half years and running as Prime Minister of India. This is a unique phenomenon with few parallels—not just in India, but for any democratic polity across the world.

In between these twenty years, Modi has contested five elections in which he was on the ticket and his own future was at stake—in the state of Gujarat in 2002, 2007 and 2012 as Chief Ministerial candidate and then in 2014 and 2019 Lok Sabha (directly elected house of Parliament) elections as Prime Ministerial candidate. Not only has he remained undefeated in each of these polls, but his popularity has also soared with each election within the country and he routinely polls as the most popular serving world leader with approval ratings in the high seventies.

In the run up to 2014 national elections, India had not returned a full majority national government for over three decades. The commentariat consensus was that the same will hold true in 2014 as well, when PM candidate Modi first put himself on the ticket. But a three-decade pattern also did not prove to be a stumbling block for Modi. For the first time ever, his party, the BJP , attained a single party full majority in the Lok Sabha. His critics dismissed this result as a one-time fluke. The detractors declared that the result was driven more by the hope generated by Modi than something which would be matched by his delivery. After completing a full term in 2019, Modi was re-elected with an even bigger majority, becoming the first Prime Minister in almost fifty years to achieve this feat. The verdict this time was driven not just by hope but by his demonstrable delivery. During these years, riding on Modi's popularity, the BJP also broke new ground and got elected in states where it had no previous presence of any consequence.

Almost everything that one took for granted for achieving any political success in India did not apply to Modi. He came from an underprivileged social and economic background, had no family or dynastic privilege, did not go to elite colleges, was not part of the network of elites who governed India before him and had no money power backing him. Before 2001, Modi had not even held a local elected office and was content working in the background, building his parent social organization—the Rashtriya Swayamsevak Sangh (RSS) and later his political party the BJP. And yet, twenty years later, Modi remains undefeated in not just the electoral arena, but also in terms of mass popularity, public acclaim, governance paradigm, and most importantly in being the most trusted public personality that India has seen post-Independence. Such is Modi's presence in India's political landscape that he becomes the focal point of contest in every debate and every election of India—from a local municipal election to the national elections.

In 2014, Modi became the first elected Prime Minister to assume the office through public acclaim. Before Modi, no other Prime Minister had assumed the office for the first time after a popular, full majority verdict was delivered in his or her name. Other Prime Ministers before him had either been nominated to their posts for the first time and later won elections or had simply been compromise candidates post fractured verdicts, or had failed to get full majority. Modi is the first Prime Minister in independent India to have been announced as a candidate before elections and then got elected to that post through popular votes.

What could be the reasons for this sustained mass popularity of Modi that cuts across class, gender, regions, demography and age? Is it the 'Gujarat Model' that became synonymous with good governance, and was later replicated at the national scale, that explains his success? Is it Modi's famed execution abilities when faced with complex governance challenges that make him stand out? Is it his emphasis on participative governance—Jan Bhagidari—that makes him connect with the people at a plane unreachable for other politicians? Can this success be explained by Modi's motto of 'Sabha Saath, Sabka Vikas' ('Together, for everyone's growth, with everyone's trust') that has completely changed the governance paradigm in India and has, for the first time, built an implicit trust between the people and the Central government?

These are fascinating questions that have no set or defined answers. It is this quest for understanding the phenomenon of Modi, as the 20th anniversary of him assuming elected office approached in 2021, that we first began thinking of a book. However, soon we realized that if we have to seriously broach this topic then it would be no ordinary book. And this is because of one simple reason. Who could claim to completely define and capture the work of Modi in these 20 years and then answer the question why the Modi phenomenon works? Ask an academic and she may give an answer at complete variance with what a wealth creator may say which, in turn, may be different from the views of a mass politician and all of them may differ from how an ordinary voter thinks about Modi. And yet, each of them would be right in their own way, for how could only one view define a phenomenon like Modi?

Soon it became clear to us that the book could not be the view of just one person for no matter how insightful, it would still fall short. That is when the idea of an anthology came up. What if we could get together a group of eminent people in their respective domains and request each of them to write on their subject matter? They would bring with them their expertise and credibility and together produce a work that has both analytical and academic framework as well as personal anecdotes of working with Modi that will give an insight into Modi's mind. In its entirety, the book will then become the only work of its kind to understand why Modi works?

In theory this seemed like a great idea and so we got down to work. And for once, practice trumped theory. The end result, this book, could not have assembled a better set of people to explain these twenty years.

The book comprises five sections and twenty-one chapters. Each chapter is written by a renowned domain expert. The chapters discuss their respective topic in a holistic framework, covering the entire twenty years pertaining to that topic in a seamless narrative.

Section 1 is about the social impact of Modi. Double Olympic medallist P.V. Sindhu writes on youth connect, Shobana Kamineni of the Apollo Group analyses women empowerment and economist Surjit Bhalla deploys an academic framework to understand the impact of Modi's policies in terms of its reach to those at the bottom of the pyramid and in eradicating poverty.

Section 2 deals with the political impact of Modi. One of India's foremost authors, Amish Tripathi, writes on the cultural revival under Modi. Who could be a better person than Home Minister Amit Shah to take us through the political journey of BJP under Modi. And so, he does as he provides a fascinating account through his writing. The last chapter in this section is by Pradeep Gupta, one of India's most reliable psephologists, who tells us through numbers and data how Modi has forever changed the way elections are contested in India.

Section 3 is on the economic policy of Modi. India's Chief Economic Advisor Anantha Nageswaran discusses the unique ability of Modi to think big and then execute it at scale. Professor Arvind Panagariya, among India's most respected economist, deep dives into the process of economic reforms under Modi and the way they have been done. Dr Shamika Ravi, a distinguished economist and author, brings her unique data analysis skills to bear in the chapter on microeconomics and how Modi empowers the poor. Uday S. Kotak, India's leading banker, writes the last chapter in this section which deals with the philosophy of respecting and encouraging wealth creators.

Section 4 is about a new paradigm of governance brought about by Modi. Ajay Mathur from the International Solar Alliance explores the frictionless interplay between development and environmental protection that has been the hallmark of Modi years. Anupam Kher builds a persuasive case of why Modi, contrary to conventional wisdom of not trusting a politician, is the most trusted man in times of crisis. India's foremost agricultural scientist, Professor Ashok Gulati, writes on the management of farm sector. Dr Devi Shetty, India's leading medical professional, analyses the governance response in managing the COVID-19 pandemic. Nandan Nilekani, a pioneering technical mind, brings in his own personal anecdotes to tell us how Modi integrated technology into day-to-day governance and made it an indelible tool of governance. There could be no one better than Nripendra Mishra, Principal Secretary to Modi in his first term, to explain the dynamics of what goes into the famed execution abilities of Modi. To explain the processes of mass movements as force multipliers in governance, we needed a spiritual master who understood the mechanisms of mass movements and when, how and why they work. We are indebted to Sadhguru Jaggi Vasudev for having agreed to write this chapter. The beautifully narrated story in the chapter 'Winds of Change', which mirror the changes that happened in the Modi years, could only have been written by one of India's most loved and prolific writers, Sudha Murty.

Section 5 is about how India deals with the rest of the world under Modi. National Security Advisor Ajit Doval brings in his first-hand experience of dealing with national security matters under Modi in this first of its kind chapter, rich in detail and conceptual expanse. Manoj Ladwa from Britain and Bharat Barai from the United States, two people who have personally known Modi for almost three decades, narrate through personal anecdotes the method behind the unique diaspora strength that Modi has been able to muster. Finally, India's External Affairs Minister, Dr S. Jaishankar, lays out the foreign policy of Modi as it has panned out since 2014 and the future vision about India's place in the community of nations.

We at BlueKraft Digital Foundation feel privileged to have been able to bring together such distinguished personalities on one platform to contribute to the academic literature on the early decades of this century. We hope that this book will be a useful addition in the public discourse of not just understating what makes Modi work but also as a commentary of the first two decades of a new century and the emergence of a New India.

Former President of India Dr A.P.J. Abdul Kalam once famously said, 'You have to dream before your dreams can come true.' If there is one undisputed reality about the twenty years of Narendra Modi in public office in this new millennium, then it is that he not only dreamed big along with all of us, but he also helped deliver many of those dreams collectively. We hope that you enjoy reading *Modi@20: Dreams Meet Delivery* as much as we enjoyed putting it together.

Happy reading. Over to you!

BlueKraft Digital Foundation
20th February, 2022.

SECTION ONE

PEOPLE FIRST

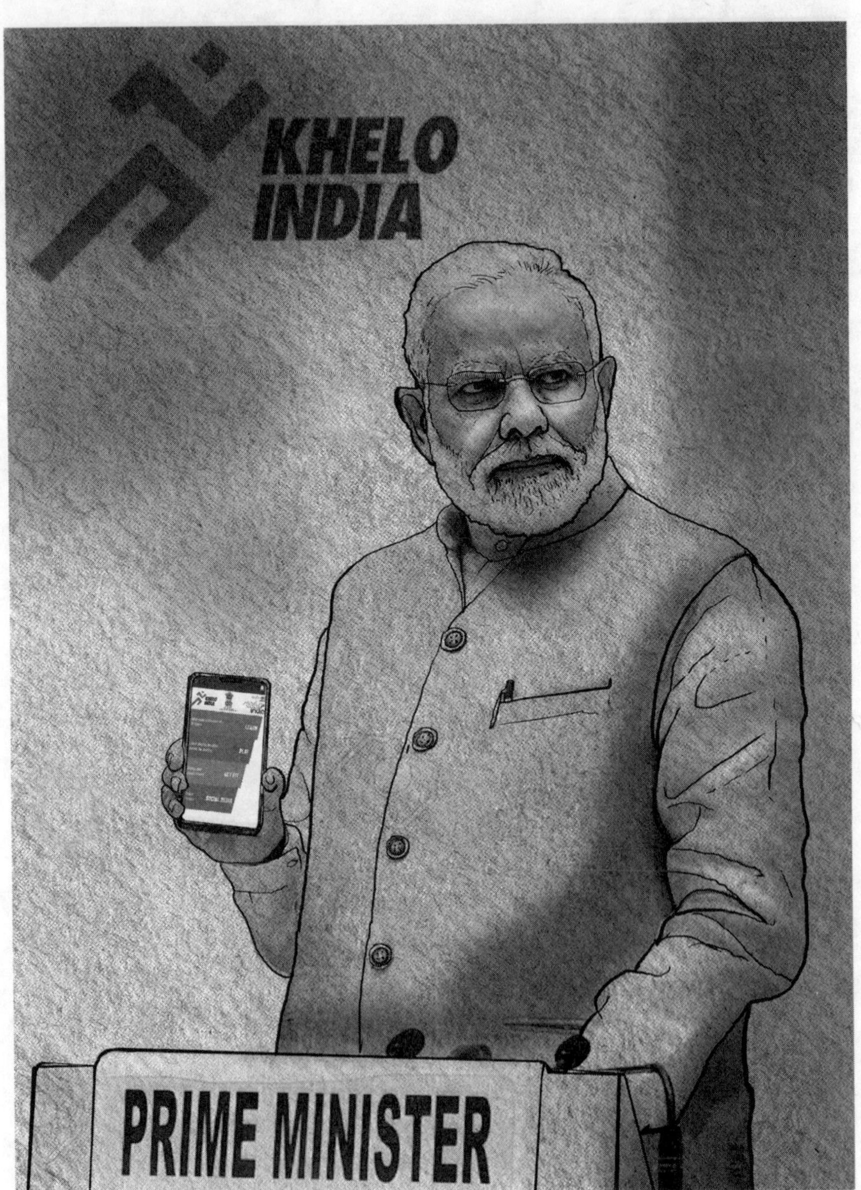
KHELO
INDIA
PRIME MINISTER

WHY MODI IS THE UNDISPUTED YOUTH ICON

P.V. SINDHU

Prime Minister Narendra Modi is among the very few undisputed youth icons of India. On that there is no debate. Or let me put it differently. If ever there had been a debate on who is among the most widely accepted, respected and recognized youth icon in present-day India, then that debate has been conclusively settled many times over, and Modi has left all his contenders far behind.

But as I began writing this chapter, the question that struck me was this: Why is that so? After all, if we go by the conventional wisdom about who can be a youth icon, then Prime Minister Modi defies the entirety of that wisdom. He is not young. He does not come from the domain of sports or cinema or popular culture or other such fields conventionally associated with youth attraction. In fact, politics—the lifelong activity that Modi has chosen as his service—is rarely associated with youth icons, at least in more recent history. And yet, he has now for almost two decades enthused the youth of our country, first in Gujarat and then the entirety of India. And he continues to do so.

I mulled over this question for many days, but the answer eluded me. While I thought and researched, one of Modi's quotes continued to reverberate in my mind. Speaking from the ramparts of the Red Fort on Independence Day in 2017, the Prime Minister had said, 'We have to leave this "*chalta hai*" attitude. We have to think of "*badal sakta hai*". This attitude will help us as a nation. We should have this confidence that with sacrifice and hard work and a resolve to do something, we will get necessary resources and the ability to do it and then a big transformation will happen, and our resolve will convert into accomplishment.'

WHAT DEFINES THE ATTITUDE OF YOUTH?

Eventually, I changed the way I was approaching the question, and then the answer seemed so natural. What is that one defining character that we most associate youth with? Age certainly, but that is biological and not necessarily a characteristic or an attitudinal quality. If I were to identify the one quality—the one attitude—that most defines youth, it would be 'fire in the belly' and the audacity to change the situation rather than compromise with it. 'How will this not happen? *Hoga kaise nahin*?' is the preeminent characteristic of any young person. It is what makes them push the boundaries, dream the impossible and make it happen.

Since millennia, it is the youth who have predominantly pushed the boundaries of human endeavour and advanced human achievements. Age certainly makes it possible to have the attitude of 'how will this not happen?' While one is young, there have not yet been too many life experiences to dim this audacity. There is time in hand to try and fail without irreversible repercussions and, therefore, try again and again till success is achieved. The boundless energy of a fresh engagement with the world, unencumbered by any past, adds further fillip to the spirit of going out there and shaping the world the way you want.

The life experiences till that age, however small they may be, further embolden the audacity. For, during adolescence and teenage, almost all the challenges that once seemed formidable—from learning to walk and talk, or mastering Maths, to playing a sport or making friends—were eventually surmounted and with a good degree of success. So, why should a youthful person not have the attitude to face the world and its problems and think of a seemingly impossible solution and then say '*hoga kaise nahin*?'

I remember my own experience when I was still in my teens—a young 18-year-old around 2013–14. This was the same season that I had won the bronze medal at the World Championship, and after the event I was asked to spell out my five-year target. I announced, with the typical confidence that comes at that age, that I want to be among the top-ranked players of the world. Many eyebrows were raised on my statement. But there I was, believing in my ability to make it happen. And I did make it happen!

However, as age advances, multiple things happen that either diminish or dim or, in some cases, completely extinguish the spirit of 'how will this not happen?' Think of a sportsperson like me. We eventually retire in what is still a relatively young age. Because, what we could do at 21, we are not able to do at 35. The same person, the same skills, better experienced, better trained. And yet the body does not support the mind and its attitude. In other cases, the vagaries of life make people adjust their ambitions, lower their expectations, compromise with situations or just learn to live with the reality of their present life. Risk-taking also diminishes with age—a person at 21 has nothing to lose, unlike a person at, say, 45 who perhaps has to think of his or her reputation built over decades, the family situation, job security and multiple other factors before taking a risk that the same person would have happily taken at 21. In essence, the experience of life moderates the spark of youth.

MODI'S IMPOSSIBLE ACHIEVEMENTS

Now think of Prime Minister Modi and some of the work he has been able to do for the nation. When he assumed office in 2014, he would have been briefed about the long pending, chronic problems that India faced since Independence. He could have also been daunted by them and given up any hopes of solving them in the near term, for they had defied solution for decades.

Not every school in the country had toilets, let alone separate toilets for girls. Not every village was electrified (18,000 plus un-electrified), let alone every house. Not every household had at least one bank account (only 58 per cent of adults had bank accounts in 2014), let alone every adult in the country. Not even 50 per cent of India was covered by safe sanitation, let alone 100 per cent. Not even the middle class was secured by accidental and life insurance, let alone the poor. Millions of poor people lived without a roof over their head. Our soldiers had been waiting for One Rank One Pension (OROP) for over four decades.

In the first year of his tenure after assuming office in 2014, toilets were constructed in every school, with separate toilets for girls. Not only every village but almost every household is now connected to the power grid. More than 108 million toilets were built by October 2019, taking safe sanitation coverage to almost 100 per cent. By the end of December 2021, Jan Dhan universalized bank accounts for the entirety of India, with the opening of over 442 million new accounts and the enrolling of over 268 million people under the Jan Suraksha Yojana by December 2021. More than 21 million concrete roof houses have been made since 2014. OROP became a reality almost five years ago.

The question I often ask myself is this: What would Modi have said in the meetings when presented with these problems? Would he not have said, 'How will these not happen—*Hoga kaise nahin*?' And then set out to chalk a detailed plan to get them done in a time-bound manner? For what other quality could have made possible such achievements and at such a scale in such a short period of time? It is not just these 20th century problems—that should have been solved long back—that Prime Minister Modi solved within just a few years of assuming office, but he has displayed the same attitude towards the 21st century issues as well.

People did ask him in 2016: How will you become the number one country in digital payments in the world when the country is poor and there is not even electricity to charge mobile phones? But India overtook China in 2018 itself to become the number one country in the world and will close 2021 with almost double the volume in millions of transactions as compared to China. Compare this to 2011, when China was ahead of India by almost four times! UPI, completely homegrown, as a digital payment ecosystem is so good that even Google recommended the US Federal Reserve to develop a similar payments ecosystem for digital payments.[1]

These are just some of the examples of what was hitherto considered impossible but has been made possible within the span of a few years during Modi's term as Prime Minister. Present to him a challenge which must be met, and he never compromises with a suboptimal result but goes for the top prize with the attitude, '*Hoga kaise nahin*?' It is this attitude—that is so unique to him—even at this age, that makes him instantly connect with the youth. The youth find in him a resonance of their self-belief, their self-image. Is there then any doubt that he has been an undisputed youth icon so consistently and for so long?

HOW IT ALL STARTED

Representing India and playing for the country in the Olympics is a rare opportunity for any sportsperson. My physical condition before the Rio Olympics was grim. From February to August 2015, for almost seven months, I was recovering from stress fracture in my left foot, and due to a foot-cast I was completely confined to the bed. During this phase, I spent many sleepless nights thinking about my condition. Many times, I would start practising impromptu, sitting on a chair, or with a Swiss ball! After my rehabilitation between September 2015 and March 2016, I participated in 22 tournaments to improve my world ranking and finally earned the thirteenth place among the top sixteen athletes who had qualified for the Olympics.

However, not once during this entire period did I ever lose the fire in my belly. The determination to rise once more and be among the best in the world had not died down. My resolve to participate and win a medal for my country kept me going. As you are all aware, I just entered the Rio Olympics as an underdog and finally ended up with the silver medal. This entire episode, in hindsight, reminds me of Prime Minister's attitude of *'hoga kaise nahin?'* whenever presented with a seemingly impossible task to achieve.

Having set my target to be the world champion, I continued my efforts in that direction and had won another silver medal at the World Championship of 2017. Over the span of a few months, I won seven silver medals in all the Super Series where I was a participant during 2017-2018. People began calling me 'Silver Sindhu' for not winning Gold! But my determined efforts yielded results, and in 2018 I won a gold medal at the prestigious World Tour Finals.

Despite my all-time record of four wins at the World Championships, the gold medal had still eluded me, and this pushed me to work out new strategies in my practice sessions. Ultimately, I won the World Championship gold medal during August 2019, thus fulfilling my long-cherished dream.

I narrated this personal experience only to elucidate the point that as youth, we have to dream big and at the same time give our best in order to achieve our dreams. And if we do both in the right measure, nothing is impossible.

After my silver medal win at the Rio Olympics, I met Prime Minister Modi on a couple of occasions, and each of those meetings was inspiring and motivating.

An incident that PM Modi narrated to me during one of these meetings from his early life is pertinent. This is from the late 1970s, after the Machchhu Dam-II failure, or the Morbi floods as it is commonly known. This disaster occurred on 11 August 1979, in what is now the Morbi district of Gujarat. Morbi was an industrial town and the flash floods induced by the dam collapse had wiped out the industrial base of the city, and with it the jobs.

As a young Swayamsevak, Modi saw the natural disaster from close quarters and had an opportunity to work with the people and help them. He had gone and camped there. In the town, he saw a pervasive sense of despair and hopelessness. In this despair, everyone was waiting for the government to do something. But Modi, even at that age, was a believer in self-reliance and in the power of bringing people together.

What he did next was amazing.

He wrote a heartfelt and inspiring letter to the people of Morbi, saying that this was their town and they had to take the lead in the aftermath of the of the disaster. He started distributing the letter door to door. Everyone knows how well Modi can inspire people with his words now, but even back then he had this gift. So, within a day, a huge number of youths were ready to take the lead in rebuilding their town. This way, Modi mobilized the power of the people. IAS officer H.K. Khan, in-charge of the flood relief effort from Gujarat government, personally praised the young Modi for his work in mobilizing the people. But Modi did not stop at just mobilizing. He ensured that the youth found a suitable role in rebuilding their own city through their voluntary efforts.

As the Prime Minister told me, he learnt at that very young age that those in power or office must trust the youth to deliver and make them a part of the delivery system, and then see the transformation they can bring. It is a lesson that he has been carrying with him since.

THE GUJARAT YEARS: HOLISTIC DEVELOPMENT

When Modi became Chief Minister of Gujarat in 2001, the youth was his special focus. Let me quote from his famous SRCC speech of 2013, which I had then watched and heard in rapt attention. 'In the education sector, we have seen a lot of growth too. When I assumed office, there were eleven universities. Today, there are 42 universities.' The *first* Forensic Science University, the *first* Raksha Shakti University and an Indian Institute of Teachers Education were some of the other major initiatives that Chief Minister Modi listed in that memorable speech. What was impressive about that address was not just the scale and breadth of the achievements that Modi listed in the education sector, but the deep thinking that went into each initiative.

My favourite initiatives from his chief ministerial days, though, are two others. The first is the Kanya Kelavani Mahotsav. Driven by his belief that 'my future was sculpted by government primary school teachers', Modi started the Kanya Kelavani and Shala Praveshotsav campaigns between 2003 and 2004. At the beginning of his tenure as Chief Minister, only three-fourth of the eligible students enrolled in local schools and just about 33 per cent of the total students completed primary education. The situation was even more dire for the girl child, with lack of basic amenities like separate toilets further adding to the woes. How could the youth in their prime, display the spunk of '*hoga kaise nahin*?' when they were not even getting basic education? And thus were born the two programmes.

Taking the learnings from his early life, Chief Minister Modi built a mass movement. Every year, in the peak summer of mid-June, the entire government machinery would move to villages, including the Chief Minister. The sole aim was to achieve the common goal of maximizing enrolment to 100 per cent, besides inspecting, marking and ensuring compliance for creating basic amenities, reducing the dropout rate to the minimum and offering a special focus on the girl child. More than 18,000 villages were covered during this campaign. The results were stunning: 100 per cent enrolment at primary level, including for girls; dropout rates touched almost zero. Within just a few years the focus shifted to improving learning outcomes and teacher quality with initiatives like the Gunotsav campaign.

The second initiative was the establishment of a Children University with the aim to develop the academic system and lifestyle on the principle of '*panchakosha*'. That the *Bhartiya* culture and *Sanskriti* were being given prime importance while still being embedded in the modern pedagogy was really inspirational.

Of course, how can I miss mentioning what Chief Minister Modi did for sports in Gujarat? Traditionally, the state has not been known for sports. But the Khel Mahakumbhs, the sustained focus on building top-class sports infrastructure across the state, the financial incentives to sportspeople including para-athletes and the personal attention that he gave to sports not only turned the state around but has immensely benefitted Indian sports, as the recent Olympics bear testimony.

But in my view, the broader reason for Modi emerging as a national youth icon, which in part helped him catapult to national leadership in 2014, was not just the work that he did for the youth in Gujarat, but something else. When Modi took over as Chief Minister in 2001, Gujarat was traditionally known as a trading state. By the end of his term—a little over 12 years—Gujarat had established itself as a manufacturing powerhouse, a global investment hub, an agricultural miracle state, an urban infra model state, the state with double-digit GDP growth rates for almost a decade, the state with the highest rankings in ease of doing business and the state that had one of the lowest unemployment rates in the country. If you dare to dream and work hard every day, then nothing is impossible! Why would Modi not become the youth icon? Or who else, other than him, would have become the youth icon?

THE PRIME MINISTER YEARS

I am not a policy person or someone who can dive deep into the intricacies of policy formulation. But I do understand the value of sustained hard work behind the scenes, away from the cameras, day after day. The world does see the final match in an Olympic contest but what the world perhaps does not see is the years of preparation that go into being able to get there to play that one match.

I remember a very special conversation about the National Education Policy that came out in 2020. The policy was in the works for almost five years. For it was about the future of our country and our youth. Why should only a few 'experts' sitting in the national capital decide what should be a national policy, and that too on such a vital subject such as education? Prime Minister Modi chose a method of consultation that was completely novel and revolutionary. More than 300,000 local elected bodies—panchayats, block-level councils, zila parishads and state governments—were consulted in what was a unique bottoms-up consultative process to frame a national policy. The process was so exhaustive and so intense that every region of the country and every stakeholder was consulted multiple times over. Prime Minister Modi himself undertook 23 detailed meetings on the issue. During the period, many ministers changed but the focus remained unwavering.

The result was a National Education Policy (NEP) which has been universally acclaimed and is futuristic—since it amalgamates our traditional strengths and cultural moorings with modern impulses. Moreover, the policy has not generated any controversy, whatsoever. It became possible because of the years of hard work, behind the camera, that went into making the NEP.

Or, consider the Target Olympic Podium Scheme (TOPS), launched soon after Modi assumed office as Prime Minister. The world has seen the stupendous results at the Tokyo Olympics, where India recorded its largest Olympic medal haul ever, and the Tokyo Paralympics—where it won more medals than all the previous medals combined. But before that, did the world really know what TOPS was? Of course, the players knew. Every aspect of a sportsperson's routine was fundamentally bettered by TOPS, but most importantly the funding and the support available for top-class training anywhere in the world, enabled by the TOPS, made a big difference. I have not yet met an athlete who does not have a good word to say about TOPS.

The institutional support that TOPS provides is of course matched in equal measure, if not bettered, by the motivational support that the Prime Minister himself provides.

For a sportsperson, there is nothing more inspiring than the Prime Minister of the country addressing him/her online or meeting him/her in person, and nudging each on of us to do better. Prime Minister Modi did it with all the Olympians, and fortunately with my parents too. Modi motivated me to give my best in the game before the Tokyo Olympics, with an added incentive that we would have ice cream on my return!

As promised, he rang up and congratulated me immediately after my bronze medal win and reminded about the ice cream when I returned. Eventually, I had that ice cream! However, like a true leader, Modi motivates not just medal winners but every sportsperson.

After winning the bronze medal at the Tokyo Olympics, I met the Prime Minister with my South Korean coach Park Tae-sang. Modi had mentioned about the historical links between Ayodhya and South Korea and encouraged my coach to visit Ayodhya. According to Korean legends, Princess Suriratna of Ayodhya had travelled to Korea some 2,000 years ago and married Kim Suro, becoming Queen Heo Hwang. The remark showed Modi's love for the roots of our culture and history.

MODI'S APPROACH TO YOUTH

It is not as if Prime Minister Modi is the only one who realizes the value of encouraging youth. Other leaders in India and abroad have also from time to time devoted their efforts in promoting youth or working/framing policies for the youth. But there is one difference that sets apart Modi's approach to the concept of youth empowerment as compared to the traditional ideas.

Conventionally, the youth are encouraged to give ideas, make suggestions, take part in discussions. However, very rarely, if ever, do they become part of the decision-making process itself or part of the system that implements those ideas. Think about it. The person most passionate about an idea is not part of the execution machinery of that same idea. Would it not likely end in below par results if not outright failure? In sports, the opposite is true. The person framing the tactics—of how to play a game or how to execute a ploy—is also the person tasked to actually execute that task. But in the world of policy and real life, things take a different turn. Youth have to inordinately wait their turn.

Modi, on the other hand, due to the learning that he got during his Morbi mass movement, has strived to bend the curve. Reversing the paradigm of only encouraging youth to voice an opinion, he has, wherever possible, put youth in decision-making positions—making them part of the system and the process.

This considered approach—of integrating youth within the system manifests itself in all domains. A few years ago, NITI Aayog organized a full-day conference where only young people were invited to present solutions to various issues confronting the country. Prime Minister Modi sat through the entire day, listening to the suggestions. This in itself would have been commendable, but it would have been a one-off effort. Instead, the best ideators among the attendees were then introduced to respective departments and secretaries to work out the ideas they presented. From merely voicing ideas, they now had a hand in shaping their execution as well.

From key appointments within his political party, the BJP, to appointing key ministers and Chief Ministers and from giving responsibilities to key lateral professionals to institutionalizing young professionals' entry into policymaking, the trust placed on the youth is unmistakable.

EXPANSION IN CAPACITY

Trust in the youth goes hand in hand with creating the right environment to train and educate our youth so that more children are equipped to compete with the best in the world.

The expansion in capacity in the past few years, with this thought in mind, has been compelling. There were sixteen IITs in the country in 2014; there are twenty-three now. As of 2014, there were only nine IIITs; in the subsequent years, sixteen IIITs have been established. Since 2014, seven new IIMs have been established. Similarly, there were only seven branches of AIIMS till 2014. Since 2014, fifteen more AIIMS branches have been approved.[2]

Over 8,700 Atal Tinkering Labs have been established under the Atal Innovation Mission, ensuring education and exposure to cutting-edge science and technology. At least 15,000 new model world-class schools under NEP, a hundred new Sainik Schools and 750 Eklavya Model Residential Schools are being set up. Expansion of the ITI network, the backbone of skill education has now reached 14,939 centres.

The Fit India Movement and the Khelo India University Games, following the Khelo India Youth Games,[3] have inculcated the concept of both the fitness and the importance of sports as a viable career in thousands of youths and both the programmes have been immensely successful.

THE FUTURE

As we look towards the future beyond the pandemic and the role that India can play at the world stage, I would like to quote Modi on the potential our youth. Speaking in 2013, before he became the Prime Minister, Chief Minister Modi said, 'Fifteen years back, I went to Taiwan for a tour. My interpreter hesitantly asked me if we were really a land of snake charmers. I replied that we no more have the courage to hold snakes and, therefore, we are now a land of mouse charmers. With the click of a mouse, our youth are able to reach the remotest corner of the world, and it is these young citizens and not politicians who have brought laurels to motherland. The world is now looking at India with a fresh lens.'[4]

Traditionally, we have believed that all that our youth need is an opportunity and they can be the best in the world. That is certainly true. But let me add a qualifier. If led by a leader, who thinks and acts like the youth—who has the fire in the belly like a young person—then not just the youth but the entirety of India has what it takes to be the best in the world.

Just look at what we have achieved when we put our mind to it.

1. The largest start-up ecosystem in the world with maximum unicorns in 2021—more than any other country in the world.
2. The largest vaccination drive in the world to combat the COVID-19 pandemic and setting the largest single day record for administering vaccine doses—over 25 million.
3. Successfully ending the dividing line of Article 370 and uniting our lands while keeping the world opinion on our side.
4. The world's best digital architecture—from DBT funds during the pandemic to vaccine certification.
5. The rising profile of Indian sports—from athletics, badminton, hockey to cricket—that have grown in leaps and bounds over the years.

All of this was achieved by the hard work of our scientists, sportpersons, security forces, innovators, medical professionals, doctors, engineers, and our youth.

The Prime Minister has given a special task to us sportspersons as well. During the breakfast meeting at his residence, he took a promise from all the Olympians—that all of us will visit at least 75 primary schools and colleges each by the Independence Day in 2023, spread the message of awareness against malnutrition and play a sport with schoolchildren so that they feel inspired.

His message focuses the importance he has given to the nutritious diet of youth—our future nation-builders. Similarly, by playing and mingling with them, we will motivate them to do their best in their given fields. This clearly shows Prime Minister Modi's commitment and vision for the youth of this country, to inculcate in our youth the feeling that they can be the best in the world.

As the world looks at India with fresh enthusiasm after the pandemic, the energy of our youth and the vision of our 'young' Prime Minister holds immense potential in what I believe will be the best years for India.

NEW GRAMMAR OF WOMEN EMPOWERMENT

SHOBANA KAMINENI

'Beti Bachao Beti Padhao.' These four words are set to create a staggering impact and have the potential to unlock the next wave of unparalleled growth in our country. As Indians, over the years, we have achieved so much to be justifiably proud of. However, it's also true that millions of women of our country are yet to reach the potential that they are capable of.

Historically, women have had to fight an uphill battle for their rights and recognition, across the globe, and especially so in our country. But now things are changing rapidly and generations of brave and talented women are forging ahead on the road to equality with vision, talent, courage and hard work.

Prime Minister Narendra Modi's mission to nurture a brighter future for women is a massive fillip in this long march of women empowerment in India. The timing could not be more perfect—as India charges ahead to becoming a democratic and inclusive superpower, a model that the world will emulate, we need our women to be creators, entrepreneurs, achievers and leaders.

WHY EQUALITY IS NON-NEGOTIABLE

Why is it desirable that women should be empowered? There are several reasons, but the most compelling are moral, biological, economic and legal. Women have been discriminated against for thousands of years. Society now has the knowledge and the moral responsibility to reverse those historical wrongs. Women bring human life to our planet and nurture that life to become productive members of the society. This is a powerful reason by itself. On a fundamental level, women form almost half the world population and should, therefore, be contributing proportionally to the world's economic well-being.

#NARI SHAKTI

Prime Minister Modi invoked the indomitable spirit of Nari Shakti by reaffirming how India fully endorsed the United Nations in its 'think equal, build smart, innovate for change' motto with regard to women empowerment. He added, 'whenever women got an opportunity, they made India proud and further strengthened it.' Take, for example, the Olympics held in Tokyo in 2021; P.V. Sindhu, Saikhom Mirabai Chanu and Lovlina Borgohain made India proud by winning medals at the Olympics. Though the Indian hockey team narrowly missed the bronze medal, they made a mark in world women's hockey with their gritty performance.

India is now determined to provide equal opportunities for self-employment and employment to women. Today, women work in coal mines, fly fighter planes and there is no area that is beyond their reach. The Prime Minister sent out a strong message that, for him, good governance was all about walking the talk, tackling the issue at hand head-on, with no ifs and buts. Whatever needed to be done had to be done, and without the fear of criticism.

A COURAGEOUS LEADER

Modi ji has demonstrated immense focus on championing the development of women. At times, he has been vociferously critical of traditional, entrenched attitudes. Despite being a political figure who may face a backlash if traditionalists feel offended, he has gone ahead and spoken his mind. In this world, where political opponents take advantage of ancient entrenched positions, he has shown immense courage by speaking his mind. Even as Chief Minister of Gujarat, he led mass movements to end the malpractice of female foeticide. To address it in a concerted manner, soon after he took charge as the Prime Minister of India, on the occasion of International Day of the Girl Child on 11 October 2014, he described female foeticide as a 'matter of deep shame' and asked the people to pledge to end gender-based discrimination and create an atmosphere of equality for girls.

He had also invited people to share their ideas for the 'Beti Bachao Beti Padhao' campaign on the MyGov website, and added that we must celebrate the achievements of our daughters, from classroom to sports so that they shine everywhere. He also tweeted and asked India to pledge to create an atmosphere of equality for the girl child to ensure there was no discrimination based on gender. He believed that we must work together to remove this menace from the society[1].

In 2014, this marked a new beginning that started with a clarion call from a leader elected with an overwhelming mandate. It ushered in a paradigm shift in saving the girl child, and the results speak for the success of the measures undertaken so far. The sex ratio of India has witnessed a substantial rise in urban areas. The corresponding ratio was 922 in 2011–12 which rose to 965 in 2017–18. Out of 640 districts covered under the Beti Bachao Beti Padhao (BBBP) Scheme, 422 districts have shown improvement in SRB (sex ratio at birth) from 2014–15 to 2018–2019. The first trimester antenatal care (ANC) registration has shown an improving trend from 61 per cent in 2014–15 to 71 per cent in 2019-20. The institutional deliveries show an improving trend from 87 per cent in 2014–15 to 94 per cent in 2019–20.

EDUCATION FOR THE GIRL CHILD

Education lays the foundation for the economic development of a nation by empowering people and creating a strong, skilled workforce. This is especially true when it is about educating the girl child, since education gives them the knowledge to make informed decisions, boosts their confidence and independence by providing skills to change their lives, helps them earn a living and support themselves. Education of the girl child also leads to a reduction in gender violence and is a stepping stone to ending gender-based discrimination and inequality.

Modi ji's focus on educating the girl child has been evident throughout his service to the state of Gujarat and the country. As Chief Minister, he had given the concept of 'Panchamrut' as a path for future development. Derived from Sanskrit, 'Panch' meaning five and 'Amrut' meaning nectar of the gods, he emphasized the power of knowledge or gyan shakti as one of the five key ingredients in his Panchamrut for development. This insight provided the impetus for the launch of several innovative programmes such as the Kanya Kelavani Nidhi (Girl Child Education) and Shala Praveshotsav (School Enrolment Drive) to promote girl child education in Gujarat.

His drive and hands-on approach was visible in his not being content with guiding policies, but personally ensuring their implementation on the ground. Over three days in June 2011, nine years after the launch of the programmes, Chief Minister Modi ensured that, along with himself, other ministers, secretaries, government officials and people's leaders visited schools in 18,000 villages, 151 municipalities and eight municipal corporations to further encourage education[2]. Before leaving Gujarat to take up the mantle of the Prime Minister of India, he set a personal example by donating ₹21 lakh (₹2.1 million) from his personal savings to create a corpus fund for educating daughters of drivers and peons working with the Gujarat government[3].

Beti Bachao Beti Padhao was envisaged to protect the girl child from foeticide and also provide her with a life of dignity and opportunity. Launched in 2015, the scheme with multi-sectoral District Action Plans as well as innovative social media initiatives like 'Selfie with Daughter' has shown positive results, with much progress in ensuring a transformational shift in the way society looks at the girl child. The Sukanya Samriddhi Yojana, launched as part of Beti Bachao Beti Padhao initiative, to facilitate the education of the girl child, has already reached out to more than three crore (30 million) aspirational young women.

The Swachh Bharat Mission under his leadership has resulted in 1,467,679 schools now having a functioning girls' toilet, an increase of 4.17 percentage points in comparison to 2013-14[4], giving an impetus to the enrolment of girls. The Ministry of Human Resource Development has also sanctioned 5,930 Kasturba Gandhi Balika Vidyalayas, or residential schools for girls that gives a larger number of girls access to quality education.

The Constitution (Eighty-sixth Amendment) Act, 2002, had resulted in the addition of Article 21A to the Constitution of India to provide free and compulsory education of all children in the age group of six to fourteen years as a Fundamental Right. It has been over a decade now since the Right to Education (RTE) Act came into being, and there has been significant progress, seen especially under Modi ji's guidance. As per the Annual Status of Education Report (ASER) Survey, the percentage of girls out of school between the ages of eleven and fourteen years has shown a steady decline from 10.3 in 2006 to 4.1 in 2018[5] and falling further even in a pandemic year to 3.9 per cent in 2021.

The same holds true for the girls of ages fifteen to sixteen years, with the out-of-school percentage falling from 20 per cent in 2008 to 13.5 per cent in 2018, and further to 7.1 per cent in 2021. The ASER Survey 2020 also shows a rise in girls' enrolment in government schools—with the percentage rising from 70 per cent in 2018 to 73 per cent in 2020[6]. The National Education Policy, 2020, now proposes to increase the ambit of the RTE Act for children from three to eighteen years of age.

With the Prime Minister saluting the girl child #DeshKiBeti (daughter of the country) on National Girl Child Day in 2021, we can rest assured that the drive to educate the girl child will continue under his progressive leadership.

ENABLING EQUALITY

As a champion of gender equality, Modi ji has not shirked from leading from the front, and he has been cognizant of the fact that empowering women is not just about gender equality and gender justice. It also means more jobs, equal opportunities for growth and entrepreneurship, higher safety, protection of the children and, most importantly, just 'letting women be'. If there is one leader who has recognized women for what they are and who they are, it is Prime Minister Modi. Whether it is by providing free cooking gas via the famous PM Ujjwala Yojana, or by financial inclusion, or by enabling women to leverage technology, a slew of schemes have been launched in recent years to empower women on the path of self-reliance.

Likewise, unleashing the entrepreneurial spirit within women has been a cornerstone in his vision for women-led development. As Chief Minister of Gujarat, he declared that women power would drive growth. He has been the enabler of women's financial empowerment. The zeal for promoting women entrepreneurship increased in scale upon his becoming

Prime Minister. Programmes such as the Jan Dhan, MUDRA and Stand-Up India have given a big boost to women entrepreneurship over the years.

Noticing that the women of India, especially the poor, suffered from financial exclusion, he took it upon his government to ensure that this anomaly was rectified with the launch of Jan Dhan Yojana (JDY). Since 2014, more than twenty-four crore (240 million) bank[7] accounts have been opened for women, giving them financial independence and enabling them to access formal credit and other services of the banking system. The success of JDY was also witnessed during the lockdown when the government was able to swiftly transfer money into women's accounts under the Direct Benefit Transfer (DBT) Mission.

Another noteworthy initiative which was launched in 2010, when he was the Chief Minister, was Mission Mangalam, an endeavour to integrate self-help groups (SHGs) with the corporate value chain[8]. Never before has a state been witness to a programme like this. It helped congregate self-help groups to strengthen their administrative structures and engage with credit institutions to enhance their livelihood prospects. This one-of-a-kind initiative in the country not only sought to ensure that women SHGs were formed to provide livelihoods for women, but it also meant to help them thrive by creating industry linkages for SHGs[9]. It was a forerunner to the MUDRA scheme.

Modi ji's efforts have always been on removing roadblocks that inhibit the growth of female entrepreneurship and their participation in the Indian economy. Amongst the many big-bang reforms, one that stands out for its sheer scale, size, reach and the manner in which it has revolutionized the lives of millions of Indian women is the Pradhan Mantri MUDRA Yojana (PMMY). About 70 per cent[10] of the beneficiaries are women, especially those belonging to the marginalized sections of the society. The scheme has helped in generating sixty-nine lakh (6.9 million) additional employment positions for women from 2015 to 2018[11]. But nothing explains the success more than some of the real-life stories available in the public domain. One such story is of Kiran Kumari from Bokaro, Jharkhand, who was once a hawker and is now a proud owner of a toy-and-gift shop after receiving a loan of ₹2 lakh[12] or ₹2,00,000.

Similarly, Stand-Up India was launched to boost entrepreneurship and as of early March 2021, 81 per cent of its beneficiaries were women[13]. An important aspect of the Modi ji government's flagship schemes—be it Jan Dhan, MUDRA or the Awas Yojana—is the overwhelming participation of women. This has secured socio-economic dignity, providing women with a strong foundation to make their own destiny. Provisions to ensure more credit access to SHGs, MSMEs and start-ups, laws ensuring safer workplace and fair wages have eased the way for women to enter into workforce and take up jobs of their own choice.

HEALTH AND WELL-BEING OF WOMEN

It is a fact that healthier women are pivotal contributors to healthier economies and, therefore, it is paramount that a nation perseveres to safeguard their health and well-being. Moreover, belonging to a pioneering healthcare family, I have witnessed the devastating impact of ill-health up close, and I am well aware of how the untimely loss of a woman disrupts an entire family.

It was an unfortunate reality that in certain segments of Indian society, the health of the women in the household was often not given the priority it deserved. But thankfully, over the past few years, there has been a decline in such retrogressive practices with women today shining nationally as well as internationally and bringing laurels to the country. A similar positive change is reflected in their health indices as well.

While, earlier women's health only received attention during pregnancy and immediately after delivery, there is now a shift to a 360-degree approach that addresses all health concerns of women, encompassing not just maternal health and nutrition but also menstrual health, sanitation, access to clean air and basic clean sanitation.

The government's efforts under the leadership of Prime Minister Modi have led to remarkable improvements in women's health, especially and access to sanitation. In his Independence Day address to the nation in 2020, he once again offered his insights into different aspects of women's health when he spoke about enabling access to menstrual hygiene products. Not restricted to words alone, this was followed by action on the ground with over 111 million sanitary pads delivered to poor women, from more than 8,578 Janaushadhi Kendras (as of mid-December 2021) at just ₹1 each[14].

The government's policies and programmes have also taken into account the worldwide change in issues affecting women's health with non-communicable diseases (NCDs) becoming the leading cause of death for women worldwide[15].

Ayushman Mahila was launched to encourage women, especially from rural areas, to come forward for screening of diseases such as cancer. This will help in early diagnosis and contribute to reducing morbidity and mortality from NCDs. With the creation of Health and Wellness Centres across the country, over 14.8 crore (148 million) women have benefitted from this initiative.

Modi ji also addressed an issue that had been ignored for many decades: the health hazards faced by women who cook in poorly-ventilated kitchens using wood, cow-dung and charcoal that emit hazardous gases and chemicals which have an adverse impact on health. The Ujjwala Yojana has ensured clean fuel and clean air within homes, thereby, enabling women to work without the fear of developing respiratory and other illnesses.

While these progressive initiatives have ensured that aspects of women's health ignored for decades are addressed, the basic issues of maternal health continue to be strengthened. In 2017, the Pradhan Mantri Matru Vandana Yojana (PMMVY) ensured that a direct benefit transfer (DBT) scheme for pregnant women and lactating mothers supported them in meeting their enhanced nutritional needs. In FY20, the scheme achieved a momentous milestone by benefiting one crore (10 million) women. Multiple supplementary nutrition programmes under the Poshan Abhiyan (Nutrition Campaign) were merged, and Poshan Abhiyaan 2.0 was launched to strengthen nutritional delivery.

Making safe pregnancy a mass movement, the Pradhan Mantri Surakshit Matritva Abhiyan has ensured safe and healthy antenatal care with private doctor services for free check-ups each month. This allows early detection of issues and risks relating to pregnancy. Over 3.02 crore (30.2 million) antenatal check-ups have been conducted at healthcare facilities across the country with the identification and treatment of 25.46 lakh (2.546 million) high-risk pregnancies, as of early December 2021. These initiatives have resulted in the Maternal Mortality Rate (MMR) falling from 167 per 100,000 live births in 2011–2013 to 113 per 100,000 live births in 2016–18. Mission Indradhanush launched in 2014 has also ensured targeted vaccination of women and has set a new paradigm in preventive healthcare. All these decisive steps and investments in women's health are improving access to healthcare for Indian women. What was once a distant dream is now becoming a reality!

DIGNITY, FULCRUM OF EMPOWERMENT

One of the fundamental rights of every woman is the right to live in dignity, free of fear of violence, coercion or discrimination on account of gender. Prime Minister Modi was refreshingly unique in reiterating that violence against women was not inevitable and that it required families and communities to change their social norms and attitudes.

In his very first Independence Day speech in 2014, he ushered in the need when he said, 'I want to ask every parent that if you have a daughter, you are always on the alert; every now and then you keep on asking her, "Where are you going?" or "When will you come back?" or "Inform immediately after you reach". Parents ask their daughters hundreds of questions, but do parents ask their son as to where he is going, why he is going out, who his friends are? This is important as man who commits a crime against a woman is also somebody's son and, therefore, the change must begin with parents.'

Clearly, since 2014, the country has witnessed a lot of change, and Prime Minister Modi has changed the lens through which women's issues are traditionally looked at. He has worked to expand the basket of rights entitled to women across all areas. From empowering Muslim women by criminalizing triple talaq to scrapping discriminatory provisions against women in Jammu and Kashmir with the abrogation of Article 370 and 35A and enforcing laws against child marriage in Jammu and Kashmir, he has worked to bring women on an even keel with respect to rights guaranteed to them under the Constitution. Further, the rights of pregnant women have also been expanded with Medical Termination of Pregnancy Act (Amendment) Bill, 2020, raising the upper limit for abortion to twenty-four weeks for particular categories of women. By allowing abortion up to twenty-four weeks of gestational age for vulnerable categories of women and with no limit of gestational age in case of pregnancies with substantial foetal abnormalities, a medical solution that women in our country have long sought for decades has finally been provided.

WOMEN-LED DEVELOPMENT

In charting new India's growth story, Prime Minister Modi has emphasized that India was transitioning from women's development to 'women-led development'.

The newly-passed labour laws include provisions that enable female employees to work in various kinds of roles and also in night shifts with adequate protection. Equal wages to women have also been guaranteed under the Labour Code on Wages. In a major step that enabled women to find a proper work-life balance, the Maternity Benefits Act was amended by the Modi government to raise fully paid maternity leave from twelve weeks to twenty-six weeks for women working in the organized sector, thus enabling them to recuperate fully before coming back to work[16].

Alongside this, to promote gender equality in the workplace, the 2013 Companies Act made it compulsory for all publicly listed firms in India to have at least one female director. In the past five years, the median number of women on Indian boards doubled, and this increase in diversity has not been restricted only to corporate India. After the recent Cabinet reshuffle in the country, there are eleven women ministers in the Modi government. This underlines a commitment to include diverse perspectives, and walk the talk.

One of the first principles of managing a business that I learnt and imbibed from my father, Dr Prathap C. Reddy, founder-chairman of Apollo Hospitals, is that addressing the challenges of the nation was just as much the responsibility of corporate leaders as it was of the administrators. I carried this lesson with me even in 2017, when I took the helm as the first woman president of the Confederation of Indian Industry (CII), which was instituted 125 years ago. It was a great honour and an equally great responsibility. To chart the course ahead, I knew that the path would have to be forged with the immeasurable power of partnerships of working with the government.

Therefore, the focus was 'India Ahead, India Together and an Inclusive India'[17]. One of my very first priorities was to realize the potential of women in the Indian economy. I suggested measures for the addition of 25 per cent of women to the workforce, as I believed that the move could create a $750 billion increase in India's GDP. As president of the industry body, I had the privilege of meeting PM Modi at several events and observed that he was so passionate about creating greater access for the women of India[18].

In the present day, it is a matter of pride that Indian women have been granted permanent commission in all branches of the Armed Forces and have been inducted as fighter pilots in both the Navy and Air Force. In May 2021, the Army inducted the first batch of women into the Corps of Military Police, thus enabling women to serve in combat positions[19]. On Independence Day 2021, the Prime Minister also said that girls would now be given entry into Sainik schools across the country[20].

It is a matter of great pride that our women are in the forefront of science and technology. The recent Chandrayaan-2 mission was a case of women-led development, as it was headed by two of our eminent space scientists, Muthyya Vanitha as project director and Ritu Karidhal as mission director. This marked a first for the Indian Space Research Organisation (ISRO). 30 per cent of the Chandrayaan-2 team was constituted by women[21].

On the morning of 31 August 2021, Justices Hima Kohli, B.V. Nagarathna and Bela Trivedi were sworn in as Supreme Court judges, marking a first in Indian history that three women judges were elevated to the Supreme Court together. Further, it improves the likelihood that we may get the first female Chief Justice of India in 2027—from among these three legal icons. The appointment of the trio provided a major boost to the number of women judges at the Supreme Court. It was a celebration of female representation at the highest judicial body and also the highest court of India.

WAY FORWARD

An exciting vista is opening up in front of us and women are playing their role in building this great nation. Modi ji's vision recognizes that women-led development holds the potential to create positive outcomes across multiple sectors. In a sense, the achievement of the targets under Sustainable Development Goal 5: 'Gender Equality', also facilitates the realization of other SDGs and, thus, ensures multi-pronged holistic development.

Ultimately, the finest barometer of leadership is the ability to create lasting change, usher in transformation that will resonate for generations and Prime Minister Modi's efforts are a gold standard against this metric.

बेटी बचाओ
बेटी पढ़ाओ

SUCCESS OF PEOPLE-CENTRIC APPROACH

SURJIT S. BHALLA*

Narendra Modi has won every major election he has contested—three as Chief Minister of Gujarat, once as a prime ministerial candidate and once as incumbent Prime Minister.

In his first Gujarat elections (September 2002), it was widely conjectured, if not expected, that he would lose post the Godhra riots. In the end, he won with large majorities (two-thirds of the seats) in the election, and repeated the performance in 2007 and 2012.

It is noteworthy that in the two national elections (2014 and 2019), he was not considered a favourite. His candidature was met with considerable doubt—whether his Gujarat success could be repeated on the national stage. Indeed, a few months before the May 2019 elections, there was a widespread belief that even if the BJP won a plurality of votes, he would be replaced as Prime Minister. (My book, *Citizen Raj*, published two months before the 2019 election had correctly and boldly forecast that Modi would win the election on his own strength). He not only won handily but also became the first incumbent (since 1971) to win a national re-election with a majority of his own.

The Modi phenomena is what we wish to examine in this chapter. What are the determinants of his success? Is there a pattern, or a consistency, to his vision? What are the lessons that historians will draw from his now nearly two-decade old political tenure in the top echelons of the Bharatiya Janata Party? This chapter will not provide answers to all these

*Executive Director, IMF, for India, Bangladesh, Bhutan and Sri Lanka

questions, but it is a beginning towards exploring the exceptional nature of his political success.

A key feature of his tenure, both at the state and at the Centre, has been his concentration on development and programmes for the poor. The poor have theoretically been at the centre of policy for most of India's Prime Ministers; remember that *garibi hatao* was Indira Gandhi's calling card. The difference between Modi and other Prime Ministers has been that the theory has been put into *effective* practice. This may be the most important factor behind Modi's extraordinary political success.

This aspect needs documentation and we provide that from the evidence obtained from his Gujarat and national tenures. Modi was Chief Minister of Gujarat from October 2001 to May 2014.

Education, water, girl child, sanitation, poverty reduction—all have been targets of Modi and all with an over-arching emphasis on delivery.

A broad brush reveals the following about Modi. His humble background shaped him to think more, and act more, on behalf of those less fortunate—let us say the bottom half or bottom two-thirds of the population (hereafter Modi's target constituency). Every one of his initiatives, from Beti Bachao Beti Padhao to demonetization to formulation of long overdue farm laws, has the target constituency in mind. That has been the litmus test of his economic policies. In 1985, then Prime Minister Rajiv Gandhi famously (and correctly) declared that only 15 per cent of the monies (food) meant for the poor reached the poor (via the public distribution system (PDS) of food grains). Under Modi, the successful targeting of the beneficiaries through Aadhar, long delayed implementation of One Nation One Ration Card (ONORC), and the use of direct benefit transfers (DBTs) has meant that leakage is no longer a sink for government programmes meant (but not delivered) to the poor.

There is a belief that runs through his policies, mingled with a strong dose of confidence. As observers we can speculate as to where the belief and confidence comes from. In terms of background, note that Modi is the second non-elite, non-Brahmin to assume the premiership (Deve Gowda was the first) unlike Nehru, Shastri, Indira Gandhi, Rajiv Gandhi, V.P. Singh and Vajpayee. If the leaders were not Brahmin (like V.P. Singh, Manmohan Singh) they were part of the 'ruling elite'. Modi has the confidence because he, unlike the other Prime Ministers, identifies with the people; he understands their trials, their poverty, and their aspirations. And that is almost a guarantee for political success, and success as a leader whom people want to follow.

In the next few sections, we will let his record of delivery and targeting speak for itself. We first document his experience as Chief Minister of Gujarat, and how a study of Gujarat administration is necessary for guidance towards his success as Prime Minister. His policies have emphasized on the delivery of benefits to the poor and those who have been discriminated against—women. Hence, the observation that women have been the prime beneficiaries of Modi's development programmes. We next document how the post-pandemic response of the Modi government was to provide large income (food) transfers to the poor, and how these transfers were likely enough to keep individuals from dropping into extreme poverty. Next, we discuss how PM Modi's government instituted major economic reforms during the pandemic crisis—and how they were one of the very few countries to do so. We then assess India's efforts, and performance, on climate mitigation.

POOR AND WOMEN AS TARGETS

If the poor are targeted, then it has to be the case that women have to be doubly targeted. Because throughout history, and around the world, women have been discriminated against. In India, the discrimination has also taken uglier forms, in the form of female infanticide earlier, and lately, starting in the mid-eighties, with the availability of technology, female foeticide.

Very early on as Chief Minister of Gujarat, Modi initiated the Kanya Kelavani scheme—education for all, and especially for the girl child. Boys also lacked education, but girls lacked it more. The Periodic Labour Force Survey of 2019-2020 (the re-named NSSO survey) reports that the average educational attainment of females aged 15-24 years was 9.7 years—and that of males of the same age was 9.7 years. Just thirty years ago (1993/94) young men had an average educational attainment level of 6.3 years, two years more than the attainment of young women. A decade earlier, in 2011-12, the gap was 0.7 years. In 2018, there were more women college students than men in India. This progress/development is the biggest transition known to man or womankind.

A combination of both goals—education and attack on girl foeticide—came in the form of the *Beti Bachao Beti Padhao* national campaign launched from the Red Fort as a major focus of his *first* Independence Day Speech as Prime Minister. Are there any clues (leading indicators) for the policy initiatives undertaken by Modi as Prime Minister from his experience as Chief Minister?

Yes—and we obtain evidence from the Modi policies in Gujarat from 2002 to 2012. Recall that he won three successive terms, and each with a resounding majority. It stands to conjecture that the people benefitted, therefore applauded, and re-voted Modi as Chief Minister. How much difference the Modi initiatives made in Gujarat governance and development is provided by the data presented in Table 1. The data are based on state-level data for the nine-year period prior to Modi assuming his role as Chief Minister in 2001, 1992–2001, and the eleven-year period post his arrival, 2002–2012. The dates are chosen to also conform with the availability of National Sample Surveys for 1993, 1999, and 2011–12 (used for analysis of trends in absolute poverty). This is a state-level analysis, and our goal is to assess Gujarat's performance in the period when Modi was not the Chief Minister versus when he was at the helm in Gujarat.

Development is a complex phenomenon and various factors, besides leadership, affect change. Nevertheless, as students of policy, we have to both understand and evaluate performance in order to glean inferences about economic change (which automatically leads to inferences and understanding) of political change. We want to understand the basis of Modi's popularity, which in a democracy, is based on his performance as perceived by the people. And people by and large are swayed by evidence.

So, what does the evidence show? Gujarat under Modi performed significantly better on all the living standard indicators than Gujarat not under Modi, since we are interested in the rate of change in indicators for the two periods, we have to consider the possibility that the whole class does well—as it did between 2002 and 2012. So how is 'better' defined in these circumstances? By looking at excess growth, i.e. the difference in growth between Gujarat and states composed of two other classifications, and excess growth with two other comparators. The two comparators are (i) all Big states excluding Gujarat, and (ii) five 'progressive' and/or rich states: Haryana, Kerala, Maharashtra, Punjab and Tamil Nadu.

Per capita growth in state domestic product—this is considered to be the most important test of performance—during his tenure, growth exceeded others by a hefty margin (1.7 per cent per year over other Big states; and 1.4 per cent a year over comparable states). In the earlier non-Modi period, Gujarat lagged comparable states by 0.3 per cent a year.

Extreme Poverty (defined as per the Tendulkar poverty line, also equal to World Bank $1.9 a day per person in 2011 PPP). Poverty declined by less in Gujarat in the earlier period (and consistent with the experience on growth). In the second period, all states do well with poverty reduction, but in comparison with other Big states, there is significantly greater decline in the Modi era especially for the poorest—SC/STs and Muslims.

Living standard indicators—sex ratio at birth, fertility, and infant mortality decline for boys and girls—improved in Gujarat and especially so in the Modi period. Sex ratio at birth—all states show an improvement in the sex ratio (improvement is equal to less foeticide).

I-DAY SPEECHES AS HARBINGERS OF CHANGE

A good predictor of what Modi will do are his Independence Day speeches. The first one in 2014, launched the Beti Bachao Beti Padhao (save the daughter, educate the girl child) programme. It was explicitly aimed at changing the centuries old practice of foeticide, infanticide, sex-selective abortions and large-scale discrimination against girls (and women) in India.

Two years later, this vision was formally articulated in Modi's 2016 Independence Speech.

'If we ensure two things for our mothers and sisters, i.e. economic empowerment and empowerment against health problems and we educate them, you can take it as an assurance that if even a single woman is educated in the family, if she is strong physically and independent economically, she has power to pull the poorest of the poor family out of poverty and therefore *we are working with emphasis on empowerment of women, health of women, economic prosperity of women, physical empowerment of women in our fight against poverty*.'

Hence, it is not surprising that most of the major and most successful schemes of the Modi government are targeted at easing the lives of the poor, empowering them, and removing hurdles from their path to reach their full potential. And the major schemes of the Modi government have women as the prime beneficiaries.

Caste and gender, a new paradigm, as well as poverty and gender—not that caste is not relevant but it explains little; gender perhaps explains a lot. The way to political victory is through the vote of the not so well off and women!

In his first speech as Prime Minister, Modi shocked the audience by openly talking about open defecation. This has long been a concern of health experts, and women. For long it was noted by scholars that India's young had a worse record on health indicators like stunting and wasting than many of the considerably poorer countries of sub-Saharan Africa. Both logically and empirically, there is a strong link between health and sanitation. Yet this link was ignored by all the previous Prime Ministers, and sanitation reform was *not* considered a policy option by many (indeed all) of them.

This link was soon anchored through the Swachh Bharat Mission (SBM). The Swachh Bharat programme is another empowerment programme which primarily benefits women.

The major goal of this programme was to make India open defecation free (ODF) by 2 October 2019, the one hundred and fiftieth birth anniversary of Mahatma Gandhi, the original proponent of a Clean India. (Unfortunately, the political leaders had forgotten Gandhi's message as they proceeded to make India modern and prosperous but without considering improvements in sanitation. Toilets were clearly not considered vote-worthy.)

Performance of Gujarat versus other Big States: 1992-2012

	Big States	Comparable States	Gujarat	*Excess Growth Gujarat* Big States	*Comparable*
Per Capita GDP growth					
Period 1 (1992-2001)	2.9	3.7	3.4	0.5	-0.3
Period 2 (2003-2012)	6.2	6.5	7.9	1.7	1.4
Extreme Poverty change (All)					
Period 1 (1993-1999)	-3.9	-8.5	-1.8	2.1	6.7
Period 2 (1999-2011)	-18.3	-16.7	-19.6	-1.3	-2.9
Extreme Poverty change (SC+ST)					
Period 1 (1993-1999)	-4	-10.8	5.8	9.8	16.6
Period 2 (1999-2011)	-24.1	-23.3	-27.9	-3.8	-4.6
Extreme Poverty change (Muslims)					
Period 1 (1993-1999)	-8.5	-6.5	-3.6	4.9	2.9
Period 2 (1999-2011)	-21.4	-28.2	-28.1	-6.7	0.1
Sex Ratio at Birth (percent Change)					
Period 1 (1992-2001)	-0.31	-0.32	-0.32	-0.01	0
Period 2 (2003-2012)	-0.42	-0.49	-0.55	-0.13	-0.1
Fertility Rate Decline					
Period 1 (1992-2001)	-1.7	-1.7	-0.8	0.9	0.9
Period 2 (2003-2012)	-2.4	-2	-2.1	0.3	-0.1
Infant Mortality Rate Decline (Male)					
Period 1 (1992-2001)	-2.6	-3.9	-1.8	0.8	2.1
Period 2 (2003-2012)	-4.1	-4	-4.2	-0.1	-0.2
Infant Mortality Rate Decline (Female)					

Period 1 (1992-2001)	-1.8	-1.2	-0.4	1.4	0.8
Period 2 (2003-2012)	-3.8	-4.8	-5.3	-1.5	-0.5

Notes: Period 1 is when Modi is not Chief Minister of Gujarat; Period 2 is when he is CM of Gujarat.

Extreme Poverty is defined as poverty according to the Tendulkar poverty line (also $1.9 a day in 2011 PPP).

All rates are averages of annual percent changes; poverty change is in terms of change in percent poor.

Comparable states are Haryana, Kerala, Maharashtra, Punjab and Tamil Nadu.

Both socially and politically, the ODF India initiative was a bold one. It was a surprise to all—the fact that a word that is taboo in everyday conversation—'defecation'—was openly discussed, and by the PM no less. This was not what the elite, especially the upper-class elite belonging to the 'in the name of the poor' group, had discussed even in private, let alone in public. Hence, policies to reduce open defecation were not, and had not been, on the agenda. That more than 60 per cent of rural India 'went' in the open was also a relative unknown; also not studied was the link of modern sanitation systems to infant mortality, stunting, wasting, etc.

Considerable progress has been made since the inception of the Swachh Bharat programme. Open defecation numbers were in a very slow decline, and in 2014, the estimate of ODF was close to 50 per cent. The most recent estimates of those not having toilets range from close to zero to around 10–20 per cent. Some claim that the government figures are over-estimates of true success. Regardless, the fact remains that this initiative of transforming poor livelihoods had not even been considered before Modi arrived on the scene—and that radical unprecedented improvement has occurred since his arrival.

TOILETS, A GAME-CHANGER: FOR LIVES, AND POLITICS

That toilets changed lives for the better is obvious. What's more difficult is an assessment of political gains resulting from this pro-poor policy. One pointer to the possible Modi success in the May 2019 election was available in a dominantly scheduled caste village near Guna, Madhya

Pradesh, in December 2018. Possibly my most heart-warming experience in my work as a (development) economist happened then. On a visit, I was confronted by six angry young women. They were vocal and self-assertive (in a very positive way). They were demanding their rights. What rights? The right to have a toilet, as some of their neighbours already had. India has always had subsidies in the name of the poor, but for the first time, I was able to witness these subsidies at work. Hence the loud complaints (my neighbour has a toilet—why not me?).

Some toilets had been built with government funds (Swachh Bharat), but it seems not without a down-payment to the sarpanch of the village who handled the interaction with government authorities. (Upon a photo verification of the toilet, ₹12,000 was deposited into a woman's bank account). How are poor people going to obtain the few thousand rupees necessary for construction to start, the women asked? Not all deserving people in Indian villages (the bottom 50 per cent) can be the first to get their toilets and houses built (costing ₹2.5 lakh or ₹250,000 per house and paid by the government).

There was a queue, and those whose turn had not yet come were complaining. Then, with toilets, there was a water shortage—and the women were complaining because they had to fetch the water from some distance away. Genuine, legitimate complaints. (Awareness of water problems gave further impetus to the plans for tap water for every household.) But the same women were sending their children to school and were proud of their girls for doing well in college. And yes, those who had the toilets were using them, especially the women.

Transformation. Women's rights. Rights of poor women. All correlates of Modi's initiatives. The success of the Swachh Bharat venture has led to other related initiatives, which also improve the lives of the poor, especially poor women. The piped water supply policy, for example. On 15 August 2019 (another important Independence Day policy), only 32.3 million rural households had tap water supply; by mid-December 2021, this number increased to 86.7 million households, or 45 per cent of rural households.[1]

Another Modi policy was the provision of liquefied petroleum gas (LPG) cylinders for poor women, so that they don't cough, or die, from smoke inhalation. The Ujjwala programme started by PM Modi has now delivered more than 82 million LPG connections—that is a little less than one in every three households in India. If such LPG stoves are going towards rural India, then by the time of the 2024 election, there will be very few households working with *chulahs*.

Toilets. Tap water. Gas cylinders. Add to that, bank accounts and financial independence. According to the National Fertility Health Survey (NFHS), women having a bank account that they themselves use increased from 53 per cent to 81 per cent in just four years—2015/16 to 2019/20.

The list of female empowerment measures in the Modi years is long. It is not that progress was not being registered earlier; it is that progress has accelerated, and substantially so, since 2014. 'In the name of the poor' has been a political slogan of all Indian governments from the start. Very few have practised it, and none have had the poor at the centre of their attention. Perhaps it was the elitism of the urban upper-class PMs of the past that they never considered pro-poor policies like toilets as being both politically correct and politically successful.

EXTREME POVERTY IN INDIA POST-PANDEMIC

Confronting low-end poverty has been one of the major goals of the Modi government—and we saw how he had made a difference to Gujarat's poverty performance between 2002 and 2012. One of the strong responses of the Modi government to the pandemic was to significantly increase the distribution of free food to the poor. Starting March 2020, this free allocation was increased from 5 kg of grain per person per month to double that amount. This increase was to all 800 million individuals eligible for the PDS. Further, the policy of One Nation One Ration Card was introduced, which provided subsidy to the entire poor population regardless of their movement from the place of their primary place of residence. Since food is a major fraction of the extreme poor (upwards of 60 per cent of total consumption), it was expected that the consumption levels of the poor would be protected.

Food subsidies are *not* included in Indian (or other countries) survey estimates of consumption. Household consumption surveys only report the actual prices paid, and quantities bought, by each individual (household). But when you get your entire cereal consumption at just ₹1 per kg, the food subsidy per person per month amounted to be nearly ₹270 per month or ₹9 per day. The Tendulkar poverty line in 2020–21 is estimated as ₹50 per person per day. For those close to the poverty line, the food subsidy alone amounted to an increase in consumption of almost 20 per cent. Thus, it is more than apparent that the Modi government's COVID-19 policy response did shield the extreme poor from an increase in their already low pre-pandemic rate of poverty. Extrapolating from the 2011–12 National Sample Survey, consumption and poverty levels (just 14.7 per cent of the population), consumption growth over the eight years, 2011/12 to 2018/19, imply a poverty rate of just 3 per cent of the population.

ECONOMIC REFORMS: NEVER WASTE A CRISIS

Modi was one of the very few political leaders who reacted to COVID-19 with the policy of 'Never Waste a Crisis'. Only a handful of countries undertook structural reform in the year of COVID-19, and India instituted more reforms than the *cumulative* set of reforms by other countries (for example, Indonesia, Greece, Brazil, etc.). These structural reforms may have an effect with a lag, but an effect they do have.

Today, privatization is no longer a four-letter word. Along a long and winding road, and one which allowed India to contribute a word to the English language—disinvestment—the Union Budget of 2021-22 began the process of withdrawal of the state from its extended stay.

Consider one of the most fundamental economic reforms introduced by PM Modi—agricultural reform. Farm laws will allow the rich farmers to proceed as they were—plus allow economic freedom for many small farmers. The poor farmers will no longer be at the mercy of a regulated market. But this reform got stopped (at least delayed) by farm protests. The Congress party joined the protests, even though they had advocated broadly the same farm laws as Modi (in their 2019 election manifesto!) Normally, protests are for rights and welfare of the downtrodden. But the farmers who protested for their rights are the largest and richest farmers in India—and supported by some of the richest middle-men in India (the *arthiyas*).

The fight for the poor goes on, despite obstacles.

CLIMATE CHANGE EFFORTS: POLICIES AND EVIDENCE

Everyone recognizes climate change as the ultimate public bad, and most countries in the world have subscribed to the 2015 Paris Agreement. India is also a signatory. In his 2021 Independence Day speech, Prime Minister Modi signalled the importance of climate change mitigation efforts.

India has repeatedly reiterated that emissions should be looked at broadly in per capita terms. And that large past emitters have to share part of the historical blame. This stance has not prevented India from being a leader in climate mitigation. In terms of performance (success of climate mitigation measures), India has been ranked as a top 10 performer for the third consecutive year.[2] In the latest 2021 ranking, India was ranked tenth and top-ranked Sweden was ranked fourth. (No country was ranked higher than four so effectively India was ranked seventh). China was ranked thirty-third and US last at the sixty-first position.

India's solar capacity has grown from 2.6 gigawatts (GW) in 2014 to 36 GW in 2020. *Our renewable energy capacity is the fourth largest in the world*. With solar and wind energy at the heart of India's climate goals, the country aims to install an ambitious 175 GW of renewable energy by 2022 and 450 GW by 2030—20 per cent more than India's current electricity grid capacity. India is halfway towards meeting its 175 GW by 2022 goal, with renewables reaching 88 GW, representing 24 per cent of India's total installed capacity. Even with the COVID-19 economic downturn, India remains committed to achieving its nationally determined contributions (NDC).

CONCLUSION

One important consequence of the Modi approach to development is that there is a radically changed political landscape in India. The first sixty-seven years of India's development saw one-party-one-family rule for all but fifteen years. In the short span of five years, this party was reduced to less than 10 per cent of seats—and the same low number in two consecutive elections. Regardless of the merits or demerits of the Congress party and its lost leadership, the story of Modi's success has a lot more to do with his (and his party's) merits than with the demerits, and/or failure, of the Opposition.

The extraordinary political success of Modi is a pointer to other changes occurring in India, especially in the political dialogue surrounding his ascent and premiership. Around the world, and in India, discussion of policies, and political leaders has always been of a comparative nature. How much (more effective) is one policy compared to another? Or how does one political leader compare to another; or what would X have done when faced with the same circumstance as Y?

Now, strangely and surprisingly, the critics assess Modi on an *absolute basis*, not relative. For example, the view is that yes, bank accounts have been opened for the poor, but why doesn't everybody have a bank account? Or that toilets have been provided, but there are still those who don't have toilets in their homes. Or that women are more educated than before, and the same as men for the age group of 15–24 years, but they are still discriminated against in the job market and some continue to be mistreated at home, and some continue to encounter sexual violence. There is a lot of progress on the ground still to be covered in India—and this movement towards 'absolutism' in Indian expectations is a tribute, rather than a critique, of Modi.

In the next national election, we will find out how important some of the genuine transformations brought about by Modi in the Indian landscape were—one nation with equal rights for all (no more Article 370) and the possible transformation with the likely enactment of the Uniform Civil Code. Regarding equal rights for all, it should be remembered that it was in Modi's tenure that the Supreme Court reversed its long-standing objection to hearing the case about gay and lesbian rights. On 6 September 2018, with co-incidentally Modi as Prime Minister, the court ruled unanimously that Section 377 was unconstitutional 'in so far as it criminalizes consensual sexual conduct between adults of the same sex'.

A basic accounting of the Modi years shows that what the elite took for granted is now also the experience of the poor. Bank accounts have been opened for the poorest; gas connections have been provided to those who could only dream about this *health* necessity before. For many (a majority of rural residents), toilets were provided to those who never thought of such a luxury in their lives. And education has come to all.

Modi's first term will be remembered as the development years; his second term as when development took the next major step forward towards India being a major player in the world economy.

SECTION TWO

POLITICS OF UNITY AND DEVELOPMENT

MODI, THE BHAGIRATH PRAYAASI

AMISH TRIPATHI

The legend of the great King Bhagirath is familiar to us all: a noble ruler of the celebrated Ikshvaku dynasty. He was an able administrator and a just monarch; he is honoured to this day in Bharat, that is India. He is most well-known for bringing the celestial river Ganga ji to earth. And, Mother Ganga has been at the heart of Indian identity for millennia.

Bhagirath-prayaas is a phrase used to describe a formidable, paradigm-shifting task; much like the word Herculean in the West. Prime Minister Narendra Modi has undertaken such an effort, a Bhagirath-prayaas for Indian civilization.

Let me elaborate.

CIVILIZATIONAL STATE, NOT JUST A NATION STATE

India is among the few civilizational states in the world. It is perhaps the only continuous civilization with roots in the pre-bronze age era. Every other pre-bronze age civilization, from Pharaonic Egypt to Sumerian Mesopotamia, have lost their prana, i.e. their life energy. They are museum pieces now. But we continue, still vibrantly alive. Even today, we practice rituals that go back to the Indus-Saraswati civilization, and even further back in time. We celebrate stories that were chronicled at the dawn of human civilization. We chant hymns and mantras that were composed thousands of years ago.

A civilizational state is fundamentally different from a nation state. Scholars hold that nation states emerged from the Peace of Westphalia in the seventeenth century CE. A nation state controls, runs and manages the affairs of a nation. And, a nation is normally defined as a land comprising a common ethnicity, religion, language and culture. A civilization is a much bigger agglomeration and a far more refined concept. It is the largest aggregation of human beings that is possible; the only bigger aggregation is humanity as a whole.

Christendom fits the definition of a civilization but it is broken into many different nations. So is civilizational Islam. China is a civilization and also a state and, hence, is a civilizational state; though some tendrils of Chinese civilization extend into other lands, such as Taiwan and Singapore, among others.

India, too, is a civilizational state, but many post-Independence leaders were chary of seeing it as one. Prime Minister Modi has broken that mould. I have had the honour of meeting him on many occasions. At one such meeting, he quoted an ancient couplet from the *Vishnu Purana*:

Uttaram yat samudrasya, Himadreshchaiv dakshinam,
varsham tad bharatam nama, Bharatee yatra santatihi

(North of the Ocean, and south of the Himalaya
Is the country of Bharat, and there-in live the Bharatee)

The *Vishnu Purana* was written around 1,500–2,500 years ago. It was probably composed a lot earlier. And the couplet above clearly suggests that Bharat, that is India, was a living entity in the ancient era.

Many Indians of the modern day have forgotten too many things. These Indians include the ruling elite who governed post-independence India. These lines from the *Vishnu Purana*, for instance, are untaught and virtually unknown. Instead, our education system has fostered the erroneous understanding that India didn't exist before it was sewn together by the British after they conquered most of the Indian subcontinent.

Many of the leaders of post-independent India rejected the civilizational memory of our land. And, our educational and cultural worldview ensured that educated Indians were cut off from our ancient ethos. It was as if the elite of the Indian state was presiding over a civilization and yet, attempting to set aside and erase that very civilization. Indians either forgot or became uneasy with the vague memory of who they were.

Milan Kundera had said, 'The first step in liquidating a people is to erase its memory. Destroy its books, its culture, its history… Before long the nation will begin to forget what it is and what it was.'

In contrast to many earlier leaders, a clear message from Prime Minister Modi is: *We must remember who we are.* It is a message that most common Indians instinctively resonate with, even if they cannot formulate it into words. We are the inheritors of a great civilization, with roots that go back before the beginnings of historical time. We are the only ancient pre-bronze-age civilization that still throbs with life. And the stream that unites our land is dharma. Dharma, in fact, is the string that holds together the garland of multiple different flowers in our subcontinent.

Yes, India defines the phrase, unity in diversity. But it is dharma that makes this unity possible.

And we must understand, dharma is beyond and above any religion or ritual. It is a law of life. Dharma is that which binds and sustains.

If we forget dharma, our land will succumb to inevitable fissiparous tendencies. Without dharma, our civilization will be scattered, like dust in the wind.

We have a living example next door: Pakistan, a nation severed from the womb of Mother India. In his magisterial book, *Creating a New Medina*, Venkat Dhulipala writes that Islam was visualized as the glue that would bind our neighbouring country together. A logical requirement for that strategy to succeed was that dharma, and the ancient Indian way, must be erased from their collective consciousness. In the absence of dharma, the glue did not work. Within less than twenty-five years of the creation of Pakistan, its eastern-wing rebelled, broke away, and became Bangladesh.

In their popular imagination, Pakistanis first saw themselves as descendants of the Turko-Mongol Mughals, then Persians, then Arabs. Now it would seem that it is back to the Turks. It is sad to see a country's elite gatekeepers change fathers so frequently in search of something that would stick, even as they reject their obvious origin. Recent genetic research is laying bare these origins: that the overwhelming majority among them have descended from Indian Hindus and Buddhists. This absence of grounding in their own land and civilization has led the cultural narrative of Pakistan astray; it has, frankly, hurt their national interests and global standing.

This is very different in the case of Indian Muslims. A recent Pew Survey (published in 2021) clearly outlines their comfort with and respect for different religions, Gods and Goddesses, and the concepts of karma and dharma. Indian Muslims follow their religion with pride and also practice dharma and peaceful coexistence. Our country is united by a strong and yet, counter-intuitively, light touch. The touch of dharma.

For the country to remain united and become stronger, dharma must be revived institutionally. Our traditions and cultures must be embraced by our governing apparatus and cultural elite.

Prime Minister Modi understands this. Indians must be clear and unapologetic about their roots for that will forge a confident country and State. Reviving our cultural comfort with our great ancient past is similar to the tapasya and scale of work that King Bhagirath undertook to bring Maa Ganga down to earth; it revived our land.

Once we understand this overarching objective, many moves that Prime Minister Modi makes in the cultural space begin to make sense. For this is his tapasya: to rejuvenate our culture and connection to dharma. Prime Minister Modi is reviving the Ganga of our culture in slow, gentle steps.

Why slow and gentle?

Remember the story of King Bhagirath. He prayed to Lord Shiva to help slow the fall of Ganga ji as she descended to earth, otherwise there could have been devastation from the fast flow and change. Similarly, we, too, must exercise restraint and be slow and gentle in reviving our culture in modern times.

Change must be evolutionary in a civilizational state like India. It must be gradual. It must take current realities into account. And, it cannot be nihilistic. It must build on what already exists. It must be adaptable. In that sense, both the right wing and the left wing (concepts drawn from the Western paradigm) are out of step since they want quick revolutionary change, usually with a desire to trump over the other side. An incremental process ensures that we build on existing traditions and patterns; clearly, if they have lasted so long, they must serve some purpose. Also, it reduces unnecessary dissonance and friction. In India, agents of change must have humility and patience.

Prime Minister Modi's vision extends beyond the divisions of the left wing and right wing. He works for the Mother India Wing, and there is quiet support for this effort, even across political party lines.

PRIME MINISTER MODI SERVING INDIA, THE LAND OF PILGRIMS

In the space of temples and spiritual centres, his government has made steady but dramatic progress through patient transformations. Once the courts pronounced their judgment on Ayodhya, the government constituted the Shri Ram Janmbhoomi Teerth Kshetra Trust, which is now tasked with building the Ram Mandir. The Prime Minister himself conducted the temple complex's Bhoomi Poojan. Contributions were raised from across India so that common people would carry the sweet sentiment in their hearts, remembering that they played a role in rebuilding this great temple to Ram Lalla. The infrastructure is being improved substantially in the holy city of Ayodhya, which will positively impact the pilgrim's experience.

We are not just rebuilding a temple that had been destroyed by invaders centuries ago. With this endeavour, we are also confidently moving in the direction of reviving our culture and uniting everyone as part of a civilizational stream of humanity.

Harvard scholar and professor, Diana Eck, has written that India is united at its sacred core, 'not by the power of kings and governments, but by the footsteps of pilgrims.' India is knitted together through the thread of devotion and an impulse to seek answers to the meaning of life and the cosmos—through a dharmic prism. Pilgrims and their stories have bound our land together. It is no surprise that foreign invaders, from Mahmud Khilji to Aurangzeb to Portuguese inquisitors, fought pitched battles to destroy our temples, viharas and gurudwaras. They were not just attacking our religion and way of life, but also the glue that binds the people of the subcontinent together.

Rebuilding the Ram Janmbhoomi temple is a single step, large though it may be. The Modi government has also built the Kashi Vishwanath corridor, a massive project that reinvigorates the splendour of the temple and its surroundings, once again giving devotees of the Mahadev a direct path and view of the Ganga ji from the temple. The improved facilities at the Vishwanath ji temple complex will greatly enhance the pilgrim's journey. Infrastructure-wise, Varanasi's face is changing rapidly. Improved roads, waste management and electricity connections are accompanied by beautification efforts that bring tears of pride to one's eyes. It was long overdue. This is Kashi. Our civilizational cradle.

There is more. The PRASHAD scheme to rejuvenate Kedarnath Dham—as well as the hill town—is moving apace under the personal supervision of the Prime Minister. The redevelopment of Badrinath Dham, under the same PRASHAD scheme, will sweeten the pilgrim's journey to the devabhoomi of Uttarakhand.

Along with the enhancement and beautification of the temple complexes, we also need to improve access. It must be made convenient, safe and cost-effective for the pilgrims. A lot of quiet work has been done in this area as well. The ambitious Char Dham project, progressing at lightning speed, will ensure all weather connectivity. Rail connectivity to the Vaishno Devi shrine in Katra has greatly improved with the Vande Bharat trains, easing access for lakhs of pilgrims. The Kashi Mahakal Express connects the important Jyotirling temples of Omkareshwar ji (near Indore), Mahakaleshwar ji (Ujjain) and Kashi Vishwanath ji (Varanasi). A corridor was opened to Sri Kartarpur Sahib, making the pilgrimage much easier for Sikh and Hindu devotees. Under the PRASHAD Scheme, tourism-related infrastructure for the following holy places has also been redeveloped and further augmented:

- Ajmer (Rajasthan)
- Amritsar (Punjab)
- Amaravati, Srisailam and Tirupati (Andhra Pradesh)
- Dwarka (Gujarat)
- Gaya (Bihar)
- Kamakhya (Assam)
- Kanchipuram (Tamil Nadu)
- Varanasi, Mathura and Ayodhya (Uttar Pradesh)
- Puri (Odisha)
- Vellankani (Tamil Nadu)
- Belur (West Bengal)
- Deoghar (Jharkhand)
- Guruvayur (Kerala)

- Hazratbal and Katra (Jammu and Kashmir)
- Omkareshwar (Madhya Pradesh)
- Somnath (Gujarat)
- Trimbakeshwar (Maharashtra)

We saw early signs of Prime Minister Modi's focus on culture even during his tenure as the Chief Minister of Gujarat. The restoration and reconstruction of the two-hundred-year-old Lakhpat Sahib Gurudwara in Kutch was undertaken by the Government of Gujarat after it was damaged during the 2001 earthquake. The project received a grant from the Archaeological Survey of India (ASI) and had the cooperation of the United Nations Volunteer Programme. Laudably, the cultural activities department undertook the task through people's participation. It was an award-winning effort. UNESCO awarded it the Award of Distinction in 2005. The judges, in fact, praised the 'sophisticated understanding demonstrated in both technical and social aspects of conservation process and practice[1].'

THE BROTHERHOOD OF DHARMA

The 550th Prakash Parv of Sri Guru Nanak Dev ji was marked by great enthusiasm in India. Also, since the Sikhs are among the most globalized Indian communities, all the Indian embassies and missions across the world, supported by the ICCR (Indian Council for Cultural Relations), mobilized to mark this great occasion in a grand manner. The National Book Trust released three texts—*Guru Nanak Bani*, *Nanak Bani* and *Sakhian Guru Nanak Dev*—to spread the message of Sri Guru Nanak Dev ji further. The 350th Prakash Parv of Sri Guru Gobind Singh ji was also marked with immense fervour, and the Prime Minister took part in the official celebrations in Patna in 2017. The four-hundredth Prakash Parv of Sri Guru Tegh Bahadur ji, a symbol of compassion and bravery, was celebrated in India and across the world through Indian government establishments in 2021.

The Buddhist pilgrimage circuit is being promoted since 2015 under the Swadesh Darshan scheme; infrastructural and cultural projects are being developed[2] with heavy investments. Pilgrimage connectivity has been vastly improved with the launch of trains, like the Mahaparinirvan Express covering the Buddhist circuit around Bihar with off- and on-board services[3], commencement of the international airport in Kushinagar, Uttar Pradesh, and direct flight service between Colombo and Varanasi, the place of Lord Buddha's first sermon[4]. Several Buddhist festivals were added to the calendar of national celebrations like Buddha Purnima, Lumbini Festival, Losar Festival and Sangha Day. A school for Buddhist studies was set up under the Dr Ambedkar International Centre at a cost of nearly ₹200 crore[5] (₹2 billion). ICCR initiated festivals, such as the Ladakh Festival, to promote indigenous Buddhist culture. ICCR is also hosting the first-ever (in modern times) International Buddhist Conference in November 2021.

Under the Swadesh Darshan scheme, the Tirthankara Spiritual circuit is being developed to further popularize and promote spiritual places associated with the holy tirthankaras and Jainism. This circuit covers Vaishali-Arrah-Masad-Patna-Rajgir-Pawapuri-Champapuri in Bihar[6]. States like Gujarat, Bihar and Karnataka are also developing Jain spiritual circuits in their states. Prime Minister Modi participated in Mahamastakabhisheka of Lord Bahubali Gommateshwara at Shravanabelagola in 2018 and sought the blessings of Gommateshwara ji. During this occasion, he inaugurated the newly-laid 630 steps to Vindhyagiri hill (where the 58-foot-tall murti of Gommateshwara ji stands) and the Bahubali General Hospital[7].

In the past few centuries, only the great Maratha queen, Ahilyabai Holkar, did more to revive temples across India. Now this has happened under the aegis of our Prime Minister.

While temples and spiritual centres are critical to the revival of our ancient culture, there is more to it.

INDIA: THE GLOBAL CAPITAL OF RELIGIOUS HARMONY

Zoroastrianism: Soon after being sworn in, Prime Minister Modi invited Vada Dasturji Khurshed Dastoor to New Delhi to discuss plans to transform Udvada into a global spiritual and cultural heritage site for Parsis and non-Parsis alike[8].

The global-scale Iranshah Udvada Utsav (IUU) took off after the organizers were urged by Prime Minister Modi to organize a festival—preferably an annual, failing which, a bi-annual one—where community members from all over the world could congregate in Udvada. India has protected the Zoroastrian heritage, which had lost its historical homeland in Persia many centuries ago. Parsis, who follow the Zoroastrian faith, continue to remain cherished and valued citizens of India.

Islam: Many places of deep religious significance to Indian Muslims have benefited from the implementation of the PRASHAD scheme for developing tourist infrastructural facilities such as Ajmer (Rajasthan), Cheraman Juma Mosque (Thrissur, Kerala), Hazratbal (Jammu and Kashmir)[9]. Prime Minister Modi has reached out to Muslim scholars and visited religious places to support inter-faith dialogue and harmony. 'Chadar' was regularly offered at the dargah of Sufi saint, Hazrat Khwaja Moinuddin Chishti, at Ajmer Sharif for the annual Urs[10,11]. He met a delegation of Barelvi Sufi scholars in 2015[12] and addressed the World Islamic Sufi Conference, a global meeting of Sufi saints in 2016[13]. He visited the renowned Saifee Masjid in Indore to mark Muharram with the Dawoodi Bohra community in 2018[14]. He has made regular efforts to showcase Indian Islamic art and culture to global leaders. He took the Japanese Prime Minister, Shinzo Abe, to the Siddi Saiyyed Jali Masjid in Ahmedabad[15]. A replica of the Cheraman Masjid (believed by many to be the second-oldest mosque in the world) was gifted by Prime Minister Modi to the King of Saudi Arabia in 2016.

In Iran, Prime Minister Modi gifted the Grand Ayatollah, Sayyid Ali Hosseini Khamenei, a specially commissioned reproduction of a rare seventh century manuscript of the Holy Quran attributed to Hazrat Ali, to the fourth caliph. The Prime Minister also gifted the Iranian President, Dr Hassan Rouhani, specially commissioned reproductions of Mirza Asadullah Khan Ghalib's collection of poetry in Persian and *Kulliyat-e-Farsi-e-Ghalib*[16]. Strenuous efforts have been made to improve the socio-economic status of Muslims through the PMJVK (Pradhan Mantri Jan Vikas Karyakaram) in the identified minority concentration areas (MCAs) of the country.

In the past seven years under the PMJVK, more than 43,000 basic infrastructure projects including education, health, skill development, women-related projects, sports and sadbhav mandaps, etc. have been sanctioned in minority concentration areas. More than ₹10,000 crore (₹100 billion) has been sanctioned and ₹8,000 crore (₹80 billion) has been released to the states/union territories for the implementation of these projects. During the COVID-19 pandemic, the government approved 186 health projects of ₹512.25 crore (₹5.12 billion) for MCAs.

Christianity: The PRASHAD scheme has improved the infrastructure and facilities at many important religious pilgrimage sites for Indian Christians such as Velankanni (Tamil Nadu), St Thomas International Shrine (Malayattoor)[17] and churches in Goa. The government has worked hard to preserve the cultural ties of Christianity with the rest of the world. For example, India gifted the holy relics of seventeenth century St Queen Ketevan to the Georgian government, nearly sixteen years after they were found in Goa[18]. The Prime Minister visited St Anthony's Church in Colombo, which had been targeted by terrorists, as a mark of solidarity[19]. He played a pivotal role in the St Jacob's Orthodox Church dispute between opposing factions to find a middle ground. The government has consistently seen itself as a guarantor of security to Indian Christians should they be caught in tumultuous external events. For example, forty-six Christian nurses were rescued from Iraq in 2014[20]. In 2015, Father Alexis Prem Kumar, a Roman Catholic priest from the Jesuit Refugee Service, was rescued from Afghanistan[21]. Father Tom Uzhunnalil, an Indian priest who was kidnapped by ISIS militants in Yemen, was rescued in 2017[22]. The Prime Minister and the government continue to engage with the Christian community on cultural and developmental issues.

INDIAN FESTIVALS, ARTS AND HANDICRAFTS

Acknowledging and celebrating our cultural festivals is crucially significant for Prime Minister Modi. Even as Chief Minister of Gujarat, he made steady efforts to promote the culture of the state by organizing festivals, developing facilities and promoting arts and handicrafts.

Transformation of the UNESCO Heritage Site Dholavira was undertaken by Chief Minister Modi[23]. The scale of his vision was noteworthy, and it is worth emulating. He did not see the development of Dholavira in isolation, and also developed the surrounding infrastructure, paying attention to protecting local flora and fauna as well as integrating local communities.

The Buddhist Circuits in Gujarat were developed. A Memorandum of Understanding (MOU) was signed with the Sri Lankan government, whereby, Sri Lankan Buddhists could travel to Gujarat while Gujaratis could do the Lord Ram Trail in Sri Lanka.

The Rann Utsav was conceived to promote Kutch as a tourist destination with the help of an innovative PPP (public-private partnership) model, while simultaneously generating income earning avenues in an earthquake-devastated region[24]. The success of the festival has no comparison today. From a thirty-day event it has now become a ninety-day extravaganza with advance bookings; it generates infectious enthusiasm every year.

The Gujarati Garba resonates globally today[25]. As the Gujarat Chief Minister, Narendra Modi promoted the Garba Festival, both domestically and internationally, to showcase Gujarat's culture to the world. Today, the Navratri dance festival is a major international event.

The Government of Gujarat undertook renovation of the Shamlaji temple complex in Sabarkantha district under Chief Minister Narendra Modi[26]. It provided better facilities to the pilgrims and created job opportunities in the surrounding tribal areas at a cost of ₹70 crore (₹700 million).

'Hunar Haat', launched in 2016, provided market and employment opportunities to artisans and craftsmen. More than 550,000 artisans and craftsmen, along with associated people, have found employment and employment opportunities through 'Hunar Haats' organized in different parts of the country.

OUR CULTURE IN OUR EDUCATION SYSTEM

Our education system has been the primary culprit in the attempts to erase our civilizational identity. A new NEP (National Education Policy) was finally launched in 2020, heralding reforms in our education system which will help reconnect students to their roots. The biggest change in NEP is the equivalence (not superiority) given to education in the mother tongue of the students (the servitude towards English will finally be neutralized). It is a matter of shame that Indian universities have been teaching all other religions without offering a degree course in Hinduism. A student aspiring to formally study Hinduism had to knock at the doors of foreign universities such as Oxford. Now, Banaras Hindu University (BHU) has recently launched India's first degree course in Hinduism.

The two-year course, under the philosophy department of BHU, will teach the scriptures, architecture, art and history of Hinduism. Undoubtedly, more universities will follow this example in times to come. Most critically, the Central Sanskrit University Bill was passed in 2019[27] to support the revival and propagation of our ancient classical language. The Modi government also launched the 'Study in India' programme in 2018. It offers short-term educational courses in Indic subjects like yoga, Indian history and culture, and in classical languages like Sanskrit. ICCR launched the first ever gamified Sanskrit learning application called 'Little Guru', to help the youth study Sanskrit in a context that appeals to them. ICCR has also launched a UTIKS (Universalization of Traditional Indian Knowledge Systems) Platform, through which online educational/training courses will be offered on various aspects of Indian culture such as culinary and cuisine traditions, flora and fauna in India, the Indian Freedom Struggle, etc.

India, through the ICCR, has also set up academic chairs in several universities across Southeast Asia and so far, has held six international Buddhist conclaves at prominent religious sites. An MoU has been signed between Cambodia and India to continue the chair for Buddhist and Sanskrit studies in Cambodia[28]. Scholarships and grants for international academic enthusiasts to pursue Buddhist studies in India have been disbursed[29] and India extended a $15 million grant to Sri Lanka for the promotion of Buddhist ties with the island nation[30]. Four autonomous schools and institutes for Buddhist studies in Ladakh, Arunachal Pradesh, Varanasi and Nalanda are now operational[31].

The government has also implemented initiatives to revive the study of traditional Indian medicine systems in India. The Deemed to be University status has been conferred upon National Institute of Ayurveda, Jaipur and a status of Institute of National Importance has been given to the Institute of Teaching and Research in Ayurveda (ITRA) at Jamnagar, Gujarat. A web portal 'AYURVEDA GRANTHA SAMUCCAYAH' has been developed to bring all major classical compendia of Ayurveda on a single platform. To streamline the Ayurvedic education system, the National Commission for Indian System of Medicine has been constituted in place of the Central Council of Indian Medicine (CCIM).

SPORTS AND PHYSICAL FITNESS ARE PART OF OUR CULTURE TOO!

While spiritual places and education are central to the revival of civilizational heritage, culture encompasses a lot more. Successful civilizations believe in themselves and have the self-image of winners. Sports and physical prowess are important elements of this vision.

The government dramatically increased the sports budget—almost threefold as compared to 2014—to ₹2,596 crore (₹25.96 billion) in 2021-22. Sporting associations have been spruced up and professionalized. The Prime Minister launched the Khelo India School Games in 2018. The following year, Modi ji also launched the Fit India movement. As he said on the occasion, 'Sports has a direct relationship with fitness. However, the Fit India Movement that we have launched today aims to go beyond the world of sports. Fitness is not just a word; it is a necessary condition towards a healthy and prosperous life.'

When more Indians are physically robust, a larger pool of sportspersons will emerge. Admittedly, many may not become sportspersons, however, their physical health will ensure that they lead a productive and happy life.

Parallel to this, many initiatives were carried out to support our sportspersons. Infrastructure was improved across the board, e.g. at the Major Dhyan Chand National Stadium in New Delhi. Target Olympic Podium Scheme (TOPS) was launched to support our athletes[32]. A new incentive structure was announced to fund five hundred private academies. Twenty new disciplines were made eligible for government jobs under the sports quota. The prize money of the National Sports Awards was enhanced. A thousand Khelo India centres were set up to help retired sportspersons who can scout new talent as well. Khelo India athletes received financial assistance as support during the pandemic. A simple but very effective step was the rationalization of diet and food supplement charges. Financial assistance towards diet and food supplements was made available to all athletes: senior, junior and sub-junior.

The results are visible. India just had its best Olympics performance ever with seven medals (one gold, two silver and four bronze medals).

Significantly, our sportspersons were on the threshold of winning medals in many other disciplines. Many reached the quarter-finals or the heats. They are knocking hard at the doors. There will be many more medals in future Olympics. Prime Minister Modi honoured these sportspersons with fanfare and a pride-filled heart. And, more importantly, sensitivity. He hosted a reception for *all* our Olympic participants at his residence. He explained one of the profound philosophies of the *Bhagawad Gita* in his own earthy way: '*Jeet ko sar par chadhne na do, haar ko man mein basne na do* (Do not get arrogant in victory and do not get bogged down by defeat).'

The Prime Minister went further. Felicitating the athletes was not an end in itself. He requested each sportsperson to visit at least seventy-five schools before Independence Day, 2023 to encourage the next generation of sportspersons. He requested them to contribute some memorabilia like the javelin of gold medallist Neeraj Chopra, which could be auctioned to raise money. He showcased the different parts of India that the sportspersons were from, in a message of unity.

By interacting with these sportspersons, the Prime Minister sent a missive to India's youth, saying that Mother India will encourage and support her children from all corners of the land. And, most importantly, that we, the children of Mother India, can be tough competitors.

And winners.

History has been taught to us in the colours of defeat. The subtle message that came across through our history books was that we are civilizational cowards whose ancestors repeatedly lost to foreign invaders over the last millennium. But that is erroneous. We lost some battles, but we won some as well. That is the reason we are still around. Or else, like many other ancient cultures, we too would have been overwritten and obliterated. We too would be museum pieces by now. Prime Minister Modi told the youth of India that they are winners, that they can beat the world. Be the best. Not just in sports, but in all fields. Believe in yourself, work hard, and compete. The nation is behind you.

And, he did this in his own gentle way. Remember: slow and incremental improvements.

SHOWCASING OUR CULTURE TO FOREIGN DIGNITARIES

But culture and civilizational issues are not just about how we see ourselves; it is also about how the world sees us. Prime Minister Modi has put thought and energy into this dimension as well.

Visits of foreign leaders to India come to mind. These naturally entail that media from those countries also cover us. Many Indian leaders in the past were reluctant to showcase Indian culture, temples and traditions to the world. Some cast a poor light, along with a curious sense of embarrassment. They often projected a break from the past and gave a message that India is modernizing. Modernization is good. It is necessary. But modernization does not entail disrespect for the past and dismissal of traditions.

Narendra Modi wears his cultural pride on his sleeve, and he never misses an opportunity to showcase India's culture to visiting dignitaries. He took the Australian Prime Minister to Akshardham in Delhi; he celebrated Diwali in Ayodhya with the First Lady of Korea; the latter in understated remembrance of the story of Queen Heo Hwang-ok, also known as Suriratna, an Ayodhyan princess who married into the Korean royal family in the ancient past. More than six million present-day Koreans trace their lineage from this queen who came from India. He took Afghanistan's President to the Golden Temple in Amritsar, and escorted the Prime Ministers of Japan and Israel and the President of France to Kashi, where they all experienced the magical Ganga Aarti. He showcased Mahabalipuram to the Chinese President and subtly reinforced that India's trade routes covered most of the known world in ancient and medieval times. ICCR took numerous foreign ambassadors and dignitaries as well as delegates (of the Pravasi Bharatiya Diwas) to the Kumbh Mela in Prayagraj in 2019.

REJUVENATING OUR HERITAGE ABROAD

The Narendra Modi administration has put great effort into rejuvenating and restoring our cultural heritage across several countries and, thus, into reinforcing India's contributions to their legacy. The Prime Minister inaugurated the renovation of the two-hundred-year-old Shreenath ji temple in Bahrain's capital, worked with our friends, the Abu Dhabi government, to allow the building of Swaminarayan ji temple—the first traditional Hindu temple in the UAE—and aided Vietnam in restoring the UNESCO Heritage Cham Temple Complex. The ASI and the Ministry of External Affairs have worked to restore the Ananda temple in Myanmar's Bagan heritage zone and the Laos' Khmer temple of Vat Phou. In Indonesia, India is working with their government towards the preservation of the Borobudur and Prambanan temple. India is involved with the conservation of Pashupatinath ji temple and renovation of Bala Tiripurasundari ji temple in Nepal.

India has worked with the Sri Lankan authorities towards the preservation of the Thirukuteeshwara ji temple and is also active in Bhutan on significant projects like the restoration of Rigsum Goenpa Lhakhang, Lingzhi Dzong Conservation Project and the construction of Sarpang Dzong, among others. Rebuilding the Ramna Kali ji temple and Sri Sri Joy Kali Matar Mandir in Bangladesh has also taken place with Indian support. The ICCR has worked at installing Lord Buddha statues in Buddhist countries, such as South Korea and Bhutan.

When travelling abroad, Prime Minister Modi does not miss an opportunity to visit temples. The pride and sense of oneness this instils in Indic communities (more often than not, among minorities in those regions) is unparalleled. In Bangladesh, he has visited and prayed at Thakur Bari ji, Jesoreshwari ji and Dhakeswariji on occasion. He offered prayers at Naguleswaram ji temple in Sri Lanka, Ganga Singh Sabha ji Gurdwara in Teheran, Iran, and the Pashupatinath ji temple and Muktinath ji temple in Nepal. In Canada, he prayed at the historic Vancouver Gurdwara and Lakshmi Narain ji temple. He has performed a puja at the historic Lord Shiva temple in Muscat, Oman.

And these are just a select list of all the temples, viharas and gurudwaras he has visited across the world as the Prime Minister. Delicately, he has showcased that India and Indians have left a footprint across the world, from ancient times to the modern day. And, most importantly, that Indians have been a positive addition to the countries they have immigrated to. They do well economically and educationally and have a far lower incidence of crime as compared to some other immigrant communities. This was exhibited extravagantly during massive events with overseas

Indians that Prime Minister Modi presided over in many countries. I live in London currently, and I have been told by British politicians that they struggle to fill up the Wembley Stadium with crowds. Prime Minister Modi did it with elan when he visited the UK. At many such events across the world, overseas Indians from all religions, regions and communities gathered with pride and displayed Indian culture and their economic successes. They were noticeably inspired by Prime Minister Modi, whose message to the overseas Indians was consistent: be proud of your Indian heritage, but also contribute strongly to the country that you now live in.

GIFTING AS AN ART FORM!

Prime Minister Modi's gifts to foreign dignitaries have been extensively covered by the international media as well. Never to lose an opportunity to reinforce our traditional culture, he does this with thoughtful selection. He presented a copy of the *Bhagawad Gita* and a rare Rogan painting—made by a Khatri Muslim family from Gujarat—to Former US President Barack Obama. He gifted a copy of the *Bhagawad Gita* to Japanese Prime Minister Shinzo Abe. He gave a handmade Sirumugai silk shawl to Chinese President, Xi Jinping, and a Pashmina shawl from Jammu and Kashmir—inscribed with Gurudev Rabindranath Tagore's poems—to President Park Geun Hye of South Korea. A Kashmiri shawl, a Himachali silver bracelet and a Sheesham wooden chest from Punjab was gifted to President Donald Trump and first lady, Melania Trump.

The Prime Minister gifted Australian lawyer John Lang's 1854 petition on behalf of Rani Lakshmi Bai (also spelled Laxmi Bai) against the East India Company to his Australian counterpart, Tony Abbott[33]. He gifted two hundred cows to villagers in Rwanda in support of President Paul Kagame's ambitious initiative towards poverty reduction and for tackling childhood malnutrition. The cultural import of this gift was memorable, highlighting a common heritage value shared by the two countries[34].

He gifted a gold-plated replica of the ancient Cheraman mosque of Kerala to Saudi King Salman bin Abdulaziz in 2016[35]. The Cheraman mosque is believed by some to be the second-oldest mosque in the world, built even before the mosque in Mecca. It is symbolic of a thriving relationship of spiritual confluence and commerce between India and the Arab world since the beginnings of Islam. It is an emblem of religious harmony.

In Iran, Prime Minister Modi gifted the Grand Ayatollah, Sayyid Ali Hosseini Khamenei, a specially commissioned reproduction of a rare seventh-century manuscript of the Holy Quran attributed to Hazrat Ali, to the fourth caliph. The Prime Minister also gifted the Iranian President, Dr Hassan Rouhani, specially commissioned reproductions of Mirza Asadullah Khan Ghalib's collection of poetry in Persian and *Kulliyat-e-Farsi-e-Ghalib*, and also Sumair Chand's Persian translation of *Ramayana*[36].

He misses no occasion to display our great culture. And these thoughtful sentiments were ably reciprocated by world leaders.

The German Chancellor, Angela Merkel, gifted Prime Minister Narendra Modi an original first edition print of German philologist Max Mueller's book on spiritual leader Ramakrishna[37]. President Barack Obama gifted the Prime Minister a rare book: *The World's Congress: Religions at the World's Columbian Exposition*, a book on the 1893 summit of World Religions where Swami Vivekananda made a mark on the global stage[38]. The British Queen, Elizabeth II, gifted Prime Minister Modi a handcrafted cotton lace that Mahatma Gandhi had spun from cotton yarn[39].

The Prime Minister's attention extended into the intangible dimension as well, when it came to maintaining cultural ties with global leaders. When the Chinese President, Xi Jinping, visited Gujarat, he was told by Prime Minister Modi that his birthplace has a special connection with President Xi's birthplace in China[40]. The Chinese traveller, Hiuen Tsang (also spelt as Hsuan Tsang and Xuan Zhuang), stayed at Vadnagar when he visited India. On returning home, he stayed in Xian, the hometown of Xi. President Xi later hosted Prime Minister Modi in Shaanxi[41] in 2015.

RETRIEVING LOST AND STOLEN ANTIQUITIES

The world draws lessons from the messages from India and the Indian government. Our priceless treasures and antiquities have been looted for centuries. Sadly, this continued post-independence. But now, the attitude of many foreign governments is changing. India is making it clear across the world that our heritage is important to us and we want it back.

Countries are, in fact, helping us recover our stolen heritage. In just the past seven years, nearly 250 such stolen artefacts have either been returned or are being returned[42,43]. Compare that to the return of just one stolen artefact in the ten years from 2004 to 2014!

No theft has been reported from any centrally protected monument or site museum under ASI in the past few years, indicating a serious shift in the protection of India's heritage. In the presence of Prime Minister Modi, the US committed to return two hundred artefacts to India valued in excess of $100 million in the international market. These included some antiquities dating back two thousand years. Further, the National Gallery of Australia had, in July 2021, announced its plans to return stolen artworks worth $2.2 million to India.

MAKING YOGA A GLOBAL MOVEMENT, LED BY INDIA

All that has been stated would be woefully incomplete without recalling the yeoman service of the Modi government in the cause for yoga. This ancient Indian tradition in pursuit of physical, mental, emotional and spiritual well-being, had slowly popularized itself in the West. But yoga had almost been successfully disconnected from its roots. It was shocking to Indians, but many in the world had begun to think of yoga in dissociation from India and its spiritual reality. Some even claiming, bizarrely, that yoga's roots lay in parts of modern Europe!

The Modi government symbolically established Indian ownership of the tradition by working with the United Nations to have 21st June—the day of the Summer Solstice—declared as International Day of Yoga. It saw great support and enthusiasm, and a huge number of countries supported this initiative. Since then, year after year, the world erupts in enthusiasm for yoga. This has had a lasting impact on India's soft power across the world. And, of course, it has ensured that yoga and India are inextricably intertwined in the world's imagination. Yoga has become a force for unity across the world.

As Prime Minister Modi said:

> 'The whole world observes International Day of Yoga. In a very short time, 21st June has got worldwide recognition and is connecting

> people. At a time when divisive forces are raising their ugly heads, this has been India's great contribution to the world. We have successfully unified the whole world through yoga. Just as yoga unifies mind, body and soul, it is also unifying people across the world[44].'

Clearly, Indian leaders in the past have practiced yoga and been aware of its benefits. And yet, yoga was not mandated to be taught in schools. Yoga remained closeted within a few minds, practised, but not preached. Today, we see a proud acknowledgement of it across the land. It is now a mass movement.

TWO OTHER, LESSER ACKNOWLEDGED, BUT IMPORTANT CONTRIBUTIONS

There are two more things I'd like to speak about, which don't really fit into any traditional category for a review, but I believe are important for an inclusive India. Firstly, by not being apologetic about his lack of command over English, Prime Minister Modi has given a powerful message that to be in a position of power and serve the country, you don't need to be from the Indian 'Anglosphere'. It doesn't matter how good your English is; what matters is your capability and your desire to contribute to the motherland. The recent 'controversy' over Union Health Minister Mansukh Mandaviya ji's English is a good indicator of how crucial, but difficult, this battle is.

The second is the intense focus on India's northeast. Of course, the infrastructure has improved dramatically. It is unfortunate that it took seventy years for some parts of the northeast to finally get railway connections, modern highways and bridges. But even more important has been the emotional integration. The celebration of sporting accomplishments from the northeast, and the national focus on leaders and achievers from the region, have been among the highest that has ever been seen. It is notable that one of the most popular young leaders across India today is from the northeast. A most heart-breaking narrative is the trope that the region is different from the so-called 'mainland' of India. All of India, including the northeast, is mainland India. We are one. The Prime Minister has driven and reinforced this message through words and deeds.

This chapter has been my concise effort to present the sheer breadth of activities and range of areas, within which the Modi government is working on Mother India's cultural agenda. A lot more must be done. But there is no denying that the work has begun in earnest, without any shilly-shallying.

Not just India, but the world stands to benefit from our ancient ways of life. The wisdom of our ancestors can illuminate minds and invigorate hearts. On the other hand, without cultural grounding we will scatter, like dust in the wind.

Culture is upstream of all else. The culture of a nation cascades down to politics, business, international relations, even interpersonal relations. Culture is like the sacred Gangotri. Whatever is mixed into the waters at the Gangotri will descend as the mighty flow of Mother Ganga. And through Ganga ji, the water will be consumed by all who receive Her blessings.

Gangotri impacts all who live on the plains of Ganga ji. Similarly, when you impact culture, you impact everything.

As the Ganga Stotram says: पतितनिवारिणि त्रिभुवनधन्ये

> Or, '*Mother Ganga, you save the fallen and bring prosperity to the three worlds.*'

We revive our culture to honour our ancestors. We revive our culture for the love of our motherland. Ultimately though, we revive our culture for ourselves, for we are its primary beneficiaries.

And, let us honour the Bhagirath-prayaas of our Prime Minister Narendra Modi who is bringing our culture back to the centre of our lives and consciousness.

May Mother India and Mother Ganga bless us all.

DEMOCRACY, DELIVERY AND THE POLITICS OF HOPE

AMIT SHAH

As Narendra Modi completes twenty years in executive office—first as Chief Minister of Gujarat from 2001 for thirteen years and now as Prime Minister of India from 2014 for seven years—it is imperative to encapsulate his epoch and milestones on his rare and remarkable journey. How does one assess this 20-year period at the head of governance? The answer is simple yet complex, since there are multiple and alternative lenses to view his contribution to nation-building.

The past two decades have been a period of enormous achievements in politics and policy for Narendra Modi, or Narendra bhai as I've always addressed him. He has worked tirelessly for the people with an awe-inspiring and all-consuming dedication. He has built a stronger and equitable economy, in both Gujarat and the country as a whole. He has helped create a cleaner and transparent polity and an administrative system, not just by personal example but by institutionalizing and future-proofing best practices. He has come to symbolize good, honest and responsive governance.

The changes brought about by Narendra bhai during these years are the most visible aspects of his leadership. However, there is a lot more to him and his journey. He began life as a child in a struggling, working-class Indian family, and has today become the paramount and most popular Indian leader—among the tallest global statespersons. The exponential increase in the Prime Minister's personal appeal in politics has been mirrored in the BJP's geographical and social expansion. He is the catalyst who has driven and accelerated the popularity of the party across India.

The BJP's pan-India growth in the past seven years is unmatched by any party in the country's post-Independence history. There are few, if any, examples like this in democracies of the world. Narendra bhai's popularity, performance and credibility have not only translated into political victories in presidential or presidential-style contests, but also enabled a sustainable accretion and structural long-term advantage for the party.

As a person who has been fortunate to have known, observed and learnt so much from Narendra bhai, I do wonder whether this 20-year bracket does justice to his accumulated wisdom and the enormity of his acumen. I see it as part of a longer yatra that began much earlier, in the 1970s, when he was a young RSS activist, and then continued through the 1980s as a BJP worker. The insights he gained into the lives of ordinary people during those formative years became the building blocks of his leadership in government; together, the two form a continuum like no other in contemporary Indian public life.

My dilemma is: Where do I begin this story? In 1987, when Narendra Modi was given charge of the BJP campaign in the Ahmedabad Municipal Corporation elections, his first independent electoral assignment, and the first of the many unprecedented victories that he has crafted for the party? Or, in the 1990s, when he was responsible for managing the party's election campaign in a clutch of states, including Punjab, Haryana, Himachal Pradesh and Jammu and Kashmir? Or should one begin with 2001, and Modi taking over as Chief Minister of Gujarat at a juncture when the consequences of the devastating Republic Day earthquake still confronted us? I will take the easiest option and commence with the Lok Sabha election of 2014.

◆

Everybody now recognizes that the 2014 election marked the most decisive shift in the history of Indian politics. This was obvious from the nature of the mandate for Narendra bhai and the party: the BJP became the first party in thirty years to get a majority on its own, and the BJP-led National Democratic Alliance ended up with a two-thirds majority.

Since 1984, no party had won an absolute majority in the Lok Sabha. During the general elections between 1951-52 and 1984, parties and Prime Ministers that had won majorities had done so on the basis of goodwill generated during the freedom movement, family legacy, anger against the incumbent government (1977), a mix of fear and sympathy (1984), with dollops of appeasement, sectional prejudice, empty sloganeering ('*Garibi hatao*', 1971) and vote bank mobilization. There had been no mandate for hope—and no mandate that was simply a reward for tested performance.

For the twenty-five years between 1989 and 2014, India had been governed by coalitions. Coalitions by their very nature are a compromise. They are a compromise of political interests and a compromise of policy outcomes. Fatalism had set in among ordinary citizens. They too had come to compromise with aspirations—whether for themselves and their families, or for the India of their dreams. There was a feeling that policy paralysis, administrative confusion, quarrelling ministers and blackmailing allies, corruption, insecurity and vulnerability to terrorism, and weak and indecisive Prime Ministers—who acted more as managers than leaders—were built into the coalition system. These had become a permanent curse on Indian democracy.

A low-level equilibrium of expectations had set in. India had taught itself not to think big and think ambitious. The ten years between 2004 and 2014 represented the pinnacle (perhaps 'nadir' is a more appropriate word) of this national listlessness and despondency. Popular morale was low, India's people were dejected. It was against this backdrop that Narendra Modi emerged as a compelling all-India candidate for prime minister. He took the BJP into new areas, constituencies and social groups. More than that, he ignited hope.

How did Modi become so popular and well-known across the country, and in such a short period? Was it the result of one blockbuster election campaign? Or was it because of a message taken to every street, every galli and every mohalla by not just the BJP's untiring workers, but also by millions of non-political volunteers? Or was it due to the idealistic men and women and young people who came to believe in Modi? Or did it happen with the aid of the force multiplier of technology? These were the mediums, but what was even more magnetic and forceful was the substance of the Modi message. That message itself had been written earlier, in the years of perseverance and striving, and of economic and social attainment in Gujarat.

I first met Narendra bhai in Ahmedabad in 1987. He had recently been assigned to the BJP Gujarat state unit as General Secretary (Organisation). The Ahmedabad Municipal Corporation elections had just been announced. The context of this election needs to be appreciated. The Congress was the dominant party in Gujarat and across the country. It had won massive mandates in the Lok Sabha and Assembly elections in 1984 and 1985. The BJP, as a political and electoral force, was at the foot of a mountain and had a long climb ahead. With about a dozen seats in the outgoing Ahmedabad Municipal Corporation, our party was hardly in the reckoning.

After being given charge of the election, Narendra bhai taught us to aim high and plan methodically. In many ways, he helped us re-think and re-imagine elections and electioneering. As secretary of the BJP city unit in Ahmedabad, I listened and observed him from close quarters and then began implementing what he told us. The basic premise of the Modi strategy was simple: mobilize and optimise the strengths and capacities of the party and the Sangh network for the election. The outcome was stunning. The BJP won a majority of municipal seats as well as the Mayor's office.

Now there was no holding back. In 1988, a state-wide membership drive was launched. What would have otherwise been a routine event was transformed by Modi into a 'Sangathan Parva' (organization festival). He was clear that he wanted it to be a 'festival' owned and energized by the people and their mass participation, and not a sterile party function by and for party functionaries. He instructed that the enrolment of members would be numbered and recorded in registers. The registers would be available at the tehsil and zilla level for random checks and audits. Like many others, I was assigned districts that I would have to visit to verify the registers and names listed.

I accompanied Narendra bhai on two long tours of the state. His pace of work, acuity of observation and eye for detail were mesmerizing. I absorbed all that I could. One piece of advice particularly stayed with me. Narendra bhai told us every village was likely to have had two major candidates in the preceding sarpanch election. The winner would invariably be from the Congress or the Janata Dal, the two leading parties in Gujarat at the time. The loser would be sidelined and forgotten. Modi asked us to target the runner-up as part of the party membership drive.

The rationale was razor sharp. The loser in the sarpanch contest, he said, would have 30-40 per cent of the vote. This was not enough to win, but still estimable. Modi asked us to approach all such persons and invite them into the BJP with dignity and after an honest conversation about our party's positions and philosophies. If the match worked, it added a sizeable number of voters, at the village level, to our existing core. It also gave us a notable micro-level leader of some influence.

This is how Modi built the party organization in Gujarat, being clear that the expansion of the party and its electoral competitiveness had to go together. Governance would be the third angle, and in 2001 Modi was given the chance to complete the triangle, of course while retaining the BJP's ideological distinctiveness.

◆

In his thirteen years as Chief Minister, Narendra Modi transformed Gujarat. From an early-stage industrial and commodities economy, the state evolved into a manufacturing and services powerhouse. He converted handicaps into opportunities. Piped water reached every home and technology-assisted soil health cards enabled small farmers. A dairy revolution in tribal areas and a reimagining of Kutch—which rose from the debris of the earthquake to become a modern industrial economy—changed lives and livelihoods in the state.

From seismic-appropriate housing to twenty-first century infrastructure, the Modi momentum was unstoppable. I have provided only a snapshot of Narendra bhai's chief ministerial years. Other chapters in this book discuss and describe the many achievements in much greater detail.

Beyond individual projects and statistics, what Modi brought to Gujarat was a new scripture of public service, and a new paradigm of governance. He was undeterred by the widely-held perception that 'anti-incumbency' and voting out governments was an instinctive and unthinking habit in Indian electoral life. He had faith in the sense and sensibility of voters. He trusted them to tell right from wrong; and good, long-term intent from short-term gimmickry.

Many of his programmes in Gujarat—the bringing of the Narmada's waters from south Gujarat to Saurashtra, for instance—were conceptualized with a long view. Their gestation period ran into more than one electoral cycle. Modi worked for not just the next election, but the Gujarat of the next decade and next generation. Expectedly the BJP too became the political vehicle of Gujarat's development and aspirations for the next decade and the next generation.

Modi's reasoning and his very approach required constant and direct communication. He was not shackled by the Secretariat in Gandhinagar. Week after week, he travelled up and down the state. He conveyed the benefits of government programmes to different audiences and stakeholders, to varied people and communities. He encouraged the BJP to do likewise—talk to people rather than speak just to the media.

He used the demonstration effect with finesse. He offered evidence of how a project was helping some populations and sub-regions to give an idea of what would happen to other sub-regions and populations as the programme was taken to its logical conclusion. At election time, he spelt out not just fresh promises, but a report card: of what he had delivered against what he had promised five years earlier.

Modi is not the type of politician who forgets his party's manifesto. He has an emotional attachment with the party that is rare and touching. More than once—most memorably in his speech at the Parliament House in May 2014—he has said that he looks upon the party as a 'Mother'. The BJP is the Mother that has nurtured him and given him his essential identity. As such, the party's manifesto is to him his Mother's word. It is sacred to him, and he is responsible for honouring it.

As Modi put such sentiments into earnest action, Gujaratis experienced a new political and public service culture. No longer did their Chief Minister speak or think in terms of caste coalitions and acronyms; he spoke and thought for all the people of Gujarat, for every Gujarati. Modi's programmes were universal in their desirability, design and delivery; they touched every family. Every part of the state—irrespective of its voting history and caste or community algebra—felt the firm and yet gentle hand of Modi sarkar.

This culture is Narendra Modi's great legacy in Gujarat. It is no surprise then that the state has not turned its back on the BJP since the mid-1990s. The BJP unit's identification with Gujarati society and its hopes and dreams is absolute. This is exactly the Gujarat model that was scaled up to all of the country after 2014. As the election that year approached, the discrepancy between the two models—the Gujarat model and the coalition-Congress model—became too apparent to ignore. The breathtaking pace of development in Gujarat had coincided with the floundering and failures of the UPA government in Delhi. India woke up to the Modi proposition.

Gujarat has always drawn people from all parts of the country. As the state's economy grew and diversified under Modi, it became an even stronger magnet for workers and investors from other regions. They came from across the length and breadth of India: from eastern India to the southern states, from Delhi and the National Capital Region to the Mumbai-Pune-Thane mega region, and from Aizawl to Alappuzha. As they experienced Modi's governance, a curiosity and then admiration began to form. Their pulse quickened. Could this be, they asked themselves, could this just be the future of India?

These guest workers, investors and stakeholders in the rejuvenation of Gujarat became Narendra Modi's ambassadors. They amplified the Modi message. They took with them individual Modi stories—of his absolute and unbending identification with India and with national pride; of his hard work, his restless energy, his incorruptibility and foresight; his government's welfare programmes, social sector delivery and visionary economic projects.

They discussed it on trains and in buses, in dhabas and chai shops, with friends, acquaintances and even strangers as well as in gatherings at home with family members across innumerable small towns and villages. Line by line, example by example, anecdote by anecdote, across India, across communities and castes—including among individuals who had no first-hand experience of Gujarat—the Modi legend grew. In time the buzz got simply too loud to be missed.

Initially, the national media didn't notice, or perhaps pretended not to notice. Looking back, there were four stages of media response to the Modi phenomenon at that point: obliviousness; dismissal; denial; and finally grudging and fitful acceptance. The so-called national media almost completely missed the undercurrent. Nevertheless, even within those who lived far away from Gujarat and were not voters or immediate stakeholders in Gujarat, that question emerged: was Modi the man India awaited? Had our country, people whispered to themselves, finally found the leader who would repair broken dreams and restore India to the prosperity and primacy that was its once and forever destiny?

The upshot was an emotional explosion, a mandate of a billion aspirations, and a cry from the soul for 'Abki baar, Modi sarkar'. Constituencies, groups, communities, families and individuals who had never previously voted for the BJP turned up at polling stations with a spring in their step and hope in their hearts. Together they gave India a fresh start.

◆

The numbers spoke with clarity. The BJP, led by prime ministerial candidate Narendra Modi and the promise of a Modi sarkar, won 282 Lok Sabha seats and 31 per cent of popular votes. This was 100 seats more than the BJP's historic best in a Lok Sabha election—182 seats in 1999. The comparison with the 2009 election—when the BJP had won 116 seats and 18.8 per cent of the vote—denoted the Modi increment.

In 2009, the BJP had won Lok Sabha seats in seventeen of India's then thirty-five states and union territories[1]. In 2014, Modi led the party to Lok Sabha seats in twenty-seven of thirty-six states and union territories[2]. By way of comparison, in 1996, when a BJP government was sworn in for the first time, the party had won Lok Sabha seats in twelve of the then thirty-two states and union territories[3]. Looked at another way, this meant the BJP had won seats in 37.5 per cent of India's states and union territories in 1996. In 2009, this had climbed to 48.6 per cent; in 2014, the first Modi wave took it to an astronomical 75 per cent.

Among the most complex and indicative parameters of Indian elections is the women's vote. Women are the sheet-anchors of our families and our society. How they vote, their choices and preferences, points to their individual aspirations but also to several other concerns that touch the voter. A woman's vote is implicated by economic worries—such as inflation or jobs for members of the family—security and law and order, educational opportunities, and a quest for honesty and ethical benchmarks.

That women voters were putting their faith in Modi was apparent from the high turnout in 2014. In 2009, while 60.2 per cent of male voters had got to the polling station only 55.8 per cent of female voters could make it to the booths[4]. Five years later, the idea of a Modi government was enough to push women's turnout up by 10 percentage points. In 2014, as much as 65.54 per cent of female voters voted[5].

In 2019, as the promise of candidate Modi translated into the performance of Modi sarkar, the enthusiasm was even higher. This time 67.18 per cent of women voters came forward. For the first time, they outpolled men (67.02 per cent turnout)[6]. Women voters had come to identify with the ideals and the implementation of Narendra bhai's programmes. Family after family came to be counted among the BJP's most loyal voters.

In 2019, of course, Modi's five years as prime minister were appreciated and acknowledged by an even larger number of voters. The BJP won 303 Lok Sabha seats and 37.3 per cent of the popular vote. In those five years, Modi changed the reference points of governance, and changed India. In the process, he took the BJP to new social and regional frontiers. It was a perfect synergy of governance and electoral politics, individual leadership and party rigour, economy and welfare, social equity and nationalism, reassurance at home and security at the border.

How did Modi do it? Typical of his approach and outlook, and his thrust for decentralization and democratization, the answer lies not in Delhi—or certainly not solely in Delhi. It lies in the many and diverse states of India.

◆

The Modi impact on the Indian voter *outside* Gujarat began to be tracked from December 2013. Narendra bhai had been chosen as the BJP's prime ministerial candidate only a few weeks earlier. The first set of state elections after that event had a certain significance. The party won absolute majorities in large states like Rajasthan, Madhya Pradesh and Chhattisgarh.

Before the December 2013 elections, the BJP had four chief ministers in different states. One other chief minister belonged to an allied party and led an NDA government. All over the country, the BJP had 773 MLAs. In May 2018, the figures peaked at 1,460 MLAs and 15 BJP chief ministers. As I write this (in October 2021) the BJP has 12 chief ministers of its own, six chief ministers of allied parties, and a total of 1,389 party MLAs in different states.

That the BJP continues to have such a wide and deep legislative and political presence even seven years into the Modi government, defying standard predictions of voter fatigue and anti-incumbency, is telling. It offers a yardstick of how Modi's leadership has expanded the party's social and geographical landscape.

Since December 2013, BJP has won majorities and formed governments in states it had previously won as well as states where it had been relatively weak. In 2017 it won the biggest mandate in the history of Uttarakhand. The three-fourths majority in Uttar Pradesh (2017) was the largest in any election in that state since 1977. It had been widely predicted that Haryana's caste arithmetic would never support the BJP. In 2014, the party won a majority in the state and was subsequently re-elected. In Maharashtra, the BJP won in 2014 and is currently the primary and pivotal party. The politics of the state revolves around it. Jharkhand has a similar story.

It was said the BJP would not get traction in the Northeast. In contrast, the party and its allies have won elections in Arunachal Pradesh, Assam and Manipur. The electoral victory in Tripura, against an entrenched Communist government the writ of which had run for some 25 years, was especially satisfying. The hard-earned reward of determined and diligent canvassing led by Narendra Modi, it represented an ideological triumph. The party won because it articulated the aspirations of local communities. Our rivals couldn't go beyond the virtues of Marx and Lenin.

The importance of the BJP's victory in a one-to-one battle with a Communist party was not lost on political analysts. Communist parties had been unseated earlier in India, in other state elections. Yet, they had been defeated and replaced by political forces and groups that offered only variants of Communist thinking and autocracy. The BJP had won in a genuine contest of ideas and world views—between suraaj and swaraj on the one hand, and cadre raj on the other.

Today, the BJP is in the reckoning in elections in virtually every state and union territory—from Jammu and Kashmir to Puducherry, and from Nagaland to Goa. Even in state elections that the party did not win, the Modi dynamo has taken the BJP vote to highest-ever levels. West Bengal, Odisha and Tamil Nadu are examples of this. An indicator of just how competitive the party has become was the Greater Hyderabad Municipal Corporation election of 2020. The BJP finished second with

48 of the 150 seats. Its tally had gone up an astounding 12 times since the previous polling.

This appreciable expansion, and that too in such a short duration, has no match in India's electoral politics. It has happened alongside the enhancement in Narendra Modi's stature and popularity, which itself has been bolstered by his efforts as the Prime Minister, as party leader and as campaigner. What is even more exceptional is that he has done it—and continues to do it—without a well-recognized family surname or a dominant caste identity to exploit, and around which to mould his politics.

In many states the BJP had a past history. In all states it had a bed-rock of leaders, activists and functionaries with public goodwill and grassroots service. Modi was the X factor, the extra something that made the difference between a marginal contest and a comfortable one—or between a narrow victory and a ringing endorsement.

Modi's role in state election campaigns is substantive. He is not just an add-on, or a mascot flown in for a few events and rallies. He embraces state campaigns, issues and idioms, each with its individual flavour. He complements the deep understanding of local politics and concerns that state BJP units and leaders bring to the table. This is very different from the supposed national leaders of other parties. They are fly in-fly out visitors, with no sense of the ground reality.

The personal connection with every state and every region is a precious gift. To understand it, one must go back to Modi even before 2001, to his apprenticeship and to the ceaseless, untiring Bharat Yatra of that period, with a watchful eye, a listening ear, and an open mind. That tapasya was his real-life university.

◆

How does one define a national leader? In the India before Modi, this question engrossed and puzzled many serious students of politics and society. In the immediate aftermath of 1947, national leaders were identified by their name recall across regions and states because of their participation in the freedom struggle. In succeeding decades, however, notably at the height of the coalition era, the expression 'national leader' came to be much abused.

It was a status generously distributed by the Delhi media to its friends and favourites. The label was handed out even to politicians of no proven merit, and only capable of winning a Lok Sabha election from one or two safe seats. They were very visible in news television studios, but unknown in villages merely 25 km from Parliament House. After Modi and 2014, such facile and insincere manufacturing of 'national leaders' was shown up for what it was. Narendra Modi is now the template for what it means and what it takes to be a national leader.

At the simplest level, a national leader is somebody who connects with a citizen not only on big, national issues—such as defence or foreign policy—but on subjects of immediate concern to the individual and his or her family, neighbourhood, town or village, state and region. During elections, national-level campaigners make an attempt to emphasize such a connection. Sometimes they are handed notes on local matters as they are preparing to deliver a speech. This is a crude method. More organized political leaders and parties have a system of research and a constant stream of inputs.

The receptivity of the person who is reading the inputs and absorbing the research material is a critical determinant. How much does the national leader in question already know? How sharply can he or she cut through the fog and get to the heart of the voter? How acquainted is such a leader with the state or region even independently? The best teacher here is travelling to ordinary places, meeting ordinary families, sharing ordinary experiences, and doing all this by ordinary means. Narendra Modi has done so with greater frequency and perseverance than any politician in the past 75 years.

As a young political activist, travelling by trains and buses, Narendra bhai visited virtually every district of the country and thousands and thousands of villages. In fervent travel spells, he rarely slept two successive nights at the same place. Even as prime minister he has often astonished state-rung BJP functionaries by offering them intimate details of micro-level issues. In some cases, even they have not been entirely conversant with the subject, or at least not with a matching granularity.

This is a consequence of Narendra bhai having seen the issue in person, and of embedding it in his memory. It gives him a gift that only a select few in history have—of being able to speak to the single individual in a large audience and bonding with him or her as if they were communicating one-to-one. He does so not just with oratory, but by conveying an understanding of the substance of a person's specific sentiments and everyday emotions, in his or her social, cultural and geographical contexts.

This experiential learning is Narendra bhai's cognitive base. It has given him an enormous understanding of India as a bottom-up—rather than top-down, imposed-from-above and Delhi-centric—national leader. It has allowed him an astute and accurate insight into how our states and regions have common challenges, but also unique ones. Inevitably much of what he has seen and learnt has influenced his policies in government.

One example is the deeply-felt desire, especially among women, for LPG cylinders that would help their kitchens transition from uncomfortable and unhealthy coal fuel. The importance of toilets is another. Only a national leader who knows his nation and his people will make such issues central to his agenda. The Pradhan Mantri Ujjwala Yojana and the Swachh Bharat Mission were ideas swirling in Narendra bhai's mind since those early days of relentless travel. He waited for the moment; as soon as he became Prime Minister, he grabbed it.

◆

Narendra Modi's knowledge and empathy have helped the BJP much more than just election time. He has guided our state governments with precision and focus as they have incubated and rolled out welfare and economic programmes. The Prime Minister effortlessly shifts from the large canvas to the microscopic view. All this has enabled BJP governments and ensured better delivery. In turn, the party has used its governance record to sustain its expansion into new social groups and areas, and win second or successive terms.

Narendra bhai is practical to an exacting degree. Even in the aftermath of electoral success, he is not swayed by triumphalism. With realism and keen observation, he is ever aware of gaps that remain. A few weeks after the parliamentary election of 2014, I was appointed as the BJP national president. In 2015, I went to the prime minister and said we were planning a party membership drive. His immediate response was that if we did it the old-fashioned way it would serve no purpose. We would easily and lazily enrol more and more members in geographies where we were already strong.

How will this expand the BJP, he asked? What is your strategy for states and areas where we are relatively absent or have very few members? He gave me concrete examples of not just states, but regions within states. Low membership had led to limited party capacity, and limited party capacity had meant membership stayed low. How would we break out of this cycle?

Having raised the bar, Narendra bhai advised us on how we could overcome it. Use technology, he said, begin a membership drive on the basis of a missed call. Anybody who gave a missed call to a pre-publicised number was immediately enrolled as a member. This would make it easier for a silent supporter of the BJP, who was attracted to it but didn't quite know how to physically interact with the party organization, to sign up.

The next step, Narendra bhai cautioned, would be harder. Invoking the lesson from the verification of membership registers in Gujarat in the 1980s, he said every missed call needed to be followed up on the ground. How many of the callers were serious and how many had made that call on a whim? The new members would need to be contacted and introduced to the party, its structures and its thinking. He urged me to prepare the party for this second stage, even while the missed call exercise was on. The follow-up stage would be crucial to convert well-wishers into full-time party insiders—'Shubhchintak se karyakarta tak', is what we called it. In time, it would catalyse the raw passion of 'missed-call members' into a long-term institutional architecture.

The challenge, Narendra bhai warned, would be toughest in regions and states where the party had so far been less visible. It was precisely here, because of the lower base, that the incremental political and electoral benefits would be highest. He was absolutely right. In terms of membership numbers, the campaign made the BJP the largest party in any democracy. It galvanized our expansion into regions and among communities that had so far been harder to access.

Narendra bhai's absolute involvement in the party and his commitment to its growth has not diminished an inch after he became Prime Minister. He has not sacrificed party interests for tactical gains in government, but in fact sees them as symbiotic. Like a disciplined soldier, he makes himself available for party meetings and assembly elections. He respects the judgement of the party president and leadership, and abides by schedules finalized by those responsible. Unmindful of how physically taxing this may be, he is always there for public meetings and campaign rallies. He never says no.

Quite to the contrary, he goes beyond the call of expectation. I still remember the final days of the Uttar Pradesh election of 2017. We were in Varanasi and Poorvanchal (eastern Uttar Pradesh) for the last stage of what had been a gruelling campaign. Modi got down to street-level, house-to-house canvassing, like any other constituency MP and party activist. This was inspirational for BJP workers who now redoubled their efforts. The commander had come down to the trenches, and he led us to a famous victory. The national leader's local impact was there for all to see.

◆

The most salient confirmation of the BJP's expansion under Narendra Modi came in the 2019 Lok Sabha election. Not only did the party consolidate its considerable gains of 2014, it actually widened its horizons. A greater vote share in constituencies reserved for Scheduled Castes and Scheduled Tribes, and across the Northeast was indicative. There was also the dramatic rise in seats in Odisha (one seat in 2014 to eight in 2019) and West Bengal (two seats to 18).

Even in states where the BJP had suffered a setback only a few months earlier—Rajasthan, Madhya Pradesh and Chhattisgarh had voted for new legislative assemblies in the winter of 2018—the Modi sarkar was firmly and emphatically re-elected. This suggested a remarkable satisfaction with the Modi-led BJP. The change of government in 2014 had delivered a genuine change of regime. The BJP had matured into India's natural party of governance.

Between 2014 and 2019, Narendra bhai harmonized interests and broke silos in policymaking. No longer were economic growth and welfare seen as distinct and separate. No more was technology or entrepreneurship, or even the idea of economic reform, restricted to educated urban elites, as it had been since 1991. Rather, these were widened and made more inclusive. In Narendra bhai's India start-ups have created technology-driven unicorns. Equally Narendra bhai's start-up culture has promoted bottom-of-the-pyramid enterprise.

Easier seed capital (MUDRA loans, Start-up India, Stand-Up India) and the use of technology as a business multiplier—including e-commerce windows—have added to the convenience. The formalization of the economy by bringing over 400 million people into the banking system and leveraging the JAM trinity (Pradhan Mantri Jandhan Yojana, Aadhar biometric identity, and mobile phone number) was revolutionary. Narendra bhai has expanded the logic of liberalization and accommodated India's vertical and horizontal diversity.

Narendra bhai has brought a similar enlightenment to social sector spending. Previous governments and ruling parties treated welfare as a hand-me-down. They offered giveaways, loan write-offs, even consumer goods and durables for votes. They made such delivery contingent on electoral support. Narendra bhai is different. He has combined welfare with GDP growth. His programmes have created sustainable, long-term infrastructure, been executed at scale, and been sculpted for universal delivery. They represent sizeable capital investment that kick-starts a virtuous cycle of economic demand and multigenerational social benefit.

Consider some statistics. In the period since 2014, 113 million toilets have been built under the Swachh Bharat Mission. The Pradhan Mantri Awas Yojana has built houses in both rural India (over 15 million houses) and urban India (five million houses). Announced on 15 August 2019, the Jal Jeevan Mission will take piped water to over 190 million rural households by 2024 (from a base of 33 million households). The outlay for this is ₹3,50,000 crore or about US$ 50 billion.

The Namami Gange Mission is not limited to cleaning the sacred river in Varanasi and one or two iconic cities. It is a holistic, basin-wide rejuvenation programme. It tackles pollution, pushes tourism, facilitates inland waterways and generates enormous economic activity, while nurturing Ma Ganga as the cultural and economic lifeline of India's heartland. The reconstruction of the revered Shri Ram Janmbhoomi Mandir in Ayodhya is being accompanied by connectivity, infrastructure and urban renewal projects on an extensive scale in Ayodhya and surrounding areas of central and eastern Uttar Pradesh. The blessings of Lord Ram will be available to the entire population living in the wider radius, to worshippers and non-worshippers alike.

All of these programmes require massive spending on cement, iron and steel, water pipes, building material, sanitary equipment, power lines and LED bulbs, and other feedstock. They generate jobs in construction, manufacturing and services. They are investments in human capital. They provide incalculable long-term capacity augmentation in the form of better health outcomes. They enable a citizen's human dignity, economic needs and personal fulfilment.

Such programmes are foundational for twenty-first century India, for New India, for Modi's India. They are not short-term freebies; they offer a combination of welfare and GDP spending. They create sustainable assets for the family and for the nation, and they will be remembered for decades to come. The people of our country understand and appreciate this as GDP growth with human development, and with a humane touch. That is why they repeatedly put their faith in Narendra Modi.

Unlike the transactional welfarism of previous governments and political cultures, Narendra bhai's 'GDP plus welfare' model does not discriminate between groups, communities, castes and religions. If a road is built, it is built for use by all. If a programme is to support people who meet a given criteria—income, age, gender, geographical location and so on—anybody who answers to those parameters is covered.

The party organization disseminates the news of these programmes far and wide into society. It encourages people to access their rights and benefits. The party acts not as an intermediary or a broker—but as part of what Narendra bhai once called the 'dharma chakra of development'.

The logic of the dharma chakra is disarmingly simple. Citizens communicate their wishes and hopes to the party and its countless activists. The party incorporates these inputs into its programme and governance agenda, and is elected on the basis of promise of delivery. The elected BJP government then implements this programme to the benefit and satisfaction of the people. The party then goes back to the people for their revised feedback. The chakra is complete.

As would be apparent, the party is not a one-way communicator; it is an interface. Its constant engagement with local people and communities is used to identify demands and gaps in the lives of Indian families. The flow of suggestions is constant and unremitting. It crystallizes into a dataset of real-life, real-time information for the party to analyse and process—and adopt and adapt for its state and national election manifestos. The party then holds the government to account for fulfilling these promises. Narendra bhai's feedback loop is complete. The BJP's social and electoral expansion is a natural corollary.

◆

The Indian ethos is essentially democratic. Through history, going back millennia, our civilization and society have embellished democratic philosophies and experimented with forms of democratic practice. Institutionalized examples of elections and elected government are available in our past. From village panchayats to large empires, from merchant guilds to religious complexes, charters of rights for citizens and stakeholders, and of responsibilities, obligations and trusteeship on the part of kings and administrators are instilled in our collective memory.

Since 1950, our nation has been a constitutional democracy. Indians are proud of their democracy and their franchise. The power and privilege to reward and punish governments on polling day is cherished by hundreds of millions of voters. Notwithstanding this pride, it was inevitable that questions sometimes arose as the administrative system underachieved even when asked to deliver basic public goods and services. The flux of the coalition era and the messy implosion of the UPA decade didn't help.

Narendra bhai's years in office have served as a refreshing affirmation that democracy can deliver public goods, economic development, and social sector services—and do so with transparency, equity and efficiency. The Modi government has deepened and renewed faith in democracy. It stands out as a case study that the democratic model can work and can bring about large-scale and positive transformation in a society of 1.3 billion people. There are obvious implications here for India and the world—a world where thinking people are constantly comparing and evaluating political and governance models.

This renewal of democracy has drawn from trust in Prime Minister Modi's intent, abilities and wisdom, and admiration for his personal attributes. His integrity and incorruptibility are held up as an example within the society. He is offered as a role model to one's children. Combined with his tireless, 24/7 work ethic, this has made him a folk hero for Indian families.

The belief that Modi will think of the best for my country, my family and for me is widespread and unshakeable. This belief, in fact, is not limited to BJP adherents and Modi voters. Even among many who are disinclined towards our party—or indeed towards politics at all—there is acknowledgement of such qualities and of the sheer passion and velocity that Narendra bhai has brought to the Prime Minister's office.

'Modi pe bharosa' (faith and trust in Modi) is an abiding principle—whether during an economic churning, a natural disaster, a pandemic, a terrorist attack or a threat at the border. For hundreds of millions of Indians, Narendra Modi is the family patriarch, the sagacious uncle, and the dependable older brother. He is the national statesman, and in him are invested India's hopes and aspirations—and its people's incredible expectations.

If any Indian is in trouble, anywhere in the world, there is a calming sense that Narendra Modi will stand by me, that his absolute attention is only a tweet away. There is confidence that Modi will do his utmost, that he will stretch every sinew, squeeze every minute and give it his all. He is much more than the Prime Minister; in the popular imagination, he is India's sentinel.

The COVID-19 pandemic is modern India's greatest challenge. It has tested our people's fortitude and it has tested Narendra bhai's leadership. Neither flinched, nor faltered. Upfront, honest crisis communication between the Prime Minister and his fellow citizens saw our people conform to the discipline of a complete lockdown at short notice. Instantly, they recognized the urgency that the head of government's words conveyed.

Narendra bhai didn't let them down. The 400/800 response—cash transfers to over 400 million individuals and food transfers that covered over 800 million people—brought essential supplies to doorsteps[7]. Targeted delivery and adroit use of digital technology, whether for cash transfers or eliminating potential leaks and discrepancies, built on the welfare and public services platforms and pipelines that Narendra bhai had so carefully put in place. The ongoing vaccine rollout is among the largest in global history, and the quickest for any developing country. Narendra Modi will settle for nothing but the best for his people; they feel it, they know it, and they pin their innermost emotions on him.

Narendra bhai's role in the BJP's expansion cannot be weighed in votes and seats alone. Its true metric is intangible. It lies in the respect that he and his administration have earned for the BJP even among those who have never voted for our party. Many years ago, in a thoughtful moment in Gandhinagar, I remember him telling me, 'One day our party has to come to office in Delhi with a Lok Sabha majority of its own. Only then can we show the world what the BJP's model of government can achieve.'

Over the past 20 years, in Gujarat and then across India, Narendra bhai has been true to his ideals. He has established the BJP not just as the premier and largest political party in the world's biggest democracy, but as the pan-Indian embodiment of national interest. Take it from me, he is far from done. The decade has just begun. Watch for where it takes Narendra Modi, where Modi takes the BJP—and where the BJP and Modi take India.

CHANGING ELECTIONS AND ELECTIONEERING FOREVER

PRADEEP GUPTA

The art of winning elections is about winning the hearts of the people, and nothing in this can be fake. For the longest time, politicians resorted to strategies and tactics for electoral success. Coalitions were cobbled to form governments by any means. Essentially due to this, people gradually lost faith in politicians and politics became a dirty word; those in white-collar professions chose to stay away from politics. The very image of a politician was one of a tainted goon who flaunted money and muscle power.

Narendra Modi's meteoric rise can be attributed to the paradigm shift that he lent to modern politics in India. He kept looking for ways to rid Indian politics of tactics and quick-fix strategies merely to win elections. He used his understanding and insights into political processes and experimented at the local body polls in Gujarat in his early years. After being inducted into the BJP as general secretary (organization) in Gujarat, Modi was in charge of the Ahmedabad Municipal Corporation elections in 1987. The party had won in Rajkot and Junagadh corporations earlier but had no such luck in Ahmedabad. Successive electoral defeats had demoralized the party cadre, and they lacked a crucial element for an election victory—conviction.

Modi encouraged the party cadre to focus on telling people about the party's strong intention of transforming the city's governance. He told them that, if they managed to effectively communicate this message, nothing would be able to prevent the party from emerging victorious. The meticulously planned campaign harnessed the prevailing discontentment against the Congress, and the BJP managed to win the election.

Politics is a science that needs understanding and insight into the psyche of the common man. Human psychology is driven by needs, expectations and aspirations, which in turn are the reasons behind one's choices and decisions. To enter politics and elections with a scientific temperament and to connect with people to get their acceptance, is not merely election management but an evolved human resource mechanism. It needs a deep understanding of human psychology. Social groups and segments of the electorate that supported the Congress party for years shifted, one by one, tying their allegiance to Modi, who made innovative experiments and was rewarded continuously with a string of electoral successes. Modi understood that elections are not merely the outcome of politics but are a part of social science. Politicians may be the faces of political parties; their wins or losses might seem like a simple pass or fail, but there are reasons why people make them win or lose. The decision is entirely in the hands of the masses, and the reason they choose or reject a particular politician usually has a simple answer—people connect.

Modi has also been conscious that politics and elections can often escalate rather than reduce social divisions and tensions. Ensuring that politics does not harm social relations and instead strengthens grassroots politics, has always been the foremost priority for him.

Here is an example. In the mid-1980s, Gujarat was witnessing intense inter-group animosity, particularly among caste groups, due to the active anti-reservation movement in the state. Local elections often create tension within the village; even next-door neighbours find themselves on opposing sides. When Modi was around twelve years old, he often heard Sarvodaya leader Dwarakadas Joshi mention how elections created rifts at the village level. His words remained etched in Modi's memory and became the inspiration behind the Gujarat government's Samras Gram Yojana. Under the programme, villages are given special incentives if they unanimously elect a sarpanch[1]. Over six stages, more than 3,700 panchayats across the state have unanimously elected their sarpanch and become 'Samras'[2].

Candidates in any election should study the responses of the people for an accurate analysis of voter choices, the whys and wherefores underneath those choices. It is only then that candidates will be able to fashion themselves, their party and the right issues in such a manner that a positive response with respect to electoral success can be guaranteed.

Be it the local body elections or national and assembly polls, Modi has been the 'guarantee' of every election, not because he is an election machine but because he knows the art of ruling the hearts of the people. His instant connection with the people he speaks with—be it at rallies, smaller interactive sessions or those he crosses paths with in various capacities—has won him a following like none other.

HUMANE POLITICS: MODI'S MANTRA

Mahatma Gandhi was a pioneer in the art of winning hearts, and now in the twenty-first century, Modi has taken it a notch further. He has practised humane politics. This may sound like an oxymoron to many—who has ever been humane in this cut-throat profession? But it is a reality. This, I feel, is his mantra that has helped him win elections for two decades despite a relentless Opposition. He has remained the blue-eyed boy of the country, no matter what his political rivals say or do.

By paying heed to Gandhi's talisman—always take decisions keeping in mind the last man in the queue—Modi delivered transformative schemes during his very first tenure as Prime Minister. Humanity has been the core of his leadership: for instance, he understood the plight of women who had to bear the humiliation of open defecation or suffer in smoke-filled kitchens. Toilets in every house under Swachh Bharat and gas connections under the Ujjwala scheme were game changers for him because the very women he looked out for, blessed him with thumping majorities.

Of course, empowerment of any section of the society does not come from mere announcement of schemes. Foolproof implementation minus pilferage is what finally reaches that last person in the queue. While previous governments promised empowerment of women, Modi made it a reality by opening Jan Dhan accounts that enabled them to receive direct cash transfers. Women could have cash in hand that they could call their own and spend according to their wishes. Women became the proud owners of their homes under the Pradhan Mantri Awas Yojana. They were no longer at the mercy of the men in their house. Their position was elevated significantly in their homes and, by extension, in society. Everything that was in the files and works, became a reality in the very lifetime of these women.

Modi has an incomparable connect with the masses. During the Uttarakhand flash floods tragedy in 2013, after watching the rescue operations, he personally landed up in Dehradun to rescue thousands of Gujaratis from the wreckage and send them home. In yet another instance of his warmth, Modi celebrated the Diwali of 2020 with the jawans along the border at Longewala in Jaisalmer. Is it still a mystery why he has won and keeps winning millions of hearts?

With his sharp political acumen and wit, Modi does not let go of any opportunity to remind the Opposition of its mistakes. The distasteful jibes of 'chaiwala' or '*maut ka saudagar*' levelled against him were effectively countered. Modi's speeches rise above petty personal attacks even as he trains his guns at the Opposition regarding how it robbed the nation of its resources and a better future for its citizens. He has shifted the tone of election speeches from personal jibes to a comparative analysis of the performance of his government *vis-à-vis* previous governments or those led by other political parties in various states. It is a simple 'my report card versus your report card' narrative. He strictly sticks to issues that affect the common man, which may not impress the elites and the privileged sections of the society, but Modi sure has the full attention of the common man. These are probably his hard-earned learnings from his early years and could be a guide for future generations of aspiring politicians.

Modi has repeatedly sought accountability from other governments while he freely reveals what his report card looks like. By giving proof of his own performance, he puts the Opposition in the dock. The entire election system has become more accountable and transparent in an environment where the ruling party at the Centre leads by example.

For the first time, a Prime Minister chose to call himself 'Pradhan Sevak'. With this, he has created a new equation with the people. It is no longer a relationship between a ruler and his subjects, but of one pressed in public service and his own people. That is the magic, humane politics that is Modi's strength. It cannot be an eyewash because holding up pretenses for two decades is not possible. Pradhan Sevak is no longer an idiom but a reality that the entire nation is not only a witness to, but has also endorsed, time and again.

POLITICAL JOURNEY THROUGH YATRAS

When in 1915, Mahatma Gandhi came back to India from South Africa, as a first step towards spearheading the freedom struggle, he travelled the length and breadth of India. He took it as an exercise to familiarize himself with the masses, to learn what actually affected them and what their aspirations and expectations were—if one day swaraj (self-rule) became become a reality. A barrister, who could have easily afforded the comforts of first-class, chose to travel in second-class compartments of Indian Railways for two full years. This was a deliberate move to be among the masses, who may have been voiceless until then, but would soon turn out to be the agents of change and creators of history. Gandhi, not only educated himself on the ground realities of this vast and diverse country through his yatras, he also empowered the people to reimagine a world where swaraj was not merely an audacious dream.

The more Gandhi scaled himself down in the conventional terms—from crisp suits to a dhoti, and from luxury to austerity—the larger his image grew in the eyes of the people. Gandhi soon realized the disconnect between the people and the Congress party leaders, who were mostly elites. In a gradual transition, he took the freedom struggle out of the hands of these elites and made it a people's movement. And, the rest is history.

Post-Independence, Gandhi had advised that the Congress should become a Lok Sevak Dal and work for the people. He called for a reimagining of the Congress party's role in a changed context. But Congress leaders rejected the idea, and once again, the Congress became a party of elites. For seventeen years, Nehru, who led the nation, remained a dreamy-eyed leader. He was far removed from the ground realities. The legacy that he left behind and the dynasts following in his footsteps could not break out of the mould of privilege. Generations of privileged leaders at odds with the very people they were representing, cut off from the realities of the masses, have left the Congress redundant.

The political backdrop of the first few decades post-Independence was that of the freedom struggle. The focus was on building a new nation. The next few generations ushered in social revolutions, but the Emergency in 1977 throttled these leaders and their social revolutions died a silent death. The leaders, who came up in the following years, did not have any social relevance and failed to create a lasting impact in the minds of the people.

At seventeen, while his peers had different dreams and aspirations for themselves, Modi decided to leave home and travel across India. Though this shocked his family, they soon accepted it. On the day of his departure, his mother prepared a sweet dish that is cooked on special occasions and applied the customary tilak on his forehead, sending him with her blessings.

He travelled to the Himalayas, where he stayed at Garudachatti, Ramkrishna Ashram in West Bengal, and even the Northeast. He traversed the expansive landscape of India, exploring the diverse cultures in various parts of the country. It was also a time of spiritual awakening for him that connected him further to a man he always admired—Swami Vivekananda.

Like Gandhi, it was Modi's turn to see Indian society from close quarters and understand the fabric of this nation. Gandhi's follower, Vinoba Bhave, too, had his influence on Modi, helping him develop clear goals early on. The travel in the following months and years was Modi's window to the world and left a lasting impression on him. He then understood the real essence of the early Congress leadership that helped India gain freedom and dignity. He turned into a student and minutely observed the common man and his needs, hopes and aspirations, discontent and worries. This would go on to become the very foundation of his deep understanding of the masses and the bond that he managed to create in all his years in office. When, during the 2014 election rallies, audiences scaled walls and towers just to get a glimpse of Modi and chanted slogans like frenzied cheerleaders, several within his own party and the Opposition failed to comprehend the reason behind his intoxicating appeal. Mahatma Gandhi was possibly the last leader who drew such a passionate following. The 'Modi wave' could rightly be called the subsequent chapter to Gandhi's social connection.

Essentially there are two types of journeys: *naam ki yatra* and *kaam ki yatra*. The first is an advertising and outreach effort and it is commonly seen in today's politics. The latter is a more meaningful and purpose-driven undertaking. It helps in connecting with the masses and understand their needs and desires. Though it is rare in the fast-paced politics of the twenty-first century, this is what helps mobilize party cadres and bring effective long-term change.

In his long and illustrious political career, Modi has planned and undertaken numerous yatras. These have played an integral role in raising public awareness about critical issues and helped the BJP in electoral mobilization. As the general secretary of Gujarat BJP, he was the brain behind two yatras that laid the foundations of the party's political domination in the state. In the mid-1980s, Gujarat suffered from three consecutive years of drought. Modi meticulously planned and launched a Nyay Yatra across the state in 1987 to mobilize citizens on the issue of drought relief and create awareness about the BJP in the hinterland. The journey passed through 115 tehsils and more than 15,000 villages across the state[3].

Another yatra planned by Modi, and one that changed the course of Gujarat politics, was the Lok Shakti Yatra in 1989. A Rath Yatra was planned across the state to expand Keshubhai Patel's support base and widen his acceptability beyond Saurashtra and Patels. The Lok Shakti Yatra successfully made Keshubhai Patel a well-known face across the state and paved the way for him to become the Chief Minister a few years later. Both journeys prepared the ground for the BJP's meteoric rise in Gujarat—from winning merely eleven seats in 1985 to securing a two-thirds majority in 1995, and holding power for more than two decades.

During his tenure as Gujarat's Chief Minister, Modi initiated numerous yatras that focused on mobilizing people for the state's development rather than partisan goals. For instance, in 2012, Narendra Modi undertook a month-long Swami Vivekananda Yuva Vikas Yatra that started on 11 September—the anniversary of Swami Vivekananda's landmark speech at the World's Parliament of Religions in Chicago.

In a democracy, elections are a strong medium to choose one's representatives. Modi understood the nitty-gritty of contesting and winning elections and of making and breaking governments. He kept studying the democratic processes and experimenting with ways to make the entire system error-free and pro-people.

Issues, people and contexts are dynamic and keep changing over the years. Leaders who manage to adapt themselves to these dynamic shifts and prove themselves useful in the current context are the only ones that survive. If you buy a pen and that pen fails to write, will you not dump it in the bin? Similarly, people elect a representative, expecting him/her to perform. But if the representative fails to deliver, is it not obvious that he/she will soon be rejected? Now among all the pens that work, which is the one that is the most favourite? In the political context, what makes a leader stand out from the others? I would say it is humane politics, because as humans we are ruled by the basic instinct of humanity. A touch of kindness supersedes all the luxuries of the world.

FOREVER A STUDENT

In 2001, an unexpected phone call from the then Prime Minister, Atal Behari Vajpayee, changed Modi's life and the face of Indian politics forever. Modi was at a funeral of a senior cameraman, Gopal Bisht, who was among the journalists killed with Madhavrao Scindia in an unfortunate plane crash, when he received that call. Vajpayee asked him to come to his residence that evening, and the rest is history. Modi was sent back to Gujarat to take charge as Chief Minister; he had not served even as an MLA before that. On 7 October 2001, he took over the reins of the state and went on to become Gujarat's longest-serving Chief Minister—a record four times until he moved to national politics in 2014.

He may have been a newcomer in the Gujarat Assembly in 2001, but Modi was no novice. He had already spent years in the BJP organization, where he came to be recognized for his organizational skills. In 1990, he was in the core team to strategize for the Gujarat Assembly polls. The results of the elections brought an end to a decade of Congress rule. From 141 and 149 seats in 1980 and 1985 respectively, the Congress was down to 33 seats and the BJP won 67 seats, and they joined a coalition government with Chimanbhai Patel. The alliance may not have survived the full term, but the BJP emerged as a formidable force in Gujarat.

In 1995, when Modi was actively involved in the campaign for the Assembly polls, the BJP decided for the first time to contest all 182 seats. In a historic outcome, the party won 121 seats and formed the government. A year later, he was summoned to Delhi as the national secretary of the BJP and was given the charge of key north Indian states such as Punjab, Haryana, Himachal Pradesh and Jammu and Kashmir. The BJP formed a government in Himachal Pradesh on its own in 1998 and formed coalitions in Haryana (1996), Punjab (1997) and Jammu and Kashmir. He worked closely with leaders like Parkash Singh Badal, Bansi Lal and Farooq Abdullah. The Chandigarh Municipal Corporation elections in 1996 was particularly noteworthy for Modi. It was the first municipal corporation election in the city and Modi wanted the BJP to set an example for other cities. He ensured that ticket distribution was conducted in an inclusive manner, and the BJP became an avenue for eminent citizens, like Air Marshal (retd.) R.S. Bedi, to participate in politics. Late Neerja Bhanot's father, Harish Bhanot, was nominated to the municipal corporation as the BJP emerged victorious by winning thirteen wards out of a total of twenty, and independent candidates won four and the Shiromani Akali Dal (SAD) got two wards; the Congress could win only one ward.

Even in Gujarat, Modi encouraged professionals and eminent citizens to join politics through the BJP. Since 2014, Modi has facilitated the entry of innumerable professionals and technocrats in active electoral politics.

In 1998, Modi was entrusted with the role of general secretary (organization), a key position previously held by stalwarts like Sundar Singh Bhandari and Kushabhau Thakre. As general secretary, his role in the 1998 and 1999 Lok Sabha campaigns was crucial. The BJP became the single-largest party in both the polls and formed the government under the leadership of Atal Bihari Vajpayee. Since the very beginning, Modi stressed on strengthening the sangathan (organization) as he realized that a great brand equity at the top level needs support to convert it into a mass hit.

His stint as Gujarat Chief Minister was challenging in more ways than one, but he hit the ground running. His lack of experience in governance notwithstanding, he played it by the ear, and how! Strong roots bear sweet fruits. All the years spent among the people and his deep understanding of the social fabric of the country gave him a head start when he assumed office. Modi's first hundred days in office saw an unconventional approach to reform governance. He proposed several out-of-the-box ideas to break out of stagnation. He worked closely with the bureaucracy in Gujarat to cut down administrative red tape and simplified procedures in order to speed up the rehabilitation efforts in Kutch after the devastating earthquake. He spent the eve of Diwali in Kutch with the victims of the earthquake and led the rehabilitation efforts on a mission mode.

He also did away with wasteful spending and, possibly for the first time, brought in austerity measures. He led by example, tried to be a good listener and a fast learner. Modi's Jyotigram initiative to reform the power sector of Gujarat was yet another revolutionary idea to deliver 24x7 electricity across the state, from the mega cities to the remote tribal villages. It met with stiff protest from farmers and despite a long-drawn stalemate with farmer lobbies, Modi refused to budge from what he had envisioned for his state. Jyotigram went on to become a statewide success and Modi proved that persistence and an inclusive approach could change the fortunes of every stratum of society. That apart, by prioritizing the education of the girl child, incentivizing villages with development funds, empowering people of the state by making them partners in their own governance, all could be seen as the early seeds of his now popular chant of self-reliance.

However, Chief Minister Modi's path was strewn with challenges right from the beginning. It was baptism by fire for him. He took charge in October 2001, and four months later, the Godhra riots created an environment of uncertainty and pulled him a few steps back. Since Independence, rarely has any politician been the target of such strong criticism from the Opposition. Had there been any other leader, he would have had to vacate office on account of the crisis, but Modi powered through those difficult months.

Of course, he had the blessings of the people, which was evident when he had to face the Assembly polls a year later in December 2002. The people's verdict was loud and clear. They stood firmly behind Modi. He improved the BJP's previous tally by ten seats, winning a comfortable majority with 127 seats. Pulling off such a performance would have been an uphill task for even a political veteran, and here he was—a first-time MLA and Chief Minister. He went on to repeat this feat in 2007 and 2012 consecutively, on the shoulders of a fulfilled promise of 'Vibrant Gujarat'. Modi pulled Gujarat out of its crises with a focus on the politics of development and good governance, essentially the pillars of the famed 'Gujarat Model'.

In 2013, when the BJP and the RSS leadership decided to enter the big battle of 2014 general elections under the leadership of Modi, the decision surprised and shocked many. Several leaders within the party found it unacceptable.

When Modi arrived in Delhi to start his new innings, few had imagined that he would remodel the very face of national politics. With the Gujarat Model on his curriculum vitae, he brought the question of ideology back to the fore of national electoral politics. He presented 'nationalism' and 'development' (vikas) as the pillars for the reconstruction of a new India. In India, Modi revived the idea of nationalism. He reiterated the need for strong borders and pushed for indigenous products at the international level through his 'Made in India' campaign and his soft diplomacy efforts. Never before had there been such emphasis on marketing and publicizing of indigenous products at the international level. Every time Modi reached out to the Indian diaspora, he was met with jam-packed auditoriums abroad and Indians back home swelled with pride. Visuals of the Chinese premier, Xi Jinping, and Modi sitting on a traditional swing on the Sabarmati River front in Ahmedabad in 2014 have lived on in the collective memory of the nation. Modi's surprise visit to Lahore on the birthday of then Pakistan Prime Minister, Nawaz Sharif, was a heart-warming gesture towards a neighbour, for which he will be known in history. His firm yet friendly foreign policy has been one of the highlights of his tenure so far.

This came as a new perspective for the people, especially the youth who had grown tired of political tactics and rampant corruption in the system. Modi came as a breath of fresh air because he offered a promise of a new way of life in politics and governance to the people. In turn, he also forced other political parties to rise above political tactics and engage in ideological politics.

This political strategy was no mere chance, but a well-thought out one to put the Congress in a spot. What is often called the 'Modi wave' has swept the Congress out of many states. This is unprecedented. In 1977, 1889, 1996, 1998 and 1999, Congress lost elections and sat in the Opposition benches, but they soon recovered lost ground and won handsomely in next polls. Prior to 2014 general elections, the BJP's best performance was 182 seats with a vote share of 25.6 per cent in 1998, and in 1999 again, it was 182 seats with a 23.75 per cent vote share.

On the other hand, the Congress' best performance ever was with

414 seats and a 47 per cent vote share in 1984, post Indira Gandhi's assassination. The Congress never secured less than 114 seats, even when they could not form the government and sat in the Opposition benches. As for the vote share, the party had never secured less than 26 per cent.

Since 2014, the Congress has been decimated in the Lok Sabha in such a manner that it did not even have the numbers to have a Leader of Opposition. With Modi declared as the prime ministerial candidate during the historic BJP adhiveshan in Goa in 2013, the BJP won 282 seats on its own, with a 31 per cent vote share. It was after thirty years and seven general elections that a single party had the majority and formed a stable government. It is often said that coming to power for the first time is due to non-performance of the incumbent government, but for a repeat, the sole factor is the performance of the incumbent. In 2019, the BJP surpassed its previous tally and won 303 seats with a 37.36 per cent vote share, several notches higher than its 2014 figures.

In 2014, with forty-four MPs, the Congress had less than 10 per cent of the total house strength. In 2019, the party won just one seat each in the states of Maharashtra, Madhya Pradesh, Uttar Pradesh, Karnataka, Bihar, Jharkhand, Meghalaya, Odisha, Goa, Puducherry, and Andaman and Nicobar. In West Bengal and Chhattisgarh, it won two seats. In Assam and Telangana, it won three seats. Its main representation came from three states—Punjab and Tamil Nadu (which sent eighteen seats); and Kerala with fifteen seats—where there is no direct contest with the BJP at the state level. The Congress drew a blank in eighteen states and union territories—Rajasthan, Gujarat, Haryana, Uttarakhand, Himachal Pradesh, Jammu and Kashmir, Andhra Pradesh, Delhi, Assam, Arunachal Pradesh, Nagaland, Manipur, Mizoram, Tripura, Meghalaya, Chandigarh, Dadra and Nagar Haveli, and Lakshadweep.

The people's mandate was clear. They demolished the principal Opposition in Parliament. The magnitude of the 2014 and 2019 victories for BJP indicates that the people were desperately awaiting an alternative and now that they have one, there has been no looking back. It is possible that in the past seven decades, if the same people had such an alternative, they would have delivered the same verdict even then. There has been no alternative to Modi since 2014, and there is none in sight now either.

In the national elections, Modi coined his slogans very carefully. '*Achche din aane wale hain*' (2014), '*Modi hai toh mumkin hai*' (2019) enthused people and were reminiscent of the popular Atal Bihari Vajpayee-era slogans of '*Singhasan khali karo ki janata aati hai*' and '*Ab ki baari Atal Bihari*'. These struck a chord with both the young and the elderly. The student of politics had arrived at the national podium, this time as the master.

MODI, MASSES AND MEGA RALLIES

Modi reintroduced mega public rallies as a critical element of election campaigns in India. Since the 1990s, the salience of mega rallies in election campaigns had waned, and their relevance was expected to decline further due to the rapid expansion of media coverage and social media platforms. However, this changed in the run-up to the 2014 Lok Sabha elections. Modi addressed many huge public rallies as the BJP's prime ministerial candidate, and attracted massive crowds across the country. Between September 2013 and May 2014, Modi addressed more than four hundred rallies and public events and covered over 300,000 kilometres[4,5].

The first among these was an ex-servicemen rally in Rewari in Haryana[6]. Modi's choice of Haryana for his first rally as the prime ministerial candidate bewildered many. The BJP had grim prospects in Haryana back then. In 2013, the BJP did not have a single MP from the state, had merely four MLAs, and was a distant third behind Congress and the Indian National Lok Dal (INLD). The Modi wave in Haryana, which started from the Rewari rally, swept the state eventually. The BJP, in alliance with the HJC, won seven seats in Haryana in the 2014 Lok Sabha elections and secured a majority on its own in the Assembly elections.

A monumental rally in the run-up to the 2014 elections, which will remain etched in the history of Indian politics, is the Hunkar rally in October 2013, in Patna's Gandhi Maidan. The massive crowds brought back memories of significant rallies at the historical venue in the past. Despite a series of bomb blasts at the venue, Modi maintained his calm and conducted himself impeccably. In his post-campaign blog, he wrote, 'The events of Patna will remain etched in my memory—there were live bombs on one side but the resolve of the people prevailed. Nobody left the venue of the rally[7].' For avid political observers like me, the rally was the first signal of the brewing Modi wave. It seemed that the BJP's prospects in Bihar were bright despite the JDU's exit from the NDA alliance. The BJP won twenty-two Lok Sabha seats in 2014 and swept the state along with allies, the RLSP and the LJP.

The thrust for the 2014 election victory came from nearly two hundred Bharat Vijay rallies addressed by Modi from March to May 2014. After blessings from Mata Vaishno Devi on March 26, Modi started addressing the Bharat Vijay rallies across the country. Through these rallies, he took his promise of ushering 'Achche Din' to voters across the country. At the end of the campaign, the massive victory seemed like an appropriate reward for Modi's extraordinary efforts over almost nine months.

Apart from mega rallies, Modi used smart innovations to connect with the masses. Usually, campaign events involve a trade-off between two-way communication and the level of mass outreach. During the 2014 election campaign, Modi overcame this trade-off and directly communicated with voters across the country through his Chai pe Charcha campaign. A series of events were organized, in which Modi discussed various issues of national importance. Screens were installed at hundreds of public tea stalls across the country. Modi directly interacted with citizens from selected locations, heard their views, and answered questions on the designated issue. Over multiple rounds, several Charchas were organized at close to four thousand sites across twenty-four states. Events were also held abroad in close to fifty locations in fifteen countries[8].

Another major innovation in the 2014 Lok Sabha elections was Modi's 3D hologram rallies. In the 2012 Gujarat Assembly elections, he had conducted a few 3D hologram rallies—the first application of 3D hologram technology in election campaigns globally. The positive response from voters and the ability of new technology to generate excitement and curiosity among voters about an election campaign event may have led Modi to scale up its use in the 2014 Lok Sabha elections. The special projectors required for the 3D hologram rallies were installed at numerous locations for each round of 3D rallies. Modi connected through a satellite link and simultaneously, he addressed all 3D hologram rallies spread across the country from a special studio in Gandhinagar. The 3D rallies were a hit and increased Modi's public outreach exponentially. During April and May 2014, he addressed citizens at close to 1,350 different locations over twelve rounds of 3D hologram rallies. The 3D hologram rallies allowed

Modi to reach out to and address voters in constituencies where he could not visit for campaigning[9].

Campaigning and advertising works when there is substance in the product. The brand that Modi brought to the table fired the collective imagination of the nation.

THE MODI EDGE

From coalition politics to big legislative moves, Modi has dared to do the unthinkable. He gave a new angle to coalition politics by stitching together some of the most uncanny coalition governments without compromising on his party's ideology or his own ideals. The BJP-PDP government in Jammu and Kashmir with Mehbooba Mufti as Chief Minister, the alliance with Nitish Kumar in Bihar and several others in the Northeast and south India are examples of his out-of-the-box thinking. While parties earlier did cobble alliances, they also had to compromise on their agenda since the alliances were unstable. Modi, however, stood his ground in each of these alliances, and when they did break up, the BJP came back stronger. Be it Jammu and Kashmir or Bihar, the party gained electorally in the subsequent polls, solely due to Modi's delivery at the national level.

At a time when national politics was devoid of any ideological standpoint, he reintroduced the BJP's promise of Hindutva. Despite a backlash from the Opposition, he remained firm on his own ideology, so much so that the Opposition had to adopt a new, soft Hindutva approach. As popularly described by the media, the 'temple run' of senior Congress leaders just before every big and small election, exposed their lack of commitment to the issue. It was a sham that no one bought. Meanwhile, Modi earned the unflinching trust and support of millions who backed him for his honesty.

It turned out to be a two-way street for Modi and his followers. Voters gave Modi strong mandates one after the other, and Modi delivered on his promises. Be it the construction of a Ram Mandir in Ayodhya, the abrogation of Article 370, the abolition of triple talaq or demonetization to counter black money, Modi took tough calls and pushed through reforms that were long pending. In each of these, he was further backed by the people and rewarded for ushering in bold and progressive changes. During demonetization, even the long queues outside banks did not bother the people, who smilingly bore the hardships that a sudden note ban had imposed on them. They were of the view that, if Modi was attempting to reconstruct a fair and honest system, they should participate in it as part of their contribution to the nation. This is the ever-changing context of nationalism that Modi introduced and it has been a successful experiment. The Opposition remains powerless in the face of such overwhelming support from the masses. The acceptance of Modi can also be read as an outright and conclusive rejection of the Opposition.

Demonetization was also proof that Modi did not blindly back the rich and big businesses, as alleged by the Opposition. It came as the great leveller, where the poor and underprivileged watched from the galleries as the rich had to part with their ill-gotten spoils. There was yet another intangible benefit from the note ban gambit—the youth realized that money which stays out of the system could turn into dust at any moment.

The record GST collections in March 2021 that exceeded ₹1.23 lakh crore (₹1.23 trillion), despite major contributors like travel and tourism, gems and jewellery, sale of luxury item and real estate being at their all-time low in the aftermath of COVID-19. This figure surpassed the pre-COVID-19 level, thanks to demonetization. Modi had promised to bring back black money, and this was his way of fulfilling that promise. The high point was when Modi's elderly mother stood in the queues like the common man; it came as a gentle reminder that Modi had no personal baggage. Right from the beginning, Modi's image—as a single man focused on his service to the nation—has worked immensely for him. Why would an ascetic need to steal? And even if he does, who would he leave fortunes for? It was in stark contrast to the Congress and several other parties that are dominated by political dynasties and are hence, viewed more as family businesses rather than governments dedicated to public service.

Elections in India have, for the longest time, been associated with money and muscle power. By lending an ideological foundation, Modi has gradually shifted the focus to real issues. He came to power by toppling a government that was perceived to be corrupt, and his selection of party candidates showed that he wanted to introduce professionalism into his government. He roped in industry experts, former bureaucrats and sporting talent to work as part of his Cabinet, infusing a freshness in the power corridors that were ridden with red tape and a crippling lack of professionalism. The early days of his first tenure saw strict vigilance to pull bureaucrats out of their lackadaisical attitude as Modi himself checked on his ministers and senior officials during their working hours in office. The ministries witnessed massive transformation with an emphasis on biometric attendance, which paved the way for punctuality and diligence in government offices.

Modi has empowered democracy in a new way. Along with ideology, he has used technology and communication in a commendable manner that has given him an image of a modern and progressive statesman. What was introduced during demonetization as a mandatory shift to digital transactions prepared an entire nation and came in handy when we were faced with the unexpected emergency during COVID-19.

Modi's honest and direct communication skills has been one of his major strengths. His passionate speeches at election rallies leave his audiences mesmerized, but he also manages to convey his ideas convincingly. His confident and persuasive oratory inspires confidence in his promises and decisions. The pause and pitch, modulation and depth influence his audiences in ways that few other politicians have managed. He has the key to what it takes to make a difference in today's social and political context—a key that he may have discovered when he set out as a seventeen-year-old to peep into the hearts and minds of this incredible nation.

The path that Gandhi set for this nation was lost somewhere over the years. The state of our farmers, healthcare and education is appalling to say the least. If 70 per cent of school going children go to government schools and their education level does not make them employable, it calls for some deep introspection. Who is accountable for this, and why has no accountability been fixed?

The sharp divide between the rich and poor is not the nation Gandhi had foreseen. If, in less than two terms, Modi can bring sweeping changes like har ghar nal (taps in every home), toilets, gas connections and bank accounts for everyone, he sure has outperformed the expectations of his own chair. These are big shoes to fill for the future generation of leaders. It is evident that elections and electioneering has witnessed a dramatic change and a new template has been set. There is an expectation from the future leader to meet the benchmark set by Modi—a touch of humanity, accountability, transparency and sheer dedication to transform a billion lives.

SECTION THREE

JAN DHAN: AN ECONOMY FOR EVERYONE

THINKING BIG AND EXECUTING IN SCALE

ANANTHA NAGESWARAN

India is a vast country, but it is also a fragmented one. We are not talking about social, economic and cultural differences here. Arguably, those differences constitute India's strengths and are part of its riches as much as they are part of its challenges. India's units of production—farms or factories—are too small and fragmented. Take the Annual Survey of Industries (ASI) report. Nearly 40 per cent of the 242,395 factories that reported to the ASI in 2017-18, had less than fifteen employees. About half of them were either sole proprietorships or partnerships. The proportion of factories with five hundred or more workers was less than 5 per cent.

Take the example of India's farms. More than two-thirds of India's farm holdings are less than a hectare. As per the Sixth Economic Census, India had 58.5 million agricultural and non-agricultural establishments. Nearly 99 per cent of them had less than ten employees. Ditto for the Indian corporate sector. India is big, but the burden of supporting and growing its economy falls disproportionately on small farms, firms and factories. They are not capable of generating millions of jobs that are needed to support India's aspiring young population.

Enter Narendra Modi.

In his two decades in public office, thirteen of them as the Chief Minister of Gujarat and seven as the Prime Minister of this large nation, he has sought to transform the fragmented Indian economy into a productive and efficient economy capable of transforming the lives of millions and propelling the country into a higher and more developed orbit.

His vision for India grasped the need for scale and size—not because big is beautiful but because big is essential to serve the needs and ambitions of a country of 1.4 billion people. Importantly, his vision and mission were not confined to economics but also to social and human resource development. Equally, his vision straddled the entire spectrum from the 'Statue of Unity' to toilets. His vision for a 'Sreshtha Bharath', therefore, encompassed thinking big and executing in scale across social and human resource dimensions as well as in economic aspects.

The list of concrete examples of his approach—thinking big and executing in scale—is long and enduring. It is difficult to know where to begin. However, begin one must for the learnings from his leadership approach to steering the country and the state are manifold.

THE ORIGINS OF THINKING AND DOING BIG

As the Chief Minister of Gujarat and as the Prime Minister of India, Modi has relished painting on a large canvas. He had figured out, by looking at how the West prospered and China successfully emulated them, that India cannot be a prisoner of its past. Therefore, it would be useful to dwell briefly on the intellectual origins of the Prime Minister's policy framework.

In the wake of the industrial revolution, the mode of production shifted from labour to capital. Consequently, China and India, two labour-intensive economies, surrendered their dominance to the West. The last two centuries belonged to the West. Sometime in the second half of the last century, things began to change. First, China began pursuing capitalism with Chinese characteristics in 1979. It embraced scale and the need for capital that the exercise entailed. Its massive domestic savings financed the required investment. While India and China had similar per capita income in the beginning of the seventies, China began to pull away by the end of that decade. By 2020, China's per capita GDP was around eight times greater than that of India. Of course, the exact gap between the two is arguable not only because China's GDP statistics are questionable but also because of the amount of debt it has taken on its books in the process.

As Chief Minister of Gujarat, Narendra Modi was impressed by what he saw in China. He concluded, correctly, that India had no choice but to pursue scale. It was consistent with his natural inclination to paint on a large canvas. The one important change he made was that he wanted to do it the fiscally-sustainable way. Indeed, notwithstanding the impact the pandemic has had on India's public finances, India's GDP adjusted for debt exceeds China's GDP adjusted for its debt.

Did Prime Minister Modi take off from where Chief Minister Modi left? Let us start our journey from Gujarat, where it all began.

FROM EARTHQUAKE RELIEF TO ECONOMIC REJUVENATION

Early signs of his ability to think big and execute in scale were evident when he confronted the ravages of the massive earthquake that struck the Bhuj region in 2001. In fact, when it happened, Narendra Modi was neither based in Gujarat nor was he its Chief Minister. As a volunteer, he supervised the relief efforts, and as soon as he became the Chief Minister of Gujarat in October 2001, he announced that the rehabilitation of earthquake victims and reconstruction of the devastated regions would be his top priority.

The earthquake measuring 6.9 on the Richter scale had its epicentre near the Chobari village, 30 kilometers away from Bhuj. It had affected an area of more than 1.8 lakh (180,000) sq. km—more than the geographical area of Assam and West Bengal combined. Its physical and psychological impact on the people was immense. To create a sense of kinship among the people and show that the state shared their pain, within days of taking office as Chief Minister in 2001, he announced that the government would not celebrate Diwali.

In her book, *Modi, Muslims and Media*, published in June 2014, Madhu Kishwar wrote, 'Modi not only re-oriented and re-energized the bureaucracy, as with everything else, he tapped into the inner strength and creative energy of his own Gujarati society.' She added, 'Chobari has acquired the characteristics of a planned little township, instead of the old-style congested village. With sharp rise in incomes, in the past eight to ten years, the living standards of these families had also risen dramatically.'

Change did not come to Chobari alone. It visited Dhordo too, under Modi. Dhordo is a village located about 86 km from Bhuj, the district headquarters which withstood the worst of the 2001 earthquake.

Bhungas, the traditional round houses of the Kutch region present in Dhordo, did not collapse during the devastating Gujarat earthquake, thus saving many lives. Now, these life-saving houses are a major hit among the visitors at the ongoing Rannotsav, set amidst the pristine white salt deserts of the Great Rann of Kutch bordering the now internationally famous Dhordo village. In 2005, Modi decided to host an annual Rann Utsav (Festival of Rann) and promoted it through a very creative and high-profile advertisement campaign anchored by Amitabh Bachchan on TV and other media platforms. More importantly, the village now has a ring road all around it. Most important of all, it has enough stored water to last two years, because in 2008 several large water-harvesting talaabs (ponds) had been constructed.

GUJARAT'S OWN DOCKLANDS

No less remarkable has been the transformation of the river Sabarmati. In 2012, global consulting firm KPMG had named the Sabarmati Riverfront Development Project as among the hundred innovative projects that aim to make cities liveable and sustainable, globally. It was among the six upcoming infrastructure projects selected from India then[1]. It was sustainable in another sense. The Sabarmati riverfront development posed a rehabilitation challenge since many were living on its banks for years. Chief Minister Modi ensured that they were accommodated in more comfortable housing that was conveniently located. Thus, modernization and development went hand in hand. By 2015, it had become a reality.

Shramana Ganguly wrote in *The Economic Times* in January 2015: 'In 2005, Sabarmati was nothing but a parched river bed—sometimes used for farming—with puddles of industrial effluents and sewage. Today, the Sabarmati in the heart of the city has been beautified. The river has been channelled to a uniform width of 263 metres, with parts of the river bed reclaimed and a waterfront developed along both banks, each covering a distance of about 11 km[2].'

VIBRANT GUJARAT WAS NOT JUST A SLOGAN

Modi launched the 'Vibrant Gujarat' investor summits. 'Vibrant Gujarat' was not just a slogan to woo investors. It established the brand, Gujarat. That was Modi's genius. When the state was formed in the sixties, it was mainly a marshy desert land. Chief Minister Modi transformed agriculture and manufacturing in the state and made it vibrant.

Well-known columnist, Swaminathan Aiyar, wrote in July 2009[3] that the secret of Modi's electoral success in 2007 was his transformation of Gujarat's agriculture. He cited the study by Ashok Gulati, Tushaar Shah and Ganga Sreedhar, 'Agricultural Performance in Gujarat Since 2000', which highlights something few people know—that Gujarat's agricultural performance is by far the best in India'.

Aiyar went on to add, 'Between 2000-01 and 2007-08, agricultural value added grew at a phenomenal 9.6 per cent per year (despite a major drought in 2002). This is more than double India's agricultural growth rate, and much faster than Punjab's farm growth in the green revolution heyday. Indeed, 9.6 per cent agricultural growth is among the fastest rates recorded anywhere in the world. That drives home the magnitude of Gujarat's performance. ...The IFPRI (International Food Policy Research Institute) study says that 10,700 check dams were built up to 2000, and helped drought-proof 32,000 hectares. That sounds like a lot. But subsequently, under Modi, Gujarat has built ten times as many check dams! ...Research shows that rural roads are the most important investment for agriculture. Gujarat has one of the best rural road networks in India, and 98.7 per cent of villages are connected by pukka roads...'

Modi's efforts did not only succeed in making the Kutch region flourish in farm production but also transformed other areas. The Kutch region exports power to neighbouring states. Further, the Kutch region and the state of Gujarat lead in solar and wind energy as well.

Success begets success. Gujarat's farm productivity surge attracted companies to enter agro-exports, agro-processing, organized food retail in the state and catalyzed rural infrastructure development.

In his thirteen years as Chief Minister, Modi showed that democracy was no impediment to development. Second, he ran a policy-driven government. Policies were not adopted and dropped on whim. Investors felt comfortable and confident that they could do business under his administration. He carried this confidence with him to Delhi.

A leader with such a lofty vision and big on execution needed a bigger stage. The benefits of his leadership must accrue to a much larger population and not just be limited to Gujarat. The stage was thus set for the arrival of Narendra Modi in Delhi in 2014 as the Prime Minister of India.

GANDHINAGAR TO DELHI: SCRIPTING EPIC VICTORIES

This chapter may be about his public policy decisions in the economic sphere. However, an important political achievement cannot be ignored. No one in his own political party and among the punditry gave the Bharatiya Janata Party under his leadership much of a chance to form a government on its own. Modi, however, believed in the possibility and guided his party to an absolute majority in 2014. To show that it was not chance but the result of deliberate planning and execution, he bettered his own record in the 2019 elections. These two were big instances of not only thinking big, executing in scale, but also of achieving in scale and in style. Now, back to public policy.

Let us move back in time from the present. In the last year and a half, the government has responded rather well to the economic and social impact of the pandemic, even with the relatively limited fiscal resources at its disposal. One of the remarkable features of the government's response to the pandemic has been the spectacular success of the Direct Benefit Transfer Mission.

DBT MISSION AND THE JAM TRINITY

Sumita Kale and I wrote in *Mint* recently: 'In general, over the last 18 months, while there have been very few silver linings in the macrocosm of the economy and the microcosm of families, one of them has been a demonstration of the effect of the JAM (Jan Dhan Yojana-Aadhaar-Mobile phone) trinity in keeping millions of Indians away from starvation. It is not much discussed, but the success of the Direct Benefits Transfer (DBT) Mission is indisputable. One of the memorable recollections one associates with former prime minister Rajiv Gandhi is his candid admission that the ordinary citizen received only 15 paise of every rupee that the government tried transferring to her. If he were alive today, he would perhaps revise that number upwards substantially. Between benefits transferred in cash and kind, government welfare transfers amounted to ₹5.52 trillion in 2020-21, compared with a mere ₹7,367 crore (₹73.67 billion) in 2013-14[4].'

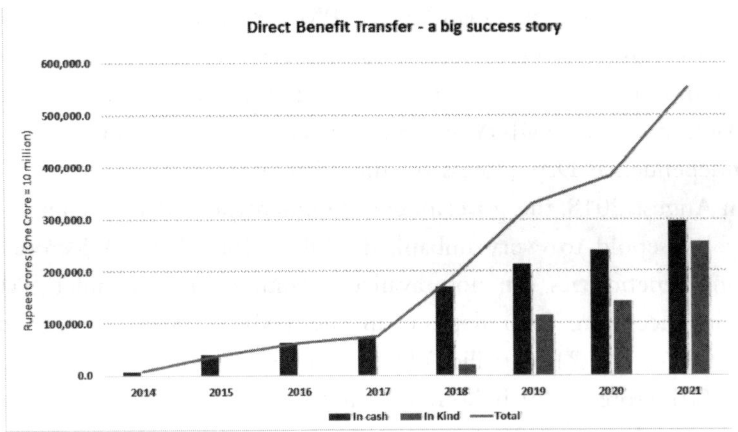

Source: www.dbtbharat.gov.in (landing page accessed on 26 June 2021)

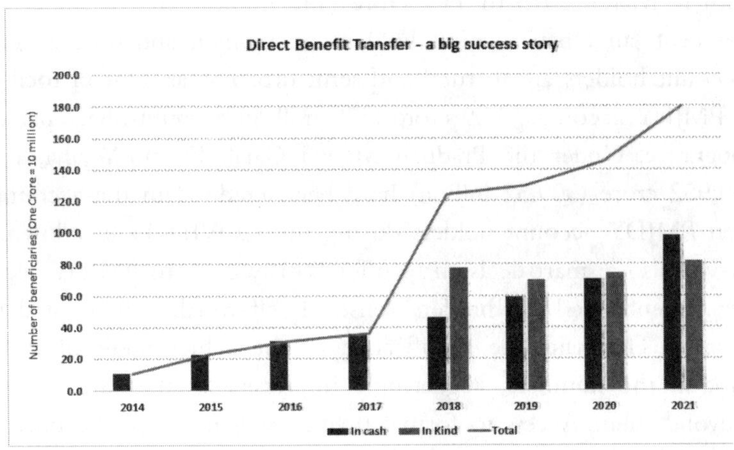

Source: www.dbtbharat.gov.in (landing page accessed on 26 June 2021)

What made the DBT so successful? It built on the success achieved with the realization of the potential of the JAM trinity—Jan Dhan Yojana, Aadhaar and mobile phones. The Jan Dhan Yojana was one of the first initiatives of the first Modi government in New Delhi in 2014.

Recently, the Pradhan Mantri Jan Dhan Yojana (PMJDY) celebrated its seventh anniversary. On the occasion, the Ministry of Finance provided evidence of the impressive progress that the scheme has been able to achieve with respect to its primary goal of financial inclusion.

Some important highlights from the press release[5] are as follows:

Pradhan Mantri Jan Dhan Yojana (PMJDY) is a national mission for financial inclusion to ensure access to financial services, namely, banking/savings and deposit accounts, remittance, credit, insurance, pension (in an affordable manner). PMJDY was announced by Prime Minister Modi in his Independence Day address on the 15th of August, 2014.

In August 2018, the government extended the PMJDY scheme from 'every household to every unbanked adult'. More than 44.2 crore (442 million) beneficiaries can now avail of banking services under PMJDY since its inception. Total deposits in the PMJDY accounts amount to ₹1,50,939.6 crore (₹1.50 trillion) by the end of December 2021, compared to ₹22,901 crore (₹229 billion) in August 2015. That is a compounded annual growth rate of 36 per cent over six years.

PMJDY accounts have grown threefold from 14.72 crore (147.2 million) in March 2015 to 44.2 crore (442 million) in December 2021. 55 per cent Jan Dhan account holders are women and 67 per cent of the account holders are in rural and semi-urban areas. Out of total 44.2 crore PMJDY accounts, 37.9 crore (379 million accounts, 85.7 per cent) are operative. Under the Pradhan Mantri Garib Kalyan Yojana, a total of ₹30,952 crore (309.52 billion) have been credited in the accounts of women PMJDY account holders during the COVID-19 lockdown.

It was also a smart decision to offer RuPay cards to PMJDY account holders. It enhanced the holders' sense of self-worth and boosted their self-respect. That said, the significance of the achievement of PMJDY lies not in the numbers, staggeringly impressive as they are, but what lies beyond them. Access to formal finance will make all the difference between a life of dignity and a life of struggle for many millions.

Independent academic research confirms this; this must be a matter of satisfaction to the Prime Minister and his government. Prasanna Tantri, Yakshup Chopra and Nagpurnanand Prabhala went through proprietary data from bank account statements and confirmed that the PMJDY resulted in a significant uptake, usage, usage growth and balance accumulation in the accounts. They further observed that activity levels increased over time and converged towards those in non-PMJDY accounts even though PMJDY account holders were poorer on average and unfamiliar with banking and had undergone no financial literacy training[6].

Let us take the second element of the JAM Trinity—Aadhaar. In August

2021, NASSCOM brought out an important publication titled, *Digital India: Digital Public Goods Platformisation Play*[7]. Aadhaar is a 12-digit individual identification number issued by the Unique Identification Authority of India (UIDAI) on behalf of the government. The number serves as a proof of identity and address, anywhere in India. It was launched in 2009. It is a reliable biometric identity proof for Indian residents. An important benefit for the government is that it enables the government to include those who may not have any other traditional identity documents, i.e. proof of residence.

Aadhaar is a testimony to Prime Minister Modi's intellectual flexibility. Even though it was an initiative of the previous government, as soon as he came to office in 2014, he gave the green signal for the project to be completed, for enrolment to begin and for a unique biometric ID to be issued to billions of Indians. In fact, Modi resolved the inertia that had crept into the project, which had caused much confusion in the previous government on whether they should proceed with Aadhaar—the Unique Identifier—or the population register. After ascertaining that Aadhaar could do what the population register could, and on top of it offer a unique, tamper-proof biometric identification, Modi gave the go-ahead for Aadhaar. After that, there was no looking back.

Put the two together—PMJDY and Aadhaar—and one sees Modi's vision that includes formalization and inclusion. It confers an identity for many Indians who may have lacked them before. It had shut them out of the formal economy at the doorstep. Now, they are inside the portal and that opens many doors for them. With Aadhaar, one gets to open a bank account. With a bank account, one receives government transfer benefits, other payments, and it allows them to cultivate a savings habit, builds up savings and then other financial products such as insurance opens up for them.

The third pillar of the trinity is mobile phones. It won't be an exaggeration to say that the DBT superstructure, built on the three pillars of the JAM trinity, has meant that the shocks that the economy had to withstand in the last decade—bad debts in the banking system, slowing global growth and international trade, and then the pandemic—did not lead to widespread deprivation and misery for many Indians.

DIGITIZATION AS A PUBLIC GOOD

Indeed, Aadhaar is only one of the many digitization initiatives that have been developed by the Government of India in recent years. Eighteen of the twenty digitization initiatives featured in the NASSCOM report, cited earlier, have been developed since Narendra Modi became the Prime Minister in 2014. As the report notes, these initiatives have helped India improve its competitiveness index scores; they have broken through data silos and have created a shared infrastructure and, third, they have enabled the formation of multi-stakeholder ecosystems.

At least three of these—BHIM UPI (Unified Payments Interface), CoWIN (web portal for vaccination registration) and the RuPay card—are going global. BHIM stands for Bharat Interface for Money. So far, 3.2 billion transactions have taken place using BHIM. A total of 235 banks are live on BHIM and the value of transactions has exceeded ₹600 billion. RuPay cards are available at least in nine other countries.

The 'Retail Payments Statistics on NPCI platforms' released by the National Payments Corporation of India tells the story of digitization of India. In the financial year 2014-15, financial transactions were 3.7 billion (volume) and their total value was ₹76 trillion. In the year ending March 2021, the corresponding figures were 37.5 billion and ₹165.5 trillion, respectively (see chart below).

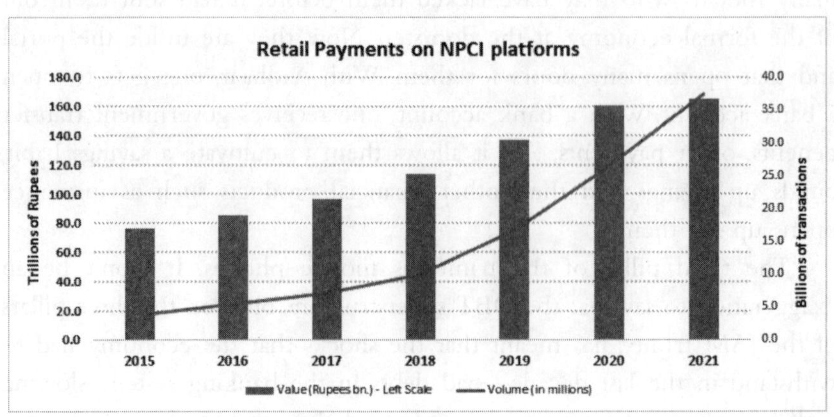

Source: National Payments Corporation of India (https://www.npci.org.in/PDF/npci/statics/RETAIL-PAYMENTS-STATISTICS-Jul-2021.xlsx - accessed on 7th September 2021). Data are for financial years ending March.

The Digital Payments Index of the Reserve Bank of India (RBI) had risen from 100 in March 2018 to 270 by March 2021. In its August 2021 monthly bulletin, the RBI wrote that the rapid formalization and digitization of the economy was evident in its index.

We can debate for a long time the causal factors behind the above numbers. Demonetization was a catalyst for, if not the cause of, the digitization of financial transactions that now offers a trail. The trail is beneficial in multiple ways. It raises the volume transacted, delivers payments faster and safely, and helps in tracking consumer behaviour. The pandemic has now come as a force multiplier for digitization.

Its objectives—stated, unstated and added—were several. Mainly, it was about discouraging the use of high-denomination notes for illegal transactions and, thus, curbing the widespread use of black money. In the process, it was expected that the ban on high-denomination notes would encourage digitization of commercial transactions, formalize the economy and boost government tax revenues.

Largely, because of this and other formalization measures that complemented demonetization efforts, direct tax collections went up by 17.9 per cent and 13.5 per cent, respectively, in the financial years 2017-18 and 2018-19. For the year ending March 2017, the number of corporate tax assessees in India was 608,836. For the year ending March 2018, the number had gone up to 841,687—a growth of 38.2 per cent. For the year ending March 2019, the number had further risen to 885,289 assessees.

Corporate income tax collection did jump for the years ending March 2018 and March 2019 to ₹5,71,202.87 crore (₹5.71 trillion) and ₹6,63,571.62 crore (₹6.63 trillion), respectively, from ₹4,84,923.86 crore (₹4.84 trillion) for the year ending March 2017.

Demonetization played an important role in stirring a debate about the entrenched informality in the economy—what to do about it and how. In that sense, it played a big role in focusing minds on the problem and, as one would expect, solutions turned out to be multi-faceted. Judgement on epochal policy decisions cannot be rendered instantaneously or in real-time. Bank nationalization is an example. At the end of the first two decades, its scorecard was positive on balance; at the end of five decades, it is mixed to negative. Historians will record that the opposite is true of demonetization[8].

REFORMING GOVERNANCE: GEM

The unique feature of the Prime Minister's ability to think big and execute in scale (and in style, if I may add) spans both social and economic initiatives. GeM, or the Government eMarketplace, is one such initiative. It may not register in public consciousness for it is about procurement done by government departments and ministries from private suppliers. But it is a godsend for many small suppliers who have been often at the mercy of bureaucrats for getting empanelled as suppliers and for receiving payments, etc.

The Economic Times wrote in July 2019:

> 'A growing number of vendors on the GeM platform that is revolutionizing procurement by the government. Rolled out by the NDA government in 2016, GeM is an e-commerce platform launched with the ambition to make government procurement cashless, contact-less and paperless—an Amazon for the sarkar, if you will… Until 2016, government procurement in India belonged to the analog world, with DGS&D (Directorate General of Supplies & Disposals) being the sole authority to fix both rates and specifications for every product[9].'

Sandeep Soni wrote for the *Financial Express* in July 2021:

> 'According to the GeM's latest data, the marketplace currently has 21.29 lakh sellers and service providers… The share of micro and small sellers also increased from around 1 lakh to a little over 7 lakh during the said period with a 56 per cent share in total order value… The marketplace currently has nearly 53,000 registered government departments, organizations, and PSUs as buyers procuring goods across 16,335 product categories and 172 service categories[10].'

Just two years ago, the number of registered vendors in GeM was only 2.5 lakh or 250,000. It has gone up more than eight times now.

One of the biggest government buyers is the railways. That is going to be part of the platform soon. Further, a loan application (app) called GeM SAHAY is to be rolled out for GeM sellers for loan applications at the point of acceptance of an order. This is smart and inclusive thinking.

DBT, built on JAM, was about delivering government benefits and transfers to all eligible beneficiaries without leakages; GeM was about efficient government procurement and opportunities to many small suppliers; GST (Goods and Services Tax) and IBC (Insolvency and Bankruptcy Code) were about making the economy and commerce efficient and bigger.

Modi's vision and execution spanned the entire spectrum from welfare to governance to commerce.

ONE NATION, ONE TAX AND ONE MARKET

The Goods and Services Tax (GST) unified India's befuddling mess of myriad state taxes with different rates on the same commodities and services. Central Excise Duty, Additional duties of Excise and Customs, Excise Duty levied under Medicinal and Toilet Preparation Act, Service Tax, Surcharge and various forms of cess and state taxes such as State Value-Added Tax (VAT), Sales Tax, Central Sales Tax, Purchase Tax, Entertainment Tax (other than those levied by local bodies), Luxury Tax, Entry Tax (all forms) and taxes on lottery, betting and gambling, were combined into seventeen taxes and thirteen cesses in the GST framework. The base of earlier taxes was not only a compliance mess but also a drag on efficiency. For example, entry taxes such as octroi held up freight lorries and trucks at check posts when they crossed from one state to another. If the truck traversed multiple states, then the delays, costs and the bribes paid to escape them, piled up. No surprises then that India's logistical costs were estimated at around 12 per cent to 14 per cent.

To be sure, the GST had been in the making since 2000. But it required a decisive push to become a reality. Modi's NDA government gave the finishing touches and launched it in July 2017, paving the way for one nation, one tax and one market. Undisputedly, it is a significant step forward in creating a single market in the whole country.

One of the critical success factors for the launch of GST was Modi's understanding of the concerns of manufacturing states such as Maharashtra and Tamil Nadu since Gujarat, too, had emerged as a leading manufacturing state under his leadership. He could allay their concerns. Second, his government cleared the arrears of VAT compensation, enhanced the credibility of the promises his government had made on GST compensation and convinced fence-sitting states to come on board.

Writing for *Business Standard*, V.S. Krishnan, former member of the Central Board of Indirect Taxes and Customs, noted:

'The many criticisms about the implementation of the goods and services tax (GST) must not be allowed to obscure the fact that what was implemented was a truly transformational tax reform… the abolition of "Entry 52" in the Indian Constitution has unified the common Indian market. Truck turnaround times have dropped dramatically all over the country. Our studies for the Ministry of Road Transport and Highways in collaboration with the World Bank show that the average trip time across five major goods transport corridors, including Delhi-Mumbai, Delhi-Bangalore, Delhi-Chennai, Mumbai-Bangalore and Kolkata-Bangalore has reduced by 17.5 per cent post GST… the abolition of the CST has fundamentally changed the rules in the logistic sector… Our study shows that the Marginal Effective Tax Rate for services sectors like transportation and finance dropped significantly by more than 50 per cent post GST[11].'

INSOLVENCY AND BANKRUPTCY CODE

Like GST, the IBC too has been in the making for some time. But the Modi government made it a reality. Recovery of loans under IBC has turned out to be far superior to the alternatives that lenders in India had before IBC arrived[12]. Indian businesses have an exit option and Indian lenders now have a recovery option. In the process, commercial and productive assets need not be wasted. They can be passed on to productive hands and revived.

Besides the above, there were also initiatives to end retrospective taxation. We start with the most recent evidence of 'Thinking Big'. In 2012-13, the previous government had brought a retrospective amendment to India's tax laws. India's attractiveness as an investment destination had dimmed. When Modi came to office, his government recognized the problem but also understood its dimensions clearly. It promised not to bring in retrospective amendments to tax laws. It kept its word. Second, it asserted the right of the sovereign to change tax laws prospectively and stated categorically that tax laws were a sovereign prerogative and not a topic for international arbitration. Third, at the same time it waited patiently for the arbitration proceedings, already under way when it came to office, to reach their logical conclusion.

Once the arbitration process had concluded towards the end of 2020, the government set about undoing the damage caused by the amendment made nearly a decade ago. It has withdrawn the retrospective tax claims. It is a classic instance of thinking big. The government, despite facing the stiff task of setting public finances, ravaged by the pandemic, did not hesitate to forego its tax claims and settle a festering dispute.

MONETIZATION OF PUBLIC ASSETS

Even more recent than that is the government's announcement on monetizing public assets through leasing them. The productivity of public assets, both for the exchequer and for the economy, has been far from desirable. Much ink has been spilt and numerous keyboards have been put to work recommending asset monetization. The government has set an ambitious target of monetizing government and public sector assets to realize better economic value from them for the nation. Based on the work done by NITI Aayog, the government estimates that the monetization potential is ₹6 trillion[13]. That is nearly 3 per cent of the GDP. The potential and the ambition are big. When executed, the economy will benefit at least in two ways. One is that the private sector is likely to achieve better efficiency gains from the assets than the government did. Second, the collateral benefits to Indian capital markets too will be considerable for the programme aims to pursue monetization through a collaborative approach between the public and private sectors.

AATMANIRBHAR BHARAT

The third of the most recent initiatives that are consistent with the theme of this chapter is the production-linked incentive (PLI) schemes that the government has announced in the past one and a half years for several sectors. India may have missed the 'industrial-revolution' bus because the colonial rulers were determined to deny the fruits of industrialization and use it as a source of raw materials and an import market for their finished products. The PLI scheme is aimed at fixing that historical harm done to India. It is meant to dispel the myth of India's premature deindustrialization. The PLI scheme for different sectors—automobiles, electronics, pharmaceuticals, renewable energy, electric batteries, steel—aims to achieve global scale in production. It aims to make India a centre for global manufacturing hub in several areas.

Post-independence, stung by the experience under a foreign ruler, the government opted for import substitution and support to small-scale industries through reservations. Thus, India's industrialization was further delayed. Hence, rectifying it was not going to be easy. Beginnings were made in the eighties through broad-banding of licenses and later through de-licensing as part of economic liberalization pursued by Prime Minister P.V. Narasimha Rao in the nineties. But these did not go far enough to establish India as a global manufacturing centre for specific products. The PLI scheme reflects the courage to think bigger, on a global scale.

As research ('From '*Make-in' to 'Self-Reliant'—A Primer on India's Manufacturing Push*', 16 August 2020) from Citigroup (India) puts it, the new pillars of the PLI scheme were explicit fiscal incentives, import restrictions, less focus on exports and a greater desire to attract the shifting supply chains to India, in the light of the pandemic. Although electronics has been a focus area since 2012, India announced a new policy on electronics manufacturing in 2019.

India's electronics exports have nearly doubled to $11.1 billion in just nine months of 2021-22 from $6.4 billion in 2017-18. The story repeats itself in the pharma sector. India's pharma exports doubled too in the last decade from $9.0 billion to $24.4 billion in 2020-21. Seeking to emulate the success achieved with incentivizing domestic production of electronics and pharmaceutical ingredients, the government has announced an ambitious scheme to become the global hub for mobile phone manufacturing.

Several international manufacturers have responded to the government's PLI scheme for mobile phones. According to a report[14] in *Business Standard*, Apple, Samsung and domestic players such as Lava Group are set to make India a major export hub for mobile device manufacturing[15].

Eminent economist Indira Rajaraman called the PLI commendable:

> 'Another commendable move has been the performance-linked incentive mechanism for manufacturing, extended to three sectors

> so far: domestic production of electronics hardware; medical devices including protection equipment and testing kits; and active pharmaceutical ingredients presently imported from China. These are very promising initiatives at a time when pharmaceuticals and medical equipment are the only buoyant sectors in a dismal global trade scenario. These kinds of nuanced initiatives with sunset dates are likely to have more stimulus content than a more aggregate expansion of the fiscal outlay without attention to the allocation and absorption aspects of its constituents[16].'

The PLI schemes are testimonials to the notion of Atmanirbhar Bharat being a pursuit of excellence rather than a pursuit of isolation. It is about making in India for the world.

THE WORLD'S LARGEST VACCINATION DRIVE

Given that we are dealing with the fallout of a pandemic that has killed nearly 5.4 million people globally[17]—and still counting, India's vaccination programme is one of the largest in the world. By the end of December 2021, more than 817 million people had been administered a single dose[18] while more than 601 million people had been fully vaccinated[19]. The CoWIN app, developed by the Ministry of Health and Family Welfare of the Government of India, and creative campaigning have contributed to the record number of vaccinations.

It is worth contemplating the extent of damage that the pandemic would have wrought but for the Swachh Bharat Mission that Prime Minister Modi launched seven years ago. The urban component of the mission has witnessed construction of nearly 6.3 million individual household toilets and 616,000 community toilets in urban areas in addition to 10.7 crore toilets in rural areas. By the end of December 2021, out of the total 4,520 cities, 4,371 were open defecation free (ODF) cities[20].

SUPPLY-SIDE STRUCTURAL REFORMS

There is a perception that the NDA governments in 2014 and 2019 under Prime Minister Modi have lacked a clear economic strategy. Dig deeper and one would realize that the criticism does not have much substance. The first flush of economic reforms launched hesitantly first in the eighties and then revived in the wake of the 'Balance of Payments crisis' in 1991 had focused largely on the external sector and on the financial sector. It had plucked many low-hanging fruits. But nearly a quarter century later, when he came to office, Modi realized that it was the supply-side of the Indian economy that needed addressing.

Supply-side reforms are not fun, but they are essential if India were to escape the low growth-high inflation and inefficiency trap. Many see it as formalization of the Indian economy at the expense of the informal sectors—the rural sector, daily wage labour and the farm sector, etc. On the contrary, it is about formalizing the informal sectors even while nursing them and supporting them through the transition. Without formalization, they would not enjoy the fruits of access to credit and market that firms operating in the formal sector enjoy. His concern for alleviating and even eliminating the pain associated with the formalization is evident in the emphasis put on DBT.

Many of his economic policy decisions since 2014 are consistent with this overall philosophy of formalizing the Indian economy and fixing the supply side. Who can blame him? Western economies see every structural problem as an issue of aggregate demand shortfall and have continued to provide monetary and fiscal stimulus. Consequently, they face an unsustainable debt burden and an uncertain future in its wake.

His reforms—GST and IBC—must be seen in that light. The bold tax cuts of September 2019 and PLI schemes are consistent with the supply-side approach. But the crowning pieces of such a supply-side approach to the economy were to be seen in three initiatives that he undertook. One in the first term and two in 2020.

First, soon after becoming the Prime Minister in 2014, Modi undertook visits to several foreign countries. They paid rich dividends especially at a time when domestic capital formation was struggling due to the ongoing problems in the banking sector. Foreign direct investment into India picked up significantly from 2014. Even after accounting for foreign direct investment out of India into other countries, net FDI into India (net of India's FDI into other countries) has exceeded US $30.0 billion every year since 2014. In recent years, it has exceeded US $40.0 billion. These figures were never seen before 2014.

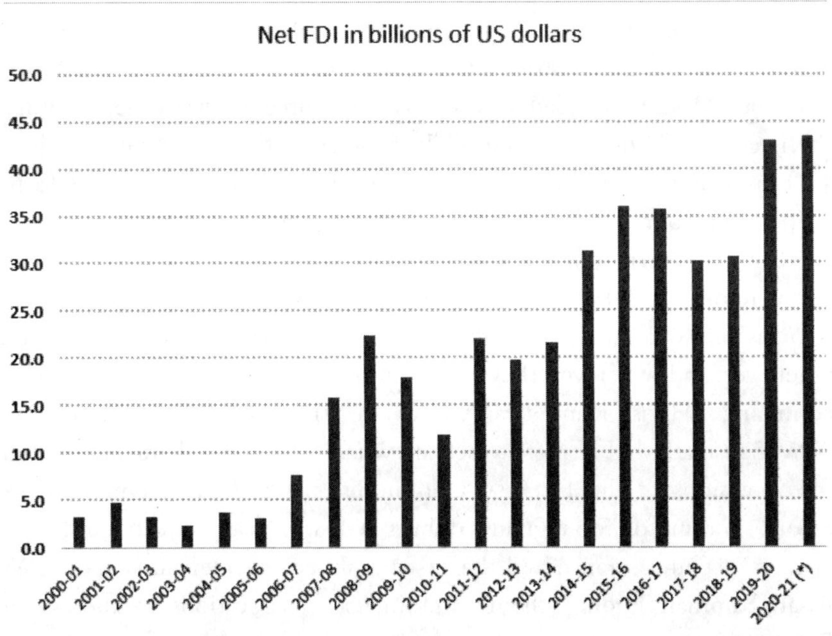

Source: Table 148: Foreign Investment Inflows, Handbook of Statistics on the Indian Economy, Reserve Bank of India. (Figures for 2020-21 are provisional)

Investors do not trust a foreign country with their funds merely because a Prime Minister goes scouting for investments. In Modi's case, the trust was established during his days in Gujarat; as mentioned earlier, he would offer a transparent, policy-driven and not discretionary or arbitrary governance. Demonstration came early in his tenure when he conducted transparent e-auctions for coal and other mining blocks. Indeed, we can safely assert that the unresolved issue of retrospective taxation did not deter foreign investors because of their overall confidence in Modi, based on his performance and governance in Gujarat. They expected that to continue even after he moved to Delhi and he did not disappoint them.

In his book *Modi Effect*[21], Lance Price writes about Prime Minister Modi lauding India's Mars Mission, Mangalyaan, which launched a spacecraft orbiting Mars since September 2014. At the Madison Square

Garden speech in New York in September 2014, Modi pointed out that India had just sent a spacecraft to Mars for ₹7 a kilometre, when it cost ₹10 a kilometre to cross Ahmedabad in a taxi!

Fast forward six years, and the spirit of frugal innovation was still intact. This time, in the policy space. During the pandemic, unlike the developed countries, Modi husbanded its scarce fiscal resources to direct them towards the neediest and the deserving while converting the pandemic crisis into an opportunity to chart a path to long-term prosperity. Two reform proposals: labour reforms and farm sector reforms stand out.

Eminent agricultural economist, Ashok Gulati, called India's farm sector reforms the 1991-moment for agriculture because the farm sector reforms allowed farmers to effectively sell to whomsoever they want, whenever and wherever they want and at whatever price they could command[22]. Harish Damodaran wrote[23] that the government scrapped the APMC Act, allowed farmers to sell anywhere and everywhere and diluted the provisions of the Essential Commodities Act (ECA). It procured a record amount of food grains, disbursed loans, made direct transfer to farmers' accounts, transferred the first instalment payment under the PM Kisan Samman Nidhi Scheme and increased allocations to the Rural Employment Guarantee Programme (MGNREGA).

Damodaran notes that the amount the Government of India had spent on the rural economy amounts to ₹1.5 lakh crore (₹1.5 trillion) and that too in a space of three months. Annualized, it worked out to almost 3 per cent of the GDP—all in the middle of a nationwide lockdown, in the middle of the pandemic. That is why, despite millions of migrant workers trudging back to their homes in villages, India did not experience famine or starvation related sufferings[24].

Recently, the government beat a tactical retreat on the farm sector liberalization by repealing the new farm laws. But, the Prime Minister has kept the door open for a better legislation to be enacted through a different and more consultative process. While this may appear to be a setback, the debate that the farm laws triggered and the liberalization that it promised have set off a positive dynamic that may be hard to roll back, even if the laws have been repealed for now.

On the labour reforms initiated by the government, economists from the Credit Suisse wrote:

> 'In a culmination of several years of work, 41 central labour laws have been reduced to four (12 repealed 2016-19, and 29 now subsumed). The number of sections fall by 60 per cent (1,232 to 480), one registration is now needed instead of six, one license instead of four, and decriminalisation of several (though not all) offences. Codes have been made contemporary (e.g. penalties raised; fixed-term employment introduced as 69 per cent of incremental factory workers [in] 1998-2018 were contractors; social security introduced for gig workers), and firm-size thresholds raised to further ease compliance burden: from 10 to 20 to be called a factory, 20 to 50 for contract worker laws to apply, and 100 to 300 for standing orders (including for layoffs)[25].'

That brings us to an important point and the final section of this chapter. Many of the reforms that the two Modi governments initiated have to be implemented by the states, whether it is farm sector liberalization, or labour law reforms or reforms to India's higher education. But Prime Minister Modi had set the ball in motion and shifted the terms of the debate. They will one day be implemented all over India. But the first and the big leap had been taken by Narendra Modi.

WHAT NEXT?

While the Prime Minister can look back at the two decades of public life with pride and satisfaction, he is not one to rest on his laurels. He will be thinking of the nation-building agenda for the next decade and beyond. Three areas of concern come to mind.

The security atmosphere in the neighbourhood has changed with the takeover of Afghanistan by Taliban. Consequently, he will be considering how to secure India in the face of the possible loss of strategic depth in Afghanistan for the time being. That requires thinking big and thinking differently about security. Economic and physical security will have to be pursued simultaneously for the former does not guarantee the latter.

The second big challenge is to put India's micro, small and medium enterprises (MSMEs) on a sustainable path. India has far too many micro-enterprises and is missing small and medium enterprises. Prime Minister

Modi, in his seven years of tenure, has done a lot to improve the business and credit conditions for MSMEs. GeM is a prime exhibit in this regard. More remains to be done to make sure that they are freed from the clutches of the 'License, Compliance and Inspection Raj' at all levels of the government. They await their moment of independence.

The third and the biggest of them all—right up his alley—is constitutional reforms. The Seventh Schedule of the Constitution that divides responsibilities between the union territories and the states and some for both needs a radical rethink and overhaul for the twenty-first century.

Nobel Laureate Daniel Kahneman had said that human beings were incapable of comprehending very large or very small numbers. He might have made an exception for Narendra Modi if he had known of the evidence presented in this chapter. The numerous policy initiatives and the evidence of the transformation that they wrought on the ground clearly establish Narendra Modi comprehended large numbers better than most. That augurs well not only for his place in Indian political and economic history, but also for India.

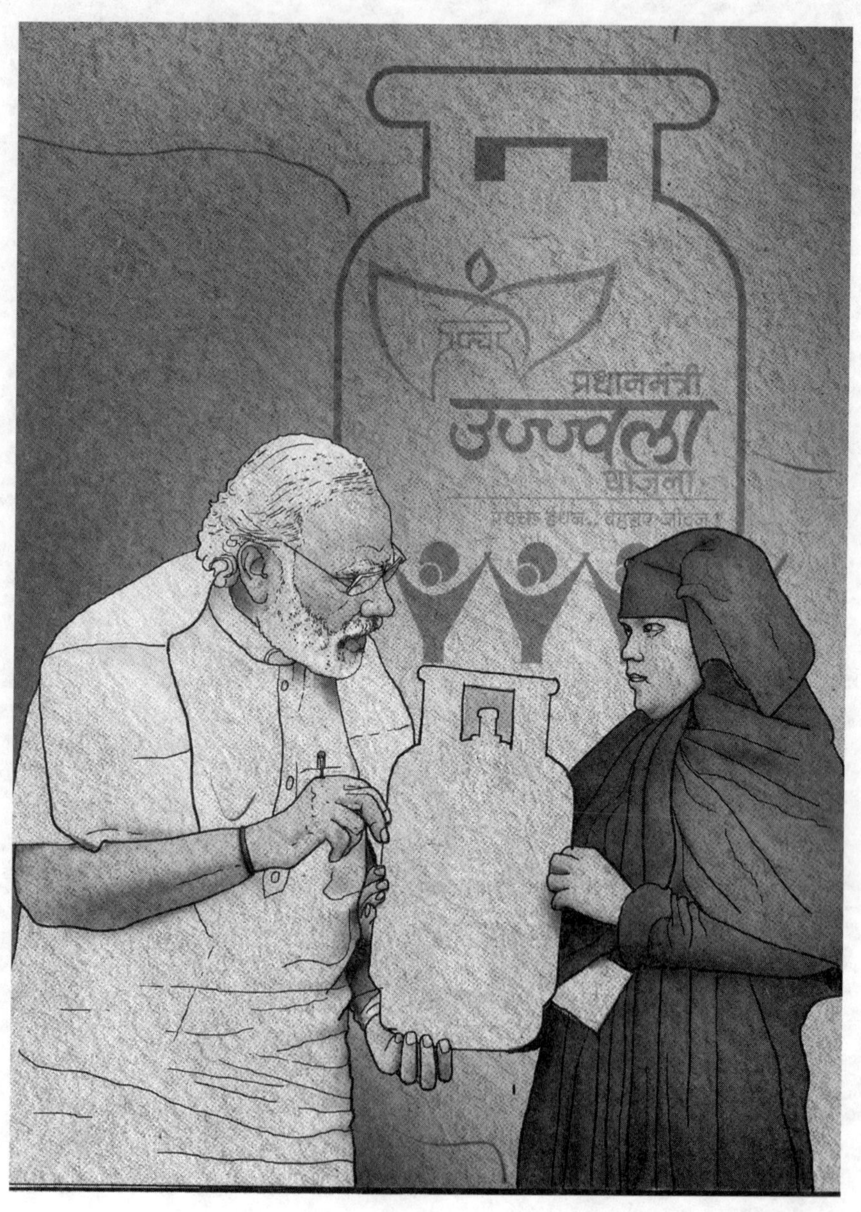
प्रधानमंत्री
उज्ज्वला

TOWARDS A PROSPEROUS INDIA

ARVIND PANAGARIYA

In 2012, speculation that the then Chief Minister of Gujarat, Narendra Modi, may make a bid for the office of India's Prime Minister had led to a lively debate on the performance of Gujarat under him. At the time, I had been studying the economic performance of the major states of India as a part of a three-year research project, which I had been directing at Columbia University. To me, data were unequivocal that the economic performance of Gujarat under Chief Minister Modi had been outstanding.

I went on to articulate this message in my monthly column in the *Times of India* in September 2012. I pointed out that with its Net State Domestic Product (NSDP) growing at the annual average rate of 10.5 per cent during 2002–03 to 2009–10, Gujarat had been the top performer among the major states of India. Its nearest competitor, Maharashtra, had grown at the annual rate of 10.1 per cent during the same years. Starting sixth among the larger states in 2002-03 in per capita NSDP ranking, the state had climbed up to the third rank in 2005-06, outperforming Tamil Nadu, Kerala and Punjab. In 2012, it retained that rank.

I further noted in the article that, while the media had paid disproportionate attention to Gujarat's performance in agriculture under Modi, the real key to its impressive performance had been in manufacturing. It accounted for 27.4 per cent of the state's NSDP compared with India-wide average of just 15 per cent. The high growth had translated in a nine percentage point reduction in the poverty ratio between 2004–05 and 2009–10. In 2009-10, the poverty ratio in the state stood seven percentage points below India-wide average.

This economic performance had, of course, been the result of concerted all-around policy initiatives, diligent implementation and corruption-free governance at the top. The Chief Minister had made particular effort to create a business-friendly environment in the state by building high-quality roads and well-functioning ports, provision of uninterrupted electricity, reduced inspector raj through greater reliance on self-assessment by enterprises, speedy disposal of labour disputes and initiatives such as the Vibrant Gujarat Summit.

Above all, as I learned later, he had had been exceptionally far-sighted in making labour markets more flexible in the Special Economic Zones (SEZs) in Gujarat than in any other state. Through an amendment of the Industrial Dispute Act of 1947 in March 2004, he had restored the right of enterprises of all sizes in SEZs in Gujarat. All they had to do was to pay the terminated worker forty-five days' worth of wages for each year they had worked. This reform contributed to the enormous success of SEZs in Gujarat. They came to account for a hefty 49 per cent of all exports by SEZs in India between 2008 and 2015. Considering that exports by all SEZs in India accounted for more than a quarter of India's total exports between 2010–11 and 2014–15, which had themselves seen exceptionally rapid growth from 2003–04 onward, this performance was doubly impressive.

My article in the *Times of India* caught the attention of the Chief Minister and brought me in direct contact with him. I first met him in November 2012, for an hour in his office in Gandhinagar. During that one hour, I learnt first-hand about his distinct governance style and the numerous initiatives he had taken in all sectors of the economy. Subsequently, as his bid for the office of the Prime Minister gathered momentum, I had the unusual opportunity to interact with him on India's economy on multiple occasions. During these interactions, we discussed in detail the reforms necessary to relaunch India into a high-growth trajectory. The Chief Minister's energy in these interactions was breathtaking. On one occasion, he had me going with my multiple presentations for almost seven hours!

ON THE NATIONAL STAGE

In the event, Modi scored a decisive victory in the parliamentary elections and became India's Prime Minister, a position he continues to hold seven years later. In 2019, he scored yet another victory with the number of parliamentary seats for his party and the coalition exceeding those in 2014. During his first term, I was privileged to work as the first vice chairman of NITI Aayog, an institution he created to replace the erstwhile Planning Commission. This was the first time in more than sixty-five years of India's post-independence history that a prime minister had shown the courage to appoint an individual fresh from abroad in the rank of a cabinet minister[1]. The position provided me the opportunity, rare for an academic, to shape the new institution and contribute to the making of national economic policies. The two-years-and-eight-months that I spent in this position remain the best of my entire professional life spanning forty-three years since the completion of my PhD degree at Princeton.

During the first five years of Prime Minister Modi's tenure, the economy grew at the average annual rate of 7.4 per cent, with inflation staying below 5 per cent, current account deficit held below 2 per cent and fiscal deficit declining every single year. By all standards, this was an impressive comeback for an economy that had been in near crisis during the last two years of the outgoing United Progressive Alliance (UPA) government[2]. But this is not the impression one would get from the media coverage either in India or abroad, which selectively focuses on the last two years when the economy performed poorly.

Growth during the last two years has decidedly been a setback, with the GDP rising just 4 per cent during 2019–20 and then declining an unprecedented 7.3 per cent during 2020–21. The low growth rate in 2019–20 was rooted in considerable weakening of the balance sheets of both corporations and public sector banks (PSBs) in the wake of reckless borrowing by the former and lending by the latter during 2008–14. A delay in corrective action by the Modi government added to the woes it had inherited.

Unfortunately, while corrective action was still underway, India and the world economy were hit by COVID-19. Given complete lack of knowledge of the virus and lack of preparedness against it, India took the prudential step of a severe lockdown in the first quarter of the pandemic. The result was a decline of 24.4 per cent in GDP in that quarter (April–June 2020) and 7.3 per cent in the full fiscal year 2020–21. Nevertheless, the economy made impressive recovery in the second half of 2020-21 in spite of the continuing COVID-19 crisis. The GDP during this second half of the year exceeded that in the corresponding (pre-COVID-19) period a year earlier.

Prospects for a return to normalcy are getting brighter by the day since India is making rapid progress in vaccination drives. Within a short period, the country has administered an astonishing 1.45 billion doses of the vaccine. Already, by the end of December 2021, over 90 per cent of the adult population had received at least one dose and 60 per cent both doses. The supply of vaccines has been rising every month and currently stands at approximately 250 million doses per month. That said, the importance of complementary protective measures such as the use of masks and avoiding large gatherings can hardly be understated. Evidence from Israel, the United States and the United Kingdom is unequivocal that even full vaccination of two-thirds of the entire population is insufficient protection against the Delta variant of the coronavirus.

Once normalcy is restored, India has excellent prospects for sustained growth at 7–8 per cent for two or more decades. The reason for my optimism is three fold. First, average labour productivity in India, as reflected in its low per capita income of $2,000 per annum, lags far behind comparator countries such as China, South Korea and Taiwan. This means that India has substantial scope for growth through the absorption of existing technologies alone. Second, at 30 per cent or less, India's current savings rate remains well below its past peak of 37 per cent in 2007–08. Therefore, there is considerable scope for raising the savings rate in the coming years. Finally, and most importantly, the Modi government has introduced numerous reforms in the past five years. Due to the slow pace at which Central and state government bureaucracies implement new laws, there is considerable lag between the enactment of reforms and the realization of their full beneficial effects[3].

Because the current slowdown has created an atmosphere of pessimism, it is important to recall some of the key economic reforms and related measures that have been introduced during the Modi era. It is only by viewing them in totality that we can gain full appreciation of their depth and breadth and, hence, their promise for future growth.

BIG-TICKET POLICY REFORMS

There are at least six major reforms that had been talked about for ten to twenty years but no previous government could muster the courage to enact them. Modi has not only enacted these reforms but also taken their full ownership. To quote him from a speech he delivered on 11 August 2021 at the Confederation of Indian Industry, 'We have taken bold decisions. Reforms continued even during pandemic. The government is doing reforms not out of compulsion but out of conviction.' From the phrase, 'There is no consensus on reforms, which many past leaders invoked to justify their lack of action, this transition to 'reforms by conviction instead of compulsion' is a refreshing change.

A modern bankruptcy law: The first big-ticket reform the government has introduced is a modern bankruptcy law through the Insolvency and Bankruptcy Code of 2016. For the first time, creditors can sue borrowers in default of their payments in a bankruptcy court and expect a time-bound resolution within 180 days, with the possibility of an extension by another ninety days. Though this deadline has not always been met, the speed of resolution and magnitudes of recovery have seen a jump that had for long seemed impossible in India.

In the past, when resolution took many years extending to a decade or more, most assets of the borrower (other than land) would become valueless. Faster resolution has now paved the way for recovery of significant value as well as revival of the enterprise, subject to bankruptcy proceedings. The prospect of a challenge in the bankruptcy court by creditors has also begun to banish the corporate culture of delinquent payments by borrowers. In the longer run, this promises to greatly strengthen the financial sector.

Apart from the obvious facts that a well-functioning bankruptcy code helps preserve the value of assets of outgoing enterprise and enhances the prospects for its revival, the biggest long-run benefit of the law flows from reduced risk of entering new businesses and consequent push to new investments. When entrepreneurs face a business environment in which exit is long drawn and costly, they are extra cautious in undertaking investments with high risk of failure even if they promise high returns. Creditors are also reluctant to finance such investments. The result is that only investments subject to minimal risk of failure over a long period of time are undertaken. Projects that require large capital investment and promise high returns are not undertaken even if they carry a moderate risk of failure. A well-functioning bankruptcy law overcomes this problem.

Goods and Services Tax: The Modi government has replaced a plethora of indirect central and state taxes by a single nationwide Goods and Services Tax (GST). The effort to replace the excise duties by VAT had begun as early as the second half of the 1980s. Even the idea of a single nationwide VAT on a given commodity had been mooted two decades ago in 2000. But neither the Vajpayee government nor the UPA was successful in forging consensus necessary to enact this difficult reform. It took concerted effort and careful negotiation with the state governments by the Modi government to bring it to fruition. The reform had required the enactment of as many as four distinct Central laws and a constitutional amendment that had to be approved by the Parliament and eighteen state legislatures.

Apart from eliminating the economic cost of distortions associated with the past regime of multiple taxes, GST has greatly simplified the indirect tax system, made tax evasion difficult and begun to bring more and more enterprises into the tax net. Given that the tax base for direct taxes in India remains narrow with rather poor prospects of substantial broadening in the medium term, a robust indirect tax system is a necessity. Being effectively a consumption tax on the purchases of final goods and services, this is the only tax that is paid by nearly all the citizens. As such, it promises to be the major source of revenue in the long run. Already, even though economic activity has not fully recovered from the shock of COVID-19, GST revenues have reached well above the pre-COVID-19 peak and are rising at an unprecedented rate.

In the past, multiple points of taxation, frequently spread over multiple states, used to greatly slow down the movement of goods on the road. They were also a source of corruption among those guarding different check posts along transportation routes. By replacing taxation at multiple points by a single nationwide tax, which is paid digitally and requires minimal interaction between the taxpayer and tax collector, GST has helped contain corruption and speed up transportation of goods, especially when they have to cross multiple state borders.

Labour law reforms: Until recently, India had as many as twenty-nine disparate and occasionally contradictory Central labour laws. The Modi government has now replaced them by four labour codes that are internally consistent and coherent. In addition to simplifying and rationalizing the old labour laws, the codes also reform them to lend greater flexibility to labour markets and bring better balance between the rights of employees and employers. Among other things, the code on industrial relations restores the right of manufacturing enterprises with three hundred or fewer workers to lay off workers upon appropriate compensation for each year worked. Earlier, only manufacturing enterprises with one hundred or fewer workers had this right.

Critics rightly argue that the revised ceiling is still low and should be set at a much higher level, even abolished. But on the positive side, the revised code explicitly empowers states to raise the ceiling to any level they desire through a notification. Moreover, the code also introduces a provision for fixed-term employment, which can be renewed as many times as the enterprise desires. This provision provides enterprises with more than three hundred workers considerable flexibility in expanding the size of their workforce without the fear of having to keep new workers in perpetuity. Additional reforms contained in the new codes include the removal of restrictions on women to work night shifts, increased threshold of enterprises exempt from having to file compliance reports, greater transparency in the union's right to bargain and simplified procedures for filing compliance reports relating to labour laws.

Rigidity of labour laws in India has been a key contributor to the dwarfism of Indian enterprises relative to their counterparts in economically successful countries such as South Korea, Taiwan and China. It has also contributed to the poor performance of labour-intensive sectors such as apparel, footwear and other light manufactures. These sectors are the primary engine of well-paid jobs for workers with limited skill in developing countries. In the early stages of development, all countries with an initially large proportion of the workforce in agriculture transformed themselves into modern economies through the creation of large volumes of jobs in these labour-intensive sectors. With labour laws substantially reformed, combined with a well-functioning bankruptcy law, prospects for accelerated job creation for workers with limited skills in India are significantly better today.

The Farm Laws: To ensure that farmers are not denied indefinitely the rights to sell their produce at the best price they can get and are able to enter contracts with buyers of produce, such as food processors and exporters at pre-specified prices, the Modi government took the courage to use the powers provided under the constitution and enacted the reforms through Central laws. Additionally, it enacted an amendment to the Essential Commodities Act, which had also been on the policy agenda of earlier governments but no action had been taken.

Unfortunately, however, these long-awaited pro-farmer reforms had to be withdrawn due to prolonged agitation by farmers from two states, Punjab and Haryana. The decision to withdraw the laws was a difficult one for the Prime Minister. As he put it in the address to the nation while withdrawing the laws, he brought the laws in the interest of farmers and he was withdrawing them in the interest of the nation.

Simplification of and reduction in corporate profit tax: In India, corporate profit tax rates have been extremely high in relation to comparator countries. Moreover, a variety of exemptions open the door to corruption and tax evasion. High taxes also translate into less retained earnings and, therefore, lower volume of corporate savings that translate into relatively more productive investments on average.

The Modi government has greatly simplified and lowered the corporate profit tax rates. It has cut the tax rate on corporate profits from approximately 35 per cent to 17 per cent for new investments in manufacturing, and to 25.2 per cent for all other investments with no exemptions permitted. The reform has thus ended a host of complex and arbitrary exemptions and realigned the effective tax rate to international standards. Within India's polity, with the ghost of socialism omnipresent, this a bold reform.

The reduction in the corporate profit tax effectively translates into larger corporate savings and investment. As such, it can be expected to increase the overall rate of private investment. It would also attract foreign investment in larger volume. The lower tax rate on new manufacturing investments would be particularly helpful in raising the share of this sector in the total private investment. Prospects for this shift look doubly good when we take into account other complementary reforms: Insolvency and Bankruptcy Code, reforms of labour laws and GST.

End to Indian Medical Council Act of 1956: A final difficult-to-navigate area of reform in India has been medical education. UPA had repeatedly tried to replace the highly corrupt Medical Council of India (MCI) by an alternative regulatory body but failed. The present government has successfully replaced the archaic Indian Medical Council Act of 1956 with an entirely new legislation. The latter modernizes the regulatory regime governing medical education and removes many barriers to its rapid expansion at all levels. In parallel, similar legislations have replaced the old laws governing regulatory regimes in education in homeopathy and Indian systems of medicine.

The impact of the new legislation on medical education is being already felt. Under the old regime, MCI kept a tight control on the expansion of both new medical colleges and the number of students permitted in the existing medical colleges. As a result, the supply of doctors grew slowly for many decades and remains well short of the country's needs today. Since the abolition of MCI, the government has successfully sped up the expansion of medical colleges. The new law also opens doors for shorter courses to produce qualified practitioners of basic primary healthcare. In the medium- to long-term, this latter provision will help replace the large number of wholly unqualified practitioners in rural areas currently by qualified ones.

OTHER ECONOMIC POLICY REFORMS

Prior to the 1991 reforms, some sectors were the exclusive preserve of the public sector while others were subject to licensing. Most sectors were also off-limits to foreign investors. The New Industrial Policy of 1991 had aimed to remove all these restrictions. Yet, after twenty-five years of reforms, some sectors had remained off-limits to the private sector while others were still to be opened to foreign investors. The Modi government has made progress in liberalization along both dimensions while also raising the caps on foreign direct investment (FDI) in sectors otherwise open to foreign investors.

Opening previously closed sectors to private entry: Concerning private entry, for the first time, the railways have been opened to private players. Initially, the Railway Ministry invited private entities to redevelop railway stations. More recently, it has decided to permit private trains. Though an initial auction for such trains did not produce any positive results, it is only a matter of time that such trains will become a reality.

The government has also introduced commercial coal mining with no restrictions whatsoever on the sale of coal. In November 2020, a total of nineteen mines were auctioned under the programme. In the second round, thirty-four bids for another nineteen mines had been received by July 2021, while in the third and fourth rounds, 88 and 99 coal mines were put up for auction by December 2021. The reform has finally cleared the way for the emergence of a genuine private market in coal where prices are determined by the forces of demand and supply with no restrictions on buyers placed in terms of end use of coal. In the past, either government mines supplied coal to specified firms at specified prices or mine auctions were restricted among specific firms, such as producers of steel or power. Two other sectors to which private entry has been opened for the first time are space and atomic energy. Private entry into these sectors, especially space, promises to multiply manifold the benefits of India's low-cost manufacturing and innovation in space-related defence and communications equipment.

Opening previously closed sectors to foreign investors: The government has also opened certain sectors to FDI that had remained closed to it under previous governments, and this was despite the passage of twenty-five years since the original decision to open Indian economy to FDI. These sectors include defence, railways, coal mining, e-commerce marketplaces and agriculture. In other sectors, the government has gone on to liberalize FDI caps on the share of foreign investors in the total investment. One important sector in this category is insurance. Despite a long-standing demand of foreign investors, this opening did not take place for ten years under UPA.

The Modi government has now raised this cap not just to 49 per cent, as sought by the investors, but to 74 per cent. In defence, 74 per cent FDI is permitted through the automatic route and 100 per cent through the approval route. Foreign investors can also own 100 per cent stake in retail trading in food products produced in India, high-tech and capital-intensive activities in the railways and manufacturing of medical devices. The liberalizing steps and expectations of high returns have led to an increase in the total FDI flow from $36 billion in 2013–14, the last full year under UPA, to $81.7 billion in 2020–21. Even though 2020–21 saw a 7.3 per cent decline in GDP due to the COVID-19 shock, FDI in this year grew by 10 per cent over that in 2019–20.

End to retrospective taxation: The introduction of retrospective taxation in 2012 empowered the government to collect taxes on transactions completed several years earlier, even though such taxes were not due under the tax rules prevailing at the time of those transactions. Because the law was used to assess billions of dollars' worth of new taxes on a set of foreign firms, it sent the morale of foreign investors into a tailspin.

One of the early acts of the Modi government in 2014 was to assure these investors that no new cases under the law would be initiated. In cases that had already been initiated by the UPA, the government took the judicious path of not pursuing them further once the High Court ruled in favour of the defendant. The assurance led to a much more predictable taxation for new foreign investments. Nevertheless, since the law empowering the government had not been repealed, fears of its use by a future government had remained. Luckily, the Modi government has now repealed the law as well recently and, thus, has given added assurance to investors. Foreign investors have uniformly hailed the repeal as an important development towards a more predictable taxation regime in India.

Real Estate (Regulation and Development) Act of 2016: The Real Estate (Regulation and Development) Act, RERA, which was passed by the Parliament in 2016 and came fully into force on 1 May 2017, promises to make real estate transactions transparent, curb corruption and better balance the rights of builders and buyers. The RERA requires each state and union territory to appoint a regulator and frame rules and regulations that would govern the functioning of the regulator. It provides for a unified legal regime for the purchase of flats and seeks to standardize the practice across the country.

The Act mandates the establishment of a real estate regulatory authority in each state and union territory. The authority is required to protect the interests of the stakeholders, create a data repository and provide an effective grievance redressal system in a time-bound fashion. The maximum time for the disposal of complaints is set at sixty days. In case of delays, the authority must record the reason for it. Under the Act, each state and union territory must also appoint a real estate appellate authority to serve as the forum for appeals.

End to petroleum subsidies: Subsidies, once put in place, are politically difficult to remove and have had a history of continuing even when no rationale for them is left. But the Modi government has successfully put an end to nearly all petroleum subsides. Diesel and petrol prices were fully deregulated by 1 January 2015. Cooking gas subsidy to urban consumers, who fall in generally well-off category of households, has also been fully eliminated. This subsidy has, instead, been redirected to below poverty line (BPL) households in rural areas. Finally, beginning in March 2020, the government has successfully eliminated the subsidy on kerosene, a fuel that is damaging to the health of its users as well as the environment.

To eliminate cooking gas subsidy, Modi deployed the novel technique of reform by persuasion. Early in his first term, under a 'Give It Up' campaign, he called upon richer beneficiaries to voluntarily opt out of the subsidy programme. As many as 10.3 million households responded positively to his call. For the remainder of the beneficiaries, the government eliminated the gap between the market and subsidized price through several small steps, reducing the subsidy by a small amount each time. By May 2020, the subsidy bill on this count had dropped to nil.

Micro, small and medium enterprises: Enterprises in India have shown a tendency not to grow in size. This tendency is partially, though by no means wholly, due to tax incentives and subsidies that are withdrawn as micro enterprises graduate to the small-enterprise category, small enterprises to the medium-enterprise category and medium enterprises to the large-enterprise category. To alleviate the problem, at least partially, the government has changed the definitions of the three categories to widen each of them. Until recently, these enterprises have been defined by investment ceilings with the ceilings being higher for manufacturing than services enterprises in each category. New definitions have eliminated the differences in ceilings applicable to manufacturing and services enterprises. More importantly, they have raised the investment ceilings. This means that enterprises in each category can now grow larger up to the new, higher ceiling without losing the tax incentives and subsidies within that category.

SOCIAL SPENDING WITH A DIFFERENCE

All governments in India have devoted public expenditures to social causes. But social spending under Modi has had two distinguishing features. First, he has launched schemes on scale and completed them in a time-bound fashion. And second, he has plugged many of the leakages in the schemes, thereby, delivering a larger bang for the buck for the beneficiary.

Schemes on scale: I offer four examples of time-bound completion of large-scale schemes. First, in his first Independence Day speech on 15 August 2014, Modi announced his intention to bring bank accounts to all Indians under a new initiative he called the Prime Minister's Jan Dhan Yojana (PMJDY). The initial target under the scheme was set at covering all households with no bank account, estimated to be seventy-five million as of 26 January 2015. The government managed to open as many as eighteen million accounts in just one week between 23 August and 29 August in 2014, a feat that found a place in the Guinness Book of Records. By 26 January 2015, the total number of PMJDY accounts reached 125.4 million, exceeding the original target by a wide margin. On 29 December 2021, the number of these accounts stood at over 442 million.

In the same Independence Day speech, Modi also announced the Swachh Bharat Mission (SBM) under which he set the target to turn India open defecation free (ODF) on 2 October 2019, the one hundred and fiftieth birth anniversary of the father of the nation, Mahatma Gandhi. Given that only 38 per cent of the rural households had access to toilets at the time, this seemed to be an impossible target. Yet, the government was successful in bringing toilets to substantially all households by the deadline in at least rural India. In a speech, appropriately delivered at the Sabarmati Riverfront in Ahmedabad on 2 October 2019 to 20,000 SBM activists from around the country, Modi said that the number of those practicing open defecation in India had gone down from 600 million in 2014 to negligible.

The programme for electrification of rural India had been underway since independence. But as of 1 April 2015, a total of 18,452 villages still remained without electricity. On 15 August 2015, Modi promised in his Independence Day speech that he would electrify all remaining villages within the next thousand days. The deadline mobilized all stakeholders and the target was met. On 28 April 2018, electricity had reached all census inhabited villages that had been previously unelectrified.

The fourth and last example of programmes undertaken on scale by Modi is the Jal Jeevan Mission (JJM). Announced on 15 August 2019, this mission promises to bring safe and adequate water, mainly through water pipelines, to all rural households by 2024. Though interruptions due to COVID-19 set back the progress of this mission, it has made impressive progress. At the time of the announcement on 15 August 2019, only 32.3 million out of a total of 192 million households had tap water connections. By 20 December 2021, households with tap water connection grew to 86.7 million. Therefore, the proportion of such households in the total number of households has risen from just 16.85 per cent to 45.1 per cent within two and a half years. More households have received piped water in the last two years than in the entire preceding post-independence period.

Plugging leakages through direct benefit transfer: An important initiative on scale, not included above, that the Modi government completed early in its first term was to give a biometric identity, known as Aadhaar, to all citizens. The programme had been originally introduced by the UPA government but progress picked speed only under Modi. By 29 August 2021, a total of 1.3 billion Aadhaar cards had been issued.

The biometric identity has given the government the ability to eliminate millions of ghost beneficiaries in whose name benefits were being drawn previously under its numerous schemes. The identity, bank accounts and digital payments platform have also given the government the power to make cash transfers directly to beneficiaries with no intermediaries involved, whatsoever. The government now routinely makes these transfers. Most recently, it began using this to deposit the payment for grain it procures from farmer under the minimum support price (MSP) programme directly into his/her bank account. In the past, the government used to pay this amount to the intermediary who sold the produce to it on behalf of the farmer. But this used to leave the farmer at the mercy of the intermediary.

DIGITAL PAYMENTS SYSTEM

While notable progress has also been made in various areas of physical infrastructure such as roads, railways, ports and bridges, it is the progress and innovation in digital payments infrastructure that deserves special mention. For India has developed a unique digital payments system that allows individuals to transfer funds to each other using mobile phones, regardless of whether they have accounts in the same or different banks. Moreover, the transfer takes place instantly and at near-zero cost. Known as the Unified Payments Interface (UPI), the platform has been hailed as the most efficient in existence by experts around the world.

Traditional mobile wallets function by taking a specified sum of money from the payer bank account beforehand and storing it in its own account to affect transactions in the future. This feature permits transactions only between users of the same wallet. In contrast, UPI does not require any prior transfer of funds to a different account and lets the payer and payee transact from their respective bank accounts directly. The government has also created an Unstructured Supplementary Service Data protocol, which allows customers lacking smartphones to transfer funds using feature phones via the UPI platform.

The number of banks on UPI platform has risen from just twenty-one in April 2016, when it began operation, to 216 in April 2021. All major wallets including Google Pay, PhonePe, Paytm and Amazon Pay now operate through UPI. In the month of December 2021, UPI processed a record 4.56 billion transactions with a value equivalent to a hefty ₹8.27 trillion. These transactions and their value represent 98 per cent and 91 per cent increase over those in the month of January 2021!

EASE OF LIVING FOR CITIZENS

The Modi government has also taken steps to improve citizens' access to publicly provided services. Some examples illustrate the point.

In the past, when submitting affidavits or applications to government agencies, individuals had to find a senior government officer or a senior member of judiciary to have the copies of their diplomas and degrees certified. This was a rather costly affair especially for those residing in rural areas. The Modi government has done away with this practice, permitting self-certification of copies of diplomas and degrees when submitting affidavits or applications.

Tax assessment and appeal mechanism is another area in which taxpayers face harassment from tax inspectors. On many occasions, the latter resort to such harassment to extract bribes from honest taxpayers. To alleviate this problem, the Modi government has adopted entirely faceless audits whereby the tax inspector must interact only digitally with the taxpayer. With no physical contact permitted, demanding bribes becomes tricky and receiving it becomes risky since it would necessarily create a paper trail.

The third example of ease of living concerns pensioners. Under the old practice, each November, a pensioner had to visit a bank, post office, Life Insurance Corporation of India (LIC) office or an Employees Provident Fund Organization (EPFO) office to provide proof that she was alive to continue to receive her pension the following year. To relieve the elderly of this hardship, the Modi government introduced the Jeevan Pramaan scheme in 2014. The scheme now allows the pensioners to certify their existence digitally.

The fourth and final example in this category relates to the process of renewal of passport. In the past, each time an individual went for the renewal of her passport, she had to get a police report. The Modi government has done away with this provision. It has also digitized the process of application for the issue and renewal of passport.

SOME GOVERNANCE REFORMS

Modi has endeavoured to improve governance holistically. The drive for digitization to improve the ease of living, direct benefit transfers and initiatives to combat corruption have been a part of this effort. Notably, his initiatives in the first term to improve business environment led to an improvement in India's position in the World Bank's 'Ease of Doing Business' rankings from 142 in 2014 to 63 in 2020.

An important long-pending change the Modi government brought about was the end to planning. India had decisively switched from the socialist-era planning model to the market model beginning in 1991. Yet, as a matter of habit, the government continued to write five-year plans. Even Prime Minister Manmohan Singh raised this issue as he was ending his term in 2014. The Modi government has finally completed this important reform. As a by-product of this reform, the long-standing artificial distinction in the budget between plan and non-plan expenditures has also come to an end.

Among governance reforms, perhaps the most important one is the reform of the civil service. Its significance has been recognized for a long time with multiple administrative reform commissions submitting their reports in the past but with no actual action being taken by previous governments. The Modi government has taken some modest steps in this area as well. For the first time, it has opened the door to later entry to outsiders for substantive and meaningful positions of joint secretaries. Admittedly, the number of entrants has been small so that the significance of the progress along this dimension has been more in establishing the principle rather than of substantive difference. Clearly, the door to outside entry needs to opened much wider. But Modi has made more substantial progress in breaking the monopoly of Indian administrative service officers on the senior positions: he has appointed an unprecedented number of officers from other services such as the Internal Revenue Service, Indian Customs and Central Excise Services and Indian Railway Service to senior positions, notably to the position of the joint secretary.

Modi has also ended the tradition of a separate budget for railways and merged it with the Union Budget. A separate railway budget probably had a rationale during earlier decades when Indian Railways had accounted for a very large proportion of the total government expenditure. But this is no longer the case and it made little sense to continue undertaking the budget exercise each year, thereby, using up a vast amount of public's time and media space wastefully.

The Modi government has made the use of Public Finance Management System (PFMS) mandatory for the Centre as well as the states for undertaking any financial transactions. This has helped speed up payments while also creating greater transparency. In particular, this has allowed the transfer of funds under various Central government programmes to not only state governments but also households with full accounting and no leakages.

An apparently small reform, but one that has had major impact on developing the solar energy market in India, was the introduction of reverse auction in solar energy. Under this auction, pre-qualified potential solar power developers bid on tariff at which they would supply a specified quantum of solar power to the government. Prior to the introduction of reverse auction, the first 150 MW solar power project was tendered under the National Solar Mission at the average tariff of ₹12.16 per kilowatt hour. Reverse auction successfully brought this tariff down to ₹3.30 per kilowatt hour at the Rewa Solar Park. This price has allowed the government to expand solar energy at a much faster pace than would have been feasible otherwise given its limited revenues.

BIG TICKET REFORMS ON THE TABLE, AND THOSE THAT SHOULD BE

The Modi government has several big-ticket reforms currently on the table. These include privatization of all public sector enterprises (PSEs) in sectors identified as non-strategic, and of two public sector banks (PSBs); a ₹6 trillion worth asset monetization programme; replacement of the archaic University Grants Commission Act of 1956 by a National Higher Education Commission Act; and entry of private companies in the electricity distribution sector. These are all extremely important reforms that will go a long way towards raising the productivity of the economy while also placing the finances of the government on a sounder footing.

There are three additional reforms that I consider necessary, which are not on the current agenda of the government. First, and indeed most important, India needs to reverse its recent turn to protectionism and begin reopening its economy to international trade. The Modi government has raised tariffs in a large number of sectors with the result that tariff lines with 15 per cent or higher rates have gone up from 13 per cent of all tariff lines in 2015 to 25 per cent in 2020–21. Despite having less than 3 per cent share in the world merchandise imports, India is also the second most frequent user of anti-dumping as measured by the number of actions in place. The country cannot create good jobs for the masses without conquering the global markets in manufacturing, especially in labour-intensive sectors, and that requires an open economy. A recent announcement by the Commerce Secretary to negotiate free trade agreements with the United Arab Emirates, the European Union, the United Kingdom, Canada and Australia is an extremely positive development in this respect. However, till date, the follow up to such announcements has been less than encouraging.

The second reform concerns a more aggressive push to privatization of PSBs. With the IBC in place, the major remaining weak link in financial markets is the poor performance of these banks. There is an inherent contradiction between the government owning these banks while also regulating them. Government employees who serve as the CEOs of these banks also lack appetite to finance risky projects with high expected returns as well as the expertise to assess complex projects. The banks also remain outside the reach of some key regulations of the Reserve Bank of India. In principle, it is possible to place PSBs at arm's length from the government as recommended, for example, by the P. J. Nayak Committee, and place their regulation fully in the hands of the Reserve Bank of India. But in practice, bureaucratic hurdles to such a reform are unsurmountable, as evidenced by the fact that no movement towards such a reform has taken place despite committee after committee recommending it. And short of it, privatization is the only way the banks can be turned into genuine commercial entities and brought under full regulation of the Reserve Bank of India.

Finally, the government must also give serious thought to a major revision of the Right to Education (RTE) Act. In its current form, the act gives teachers all the rights but provides no mechanism for the enforcement of their duties. The result has been rampant teacher absenteeism, dereliction of duty and poor delivery of service in public schools. Unsurprisingly, parents have been steadily moving their children out of public schools to whatever private school they can afford. The outcome has been hollowing out of public schools with nearly 70 per cent of public elementary schools now left with only five to seven students per class on average. Such small classes are not only pedagogically inefficient, they also cost more than ₹40,000 per pupil per year in just teacher salaries. This is a dire situation that needs to be addressed through appropriate reform of the RTE Act.

IN CONCLUSION: LOOKING AHEAD

What would the Indian economy look like post-COVID-19? A set of mutually reinforcing reforms such as the end to investment licensing, opening up to foreign trade and investment, opening of telecom sector to private players, expansion of infrastructure, liberal entry to private banks and deregulation of interest rates under Prime Ministers Rao and Vajpayee had kicked off a virtuous cycle of investment and output to deliver more than 8 per cent growth for almost a decade beginning in 2003–04. Similar mutually reinforcing reforms of labour laws, bankruptcy system, corporate profit tax and indirect taxes, complemented by rapid expansion of infrastructure and digitization, under Modi promise to unleash 8 per cent plus growth in the post-COVID-19 era. Unless future governments return to anti-growth policies of the kind that the UPA enacted in its second term, this growth will likely sustain for two decades. Of course, if the government additionally liberalizes trade and privatizes large proportions of PSEs and PSBs, it can count on bumping up this growth rate to 10 per cent.

In a nutshell, India has excellent prospects of achieving a per capita income of $8,000 or more in 2020 dollars in less than two decades. At this per capita income, it can ensure a prosperous life for nearly all its citizens. Such prosperity will also guarantee it a place among the top three global powers and return to it its lost glory of yesteryears.

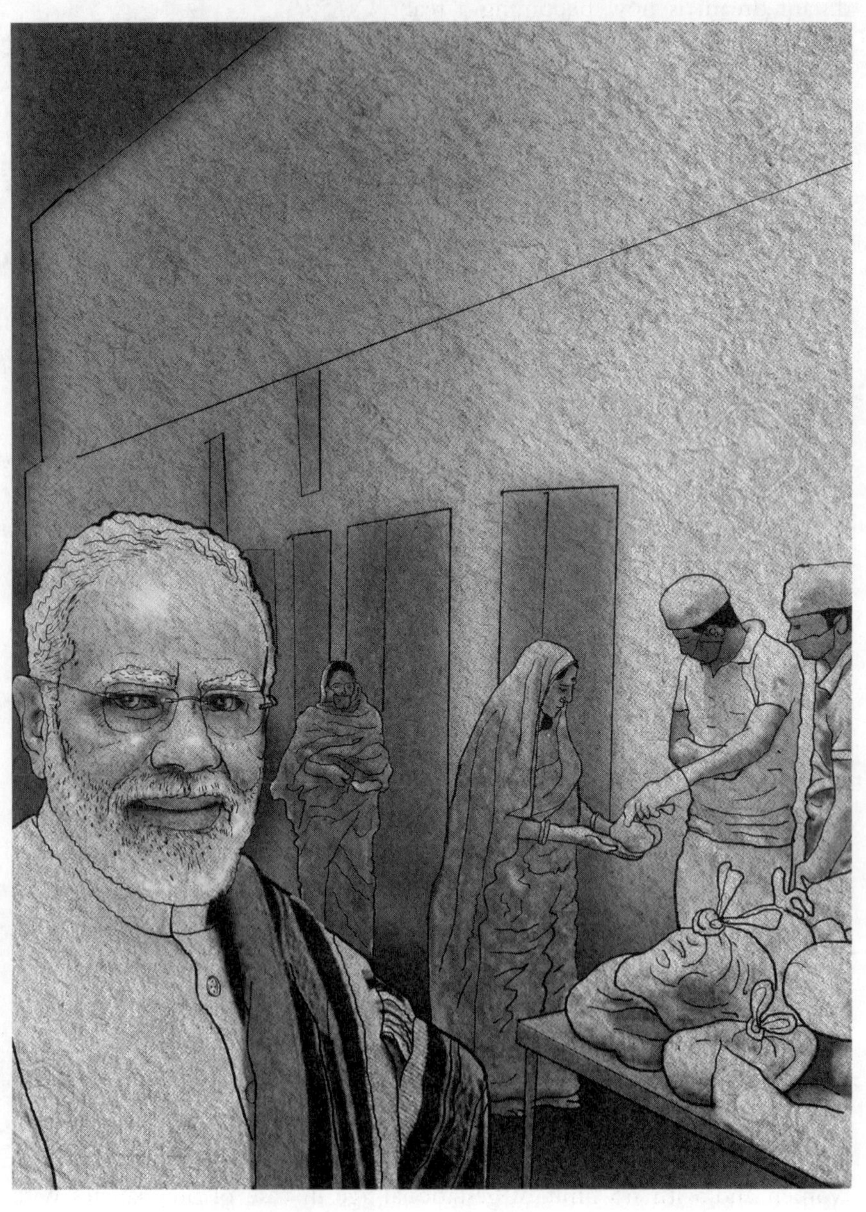

MICRO-REVOLUTIONS THAT IMPROVED THE LIVES OF ORDINARY CITIZENS

DR SHAMIKA RAVI

A fundamental challenge before democratically elected leaders is the task of balancing economic growth with development. This is particularly challenging in dynamic economies, which are liberal plural democracies. Transformative leadership, however, can steer nations through complex challenges and attempt bold, innovative ideas. This essay presents five critical successes of Narendra Modi's administration that signify micro-revolutions within the modern Indian economy. Each of these five phenomena is fundamental to transforming the lives of ordinary people for the better across the country. Using rigorous empirical analysis of publicly available data, the article highlights the evidence of widespread and significant impact on development outcomes in India.

The five key successes that are highlighted here are: (1) Strengthening India's welfare architecture; (2) Improving health, hygiene and safety through access to toilets; (3) Having an emergency and agile response to a global pandemic; (4) Empowering women leaders; and (5) Showcasing the Gujarat experience of growth with development.

These do not constitute an exhaustive list of developments but have been curated based on research interests and data availability. For each highlighted phenomenon, evidence is provided from independent scholarship and empirical analysis of publicly available data from different sources. It is essential to study and evaluate the evidence beyond official government statistics. At the same time, the narrative that one often hears in the popular press needs independent and constant scrutiny. So, this essay is also meant to encourage younger scholars to replicate and verify these results.

Strengthening welfare architecture

Indian households, across all states and union territories, have witnessed significant improvements in connectivity since 2014. While this is palpable in terms of hard infrastructure such as roads and electricity, which are widely observed and recognized, I have focused on connectivity in terms of something less obvious but equally important. The presence of average Indian households on the JAM (Jan Dhan, Aadhar and Mobile) platforms has created a foundational core for India's future economic growth and welfare architecture. One can study the strength and coverage of this platform by looking at official data from the institutions concerned, or one can look at self-reported data from household surveys across the country. As per the latest data from UIDAI*, approximately 132.3 crore individuals hold Aadhaar cards in India. This amounts to approximately 95 per cent of the country's population.

Similarly, one can look at access to bank accounts, propelled by the gargantuan PMJDY drive in 2014. As of December 2021, more than 44.2 crore bank accounts have been opened, and most are for women (55 per cent)**. In terms of mobile phone connectivity, TRAI data[1] shows more than 1.19 billion subscribers as of November 2021.

The official data on JAM connectivity is closely mirrored in household surveys. The National Family Health Survey 2015-16 (NFHS-4) data showed (Figure 1) that on average more than 90 per cent of households reported access to a bank account, mobile telephone connection, and having an Aadhaar card across states in India. Four years since the NFHS-4 was collected, these numbers are significantly higher today as reported in the latest round of NFHS-5 (2019-20) published recently. While unit level data of NFHS-5 is still unavailable publicly, we know from the published report that 93.3 percent households have mobile connections and 95.5 percent have bank (or post office) account. The outreach is comparable across rural and urban areas with 96% and 95% bank (or post office)

*Reported on 31st December 2021

**https://www.pmjdy.in/account - as of 8th December 2021

account coverage respectively. In terms of mobile phone connectivity, urban households have near universal coverage at 97% while rural households have slightly lesser coverage of 92%. So if we recreate Figure 1 with NFHS-5 data (when available), we expect the average figures to rise but the variation is likely to fall significantly. This is because most efforts in the last five years were targeted towards under-served states across the country. In absolute terms, the JAM outreach reflects unprecedented scale and speed of connectivity, not observed anywhere else globally.

Figure 1: JAM Connectivity (2015-16)

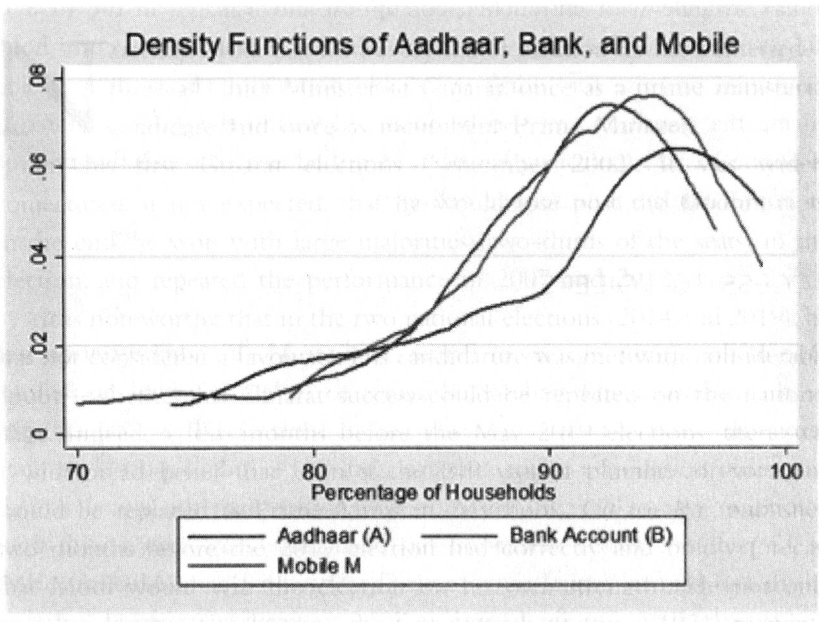

Source: National Family Health Survey 2015-16 (NFHS-4)

It is important to highlight that of the JAM trifecta, while access to Aadhaar and bank accounts has improved on government efforts, improvements in mobile telephone connectivity have been primarily due to private enterprises. Enhanced connectivity is leading to rapid improvements in the quality of life for average citizens across the country. This is happening through both expanding access to markets and improving access to government welfare support. Numerous new market solutions are being made available, including agri-tech services, financial services, media, and entertainment services. Simultaneously, the JAM platform is being used to implement direct benefit transfer through numerous schemes to the vulnerable population across the country. The latest data from the end of December 2021 show that direct benefit transfers were being carried out for 310 schemes through 54 ministries[2]. Rigorous research has shown a significant reduction in corruption and leakages by linking major welfare schemes to JAM. In the instance of India's largest welfare scheme, the public distribution system (PDS) scheme, this reduction in corruption was estimated to be significant[3]. This is remarkable in the backdrop of India's struggle with entrenched corruption and leakages in the PDS in the past decades. The move to a more efficient welfare architecture holds long-term promise for India's vulnerable population. Fears of exclusion during the transition can also be addressed within the JAM architecture as phone-based monitoring has been identified as a cost-effective method of improving last-mile service delivery[4].

ACCESS TO TOILETS

One of the lasting legacies of Prime Minister Modi's administration will be the improved and widespread access to toilets for rural households across the country. Despite a steady rise in India's GDP per capita, open defecation remained a major concern until 2014. India reported an open defecation rate of over 40 per cent, way higher than the global average of 12 per cent. Open defecation has been closely associated with poor health and human capital outcomes[5]. The Swachh Bharat Mission (SBM) was launched on Gandhi Jayanti in 2014 to provide universal access to toilets for rural households. Successive governments had in previous decades made several attempts to improve toilet access but with limited success.

In comparison, the SBM was able to achieve rapid success due to widespread momentum throughout the country. To understand this sanitation transformation, research was done using a theory of change grounded in behaviour-centered design. It shows that disruptive and transformative political leadership galvanized government bureaucracy nationwide, informed and motivated the public at large, and set new norms of ethical behaviour[6]. Within five years, approximately 98 million toilets were constructed across India achieving universal coverage by 2019[7]. It is now recommended that governments that wish to achieve the objective of sustainable development goal of universal access to safe sanitation can learn from the success of India's Swachh Bharat Mission.

Scholars have rigorously studied the impact of access to toilets over the past few years. There is overwhelming evidence to support that it has led to significant improvements in health and hygiene outcomes of ordinary Indians[8]. Perhaps what is relatively unknown is the significant impact of SBM on the safety of women and girls in rural areas. Having easy and close access to toilets near their homes, reduces the exposure and vulnerability of women to crime. Combining data of toilet construction with the National Crime Records Bureau (NCRB), scholars have done careful empirical research to find that this scheme led to a 22 per cent reduction in sexual assault and a 14 per cent reduction in rapes within the first few years itself[9]. While such findings have not found their way into popular media discussions, they signify a fundamental improvement in the quality of lives of people, especially women and children in rural India.

AGILE RESPONSE TO GLOBAL PANDEMIC

The COVID-19 pandemic has been the worst global health disaster of the century. It has destroyed lives and livelihoods, and curbed civil liberties in many parts of the democratic world. While little credible data is forthcoming from authoritarian countries such as China, we know that democracies worldwide have witnessed protests and upheavals on a mass scale. This is particularly true of affluent Western nations with access to high-quality health infrastructure and timely access to vaccine distribution. India remains an exception, and her performance is especially remarkable for a resource-poor economy with limited health infrastructure. India is clearly punching well above her weight.

In terms of COVID-19 tests per one thousand population (see figure 2), the latest data show that India has tested far more than any country in the neighbourhood. But perhaps more noteworthy is the fact that India has tested significantly more than richer nations like Mexico, South Africa, Brazil, and Thailand. Making tests affordable and readily available across the country has been an important part of the pandemic management strategy. This is not merely important for timely detection and containment of the infection, but it also plays a critical role in assuaging people's fears. Risk management under uncertainty also demands managing people's expectations and fears.

Figure 2: COVID-19 Tests per 1,000 population

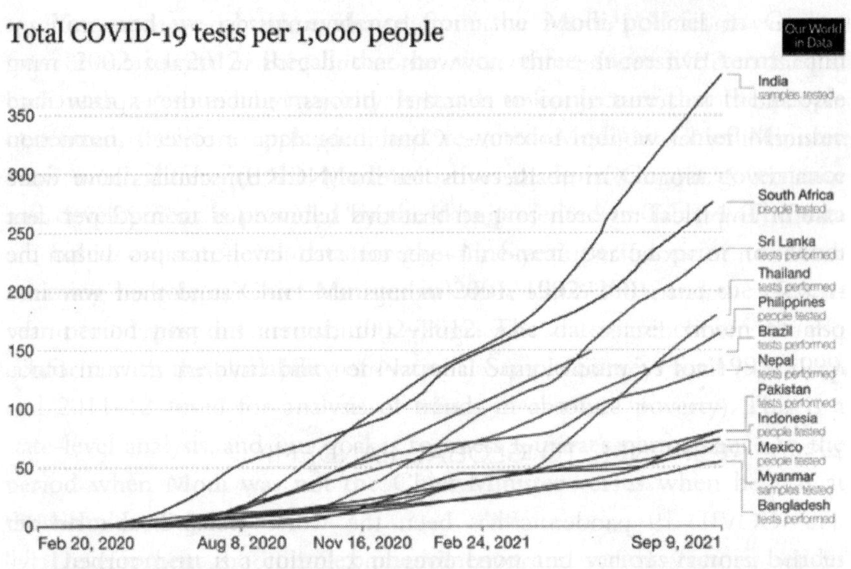

While governments globally continue to experiment with containment strategies of lockdowns and social distancing, it is now well accepted that the only durable solution to the pandemic is widespread vaccination drive among their population. Outside of the rich OECD (Organisation for Economic Co-operation and Development) countries, India is the largest producer of vaccines and among the very few developers. With the discovery of the vaccine, COVID-19 has morphed into the traditional problem of global inequality. Amid escalating vaccine nationalism and jostling for international market share among pharmaceutical majors, India has not only supplied significant doses to the world community, meeting past commitments but has also quietly inoculated over 90 per cent of the adult population with at least one dose. The absolute numbers are staggering—more than 817 million individuals and over 1.45 billion doses by the end of December 2021. The task remains unfinished, but the country is poised to meet the goal of vaccinating all eligible populations by mid of 2022. Recent spurts in daily vaccination—with several days of over 10 million doses and once even achieving 25 million in a single day —signal a pick-up in speed. This is the driving factor behind the International Monetary Fund's high growth projections for India even during the pandemic[10]. The latest projection (January 2022)continues to peg the country as the fastest growing economy globally for the current and next fiscal years. It is well appreciated that a robust vaccination drive and ready availability of health infrastructure (testing, hospital beds, oxygen, etc.) will determine India's economic recovery from the devastating global pandemic.

Figure 3: Vaccination Doses Administered

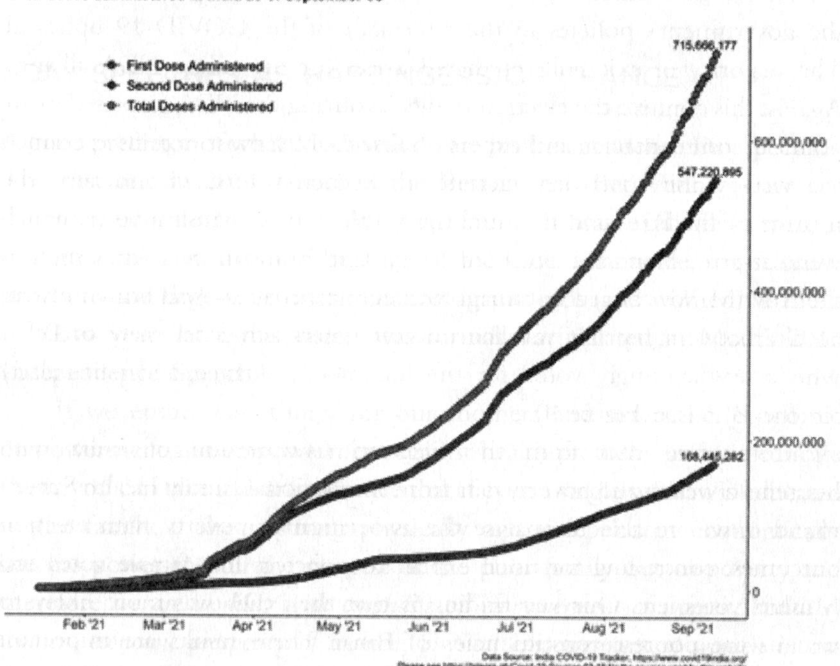

Beyond managing the infection outbreak and vaccination drive, an equally important aspect of the pandemic response is the real-time humanitarian support to vulnerable populations across the country. The pandemic caused significant economic disruption in the early months as country after the country went into national lockdowns. India's nationwide lockdown was hard on the poor, and their hardships have been well documented[11]. Sensing the emergency, the early nature of government interventions during the national lockdown was primarily focused on humanitarian support to the poor, affected households. Among others, relief measures included direct cash transfers to construction workers, farmers, the elderly, and women in self-help groups. Widespread emergency distribution of food-grains through the PDS was carried out across all the states of the country.

The timely and pre-emptive national lockdown witnessed extensive reverse migration of informal workers from industrialized states to their home states. Bihar had a significant reverse flow of people in the months following the national lockdown, from different states of the country. Therefore, the State Assembly elections in Bihar became a litmus test for the government's policies in the aftermath of the COVID-19 upheaval. The majority of exit polls predicted a loss for the ruling NDA alliance. Against this context, the election results favouring the NDA surprised many political commentators and experts. Subsequently, most experts explained the victory using two key factors: (1) women voters, who recalled the misrule of the RJD and favoured the NDA; and (2) Muslim votes, which were diverted from the RJD-led Maha Gathbandhan by parties such as the AIMIM. We carried out a rigorous econometric analysis which reveals an alternative story[12]. It was the poorest voters across the state of Bihar who overwhelmingly voted for the incumbent alliance, and particularly for the BJP (see Figure 4).

Combining data from the Election Commission of India with household wealth and poverty data from the National Family Health Survey, round 4, we are able to analyse the association of poverty with election outcomes, controlling for usual explanatory factors like female votes and Muslim votes, etc. Our key finding is that the NDA was more likely to win in the poorest constituencies of Bihar. These results are important because the Bihar Assembly elections were held during the COVID-19 pandemic, severely affecting the poorest population. Bihar is the poorest state in India, so the relevance of these results is especially noteworthy.

Figure 4: Odds Ratios of Winning a Constituency in the Bihar Assembly Elections 2020

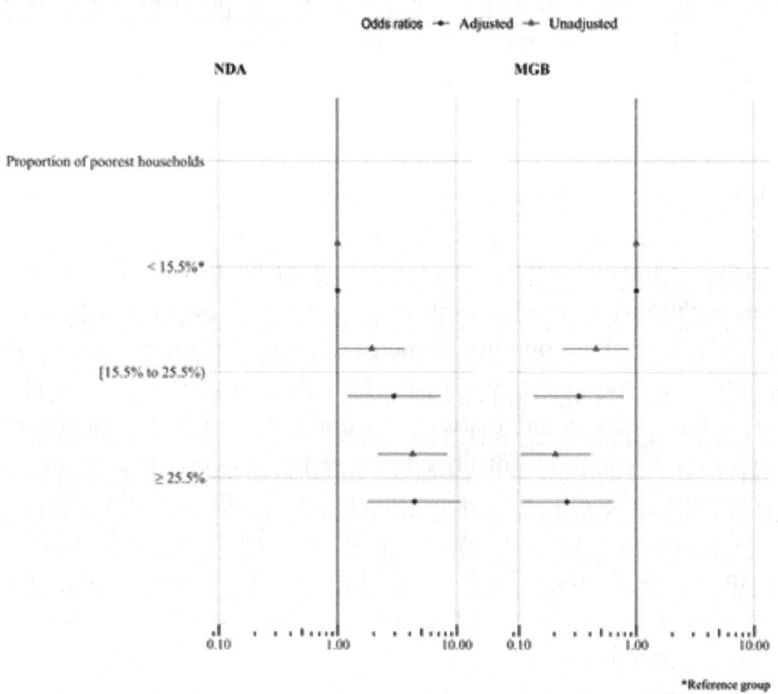

Graph Source: TechTank, Brookings Institution[13]

Note: 1) The odds ratios are computed by running a logistic regression at the constituency level where the dependent variable takes a value of 1 if NDA/MGB won the election in the constituency and takes a value 0 otherwise. 2) For adjusted odds ratios the model has been adjusted for a sex ratio of the electorate in the assembly constituency, the proportion of Muslim, general caste and rural households in the district where the assembly constituency is located, the AIMIM and the LJP factor.

EMPOWERING WOMEN LEADERS

Much has been written on the policies of the Modi administration, which have greatly benefitted women. These include the impact of improved availability of LPG cooking fuel through the Pradhan Mantri Ujjwala Yojana (PMUY), on women's health and the effect of improved access to toilets under SBM on the health and safety of women. Besides, the fact that the majority of beneficiaries of the PMJDY are women account holders adds to the empowerment of this important section of our society.

There are, however, 'silent revolutions' unfolding that have gone relatively unnoticed. Among these, we study the performance of women leaders in India's Parliament in the recent years.

The fundamental job of leaders in a democracy is to represent the concerns of their constituents and persuade the government to improve accountability. Therefore, an essential feature of parliamentary democracy is that the elected MPs question the government, irrespective of political affiliation, caste, gender, etc. It provides a check on the power of the government and makes the government accountable to the will of the people. While traditional approaches to measuring women's political empowerment have been limited to counting women leaders in Parliament and Legislative Assemblies, we measure it by analysing how they engage in both the Houses, *vis-à-vis* their male counterparts. Are women MPs, whether of the ruling party or the Opposition, equally empowered when compared to their male counterparts to question the government on the floor of the House?

Women's political empowerment is essential to strengthen civil and human rights (United Nations 2011)[14]. In this regard, the academic literature on the global and the Indian context has focused mainly on gaps in the number of women in Parliament[15], women as political leaders and their impact on social outcomes[16–20] and the rise of women voters (which we dubbed as a 'silent revolution' in India)[21–23]. However, there has been minimal discussion on whether a woman political leader, elected as a Member of Parliament, is empowered to raise concerns of the constituents she represents (most likely the weaker sections of society—women and children) on the floor of the House. This is an important measure of the political empowerment of women leaders within democracies.

For our analysis, we use publicly available data on the fifteenth Lok Sabha (18 May 2009 to 18 May 2014) and the sixteenth Lok Sabha (18 May 2014 to 23 May 2019) from the PRS Legislative Research, commonly known as PRS[24,25]. PRS tracks data on the functioning of the MPs of the Lok Sabha and the Rajya Sabha. It provides detailed information on gender, age, the state, and the constituency in the case of elected members and the political party of MPs. In addition, for each MP, there is data on the attendance across Parliament sessions, the number of questions they have asked, the number of debates they have participated in, and the number of Private Members' Bills they have introduced. Our focus will be on the number of questions raised by the MPs. We compare the median*** number of questions asked by MPs across gender and political affiliation (Bhartiya Janata Party) and Indian National Congress). In the fifteenth Lok Sabha, there were sixty-four women MPs, of which fourteen belonged to the BJP (12 per cent of BJP MPs) and twenty-five belonged to the Indian National Congress (12 per cent of INC MPs). In the sixteenth Lok Sabha, there were sixty-eight women MPs, of which thirty-two belonged to the BJP (11 per cent of BJP MPs), while only four belonged to the INC (8 per cent of INC MPs).

Overall, we find that in the fifteenth Lok Sabha, women MPs asked significantly fewer questions than their male counterparts (135 versus 250). However, in remarkable contrast, their engagement was at par with male MPs in the sixteenth Lok Sabha (218 versus 219) (see Figure 5a). A closer look at these results by the party affiliations of women MPs reveals a striking feature (see Figure 5b). In particular, the median number of questions raised by women MPs from the BJP (leading Opposition party of fifteenth Lok Sabha) was 355. In contrast, the median number of questions asked by female MPs from the Congress (leading ruling party of fifteenth Lok Sabha) was merely fifty-eight.

When the BJP came to power in the sixteenth Lok Sabha, the female MPs from the party asked the highest number of questions (346) to their own government! An important implication of these results is that when the Congress was the ruling party, its women MPs asked their government the least number of questions. The contrasting behaviour highlights the core empowerment of female MPs within the BJP under the leadership of Prime Minister Modi in Parliament. Women MPs of the ruling party asked a significantly higher number of questions to its own government

***We use median for our analysis because of the presence of extreme values or outliers. There are some MPs who have asked zero questions in the Parliament, while there are others who have asked more than one thousand questions. To prevent our analysis from being influenced by outliers, we use the median instead of the mean. However, our analysis remains similar if mean values are considered instead of the median.

on important issues such as health, education, roads, and MSMEs. These reflect the larger concerns of people, especially the weaker sections of the society—women and children (see figure 6).

Figure 5a: Median number of questions asked by MPs

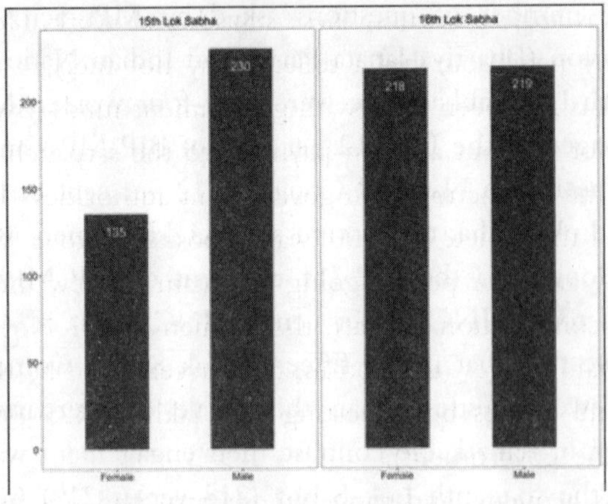

Source: PRS Legislative Research

Figure 5b: Median number of questions asked by MPs

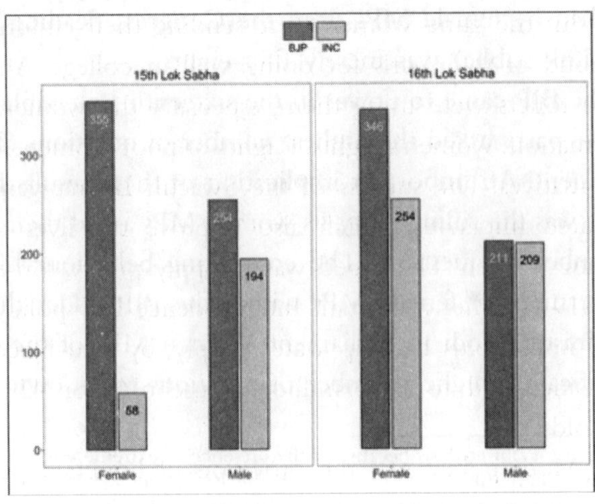

Source: PRS Legislative Research

Figure 6: Significant Difference in Questions raised by Female and Male MPs to Ministries

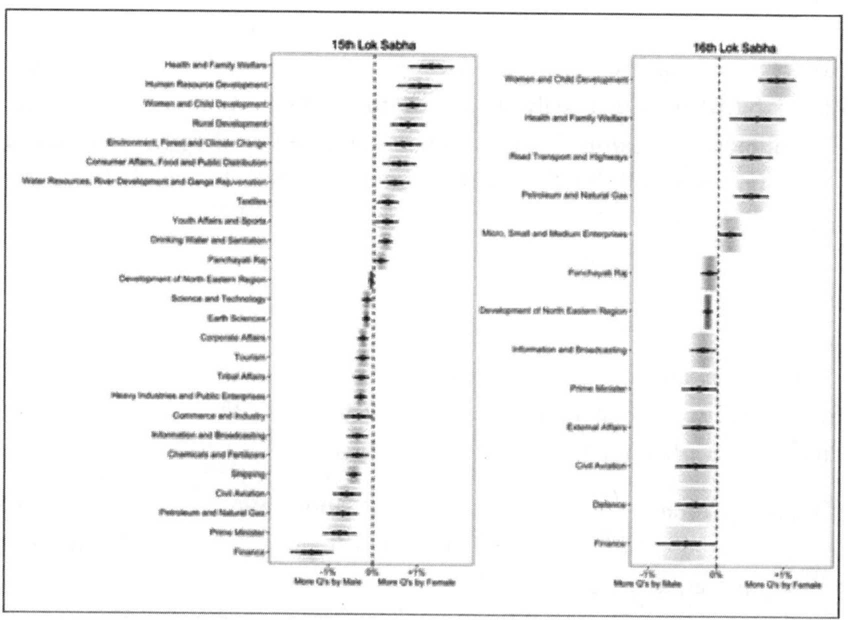

Source: PRS Legislative Research

THE GUJARAT EXPERIENCE

Balancing economic growth with improved quality of life, measured in terms of social indicators, is the most important yet challenging goal for any democratically elected leader. Gujarat is commonly cited in India's modern 'Miracle States'[26], and several scholars have analysed its rapid economic growth since 2000. What is perhaps less known is the performance of the state on key development indicators relative to other major states of India. In this section, therefore, we explore the relationship between economic and social development across the states of India from 2001 to 2018 to highlight the performance of Gujarat.

In particular, we study the performance of fifteen large states****,

****Andhra Pradesh, Assam, Bihar, Gujarat, Haryana, Karnataka, Kerala, Madhya Pradesh, Maharashtra, Odisha, Punjab, Rajasthan, Tamil Nadu, Uttar Pradesh and West Bengal. These fifteen

which represent approximately ninety per cent of India's population, by analysing (a) per capita net state domestic product at factor cost at constant prices (the base year 2011-12), and (b) the neonatal mortality rate (NMR), which is defined as the number of deaths during the first twenty-eight completed days of life per one thousand live[27]. Our choice of the NMR was primarily driven by the fact that it is one of the key development indicators being closely monitored under the Sustainable Development Goals (SDGs) of the United Nations, of which India is a signatory. Reducing NMR to 12 per one thousand live births by 2030 is one of the SDGs of the UN[28], and the data from 2017 shows that India accounts for more than 25 per cent of 2.6 million neonatal deaths worldwide[29].

We compare changes in per capita net state domestic product (NSDP) from 2001 to 2018 with changes in NMR during the same period. We divide these fifteen states into four quadrants:

(a) Quadrant 1, low growth in NSDP and low reduction in—NMR where NMR reduces by less than 50% and the NSDP increases by less than 200%
(b) Quadrant 2, high growth and low reduction in NMR—where NSDP increases by more than 200 per cent, but the NMR reduces by less than 50 per cent
(c) Quadrant 3, low growth and high reduction in NMR—where NSDP increases by less than 200 per cent, but the NMR reduces by more than 50 per cent
(d) Quadrant 4, high growth and high reduction in NMR—where NSDP increases by more than 200 per cent, and the NMR reduces by more than 50 per cent.

From an overall state perspective, it is desirable to be in Quadrant 4 to have high economic growth in terms of increased per capita NSDP and

states were selected because the neonatal mortality data (NMR) for 2001 and 2018 was available only for these states. Data for NMR at the state level is available from the Sample Registration System (SRS), Office of the Registrar General & Census Commissioner, India (https://censusindia.gov.in/2011-Common/Sample_Registration_System.html). Data on per capita net state domestic product at factor cost at constant prices (the base year 2011-12) is available from the Handbook of Statistics on Indian Economy, the Reserve Bank of India (https://rbi.org.in).

a high reduction in NMR. The analysis reveals that only three states—Gujarat, Maharashtra, and Tamil Nadu—have tripled their per capita NSDP and simultaneously reduced their NMR by more than 50 per cent from 2001–02 to 2018–19. Overall, we also find a positive association between reduction in NMR and increase in per capita NSDP (see figure 7).

Gujarat's economic performance under Modi has been remarkable and well documented in the academic literature. Our results, however, highlight the relatively lesser-known fact about the state's noteworthy performance on critical development indicator.

Figure 7: Increase in per capita Net State Domestic Product at Constant Prices (base year: 2011-12), and reduction in Neonatal Mortality Rate (NMR) from 2001 to 2018

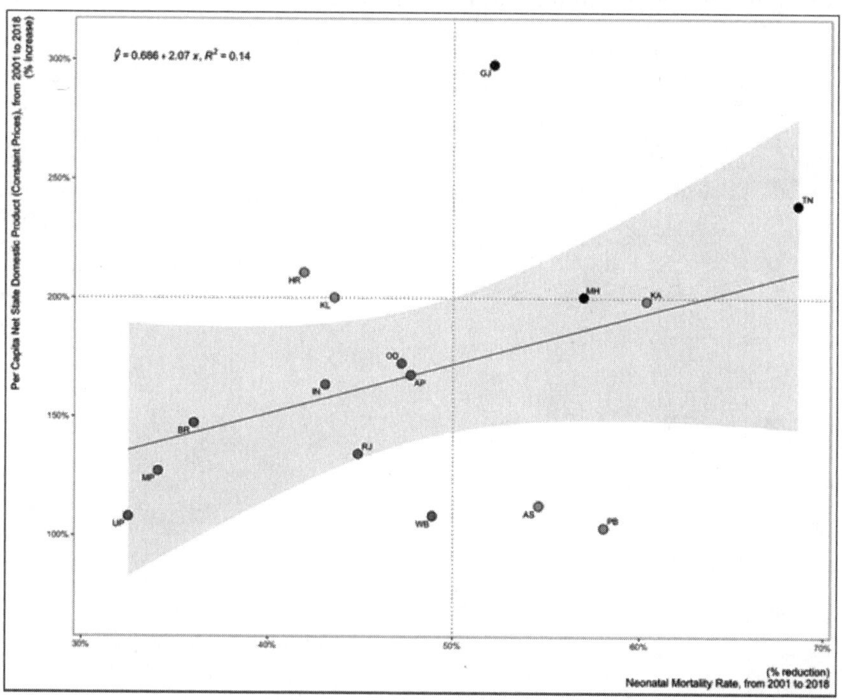

Source: Data for NMR at the state level is available from the Sample Registration System (S.R.S.), Office of the Registrar General & Census Commissioner, India (*https://censusindia.gov.in/2011-Common/Sample_Registration_System.html*). Data on per capita net state domestic product at factor cost at constant prices (the base year 2011-12) is available from the Handbook of Statistics on Indian Economy, the Reserve Bank of India (*https://rbi.org.in*).

CONCLUSION

This essay presented five key successes of the Modi administration, which have transformed the lives of ordinary citizens across the country. Using rigorous empirical research of publicly available data, we explain the significance of each of these five phenomena. These include the major strengthening of India's welfare architecture (JAM), near-universal outreach of toilet facilities, emergency and agile response to the global pandemic, empowerment of women leaders, and the experience of Gujarat that combined economic with social development. These key successes are akin to micro-revolutions that are quietly transforming the lives of ordinary Indians. These are regrettably missing from the popular media and economic discourse, but they are indeed critical gains that constitute the core foundations for India's future sustainable growth and development.

MAKE IN INDIA

PRIVATE ENTERPRISE AND NATION-BUILDING

UDAY S. KOTAK

'Those who create wealth for the country, those who contribute in the nation's wealth creation, are all serving the country. We should not doubt our wealth creators[...]

'Those who are making efforts to create wealth, according to me, they themselves are an asset to the nation and must be empowered.'

Prime Minister Narendra Modi's ringing endorsement of India's entrepreneurs from the ramparts of the Red Fort in the Indian capital city of Delhi on 15 August 2019 (the seventy-second anniversary of India's independence) underlined the importance his government places on the role of the private sector and entrepreneurs in nation-building. He emphasized the government's unstinting support to the private sector and exhorted it to partner with his government in the country's economic progress.

I felt a sense of pride at the Prime Minister's recognition of the contribution of entrepreneurs to nation-building. It is not often that entrepreneurs are applauded for their contribution to the economy and society at large. I also believe that Modi's compliment to entrepreneurs would encourage youngsters to look at entrepreneurship more favourably and propel the next generation of Indian entrepreneurs to start more interesting businesses in new areas.

This new 'contract' between the government and the private sector recognizes the important role private enterprise plays in achieving the national objectives of equitable, sustained and sustainable economic development. As Modi said in his interview with *The Economic Times* in August 2019, 'I consider entrepreneurs as India's Growth Ambassadors. I want to tell them that our government will leave no stone unturned to make India a better place to do business in all aspects. We want entrepreneurs to get better productivity and better profits. We want our industries to grow in speed and scale. We want our businesses to get access to bigger markets, both at home and abroad. We want our investors to earn more, invest more and create more jobs.'

As India progresses towards a confident, self-reliant nation, the Prime Minister's vision for moving to a $5 trillion economy is propelled by three factors: one, he foresees that for creating prosperity for Indians, we need to increase the size of the cake; two, private enterprise is the engine that can get us to that point efficiently and effectively; and three, for India to have a presence on the world stage, the size of India's economy matters, especially when you meet and negotiate with world leaders.

VISION AND EXECUTION

I have had the privilege of interacting with the Prime Minister over the past twenty years of his governance, first as Chief Minister of Gujarat and later as Prime Minister. His visits to different parts of the world as Chief Minister of Gujarat were marked by a keen desire to adopt best practices and creative ideas for implementation in India. In a meeting that followed his visit to Japan, he narrated several experiences with keen admiration and remarkably detailed observations. He recalled walking on the streets and around stations in Japan, and noticing yellow textured pavers or Braille blocks assisting the visually challenged. On his return, he soon replicated the tactile blocks at Kankaria Lake Front in Ahmedabad.

Something that has also stayed with me regarding the Prime Minister is his phenomenal memory and personal touch. I met him during one of my visits to Ahmedabad, when he was the Chief Minister of Gujarat, along with a colleague of mine, whose family hails from Modi's home town of Vadnagar. Modi remembered my colleague's father's name and narrated specific instances from his early days. Naturally, my colleague was floored.

Similarly, my meetings with him at the Vibrant Gujarat Summits left a deep impression on me. His intense passion to change India for the better and his abiding conviction in India's private sector as an engine for sustained growth was very encouraging.

In recent times, Modi has been open to bolder ideas for the rapid transformation of India's economic landscape. His ability to grasp both the big picture and finer details is remarkable.

India's rapid ascent in the World Bank's *Ease of Doing Business* ranking in the last four years is testimony to the efforts of the Modi government to make India an attractive investment destination. India now stands at number 63, up from the 130s during 2013-17. India's ranking in the Global Innovation Index has improved to 46 in 2021, up from 66 in 2016.

The government's efforts have encompassed all of India's private enterprises, from large companies to small units to start-up enterprises and small farms. Its broad-based investment reforms have rekindled the spirit of enterprise among entrepreneurs, big and small, new and old. Its specific programmes, tailor-made for large, medium, small or micro enterprises (as the case may be), will help meet the government's larger objectives of self-reliance, investment and job creation, while providing sufficient incentives to the private sector to invest. It is a win-win situation for the country and its entrepreneurs.

In his earlier stint as the Chief Minister, Modi had created a favourable environment for entrepreneurs in his home state of Gujarat through his Vibrant Gujarat initiative. The Vibrant Gujarat Summit was launched to make the state a world-class destination for investment by both Indian and foreign companies. Gujarat was the first state to do it; thereafter, most other states have followed suit. Modi demonstrated a great deal of energy and enterprise to showcase his home state to global and domestic companies. I had no doubt that his personal commitment and involvement would lead to large-scale investments in Gujarat and higher growth rates for the state, especially in manufacturing. We now know that the Vibrant Gujarat Summit was a great success, with Gujarat becoming a major manufacturing hub for automobiles, chemicals, petrochemicals, renewable energy, refining and textiles. The manufacturing component of Gujarat GSDP grew 11.3 per cent through the financial years 2003-14, roughly the period of Modi's tenure as Chief Minister. A similar story is unfolding across the length and breadth of the country under his leadership as Prime Minister, with the unleashing of the intrepid spirits of entrepreneurs. The time for a vibrant India has arrived.

The Modi government's biggest achievement in the area of investment has been to create a stable business climate through simple, stable and transparent policies and regulations. It has managed India's economy prudently, implemented major reforms in every factor of production (capital, labour, land and resources), opened up India's economy to foreign investment and simplified India's investment approvals and taxation systems. I believe that the framework for the next decade of growth is in place.

Modi has a proven track record on reforms. The conviction and commitment to reforms is visible in the way he has addressed various issues related to ease of doing business that were holding back India's economic development. In a short span of seven years, his government has implemented path-breaking economic and social reforms. On the economic front, the Modi government has: (1) simplified India's taxation system for both direct and indirect taxes, (2) implemented PLI schemes to encourage domestic manufacturing and increase self-reliance, (3) simplified India's labour laws, (4) established a bankruptcy resolution framework and (5) deregulated several sectors to highlight some of the major reforms.

India's fiscal situation and inflation have been fairly stable and the Indian rupee has depreciated modestly versus other currencies over the past few years. A stable macro-environment is a prerequisite for investment by the private sector. Several emerging countries have gone through periods of very high inflation and even hyperinflation, which renders all plans for investment redundant. India's fiscal stability and contained inflation over the past seven years was punctuated by high inflation in the second half of the calendar year 2020 due to supply disruptions arising from the COVID-19 pandemic. Otherwise, India has broadly tamed inflation. Average CPI (Consumer Price Index) inflation over the past seven years is 4.8 per cent, significantly lower than 9.8 per cent through the financial years 2009-14. Also, India's external position has been very healthy at present with foreign exchange reserves of US $633 billion (as of December 2021), external debt-to-GDP at 20.1 per cent (as of September 2021) and foreign currency reserves sufficient to cover fifteen months of imports.

COMMITMENT TO REFORM

India's labour reforms will benefit large and small enterprises alike through easier compliance and flexible hiring options. India's simplified labour laws should facilitate more private sector investment in manufacturing, which has otherwise been a problem in India for decades. Twenty-nine labour laws have been collapsed into four labour codes and 2,400 sections have been reduced to less than four hundred. Complex and rigid labour laws had hampered the growth of labour-intensive manufacturing units. On the one hand, large companies pursued capital-intensive industries and ignored labour-intensive ones, exacerbating India's employment challenges.

On the other hand, micro, small and medium (MSME) enterprises chose to stay small rather than grow in order to stay outside the purview of the erstwhile labour laws, with their high associated compliance costs. Even very small companies with less than ten employees had to comply with the Factories Act, 1948, while those with more than hundred employees were subject to the Industrial Disputes Act, 1947. These laws had outlived their utility given the evolution of India's economy. The government has adapted these outmoded laws to the new economy without compromising on the rights of workers.

The opening of all relevant sectors to foreign direct investment (FDI) has already started to yield results with a huge increase in FDI over the past few years. India received US $82 billion in FY 2021 of gross FDI versus US $36 billion in FY 2014. Almost all sectors are now open to FDI with 74-100 per cent FDI allowed under the automatic route. A large part of the FDI is now going into India's vibrant start-up economy, resulting in the emergence of a new crop of highly passionate and fearless entrepreneurs, creation of new business models and rapid employment generation.

The government has addressed one of the biggest issues for investors through a complete and radical overhaul of India's taxation system. Both direct and indirect taxation have seen significant changes in the past five years. The government, as recently as August 2021, gave an unequivocal signal to domestic and foreign investors by introducing a bill in the Lok Sabha to remove the dreaded retrospective taxation system.

Prior to this, the government implemented the Sabka Vishwas legacy scheme in 2019 to settle pending indirect tax disputes and the Vivad se Vishwas scheme in 2020 to similarly settle pending direct tax disputes. The scrapping of the retrospective taxation system and tax dispute resolution mechanism resonates with the basic objective of the government—maximum governance, minimum government. As Prime Minister Modi had said on 11 November 2020, 'The change from tax terrorism to tax transparency has happened because we have propagated the concept of reform, perform and transform'.

In the case of direct taxation, the government has implemented an alternative taxation structure for companies and individuals that do not want to avail various deductions and exemptions. The FY 2021 Union Budget simplified personal tax. Individuals can avail of an alternative personal taxation regime with lower personal income tax rates (for income up to ₹15 lakh or ₹1.5 million) after foregoing deductions and exemptions. This has made the filing of taxes fairly simple for a vast majority of individual filers. The government had previously simplified corporate taxation in September 2019, by introducing an alternative tax structure for companies, which effectively resulted in a reduction in the effective tax rate to 25.2 per cent from 34.9 per cent for the larger companies (taxable income more than ₹10 crore or ₹100 million).

At the same time, the government reduced the corporate tax rate for new manufacturing units to 15 per cent (17.2 per cent including surcharge and cess), which is amongst the lowest in the world. When this happened, I got a great deal of confidence that India would achieve its objective of self-reliance with Indian companies doing world-class manufacturing in India. Indian companies finally have a tax rate that is competitive vis-à-vis other countries. For long, India has been dependent on imports for hi-tech products. My confidence has increased further with other measures such as labour reforms and production-linked incentives. Lastly, higher profits for companies through lower corporate tax rates will encourage them to invest more aggressively in their businesses and further meet the nation's objectives of job creation and strong and sustainable growth. This is again a strong signal of the government's willingness to see private companies make higher returns from their investments.

In the case of indirect taxation, the Goods and Services Tax (GST) system, in force from July 2017, has replaced a patchwork of national, state and local taxes. This has reduced taxation complexity and also widened India's taxation base. The number of monthly filings has increased to 1.05 crore (10.5 million) from sixty lakh (6 million) at the time of implementation of GST. This broad base of India's taxpayers could allow the government to reduce the GST rates over time.

Lastly, an effective bankruptcy law provides a necessary and long overdue safety net for entrepreneurs to take risks and invest their capital. The insolvency and bankruptcy code, established by the government in 2016, provides for the resolution of bankruptcies for banks and companies in a time-bound manner and within a transparent process. In an increasingly disrupted world, a safety net is an imperative for promoters to bounce back from failures and keep trying until they succeed. Some of the world's finest entrepreneurs failed in their initial attempts, but bounced back to create highly successful companies. Today's young entrepreneurs do not fear failure, and they will be even more confident about taking risks in pursuing their passions and creating new businesses. Timely evolution of the bankruptcy law and its practice is important for India to see creative destruction at its best—a key feature of capitalism.

THE RIGHT BALANCE

Prime Minister Modi has also sought to strike the right balance among the private sector, the public sector, the government and the bureaucracy in the economy. As he stated in his webinar on privatization and asset monetization on 24 February 2021, 'It is the responsibility of the government to give full support to the enterprises and businesses of the country, but it is not necessary and feasible in today's era that the government should run the enterprises and continue to own it. Therefore, I say the government has no business to be in business. The focus of the government should remain on the welfare and development projects of the people.'

In light of the government's stated policy to reduce the role of the public sector in the economy, there is a need to explore the role of private companies in ensuring a better future for the larger public sector undertakings (PSUs) as well. The government has many large PSUs that operate in challenged and challenging industries. They are quite valuable currently, despite the steady erosion in their market capitalizations over the past few years. The markets have become increasingly concerned about the fate of the PSUs in a disrupted world. The government has announced ambitious plans for the privatization of PSUs in non-strategic areas, and has chosen to retain one or two PSUs in certain strategic sectors. The government may want to review the 'strategic sector' definition given the rapid disruption across sectors.

For example, coal, petroleum, power and other minerals have been classified as strategic sectors even though India imports a large portion of its petroleum requirement. More importantly, fossil fuels are facing growing irrelevance in light of a global movement towards green energy and technological developments in renewable power, electric vehicles and battery technology. PSU companies may not be in a position to reinvent themselves and reorient their business models on the lines of these fast-changing realities. A private company could be in a better position to do so and, thus, could prevent the loss of value for the PSUs and the government.

The Modi government came to power in May 2014 at a time when confidence in the private sector was at its lowest. Private enterprise was reeling under investigations by various government agencies into the awarding of 2G spectrum in 2008 and coal blocks over 1993-2010. A downturn in global commodity cycles and the inability to procure resources for downstream power and steel plants compounded problems for companies, eventually leading to several bankruptcies in power, roads and steel sectors. There was a steep increase in non-performing assets (NPAs) in the Indian banking system, which peaked at 11.6 per cent of loans in FY 2018. The fallout was a steady retreat of the private enterprise and the plateauing of private sector investment.

Over the past few years, the Modi government has followed a systematic approach to solving various issues that plagued domestic manufacturing. Among its most notable achievements, it has simplified India's labour laws and taxation systems, brought about transparency in the allocation of natural resources and implemented the productivity-linked incentive (PLI) scheme. These measures will restore confidence of the private sector and establish the primacy of a rule-based system, two key requirements for private investors to put in their capital.

Two developments have been particularly good for large enterprises: (1) the establishment of a transparent auction system for natural resources such as mineral blocks and telecom spectrum and (2) the implementation of the PLI scheme for manufacturing.

The Modi government has ensured fair access to the country's natural resources through transparent auction processes that ensure market prices. The new auction system has allayed concerns about any negative retrospective action against the winners of such auctions. Exploitation of minerals or setting up of telecommunications operations requires large amounts of capital. Many developing economies have faced serious challenges in the allocation and exploration, facing charges of corruption, crony capitalism and environmental degradation. India was no exception until recently. The upfront or staggered payments received by the government from companies can be used for national objectives. After all, natural resources belong to the citizens of a country and the government is a guardian of the same on behalf of the citizens.

The PLI scheme could lead to a manufacturing renaissance in India. The share of manufacturing in real GDP has languished at 17 per cent for the last several years, especially compared to the 26 per cent in the case of China. The manufacturing sector can create millions of high-paying jobs, resulting in rapid growth in household incomes and upward movement of low-income households to middle-income households. Very few countries have developed without a robust domestic manufacturing base. Our research estimates that the PLI scheme, with an outlay of ₹2 lakh crore (₹2 trillion), can result in investment of ₹2 to ₹2.5 lakh crore (₹2 to ₹2.5 trillion) and value addition of ₹10 to ₹13 lakh crore (₹10 to ₹13 trillion). Besides, the PLI can push the share of manufacturing in GDP to 20–22 per cent by 2030.

The scheme will provide additional incentives to both Indian and foreign companies to invest in manufacturing sectors, which is where India has little or no presence. The scheme is focused on new areas, such as advanced chemistry cell batteries, photovoltaic solar modules, semiconductor fabrication units and telecommunications equipment, among others. These areas entail far higher amounts of risk for the private sector as India does not have adequate technological capabilities in these areas. The government has rightly chosen to provide additional 'risk capital' to companies in the form of incentives to manufacture these items and reduce dependence on imports.

India has limited manufacturing capacity in these industries currently and, therefore, runs the risk of increasingly relying on imports without a domestic manufacturing base, especially as the demand for these products grows exponentially in the future. However, India can transform its economy if it can invest successfully in emerging disruptive technologies. An example may help illustrate this point. India currently relies on large imports to meet its energy requirements. In fact, it imports 85 per cent of its oil requirements. Energy is India's biggest import item, accounting for 25 per cent of its total imports currently.

However, the country is blessed with the right geography—it has abundant sunshine—even if it is cursed by geology in terms of inadequate oil and gas reserves. It can make the transition to renewable energy from conventional energy and reduce its reliance on imported energy. But this would entail investments not just in renewable power generation but also in renewable power generation equipment, such as photo-voltaic (PV) modules and storage batteries, which it does not produce at present. India runs the risk of replacing current energy imports with future imports of solar PV equipment unless it starts manufacturing the same. The government's PLI scheme will help correct these types of imbalances in India's trade today. At the same time, this will present a completely new opportunity for Indian companies to exploit and create market capitalization in the process and achieve the country's clean energy and climate change objectives.

ENERGISING MSME, START-UPS

MSMEs are an important part of the Indian economy, contributing to around 30 per cent to India's GDP and employing over eleven crore (110 million) workers in the non-agriculture sectors. The last MSME survey pegs the number of MSME units in the country at 6.33 crore (63.3 million units, out of which 63 million are micro enterprises and 300,000 are small and medium enterprises). In FY 2021, the sector's share in exports was around 50 per cent. Evidently, a large part of India's growth and development trajectory hinges on how much the MSME sector can scale up. The government has unequivocally focused on improving the financial strength of MSMEs through: (1) the inclusion of more enterprises within the MSME ambit, (2) greater financial inclusion and access to formal financing channels for MSMEs and (3) skilling.

Under the Atmanirbhar Bharat programme, the government revised the investment and turnover thresholds of MSMEs. Low investment thresholds may have perversely discouraged firms from growing so that they could continue to receive incentives for MSMEs. In the latest revision, investment thresholds for micro manufacturing enterprises have increased four times to ₹1 crore (₹10 million) and for medium manufacturing enterprises two-fold to ₹20 crore (₹200 million). In July 2021, the government also included retail and wholesale trade as part of the MSME definition. This will enable the trade sector to benefit from priority sector lending to the MSMEs.

Credit availability for MSMEs has also improved dramatically over the past few years, especially in the ongoing pandemic period where the government has rightly implemented measures to improve liquidity for the MSME sector. The government has focused on deeper financial inclusion as well as greater formalization of business financing to ensure that the MSMEs are not constrained by limitations of informal financing channels. It has focused on three key areas: (1) MUDRA loans and Jan Dhan accounts, (2) MFI (microfinance institutions) loans and (3) support through ECLGS.

The Pradhan Mantri MUDRA Yojana (PMMY), started in April 2015, aims to disburse loans up to ₹10 lakh (₹1 million) to non-corporate, non-farm small/micro enterprises. Banks have disbursed around 5.1 crore (51 million) loans worth ₹3.2 lakh crore or ₹3.2 trillion in FY 2021 (similar to FY 2019 levels), a steep increase when compared to the ₹1.4 lakh crore or ₹1.4 trillion in FY 2016 through 3.5 crore (35 million) loans. Additionally, 2.9 crore (29 million) loans worth ₹1.8 lakh crore or ₹1.8 trillion have already been disbursed in FY 2022, by the end of December 2021. A major portion of the outstanding loans is directed at women entrepreneurs (two-third of loans sanctioned). Even before the government focused on easier credit availability for MSME entrepreneurs through the PMMY, it initiated the Jan Dhan Yojana programme in August 2014 to provide banking to the unbanked. Over 44 crore (440 million) accounts have been opened with outstanding deposits of ₹1.5 lakh crore or ₹1.5 trillion by the end of December 2021.

Along with the MUDRA scheme, the private sector micro-finance industry has also done a commendable job in supporting entrepreneurs at the grass-root level. As of September 2021, around ₹2.43 lakh crore or ₹2.43 trillion loan is outstanding as of Q2FY22 (July-September 2021) with an average ticket size of around ₹36,000. Banks (including small finance banks) dominate the share of lenders, at around 41 per cent of the loans. In the wake of the second wave of the pandemic, the government announced a credit guarantee scheme (up to ₹7,500 crore or ₹75 billion) for the MFI sector to benefit the smallest borrowers. Financial institutions can lend up to ₹1.25 lakh to approximately ₹25 lakh (₹125,000 to ₹2.5 million) small borrowers as new loans, rather than as repayment of old debt. The government is to provide a guarantee for up to 75 per cent of the default amount.

The government's most recent financial support for the MSME sector came through at the start of the pandemic. The government announced a 100 per cent credit guarantee scheme of ₹3 lakh crore or ₹3 trillion (Emergency Credit Line Guarantee Scheme, which was enhanced to ₹4.5 lakh crore or ₹4.5 trillion in June 2021) to support existing borrowers (including MUDRA loans) to tide over the pandemic-led impact. Under ECLGS (subject to certain conditions), 20 per cent of the outstanding loan is available to businesses with outstanding loans up to ₹50 crore (₹500 million) and turnover of ₹250 crore (₹2.5 billion). Financial institutions have disbursed around ₹2.28 lakh crore (₹2.28 trillion) to 95.2 lakh (9.52 million) borrowers until 19 December 2021. The ECLGS has been one of the most important measures for the MSMEs in mitigating the pandemic's impact. Credit disbursement to MSMEs increased to ₹9.5 lakh crore (₹9.5 trillion) in FY 2021, compared to ₹6.8 lakh crore (₹6.8 trillion) in FY 2020. Although a large part of the MSME sector, especially micro enterprises, remains outside the ambit of the formal financial channels, existing borrowers have been well supported.

One of the key challenges for the MSMEs is the dearth of skilled labour. Thus, the government provides support to the Entrepreneurship Skill Development Programme (ESDP), specifically for the MSMEs. This MSME scheme aims to provide capital grants to training institutions that operate under the Ministry of MSME for the purpose of the creation and strengthening of infrastructure and to support entrepreneurship and skill development training/capacity building programmes. The government has been running the National Skill Development Mission under the Pradhan Mantri Kaushal Vikas Yojana (PMKVY). As of December 2021, 61 lakh (6.1 million) trained candidates have benefited from the recognition of prior learning and another 45 lakh (4.5 million) have been trained under the short term training programme. However, the placement success rate remains low—around 54 per cent, with 80 per cent of these trainees finding employment and 18 per cent being self-employed. A bulk of the placements are in electronics and hardware (54 per cent), followed by apparel (20 per cent) and retailing (10 per cent).

As a result of the Modi government's initiatives, the start-up environment in India has seen frenzied activity and massive investment over the past few years, with a number of young entrepreneurs innovating with new business models. By December 2021, investors ploughed US$34 billion into Indian start-ups across more than 1,009 deals. India had 90 unicorns (market value of more than US $1 billion), with around 44 entering the unicorn stage in 2021 alone (against the nine in 2020). The government has provided both direct and indirect support to the start-up ecosystem in India.

However, the government's bigger contribution to India's thriving start-up movement may be the Prime Minister's continuous endorsement of the role of wealth creators and entrepreneurs in investment, job creation and nation-building. Notable is his special appreciation of start-up enterprises and young entrepreneurs as well as the government's broader investment reforms discussed earlier in the chapter and its specific actions that recognize and preserve the special nature of the start-up companies.

Consider the new labour codes enacted in 2019-20. These recognize the special characteristics of the gig economy and the unique nature of the employer-worker engagement model in the gig economy, which is different from the standard employer-employee engagement model of employment contracts and wages applicable to other industries. The flexible engagement model for both companies and workers in the gig economy is central to the business models of several start-up businesses, such as food delivery and ride sharing, among others. The Code on Wages, 2019, does not cover gig and platform workers, thereby, excluding them from the requirement of minimum wages, which is important for the economics and operations of such start-ups.

At the same time, the Code on Social Security, 2020, mandates that the government create schemes for gig workers and platform workers so that they can avail certain social security benefits (subject to certain conditions). This partly addresses the issue of rights of gig and platform workers who are outside the standard employer-employee model.

Global private equity and venture capital funds have contributed a bulk of the funds for start-ups but the government provides important support through its Start-up India programme in three key areas: (1) legal, IPR (intellectual property rights) support and insolvency, (2) funds and tax incentives and (3) incubation. The government has simplified the IPR application process by fast-tracking patent applications and even providing facilitators to assist in their filing. Further, the government offers start-ups an 80 per cent rebate on patent filing fees. Through the Startup India portal, start-ups have been allowed self-certification for nine labour laws and three environment laws. As per the Insolvency and Bankruptcy Act, start-ups with simple debt structures may be wound up within ninety days.

The government also provides certain tax incentives (subject to certain conditions) to recognized start-ups. These include income tax exemptions for three years and capital gains tax exemption, if gains are reinvested in the government's fund of funds. The government launched the Startup India Seed Fund to provide seed funding to start-ups. The initial corpus of ₹950 crore or ₹9.5 billion is likely to support close to 3,600 start-ups over four years, and the government has set up a fund of funds through SIDBI for investment into start-ups with an initial corpus of ₹2,500 crore (₹25 billion), to be expanded to ₹10,000 crore (₹100 billion) over four years.

India has seen a significant increase in the grant of patents, trademark registrations and copyrights over the past four to five years, which bodes well for its start-up and overall economy. In FY 2021, a total of 28,391 patents were granted versus 6,326 in FY 2016 (a 4.5X increase), 255,993 trademarks were registered in FY 2021 versus 65,045 in FY 2016 (4X increase) and 16,402 copyrights were granted in FY 2021 versus 4,505 in FY2016 (3.5X increase).

IL&FS SAGA AND DECISIVE ACTION

Founded in 1987 with the objective of funding infrastructural projects, Infrastructure Leasing and Financial Services Limited (IL&FS) has the Central Bank of India, Unit Trust of India, HDFC Ltd, State Bank of India, Life Insurance Corporation of India, ORIX Corporation Japan and Abu Dhabi Investment Authority as its main shareholders. In over three decades of operations, the IL&FS Group grew to become a financial behemoth, with a complex structure comprising 347 entities in over twelve lines of businesses, and a geographical presence spanning eleven countries.

However, the multi-layered, web-like structure with sizeable intra-group lending exposure and gross leverage at nearly 17:1 consolidated debt-to-equity ratio meant that, by September 2018, the Group's funded and non-funded balance sheet had swelled to over ₹99,000 crore (₹990 billion). Such disproportionate leverage with non-commensurate underlying revenue streams severely constrained the Group's ability to honour its repayment obligations, thereby, posing a massive systemic risk. By September 2018, the IL&FS Group's looming failure presented the imminent possibility of a contagion effect in the Indian financial markets. It was an apprehensive time with sections of the media even referring to it as 'India's Lehman moment.'

The failure of IL&FS represents a significant collective failure, built over thirty years, of its management, board, institutional shareholders, auditors, credit rating agencies and regulators.

The Modi government inherited this complex structure with all its accumulated problems. In September 2018, with a catastrophic domino effect imminent, the government moved swiftly and took decisive action. The government constituted a new Board in public interest and asked me to chair it. We were tasked with the responsibility of averting a systemic financial sector crisis and protecting national assets that were created by the Group over its operational history.

Over the past three years, the new IL&FS Board has embarked on an orderly resolution journey for the IL&FS Group, and has put in place a plan to maximize recovery for all its stakeholders. The absence of a legal framework for group insolvency resolution presented an additional challenge. The progress achieved during the IL&FS Group's resolution process has been possible due to the continuous support of the government under the leadership of Prime Minister Modi and his team, including the Ministry of Corporate Affairs, the Ministry of Finance, the Central Board of Direct Taxes, the Reserve Bank of India, the Securities and Exchange Board of India, the Ministry of Road Transport and Highways and the National Highway Authority of India. Their support and the open-minded approach has allowed the new Board to consider out-of-the-box and alternative resolution avenues, such as InvIT, which have not only laid the ground for potentially higher recovery for creditors at all levels but have also helped the new board to preserve the '*going concern*' status and value of national assets.

There have been some erroneous attempts to draw an analogy between the IL&FS and Satyam crises. The two cases are different. Satyam was a zero debt, software services and single business company; IL&FS was a multi-business financial conglomerate, with uncontrolled leverage of ₹1 lakh crore or ₹1 trillion across 347 companies. The failure of IL&FS is comparable with the failure of business groups like Lanco and Videocon, though the resolution outcome is entirely different. Notably, in the Lanco/Videocon cases, the total recovery through resolution was only a small percentage (single-digit figure) of the total debt. At IL&FS, our new board has estimated recovery, through multiple resolution mechanisms, in excess of 60 per cent of the debt across the Group.

My board and I are humbled to have been given this responsibility to protect the financial sector and restrict the ramifications of the crisis on the wider economy, which we have taken up as our national duty. The IL&FS saga also represents the Modi government's willingness to forge new solutions for unique problems that have accumulated over a long period of time, and finally, to act decisively upon them.

PRIVATE ENTERPRISE IS READY TO DELIVER

I had first visited the US in the early 1990s. I was astounded then to see the scale and presence of financial institutions, such as JP Morgan, Goldman Sachs and others, that had built a global financial sector for the US. One of the reasons for the strength and size of the US economy is its financial sector. Similarly, India's financial sector has a crucial role to play in realizing the Prime Minister's broad and ambitious vision. We must focus on a progressive and world-class regulatory framework and a coordinated approach for both banking and capital markets in order for the financial sector to be a catalyst for India's growth. An Atmanirbhar India must have an Atmanirbhar financial sector, which welcomes foreign savings but nurtures Indian savings, and Indian talent to create global quality institutions in India.

Respect for well-regulated but free markets is crucial, since markets are now becoming larger engines for financing India's growth. The government has rightly chosen a light-touch regulatory approach for the economy and adapted its role to that of an enabler for private investment. I am confident that a combination of free markets and government support for private enterprise will create a space for the private sector to innovate and invest in the Indian economy. I believe India's private sector is ready and willing to execute the Prime Minister's vision of inclusive economic development ('*Sabka Saath, Sabka Vikas*').

The ongoing COVID-19 pandemic may have slowed India's march to a ₹5 trilion economy, but it has also demonstrated the ability, resilience and resolve of the government and the private sector to, in collaboration, deal with the challenges and overcome them. The government's steps to support the economy in general and the weaker sections of society in particular, along with the RBI's accommodative monetary policy approach, have helped mitigate the economic impact of the pandemic. The pandemic also saw India's private sector accelerate digitization and adopt disruptive technologies to emerge stronger.

India has had a few leaders with the kind of vision, statesmanship and courage that create national transformation. Over the past twenty years of leadership, first as Chief Minister and now as Prime Minister, Modi has demonstrated many admirable qualities to be counted among these select few. Posterity will be the best judge. I believe this leadership bodes well for India becoming a strong economic power that transforms the future for all Indians.

SECTION FOUR

A NEW PARADIGM IN GOVERNANCE

ENVIRONMENTAL SUSTAINABILITY AND ECONOMIC DEVELOPMENT: CONVERGENCE IN PRACTICE AND ACTION

AJAY MATHUR

Prime Minister Narendra Modi is widely appreciated for transformative policies that have accelerated economic growth and development. However, a relatively less discussed aspect of PM Modi's governance model has been his focus on sustainable development, climate change and environmental protection.

Over the past twenty years as the CM of Gujarat (from 2002-2014) and then as the Prime Minister of India, Modi has undertaken innumerable measures for addressing climate change, environmental protection, wildlife conservation, and transitioning to cleaner fuels and renewable energy. For instance, under his leadership, Gujarat became the first state in the country and Asia, and fourth in the world, to establish an independent department for climate change. Rather than merely relying on traditional policy instruments and strict regulations, Narendra Modi has encouraged innovative solutions and scientific research for addressing environmental concerns and reducing our carbon footprint.

This chapter looks at PM Narendra Modi's proactive approach on environmental issues, and discusses the various initiatives that he has taken during his illustrious career in executive office including the shift to renewable energy.

MOVING BEYOND TRADE-OFFS

There is a common belief that high economic growth and environmental protection are incompatible with each other. It is claimed that policymaking necessarily requires a trade-off between both. However, a convergence of environmental sustainability and economic development has been a hallmark of all the development initiatives that Modi has envisioned.

During a discussion I had with Prime Minister Narendra Modi on sustainable development, and specifically on energy and climate change, he said that solar energy and energy efficiency were close to his heart and that his focus had been on enabling sustainable development. In fact, as Chief Minister of Gujarat, he had written in 2009, 'For me, this renewable energy is an article of faith. When it comes to solar energy, wind energy and the other experiments that I am undertaking—we are the fourth government in the world to create a climate change department.'

'Even the Indian government does not have a dedicated department for climate change, because it is my commitment that we should also watch for the interests of the future generation. Renewable energy is a sector where we should work with great finesse, and this has led to us being the first government to bring out a solar policy.'

His deeply-held 'article of faith' builds on the ancient Indian tradition of linking ecological and economic growth. The *Brihadaranayaka Upanishad* specifically says, 'The earth is helpful to all living beings, and all living beings are of helpful effect to the earth'.

The Buddha commended frugality as a virtue in its own right. Skillful living avoids waste and we should try to recycle as much as we can. He advocated a simple, gentle, non-aggressive attitude towards environment—calling for the cultivation of reverence for all forms of nature. He used examples from nature to teach. In his stories, the plant and the animal worlds are treated as part of our inheritance, even as a part of ourselves.

These thoughts are captured in many forms in political practice. In Kautilya's *Arthashastra*, the change of land use from forests to agricultural and horticultural fields is systematized, with the object of mandating optimal population density, so that carrying capacities could be maintained. In modern times, this balance has been best captured by Mahatma Gandhi, who, in his seminal but oft-forgotten work, *Hind Swaraj*, spoke of a self-governing society that balanced ecology and economy.

Modi pointed out that, in the house that Mahatma Gandhi was born in Porbandar, underground tanks had been constructed more than 200 years ago, which stored rain water. In his unique way, the Mahatma gave us an important message on water conservation, so that future generations have easy access to clean drinking water.

Over the centuries, however, the emphasis on balance moved to an extreme where economic growth was emphasized. Now the pendulum has swung to the other extreme, where environmental considerations view all economic growth with suspicion.

In his book, *A Convenient Action*, Modi wrote, 'The bounties of nature in circulating waters of streams, seas and oceans, hills, snowy mountains and forests, all have to be guarded and replenished if used, so as to yield us a sustainable amount of food, milk and other agricultural products and ultimately bestow us with splendour, strength and brilliance. Sustainability is ultimately a moral issue since it involves the protection of the interests of our future generations'.

The initiatives, embodying this thought, that have been created by him—in areas as diverse as water availability and management, clean air, solar energy, energy efficiency, and climate change—are innumerable, and their simple listing would be inadequate to express the deep commitment to environment and sustainability that underlies those programmes. In my view, the key organizing principle in all these initiatives has been their ability to bring together the betterment of stakeholders (including taking care of those who are adversely affected) with solutions that are more environmentally sustainable. And by his personal leadership, Modi has been able to convert them into mass movements which are both broad-based in terms of stakeholder involvement, and appeal to their intrinsic values and interests.

RENEWABLES & ENERGY EFFICIENCY

The first time when such an initiative authored by Modi caught my attention was in 2011, when the 1-megawatt (MW) pilot rooftop solar project on a branch canal off the main Narmada canal, was inaugurated. It was a truly innovative concept in as much as it provided clean electricity through the solar power plant. But at the same time it dramatically reduced the evaporation of the canal water. These two goals—of providing energy and water supply, while also enabling their sustainable management—have become the hallmark of the projects that I began to see emerging from Gujarat (and later from the Central government in New Delhi). The 1 MW solar canal top project was only the beginning. He then saw its extension into a 10 MW project (which was inaugurated by the United Nations Secretary General Ban Ki-moon in 2015), and later plans which included using the more than 500-km-long network of the Narmada canal across the state for setting up the canal top solar power plants.

The canal top solar power projects are in line with the larger view that Modi has continuously espoused and promoted to enhance solar power generation whenever and wherever possible. As an Indian, I was immensely proud when Gujarat under his leadership, brought out the Megawatt Scale Policy in 2009, and started providing long-term PPAs (power purchase agreements) to solar power development. Many people (including me) were apprehensive of the high tariff (of about ₹15/kWh for the first 12 years, and then coming down to ₹5/kWh from the thirteenth year to the twenty-fifth year), that was provided to the solar power developer. But the sharp drop in prices of solar power which accompanied the increasing scale of solar power generation brought to us the wisdom of this approach. The tariffs provided to the solar power developers kept declining, and showed the power of concentrating the attention of all stakeholders (solar manufacturers, developers, bankers, etc.) in a competitive manner once a large scale and predictable programme and policy was placed before them.

As Prime Minister, Modi dramatically increased the goal of the National Solar Mission from 20,000 MW of solar power to be achieved by 2020 to 100,000 MW to be achieved by 2022. This change was brought about in 2014, and immediately resulted in a sea change in the thinking of all the stakeholders, including regulators and the state power departments. Today, in 2021, we are well within striking range of achieving this enhanced goal, and have left behind the earlier goal (of 20,000 MW) long ago. Solar electricity is available today at ₹1.99 per kWh, again showing the decrease in prices that are possible with large increases in the scale of procurement. Obviously, solar electricity at ₹1.99

per kWh is available only when the sun is shining, but during this time (as of now) it is far cheaper than any other source of electricity. This has provided a strong business model for energy transition in India. The transition is powered not by regulations or banning fossil fuels, but by the increased economic viability of electricity from solar panels—which has already been achieved—and of storage batteries, which we expect will be achieved in the next one to three years.

I believe that in the time to come, when round-the-clock electricity from solar panels and storage batteries become cost effective, the financial sector will see no need to invest in any other form of electricity generation. Modi has convincingly moved us on to an economically viable and sustainable path to development. This provides the world with a great example that can be used and replicated in other countries, and especially in developing countries which are blessed with lots of sunshine but are yet to build up their electricity generation capacity in order to meet the latent demand.

A new initiative which focuses on the indigenous manufacture of solar panels could be path-breaking. This initiative, which provides a performance-linked incentive to advanced (high efficiency) solar panel technologies, has received a massive response from potential manufacturers. The incentive, which will be paid on the sale of advanced solar panels, provides manufacturers (and their financiers) with the confidence that these technologies would be competitive in the market, and therefore worth the investment.

A second area in which I have had the occasion to personally learn from Modi's approach is that of energy efficiency. In 2009, when I was with the Bureau of Energy Efficiency (BEE), I was looking at the energy efficiency performance of all Indian states, and the data from Gujarat jumped out at me. It was startling that this state, which had been seeing an economic growth in excess of 7 per cent per annum, was showing an energy demand increase of only 4–5 per cent per annum. Here, in front of us, was an example of the decoupling of economic growth and energy growth—something that the world had been talking about but had been achieved only by a few Western countries. As I went deeper into the numbers, several things stood out. The first was the improvement in the power generation efficiency, driven by a number of actions including the renovation and modernization of poorly performing power plants, increase in the use of washed coal, and the increase in the use of energy-efficient equipment.

A second factor was the greater use of natural gas in power generation. Increase in the energy efficiency of energy-intensive industry (particularly fertilizer plants) was the third factor, and increase in use of energy-efficient equipment in urban areas, piloted by projects in the state capital of Gandhinagar (and later expanded into the solar city programme) was the fourth factor. This taught me a valuable mantra regarding the public policy strategy for the enhancement of energy efficiency. Modi's approach of starting with pilot projects, trying out business models, and then introducing policies to enable the large-scale replication of these technologies and business models has been immensely effective in bringing about a change in the way energy is used, and in the way energy use is perceived by the consumers.

Soon after Modi became the Prime Minister, he personally took up the challenge of promoting energy efficiency in hotels, offices, factories, and on the streets by switching to LED lighting. This was a major initiative. In the years before 2015, the Bureau of Energy Efficiency, and the Energy Efficiency Services Limited (EESL) (a joint venture of public sector undertakings created to promote energy efficiency markets) had been trying to popularize LED lighting. But in spite of our best efforts, an LED bulb still costed ₹500 in the market, and most people did not purchase an LED bulb even though it paid for itself in about 3 years from the savings in energy bills that accrued from replacing the incandescent bulbs with LED ones.

Modi revolutionized the adoption of LED bulbs. He asked EESL to initiate programmes in every state so that LED bulbs could be sold through electricity distribution companies, and its cost would be recovered through a series of monthly instalments. I think this became very attractive because the amount of the instalments (of ₹10 per month) was less than the energy savings (of more than ₹18 per month) that consumers were able to achieve. On the other hand, as EESL initiated procurement of the LED bulbs, Modi encouraged them to secure these LED bulbs through bulk procurements. A series of bulk procurements carried out over a 32-month period between January 2016 and September 2018, brought down the price of LED bulbs to less than ₹40 each and EESL was able to sell them for ₹70 each. Interestingly enough, at this price most consumers preferred an outright purchase instead of monthly instalments. However, as the Prime Minister often mentioned, the monthly instalments provided a way for the poorest Indians to access this cutting-edge technology.

Again, the Prime Minister initiated this programme (called 'Ujala' or 'Lighting'), through a pilot project that started with his own office, and in the state of Delhi. He gave the first LED bulb to a common consumer in Delhi, and also replaced an incandescent bulb in his office with an LED bulb. After that he used his moral authority to convince a range of political leaders, including the Chief Ministers of various states, to adopt the Ujala programme. Over a period of 40 months, more than 368 million LED bulbs were sold through EESL alone, and without any subsidy. Today, the transition is complete, and LED lighting dominates the market with a share of over 80 per cent. Modi's approach had the advantage of using people's own thinking about enhancing their welfare to carry out the sustainable development agenda as well.

This has been captured in a statement that he made while inaugurating the programme in his office, when he had changed an incandescent bulb with an LED bulb. He said, 'If I ask for installation of 1,000 MW of energy, there will be many entities who will line up, but we will have to line up millions of people who could scale up energy efficiency and save 1,000 MW.'

The Ujjwala programme launched by him on 1 May 2016 addressed a similar theme—that of frugality of energy use—but for a very different stakeholder group, i.e. rural women, whose lives became immeasurably better with easy access to LPG cylinders for cooking; they earlier used biomass fuels in a dirty and polluting manner. According to the World Health Organization (WHO), about 500,000 deaths occurred in India every year due to the use of unclean cooking fuels. The then Petroleum and Natural Gas Minister Dharmendra Pradhan, echoing the Prime Minister, said that this (investment in providing LPG connections to rural households) represented a 'social investment'. The programme enabled LPG connections in 88 million BPL (below poverty line) households as of December 2021, by providing for subsidized connections for them.

When one looks at the steps adopted, the similarities in terms of actions—both at the Central and state levels—become evident. These strategies broadly align with the pillars of strategy on climate change that Prime Minister Modi has conceptualized, based on his own understanding and knowledge acquired from experts over the years.

WATER SUPPLY AND SEWAGE TREATMENT

Apart from energy, a key set of initiatives have focused on the provision of drinking water for all people. Gujarat, a state with water riots till 2001, has been transformed into a state where everyone has access to water, enabled by a Drinking Water Grid that has ensured potable water being supplied to all parts of Gujarat. This has included the construction of over 11,500 km of water pipelines, major and minor reservoir development—each of the 151 filtration and treatment plants ensures that 2,250 MLD (million litres per day) of water reaches every part of Gujarat. An additional benefit, but a major benefit from a sustainable development viewpoint has been the increase in groundwater levels as tubewell drilling was brought to a near halt.

Linked with this is the rainwater harvesting and conservation. Rainwater harvesting check dams and talawadis were built across Gujarat starting in 2004. The idea was to prevent farmer distress arising from insufficient water. The Sardar Patel Participatory Water Conservation Project allowed NGO/civil society groups to set up such structures. A portion of the cost and/or labour work was borne by them, thus making it a unique public-people partnership. Over 3.5 lakh (350,000) check dams and talawadis were developed by 2012, benefiting over 13 million people in rural Gujarat. Also, a reported 4-metre increase in the water table was observed during the same period. Combined with 350,000 hectares of land covered by efficient irrigation methods, agriculture has been transformed.

Initiatives for wastewater treatment and river revival were adopted too. This included the utilization of methane gas generated by sewage treatment which also serves the purpose of clean fuel, while also preventing emissions and pollution simultaneously. The adoption of this technique at several government establishments was a positive step. The revival of the Sabarmati River and the measures adopted to clean up the river and its banks, along with the riverfront redevelopment have served as examples for several other states and countries.

On land, the Van Mahotsavas enabled and promoted conscious afforestation campaigns run by the Gujarat government during monsoons. These measures have considerably helped increase tree cover and contributed to multiple goals of climate and wildlife conservation too. In addition, special efforts by the Gujarat government to revive and restore mangroves provided an opportunity to help make the state's coast resilient to cyclones.

At the national level, Prime Minister Modi has spearheaded measures aimed at ensuring drinking water supply to all through the Atal Mission for Rejuvenation and Urban Transformation (AMRUT) mission. AMRUT was launched as the first water-focused mission in 2015, catering to 500 major cities covering 60 per cent of the urban population. Under the mission, 11.4 million water tap connections have been provided taking total connections to 41.4 million in AMRUT cities. A total of 8.5 million sewer connections, including households, have been covered under septage facilities, taking coverage to 232 million. A total of 6,000 MLD of sewage treatment capacity is set to be developed through AMRUT, of which 1,800 MLD of treatment capacity has been developed. Further, 907 MLD capacity has been created for recycle/reuse of treated wastewater.

Through green spaces projects, as much as 3,850 acres of permeable green spaces have been added and another 1,600 acres of green area will be added. At least 2,200 waterlogging points have been eliminated, and another 1,500 waterlogging points will be eliminated as part of ongoing projects. Rejuvenation of 106 water bodies has also been taken up.

The mission has also made tremendous progress under its component of reforms. Credit rating work has been completed in 470 cities. Of which, 164 cities have received Investment Grade Rating (IGR), including 36 cities with rating of A- or above. The online building permission system has been implemented in 2,471 cities including 455 AMRUT cities. This reform has helped improve India's rank in ease of doing business in construction permits to 27, from 181 in 2018, according to the 2020 Doing Business Report (DBR) of World Bank.

Taking the transformations further, AMRUT 2.0 aims to make around 4,700 towns/cities 'water secure'. It will build upon the progress of

AMRUT to address water needs, rejuvenate water bodies, better manage aquifers, reuse treated wastewater, thereby, promoting a circular economy of water. The objective of AMRUT 2.0 is to provide 100 per cent coverage of water supply to all households in around 4,700 ULBs (urban local bodies), by providing 26.8 million urban household tap connections, thereby, benefitting around 107 million people. It will provide 100 per cent coverage of sewerage and septage in 500 AMRUT cities, by providing 26.4 million sewer connections/septage connections, thereby, benefitting around 106 million people. Rejuvenation of water bodies and urban aquifer management will be undertaken to augment sustainable fresh water supply. Recycle and reuse of treated wastewater is expected to cater to 20 per cent of the total water needs of the cities and 40 per cent of the industrial demand. Under the mission, freshwater bodies will be protected from pollution to make natural resources sustainable.

AMRUT 2.0 has several defining features. These include upscaling from 500 cities covered under AMRUT with 100,000+ population to all 4,372 cities, covering 100 per cent urban India. It will promote a circular economy of water through formulation of City Water Balance Plan for each city, focusing on recycle/reuse of treated sewage, rejuvenation of water bodies and water conservation. Digital economy will be promoted by adopting a paperless mission. Pey Jal Survekshan (drinking water surveys) will be conducted in cities to ascertain equitable distribution of water, reuse of wastewater and mapping of water bodies with regard to quantity and quality of water through a complex process. The Technology Sub-Mission for water will leverage latest global technologies in the field of water.

The mission also focuses on strengthening urban local bodies and improving water security across cities. Major reforms include rejuvenation of water bodies, rainwater harvesting, reducing non-revenue water (NRW), meeting 40 per cent industrial water demand through recycled used water, dual piping system for bulk users through building by-laws, unlocking value and improving land use efficiency through proper master planning, improving credit rating and accessing market finance including issuance of municipal bonds and implementation of the online building permission system.

A unique feature of the AMRUT 2.0 is the implementation of projects through public-private partnership (PPP) with innovative business models.

It has been mandated for cities with a population of over 1 million to take up PPP projects worth a minimum of 10 percent of their total project fund allocation on the basis of an annuity/hybrid annuity/BOT model.

WILDLIFE CONSERVATION

Modi's focus on wildlife and forest conservation has been unrelenting. A major initiative was on whale shark conservation that collaborated with community and religious leaders to bring whale shark hunting significantly under control along the coasts of Gujarat. As a result of this, the state's coastline became a natural refuge for the largest fish of the world.

Working with local populations, the government made significant efforts to help reduce mortality in vulture populations in the state by encouraging people to not use diclofenac for cattle while also contributing significantly to research on the reasons behind it. In addition, the maintenance of the Rann of Kutchh, which is home to several unique species of animals (including the iconic wild ass) and birds, has been an unparalleled success. The growth of lion population in Gujarat and the support gained from the local communities in Gir and elsewhere have meant that the lions have started to expand and reclaim old territories once again. This was rendered possible because of the engagement with local communities, who now see themselves as stakeholders gaining from conservation activities.

We also saw the complete 'undergrounding' of all cables in the Kutch region after reports of bird hits on cables in the region. This increased the cost of the transmission lines, but enabled free flight of birds in this region which attracts several unique species of migratory birds in the winter season.

These approaches—of marrying environmental sustainability to economic development, the involvement of local (and often adversely affected) communities and of starting with pilot projects and business models and then introducing policy changes for large-scale replication, as well as use of the power of the market to drive down costs to make new technology economically viable—have been the hallmark of Modi's actions. I have had the privilege of observing and learning from him, especially on the subject of energy and climate change. As I look at a variety of his other initiatives, be it the case of water management or biodiversity conservation or urban waste management and recycling, I see these approaches also flowing through their successful implementation.

CLEAN INDIA MISSION AND URBAN REJUVENATION

'A clean India would be the best tribute India could pay to Mahatma Gandhi on his 150 birth anniversary in 2019,' said Modi during the launch of the Swachh Bharat Mission at Rajpath in New Delhi. On 2 October 2014, the Swachh Bharat Mission was launched throughout the country as a national movement. The Swachh Bharat Abhiyan is the most significant cleanliness campaign by the Government of India. Modi led a cleanliness pledge at India Gate, which was joined by about thirty lakh (3 million) government employees across the country. He also flagged off a walkathon at Rajpath and surprised people by joining as a participant at the event—not just for a few token steps, but by marching a long way with the other participants.

While leading the mass movement for cleanliness, the Prime Minister exhorted people to fulfil Mahatma Gandhi's dream of a clean and hygienic India. Modi himself initiated the cleanliness drive at the Mandir Marg Police Station. Picking up the broom to clean the dirt, making Swachh Bharat Abhiyan a mass movement across the nation, the Prime Minister said people should neither litter nor let others litter. He gave the mantra of 'Na gandagi karenge, na karne denge' (We will neither litter, nor allow others to litter').

By encouraging others to do so, he also invited nine people to join the cleanliness drive and requested each of them to draw nine more people into the initiative, thus creating a chain of mass participation.

The cleanliness drive, thus, turned into a national movement. A sense of responsibility has been evoked among people through the campaign. With citizens now becoming active participants in cleanliness activities across the nation, the dream of a 'Clean India' as envisaged by Mahatma Gandhi has begun to take shape.

The Prime Minister has helped spread the message of Swachh Bharat by urging people through his words and actions. He carried out a cleanliness drive in Varanasi as well. He wielded a spade near the Ganga at Assi Ghat.

He was joined by a large group of local people, who cooperated in the campaign. Understanding the significance of sanitation, Prime Minister Modi has simultaneously addressed the health problems that roughly half of the Indians families have to deal with, due to lack of proper toilets in their homes.

People from different sections of the society have come forward and joined this mass movement of cleanliness. From government officials to jawans, bollywood actors to sportspersons, and industrialists to spiritual leaders, people from all walks of life have lined up for the noble work. Millions of people across the country have been joining the cleanliness initiatives of the government departments, NGOs and local community centres to make India clean. Organizing frequent cleanliness campaigns and spreading awareness about hygiene through plays and music are also being widely carried out across the nation. Modi lauded the participation of people via social media. The '#MyCleanIndia' was also launched simultaneously as part of the Swachh Bharat drive to highlight the cleanliness work carried out by citizens across the nation.

An estimated 108 million toilets have been built as part of the Swachh Bharat Mission, by the end of December 2021. The objectives of the first phase of the mission also included eradication of manual scavenging, generating awareness and bringing about behavioural changes regarding sanitation practices, and augmentation of capacity at the local level. The second phase of the mission aims to sustain the open defecation free status and improve the management of solid and liquid waste, while also working to improve the lives of sanitation workers.

In the second phase of the mission, there has been an increased emphasis on urban actions, especially promoting cities to become cleaner through measures, including the picking and treatment of urban garbage. A very effective instrument has been a campaign to promote measures of cleanliness and intercity competitions. This encourages cities to be in the top tier of performers, and in the process, cities have, through the support provided by the Central government, invested in the provision of better municipal services, and some cities have also made changes in growth and expansion strategies so that growth is cleaner and more sustainable.

MULTILATERAL ENGAGEMENT

I have also observed from close quarters, how Modi has influenced the international dialogue on sustainable development, and especially on climate change. This is best illustrated by his personal leadership in creating two major international initiatives—the International Solar Alliance (ISA) and the Coalition for Disaster Resilient Infrastructure (CDRI). In both of these initiatives, the emphasis has been to get a self-selected group of countries to come together, learn from each other, and help each other. And other countries are encouraged to join as they see the benefits of these initiatives. This approach to multilateralism is both effective, as well as inclusive. It also changes the focus of the debate from being an acrimonious fight between developing and developed countries to one of collaboration and cooperation of the many countries of the world who want to see a future that is both more environmentally sustainable, and promotes economic development as well. And the change is grounded on changed economic fundamentals (which increasingly favour sustainable development options), as much as on environmental considerations. The success of these organizations, and the fact that they are launched together with the developed country partners (France in the case of ISA, and UK in the case of CDRI) indicates the relevance and the effectiveness of the approach, as well as of the personal leadership of Modi in global affairs.

The ISA (with which I am associated) brings together countries into cooperative actions which make solar electricity viable. Today, in many geographies, including India, solar electricity is already the cheapest electricity—but only when the sun is shining. Modi, at the first Assembly of the ISA in 2018, spoke about countries coming together so that solar electricity from countries where the sun is shining could flow to countries where the sun had already set. He called this the 'One Sun, One World, One Grid' initiative, which would connect regional electricity grids to one another, enabling this solar electricity flow to occur, at all time of day, from countries where the sun is still shining to countries where it has already set. The endorsement of this initiative at the Fourth Assembly of the ISA in 2021, and the creation of a steering committee with countries from around the globe has now moved this initiative into an international programme.

This represents both a global acceptance of his idea—an approach developed in India, as well as a new way for promoting the use of solar energy with strong economic benefits for both the buyers and sellers of renewable energy. It highlights the approach that seems to be at the heart of Modi's view of enabling the global energy transition, i.e. of making renewable energy more attractive—financially and infrastructure wise—than access to fossil-fuel based electricity transition.

The CDRI enables countries to prepare for inevitable disasters. The traditional response—in all countries—was for the Finance Minister to seek disaster relief, after the disaster had already occurred. However, as the National Disaster Management Authority's (NDMA) experience in India, and that of the Ministry of Disaster Management and Relief in Bangladesh, have shown proactive actions—before the disaster strikes—helps in reducing the impact, both in terms of lives and physical assets. It is with this in mind that the NDMA and CDRI have focused on codes and standards that are region-specific based on the disasters—cyclones, earthquakes, etc.—which create the vulnerability in that region. The CDRI initiative to support the island countries in planning disaster management, launched at COOP-16, with the support of many countries, shows the acceptance of this multilateral approach towards internationalizing disaster resilience.

The last leadership example that I would like to cite in the area of sustainable development is Modi's efforts in drawing attention to the 'losers' of climate action, and his coining of the phrase 'climate justice', to describe efforts to address the needs of the so-called 'losers' as well. In the run-up to the 21st Conference of the Parties of the UN Framework Convention on Climate Change, he repeatedly brought up this subject in his interactions with global leaders. It was soon fully recognized as an issue, and finds place in the preamble to Paris Agreement. The importance of this issue is becoming clearer by the day as investors and workers in the fossil fuel industry, especially in the developed countries, react with anger and confusion at the uncertainty regarding their future; again highlighting the importance of climate justice in climate action.

The importance of climate justice in all climate action has been brought out by the recent experiences during the COVID-19 pandemic, which serves to highlight the importance of ensuring benefits to all stakeholders, including developing countries, in climate action. Modi's mantra of ensuring environmental sustainability with economic benefits for all is again underlined in the climate justice approach, which sees a resetting of the global agenda beyond time targets alone and incorporating an overarching social dimension to it as well.

LEARNINGS AND LESSONS

We have, as an academic principle, always been taught that self-interest is the best way of enabling change. Modi has provided us with real-life examples of approaches to convert this theory into practice, and the large number of practical initiatives that he has launched have brought the theory to life. More than anything else, he has also, by his leadership on sustainability issues, demonstrated his personal commitment to this issue as an integral part of economic development, and shown how personal and national (or global) interests can be addressed and framed in a manner that carries all people with it—and thus converts them from being personal virtues to becoming mass movements.

MODI: THE MAN INDIA TRUSTS IN A CRISIS

ANUPAM KHER

Over the past two decades, both as the Chief Minister of Gujarat and Prime Minister of India, Narendra Modi has overseen several crises like the ongoing COVID-19 pandemic and other extreme natural disasters in various parts of the country. From the Kutch earthquake in 2001 to cyclone Yaas in 2021, the location of the crisis and the magnitude of the challenge may have varied, but what has remained constant is Modi's proactive, calm and sensible approach.

Prime Minister Modi has always ensured an effective government response in times of calamities. His hands-on style of functioning ensures unwavering commitment and devotion from the entire administration in charge of the disaster response and mitigation measures.

The exponential pressure a leader faces in an actual crisis with hundreds of lives at stake and limited resources to utilize, is unimaginable. Elected leaders like Modi are expected to regularly handle crisis situations and ensure swift and effective responses. Unlike in films, there are no retakes or any scope for error and experimentation during a crisis.

Why are leaders like Modi so successful in managing situations with hundreds of lives at stake despite immense pressure, limited information and high uncertainty? While preparing for my role as Commissioner of Mumbai Police, Prakash Rathod, in the film, *A Wednesday*, I tried to understand how successful leaders managed a crisis. I found that the ability to remain calm amidst pressure is critical. Apart from this, leaders need to be dedicated entirely to their country and its citizens. This is necessary for continuing to engage in disaster relief and response despite adversities.

I will tell the story of Narendra Modi's twenty years of governance through several crisis situations faced by him in this long period. The chapter provides an overview of how he successfully overcame various situations through innovative decision-making and novel strategies. Further, I will discuss why India has immense trust in Modi's ability to manage a situation successfully.

FAITH IN HIS ABILITY

Natural disasters often have severe consequences. Loss of life and property changes countless lives overnight. In such dismal situations, people are naturally lost and need a pillar of support or a helping hand. Modi does not hesitate in playing this vital role for citizens after a natural disaster. Through his empathetic actions and words, he plays the much-needed role of a guiding elder.

In 2001, Modi decided to spend his first Diwali as Chief Minister of Gujarat in earthquake-affected pockets of Kutch. He could have been at a grand celebration in any part of the state. Instead, he chose to stay with grief-stricken families of the region who had lost life and property in the earthquake. This was a touching moment for the lakhs of affected households. Modi spoke to the locals about their plight and personally assured all possible assistance in rebuilding efforts. The care and concern demonstrated by Modi on that visit has been a rare sight in Indian politics.

Modi's solidarity generated immense trust as people from the region realized that they had finally found a leader who was not only committed to rebuilding efforts but who also looked after each Gujarati as a family member. People like to spend festivals with family members. For Modi, the entire country is his family. As Prime Minister, he has often celebrated Holi and Diwali with soldiers in various parts of the country.

Post disasters, not only governments but families and individuals were engaged in rebuilding. Overcoming the stiff economic challenges posed by loss of property and assets and personal grief due to loss of lives requires immense grit and determination. At times like these, Modi becomes an inspirational figure for those aiming to rebuild their lives.

While campaigning for my wife and Chandigarh MP, Kirron Kher, in the 2019 elections, I asked a bystander why he supported the BJP. The young boy confidently said, '*Kyunki sapne dekhna sikhaya hai humaare PM ne*' (because our Prime Minister has taught us to dream). The inspirational tale of a young boy serving tea at his father's tea stall becoming the Prime Minister of the world's largest democracy is a highly inspirational story. The title of my autobiographic play *Kuch Bhi Ho Sakta Hai* (anything can happen) perfectly captures Modi's inspiring life journey.

Moreover, Modi never asks people to become like him. He merely discusses his life journey with the simple hope that people will be inspired by his story to strive hard and work towards achieving a similar transformation. This is the kind of inspiration people need to overcome a crisis. For those affected by natural disasters, the transformative journey of Modi becomes an inspiration for rebuilding their own lives.

Over time, people of India have become used to Modi's calm and adept handling of crisis situations. They have immense belief in his ability to handle a crisis. This is not an easy achievement in a democracy because citizens are usually dissatisfied with their leaders' actions in crisis situations. Whatever the leaders do, they are constantly criticized for not doing enough. This is not the case with Modi, as most citizens trust that the country is in safe hands with him at the helm.

As an actor, I regularly travel across the country and directly interact with people. One sentiment transcends regional and social divides—'*Modi Sambhal Lenge*' or Modi will handle it. Until now, such phrases were only heard about prominent cricketers handling tricky run chases! What explains the immense public trust in Prime Minister Modi's ability to handle a crisis?

Unlike many predecessors who became passive during a crisis, Modi always steps up, takes charge and fulfils his duty. This is critical as active leadership is vital for countries to emerge from a crisis situation. In a country where people are used to politicians going below the radar whenever something goes wrong, Modi is an exception. He has never shied away from taking the responsibility of leading Gujarat and India out of critical situations.

An excellent example of this was Modi's impeccable conduct at ISRO in September 2019 when Chandrayaan-2's Vikram lander lost communication. Realizing that the hard-working ISRO team was extremely demoralized, Modi decided to stay back in Bengaluru and returned to the ISRO centre the next day. He spoke to the project team and encouraged them to forget the failure and take pride in their achievements. Embracing an emotional ISRO chief, K. Sivan, to console him remains one the most iconic moments from Modi's twenty years of governance. Modi's gesture and the raw emotions visible in the image reflected his leadership. He was fulfilling his promise by being present in both good and bad times. This sense of responsibility automatically creates a belief in the minds of citizens across the country—'Come what may, Modi will be there for us.'

In my decades-long film career, I have repeatedly seen that successful actors consistently have full houses for their premiere shows as fans eagerly await their movies. Essentially, trust and expectations stem from performance. A similar cycle of performance and confidence exists in politics as well. People trust Modi because he delivers. It is his success that has strengthened public trust in his leadership.

Since independence, India has seen many leaders who have made grand promises to deliver before elections, and engaged in heavy corruption after coming to power. Due to such experiences in the past, Indians place a significant premium on honesty and good intent. In the case of Modi, both are guaranteed. There have been both ups and downs in Modi's twenty-year journey of governance. However, what has remained constant is his intent and positive objectives. People understand that he is always looking out for them and making decisions in the national interest.

THE KUTCH TURNAROUND

The story of Modi's twenty years in governance should begin with the Bhuj earthquake in 2001. On 26 January 2001, tragedy struck Gujarat as a devastating earthquake with its epicentre at Bhuj left nearly 20,000 people dead and tens of thousands injured. Nearly twelve lakh (1.2 million) homes were damaged as tremors were felt across the state and beyond. In the Kutch region alone, six lakh or 600,000 people were left homeless due to the tragedy. An entire region of Gujarat had been left in shambles by the earthquake.

The tragedy deeply affected Modi, and due to his immense attachment with his home state, he wanted to participate in the relief work in whatever way possible. He left for Gujarat and worked on the ground as a relief-work volunteer for several weeks. In an age when political leaders leave no stone unturned to publicize even their minimal participation in relief work, here was a leader who just wanted to quietly participate in rebuilding his home state.

A few months later, amidst the crisis, Modi took oath as the Chief Minister of Gujarat in October 2001. He immediately focused on rebuilding and redevelopment efforts in Kutch. This was one of the first expositions of Modi's famous target-oriented execution. P.K. Mishra, Principal Secretary to Prime Minister Modi, mentions in his book on the Kutch earthquake that the new Chief Minister asked officials to accelerate their efforts and ensure significant progress by 26 January 2002, the earthquake's first anniversary[2]. Thus, under Modi's leadership and guidance, the Gujarat government started working on a mission mode to redevelop the region.

The Gujarat government made four thousand masons and twenty-seven thousand engineers work together to rebuild houses and public buildings. The workers removed almost seventy lakh (7 million) tonnes of debris in just eleven months. The swiftness of Gujarat's reconstruction is evident in numbers. The state government was overseeing the repair and reconstruction of 9.28 lakh and 2.15 lakh houses, (928,000 and 215,000 houses) respectively[3]. Out of these, more than 8.2 lakh (72 per cent) houses were repaired or reconstructed in the first year itself!

By way of comparison, it took four years for Japan to build 1.31 lakh or 131,000 houses in earthquake-hit Kobe region in 1995[4]. The earthquake had severely disrupted school education as close to 51,000 classrooms needed to be repaired or reconstructed. Within one year, the Gujarat state government's efforts led to the repair of 41,514 classrooms and the construction of 1,792 new classrooms. What led to these quick results?

The change in work culture initiated by Modi. Senior secretaries of the state government were assigned some of the most affected talukas and directed to visit them for three days every week, till the end of January 2002. Chief Minister Modi conducted weekly review meetings with secretaries and other officials personally[5].

From houses to classrooms, government offices to hospitals, roads to pipelines, nothing had been left undamaged by the earthquake. However, the Modi-led Gujarat government could complete most of the reconstruction and repair work within three years of the earthquake. What makes Modi different from his predecessors and compatriots is that his vision for Kutch did not end at the successful completion of reconstruction efforts. While most other leaders would have been satisfied and stopped, Modi was already looking ahead and aiming to transform the region entirely. This showcased another aspect of Modi's approach—discovering opportunities in a crisis, i.e. '*Aapda mein Avsar*'.

Over the next decade, Modi left no stone unturned to transform Kutch from a disaster-stricken region into a vibrant economic hub and tourist hotspot. The Gujarat government gave a five-year tax holiday for investments in Kutch to give an impetus to industrial growth in the region. The Gujarat government's steps led to an investment of about ₹1 lakh crore or ₹1 trillion in the region[6]. As a result, prominent companies such as Essar, Adani Group, Suzlon, Sanghi Group, Tata Power, Welspun, Videocon International, Surya Group, JP Group and Electrotherm have set up factories in the region. Apart from this, Kutch has emerged as one of the country's leading tourist destinations.

As Kutch was redeveloping, it was becoming a microcosm of Gujarat—the much-appreciated Gujarat Model was slowly taking shape. This is what one means when one talks of discovering opportunities during a crisis.

The Kutch earthquake also turned out to be a critical juncture for disaster management in India. In 2003, the Gujarat State Assembly passed the Gujarat State Disaster Management Bill. Gujarat became the first state in the Country to provide a regulatory and legal framework for disaster management. The Gujarat government's efforts were replicated by the Central government in 2005, and the National Disaster Management Authority (NDMA) was formed[7].

'MODI IS THERE FOR US'

On numerous occasions in the past two decades, Modi has found himself to be at the helm of rescue operations. Having him at the helm of affairs automatically gave a sense of security to those stranded and waiting for rescue operations. Some leaders consciously avoid dealing with crises due to a fear of failing. On the other hand, leaders like Modi step up in a crisis and lead from the front—in public interest. There is no better example of this than Modi's role in the rescue operations during the Uttarakhand floods in 2013.

As news came in on 16 June 2013, about thousands of Gujaratis being stranded at various holy places across Uttarakhand, Chief Minister Modi got into action and started planning rescue operations for them. The next day itself, he flew to Delhi and coordinated the rescue efforts from Gujarat Bhawan in the city. Camp offices were opened in Gujarat Bhawan and inside the premises of Uttarakhand government's control room. Gujarat government officials directly contacted Uttarakhand collectors, deputy collectors and disaster management officers, to coordinate rescue operations. An advertisement was circulated in the Gujarati media with helpline numbers for citizens to provide information about stranded family members and acquaintances and request evacuation.

As citizens across Gujarat started sharing information and making requests for rescue, the state government had its task cut out. Alongside, Chief Minister Modi wrote a letter to Mallikarjun Kharge, then the Railways Minister, requesting that he arrange for special trains to bring stranded citizens back to Gujarat. A special team of officers and doctors from Gujarat left for Uttarakhand the same day to oversee the rescue operations. Within a few days, the Gujarat government managed to create a formal process for rescuing its citizens stranded in Uttarakhand.

Narendra Modi led from the front and personally went to Uttarakhand on 20 June to directly coordinate the rescue efforts. His presence in Uttarakhand ensured complete seriousness and dedication of officials towards the rescue operations. He also engaged local BJP and RSS leaders and took their help in the state's rescue operations. Despite being away from Gujarat, Gujaratis knew that their Narendra bhai was looking out for their safety and working tirelessly to ensure their safe return home.

Since 2014, a similar sentiment has developed among the Indian diaspora living abroad. Having stayed abroad for a considerable time, I have realized that living abroad, especially as a fresh immigrant on a student or a work visa, is highly uncertain. However, amidst all the uncertainties, Modi has been able to assure them and create one certainty—support of the Indian government and diplomatic staff in times of need. I have personally felt a sense of security from the fact that come what may, the Indian government under Prime Minister Modi is always looking out for its citizens abroad and will be just a tweet away in times of need. In the past seven years, whenever Indians abroad have needed support, the Modi government has always been there for them.

A few weeks after entering office, the Modi government encountered a crisis situation: forty-six Indian nurses were held captive by the terror group ISIS, and were trapped in a hospital in Tikrit in Iraq. All nurses returned safely to India after twenty-three days. The rescue was made possible by extensive diplomatic efforts by the Indian government and back-channel negotiations[8]. This was the first among many diplomatic victories for the Modi government. More importantly, the incident clearly demonstrated that Modi's promise—of prioritizing national interest and doing whatever it takes to help Indian citizens—wasn't merely electoral rhetoric. Modi meant what he said.

Less than a year later, Father Alexis Prem, a Jesuit priest from Tamil Nadu, returned to India after being held captive by the Taliban for eight months. The Ministry of External Affairs (MEA) had confirmed that his release required efforts from the Prime Minister himself[9]. In 2017, the Modi government ensured the release of Father Tom Uzhunnalil, a Vatican priest from India, who had been abducted in Yemen. His release was secured through months of diplomatic negotiations by the Modi government[10].

The Modi government conducted Operation Raahat to evacuate Indian nationals from Yemen when the conflict and violence escalated in 2015. This was one of the largest evacuation operations conducted ever by the Indian government. Modi made a pivotal intervention in the rescue operation. He directly reached out to King Salman of Saudi Arabia to request safe passage for Indian evacuees and the halting of bombing operations. As former External Affairs Minister Sushma Swaraj had mentioned, it was due to his personal rapport with Prime Minister Modi that King Salman agreed to the halting of bombing for a few hours every day for a week[11]. Over 4,600 Indian citizens were safely evacuated through special flights through the immensely successful operation. India's efforts were so successful that numerous countries, including the US and the UK, sought our help in rescuing their citizens. Eventually, India successfully evacuated more than nine hundred foreign nationals from forty-one countries under Operation Raahat[12].

A few months ago, as the Taliban expanded its control in Afghanistan and regime change became apparent, numerous countries (including India), decided to evacuate their citizens and some locals. The Indian government evacuated hundreds of Indian citizens and Afghans under Operation Devi Shakti. Apart from rescuing its citizens, India fulfilled its civilizational and cultural duty and evacuated Afghani Sikhs and Hindus as well. As the threat of religious persecution was imminent, three saroop of *Guru Granth Sahib* were also brought to India. Sitting thousands of miles away in the US, my heart swelled with pride when I saw a video clip of Union Minister Hardeep Puri personally receiving the *Guru Granth Sahib* at the airport[13].

In each of these situations, an assurance that Narendra Modi was working for their safe return became a source of strength for people in tough times. They all had a shared belief: 'Modi is with us, like a family member always watching out for loved ones.' I cannot recall any other political leader in the history of post-Independence India enjoying such belief and trust among citizens.

A SUPPORTIVE UNION GOVERNMENT

Lessons learnt during his tenure as Gujarat Chief Minister have shaped Modi's prime ministerial tenure. As the Chief Minister of an Opposition-ruled state for a decade, Modi often suffered due to limited Central support during crisis situations and unfair policies of the Central government. From severe floods in Jammu and Kashmir in 2014 to cyclone Yaas in West Bengal and Odisha in 2021, cooperative federalism has ensured that the Centre and the states work together for disaster relief and redevelopment.

The Central government assists states in providing a swift response to natural disasters. Timely extension of assistance and deployment of the National Disaster Relief Force (NDRF) battalion and Armed Forces by the Modi government has saved innumerable lives on multiple occasions. For instance, a few months after Modi took office as Prime Minister in

2014, there were severe floods in Jammu and Kashmir. Realizing that the state government lacked adequately trained personnel and equipment for rescue operations, especially in challenging terrains and inaccessible areas, the Centre deployed the army and air force. The Armed Forces' commendable work and dedication for flood relief which saved thousands of lives and built immense goodwill, will be remembered for years to come.

In crisis situations, even a slight delay by the Central government in deploying the NDRF or the military can prove disastrous and cost innumerable lives. To ensure swift response and timely deployment in a vast country like ours, the Modi government has increased the number of NDRF battalions[14].

Leaders must anticipate requirements for disaster relief and act proactively. In 2016, the Puttingal temple in Kerala's Kollam district witnessed a massive fire that led to more than a hundred deaths. Modi decided to visit Kollam to review the situation immediately. To avoid disruption of medical services and rescue work, he asked the authorities to avoid the usual protocol and formalities during the visit[15]. A team of burn specialists travelled with the Prime Minister to Kerala as their assistance was required in the rescue work.

The Central government's support to states is not limited to assistance in rescue and immediate disaster relief. Apart from short-term measures, the Modi government has focused on reconstruction and redevelopment. Natural disasters are a significant economic shock for any state and could even have ripple effects beyond its borders. Based on his experience in Gujarat, Modi understands that undoing the damage and bringing the economy back on track after a natural disaster is an uphill task for state governments, and that it requires Central support. In 2018, Kerala witnessed massive floods that led to thousands of crores of damage across the state. The Central government's assistance in the reconstruction and redevelopment of the state was not limited to merely approving a Central relief package.

The Modi government went a step ahead and announced a slew of measures to assist citizens and ensure redevelopment. The Centre approved the building of damaged houses under Pradhan Mantri Awas Yojana (PMAY) and announced an additional 5.5 crore or 55 million person days under Mahatma Gandhi National Rural Employment Guarantee

Scheme (MGNREGS). Insurance companies (like the LIC) were asked to ensure a timely release of compensation to affected families. The National Highways Authority of India (NHAI) was directed to repair national highways damaged due to floods on priority. Central PSUs, like the NTPC and the PGCIL, were expected to provide all possible assistance to the state government to restore power lines. Such extensive support has been a norm rather than an exception under the Modi government.

Political differences with Opposition parties have always been kept aside to focus on collectively managing crises. The Central government's response does not depend on whether the state is ruled by the BJP, an NDA ally or an Opposition party. Irrespective of the political alignment of the state government, the Centre under Modi has announced special relief packages and extended all possible support. In the past seven years, there have been numerous natural disasters in Opposition-ruled states (but not limited to such states), such as in Jammu and Kashmir (floods of 2014), Kerala (floods of 2018), cyclone Fani (2019), cyclone Amphan (2020) and cyclone Yaas (2021). As a former Chief Minister, Modi understood the urgent need for additional fiscal support and the importance of additional resources from the Centre in such situations. The Central government ensured that relief package was released for states at the earliest so that they did not face any resource constraints in undertaking rescue, relief and redevelopment. It is evident that Modi has not only spoken about the principle of '*Sabka Saath, Sabka Vikas*' but has also followed it in policy and decision-making. Compare the Modi government's approach that prioritizes national interest, with that of its predecessor—and you get the point.

In the case of natural disasters across the country, Prime Minister Modi always preferred to personally visit the affected states and review the disaster response. Even threats to personal well-being have not prevented him from visiting disaster-affected states and helping in disaster response. In May 2020, he had visited Odisha and West Bengal and conducted an aerial survey of Amphan-affected areas. This was his first visit since the COVID-19 lockdown started in March 2020. At that time, we had limited knowledge about COVID-19 transmission and undertaking such a trip was accompanied with health risks. However, Modi prioritized his duty and undertook the visit. Irrespective of the ruling party, he has been proactive in personally reaching out to the respective chief ministers. In his visits, he has ensured that politics remains at bay and personally given reassurances of support.

Overcoming natural disasters requires close cooperation between state governments and the Centre. Both need to work in tandem, and the latter must bridge shortfalls faced by the former. PM Modi's balanced approach towards Centre-state relations is creating a paradigm shift in disaster response and relief.

TACKLING THE COVID-19 PANDEMIC

Since early 2020, the COVID-19 pandemic has been an unprecedented crisis for leaders across the globe. There was initially limited information about the disease, its impact and transmission. Due to the paucity of sufficient information, leaders were operating under severe uncertainty with little ability to foresee the consequences of their actions and policies. In close consultation with public health experts, the government has taken important decisions on countering COVID-19. Strategies for countering COVID-19, like lockdowns and general restrictions, have sharp economic costs. Policymakers find it challenging to balance competing interests and making trade-offs. In India, countering COVID-19 became the foremost priority for the Central government. I will highlight selected aspects of India's COVID-19 management strategy which have caught my attention.

First, countries need to be united while facing adversities. Collective action and cooperation among citizens is necessary for overcoming a global pandemic. Government agencies taking some precautionary measures or a small segment of citizens following COVID-19 appropriate behaviour would not have helped much. Globally, governments have realized that public messaging on COVID-19 should encourage united action against the pandemic. This was a very early realization in India, and PM Modi personally took the initiative to build a collective resolve among the masses to fight the pandemic. In April 2020, Modi urged citizens to switch off all house lights for nine minutes at 9 p.m. on 5 April and light diyas, candles or turn on mobile flashlights. The collective exercise created a moment of national unity. Crores of citizens across the country stood together at the same time and resolved to come together in the country's fight against COVID-19.

Second, India has taken a holistic approach to countering COVID-19, making it easier to balance competing interests. Like many other countries, India needed a buffer time for augmenting medical infrastructure and arresting rapid transmission of the disease. This led to the first national lockdown in March 2020. Initially, it was meant for twenty-one days, but the lockdown had to be extended multiple times as COVID-19 transmission continued. There is little doubt that lockdowns are extremely costly as many economic activities come to a standstill. Even Modi had to take the harsh decision of imposing a lockdown as he prioritized saving citizens' lives. However, the Modi government was one of the few globally that took concomitant measures to protect those adversely affected by the lockdown. PM Modi announced the Pradhan Mantri Garib Kalyan Package, which gave direct assistance and support to citizens facing economic hardships.[16] The income supplement and additional PDS transfers announced in the package were particularly beneficial for crores of poor households.

Third, while many were ruing about the economic impact of the COVID-19 crisis, Modi was preparing a blueprint for taking Indian economy to new heights. Essentially, he discovered an opportunity in the crisis, i.e. '*Aapda mein Avsar*'. Recalling the transformation of Kutch after the 2001 earthquake, he gave a clarion call for building a self-reliant India. In May 2020, Modi announced the Atmanirbhar Bharat Abhiyan, a comprehensive package for economic revival. The government also undertook long-pending economic reforms that are expected to drive the country's economic progress[17].

Fourth, for decades politicians in India used to hide their failures and were reluctant to take up challenges; they claimed that India does not have adequate capacity or achieving specific outcomes isn't possible for the country. Modi brought a paradigm shift in this mindset over the past seven years, and this has been particularly evident in COVID-19 management. Over the past eighteen months, Modi has made us realize that, if Indians resolve, they can achieve anything under the sun. From importing PPE kits and N95 masks, India has become one of the world's largest producers and a net exporter. From importing ventilators to installing domestically manufactured ventilators in public hospitals across the country. From waiting for medical breakthroughs abroad to conducting the world's largest vaccination drive through indigenously developed vaccines. A crisis has become a historic moment for the country as we have discovered a new self-belief that nothing is out of reach for us anymore.

Fifth, India's COVID-19 strategy has evolved from close consultations between the Central government and state governments. Since the pandemic started, PM Modi has personally chaired multiple review meetings with chief ministers. From the first lockdown to vaccination drive to providing medical supplies during the second wave, the Centre has discussed almost all aspects of COVID-19 management with CMs and state governments while formulating policies. On numerous occasions, issues raised by state governments have led to necessary modifications in policies. Thus, COVID-19 management has demonstrated the strength of cooperative federalism.

Sixth, despite many attempts by the Opposition to politicize the COVID-19 response, Modi has ensured that COVID-19 management does not fall prey to partisan polarization. From the distribution of vaccines to medical supplies, Opposition parties have not missed any opportunity to target Prime Minister Modi. As I wrote in *The Indian Express* a few months back, it almost seemed as if his rivals were focusing on defeating the Prime Minister instead of the pandemic[18]. However, despite the Opposition's repeated attempts at politicization, Modi has remained focused on countering the pandemic. A close analysis of COVID-19 statistics reveals that it is the Opposition-ruled states that have fared the worst. Maharashtra has the highest case count and number of deaths. Kerala has been facing a perpetual COVID-19 wave and has the highest positivity rate among large states. Punjab has the highest case fatality rate. However, the PM has never made this a political issue.

He has never made a political remark against ruling parties of chief ministers in these Opposition-ruled states for their abject failure at managing COVID-19. On the contrary, in a meeting with chief ministers on COVID-19 management, Modi urged them to increase testing and not worry about high numbers. The Prime Minister understands that we are engaged in a collective fight against COVID-19, and any single state's failure could hurt all others. In today's times, when leaders don't miss even a single opportunity for political mileage, Modi has taken a bold decision of refraining from politicizing COVID-19 management.

These are just a few dimensions of Modi's effective COVID-19 management strategy. Unfortunately, there have also been some adverse outcomes over the past eighteen months, like the migrant crisis, which could have been handled better. However, contrary to popular portrayal, Modi is a leader who is always receptive to criticism and eager to improve.

CONCLUSION

Uninterrupted governance over a period of two decades is a rare achievement for an Indian politician. During this long period, Modi has been at the helm of affairs during countless crisis situations. Through exemplary conduct in situations like natural disasters, infectious disease outbreaks and humanitarian crises, he has demonstrated his deep commitment towards the nation. For Modi, India is always first. A crisis is considered a true test of leadership and Modi has delivered. He has never shied away from leading from the front and demonstrated impeccable leadership. His ability to remain calm and maintain composure, optimistic spirit and a laser-eyed focus have ensured success. In countless crisis situations, Modi has not only ensured a swift response and extensive assistance from the governance but also inspired crores of citizens to take individual action in collective interest. Whenever the public has felt a need, Modi has delivered. This is why he remains the man India trusts in a crisis.

AGRICULTURE: GOOD, BUT CAN BE BETTER

ASHOK GULATI*

When an honest and sincere person enters political life, his purpose is to do good for the largest number of people, especially the less privileged. On his own, a person can do some good for some people based on his personal efforts and resources. But if that person gets a chance to be in power in a state, that state's policy can be oriented to bring prosperity for the masses on a sustainable basis. It is this inclusive prosperity that is the basic objective of politics in a democracy. Unfortunately, in India, only a few politicians will pass this test.

But how can one assess a politician bringing prosperity to the masses? Announcing freebies to the people from the state exchequer is the easiest route that any politician can take. And it is done quite frequently in India, especially just before elections. That's not just hollow, but it is also simply a quid pro quo for votes. In most cases, the move damages the ecosystem as it is generally unsustainable, given the limited resources of the exchequer. Further, it also makes people lazy and perpetually dependent on doles from the state exchequer. And if these freebies amount to cutting down investments, it slows down the process of growth and the people remain stuck in a low-income trap. There is an old saying: 'equipping people to catch fish is far better than giving them fish every day.' Preparing people to catch fish requires crafting a vision, chalking out a strategy, guiding

*Ashok Gulati is Infosys Chair Professor for Agriculture at the Indian Council for Research on International Economic Relations (ICRIER), and former Chairman of the Commission for Agricultural Costs and Prices (CACP), Government of India.

the implementation of various programmes and following them up all the way, till they deliver results.

It is in this context that the performance of the agriculture sector becomes crucial, because the largest number of working population in India, and in most states, is still engaged in agriculture. As per the Census of 2001, Gujarat's agriculture sector engaged 51.6 per cent of its working population in the sector, which came down to 49.6 per cent in the 2011 Census. Augmenting incomes of farmers also helps to raise incomes of landless agri-labourers via higher wages, which together create a base for sustainable demand for manufactured products, thus providing an impetus to industrial growth. Agriculture also provides food and nutritional security for the masses.

Narendra Modi became the Chief Minister of Gujarat on 7 October 2001, and then, the Prime Minister on 26 May 2014. Accordingly, we look at the performance of Gujarat's agriculture during his regime from 2001–02 to 2013–14, and that of all India from 2014–15 to 2020–21.

THE AGRARIAN MIRACLE

We have compared Gujarat's agri-performance with other states to see if the state did better or worse than most of the other major states of India. This was a test of the vision and strategy of Modi as the Chief Minister of Gujarat to benefit the largest segment of the state's population.

The best way to measure the performance of agriculture is to look at the average annual growth rate of the state-level agri-GDP. Going by this, for the period 2001–02 to 2013–14, which is a long enough time to account for variations in rainfall, one finds that Gujarat's agriculture registered the highest growth rate (of 9.2 per cent per annum) amongst all major states of India (Figure-1).

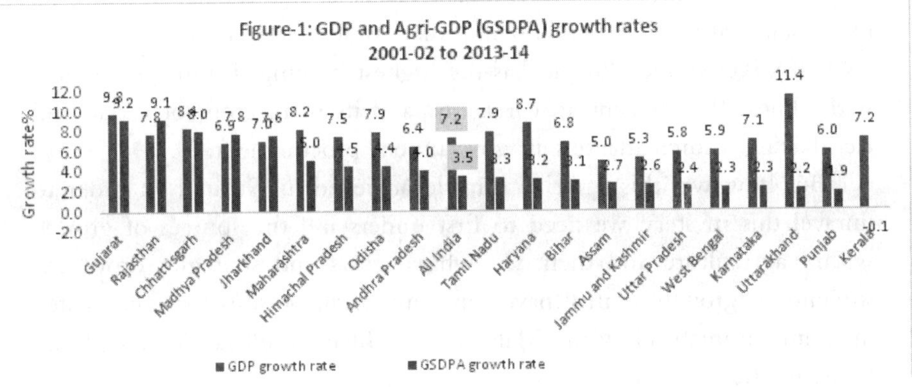

Source: Calculated from the data published by MOSPI (Ministry of Statistics and Programme Implementation)

This level of growth (9.2 per cent per annum) in agriculture, over a thirteen-year-long period is unheard of in Indian history. It was even far higher than what Punjab achieved during its heydays of the green revolution. When juxtaposed against an all India agri-GDP growth of 3.5 per cent, and agriculturally more progressive state such as Punjab (at 1.9 per cent), Gujarat's agricultural performance under Modi was nothing short of an agrarian miracle.

Interestingly, this also helped Gujarat to achieve an overall GDP growth of 9.8 per cent during the same period, next only to Uttarakhand at 11.4 per cent—but way above the all-India GDP growth of 7.2 per cent per annum. The most unique feature of Gujarat's growth story under Modi's leadership was that its overall GDP growth (9.8 per cent per annum) and agri-GDP growth (9.2 per cent per annum) were so high and so close to each other that no other state could qualify for that distinction. It is important to note this as it indicates that Gujarat's growth during Modi's tenure as Chief Minister was more inclusive than perhaps any other state. No wonder it gave rich political dividends too, and Modi was elected the Chief Minister three consecutive times. So, here is a lesson for many state leaders to follow. Focusing on agriculture can be good economics as well as good politics.

As a result of this growth in agriculture, the average monthly income of a farming household in Gujarat stood at ₹11,899 in 2015–16, which was the fourth highest (after Punjab, Haryana and Kerala) amongst all major states, as per NABARD's All India Rural Financial Inclusion Survey (NAFIS). Remember, Punjab has the highest holding size in the country, with almost 99 per cent area irrigated and its main crops of wheat and rice having assured markets in government procurement.

But how was this agrarian miracle achieved in Gujarat? In order to unravel this mystery, we need to first understand the sources of growth within agriculture and then, see what factors and strategies drove the stupendous growth. It may have some important lessons for other states, including Punjab, Haryana, Maharashtra, Bihar, Madhya Pradesh, Uttar Pradesh, etc.

The Gujarat Cooperative Milk Marketing Federation (GCMMF), with its premier brand of AMUL, is already famous for its robust and inclusive performance. Its milk procurement is the highest in the country. There is no minimum support price (MSP) for milk announced by the government, but it is negotiated within the cooperative network, keeping in mind the retail prices of milk and milk products and the costs of producing milk. Milk production in Gujarat increased from 5.9 million tonnes in 2001–02 to 11.1 million tonnes in 2013–14. However, the share of livestock in Gujarat's overall gross value of agricultural produce hovered around 26 per cent between triennium ending (TE) 2002–03 and TE 2015–16. But the real change in relative shares came from fibres (cotton), increasing from 5.9 per cent to 12.7 percent; fruits and vegetables, from 10.9 per cent to 16.7 per cent; condiments and spices from 2.2 per cent to 4.7 per cent; and forestry and logging from 2.4 per cent to 5.9 per cent during TE 2002–03 to TE 2015–16 (Figure-2).

Figure-2: Sector-wise shares in total value of output from agriculture and allied activities (at current prices)

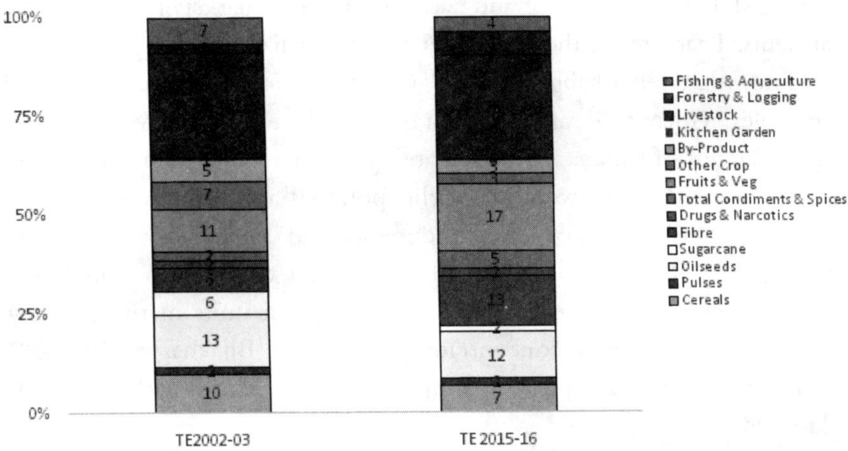

Source: Calculated from MOSPI data (see Gulati, Roy and Hussain, 2021)

Thus, the real revolution in Gujarat's agriculture came from cotton, triggered by adoption of Bt cotton. Although Bt cotton became controversial in Andhra Pradesh and Maharashtra, and some activists even held it responsible for farmers' suicides in Maharashtra, the Gujarat story was that of a great success. If one compares Maharashtra and Gujarat for the results of Bt cotton, Gujarat's cotton yields were almost double that of Maharashtra. The reason was that Gujarat was able to increase irrigation coverage to almost 57 per cent of the cotton area, while in Maharashtra it hovered around just 3 per cent. No wonder, in Maharashtra, Bt cotton involved high risk in case of monsoon failure, while in Gujarat it brought about overall prosperity to peasants.

It is well known that seeds of Bt cotton came from Monsanto-Mahyco (Monsanto has now been taken over by Bayer). By now, almost 95 per cent of cotton area in the country is under Bt. It was becaus of Bt cotton that India emerged as the largest cotton-producing count and by 2011–12 it had also emerged as the second-largest exporter cotton. Initially, much of the exports of cotton bales were going to C but lately that has been diversified to Bangladesh, Vietnam, many countries, and also into higher value exports of yarn. Narendra Modi, as the Chief Minister, had a dream of making Gujarat a hub of integrated value chain of cotton, linking farms (raw cotton) to factory (yarn, fabric, garments), fashion designing and accessing foreign markets for high-value garments. That dream, though, is yet to materialize.

The other remarkable progress was in the production of fruits and vegetables. Gujarat became the largest producer of papayas and the second-largest of banana, pomegranate and sapota. High-value vegetables such as beans (largest producer), garlic, potatoes and brinjals, saw robust growth. So did much of the condiments and spices, especially jeera (cumin). An interesting phenomenon of Gujarat was seen in dehydrated onions. Almost 80 per cent of onion dehydration units in the country were in Gujarat, mostly concentrated in Mahuva, Bhavnagar district. It reveals the innovative spirit of Gujarati entrepreneurs, with focus on value addition.

One may ask: what was Narendra Modi's contribution in all of this? Here is a list of some important things that he did as Chief Minister, which helped trigger the agricultural revolution in Gujarat.

The first was the focus on water and power, with a view to get more crop from every drop of water. It was not just expediting the arrival of Narmada waters but also significantly scaling up check dams, bori bund, khet talavadi and micro-irrigation (drip and sprinklers). In 2005, the Gujarat government launched the Gujarat Green Revolution Company Limited (GGRC) to promote micro-irrigation as an integral part of the state government's Jal Sanchay Abhiyan. It provided a subsidy on micro-irrigation to the tune of 70 per cent or ₹70,000 per hectare, whichever was less. These measures helped increase the irrigation cover of cropped area from 33.3 per cent in 2001–02 to 47.6 per cent in 2013–14—nearly a 43 per cent jump in irrigation coverage. Contrast this with the all-India picture, where the irrigation cover went up from 41.7 to 47.7 per cent over the same period, a growth of just 14 per cent. The significant increase in irrigation cover in Gujarat gave the farmers a lifeline against droughts, increased their productivity and recharged groundwater.

Gujarat is perhaps the only state where the groundwater situation improved drastically, and it was during the Narendra Modi period as Chief Minister. As per the Central Ground Water Board, there were only 97 talukas in 2004 that were safe for groundwater exploitation. This number increased to 156 in 2009 and to 175 in 2013. Simultaneously, semi-critical talukas reduced from 69 to just 9 over the same period from 2004 to 2013 (see Table-1).

Table-1
Status of groundwater development in different talukas in Gujarat (2004–2013)

	Safe	Semi-Critical	Critical	Over-Exploited	Stage of Ground Water Development (%)
2004	97 (43%)	69 (31%)	12 (5%)	31 (14%)	76%
2009	156 (70%)	20 (9%)	6 (3%)	27 (12%)	75%
2013	175 (78%)	9 (4%)	6 (3%)	23 (10%)	68%

Source: Central Ground Water Development Board

It was a remarkable success story of water conservation in a state that has 75 per cent of its cropped area categorized as arid and semi-arid. The accomplishment needs to be emulated by states like Maharashtra, Karnataka, Rajasthan, etc. that suffer from acute water shortages. In contrast, in a state such as Punjab, which has almost 99 per cent irrigation cover, the water table has been depleting at an alarming rate, almost by 30 cm a year! This is primarily caused by a policy of free power and a massive paddy cultivation on more than 3 million hectares, emitting large amounts of greenhouse gases (methane and nitrous oxide) during its growth period and carbon dioxide through stubble burning after harvest, choking millions for breath.

The comparison brings us to power sector reforms in agriculture. Gujarat, under Modi's leadership, introduced the Jyoti Gram Yojana in 2003 on a pilot basis and later, scaled it up to the state level. Before 2003, the situation on the power front in Gujarat was as bad as in most other states. There were common power lines for agriculture, households, commercial or manufacturing purposes. This often led to large leakages as the tariffs for agriculture were much lower and the share of agriculture in the state's total power consumption was accounted on a residual basis. It resulted in unreliable and poor-quality power to rural areas.

The Gujarat government separated out feeders for rural areas, supplied 24x7 power supply to rural households and rationed supplies to agriculture for eight hours a day with pre-announced schedules. This changed the landscape of power supply in rural areas.

The leakages were getting plugged, and the share of agriculture in the total power consumption declined from 36.3 per cent in 2002–03 to 25.4 per cent by 2013–14. Farmers were happy as they were getting good quality, assured supplies without interruptions for eight hours with pre-announced schedules; and rural households in Gujarat became the first ones to get 24x7 supplies. This released more supplies for commercial and manufacturing sector on a paid basis, thus improving the financial situation of the power sector. The reform in rural power supplies is an example that many other states could follow to plug massive leakages, improve the quality of power being supplied to agriculture without increasing tariffs (with rationing), and in the process, improve the financial sustainability of the power sector.

Another factor that led to the success of agriculture was the high and sustained focus on rural roads. Although the Pradhan Mantri Gram Sadak Yojana (PMGSY) was launched in 2000, linking all rural markets and paving these roads was a major task done under the Narendra Modi government. By March 2015, the length of PMGSY roads was 18,441 km, and 92 per cent of rural roads were surfaced in Gujarat, significantly higher than the national average of 61 per cent. There have been studies by IFPRI (Fan, et.al. 2007) showing that investments in rural roads give rich dividends to farmers. Pucca rural roads improve the prices for their produce through access to larger and far-off markets, while the cost of getting inputs reduces. This makes agriculture much more competitive and remunerative than the case would otherwise be with poor quality or an absence of rural roads.

Lastly, I do want to mention about an innovative model of agri-extension that was unique to Gujarat: Krushi Mahotsav. As Chief Minister, Modi placed emphasis on agri-extension, where he involved almost all agri-extension departmental people, asking them to move to villages for a month or so before the major sowing season began. Krushi raths (agri-vehicles) would visit all villages of Gujarat, and the government officials would hold meetings with farmers, telling them about the availability of latest seeds, farming practices, etc. This was a massive mobilization drive, often kick-started by the Chief Minister at the start of the sowing season. The private sector also wanted to display its latest products to farmers, and this helped bridge the gap between lab and land, resulting in improved choices of seeds and other inputs at cost-effective rates, thereby, improving productivity. Some states did try to emulate this model with varying degrees of success.

To sum up, Narendra Modi's tenure as Chief Minister saw the highest growth in agri-GDP (9.2 per cent per annum) and second-highest growth in overall state GDP (9.8 per cent per annum in Gujarat). No other state had achieved this twin balance of high growth with inclusiveness. And on top of this, his policies and their implementation improved the groundwater table in Gujarat, making agriculture sustainable and climate resilient, which is the crying need of the hour. No wonder that it came to be called the 'Gujarat Model'. It was on the basis of the Gujarat Model of economic development that Modi catapulted himself to the national scene, getting elected as Member of Parliament and then taking over as the Prime Minister of India on 26 May 2014. This was also a first—in the sense that no other state leader had directly jumped from the position of a Chief Minister to that of a Prime Minister—in Indian history.

AGRICULTURE UNDER PM MODI

Before we look at the performance of agriculture under Modi as the Prime Minister, it may be worth recalling that, as per our Constitution, agriculture is primarily a state subject. But there are certain policies related to agri-food sector that have historically been within the purview of the Union government. For example, the policy of food and fertilizer subsidy, the policy of Minimum Support Prices (MSP), the procurement of some selected agri-products, the policy of external trade in agri-commodities, etc. All these do impact the performance of agriculture. Besides these, there are policies and programmes that are often jointly handled by the Central government and the state government. For example, the programmes related to agri-research and education, crop insurance, soil testing, agri-marketing (e-NAM), etc. Nevertheless, the primary responsibility of the performance of agriculture lies with state chief ministers.

The Modi government has completed seven and a half years at the Centre. What has been its record with respect to agriculture? It is interesting to note that the growth rate of agri-GDP of India as a whole was 3.5 per cent per annum during the first seven years of Modi government (2014–15 to 2020–21). This is only marginally higher than the long-term trend of about 3.2 per cent per annum in agriculture. But one must also note that it has been achieved despite the first two years, 2014–15 and 2015–16, of the Modi government turning out to be successive drought years. Back-to-back droughts are like black swan events, which have occurred only three times in the past hundred years! So, achieving an overall average growth of 3.5 per cent per annum for seven years against this backdrop is a reasonably fair accomplishment.

But there was an important learning from these two successive droughts. The Modi government took some bold decisions to tackle the problem of droughts. First, it revamped and launched the Pradhan Mantri Fasal Bima Yojana (PMFBY) in April 2016, whereby the Centre and the states together would subsidize almost 90 per cent of the insurance premium for the farmers, with the Centre and the states equally contributing. Second, it identified ninety-nine irrigation projects that could be completed on a priority basis by 2020, ensuring that financial resources wouldn't be a constraint. Both these measures were to give protection and resilience to farmers against the risk of droughts. However, the implementation modalities of both these programmes were largely dependent on the states.

The results are somewhat mixed, indicating the complexities of operating and implementing agricultural programmes in a federal structure. In a separate paper on crop insurance, we have shown how many states deviated from the Central guidelines and were still insuring farmers when the Indian Meteorological Department (IMD) had given its first forecast about the monsoon. That nullifies the logic of crop insurance. As a result, the re-insurers kept the premiums high. While one does expect some teething problems when a large programme is started with states, some of the operational problems continue. And some states have started getting out of the PMFBY, which does not bode well for the farmers as they will be left high and dry when a severe drought hits. Progress on the irrigation front for the completion of ninety-nine priority projects is also on a somewhat delayed track, indicating that state governments cannot gear up to the expectations of the Centre while implementing these projects, or maybe the Centre has been over-ambitious.

The Modi government also initiated several new schemes, ranging from e-NAM (electronic platform for National Agriculture Market) in 2016 to APLM (Agricultural Produce and Livestock Marketing Promotion and Facilitation) Act in 2017, to Gramin Agricultural Markets (GrAM) in 2018–19, and so on. It also linked the MSP of crops to Cost A2 plus Family Labour costs, with a minimum margin of 50 per cent above cost. In 2019, the government launched the PM-KISAN (Pradhan Mantri Kisan Samman Nidhi), which is basically a direct income transfer of ₹6,000 per farming household.

And then, in 2020, the Modi government passed the three farm laws to liberalize agri-marketing in the country. These were: the Farmers Produce Trade and Commerce (Promotion and Facilitation) Act, 2020 (FPTC); the Farmers (Empowerment and Protection) Agreement on Price Assurance and Farm Services Act, 2020 (FAPAFS); and the Essential Commodities (Amendment) Act, 2020 (ECA). All these three laws needed to be assessed holistically to get the real intent behind them. But somehow a narrative was created that these farm laws were not in the interest of the farmers, and then after a year of protests by the farmers, these laws were repealed by the Modi government in November 2021.

However, if agriculture has to progress, India needs more efficient value chains for the farmers, where farmers can get a larger percentage of what consumers pay. This is especially so in the case of perishable fruits and vegetables. For that to happen, India needs to create Farmer Producer Organizations (FPOs) and invest in marketing infrastructure. In that context, it was good to see that Prime Minister Modi announced the creation of ten thousand additional FPOs and Agriculture Infrastructure Fund (AIF) of ₹1 lakh crore (₹1 trillion) for handling post-harvest produce. The responsibility of implementing this lies with NABARD and SFAC.

Some other re-organizational efforts in the agri-sphere under Modi 2.0, were the creation of a Ministry of Fisheries, Animal Husbandry and

Dairying vide its notification on 17 June 2019, showing the growing importance of these in the overall agriculture landscape, and the creation of a Ministry for Cooperation in July 2021, to give a push to the cooperative movement.

If one were to assess some notable achievements of Modi government in the field of agriculture, one may list the following:

- Pulses production, which had been a tough nut to crack, increased from 19.25 million tonnes in 2013–14 to about 26 million tonnes in 2020–21. It has helped reduce imports of pulses to almost half of what they were in earlier years. The Modi government has also done a record procurement of pulses through NAFED, which has helped farmers realize better prices for pulses.
- The Modi government has also done record procurement of wheat and rice, and scaled new peaks in grain stocks with the Food Corporation of India (FCI), which touched 110 million tonnes in July 2021. This is way above the buffer stock norm of 41.1 million tonnes, which is needed to feed the public distribution system (PDS) as well as guard against any risk of drought.
- Record distribution of grains (79 million tonnes) under PDS and *Pradhan Mantri Garib Kalyan Anna Yojana*, and record food and fertilizer subsidy bill of ₹6.52 lakh crore or ₹6.52 trillion in 2020–21, which amounts to 38.5 per cent of all the revenue of the Union government, net of states' share. This has perhaps never happened in India's economic history since independence. While one recognizes that it was a pandemic year, and millions lost their jobs and needed big financial/food support, this level of support may not be financially sustainable in the years to come. One needs to do some serious thinking about how best to reform the regime of food and fertilizer subsidies in a manner that the basic objectives of supporting poor consumers and small farmers are satisfied at a much lower cost than what is currently being incurred. Our work at ICRIER (Indian Council for Research on International Economic Relations) on these issues reflects that we need to move towards direct cash transfers, i.e. give food and fertilizer subsidies directly to the accounts of identified

beneficiaries, and let people buy grains and other food items from the markets and let farmers buy fertilizers at market prices.

- This policy switch, from highly subsidized price policy to direct income support to beneficiaries, would stop massive leakages in the public distribution system as well as in fertilizer distribution (especially urea), and would be much more efficient and cost effective than the present system. If Modi can get this right, his government can easily save minimum of ₹50,000 crore (₹500 billion) each year without compromising on the objectives of helping the poor and small farm holders. This saving can be used to increase expenditures on agri-R&D (agricultural research and development), infrastructure in rural areas, innovation funds for agriculture, and so on, which will help create vibrant and competitive agriculture besides creating higher productivity jobs and augmenting farmers' incomes.
- On foreign trade of agricultural produce, in 2020–21, India had a surplus of $20 billion, with exports touching $41.8 billion and imports at $21.6 billion. India has emerged as the largest exporter of rice at 17.7 million tonnes worth $8.8 billion, comprising more than 35 percent of global rice trade. And our agri-export basket is quite diversified, from fish to spices to sugar, and so on. However, our imports are quite concentrated. Edible oil imports alone in 2020-21 were to the tune of $11.1 billion (13.5 million tonnes) and pulses were of $1.6 billion (2.4 million tonnes). As indicated earlier, Modi government has been able to reduce the imports of pulses from 5.6 million tonnes in 2017–18 to 2.4 million tonnes in 2020–21, largely by increasing pulses production. A similar attempt is being made in the case of edible oils and the Prime Minister has announced a new mission for edible oils with focus on oil palm worth ₹11,000 crore or ₹110 billion. India has roughly 2 million hectares identified as suitable for oil palm but only about 300,000 hectares has been tapped so far. The government needs to develop a right strategy to achieve self-sufficiency in edible oils by increasing productivity, and making India a globally competitive producer of oilseeds and edible oils.

Overall, to wrap up, the performance of Indian agriculture under Narendra Modi as the Chief Minister was spectacular—almost a miracle—with 9.2 per cent growth over a thirteen-year period. But in his tenure as Prime Minister of the country for the past seven years, agriculture performance has been 3.5 per cent per annum, which is only marginally higher than the long-term trend of 3.2 per cent. Several new initiatives have been undertaken, and one can only hope that they will show better results in due course.

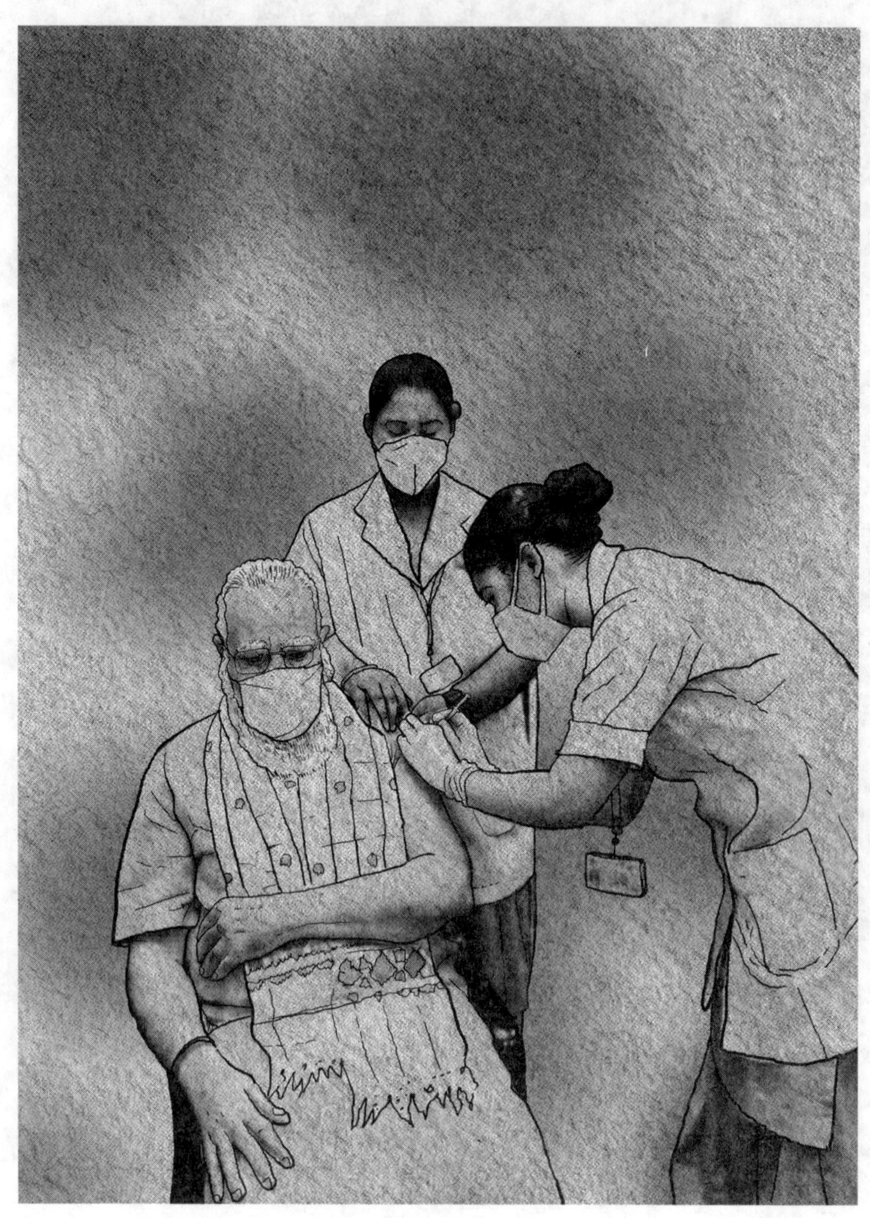

FIGHTING THE PANDEMIC: LEADING FROM THE FRONT

DR DEVI SHETTY

The COVID-19 pandemic is arguably the biggest challenge that Prime Minister Narendra Modi has faced in the two decades he has spent in elected office. It has also been the greatest challenge that we as a nation and the world have encountered in the last century. In early 2020, less than a year after Modi's second term started, a global public health threat exploded with the SARS-CoV-2 or the COVID-19 virus. The pandemic endangered countless lives across the globe. Besides, it led to an unprecedented curtailment of economic activity. It is not an exaggeration to say that everyday life as we know it, has not been the same since the pandemic took hold of the world. By the end of December 2021, more than 3.48 crore (34.8 million) Indians had been infected by the coronavirus. Unfortunately, more than 4.8 lakh or 480,000 citizens lost their lives as a result[1].

Nonetheless, a global comparison of India's COVID-19 statistics belies the dismal picture being painted by many within our country. We have fared better than many of the most developed countries. In India, there have been 24,879 cases per million citizens. This figure is more than five times that in the US and the UK—at 1,48,817 and 1,56,458 respectively. In Europe, there have been more than 1,03,728 COVID-19 cases per million citizens. Similarly, the number of deaths per million in India—340—is far lower than in other countries. In the US and the UK, 2383 and 2147 deaths per million people respectively have been recorded[2].

Over the last two years, Prime Minister Modi has worked tirelessly to overcome the unprecedented challenge. India has revamped a health system neglected for more than seven decades, provided an economic package incomparable to any stimulus given in the past, and launched the world's largest vaccination drive. To evaluate India's COVID-19 management, it is helpful to look back and recall our entire journey during the pandemic. It is important to note where did we start from and where have we reached. This chapter reflects on India's fight against COVID-19 under Modi's leadership.

TIMELY ACTION

In the case of rapidly transmitting infectious diseases, the initial response has sharp path-dependency. By ensuring a timely response and robust COVID-19 management early on, India managed to prevent a severe crisis at that time. Globally, India was one of the first countries to start regular monitoring of the emerging situation in China and planning a response strategy in the case of a potential global outbreak.

On December 31, 2019, the first cluster of pneumonia cases was reported in Wuhan, Hubei Province of China. Less than a month later, India recorded its first COVID-19 case on January 30, 2020[3]. A young student who had returned from China to her home in Thrissur, Kerala, had tested positive. But even before the first recorded case, our COVID-19 management and response strategy had been put into action.

Top government officials were tracking the developments in China and maintaining regular communication with the Prime Minister's Office (PMO). From January 2020 itself, Modi was personally overseeing the situation and ensuring an adequate government response. India's institutional response to COVID-19 had started in January itself, as the Indian Council of Medical Research (ICMR) and the National Centre for Disease Control (NCDC) started tracking returnees from China and monitoring COVID-19 testing. The World Health Organization (WHO) eventually declared COVID-19 as a pandemic on 11 March 2020[4]. By then, India already had a formal institutional mechanism for COVID-19 response, and top public health experts and medical professionals in the country were directly involved in monitoring the situation and planning the country's COVID-19 strategy.

Moreover, the government had started active measures such as screening at airports, creating awareness about COVID-19 and its related symptoms, building additional testing infrastructure, and providing isolation facilities across the country to prevent a surge in cases and reducing transmission. Imagine the state of India's COVID-19 management if we had waited too long before responding.

The Modi government had already put in place a 'whole of government' approach to overcome the emerging challenge. Apart from the health ministry, numerous other ministries were involved in managing the pandemic and the accompanying challenges. The Ministry of External Affairs (MEA) and the Civil Aviation Ministry ensured that India was among the first countries to safely evacuate its citizens from China. The Civil Aviation Ministry closely observed global response and travel restrictions and initiated action. The Home Ministry was involved to ensure the preparation for imposing COVID-19 restrictions. Various ministries like Chemicals and Fertilizers (Department of Pharmaceuticals), Commerce, Textile, and MSMEs had already been told to ensure adequate supply of essential items and achieve manifold increase in domestic production. Prime Minister Modi ensured that these ministries worked in tandem and synchronized their efforts to ensure best results.

THE NATIONAL LOCKDOWN

As the COVID-19 situation worsened globally and cases continued to rise, the Modi government imposed a complete national lockdown from March 25, 2020. A day earlier, Modi addressed the nation and announced the nationwide lockdown[5]. In March 2020, Modi reached out to various sections of the society through religious leaders, healthcare professionals, radio jockeys (RJs), journalists, etc. to create awareness about COVID-19. Cognizant about the emerging situation, he decided to refrain from participating in Holi festivities. Around a week before Holi, Modi tweeted and announced his decision of avoiding Holi gatherings.[6]

The Modi government realized that adequate preparedness and controlling the spread of infections required a lockdown. Eventually, the Prime Minister took the bold decision of imposing a hard lockdown.

A lot of people, especially from the medical fraternity, had pushed for the implementing of a lockdown. But it was not an easy decision, and there were many difficult questions. How to ensure that the marginalized would be able to sustain their livelihood? How to ensure that the supply chains keep running? How to convince people to stay at home?

Most countries made the mistake of implementing a lockdown after the virus had spread, making it difficult for everyone. India timed the lockdown perfectly, implementing it when there were only a few cases. As per an Oxford University study, India's lockdown was also one of the most stringent in the world[7].

Contrary to the narrative created by some people, the lockdown was not done arbitrarily or suddenly. Modi perhaps understands the psyche of the people better than most others. He knew that the concept of a complete lockdown was alien to citizens of this country, and that people needed to be prepared for it. And so, he announced a 'Janata Curfew' on 22 March and urged citizens to stay indoors on that day[8]. The Janata Curfew, in a way, served to acclimatize people to the concept of a lockdown. In fact, 24 states had already announced some sort of lockdowns before the Prime Minister announced the national lockdown.

The 21-day national lockdown started on 25 March. It was extended thrice and lasted a total of 68 days[9]. All economic activity except essential services was suspended. The complete lockdown disrupted everyday life for all—the rich and the poor.

We must realize that Modi and his government had absolutely no choice when they had decided on the lockdown. It was and remains the most appropriate decision given the circumstances and the availability of information at that time. In March 2020, we didn't have a complete picture of the dreadful virus and how it behaved, or affected the human body. We had glimpses of photographs from China, Italy and other COVID-19-hit countries—dead bodies left unattended along the corridors of hospitals. There was limited knowledge about the contagiousness of the disease, the disease's transmission, treatment, medical infrastructure requirements and our preparedness. Not only India but countries across the globe had similar concerns and worries. Globally, a complete lockdown was viewed as the only path for countries to arrest transmission and prepare the healthcare system. Public health experts also supported the decision and considered it to be the right thing to do.

Finally, while discussing the impact of the lockdown, we should be mindful of the unobserved counterfactual. There was a high likelihood of the situation worsening and cases rising before adequate preparations were made, if a complete lockdown was not imposed. Perhaps, the surge in cases would have started sooner and turned out to be far worse than it actually did. While announcing the complete lockdown, Prime Minister Modi clearly stated the government's priorities—'Jaan hai toh jahan hai'[10]. The objective of India's lockdown was clear. The country was ready to bear the economic costs as long as lives were protected

COVID-19 APPROPRIATE BEHAVIOUR

The high transmissibility of COVID-19 infections makes COVID-19 appropriate behaviour necessary to prevent the rapid spread of the disease. Achieving mass adherence to COVID-19 appropriate behaviour was always going to be a stiff challenge for the country. Finding practical solutions required a holistic understanding of the problem and communicating it effectively.

Anyone who has closely observed how the Prime Minister has steered India through this crisis, will realise how he has leveraged a mix of gentle nudges along with easy to understand language to sensitize and guide people's behaviour. For example, how do you explain the word 'pandemic' or the meaning of 'social distancing' to 130 crore Indians? How do you ensure social distancing in a country which has one of the highest population densities in the world? How does one keep the people of the country as well as our healthcare workers motivated during the 68 days of the lockdown? These were questions that I think Modi thought long and hard on, as it shows in his actions. He used the phrase, 'Corona Vaishwik Mahamari', to stress the gravity of the situation. He also explained social distancing through 'Do gaj ki doori', which people understood. By using 'Jaan hai to Jahan hai' and then 'Jaan bhi, Jahan bhi' the Prime Minister explained thousands of words' worth knowledge in the shortest and easiest manner possible.

Many people were surprised at and some even mocked his call to light a lamp (diya) and compliment healthcare workers by playing on utensils (thaali) and with claps (taali). Yes, these gestures weren't supposed to drive Corona away. But they acted as a binding force for 130 crore people who were stuck at homes in despondency in a once-in-a century pandemic. They helped reached the last mile in informing people about the grim situation. They helped light a flame of hope, optimism and positivity in people who did not know what would happen next. They also inspired thousands of healthcare workers to keep working hard for the people, without caring for their own families. The diya, the taali and the thaali were strong symbols of human resistance against an unknown enemy. India was perhaps at its lowest point, not sure of what lay ahead, but a true leader is who gives 130 crore countrymen hope even in such circumstances.

Since January 2020, we have come a long way in generating public awareness and sensitization. Today, even a local kirana store ensures that customers stand in a queue with some distancing. A roadside vegetable vendor allows customers to pay through a UPI QR code to avoid exchanging currency notes.

A MAKE IN INDIA SUCCESS STORY

In early 2020, India was unprepared for a large-scale viral pandemic. There was a severe shortfall of medical supplies and infrastructure from testing facilities to basic supplies like N95 masks and PPEs, from ventilators to hospital beds. The gap needed to be bridged urgently if India wanted to overcome the COVID-19 challenge. Within a few months, the Modi government managed a successful turnaround by scaling up domestic production.

RT-PCR is the standard test used to confirm the diagnosis of COVID-19. When the pandemic started, only one lab in India—NIV Pune—could conduct RT-PCR tests for COVID-19. In March 2020, when COVID-19 numbers began increasing in India, we had 52 labs to diagnose the disease[11]. Concentrated efforts by the ICMR, the Ministry of Health, and the National Accreditation Board for Testing and Calibration Laboratories (NABL) led to ramping up of testing facilities. Within a few months, there were 1,364 government-approved labs with RT-PCR testing facilities across the country[12]. Currently, we have more than 3,000 labs across the country[13]. Apart from RT-PCR tests, we have an ample supply of rapid testing kits. This has improved COVID-19 management as we can efficiently conduct random[14] testing in hotspots and crowded public places like railway stations, airports, etc. The success often gets lost in numbers and statistics, but it has been nothing but a superlative effort by all arms of the government to build capacity in such a short time.

This testing infrastructure would improve the country's healthcare in the long run. Most public hospitals, even those in small towns, now have RT-PCR testing. Post-COVID-19, these labs will detect viral diseases like Hepatitis C and HIV early, apart from genetic diseases and cancer. Early detection of these dreadful diseases can result in virtual cures with minimal cost, especially in rural India.

When the pandemic started in 2020, there was a shortage of basic supplies like N95 masks and PPE kits for our healthcare and frontline workers. I was shocked when I heard instances of young doctors in the ICU wrapping themselves with old raincoats and covering their faces with motorcycle helmets as protective gear. The domestic production of PPE suits and N95 masks was extremely low, with very few domestic manufacturers. The pandemic triggered a global shortage, and exports had ceased to arrive. India could not rely on imports to bridge the domestic shortfall. Such a severe shortfall not too long ago seems unrealistic if we compare it to the current situation. India has become the world's second-biggest producer of PPE overalls! We have become a major exporter of PPE overalls and N95 masks. Today, N95 masks are available at affordable rates, even at local pharmacies. Healthcare workers across the country have an ample supply of PPE overalls.

This turnaround did not happen overnight. Prime Minister Modi's holistic approach towards governance led to this manifold increase in production. The Ministry of Textiles focused on increasing the production of PPE kits. Ministry officials and industrial bodies actively engaged with manufacturers across the country and encouraged them to produce PPE suits and N95 masks. The government offered active assistance and support, from technical know-how to overcoming regulatory hurdles. Currently, there are more than 600 domestic manufacturers of PPE suits, unthinkable when the pandemic started last year[15].

Soon after we started treating severe COVID-19 patients, the medical fraternity realized that ICU beds with ventilators would be necessary for treating patients. This information was passed on to the Union government, and they took swift action.

At the beginning of the pandemic, the country had just about 17,850 ventilators in public hospitals[16]. The government needed to urgently ensure the installation of thousands of ventilators. However, India lacked production capacity and was almost entirely dependent on imports from Europe and China. Making matters worse, importing from abroad ceased to be an option as all countries were trying to augment domestic ventilator capacity. The Modi government was swift in considering all options and finding solutions.

In April-May 2020 itself, orders were placed for more than 50,000 ventilators, almost three times the existing capacity before the pandemic. Moreover, these were to be paid for entirely by the Central government through the PM CARES fund, and distributed to state governments for installation in public hospitals[17]. Modi had got into action and, like always, transformed the scale of public provisioning. The Health Ministry worked alongside other central agencies on a mission mode to augment the domestic supply of ventilators. A design for an indigenous ventilator was created. The public sector Bharat Electronics Limited was asked to manufacture and supply 30,000 ventilators[18]. Various private manufacturers were identified and given technical and logistical assistance in starting the production of ventilators. The government acted as a facilitator and ensured regulatory hurdles in production were cleared. Nothing short of a miracle was achieved, and free ventilators were supplied to public hospitals across the country. From 17,000 ventilators in public hospitals before the pandemic, the number rose to 50,000. Many states could successfully expand their capacity multiple times through these new ventilators.

The significant increase in production of N95 masks, PPE suits, ventilators, and expansion of testing capacity are 'Make in India' success stories. The self-sufficiency in supply has taken India a step closer to achieving Modi's goal of building an Aatmanirbhar Bharat.

THE SECOND COVID-19 WAVE

In April-May 2021, India suffered a brutal second COVID-19 wave. The highly transmissible Delta variant led to the second wave. As we have seen in the last few months, the Delta variant has wreaked havoc across the globe, including countries that had managed high vaccination coverage before the spread of the new variant. As is always the case, doctors, administrators and also the government feel that we could have done better. However, the Delta variant was a new beast altogether. India was the first to witness to its wrath, but as it spread, even the developed countries faced similar shortages and overwhelmed hospitals.

During the second COVID-19 wave, the entire healthcare system was tested as the demand for medical infrastructure and supplies increased exponentially. The Prime Minister led from the front and led the country out of the crisis. Various ministries, Central government organizations, and state governments worked in tandem to ensure necessary medical supplies.

Since the early days of the pandemic, India had institutionalized COVID-19 monitoring through the ICMR and the NCDC. The regular tracking ensured that, unlike many governments, India was not caught unawares when COVID-19 cases started rising. Being actively involved in treating COVID-19, I regularly followed government advisories and COVID-19 management decisions. A cursory look at government advisories and actions in February–March 2021 will reveal that Prime Minister Modi was consistently overseeing the COVID-19 situation. On the contrary, the Central government was highly vigilant and actively oversaw COVID-19 management to minimize transmission and protect lives. Numerous advisories were issued to states where COVID-19 infections were rising during this period. Central government monitoring teams visited many states and provided detailed suggestions on COVID-19 management. Moreover, the Centre had even deployed district-level monitoring teams to prepare COVID-19 management strategies in high case-load states[19].

Globally, the Delta variant has posed an unprecedented challenge for governments. High transmissibility of the Delta variant led to a sharp surge in infections, to previously inconceivable levels, in a very short duration. This overburdened the healthcare system and led to a severe shortfall of critical supplies.

A critically ill COVID-19 patient's medical oxygen requirement can be as high as 86,000 litres per day. Hardly any known disease requires such large amounts of Oxygen to save the life of a single person. Imagine an entire hospital filled with such patients. Healthcare delivery systems across the world are designed to serve peak demand based on experience. What overwhelms hospital infrastructure is the flooding of patients in large numbers within a few days. Even an advanced healthcare system in North America and Europe would not have been able to withstand the demand pressure witnessed during the peak of COVID-19 second wave in India and across the world.

During the second wave, there were innumerable patients with severe COVID-19 and breathing difficulties. Medical oxygen was found to be in short supply as demand increased exponentially. Modi personally oversaw the Central government's efforts for equitable distribution of scarce medical oxygen across the country. As Prime Minister, he knew that he was responsible for the entire country and had to meet the demand from all states. However, limited production capacity wasn't the only challenge the government was facing. Delivering medical oxygen to the entire country was a logistical nightmare, incomparable to anything that the country had ever seen. The production of oxygen in India is concentrated in east India. From here, it had to be transported to the entire country. Using surface transportation was challenging as oxygen tankers would take a few days to reach hospitals in north and west, where the shortfall was acute. Many of the previously stifling policies were quickly changed to facilitate the transportation of oxygen from the production site to hospitals across the country.

Modi has always been known to provide novel solutions in crunch situations. The Central government roped in Indian Railways, the Indian Air Force, and the Indian Navy for assistance in oxygen transportation. The railways launched special trains—Oxygen Express—for delivering liquid medical oxygen across the country. Starting on 24 April Oxygen Expresses delivered more than 15,000 MT of oxygen across the country in less than a month[20]. A major challenge in the transportation of oxygen was the shortfall of cryogenic tankers and cylinders. The Air Force transported empty cryogenic tankers within the country and from abroad[21]. The government's strenuous efforts to increase medical oxygen production and facilitate transportation saved countless lives during the second wave. Significant loss of life was prevented as the government took up oxygen provisioning on a war footing.

The second wave also witnessed a shortfall of medicines and hospital beds. The Central government urgently and efficiently addressed all urgent appeals for help by state governments and assisted them in augmenting supply.

Though providing hospital beds is primarily a responsibility of state governments, the Centre did whatever it could to support the states in providing more hospital beds. In April 2021, the number of isolation beds and ICU beds was almost 154 times and 40 times respectively, higher as compared to early 2020 when the pandemic had started.

During the second wave, Modi's 'whole of government approach' led to various ministries mobilizing entities under them for operating special COVID-19 care centres and makeshift facilities across the country.

Makeshift facilities and field hospitals were started in Delhi by the Central government. For instance, In July 2020, the ITBP had opened the 10,000 bed Sardar Patel COVID-19 Care Centre in Delhi—the world's largest COVID-19 care facility[22]. During the second wave, the Centre decided to reopen this special centre and ensured deployment of adequate staff and other resources[23]. Moreover, more than 2,100 beds were provided for COVID-19 patients in Delhi through Central government hospitals during the second wave. Anticipating the surge in requirement, Central government hospitals in the city increased the number of beds for COVID-19 patients in Delhi by almost four times during the second wave as compared to early March[24].

Whenever there has been any crisis in the country, the defence forces have always been at the forefront. During the second wave, the Armed Forces Medical Services (AFMS), the Defence Research and Development Organisation (DRDO), Defence Public Sector Undertakings (DPSUs) and Cantonment Boards came together to increase the availability of hospital beds[25]. Military and AFMS hospitals across the country provided beds for civilian use. The DRDO set up special COVID-19 facilities in many cities across the country, including Delhi, Lucknow, Ahmedabad, and Patna, The Indian Army also provided hospital beds and special isolation facilities across the country. The armed forces helped in overcoming the severe shortage of medical and non-medical staff[26].

The Indian Railways made an ingenious intervention to augment availability of hospital beds. Nearly 4,000 railway coaches were converted to special COVID-19 care facilities. These could be easily moved and stationed across the country depending on state government requirements.

Collectively, these provided potentially 64,000 additional beds for COVID-19 patients[27].

The second COVID-19 wave was a tragic experience as innumerable lives were lost. Yet, looking back, one can confidently say that adequate efforts were made to save as many lives as possible and reduce public suffering.

WORLD'S LARGEST VACCINATION DRIVE

India is conducting the world's largest vaccination drive. We undertook an unprecedented challenge in human history, of vaccinating such a large population with multiple doses—and within a few months. Prime Minister Modi has worked tirelessly to fulfil his promise of '*Sabko Teeka, Muft Teeka*'.

How has the monumental exercise fared in India? As of 31 December 2021, more than 145 crore (1.45 billion) vaccines had been administered across the country. To understand the enormity better, here is a statistic: India has administered more vaccine doses than entire continents such as Europe, North America, South America, and Africa[28]. Over 90 per cent of eligible citizens had received at least one dose. About 60 per cent were vaccinated with both doses.[29] Numerous states and union territories have already achieved nearly 100 per cent first dose coverage among eligible citizens, and others remain on track. Himachal Pradesh became the first state to achieve full vaccine coverage among the eligible population[30]. The mammoth task of vaccinating the entire population has been proceeding at an unprecedented pace. It took just about nine months for the country to cross the 100 crore or 1 billion milestone. The vaccination pace has been increasing steadily in India. In the beginning, it took 85 days to administer the first ten crore doses. Now, close to ten crore (100 million) doses are administered every fortnight[31]. Since the Central government took over the entire vaccination drive, the pace has increased manifold. The number of doses administered monthly has also consistently increased[32].

More recently, the government has expanded the vaccination drive by covering the young between the age of 15 and 18 years, as well as announcing a 'booster' dose for frontline workers and those with co-morbidities.

Over two decades in office, Modi has focused on utilizing latest technologies and mass participation to improve governance. This has been visible in the vaccination programme also. For instance, the ICMR introduced drone-based delivery of vaccines in remote locations in the North-East and the Andaman and Nicobar Islands[33]. Further, to maintain the high vaccination rate and fully vaccinate the entire eligible population, he launched the 'Har Ghar Dastak' (Knock every door) drive[34]. The initiative involves the Prime Minister's 'whole of government approach' as post offices, schools, Anganwadis and other public institutions have been supporting healthcare workers in expanding vaccination[35].

The COVID-19 vaccination programme has been a paradigm shift despite unprecedented constraints and hurdles. It is incomparable to other programmes as it aims to achieve universal coverage. Moreover, the vaccine requires monitoring adverse effects, making it imperative to conduct vaccination in a medical establishment rather than door-to-door campaigns like the polio vaccine drive. Starting mass vaccination for COVID-19 alongside developed countries is in itself a historic achievement for India. It is a matter of pride that we are one of the few countries globally with multiple indigenously developed vaccines and self-sufficiency in domestic supply. This includes the world's first DNA vaccine—ZyCov-D, developed by Zydus Cadilla. Moreover, the vaccine distribution is being conducted through cutting-edge digital innovations like the CoWIN portal and dashboard.

This is a welcome change for the country, as there had long delays in introducing vaccines in India in numerous instances in the past. Despite sufficient market demand, the domestic manufacturing of vaccines took even longer. For example, polio vaccination abroad started in the mid-1950s. However, in India, mass immunization for polio began only in 1978. Unfortunately, despite the high prevalence of the disease and significant demand for vaccination, the country failed to build a domestic supply chain. As a result, for decades, we remained dependent on imported vaccine doses and struggled to eliminate polio[36].

Similarly, more than a decade after global introduction in 1982, India added the Hepatitis-B vaccine to the universal immunization programme. A vaccine for measles was rolled out globally in 1963. However, vaccine manufacturing and distribution in India did not happen till the 1980s. For COVID-19, we started vaccination less than a year after the first recorded infection. The entire journey took less than a year, from encountering a completely novel virus to administering the first dose of a domestically manufactured vaccine. The magnitude of this achievement should not be understated.

What has led to this historic effort and commendable success? Since last year, the Centre has been proactive in organizing the vaccination programme. It has left no stone unturned to ensure adequate vaccine supply, from supporting research and development of vaccines through initiatives like Mission COVID-19 Suraksha[37] to facilitating expansion in production by encouraging technology transfer and making advance payments.

The government provided financial, technical, and institutional support to multiple pharmaceutical firms trying to develop and manufacture vaccines in India. Modi has personally overseen the progress on vaccine development and regularly interacts with various manufacturers. In November 2020, he visited three vaccine manufacturers[38] and held a virtual conference with another three manufacturers to oversee vaccine development[39]. Since then, the Prime Minister has personally spoken to vaccine manufacturers on several occasions to address their concerns and extended complete government support. In addition, his government has given adequate assistance for vaccine research through Mission COVID-19 Suraksha.

Launched in November 2020, the Indian COVID-19 Vaccine Development Mission was expected to enable vaccine research development. The Modi government provided ₹900 crore (₹9 billion) for these efforts[40]. Moreover, public institutions under the aegis of the Centre, such as the ICMR, supported vaccine manufacturers in vaccine research and conducting clinical trials.

The launch of Covaxin, developed jointly by Bharat Biotech and the ICMR, was a landmark achievement for the entire country, and especially the scientific community. Realizing Bharat Biotech's supply constraints, the Modi government has made efforts to increase production. The Department of Biotechnology has facilitated technology transfer with numerous companies—Haffkine Biopharmaceutical Corporation Ltd, Indian Immunologicals Ltd, Hyderabad, Bharat Immunological & Biologicals Ltd, Bulandshahar, Uttar Pradesh[41], and Hester Biosciences, Gujarat[42].

Further support has been given to vaccine manufacturers Serum Institute of India and Bharat Biotech through advance payments and orders. For instance, 100 per cent advance payment amounting to ₹1,732 crore and ₹787 crore (₹17.32 billion and ₹7.87 billion) were released to SII and Bharat Biotech, respectively, in April 2021 for vaccine supplies in May–July 2021[43]. In June 2021, the Health Ministry finalized an arrangement with Biological-E for reserving 30 crore or 300 million doses of its under-trial vaccine. The ministry has given an advance payment of ₹1,500 crore or ₹15 billion for it[44].

As a citizen of India, it is a matter of great pride for me that our country has not only been self-sufficient but has also been a major source of global vaccine supply. Under the Vaccine Maitri programme, SII and Bharat Biotech have provided vaccine doses to 94 countries and two UN entities[45]. Apart from meeting commercial export obligations, India has supplied vaccine doses by way of grants or through the COVAX initiative.

All stakeholders in the vaccination programme—from the scientists involved in vaccine development to frontline healthcare workers who are administering vaccines—deserve credit for the successful progress in COVID-19 vaccination. However, I would also likely specifically mention the pivotal role of Prime Minister Modi. A leader's ability to steer the ship is pivotal in achieving the intended outcome. Ignoring the extensive pessimism and derision about India's ability to deliver, Prime Minister Modi has remained a beacon of hope. He has remained optimistic throughout and been always willing to provide state assistance for vaccine development. His constant COVID-19 messaging has focused on vaccination and encouraged millions of citizens to get vaccinated. His personal decision to get vaccinated with Bharat Biotech's Covaxin dispelled much of the misinformation about the vaccine and reduced vaccine hesitancy. As PM Modi mentioned in an op-ed published after India crossed the historic 100-crore milestone, the last mile delivery of vaccines involves a complex logistical process. However, under Modi's leadership, the government has ensured that this process was carried without local corruption and penetration of the 'VIP culture'.

TRANSFORMING THE HEALTH SYSTEM

For seven decades, successive governments in India failed to build a robust healthcare infrastructure. For instance, public hospitals always had over 70 per cent shortage of medical specialists, and the country was always short of over one million doctors and two million nurses. Prime Minister Modi has been receptive to new ideas for improving the healthcare system and repeatedly expressed his willingness to usher noticeable changes.

His intent has been matched with action as his government has taken some critical initiatives over the last seven years. Since 2014, there has been a significant increase in medical education seats across the country. More than 35,000 undergraduate seats have been added in the country. The total number of MBBS seats increased from 51,348 seats in 2014 to 88,120 seats in 2021, a 72 per cent increase. The increase in postgraduate (PG) seats has been even more phenomenal. Currently, there are 55,595 PG seats in the country—including Diplomate National Board (DNB) seats offered by National Board of Examinations (NBE) and the College of Physicians and Surgeons (CPS) seats that offer diploma courses in broad specialties post MBBS seats. This is a 78 per cent increase as compared to pre-2014[46]. The increase in seats will be instrumental in helping India achieve the World Bank prescribed ratio of 1 doctor for every 1,000 persons.

The phenomenal increase in medical education seats was achieved through an unprecedented increase in the number of medical colleges. Close to 179 new medical colleges opened across the country between 2014 and 2020[47]. A special scheme for establishing medical colleges at district and referral hospitals has led to an increase in the availability of seats and make medical education more accessible. The Central government has approved more than ₹25,000 crore (₹250 billion) for the establishment of new medical colleges[48]. Over three phases, the government has approved the establishment of 157 medical colleges attached to existing district hospitals. It is heartening to note that the list of districts includes some of the country's most remote or economically backward districts, making medical education genuinely accessible. Through this initiative, many districts will be getting their first medical college after more than seven decades of independence. Soon, tier two and three cities in India will have vibrant public hospitals since most of them will be converted to post-graduate institutes with enthusiastic young doctors serving patients exactly like the UK's National Health Service (NHS). These new medical colleges are expected to add more than 15,000 medical education seats collectively[49].

Moreover, in the last seven years, the Central government has sanctioned 15 AIIMS in various states. The sanctioned AIIMS are on track towards timely completion and becoming functional. Many of these institutions have already started admitting students for MBBS and/or providing OPD services[50]. These institutions will offer world-class medical education and healthcare facilities and significantly impact citizens' lives.

Alongside infrastructure expansion, the government has taken some critical regulatory reforms. Last year, the government replaced the Medical Council of India with a 33-member regulatory body called the National Medical Commission (NMC). The NMC will ensure greater transparency and accountability in medical education. The Commission has focused on streamlining regulations, fulfilling the human resource requirements in healthcare, and ensuring medical education remains affordable. In July 2020, the government endorsed a proposal from the National board of examination to start a two-year diploma course in eight broad specialties to strengthen secondary and tertiary health care delivery.

The first and second COVID-19 waves have led to an important realization that large hospitals need to be self-sufficient for their oxygen requirements. This has led to concentrated efforts and approval of considerable resources to install Pressure Swing Absorption (PSA) plants. The Central government has sanctioned 1,562 PSA plants across the country. Out of these, 1,225 have been financed through the PM CARES fund and covered each district of the country. Additionally, various PSUs also contributed towards installation of PSA plants. These plants will support more than one lakh or 100,000 oxygen beds daily[51]. Also, the daily liquid oxygen production capacity of the country has increased considerably in the past year—from 6876 MT/day on 1 October, 2020 to 8778 MT/day in November 2021[52].

CONCLUSION

For healthcare professionals, the COVID-19 pandemic has been one of the most challenging periods of our careers. When cases started increasing, we realized that India was entering a tough battle against COVID-19. We will have to prioritize our professional duties over personal desires till the pandemic comes under control. All of us knew that treating a highly transmissible infection like COVID-19 was extremely risky, and there was an imminent threat for us every time we entered the hospital. However, nothing could dissuade our healthcare professionals and frontline workers' commitment to their duty. Staying away from home for weeks or close personal losses, nothing came in the way of responsibility for them.

Prime Minister Modi's reference to us as 'COVID-19 warriors' has been highly inspiring. Since the pandemic started, we have worked with the sole intention of protecting our country in this war against COVID-19. I must mention that Modi has always looked out for us and met our requests. I must also mention the commendable life insurance benefits for more than 20 lakh or 2 million healthcare workers[53].

The Prime Minister made a heart-warming gesture when he urged citizens to clap or ring bells after the end of one-day Janata Curfew in March 2020, to 'acknowledge and salute' the efforts being made by healthcare and frontline workers across the country[54]. I was overjoyed by the overwhelming public response to the Prime Minister's call. This small gesture went a great distance in strengthening our resolve to work tirelessly in India's fight against COVID-19.

The COVID-19 pandemic has certainly been a challenging phase for the entire country. However, I am glad that we have successfully overcome—and are successfully overcoming—the challenges that we have encountered. This would not have been possible without the leadership of Prime Minister Modi, whose optimism and service-oriented approach have kept us focused. Like a great finisher in cricket, Modi has always kept us on track to achieve the target. There have admittedly been numerous moments of low self-belief and dejection. But, on each occasion, the Prime Minister's words of advice and inspirational messages have helped us shrug off the negativity and focus on our duty in the fight against COVID-19.

Modi inherited a fragile public healthcare system. A system that was completely unprepared for handling the burden put by the COVID-19 crisis. Rather than ruing over the state of affairs that he inherited or playing politics over it, He focused on rebuilding and strengthening the system. A process that should have started many decades ago finally began in 2014. The Indian healthcare system is gradually transforming, and we are inching towards building a system that we always deserved and awaited.

प्रधानमंत्री जन-धन योजना
UPI
UNIFIED PAYMENTS INTERFACE

IMAGINING TECHNOLOGY AS A GOVERNANCE TOOL

NANDAN NILEKANI

Prime Minister Narendra Modi, speaking on 1 July 2021, to the beneficiaries of Digital India—an all-encompassing digitization movement envisaged by him six years ago—said that India's data and demographic dividend, along with its proven technical proficiency, will make this decade the country's 'Techade'. Both the occasion and his remarks were suggestive of his understanding of technology and its consequences for India.

From his earliest days as a social worker, to multiple tenures as the Chief Minister of Gujarat, to his journey to the pinnacle of India's polity, Modi has come to realize that it is only technology that can propel the nation forward and turbo-charge the efforts of the governmental apparatus. A glimpse of his early thinking on technology is visible in a rare television interview he gave in 1999–2000, where he spoke at length on his penchant for experimenting with new technologies and exploring the internet for hours.

Modi understands technology intuitively and sees its usage as 'horizontal'—accessible across everything he does—as opposed to it being limited to a force multiplier for vertical efforts. This explains why technology has underpinned all his works: from getting his messages across to the people of India, to directly transferring benefits to citizens, to increasing the efficiency of bureaucratic action. His use of technology has also transcended form factors. Through *Mann Ki Baat*, a monthly address to Indian citizens, he has been able to harness the humble and forgotten radio, lending the medium itself a fillip. In an ironic inversion, new-age aural platforms now host content meant for radio audiences. From architecting a Gutka Mukti Abhiyan via missed calls to engaging global audiences via video chats, he has always been open to radical experiments. His presence across social media platforms is remarkable, not only in its breadth but also in the content's relevance for varied segments. This ability of his—to match content with channels—is unique and explains his sustained leadership on these platforms.

In traversing the arc of some of Modi's trysts with technology, from his earliest days as Chief Minister of Gujarat to his second term as Prime Minister of India, readers will be able to appreciate his commitment to harness technology for the common good.

HARNESSING TECHNOLOGY FOR PUBLIC GOOD

A predominant concern for the citizens of a democracy is: when and whether their voice of concern will reach the right corridors of the government? With respect to the bureaucracy, the apprehension of citizens towards the labourious process of having their grievances lodged was something Modi sensed during his service to the people of Gujarat. In 2003, only a couple of years after being sworn in as the Chief Minister for the first time, he initiated the SWAGAT (State-Wide Attention on Grievances by Application of Technology) platform, an online grievance redressal system and became one of the earliest leaders in the country to embrace e-governance.

Furthering his intent to take this platform to the grassroots level of administration, Chief Minister Modi launched SWAGAT at the taluka level in 2009, and its village level avatar in 2011. SWAGAT's impact was both local and global. In just nine days, GRAM SWAGAT received 9,000 applications. In 2010, the SWAGAT programme was internationally recognized by the United Nations through its Public Service Award for improving transparency and accountability in public service. The UN award brought to public attention the functioning of this IT-enabled system. The organized and time-bound manner through which public grievances in Gujarat were dealt with inspired other Indian states to replicate aspects of the model.

Much of the credit for the success of SWAGAT was due to the

efficiency of the Chief Minister's office (CMO). Gujarat's CMO had acquired an ISO certification for its processes in January 2009. The certification was renewed in January 2010 as per the latest standards. For the ISO certification, the functioning of the secretariat and the public relations office, the CMO's general administration, human resources, Jan Sampark ('public interaction', where SWAGAT comes in) and, lastly, the information technology infrastructure, were overhauled. A special software called SWAGAT Lok Fariyad was developed so that complaints could be uploaded in real time. Several years later, with his becoming Prime Minister, we see the same efficiency in PRAGATI (Pro-Active Governance and Timely Implementation) as a tool for monitoring projects at the national scale, resolving bottlenecks and accelerating execution of projects.

While I only discovered the fascinating, omnipresent and demanding governmental file during my stint in government, Modi had understood the drawbacks of this paper-based governance artefact much earlier. In 2007, his government in Gujarat issued an order that abolished paper files in the Gandhinagar secretariat. All work in the thirty-four departments was to be done digitally. This gave speed and efficiency to the work undertaken by the secretariat.

Another initiative by Chief Minister Modi was broadband connectivity to all panchayats of his state. By 2010, Gujarat became the only state in the country to provide broadband connectivity to all 13,695 village panchayats. E-governance services in a number of areas were introduced. These included e-dhara for computerized land records; e-gram, e-municipality and one-day governance for delivery of citizen-centric services.

Digital tools were not only used to provide services but also to ensure effective management of utilities. Gujarat's Integrated Water-Shed Management Programme won accolades for innovative technology usage in e-governance in 2011. Gujarat became the first state to apply satellite GIS (Geographic Information System) to fully plan, implement and monitor watershed management. Satellite imagery was used to transparently identify watershed boundaries and the neediest areas for assistance. GPS (Global Positioning System) and mobile software were used to feed data and create maps to plan and monitor progress. Gujarat State Watershed Management Agency has used technology to benefit 1,048 villages, 7.08 lakh (708,000) hectares of land and 2.5 lakh (250,000) farmers, making it one of the largest interventions of its kind.

Gujarat proved to be an exciting, but somewhat bounded laboratory for many of Modi's experiments. What his chief ministerial intervention did enable was an important learning opportunity to discover the possibilities and limitations of technologies. By the time he arrived in New Delhi, Modi had developed an experiential view of how to architect technological projects, how to get the right set of stakeholders involved in the process and how to spark the imagination of the citizenry with respect to the proposed programmes.

The provision of high-speed internet to the final mile of governance in Gujarat yielded several benefits. With this experience behind him, Prime Minister Modi has been vigorously pursuing the BharatNet scheme, a middle-mile network from blocks to Gram Panchayats. Since 2014, more than 1.5 lakh (150,000) village panchayats have been connected with optical fibre networks under this scheme. This endeavour has wide-ranging implications since most country-scale initiatives assume strong connectivity till the village level.

Ensuring that essential governmental services in the fields of health, education and agriculture reach the remotest parts of the nation and deepening access to social welfare and financial inclusion schemes have been a priority for Modi's administration. To this end, Common Service Centres (CSCs) have played a vital role. CSCs are physical facilities for delivering Government of India e-services to rural and remote locations where availability of computers and internet was negligible or mostly absent. The Government has, as of August 2021, set up 3.56 lakh (356,000) CSCs across the nation to bring the state closer to the citizens.

Modi took charge of the nation when the India Stack—a bouquet of technological goods spanning unique identification, digital documentation and finance with the potential to alter the country's destiny—started coming of age. Whenever the opportunity has arisen, the Prime Minister has used his socio-political capital to further the cause of technology. I have witnessed his commitment first hand on multiple occasions.

UNDERSTANDING AADHAAR POTENTIAL

When I took on the role as the founding chairman of the Unique Identification Authority of India (UIDAI) in 2009, I decided that I would visit all the states and evangelize the idea of Aadhaar and get their feedback. I would go to each state, meet the Chief Minister and the senior bureaucrats and talk about the benefits of rolling out Aadhaar. In July 2011, I went to meet Chief Minister Narendra Modi in Gujarat.

I noticed how spick and span his office was, and it reminded me of the corporate office of Infosys! A thirty-minute meeting went on for ninety minutes as he shared stories on how he had done developmental innovations in Gujarat and the many ways he was using technology. I did not have to explain much about Aadhaar. He had grasped all the possibilities and the potential of Aadhaar. Of all my visits to various states and meetings with several chief ministers, he was the only one who had understood that the Aadhaar document would reach 1.3 billion Indian residents and, therefore, what was printed on the card was of strategic importance. There was not a single interruption during those ninety minutes and he gave me his undivided attention. I came back feeling I had met a very different kind of politician!

After the 2014 elections were held, and Prime Minister Narendra Modi and his cabinet were sworn in, there was speculation about the future of Aadhaar vis-à-vis other initiatives such as smart-card-based IDs. I had devoted five years of my life to Aadhaar before stepping down and standing (unsuccessfully) for the Lok Sabha elections of 2014 from Bengaluru. I was passionate about the value of Aadhaar to India, and after encouragement from my wife and some friends, I decided to meet Prime Minister Modi and discuss the matter.

Towards the end of June 2014, I was in New Delhi, wrapping up my home to return permanently to Bengaluru. I sought a meeting with the new Prime Minister. To my utter astonishment, I got an appointment within twenty-four hours at a time convenient to me. I went with some trepidation, as I had just stood for the election on a rival party's ticket. Modi was gracious and listened to me intently. This time, his questions were about issuing the card to residents and not citizens, and how India's fiscal situation could benefit from direct benefit transfers (DBTs) and its role in reducing corruption. He was well-informed on all issues, including the privacy case in the Supreme Court. What struck me was his openness to listen and to do what was right for the country.

Over the years, Prime Minister Modi has internalized the understanding of Aadhaar in a manner that has allowed him to intensify its utility. It was evident to him that linking an individual's mobile phone number, bank account and Aadhaar could yield several advantages to beneficiaries and to the several arms of governments at the Union and state levels that were vested in delivering benefits to citizens. At a conclave on realizing India's JAM (Jan Dhan-Aadhaar-Mobile) vision in 2015, he stated that, 'JAM is about achieving maximum value for every rupee spent, maximum empowerment for our poor, maximum technological penetration among the masses.'

While a few challenged the usage of Aadhaar for developmental purposes, he saw Aadhaar's role as liberating India's people from queues and cumbersome processes. Three hundred and twenty schemes are currently in use, transferring benefits directly into the bank accounts of the beneficiaries, bypassing any intermediaries. A cumulative amount of ₹20.23 lakh crore or ₹20.23 trillion had been transferred directly into the bank accounts of beneficiaries by the end of December 2021. This has also saved the government an estimated ₹2 lakh crore or ₹2 trillion by eliminating bogus and fake accounts, ghost beneficiaries and plugging leakages.

The point to take home here is that the government wasn't rolling out one development intervention, they were building digital public infrastructure. Aadhaar by itself could only prove your identity; however, plugging Aadhaar into multiple programmes supercharged the overall welfare delivery experience for the government and its citizens.

Aadhaar was a foundational identity system, but over the next decade, complementary digital infrastructure has been built in the space of payments and data exchange. These systems were all designed as lego blocks—they could be recombined and stacked on top of each other to create new and unique solutions. A Bank for International Settlements (BIS) report published in 2019 said that India managed to achieve due to its public digital infrastructure the kind of progress in financial inclusion that would have taken forty-seven years otherwise in seven years. The same infrastructure was used to deliver financial aid directly and rapidly to citizens when the pandemic first hit.

POPULARIZING DIGITAL PAYMENTS

In 2016, when the government decided to demonetize select currency notes, the Prime Minister saw an opportunity to steer the country towards digital payments. He took keen interest in the Unified Payments Interface (UPI), which was being developed by the National Payments Corporation of India (NPCI). He regularly enquired about the status of its development, and also christened it BHIM (Bharat Interface for Money)—a fitting tribute to Bhimrao Ambedkar, whose work was instrumental in the establishment of the Reserve Bank of India, and the concept of finance commission to distribute wealth between the Union and state governments. When he launched BHIM in December 2019, the Prime Minister said that there was a time when people used to address an unschooled person as '*angootha chaap*', but now the thumbprint can act as a person's bank, his/her identity, and even be used to run a business. This struck me as a distinctly Modi-esque framing—articulating the benefit of an empowering technology by building on the uniqueness of established Indian behaviour.

The adoption and scaling of UPI has been possible because of the government's commitment to digitize money flows in India. More than 229 banks are operational on UPI now. Every month, UPI processes several crore transactions and, in the process, creates trails which can be leveraged for other financial services. UPI, as a digital payment ecosystem, has gone on to command global attention. Google recommended that the US Federal Reserve develop a similar payments ecosystem for digital payments.

On 2 August 2021, Modi launched e-RUPI, a person-to-purpose specific digital payment solution. It is best understood as a cashless and contactless instrument for digital payment where a QR code or SMS string-based e-voucher is delivered to the mobile phones of intended beneficiaries of schemes. The e-RUPI connects the sponsors of the services with the beneficiaries and service providers in a digital manner, without any physical interface. It also ensures that the payment to the service provider is made only after the transaction is completed. Being pre-paid in nature, it assures timely payments to the service provider without the involvement of any intermediary.

The e-RUPI is expected to be a revolutionary initiative in the direction of ensuring a leak-proof delivery of welfare services. It can also be used for delivering services under schemes meant for providing drugs and nutritional support under 'Mother and Child' welfare schemes, TB (tuberculosis) eradication programmes, drugs and diagnostics under schemes like Ayushman Bharat, Pradhan Mantri Jan Arogya Yojana, fertilizer subsidies, etc. Even the private sector can leverage these digital vouchers as part of their employee welfare and corporate social responsibility programmes.

Much like the panchayat-level broadband connectivity project—conceived in and for Gujarat by Chief Minister Modi—that was taken to India-scale by Prime Minister Modi, the abolishing of paper files in the Gandhinagar secretariat proved to be one of the motivations behind his backing of DigiLocker. DigiLocker is an Indian digitization online service provided by Ministry of Electronics and Information Technology under the Digital India initiative. It is a secure cloud-based platform for the storage, sharing and verification of documents and certificates.

In a culture where citizens are often asked to produce documents to avail various services, maintaining hard copies of identification, eligibility or qualification documents can be an expensive and complex affair. By securing documents in an electronic form, which is also a recognized format, DigiLocker is doing away with the need to maintain paper formats. As of August 2021, a total of 432 crore (4.32 billion) documents have been issued through DigiLocker. This has saved citizens and authorities cost and time.

NEW LEARNING METHODS

In 2019, I had another opportunity to discuss two topics of mutual interest with the Prime Minister: education and lending. Since 2014, I have been contributing to the development of DIKSHA, a platform for teachers, students and parents, which offers engaging learning material relevant to the prescribed school curriculum. DIKSHA is based on the Sunbird Open Source software, developed by the EkStep Foundation.

It seeks to help five personas (parents, teachers, students, community members and administrators) with three scenarios (learning, helping to learn and managing the learning process) via two interactions (learning and administration). DIKSHA's building blocks cover content, curation, assessment, personalization, analytics and translation.

When the platform reached a certain size, the team working on the platform and I decided to present its particulars to the Prime Minister. An important part of our efforts had been the embedding of QR codes in textbooks to energize them. These codes help students access crowdsourced multimedia. His grasp of the concept was immediate and visceral. Having interacted with students, teachers and parents regularly—particularly on Teacher's Day (5 September) every year via videoconferencing—he understood the problems that passive content posed to the learning potential of young children across the country.

To prove that there exists a better manner to enliven content, the Prime Minister, in his book *Exam Warriors*, has linked tips for exam preparation to multimedia, quizzes and a community via QR codes. Not only did he grasp the minutiae of DIKSHA, the Prime Minister directed his colleagues to scale the effort nationally. Today, students across the country are benefitting from richer content, while parents and teachers are able to track progress—not only on an aggregate level but for every single child. Content sourcing via VidyaDaan, digital teacher training through Nishtha, and access enablement via eVidya were particularly useful in ensuring a continuity of learning during the pandemic.

While we had not ventured into the design elements of DIKSHA in our presentation, the Prime Minister understood the power and implications of the underlying framework. He casually enquired whether the same components could be used to build up-skilling and training modules for the bureaucracy. He assigned a pointsperson and a team to follow through on this vision to ensure that the Department of Personnel and Training adopted a modern learning infrastructure for the bureaucrats serving our nation.

Lending has long been a bane for the poor—particularly those without a credit history to prove their creditworthiness. With UPI, India architected a new model to deepen access to finance—in sachets, as mobile-friendly and as a speedy implementation of transactions. Volunteers from the Indian

Software Products Industry Round Table (iSPIRT), the dynamic think tank from Bengaluru, had been working to reimagine lending for small businesses and the poorest among us who have always stood at the back of the line for credit providers. In the proposed model, small businesses and individuals would be able to share their transaction histories and tax payment receipts to avail credit offers from lending institutions.

The sharing of information by credit seekers, the evaluation of credit worthiness and offers for credit by lenders and finally, in cases of a match, the disbursal of funds would all happen within minutes, over the phone. Given the Prime Minister's technocratic impulse, he immediately endorsed the idea of rewarding compliance and serving the under/un-served with the help of technology. The rapidly developing Account Aggregator framework and Open Credit Enablement Network (OCEN) are results of the government's desire and the Reserve Bank of India's continued support for the nation to leapfrog traditional methods of financial services penetration.

This interaction, over a couple of hours, reaffirmed my view of Prime Minister Modi's instinctual understanding of technological advances as India's best bet to march forward. It is due to this shared belief that the nation now has a software arsenal sought by nations across the world. It is also on account of this conviction that the last couple of years have seen initiatives as radical as Ayushman Bharat and as forward-thinking as CoWIN, which recorded 145 crore (1.45 billion) vaccinations by the end of December 2021 and has been giving vaccinated Indians a verifiable digital certificate.

Modi has not only championed country-scale programmes but also been at the forefront of using technology to connect with voters. He was one of the first global leaders to interact with voters over a video chat back in 2012. The Google Hangout hosted by him back in 2012 remains one of the most watched interactions of its sort. He was also the pioneer in live-streaming his speeches on YouTube to directly reach audiences, bypassing traditional media channels. In 2014, he introduced 3D hologram rallies and LED raths. A unique tech-based volunteer platform launched by him during the election campaign has now evolved to what is now MyGov, India's first crowdsourced platform for policymaking and governance. It is this approach to crowdsourced policymaking using technology that has resulted in the drafting of the National Education Policy (NEP) as a grassroots nationwide effort. He routinely solicits the citizenry's feedback on other contemporary issues via MyGov and the comprehensive NaMo app. While in the Silicon Valley in 2017, not only did the Prime Minister meet top tech executives, but he also made it a point to visit the headquarters of leading tech companies to understand their R&D culture and its relevance for India.

FOCUS ON HEALTHCARE, EDUCATION

Two areas in which governments have always aspired to do better—but have been the victims of their own limitations—are healthcare and education. While multiple programmes have been designed and modified several times over, outcomes in both domains continue to leave a lot to be desired. In an attempt to consolidate and upgrade these efforts for healthcare, PM Modi has envisaged the National Digital Health Mission (NDHM), a comprehensive programme with citizens and patients at its heart. The underlying objectives of the mission are to improve healthcare quality by making it accessible, affordable and reliable. It seeks to give every Indian citizen a Digital Health ID, which would contain comprehensive health records. It will be a single identifier to pull relevant health records and view these records in a non-discretionary and non-sponsored manner.

By the end of December 2021, 14.67 crore (146.7 million) health IDs had been generated and 6,803 doctors and 15,010 facilities had registered on the platform. The NDHM also aims to develop the backbone necessary to support the integrated digital health infrastructure of the country. It will bridge the existing gap amongst different stakeholders of the healthcare ecosystem, such as healthcare professionals, NGOs, hospitals, insurers, etc., through digital highways.

NDHM also seeks to create a health professional registry to search for doctors in a holistic and inclusive way through building platforms, registries and directories. This will enable the various systems and domain-specific registries to access electronic medical records through a unified health interface, similar to UPI. This will work as a link with applications and domain-specific registries to enhance visibility for the patient community and doctors, and it will encompass aspects of discoverability to enable online booking of hospitals and tele-consultations.

On the education front, digital learning has been a big area of focus for the Modi government. Early investments via the National Mission on Education have helped students access education even during the lockdowns, through ICT (information and communications technology) initiatives such as Swayam, Swayam-Prabha, National Digital Library, e-Yantra, Virtual Lab, etc. The DIKSHA portal has more than 2,300 crore (23 billion) hits, testimony to the utility of making content available online. The newly approved NEP also places huge emphasis on digital and technology-enabled learning. It proposes to set up a National Educational Technology Forum to further promote the use of technology in learning and assessment for both school and higher education. Speaking at the Shikshak Parv in September 2021, the Prime Minister stated that N-DEAR (National Digital Educational Architecture) is going to play a big role in eliminating inequality in education. Just as the UPI interface has revolutionized the banking sector, N-DEAR will act as a super connect with respect to all academic activities.

Narendra Modi's approach to technology has been inclusive in the spirit of Sabka Vikaas, with the emphasis on widening the benefits of technology to all sections. A good example of this is the National Portal for Soil Health, which has digitized the entire process through which farmers from all over India can send their soil samples for testing, track the testing process online and obtain recommendations while downloading their digital soil health cards in a language of their choice.

Aware that a number of the technology initiatives under the government were siloed, Modi launched Digital India in 2015, a flagship unifying programme with a vision to transform India into a digitally empowered society and knowledge economy. India's ability to pursue low-cost, scalable and inclusive digitization has benefited from this approach. There are a number of multi-stakeholder ecosystems now evolving which promise to alter the governance landscape comprehensively. The FasTag system for cashless highway toll payments is one such digital ecosystem that leverages radio frequency identification technology and has revolutionized toll collection along India's national highways. The speed of the rollout of FasTag stands out for the Modi government's emphasis on executing at scale. While I had come out with the original report for paving the way for a unified electronic toll collection technology for National Highways in India back in 2010, there was limited movement on this front till Modi's government decided to pursue reforms on this front.

From the trillions of rupees worth transactions on GeM (Government e-Marketplace) to the empowerment of millions of farmers registered on e-NAM (e-National Agriculture Market) to delivering simplicity to millions of taxpayers registered on GSTN (Goods and Services Tax Network), there are a number of national public digital platforms driving Digital India's distinctive forward march. GeM in particular has emerged as a game changer for public procurement empowering small and medium businesses to access buyers across India at a scale that matches Amazon's e-Marketplace. GeM Sahay is helping MSMEs get instant loans based on their orders, transaction flows and tax filings. Beneficiaries have hailed the experience as 'miraculous and magical'.

All these platforms—via citizen empowerment, increased ease of doing business and easier governance—are smoothening government-citizen engagement, increasing the government's agility and responsiveness, enhancing policy effectiveness and bolstering the integrity of the governmental ecosystem through consolidation of services. India is perhaps the only nation with such a holistic approach towards digitization. Our commitment to open standards, interoperability and scalability is now inspiring countries across the world to embrace a similar approach.

As he enters his twenty-first year in the service of the nation, Prime Minister Modi's continued commitment to Digital India will ensure that the nation leaves an indelible mark on the technological map of the world.

DISINVESTMENT
REFORMS
GST

NO SHADOW BETWEEN IDEA AND REALITY

NRIPENDRA MISRA

The country sees Narendra Modi as the Prime Minister of India. But during the time I had the privilege of working with him, I realized that it was his journey to the prime ministerial role that shaped his leadership of the country. In taking this journey, he has drawn from myriad influences within our country—Mahatma Gandhi, A.P.J. Abdul Kalam, Rajendra Prasad, Sardar Vallabhbhai Patel and international influences, such as Nelson Mandela, Abraham Lincoln, Lee Kuan Yew and Shinzo Abe. It is a journey that has taken him to every corner of our country, to others that are developed and some areas mired in poverty and to nations that are seen as development successes. His journey has helped craft key aspects of his vision for a new India, of inclusion and enablement of our weakest citizens, of gender equality and women's empowerment, of encouraging Indian global champions and of an India that stands its ground as a global leader without wasting goodwill on quixotic crusades.

It was on 20 May 2014, that I received a call from Arun Jaitley to visit Gujarat Bhavan for some interaction. After reaching there, I was told that I would be calling on Prime Minister-designate Modi at 4 p.m. During those days, I was working for an NGO committed to curbing criminal elements in the election process, and a PIL was already before the Supreme Court, which had been co-petitioned by a few other NGOs. Since I had never met Modi before, I was both nervous and uncertain. I entered his chamber and, after a few pleasantries, he spoke about Gandhi ji, the commemoration of the freedom movement and poverty. I noted his priorities for the future and took his leave. Visitors meeting the Prime Minister are always put at ease by him, and come away with admiration. It was only on 25 May 2014, that I was summoned again and conveyed personally by him about my appointment as Principal Secretary to the Prime Minister. There was a legal hitch, but his mind was made. His personality has little space for indecisiveness and his resolve is firm.

While addressing the nation from the ramparts of the Red Fort on the sixty-eighth Independence Day, Prime Minister Modi unfolded his unflinching commitment for the downtrodden: 'We take a solemn pledge of working for the welfare of mother India and particularly for the welfare of the poor, oppressed Dalits, the exploited and the backward people of our country.' He did not make any preferences for caste or religion, and his belief was the welfare of all.

As a statesman and an exceptional leader, Prime Minister Modi not only had a vision for the people, but also displayed the ability to translate that vision into reality. Within an overarching grand plan, he created small programmes—steps with viable linkages. I have the opportunity to recall a few of them in this chapter. On 15 August 2014, he laid out his transformational plans for India. His vision of a nation where women are legitimately empowered in all walks of life, where the economy is reformed for the benefit of all, where wealth generation becomes attractive because of the measures taken for promoting ease of doing business, where corruption is greatly discouraged through systemic reforms and technology, where everyone has access to healthcare, where ordinary people earn their livelihood for a better tomorrow and ease of living is felt by all sections of the society.

THE MAN AND HIS MISSION

Independent India has witnessed a host of promises claiming the transformation of the country. Electrification of all villages was one such promise. During a review of the programme, it was presented to the Prime Minister that there are 18,500 villages in the country where electric wires and poles were yet to reach. In his speech on 15 August 2015, he promised that in the next thousand days, all villages in India would be electrified. This was achieved in April 2018. He surprised both NITI Aayog and the Union Power Ministry while fixing an outer limit of thousand days for electrifying all villages. The Power Ministry effectively worked with the states and achieved the target. Modi monitored the state-wise progress on a weekly basis.

While talking about the programme and its implementation, he once explained his work ethic to me in great detail. He said that his selection of programmes had a modular approach—from small to big; but they all had links. No surprise, then, that immediately after the electrification of the villages, he announced the household electricity connection plan, at least one in each village, on a mission mode, with preference for habitations of Scheduled Castes and Scheduled Tribes. Since the launch of the programme in 2017, 2.62 crore or 26.2 million households (99.93 per cent) have been electrified.

It was then becoming evident to us that Prime Minister Modi would soon launch a programme for rural education and rural communication on the foundation of electrification. Once communication and Wi-Fi services reached the villages, tele-education, tele-medicine and banking for all would be successfully launched. As Chief Minister of Gujarat, Modi had seen the powerful impact of the spread of rural electrification through the Jyoti Gramodyog Vikas Yojana, which had multiple positive effects on the rural economy. Today, Gujarat boasts of twenty-four-hour three-phase quality power supply to all villages as a result of his leadership. The state pioneered a Rural Feeder Segregation Scheme, which is now being adopted as a model by other states. It involved creating new power infrastructure and massive investment. It was completed in March 2006. One could identify various programmes being built over an ambitious canvas even then.

Having experienced poverty himself in his childhood, he knows well how it restricts human potential. While announcing his resolve to address the curse of poverty on 15 August 2014, he was clear in his mind that anti-poverty measures should be enablers, instead of free distribution of freebies. The poor need to improve their income and well-being to break the vicious cycle. Access to basic education became his top priority. As Chief Minister of Gujarat, he had realized that education, particularly primary education, had to be bolstered. He launched two programmes—Kanya Kelavani and Shala Praveshotsav. These programmes were initially a three-day campaign, but ultimately, acquired deep roots in strengthening education in Gujarat. The stakeholders were invited to participate and own it. The government became the facilitator. The teaching process was revolutionized and more than twenty-one thousand teachers were recruited. Gujarat today has achieved unprecedented results in terms of improvement in enrolment rate (including girls), improved schooling facilities, and imparting quality education. Hundred per cent enrolment of girls in schools at a primary level has been achieved.

With that confidence of achieving success in Gujarat, Prime Minister Modi announced the National Education Policy recently, which includes education in Indian languages, value-based education, vocational education achieving functional literacy and numeracy, holistic education, the use of technology and ethics and human values. It commits to delivering high-quality education for all. Built on the foundational pillars of access, equity, quality, affordability and accountability, this policy is aligned to the 2030 Agenda for Sustainable Development.

Based on his long personal experiences addressing such problems and his deep desire to make a real change, the Prime Minister took an active interest in evolving social security programmes and their implementation. The Pradhan Mantri Jeevan Jyoti Bima Yojana, started in 2015, gives a life insurance cover of ₹2 lakh or ₹2,00,000 at a premium of just ₹1 a day for people from the age of eighteen to fifty. years The Pradhan Mantri Suraksha Bima Yojana gives insurance cover of ₹2 lakh at a premium of only ₹1 a month. The Atal Pension Yojana, focusing on those working in the unorganized sector, provides pension after the age of sixty with very low premiums to be paid in the working life of a beneficiary.

He also reached out to the farmers. The Pradhan Mantri Fasal Bima Yojana, which provides crop insurance at a nominal premium, and the Deen Dayal Upadhyaya Gram Jyoti Yojana for better supply of electricity in villages, are two other examples of schemes catering to the poor and marginalized sections of our society. Prime Minister Modi believes that schemes such as these are 'our obligation towards the poor, of compassion towards the poor. And no matter how much we develop, no matter how much we achieve if its success does not reach the poor, development is incomplete.' All these schemes have delivered social security on ground to the people in need.

His campaign against poverty continues. Housing for the poor, universal household electrification, disbursement of free ration during the pandemic, employment to poor, financial support to street vendors and programmes to finance Scheduled Caste/Scheduled Tribe women entrepreneurs are the initiatives which can be described as works in progress.

In his address to the nation on 15 August 2014, Prime Minister Modi committed himself whole-heartedly to the cause of women empowerment. To quote him, 'Has it ever pained us that our mothers and sisters have to defecate in open? Is dignity of women not our collective responsibility?' As Gujarat Chief Minister, he had noted the abysmal statistics on education of girl children. He was appalled to know that the lack of basic amenities such as separate lavatories, safe drinking water and sanitary provisions for girl students were keeping them away from schools. 'Beti Bachao Beti Padhao' was launched on 22 January 2015, and it was a call against female foeticide and for gender equality in education. 'For women', which he talked on 15 August 2014, did not remain a mere promise, but was turned into reality.

The sex ratio has improved by 16 points—from 918 in 2014-15 to 934 in 2019–20. Gross enrolment ratio (GER) of girls in the schools at secondary level has improved from 77.45 (2014–15) to 81.32 (2018–19 provisional figures) as per UDISE-data. More than ten crore (100 million) rural toilets have been built and more than six lakh or 600,000 villages have been declared open defecation free (ODF). Under Prime Minister Modi's government, India achieved hundred per cent rural sanitation in five years, from an abysmal 38 per cent in 2014.

WOMEN EMPOWERMENT

Many of the problems faced by women in India are of elementary nature, but a solution to those issues can make a fundamental difference to the lives of women. Cooking with traditional fuels such as wood was common in rural areas. Prime Minister Modi realized the health hazard that it posed to women. He often mentioned that cooking with traditional fuels was as hazardous as smoking four hundred cigarettes. He gave a solution in the form of Ujjwala Yojana, which was launched on 1 May 2016. Households under the scheme have been provided LPG cylinders at a highly reduced rate. A total of 80 million LPG connections have been released under the scheme since its launch in 2016. The second phase of Ujjwala was announced in August 2021 for an additional one crore (10 million) connections to uncovered low-income families. It will help achieve the Prime Minister's vision of universal access to LPG.

Among the many problems faced by women is unjust and unequal treatment in matters of marriage and divorce. The triple talaq practice in the Muslim community was an issue that had a highly regressive effect on women of the community. It was argued that this form of divorce was integral to the Muslim personal law or the Shariat. But there had also been strong demands to ban this practice. The passage of the Muslim Women (Protection of Rights on Marriage) Act in July 2019, banning triple talaq and making it a criminal offence, has brought greater freedom and justice to Muslim women.

Women empowerment without economic freedom would remain incomplete. Prime Minister Modi was, therefore, convinced that financial inclusion was a must. Banking services in India had traditionally left out the poor and the marginalized. Such people did not have access to bank accounts or to institutional credit at reasonable rates, which discouraged savings and opened them to exploitation at the hands of middlemen and money lenders. Financial inclusion of people, particularly women, was thus regarded by the Prime Minister as the key to their upliftment.

In order to achieve this objective, Prime Minister Modi launched the Jan Dhan Yojana, under which bank accounts with zero deposits were planned to be opened for the unbanked population. Between January 2015 and March 2015, no less than thirty crore or 300 million new bank accounts were opened successfully. Care was taken to ensure that they remained functional. Prime Minister Modi also recognized this as an opportunity to directly and digitally transfer monetary benefits to the people. It was a major institutional reform to curb corruption. Thus, the activity happening at the informal level became part of the formal economy. In terms of financial independence of women, by the end of December 2021, 55 per cent of the 44.2 crore (442 million) Jan Dhan account holders were women, having an overdraft facility of ₹5,000 to account holders of self-help groups.

Ambitious as the Jan Dhan Yojana was, the Prime Minister's financial inclusion plan did not stop at it. In order to encourage entrepreneurship among the marginalized, he launched the Micro Units Development and Refinance Agency (MUDRA), which allowed small vendors to get loans at concessional rate from banks and microfinance institutions up to ₹10 lakh (₹1 million) without any collateral. Within three years of its launch, MUDRA loans were given to twelve crore (120 million) people; 68 per cent of them being women entrepreneurs. This is in addition to loan amount sanctioned to women entrepreneurs under the Stand-up India scheme. Modi recognized the necessity of skilling women, who account for 40 per cent of the seventy-three lakh (7.3 million) candidates trained under the Pradhan Mantri Kaushal Vikas Yojana. Thus, his idea of identifying linkages to develop an integrated women empowerment programme became a reality.

His thought process to achieve a larger goal is appreciated once the programme unfolds in stages. The drive for cleanliness was announced in his address to the nation on 15 August 2014. He said, 'People wondered whether it is the work of a Prime Minister. People may feel that it is a trivial work, but for me this is a big work... By 2019, when we celebrate the hundred and fiftieth birth anniversary of Mahatma Gandhi, we resolve not to have a speck of dirt in our villages. This happens not just with the government but with public participation, and that is why we have to do it together.' He himself participated in the cleanliness drive by taking a broom early in the morning to chosen localities inhabited by the poor. He ensured broader participation by seeking cooperation of prominent people from various walks of life as ambassadors of the Clean India drive. Rural toilets, toilets in schools—particularly separate toilets for girls—and the goal of open defecation free villages became a reality when he announced that no school in India would be without toilet facilities.

His next destination is healthcare, followed by the wellness centre, and finally, ease of living. Prime Minister Modi strongly believes that poverty has linkages with health. He promised, under Ayushman Bharat, basic health facility including medicine and hospitalization to vulnerable sections of the society. The beneficiaries were identified and given Ayushman cards. By the end of December 2021, 17.21 crore or 172 million such cards had been issued to beneficiaries, enabling them to get treated at more than 22,000 hospitals across India—including approximately nine thousand private hospitals. More than two crore (20 million) free treatments have been availed under the scheme till now.

The scheme has been further strengthened by establishing outlets providing medicines at affordable prices. Ayushman Bharat Digital Mission has been launched to enable every citizen to have a digitized health record. Primary, secondary and tertiary healthcare system is being strengthened with a view to effectively serve as a wellness centre. Thus, the promise of improved healthcare has taken deep roots providing healthcare to those who cannot afford it. A sense of security and confidence amongst the poor is Prime Minister Modi's definition of ease of living.

EXPANDING THE SCOPE OF REFORMS

While the political integration of India was achieved by the efforts of Sardar Patel at the time of Independence, the economic integration of the country had remained a dream. Rules and regulations governing the movement of goods across various states of the country, especially those relating to essential commodities, had remained obsolete, regressive and opaque; often, they worked at cross purposes and prevented the economic integration of the country by making it a single market for both producers and buyers. In a few cases, the movement of goods between India and some other countries was easier than the movement of goods within the country!

Apart from this, there was the long-standing problem of a complicated indirect tax regime governing sales tax, excise tax, value-added tax (VAT), etc. that had acted as strong deterrents to economic exchange among the states. This, in turn, caused tremendous loss to the country by introducing market distortions that affected both producers and consumers adversely, while benefitting the middlemen of all sorts and encouraging corruption at all levels.

A single, integrated Goods and Services Tax (GST) for the entire country was seen as the most important step for the economic integration of India. Ever since the concept was mooted in India in 1999, it had been a subject of discussion and debate, but the problems and roadblocks in the path of GST were such that its implementation had remained only a distant dream. The principal resistance to it came from the states, which felt that a GST regime would lead to a severe curtailment of their taxing powers—through revenue losses, and the loss of their fiscal autonomy in the long run. While negotiations had continued for years, no solution was in sight.

Having been Chief Minister for thirteen years, Prime Minister Modi appreciated the concerns of the states. He even expressed reservations as Chief Minister in his communication to the Union government. As a statesman, he was receptive to the argument in favour of GST with its potential to integrate the nation financially. Honouring federal principles, he was generous on behalf of the Centre, which enjoys a dominant role in the realm of both direct and indirect taxes, and also the sovereign powers of borrowing through both domestic and international markets. The concerns of the states were met by giving guarantees to the states for a period of five years, compensating any revenue loss suffered by them because of the GST's implementation.

The scheme eliminated significantly the scope for tax evasion and corruption. It also led to an institutional evolution, where the GST Council comprising state finance ministers, under the chairmanship of the Union Finance Minister, was entrusted with the task of implementation, including the finalization of the tax structure. GST became 'one nation, one tax regime'.

Modi's fight against corruption is mainly through systemic changes, digitization and minimizing direct contact between the citizens and the governmental machinery. It has led to introduction of faceless e-assessment in direct taxes. The institutional reforms in the financial sector are largely promoted towards ease of doing business and curbing corruption. A simple but significant amendment is making self-attestation an acceptable practice in government, removing the need of attestation through public representatives or gazetted officers.

INFRASTRUCTURE, WEALTH CREATION

Infrastructure is high on Modi's agenda. He closely monitors incomplete projects. During one such review, it emerged that many roads were incomplete due to lack of coordination between the road constructing agencies and railways regarding road over bridges. He promptly introduced systemic changes, which significantly shortened the time in both design and final construction, as well as isolated the bottlenecks to coordination.

Prime Minister Modi understands well enough that real development can occur only on the strength of economic growth, entrepreneurship and wealth creation, and that the absence of any of these redistributive measures for creating a more egalitarian society will only lead to distribution of poverty—since, in order for wealth to be redistributed by the state through welfare schemes, it has to be created in the first place. And the history of the world in the past three hundred years shows that wealth creation is best done by citizens and their private enterprise, while the state creates the enabling conditions for the economic success of its citizens.

In order to encourage wealth creation by the citizens, therefore, Prime Minister Modi stresses upon improving the ease of doing business in the country. Under his leadership, the increased transparency, the abolition of obsolete rules and regulations and the massive increase in the application of digital and other technologies have helped improve India's international rankings on the ease of doing business. From a low of 144 in 2014 in World Bank's *Ease of Doing Business* rankings, India has risen to 63 in 2020. Prime Minister Modi's target is to bring it among the top 50, which is clearly within our grasp now.

The phenomenal success story in this area has been written by Prime Minister Modi himself. With a deep understanding of how unnecessary processes and clearances make it difficult for any entrepreneur—big or small—to start a business, to run it successfully or even to exit from it in the eventuality of failure, the Prime Minister has worked relentlessly to eliminate them by reducing compliances, while still ensuring accountability and transparency with the integration of the latest technology.

During his initial months in South Block, Prime Minister Modi felt that the External Affairs Ministry was spending too much time on orientation and lessons of foreign policy, leaving very little space for new initiatives. Many were under the misapprehension that Prime Minister was fresh to foreign policy. But they had not realized that he was one of the most widely travelled political leaders, having visited a large number of countries such as the US, Japan, China and many others even before entering electoral politics. Moreover, he was keen to redefine the country's foreign policy without any compromise or dilution of its basic tenets.

Prime Minister Modi considered foreign policy as multi-dimensional, with a significant impact on history. He often emphasized the fact that the countries that attained freedom in the same period as India also have issues of poverty. Therefore, he sought 'cooperation from the SAARC countries' in the fight against poverty and desired to work together on major economic issues being addressed by global institutions.

Another important aspect of his foreign policy is working closely with the developed countries in areas where there is significant complementarity. At the UN Conference on Climate Change held in Paris in December 2015, he surprised the Indian delegates by committing higher-than-expected performance indicators, thus winning recognition for India's sincerity. He played a leading role in finalizing the Paris Declaration on Climate Change.

Prime Minister Modi is broadly receptive to Free Trade Regional Agreements, which encourage bilateral trade and liberalization. However, the interest of the nation is supreme for him. During the advanced negotiations on Regional Comprehensive Economic Partnership (RCEP) being promoted by the ASEAN grouping, he extended constructive cooperation, provided that India was accommodated in structural adjustment by being granted a longer period to fulfil its commitments. However, in the final stages, he noticed rigidity from a few countries and took a well-reasoned decision to withdraw from RCEP negotiations. Even as economic development and strategic security are his main foreign policy planks, the novelty is that he can spontaneously identify significant complementarities in these areas while exchanging views with international leaders.

Prime Minister Modi has a remarkable character of not finding fault with the commanders and soldiers while a programme is under implementation. I never heard him discussing the lack of performance or inadequacy of the implementing machinery, whether it was demonetization or something else. Where he was convinced about the policy but the outcome was not matching with his expectation, he still did not criticize the implementation personnel. In the context of demonetization, he was convinced that the problem of corruption was closely related to black money. Demonetization, to Prime Minister Modi, was a purification campaign—almost Gandhian in its approach—to cleansing the financial system. He did not agree with some economists who saw the positive role of black money in GDP growth. In order to give it a body blow, the Prime Minister announced the demonetization of ₹500 and ₹1,000 notes. The citizens, particularly the poor and middle-income group, enthusiastically stood by the Prime Minister as the scheme was seen in their interest and the interest of the nation. The people promised that in spite of hardships, they were willing to make sacrifices in the larger national interest. It was abundantly clear that the financial institutions could not perform to the expectation. But at no stage was Prime Minister Modi prepared to blame the machinery.

It is evident to any impartial observer of India that in the past seven years the country has made great strides in all fields. What is most important is that an overwhelming majority of people have benefitted from his decision and delivery and have enthusiastically supported him at every turn. Prime Minister Modi has demonstrated that people of India are always willing to support leaders committed to national interest.

Looking back at the tenure of Prime Minister Modi since 2014, I am reminded in a contrarian way of some lines of the great poet T.S. Eliot, who beautifully expressed the predicaments of the human existence and the vast gap caused by them between our expectation and achievements, between our dreams and reality, and, it could be added, between our promises and their delivery:

'Between the idea
And the reality
Between the motion
And the act
Falls the Shadow'

We are lucky that, as far as Prime Minister Modi is concerned, no shadow falls between the idea and the reality.

DEMONSTRATING DEMOCRACY

The Power of the Masses and Mass Movements

SADHGURU

THE STAGE OF DEMOCRACY

To truly understand and appreciate the significance of the times we find ourselves in, we need to take a step back and view the long arc that we have come to call the Indian Civilization. Bharat, the kaleidoscope of cultures, ethnicity, languages, local flavours and regional quirks, philosophies and literatures, has for the larger part of its existence, never actually been a single political entity. However, to the external eye and the internal heart, there was always a common string that demarcated this geography into a unified identity. This was a land of seekers in pursuit of self-realization.

This deep-rooted ethos of seeking, and a profound sense of spirituality and life has left a strong samskaric imprint in the Indian psyche. This has resulted in an underlying sense of oneness and an intrinsic concern and compassion for the well-being of all. Vasudhaiva Kutumbakam is not just a catch phrase to the Indian mind, it is a felt experience. However, interestingly, through the history of this land, this felt oneness has found very little expression and manifestation as unified action. Seeking by its nature is an individual sport!

As a result, the largest part of Bharat's achievements and glory has come through individual genius and striving. The pursuit of truth in this land has found the most superlative expression in areas that deeply impact humanity such as science, medicine, mathematics, the arts and spirituality. As a consequence, it has been the scientists, artists, kings, leaders and mystics of this land who have set the highest benchmark and aspirations. The people of this land have deftly flowed in the wake of the tide created by these Greats and we have a glorious heritage to show for this. Another reason for this dearth of mass synergy is that there has never been a strong impetus for unified action in the absence of a felt external threat. Bharat has always opened its arms to external influence and 'new' has never been a threat to the Indian mind. It was only in the past thousand years that outside forces came with singularly brutal intentions and resultantly, forcibly rent the Indian Fabric. It took a Mahatma to rally the people of India to unified action against the external enemy and we witnessed, perhaps for the first time, the rise of a common national identity and the formal birth of the Republic of India in the modern era. India began its journey into democracy.

Nearly five decades of India's infancy were spent in settling into this new identity, finding our economic feet and catching up to the technological advancements of the Western World. Today, we are at a juncture where this energy for collective action that germinated in the freedom struggle needs channelling and maturity. In this phase, the challenge is a more subtle one. Humans have always been quick to join forces *against*, now it is a question of joining forces *for*—for the well-being of all, for the growth and resilience of the Nation, for collective advancement, for demonstrating inherent capabilities.

For this imminent transformation, the Indian Consciousness was seeking a leadership that would steer it to its true potential. A leader who would put the interests of the nation above all else and lead by example. India needed a politics beyond self-interest and entitlement. The need of the hour was insight, integrity and inspiration along with a very particular and personal understanding of what it means to be Indian. This longing and affirmation of a couple of generations of Indians has manifested in the form of Narendra Damodardas Modi.

UNDERSTANDING INDIA—RIDING THE TIDE

It is perhaps one of the most remarkable aspects of Narendra bhai as a leader that he understands his role in history as keenly as he is able to perceive the direction of the tide. As a statesman, he is acutely conscious of the fact that in our new avatar as a democracy, the role of the common citizen and the power of Collective Will are the primary aspects that will shape the future of this nation.

From the early stages of his political career, he has demonstrated and honed this understanding. It is common knowledge that, as a young man, he spent many years travelling the length and breadth of this country to gain insights into the heart of its people. This initial training and his own humble roots have stood him in great stead in his later roles where he has had to tap into this profound understanding of Bharat. This is the kind of 'insider knowledge' that large international corporations spend a significant portion of their R&D budgets on before venturing into new territories. In a democratic national leader, it is an invaluable asset and a critical differentiator.

ASPIRATION AND INSPIRATION

In the first years of public office as the Chief Minister of Gujarat, Narendra bhai's success, his wide acceptance and popularity was in a large part due to his ability to read the aspirations of the people and let that be the guiding light for his decisions and actions. His model of development was 'Development through Public Participation'. His transformation of Gujarat's economy was fuelled by clarity of vision and the ability to communicate this vision to fifty-five million Gujaratis and earn their trust and cooperation.

Whether it was the 2003 Kanya Kelavani literacy movement of the Gujarat government with its focus on the girl child or the Krishi Mahotsav to rejuvenate agriculture at the grassroots, the hallmark was that these movements enlisted the people's participation. Narendra bhai has always been cognizant of the power of emotional commitment. The key to the success of these endeavours was that they were not approached as dry government schemes; rather, each was aimed at transforming the mindset of the masses. For instance, with the Kanya Kelavani movement, we know that CM Modi led from the front, travelling across the state personally convincing parents of the importance of education.

In 2012, when he presided over the silver jubilee celebration of

Goddess Umiya Temple in Unjha, he took the opportunity to lament the fact that the taluk had the lowest sex ratio in Gujarat despite being the abode of Goddess Umiya, and appeal to the Kadava Patidar community to put an end to the abhorrent practice of female infanticide. This led to the community taking a vow in the holy temple that they would abolish the practice. In early 2020, the same community came together from across the world to pool resources to lay the foundation stone for what is envisioned as the tallest temple in the world. I was particularly happy to send my blessings to this monumental acknowledgment of the Divine Feminine. The shifts that can be achieved by creating awareness in Human hearts are far greater than those that can be achieved by enforcing policies or laws. Narendra Modi seems to know this, both by instinct as well as grassroots experience.

One of the hallmarks of a mature and wise people is the appreciation and remembrance we express to the greats who came before us. A nation that doesn't build on the edifice of pride and gratitude will never manage to build a truly glorious future. I remember hearing of the events surrounding the largely unsung nationalist hero, Shyamji Krishna Varma, which gave early evidence that this leader is a man who understands the power of gratitude.

Shyamji Varma was a great nationalist and freedom fighter who founded a centre called the India House in London, which was not only a meeting place for like-minded revolutionaries but also a refuge for Indian students facing racism in the United Kingdom. Before his death in Geneva in 1930, he made arrangements with the local St George's Cemetery to store his asthi, expressing the wish that the urn should be sent back to a Free India. Almost fifty-five years after India had gained Independence, Narendra bhai—then two years into his tenure as Chief Minister of Gujarat—stepped in to help fulfil this last wish. The ashes were brought home from Switzerland. From Mumbai, they were transported in a ten-day Viranjali Yatra across 2,029 km and seventeen districts to the final resting place in Mandvi in Gujarat, the birthplace of the freedom fighter. Today there is a memorial there where thousands are able to pay homage and be inspired by a great life well-remembered.

This grand gesture was remembrance, gratitude, sentiment and optics all rolled into one and speaks of a man who knows the importance of building upon the foundations of the past and inspirations of iconic leaders of yore.

HARNESSING HUMAN SPIRIT

In my early days in Mysore, along with a group of spirited youngsters, I set out on a mission to clean up our beloved city. Armed with brooms, with biscuit packets for the volunteers and paanka (lemonade) courtesy the generosity of the householders whose streets we cleaned, we set out each Sunday with tremendous enthusiasm. This enthusiasm got so infectious that there was a certain time when we had close to 30,000 to 35,000 volunteers and the city municipal workers started to work earlier than before to beat us to the task. More recently, when Mysore was declared the cleanest city in the country, a couple of my friends called me to recollect the beginnings of this transformation. I share this to register how the simple exuberance of the common citizen can transform a locality, city or nation. The strength of this administration is that it has recognized the power of participatory democracy. Whether it is the Swachch Bharat Abhiyan or the Beti Bachao Beti Padhao mission, they have each taken root because they have been people-led, with citizens as change agents. The fact that every village had at least one swachhagrahi was a masterstroke of participatory leadership.

Another astounding response from the people was when they heeded the Prime Minister's call to 'Give it up'. About one crore (10 million) people gave up their LPG subsidy, saving the government ₹4,166 crore or ₹41.66 billion every year, thereby contributing to over seven crore (70 million) connections to women and poor households that truly needed them through the Pradhan Mantri Ujjwala Yojana. Similarly, nearly forty-two lakh (4.2 million) senior citizens gave up their railway fare subsidy within nine months of the appeal. This is testimony to the enormous trust the government has managed to garner unto itself and the spirit of community it has instilled in citizens.

TRUST BEGETS TRUST

With all that is valuable in this world, you must give before you can receive. It is true of love, compassion, respect and it is true of trust. The reason Narendra bhai has been so successful in gaining the trust of the people is because he has always placed trust in them as individuals and as a collective.

This has manifested in so many different levels in his administration.

Time and again, he has demonstrated great trust in competence. This we have seen repeatedly with various levels of governance—from district collectors to members of his Union Cabinet. He has been known for his progressive lateral hiring of professionals into key governmental positions, where competence is valued over protocol.

Even as Chief Minister, he initiated the Karmayogi Abhiyan, a major exercise to build capabilities of 500,000 government employees and create a stronger administrative team in Gujarat. This strong focus on building leadership at all levels is a trait that he has carried with him to Delhi as well.

PM Modi has placed his trust not only in the governmental backbone of the country but on its citizens too. Never before has so much responsibility been conferred on the common man. Many avenues have been thrown open for the average people to express their ideas for improvement or share feedback. From systems of education to thoughts on how to rewrite our History, from ideas for alternative energy to the economy, the Indian Citizen's views are sought and heard. As the Prime Minister he has made it a point to keep directly in touch with the people. With his radio programme *Mann ki Baat,* his forthcoming communications and pervasive presence on social media, the distance between government and citizen has been greatly reduced. Such engagement cannot but result in the emergence of a truly participatory democracy.

This trust has not come easy, it has been hard won. I would say, a chief contributing factor has been the long-term impact of Narendra bhai's personal demeanour and extraordinary commitment. In his years of public office, the dedication that he has continuously exhibited has inspired and percolated into several tiers of governance and, in turn, the man on the street. Whether it is the inhuman hours he puts into his work or his impeccable personal integrity and famed incorruptibility, his sense of propriety in not using his office for personal gain or that of any relative or friend, each of these have had an impact on those around him and those who have watched his progress. When the citizenry has complete trust in the Leader's primary intentions and priorities, gaining their cooperation in even the most difficult transformational reforms becomes easier in a nation of India's complexity.

Another aspect of his politics is his keen respect for the voice of the people: His ear is always firmly to the ground and he is quick to hear and act. When he speaks of *'jan aadesh'* as he often does, he means it quite literally. I was very happy to witness this personally at the culmination of the Rally for Rivers movement. After our twenty-nine-day nationwide rally in September 2017 to garner the support of the people for the urgent cause of river revitalization, when we reached New Delhi with 162 million voices in affirmation and a 760-page *Revitalization of Rivers in India: Draft Policy Recommendation*, we found the Prime Minister anticipating us. I understood that he had been sharply following the progress of the rally and been listening to the voices of the people at every stage. I handed over the bound document to him at the culmination of the rally, and the very next day, our team received a call from the Prime Minister's Office (PMO), requesting a soft copy of the document that could be shared with and analysed by various experts and teams.

Within a month, in November 2017, the PMO formed an expert group under NITI Aayog to look into the policy recommendations. Six months later, the group had prepared a Programme for Action led by the Department of Rural Development. In his letter to all states and union territories, NITI Aayog CEO Amitabh Kant said, 'Based on the discussions, it has been decided to launch a major mission on revitalization of rivers utilizing the existing schemes and (programmes) of the government with community-led efforts.'

Subsequently, in 2020, the Honourable Minister for Environment informed me that the Union government was working on detailed project reports to implement this community-led model of river revitalization in thirteen of India's major rivers. There is indeed no other way to affect the scale of change that we need to achieve without making the Indian farmer and rural community the primary stakeholder and beneficiary. It is wonderful that this is clearly understood by the government.

To me, what was most heartening about this was the swiftness of the response. This is something we had not hitherto expected from the slow-moving behemoth that is the Indian governmental structure. The Prime Minister has managed to cut out much of the red tape and bureaucratic roadblocks and create a system that is nimble—a vital necessity in a government that aims to be porous to the aspirations of the people and move with agility to meet them.

THE POWER OF THE SYMBOL

Another essential wisdom that Narendra bhai displays is his understanding of the power of sentiment and emotion. This is particularly true in Bharat. Indians are not moved by dry logic of loss and gain, nor is it easy to box us into compliances of rules and regulations. To move India's Collective Will, it takes a stirring of the heart. This was something that Mahatma Gandhi demonstrated beautifully. Consequently, Narendra bhai has never underestimated the Power of the Symbol.

In recent years, I was particularly amused by the furore caused by the very simple proposal that as citizens we should stand for the National Anthem in theatres and such spaces. What the protestors fail to understand in their juvenility is that when a nation is making efforts to move a very large mass of people out of abject conditions, it is extremely vital that we operate on the foundation of a robust National Identity. Nationhood after all is not a god-given concept.

If a young and complex Nation has to surge ahead, it cannot be achieved without a strong national sentiment. The naysayers may have the luxury of endless debate but a Prime Minister who has this onerous task on his hands cannot afford to miss this point, and we are fortunate that he does not miss it! There may come a time of extreme prosperity and stability when we can afford to tone down our national sentiment—indeed, we look forward to that time, but that time is not now.

I was also impressed by the symbolism and thought that went into the creation of the Statue of Unity in the memory of Sardar Vallabhbhai Patel, whom we call the 'Iron Man of India'. As Gujarat Chief Minister, Narendra Modi announced a nationwide campaign to collect small pieces of iron from farmers to use in creating the statue. This can very easily be dismissed by an uninvolved outsider as just a gesture, but each one of those farmers across five lakh (500,000) villages has experienced a great sense of belonging as well as contribution.

Similarly, when the COVID-19 pandemic struck, the Prime Minister's first concern was to get the buy-in from citizens. A telling example of this was how the citizens responded to the call to stand in solidarity with our frontline health workers and demonstrate the unified will of this nation. This was extraordinarily vital because without cooperation, India would have faced a calamity of unimaginable proportions. We have neither the manpower nor the temperament as a country to keep people indoors and coerce compliance by brute force.

The now-famous clapping and lamp lighting by Indians across the board served to create awareness and simultaneously, to keep up the spirits of the people. It is difficult for non-Indians to understand the unique challenges that the Indian administration faces in dealing with the unparalleled multiplicity of this land. We can only extrapolate from the fact even the simplest communication has to go out in twenty-two official languages! India is a very organic chaos, and that is its weakness and its strength. Emotion is the only way to harness the kinetic energy emanating from this whirlpool that is Bharat.

TRANSFORMING LIFE IN INDIA

A nation can rise on emotion but to function it needs systems. Culturally, without doubt India is a magnificent place to be, but systemically, life in India has often been a horrendous experience for the common man. A Human Being should be able to live with ease and dignity even without having a chacha or mama in an elected or official position. Hitherto, the people of this country had almost abandoned hope of a life beyond the daily humiliation of having to grease the palms of people in authority even for the simplest aspects of life—from registering a birth to registering a death and everything in between. I remember a particular incident when I was working on my farm in my younger days. One particular farmer I knew had several years earlier bought five goats, mortgaging his land in the Grameena Bank. Out of these he managed to keep only two goats! One went to the bank official and the other two to the Panchayat Head who facilitated this loan. About fifteen years later, when the bank wanted to seize his land and property, he was at his wits' end, trying to tell them that he actually had received only two goats.

When I think of these hardships that a generation of Indians have had to undergo, to my mind one of the most potent ideas that the Prime

Minister has unleashed is the Pradhan Mantri Jan Dhan Yojana. With earnings, loans, flow-out from government schemes, all directly entering the bank account of the citizen, this one idea along with the larger digital revolution has the power to transform India at the grassroots.

Right now, we need to focus on creating systems that empower the citizen and harnessing the potential of individual capability instead of making the country dependent on state-run systems and infrastructure. For instance, in the Skill India Movement, we are still attempting to bolster the system through state-run centres and schemes. Instead, we should harness the already existing resource—which is the skilled craftsperson, technician or artisan. Master craftspersons or technicians across the country, from a wide variety of technical and craft specialties, can be paid and incentivized to adopt the apprentice model of skill transfer. Further, each successful student/apprentice who passes a standard skill test should earn the master further monetary bonus. This will ensure a quality transfer of both technical and traditional skills without the State having to create costly infrastructure and support systems.

I remember an occasion during the tenure of the former Prime Minister, A.B. Vajpayee, when I had visited the offices of the Ministry of Rural Development at the Parliament building because I had some concerns about rural development and rejuvenation. The Minister concerned introduced me to the IAS officers involved, who showed me all the schemes and policy documents that had been prepared. It struck me that these ideas and schemes were extremely well thought out, and the policies had been drafted by people who knew what they were talking about. As I saw it, the lacuna was the lack of groundswell of People's Enthusiasm to deliver the intended result.

At this juncture in our growth, the entrepreneurial spirit and spirit of cooperation has been ignited. Now it is important that we start to shift the onus of nation-building on its primary stakeholder—the citizen. We need a system that focuses exclusively on *Ease of Living.* We must craft a system where the common man finds everyday life a smooth and happy experience, where access to basic civic needs and growth lie in his hands.

Almost every aspect of the fundamentals of human life—from education to livelihood to ecological restoration—can be handled with mass mobilization and the support of digitization. This pioneering approach towards true democracy has the potential to transform the very way Bharat is.

This work demands an enormous degree of calibrated attention and a specialized support system within the administration. A unique Department or Ministry helmed by an elected representative with a dedicated bureaucratic structure would be ideal to ensure that each movement and powerful idea involving the masses stays fired up and on course, so that it can gather momentum and a life of its own in the shortest possible duration.

As we stand in 2021, the nation has a window of fifteen to twenty years to bring about an unprecedented transformation. We should do everything in our power to make sure this happens.

CHARTING THE FUTURE

In the Adi Parva of the Mahabharata, we have the story of King Bharata, who had nine sons but found none of them worthy of the throne. Instead, he adopted Bhumanyu, the simple forest-dwelling boy born of Sage Bharadwaja, because he saw in him all the qualities that befit a king. In many ways, I hold this to be the seed of democracy in this nation, the first demonstration of prizing competence, where leaders rise from the ground up through their ability and not through entitlement. Today in Democratic India, we see this again in the form of Narendra Damodardas Modi.

As a nation, we must make the most of this opportunity. With the most youthful population on the planet, and a surging spirit of National Pride, empowered by a capable, committed leader—this is the moment to script the transformation of Bharat. A confounding kaleidoscope Bharat may be, but a kaleidoscope can be coaxed into the most spectacular patterns and geometry with patience and application. We are at a moment in history when the possibilities of transcending limited identities of religion, region, ethnicity and caste are great because technology has made geographies porous and created the stage for a larger identity. It is now up to the people of Bharat. The synchronicity and agility with which we respond to this opportunity will determine how far we are able to walk the path to a truly Bhavya Bharat. We must respond through the power of Positive Mass Movements, as Democracy is essentially a Mass Movement.

Digital India
Power To Empower
UNICORN

THEN CAME THE WINDS OF CHANGE

SUDHA MURTY

The earliest memory of my country is the one right after the end of the British rule. There was struggle just for basic necessities. I clearly recall my father 'booking' a pale green Fiat car that took 17 long years for him to finally bring home. Prosperity, at the time, was defined by whether a person had a government job that afforded him a pension, or if he owned a car or a house, or whether he had a telephone and a refrigerator or perhaps, if he had the opportunity to travel abroad on company expenses. If a person boasted about any one of these, people thought of him or her as *lucky*.

It was also a period marked by the lack of industrialization and a particularly difficult environment for entrepreneurs. There were a few great exceptions such as the Tatas and the Birlas, but there was no one of significance from an ordinary background.

Whether in school or at home, we were taught that to be content was the ultimate goal and the source of real happiness—most likely because there was a huge lack of facilities in the country and that contentment was the only way we could rationalize happiness at the time. So most of us were delighted with the little we achieved because we never dreamt of anything too big or large or competitive or outside of the country. We never thought of travelling by air, for example. Experiencing airplanes was more about children watching the planes take off and looking at one another in awe, knowing that they would never get a chance to travel in one.

The elders of society believed that anything from the West was the best—strong remnants of thoughts that the British had left behind. The mindset was largely due to India's colonization and the oppression its people had faced over the last thousand years. Societal conditioning made us afraid to face loss, failure and others' judgements.

Slowly, but surely, things began to change. The drastic transformation came in 1991 with the economic liberalization policies. The Licence Raj disappeared, and the rupee devalued at a rapid pace. Private colleges sprang up and many budding entrepreneurs entered the arena of business. And yet, there were no angel or institutional investors, and everyone had to rely on bank loans for seed capital. Since most of the time, banks favoured the influential and the wealthy, there were numerous cash transactions that occurred among the poorest of the poor. Interactions were slow and we dreamt of a day of instant communication. City life was better than rural life but fraught with challenges; a gas connection was still a luxury, travelling on the poorly constructed roads was not easy and obtaining a television turned you into an instant community celebrity. Then, 2001 brought the disruption of technology, followed by such intense popularization of the internet that the word became a verb.

I have been working for the poor and the common people for the past thirty years. I recognize and feel the change through my own experiences. In 2000, I was planning for a week-long trip in Karnataka for philanthropic work. I preferred to stay with someone I knew, instead of a fancy hotel, so that I could experience the ground realities. So, I called a couple I knew in the area. Both were doctors who ran a nursing home together. My friends were happy and said, 'Come, Sudha, stay as long as you want. We are going on a pilgrimage, so we won't be there when you arrive. We had planned this trip months ago. But our house is open for you! Sarala, our reliable housekeeper, will be here and you will have no problems in our absence.'

I accepted their kind offer and travelled to their town as scheduled. It was a reasonably good house and Sarala was waiting for me when I arrived. She was a plump woman in her mid-30s and had a cheerful face. She lived in the helper's quarters in the compound, along with her 5-year-old daughter. Every morning, she would cook for me and pack my lunch. After I returned home in the evening, she would prepare delicious food for me. I have a habit of speaking to people, especially people around me, and those who can give me a true picture of my country—farmers, construction workers, school teachers, pandits or priests, street hawkers and others who toil every day for daily wages.

SARALA'S STORY

As I ate and spoke with Sarala, I learnt her story.

'Amma,' she said, 'My parents are coolies in a village nearby. There, I studied till the VIIth standard and then they got me married after a few years. I had my daughter. Very soon, I lost my husband in a road accident. The roads in our village are not tarred and they are horrible with many ups and downs. My husband ran over a big stone while cycling home and hit his head badly. Since there was no hospital nearby or access to ambulances, he was dead by the time we took him to the hospital. This is the same one that Madam runs along with her husband. My parents wanted me to stay in the same village and become a coolie like them, but I refused. I requested Madam for a job desperately. She was kind to me and made me the housekeeper of her home. I try and look after their house efficiently...'

'Yes, they had high praise for you when I spoke to them,' I interrupted her.

'Yes, Amma, I have to do my job well to retain it. I don't have a good education, nor do I have the confidence to go somewhere else and do well. These are caring people and have given me a place to stay. They look after my daughter's education, and they also look after our health. We don't have any health insurance and doctors' charges can be so expensive, Amma. So I am content and happy.'

'Sarala, why don't you finish your studies? Then I am sure you will get a better paying job.'

'Amma, I don't think so,' said Sarala. 'Look at my parents—they earn daily wages when they work in the fields. Compared to them, my job is very good, and I am satisfied.'

'Well, then, what do you dream for your daughter?' I asked.

'Amma, I want her to obtain a college degree. She should get hired as a receptionist in a hospital or a company. It will be a very good job.'

I was disappointed and asked, 'Is that all?'

'That is all I want for her. After graduating from college, she will get a better salary.'

'Why don't you dream about your daughter becoming a doctor or an officer? Why don't you aim higher?' I nudged her.

'I want her to do better than me. I have seen my uneducated parents and desired to do better than that. I am aware of my parent's plight in the village—there is a lack of drinking water, clean toilets, banks and medical facilities too,' Sarala said with sadness.

'Where do they keep their savings then?' I wondered out loud.

'Whatever my parents earn, they keep in a *dabba* at home. I have to give them cash if they ever need anything. Look at me now—I have opened an account in a bank and my salary gets deposited there directly. I want my daughter to have more, but I should know my limitations also. How can my daughter ever become an officer? Amma, all desirables are not achievable.'

I laughed and said, 'All achievables are also not desirable. But things have changed a lot, Sarala, and you must aim higher for your daughter. Who knows the extent of her capability? You must help her accomplish more. But come now, please will you turn the television on? I want to see the Olympics.'

She switched it on and asked, 'What is this?'

'It is the world's best sports meet. It started a long time ago, in a country called Greece, and they hold this meet once in every four years in different countries. Players from various countries go there. For all events, the best one gets a gold medal, the second gets silver and the third gets bronze.'

'What happens to the others?' Sarala asked.

'They get a participation certificate,' I said absent-mindedly.

Sarala became curious, 'Has anyone ever gone from our country? Perhaps nobody…this Olympics is the world's best, after all.'

'Of course, people have gone from India.'

'Have they won medals this year? And if so, how many?'

'I am not sure as the meet is still going on, Sarala,' I said.

'It is more than enough that they are there. This way, the participants can travel abroad, see the events and get a certificate,' she remarked.

I was sad at the way she thought that we should be happy with a certificate. In her eyes, just going abroad, even if one was not winning, was an achievement. No wonder she aimed for her daughter to become a receptionist.

The next day, as I was about to depart, Sarala gave me a box and smiled. She said, 'Amma, this is a very special dish!'

'What's this?' I said, perplexed.

'You help many poor people, Amma. I know I can't give you anything much, but this is dates *poli*. Very few people know how to make it properly, and I am one of them. Madam has taught me this recipe. Whenever you decide to eat it, pour a teaspoon of liquid ghee over it first. Then it tastes wonderful.'

'Of course, I know of this! My mother makes this too and tells me the same thing!' I thanked her, took the box, left a 'thank you' note for my hosts and went on my way.

Many years passed. Calendars changed. Saplings became trees. Leadership changed. The political atmosphere in the country improved. There was a big revolution in information technology. Meanwhile, I continued to immerse myself in Infosys Foundation's fieldwork.

MANY YEARS LATER...

In 2020, a pandemic–hit India and the Foundation became extremely alert. The first agenda for us was to save the medical fraternity and look after patients, especially the underprivileged. We became busy assisting hospitals, providing beds, distributing sanitizers, masks, gloves, dry ration and cooked food. Then came the personal protective equipment (PPE) kits. Even though the medical staff resembled astronauts while wearing them, the kits were crucial in ensuring that the virus did not enter through their noses, eyes or throats. It was critical for us to supply them with more. However, obtaining the PPE kits wasn't easy. We didn't want doctors and nurses to face patients without the kits, so we ordered some imported ones. We found out that not only were they expensive, but that they were coming too late. When the government under Modi's leadership can develop complicated homegrown vaccines at a pace comparable to the West, it gave me new hope, and I also caught the 'Make in India' bug! But who would do so efficiently, quickly, and with good quality at a reasonable price? Many hospitals were looking for these kits all over the country.

In the midst of this frantic search, one email caught my eye—it was from a young girl. She wrote, 'I have a small garment factory that employs 50 workers. We are outstanding in the manufacturing and producing of any design that you give to us. If you can provide us with raw material and an imported PPE kit, we will make comparable ones. I am from a small town and do not have working capital, even though I have the talent and knowledge. I am happy to explain in more detail if you can give me an appointment.'

Something about the email struck a chord and I remembered the time I wrote a letter to J.R.D. Tata 50 years ago, without any connections. I requested him to go through the letter even if it was from a small-town girl who was unknown to him. I saw myself in the girl's position and I called her to the office. The girl landed in my office with all the relevant documents. She was a simple girl with a no-nonsense attitude, and I drowned her with the questions I had.

'I can mimic any design you give me,' she said. 'I think that skill can be used for a good cause in these times.'

'Have you done this before?' I asked.

'Ma'am, my diploma is in design. If you are familiar with Chandni Chowk in Delhi, you know that plagiarized dresses of famous fashion designers sell there for one-tenth the price.'

'That is not my area of interest, so I cannot comment on it,' I responded.

'I am telling you, Ma'am. Give me a PPE kit, the right raw materials and I will not disappoint you. I will rip open the kit and produce the same quality product. I will even deliver it wherever you want.'

'But how will you do it? You only have 50 people in your factory currently. We need much more than you can produce,' I said with complete transparency.

'Please don't worry. I can hire more people. That is my problem to address,' she shot back.

'What if there is a difference of opinion in the quality you produce?'

'If the quality is not acceptable to you, then I will return your money in instalments, Ma'am.'

So, I took the risk, and I gave her a cheque for ₹10 lakh (₹1 million) towards the first prototype and a small order. I said to her, 'Look, I am giving this money to you personally. I hope you will keep your word and come out with an excellent product at a reasonable price. Any future orders will depend on the outcome of this pilot programme.'

She took the money with grace, thanked me and touched my feet. She said, 'You will not regret this, Ma'am.'

Confidently, she walked out.

Five days later, she brought in the first prototypes, and I compared it to the imported product. It was comparable and cheaper too. The young girl had delivered it in neat packaging, and I sent the kits to a few hospitals and reliable doctors for genuine feedback. Soon, I received their inputs—the items manufactured by this young lady's facility were better than the imported products!

Immediately, we handed her a big order from the Foundation, and she became our regular supplier. There were no complaints from the doctors or the hospitals where we donated them.

After a few months, the young girl came to meet me.

I asked, 'What happened? Didn't you get a cheque for your last shipment?'

She smiled and said, 'Everything is in order, Ma'am. I wanted to speak to you.'

'*Beta*, about what?'

'I want to give you something.' She handed me a box and said, 'This is dates *poli* specially made for you. Ma'am, if you add liquid ghee on it, the taste will be outstanding.'

'Did you make this? And how did you know about the trick of adding liquid ghee?'

'Ma'am, I am not an expert at making this. My mother made this for you.'

'How does your mother know that I like dates *poli*?'

'Twenty years ago, you stayed in a doctors' house. My mother, Sarala, was a housekeeper there and she made dates *poli* for you then. She remembered you liked it and sent this for you.'

I was delighted. 'Are you Sarala's daughter, that little 5-year-old girl?'

She nodded, 'Yes, my name is Swapna.'

I forgot about my next meeting and wanted to know more, 'Tell me about your journey, Swapna. First, why didn't you tell me that you were Sarala's daughter? I remember vaguely that your mother wanted you to become a receptionist.'

'Yes, you are right, my mother wanted that for me. When I was growing up, I realized that my passion was more important to me than holding a steady job. I have always loved designing and making things. Very early, I knew that I could easily study any design, cut the material and stitch it by hand. Knowing this, Doctor Kaka got me a sewing machine when I was still in school. I always noticed the new clothes on the mannequins in the market and I could easily stitch the exact same outfit very quickly. So, I started stitching salwar kameez and other clothes to earn extra money in high school. Then I joined a diploma course in design. I got an opportunity to do more, and I worked for a few years in Delhi.

'There, I understood that it is not the degree alone but passion and excellence that can take you to the top. I learnt the crux of running a design business and came back to the South. I took a loan from the bank, used it for seed funding and began my business supplying clothing to clients in Delhi. I earned decent money and expanded my business. I saw in one of your interviews that you were very keen to supply PPE kits to hospitals as early as possible. So, I decided to approach you.'

'But why didn't you tell me who you were?'

'I wanted to do this on my own, and I didn't want your decision or judgement to be biased. I was ecstatic when you gave me money for the pilot. I didn't want to break your trust, so I put my best into the product. I know that it is not fashionable or a designer's delight, but it will save the life of our nurses, doctors and helpers in the medical field. I grew up in a doctors' house and I understand what it means to serve people. So, I set aside my Delhi work and took this project on as a priority for our country. During these times, many shops in Delhi were shut anyway and things were delayed.'

'Does Sarala know how you are helping us?' I asked her.

'Of course! She knows. She is downstairs, Ma'am!'

'Why didn't you bring her with you?'

'I wanted to take your permission.'

'Don't be so formal. Call her upstairs, please!' I urged her.

A few minutes later, Swapna came in with her mother. Sarala was wearing a nice sari. *She must be almost 55 now*, I thought. She sat down with grace, and I could feel her confidence and happiness.'

'Amma, I really didn't know that I would meet you again like this!' she said with a smile.

'Sarala, I am happy that Swapna did not become a receptionist. She is doing very well. You must be pleased.'

Suddenly, Sarala had tears in her eyes. She said, 'I wish her father would have been alive to see her. If the roads would have been good in those days, he would have lived to see this day.'

'Yes, Sarala, I agree. India has become one of the fastest highway builders in the world in the past few years.'

'Amma, my daughter has opened my eyes. She taught me that one can work at any age if one is passionate about it.'

'What are you doing these days, Sarala?'

'As you know, Amma, I was always good at cooking. At first, I started catering for my daughter's small company, and now I run an independent catering business.'

'I am happy to hear it. How are your parents?' I asked.

'They are still in the village and don't want to move to live with us in the city.'

'Do they still save money in a box?'

'No, Amma. They have become modern. In the past few years, things have changed a lot in the village. They have their bank account now, just like the others in our village. They also do online transactions and are very happy with its convenience in their old age.'

I nodded, 'Yes, I know that India has the top spot in real-time digital payments at 25 billion transactions per day.'

'You used to travel a lot for fieldwork in your younger days,' remarked Sarala. 'I am sure you must miss travelling during this pandemic.'

'Yes, I do. I have one item pending on my bucket list—I would love to see the world's tallest statue of Sardar Vallabhbhai Patel in Gujarat. It was built in 2018 under Modi's leadership and is a stark reminder of the man who played an important role in unifying our country. I would love to visit the statue once.'

Just then, my Programme Director peeped in, 'Ma'am,' she said. 'The video team is waiting for you to provide a byte for vaccination awareness.'

'Please give me some time. I will come shortly.'

I turned to Sarala. 'I hope you and your employees are vaccinated,' I said.

'Yes, Ma'am, people in my parents' village have also been vaccinated. They also have the Ayushman Bharat Yojana health insurance scheme.'

'I am so happy to hear about the implementation of these programmes. The Ayushman Bharat Yojana is the world's largest health assurance scheme, and I just read the other day—17.2 crore (172 million) health cards have been issued and 2.5 crore (25 million) free treatments have happened till December 2021! In a country like ours, this scheme was sorely needed. The ripple effect of Prime Minister Narendra Modi's actions in the government can be easily felt in the country. Homegrown COVID-19 vaccinations and drives are only a part of the success that take us one step forward towards self-dependence. Did you know that Mission Indhradhanush has been lauded as one of the best immunization programmes? Almost 4 crore (40 million) children and 95 lakh (9.5 million) pregnant women have been covered under this!'

I was pleased about my country's achievements, and I smiled.

The mother and Sarala's daughter beamed in reaction to my enthusiasm.

'Swapna,' I said, 'The days when people only looked out for jobs are gone. Now youngsters like you are creating jobs for people—instead of taking one. It is the best way to create wealth in society and reduce poverty. Do you know India has had 60 unicorns in the past seven years? I hope to see you become the 61st.'

'Ma'am, I didn't know. I thought China was the one producing many unicorns.'

'Those are old statistics, Swapna. Today, India has produced five times the number of unicorns as China, despite the pandemic. This generation has proven that we can be the best at anything we put our mind to.'

Sarala interjected and said, 'Do you remember, you taught me what Olympics stood for? That day I said that participation itself was wonderful, but today I take back my words. It is wonderful to win a medal, preferably gold! I don't want Indians to be second best to anybody.'

I laughed and nodded.

After they left, I sat alone with my thoughts. Swapna's story was a story of change—of a woman helping herself. She represented the modern Indian generation that is determined and hardworking, and aims to be the best.

This is the India of 2021, and this is the India of the future, advancing into the twenty-first century. I felt like flying in the air, jumping into the water, gliding through the snow, drenching in the rain—all these things make me so happy.

THE NEW NORMAL

If someone had told me this story two decades ago, I would have doubted it. But it happened to me now, and I enjoy this changing world. My analytical skills kept pushing me to find a credible reason for this change. The atmosphere in our country in the past seven years has become more supportive, women are feeling safe to explore business and there is an environment conducive to the development of businesses through better roads, good education and availability of opportunities.

The governance of Prime Minister Modi has inspired another wave of transformation that has affected the lives of billions of people, including you and me—whether it is the vaccination programme, the joy we felt collectively at the success in the recent Olympics, the start-ups and unicorns set in motion by many other young Swapnas, the smokeless gas saving the tears of our poor sisters in rural areas or Jan Dhan Yojana, which has opened up the world of banking and digital payments to all my countrymen.

Gone are the days when people sent their children abroad with tears in their eyes, knowing that the children will settle there and not return to India due to financial constraints. Today, many people choose to return with the positive change in the environment back home. Some even come back with the greatest of intentions to keep the progress going. Now, Indians are no longer considered secondary to anyone at a global level. The younger generation is confident and ready to face all countries in various competitions including cricket, but also in athletics and so much more. We aim for the best.

This is possible only when there is a true leader—like Modi—who is as deeply rooted as a banyan tree. A big tree with a big personality. Every part of the tree is useful to others, much like our Prime Minister, every project is useful to us. The animals can eat the leaves, the birds can make nests, people can take fruits, bees and humans can both enjoy the honey and the aroma of flowers, and branches can be cut for wood to create a shelter for the needy. But there a good leader stands—tall and all alone without any benefit for himself or herself. These are the leaders entrenched in ground reality with an aim to transform the destiny of the country and her people.

> '*Chhayaam anyasya kurvanthi thishtanthi svayam aathape*
> *Phalanthi cha parartheshu na swartheshu mahadhrumah*'
>
> Trees stand in the scorching sun, yet provide shade for others,
> They bear fruits, not for themselves but for others.

SECTION FIVE

VASUDHAIVA KUTUMBAKAM: INDIA AND THE WORLD

TACKLING ADVERSARIES THROUGH STRONG AND EFFECTIVE NATIONAL SECURITY POLICIES

AJIT DOVAL, K.C.

INTRODUCTION

National security policymaking is a function of not just defining objectives and building capacities, but also the showing of political will to deploy capabilities to achieve identified goals. Once policies are made, what matters most is how the leadership builds systems and processes, creates national will and leads its team to walk the talk.

Prime Minister Narendra Modi's commitment to nation-building, an abiding belief in India's inherent potential and a unique leadership style have played important roles in framing strong and effective national security policies. A political leader with a vision of the future and down-to-earth experience of public service and governance, he has three traits that distinguish him from most others who occupied his exalted position. His capacity for hard work, penchant for details and fast comprehension of complex issues are extraordinary features of his leadership style. His long experience as the Chief Minister of Gujarat, a progressive coastal state with strong historical and global connects, has impacted his thinking on Centre-state relations and his worldview. These considerations have shaped the way he defined objectives, signalled intent and built capacities to strengthen national security since he took office in 2014.

Prime Minister Modi entered office after being a successful Chief Minister of Gujarat for over 12 years. His long experience in public life gives him an uncanny ability to gauge the mood and temper of the people and relate to their needs and aspirations. He also developed a keen sense of observation, an eye for detail, and the ability to analyse and correlate facts. All this was apparent in his style of functioning as a Prime Minister. When he became the Chief Minister of Gujarat, he was able to bring about radical changes in the process of governance. He understood the strengths and limitations of the bureaucracy—a resource that is useful, if imaginatively utilized and controlled. As Prime Minister, he understood that, if bureaucracy has to be led, the leader has to come up with some new ideas, innovative plans and practical suggestions to remain a step ahead in all aspects. He should also be a problem solver for them. The PM achieved this quite successfully.

Prime Minister Narendra Modi has shown the determination to push back against efforts to impose unilateral actions that adversely impact India's security interests. However, this has been done in a gradual, calibrated and responsible manner, after exploring every opportunity to resolve disputes through peaceful means. He has also made efforts to upgrade structures, evolve attitudes and build capacities to deal with both contemporary and futuristic security challenges. Most importantly, his initiatives are people-centric and defined by what is good for India and the world at large. With this approach, under his leadership, the country has developed a unique Indian way of handling national security challenges, which is a rare mix of prudence and unflinching resolve. This chapter discusses some of the key initiatives taken by him. It also looks at the following: What has changed? How has it changed? And, how Prime Minister Modi's leadership style and personal beliefs have impacted the change?

As a person who has had the opportunity to witness these changes from close quarters for over seven years, I can assert that these changes were neither accidental nor providential. They were the consequence of deep thought, deliberation and, clarity as well as PM Modi's high risk-taking capabilities.

Engaging with these questions in the seventy-fifth year of India's independence is useful for several reasons. It provides an opportunity for policymakers to review their effectiveness. It also helps determine future strategies. The Prime Minister's initiatives could be broadly classified under three headings: (1) consolidation by evolving attitudes (2) assertion of political will, and (3) bringing about transformation. These initiatives have progressed concurrently and are briefly discussed in the succeeding paragraphs.

CONSOLIDATION BY EVOLVING ATTITUDES

One of the important tasks of Prime Minister Modi has been to create a national vision of security and change the deeply-ingrained status quoist mindsets and archaic attitudes that resist all change. The key challenges included finding the right balance to leverage soft and hard power, pursuing national interests in a polarized global environment and executing outcome-driven security policies. Branding India's image globally was also important to make the country a destination of choice for investments and strategic partnerships.

Prime Minister Modi's approach has involved consultation with stakeholders, reliance on expert advice, a penchant for going into details and awareness of the peculiarities of the organizational cultures of institutions dealing with national security. This has led to strategic clarity and speedy decision-making. The fact that PM Modi was not hemmed in by the baggage of serving in the Central government brought in fresh perspectives. He insisted that important strategic reviews of national security, such as annual DGPs' (Directors General of Police) and Combined Commander's Conferences, be held outside Delhi. He was also willing to break from past precedence, take risks and rise above political considerations in national interest. The delegation of planning and execution of specialized tasks was left to the professionals.

SECURING INDIA INTERNALLY

The foundations of Prime Minister Modi's security policy flow from the belief that India will be taken seriously internationally only if it is strong internally. Efforts have been made to build a seamless, coordinated national security apparatus and intelligence grid. Focused intelligence-based operations have helped prevent and respond to threats expeditiously. This has resulted in no major terrorist attack in the hinterland beyond Jammu and Kashmir and some regions of Punjab. In a world that has witnessed heightened levels of Islamist terrorism in the past decade, India's effective countering of terrorist threats despite numerous attempts by extremist groups is a tribute to his decisive leadership.

The Prime Minister understands the complexities of security policymaking very well and approaches every problem with the goal of finding an implementable solution. He invariably adds value and suggests innovative ideas, at times leaving the security officials pleasantly surprised. Failures, setbacks and episodic surprises don't rattle him. He has always emphasized the need to create structures that can bring real-time response and inter-agency synergy. Different stakeholders dealing with terrorism have been strengthened through capacity-building and systemic improvements.

It is noteworthy that in the decade from 2004-14, one thousand people lost their lives and three thousand were injured. Also, there were twenty-five major terrorist attacks, outside Jammu and Kashmir, Northeast and the Left-Wing Extremism (LWE) affected areas. The Prime Minister had a first-hand experience of witnessing the scourge of terrorism in Gujarat when he was the Chief Minister. During the long discussions on ways to strategize an effective response to terrorism, he always gave game-changing ideas and suggestions that helped the country in combating terrorism. In addition to successful counter-terrorist operations in J&K, more than one hundred terrorists were apprehended from other parts of the country, and by and large the hinterland of the country under Prime Minister Modi has remained free from the menace of terrorism.

Under PM Modi's guidance, the security apparatus of J&K has been instrumental in ensuring development of the state's infrastructure. J&K achieved the highest road-building activity under the Pradhan Mantri Gram Sadak Yojana (PGMSY) in 2019-2020, with the completion of around 11,400 km of cumulative length. In July 2020, six bridges were inaugurated in the border areas. Civil-military fusion is being ensured by creating dual-use infrastructure, wherein the Union Ministry of Road Transport and Highways is coordinating closely with the Defence Ministry. Almost twenty-nine stretches of highways have been identified to be converted into aircraft runways in an emergency. Thirty military airfields and seven

Advance Landing Grounds have been opened for joint civil–military use. This will give a boost to Prime Minister's 'Ude Desh ka Aam Nagrik' (UDAN) regional air connectivity scheme. For the first time, a long-term and holistic approach is being taken for infrastructure development.

Large numbers of terrorist modules have been neutralized within, and also outside the country with the support of friendly countries. Groups like Jamaat-ul-Mujahideen (JMB), Sikhs for Justice (SFJ) and Jammu and Kashmir Islamic Front (Jel-J&K) have been proscribed. The entire network of Students' Islamic Movement of India (SIMI) and Indian Mujahideen (IM) has virtually been broken. Al Qaeda modules were identified by the National Intelligence Agency (NIA) in the early stages itself and thus not allowed to take roots. New intelligence posts in coastal areas have been sanctioned to increase India's maritime security. The government has also ensured justice for victims of the 1984 anti-Sikh riots and provided relief and rehabilitation, which has greatly assuaged the hurt feelings of the Sikhs.

A multi-pronged campaign against LWE was launched through focused ground operations at centres of gravity like the Dandakaranya region in south Chhattisgarh, along with measures on the ideological front. Intelligence-driven coordination between Central Forces and the State Police and action against 'Urban Naxals' has progressed simultaneously.

Infrastructure development in backward districts, LWE-affected areas and border states is being pursued with both development and security objectives in mind. The Aspirational Districts Development Programme, which covers many of the districts affected by LWE, has been executed successfully.

A combined security and development related approach has led to better communication and regional connectivity, electricity, health and education facilities in LWE-affected areas. As a result, there has been a continuous decrease in LWE violence and shrinkage in their spatial area of influence.

The Modi government has shown willingness to talk with insurgent groups and address genuine concerns of ethnic groups in the Northeast. This has led to the signing of settlement agreements with several groups such as the Achik National Volunteer Council (ANVC) in Meghalaya in 2014, the National Liberation Front of Twipra led by Sabir Kumar Debbarma (NLFT-SD) in Tripura in 2019, Bodo groups in Assam in 2020, and the resolution of the Bru/Reang issue between the state governments of Mizoram and Tripura in January 2020. The Armed Forces Special Powers Act (AFSPA) of 1958 has been removed from Meghalaya and some districts of Arunachal Pradesh. A framework agreement was signed with the National Socialist Council of Nagaland (Isak-Muivah) in August 2015. The Centre has also supplemented these with capacity-building measures in the Northeast states. Ten additional India Reserve Battalions were sanctioned in March 2018. Based on precise intelligence, pre-emptive actions against terror infrastructure across India's borders were conducted in Myanmar in 2015 without any casualties to our brave security forces personnel. As a result of these actions, there is a significant decline in insurgency incidents, casualties among our security forces and civilian deaths.

Several pending proposals to recognize the sacrifices of security personnel—civil and military—and raise morale were cleared expeditiously. The setting up of the Police Memorial, the National War Memorial and the implementation of the One Rank One Pension were accorded top priority. The inauguration of the Statue of Unity on 31 October 2018, symbolizes the value that the leadership pays to national integration and India's 'unity in diversity'. Permanent commission for women in the armed forces, induction of more women in the security forces including the fighter stream of the Indian Air Force, and enrolment of women soldiers in the Indian Army as well as in Sainik Schools are important initiatives to bring about broader inclusivity in natural security management and change attitudes towards gender discrimination.

NATIONAL INTEREST ABOVE ALL

Prime Minister Modi's approach to national security is marked by a strong undercurrent of nationalist ideology and a strategic long-term vision of building a strong India. He applies his innovative thinking to finding cost-effective solutions to high-cost security requirements. I got its first glimpse when the Prime Minister called me for an informal meeting in May 2014—a week before assuming office. For me, it was one of the most unforgettable experiences. I could observe the strength of his conviction, clarity of thinking and resoluteness to bring about transformation, regardless of obstacles. He exuded a deep sense of commitment and confidence. I found these characteristics manifest themselves in his policy approach, decision-making ability and prioritization—blended with zero tolerance for procrastination.

The most dominant of these characteristics was Prime Minister Modi's passion for furthering national interests—overriding all other considerations, including the political costs. In early 2015, he was briefed on the acute shortage of fighter aircraft faced by the Indian Air Force. The situation was getting critical with each passing year. The air force would have soon been plagued with a nearly 45 per cent shortfall in its fleet of combat-worthy fighter aircraft. The induction of Rafale fighter aircrafts, which had been selected after a long process of trials and due diligence for eleven years, had been abandoned by the UPA government just before demitting office. The Prime Minister visited France in April 2015. He got the deal revived through a government-to-government agreement on terms much more favourable than what had been envisaged in the original proposal. Ignoring all other considerations, he worked out a deal that not only best suited our national interest but also achieved it in record time.

NEW DIRECTION AND MOMENTUM IN FOREIGN POLICY

Prime Minister Modi has taken more active stands on international issues. This has resulted in a bold and outcome-driven foreign policy. Early in his tenure, he visited all Central Asian countries and engaged proactively with West Asian nations including Saudi Arabia, the United Arab Emirates, Israel and Oman. The Organisation of Islamic Cooperation (OIC) invited India's Foreign Minister to address it for the first time. In his first three years in office, he visited fifty countries. One common thread in his approach was 'India First', which allowed him to engage with partners who may have inter se rivalries or differences. His counterparts also showed sensitivity towards his approach. Besides his inimitable persuasion power, they were convinced about his strong beliefs and sincere intentions.

His personal convictions about India's role in the international system, its spiritual and civilizational roots that envisages the 'world as a family' (vasudhaiva kutumbakam) and 'happiness for all' (sarve bhavantu sukhinah) have been integrated into policymaking. This has helped him win the faith of the people including the Indian diaspora. Prime Minister Modi also follows a punishing schedule for himself. This selfless commitment has won him recognition and respect at home and abroad. The net result is that people trust him and are willing to back his initiatives.

His approach to global affairs is based on interlinking foreign policy with strong internal growth. He believes that a secure India that is confident of its place in the world will be able to deal with peers and competitors from a position of strength. A great motivator and powerful communicator, he has constantly motivated Indians to aspire for bigger things and develop capability to achieve those goals.

Reaching out to neighbours was a top priority for the Prime Minister under the 'Neighbourhood First' policy. India's South Asian neighbours attended the swearing in of Prime Minister Modi in May 2014, an unprecedented event. This was not a one-off 'out of the box' initiative. When it became clear that vested interests may stymie efforts to build a South Asian consensus, he innovated by inviting BIMSTEC leaders for the BRICS Summit in Goa in 2016. He also insisted that the member countries of the Bay of Bengal Initiative for Multi-Sectoral Technical and Economic Cooperation (BIMSTEC) should step up cooperation in the security domain. Several initiatives in port-led development, maritime security, space security, law enforcement cooperation, and climate change have been taken forward at the National Security Advisors' (NSA) forum of BIMSTEC. There has also been progress on the BIMSTEC Shipping Agreement.

On assuming office as Prime Minister, Narendra Modi made his first official visit to Bhutan. India has stood firmly with Bhutan during several crises, including the COVID-19 pandemic and its boundary dispute with China. He was the first Indian Prime Minister to visit Nepal after a gap of seventeen years. The long-delayed Land Boundary Agreement with Bangladesh involving the difficult task of exchange of enclaves was concluded successfully. India also respected the international verdict on settlement of maritime boundary with Bangladesh. This removed a major impediment in the relationship with Bangladesh and paved the way for several path-breaking initiatives to improve connectivity, transit through land, rail and inland waterways.

A new push has been given to relations with the Maldives and Sri Lanka. The trilateral maritime security initiative at NSA-level among India, the Maldives and Sri Lanka has been expanded in scope and spread by involving three more nations—Mauritius, Seychelles and Bangladesh—in an upgraded 'Colombo Security Conclave'. This will ensure greater alignment and cooperation in matters beyond the domain of maritime security to address other common security challenges including terrorism, radicalization, trafficking and organized crime, and cyber security.

In West Asia, we have long-standing interests. It is the principal source of our energy requirements and houses India's largest diaspora abroad, channelling significant amounts of remittances back home. But Prime Minister Modi's vision went beyond all this. He emphasized on relations becoming more broad-based and opening a two-way street in terms of investments, trade and enhancing cooperation in defence, intelligence, cyber, renewable energy, agriculture, space, etc. You will find that Indians, as well as industrialists from the Gulf region, are very eager to deepen investments in both directions.

The important thing is that India's relations with West Asia stand on its own footing, and have the depth to look beyond security issues alone. Both India and the Gulf Cooperation Council (GCC) states do not view this relationship only from the standpoint of Pakistan. These countries understand the impact of radicalization and terrorism on civil society. Excellent intelligence cooperation resulted in the deportation of nearly 150 terrorists and hardened criminals to India from 15 countries—mostly from Gulf nations—in the past seven years.

The growing flux and unpredictability in the global security landscape has magnified security vulnerabilities. India is approaching security relations with strategic partners, including the US and the UK with the objective of jointly meeting the emerging challenges. Security threats in the twenty-first century have become borderless and broad-based, going beyond traditional areas. Threats can no longer be tackled in isolation, and requires the cooperation of all.

Keeping the global commons secure (on which the global trade transits), opposing unilateral actions designed at challenging the rules-based international order and combating global terrorism and radicalization form the cornerstone of our security cooperation with major countries. The impact of climate change, energy security, cybersecurity, human and drug trafficking, illegal migration, cooperation in the civilian nuclear and space sectors are other areas that have been gaining prominence.

Shared global values and common challenges have enhanced strategic trust with these countries. In recent years, we have increased security and intelligence cooperation with the US and the UK. Unlike before, these countries are now more willing to share core technologies and best practices, transcending relations beyond a buyer-seller or transactional approach. The scope and frequency of bilateral military exercises have expanded to improve inter-operability. The US has designated India as a major non-NATO ally and accorded STA-I status, enabling the transfer of key technologies. There are several possibilities in the areas of artificial intelligence (Al), quantum technologies and rare earths, which are becoming indispensable for national security and long-term stability of a country.

Prime Minister Modi made efforts to develop personal equations with world leaders such as President Vladimir Putin of Russia, US Presidents Barack Obama and Donald Trump, Prime Minister Shinzo Abe of Japan, President Xi Jinping of China and heads of state/government of all major powers including France, Australia, the European Union, Israel, West Asian partners and the UK. This has been one of the most enduring features of PM Modi's style, which has reaped significant dividends for our country.

India is also no longer hyphenated with Pakistan or viewed from the prism of non-alignment alone. This does not mean we have lost our strategic autonomy, but we are invested in adroit diplomacy to suit our requirements. A major change, compared to what the situation was, say, two decades back, is that India's potential as a regional power and importance of its peninsular geography is being realized. Resultantly, major powers are approaching us with a great deal of respectability and on equal terms.

ASSERTION OF POLITICAL WILL

Prime Minister believes that national will is the most essential ingredient of national power. The resolve of the nation to protect itself against adversarial forces is the most important aspect of national security. Without this, possessing technological and military power is of little real value. At the same time, he insists that security agencies must work within the purview of international law because India is a responsible nation and an emerging power. Accordingly, several of Prime Minister's initiatives have signalled intent by actions, not words, but without compromising on his core beliefs.

DEFT AND DECISIVE PAKISTAN POLICY

The most important manifestation of political will has been in tackling cross-border terrorism. Despite the best efforts of the Prime Minister to engage with Pakistan in a bid to create an environment for peaceful engagement, India witnessed terrorist attacks that were planned and executed from Pakistan—in Pathankot (January 2016), Uri (September 2016) and Pulwama (February 2019). India scaled up its approach to deal with such incidents in a gradual and calibrated manner.

Much has been written about India's response to the Pathankot attack in early January 2016, which took place soon after the Prime Minister attended the wedding ceremony of then Pakistan Prime Minister Nawaz Sharif's daughter on Christmas day in 2015. Indian agencies were able to develop operational advance intelligence to track the movement of the attackers. This provided the security agencies an opportunity to deploy senior military commanders, mobilize counter-terrorism and anti-hostage forces both from the Army and Central Police Organizations within the Pathankot air base prior to the attack. Though, in the engagement with terrorists, India lost some security personnel, but a major terrorist attack was countered and four suicide terrorists were neutralized.

There was a new direction that was given—unless India raises the cost of cross-border terrorism, Pakistan will continue with its nefarious activities under the belief that we will not escalate matters because of the presence of nuclear weapons. India's responses to the Uri (2016) and Pulwama (2019) attacks through strikes against terrorist infrastructure within Pakistan-occupied Jammu and Kashmir and Pakistan were an assertion of political will of the top leadership to ensure that cross-border terrorism would no longer go without a response. The targets chosen, the methodology followed and the post-conflict management of these operations signalled a new normal in India's response to sub-conventional threats.

The Prime Minister had been advocating a change in response in dealing with cross-border terrorism ever since he was the Chief Minister of Gujarat. Lack of response to the numerous incidents of bombings in our major cities, and even the landmark event of 26/11, had earned India the infamous nomenclature of being a 'soft state'. The first of its kind operations after Uri enhanced India's global prestige. It caused panic in the adversary's mind and momentarily disrupted terror training and planning of more attacks. Our soldiers on the borders were also given a free hand to respond to local situations—imposing direct costs on the sponsors of terror.

In the response to Uri 2016, a few aspects stand out. One, it was a simultaneous operation by multiple strike teams at four disparate locations and extended across a vast geographical boundary. Two, it was a political call by the Prime Minister, which meant that he was taking responsibility, not only for success, but also failure. This exhibited risk-taking at the highest level—a quality shown by very few. Three, it was novel planning, in that it generated chaos, panic and confusion by creating the 'enemy is everywhere syndrome'. The then Pakistan Army leadership castigated its ground formations for failing to block even one strike team across a vast frontage, despite having a large number of forward deployed troops.

When it comes to the response to Pulwama 2019, the one key aspect of the Balakot counter-strike was that it was very different from other counter-terror counter-strikes undertaken by India. We have been responding to terror strikes in the ground domain. It was for the first time that an aerial strike was conceived and implemented with finesse, in the bargain also blowing away the myth of Pakistan's nuclear blackmail. Well, if the adversary hurts our core interests, causes disproportionate casualties, there may, and will be counters. Domain and level will not be inhibiting factors. That said, the post-Uri strikes were different, and Balakot was different from post-Uri strikes. Tomorrow, it may be different from both. This remains at the core of the Prime Minister's style of thinking and direction.

All this reflected a changed approach to Pakistan. These operations were designed to convey a credible message to Pakistan that India could create and exercise both conventional and sub-conventional options to raise costs for Pakistan to unaffordable levels. Responses to Uri 2016 and Pulwama

2019 involved new techniques and innovative methodologies. These added to India's toolkit of punitive options in a nuclearized environment. There was constant learning at all levels across segments. Course corrections were applied, wherever necessary. The political leadership showed progressively positive intent to use force, albeit in a calibrated and restrained manner. Specifically, terrorist infrastructure was targeted. There was no collateral damage to innocent civilians. India did not suffer any casualties. A clear message was sent, that inimical actions would lead to retaliation.

At the same time, focused efforts were made in the Financial Action Task Force (FATF) and the United Nations Security Council (UNSC). The FATF placed Pakistan on the grey list in June 2018, urging it to implement a 27-point action plan to curb money laundering and terror financing. Till date, Pakistan continues on the grey list, much to its chagrin.

It is for Pakistan to assess the debilitating impact of employing terror as an instrument of state policy on its economy and international reputation.

COHERENT AND CLEAR CHINA POLICY

India's approach to dealing with unilateral attempts to challenge the status quo on the Line of Actual Control (LAC) has also witnessed a change under PM Modi. India has conveyed through its actions and political intent that the status quo will not be allowed to be changed. The response has been calibrated, gradual and across the spectrum. India has made it clear that it is ready to stand firm on the boundary issue.

Prime Minister Modi has a distinctive reputation of looking at complex problems from a non-conventional vantage point and coming out with out-of-the-box solutions. This was particularly most apparent in his handling of security matters. Thinking unconventionally, he takes calculated risks, when he is convinced that it is necessary for safety and security of the country. Also, when a situation becomes complex, he frontally engages himself and often with astounding results.

A test for the Prime Minister came very early during his first term. The sixteen-day stand-off at Chumar commenced on 16 September 2014, when road extension activities by the Chinese PLA (People's Liberation Army) on the Indian side of the LAC were blocked by mobilizing 1,500 Indian soldiers in quick time.

During the stand-off, the Prime Minister seized the opportunity of President Xi Jinping's visit to India that month. During an informal tete-a-tete with President Xi in Ahmedabad, he was able to convince him about the need to ensure the unconditional and immediate withdrawal of Chinese troops. He did not bank solely on conventional diplomatic or military-to-military engagement. The Indian reaction at a time when the Chinese President was in India, highlighted the Prime Minister's political resolve to stand firm on issues of national importance. In 2015, India's responses in eastern Ladakh, Arunachal Pradesh and Sikkim were equally firm.

In June 2017, India faced a qualitatively different challenge due to attempts by the PLA to build a road through Doklam plateau close to the India-Bhutan-China tri-junction adjacent to Sikkim. The stand-off lasted seventy-three days.

Swift decision-making at the topmost level enabled timely and effective action at the tactical level—to prevent adverse occupation of an area which is sensitive and critical to our concerns. So, when it comes to protecting our vital national interests, the Prime Minister has not hesitated to swiftly employ military power. As a matter of fact, the discourse in Chinese state media and other sources post-Doklam, was abusive and intimidatory to the extreme. It mentioned that China had failed to discern the 'revolutionary transformation of the Indian psyche wrought by PM Modi' (Hemant Adlakha, *The Diplomat, Mumbai,* 11 January 2018). Opinion makers in China were pointing at India being the second-biggest threat to China (replacing Japan) after the US.

However, India showed resolve both during the stand-off and in post-conflict negotiations. After all other options had been exhausted, PM Modi personally took it up with President Xi. PM Modi showed statesmanship when he walked up to President Xi on the sidelines of the G-20 meeting in Germany for an informal meeting. I was an eyewitness to this most dramatic interaction between the two leaders, when they agreed to find an immediate solution. Eventually, after a series of negotiations, the deadlock was resolved. It would not have been possible without the Prime Minister's direct action. Both countries agreed to a mutual withdrawal to pre-16 June 2017 positions. There are numerous such episodes that highlight the Prime Minister's frontal approach to complex problems, with innovative ways to address them.

Eastern Ladakh 2020 was another instance of the Prime Minister's leadership. In contravention to all existing border management agreements, inimical forces in the shadow of a pandemic, endeavoured to challenge some of our major interests, which required a proportionate use of force. That use of force was approved with alacrity at the topmost level. It authorized freedom of action at the lowest tactical level. The leadership and troops showed the will to resist unilateral actions. Thus, during this crisis, while we have reacted in a particular manner, there were other options. Some were exercised and some more will be exercised, if vital and major interests of the country are at stake. The question to be asked is: Was the aggressor able to impose its will upon us? If the answer is an unambiguous 'no', then its actions are questionable.

India also took up focused efforts with China to list Masood Azhar as a terrorist in the UNSC's 1267 Sanctions Committee List. India unambiguously conveyed its disappointment to China about its actions to put the listing on 'hold' or 'block' on the grounds of procedural and technical loopholes. India also conveyed directly to China the likely impact of its continued ambiguity on bilateral relations. India's willingness to raise the subject in bilateral summits and multilateral engagements acted as an additional pressure point. Cooperation from P-5 members and other international partners assisted India. In May 2019, India's decade-long effort to list Masood Azhar culminated successfully.

When it comes to the Belt and Road Initiative/One Belt One Road (BRI/OBOR), India is not opposed to it as long as it does not conflict with India's national sovereignty over Pakistan-occupied Kashmir and Gilgit-Baltistan. It was due to this fundamental reason that India did not participate in the first BRI conference in 2017. India, too, has undertaken infrastructure and connectivity projects in its neighbourhood and beyond. The key aspects of our projects are trust, transparency, environment protection, absence of debt-trap diplomacy and precedence to local sentiments and ownership—as it should be with any infrastructure development project in third countries.

NEW FRONTIERS IN DETERRENCE

Several other initiatives taken by India under Prime Minister Modi's watch have strengthened deterrence. In his address on the occasion of the successful first deterrence patrol by INS Arihant on 5 November 2018, the Prime Minister emphasized that 'peace is our strength, not our weakness'. He viewed India's nuclear programme and nuclear triad in the context of India's efforts to further world peace and stability.

Yet another remarkable feature of Prime Minister Modi's approach has been his adoption of a very holistic and comprehensive view of decision-making. Security-related policies and decisions have a bearing on international relations, domestic policy, economy, acquisition and integration of technology. Whenever dealing with any security-related issue, the Prime Minister, as a reflex action, comes out with ideas on its impact on other sectors. In early 2017, the PM was briefed on how space was becoming a new frontier of future conflicts, and India's vulnerability on this count. He was also informed of the need for India to enter the elite club of a space power, by demonstrating its capability to hit objects in space. The window was short—as in the past—and there was always the possibility of an international ban being imposed by powers who already possessed this capability.

Before arriving at any decision, the Prime Minister meticulously went through its multiple implications in the minutest details—such as its internal fallout, likely controversies over space debris, the need to maintain high secrecy and impact on our defence research projects involving foreign collaboration or supply of spare parts, etc. He held three long meetings with amazing patience and attention. He finally took the momentous decision and asked me to go ahead. The Prime Minister gave several specific directions with regard to handling international reactions, maintaining high secrecy and relying on domestically available material and technology for the test. On 27 March 2019, the Defence Research and Development Organisation (DRDO) successfully conducted the Anti-Satellite (ASAT) test by hitting a target with remarkable accuracy. With this, India became a recognized space power. Prime Minister Modi assured the world that India's successful ASAT missile test was not directed against anybody. It was a demonstration of how modern technology could be leveraged to create an environment of peace and security in the region.

The Indian Navy now conducts mission-based deployments, thereby, ensuring continuous presence at strategic locations and choke points on the periphery of the Indian Ocean Region. This has allowed Indian Navy to undertake a flexible response to emergent situations including disasters and special emergencies like the pandemic. These actions were as much a statement of capability development as they were of political intent.

FOCUS ON LAST-MILE DELIVERY

Prime Minister Modi excels not only in original thinking, but also in the diligent planning of the minutest details to ensure their execution. He believes that the devil lies in the detail—not only in planning, but also in its execution.

In May 2015, he was given a detailed briefing about the state of infrastructure along our northern borders—the gross inadequacy of roads, tunnels and other facilities required immediate attention. He was also informed about the massive strides made by the Chinese in infrastructure development on their side. He was quick to grasp the strategic import of this deficiency and, thereafter, followed it up with the doggedness that no other Prime Minister would have demonstrated. Additional funds were sanctioned through his personal intervention with the Finance Minister. He also went into the smallest detail, including of a highly technical nature to understand the problems and complexities, particularly in the construction of tunnels. Today, border infrastructure is manifold stronger than when the NDA government took office in 2014. Notwithstanding, excellent work done by the Border Roads Organisation (BRO) would not have been possible without the Prime Minister's personal involvement in the matter. Similarly, indigenous production of AK-203 assault rifles in India, with 100 per cent technology transfer and no royalty clause was not possible without the Prime Minister constantly monitoring its progress—from negotiations with the Russians to the establishment of the facility in Amethi.

BRINGING ABOUT TRANSFORMATION

It is difficult to comprehend Prime Minister Modi's security policies without understanding his vision for the nation. Groomed and nurtured ideologically in a strong nationalist mode, he has a strong sense of civilizational awareness and a long-term strategic vision of India's future. He believes that a strong economy, transformed human capital, technological excellence and powerful national consciousness are guarantors of India's security. He recently exhorted fellow Indians to look at the next twenty-five years as 'Amrit Kaal' and highlighted the need for collective efforts (Sabka Prayas) to achieve the desired transformation by the 100th Independence Day. Several transformative initiatives have been launched to achieve this goal.

FURTHERING PROGRESS AND PEACE

One of the most important transformative initiatives of Prime Minister Modi was taken on 5 August 2019, by an amendment to Article 370, the only temporary article out of 395 Articles of the Constitution of India, through a Presidential Order. This ensured that all provisions of the Constitution of India would apply to J&K. The Presidential Order of 5 August, 2019, also superseded the Presidential Order of 1954, which was the basis for Article 35A. This was an important step to ensure full integration of J&K, address factors leading to alienation, discrimination and separatist mindset among the people. Ladakh was also granted Union Territory status, a long-standing demand of the people of the region. This has been followed up by strengthening grassroots democracy in J&K. For the first time, the district development council elections were held during November-December 2020. Earlier, block development council elections were held on 24 October 2019.

Several steps have been taken to ensure social harmony and inclusive growth. There was no adverse fallout following the landmark Supreme Court judgement on Ram janmbhoomi. The Muslim Women (Protection of Rights on Marriage) Act, 2019, which made triple talaq and other similar forms of talaq illegal, has provided immense solace to Muslim women. Further a 10 per cent reservation has been introduced for economically backward sections of the non-reserved category. The 14th Finance Commission has made important recommendations to increase the share of states in devolution of Central taxes. These are all transformative changes that bear the stamp of the Prime Minister, who has a vision for India's future.

DEFENCE SECTOR REFORMS FOR AATMANIRBHAR BHARAT

The National Security Council Secretariat (NSCS) has been restructured to deal with futuristic challenges. Its roles and functions have been institutionalized in the 'Allocation of Business' rules. The changes reflect a special focus on science and technology, innovation and non-traditional security including maritime security, economic security, climate change and weather warfare. Existing structures in the NSCS dealing with external, internal, intelligence, cyber and military domains have been further beefed up. Close coordination between NSCS and NITI Aayog will ensure that security and development initiatives of the Prime Minister are implemented in a coordinated manner. Defence reforms are top on PM's transformation agenda. The creation of the post of Chief of Defence Staff (CDS) with a Department of Military Affairs (DMA) will help integrate defence planning, conduct joint operations and facilitate inter se prioritization of resources between the armed forces. Joint structures in the domains of cyber, space and special operations function directly under the CDS.

The other important dimension that the Prime Minister introduced, was the tenet of integration and jointness in the armed forces. He felt that it would lead to optimization, and each theatre would by and large be self-contained to achieve their military objectives. The creation of the Defence Cyber Agency, Defence Space Agency and Armed Forces Special Operations Division were some of the other steps taken with an eye on future challenges.

Prime Minister Modi commenced the process of defence reforms in 2014 itself—by initiating measures to simplify procedures and processes of defence acquisition, encouraging the private sector and start-ups in defence production, emphasizing on co-production, cutting down project timelines, augmenting local capabilities and allowing greater foreign direct investment (FDI) in defence through the automatic route.

In line with PM Modi's vision of Aatmanirbhar Bharat, several indigenous projects have been fast-tracked to ensure self-reliance and boost Make in India. Indigenous shipbuilding has received a big boost following successful sea trials of IAC 1 (Vikrant) on 4 August 2021. Thirty-six warships are on order in domestic shipyards. Several squadrons of indigenous light combat aircraft (LCA) and its variants and the main battle tank Arjun will be procured for the armed forces. The Brahmos cruise missile has been integrated with the SU-30 MKI and the AEW&C aircraft has been inducted.

Foreign direct investment in defence has been raised from 49 per cent to 74 per cent under the automatic route. GST rates on domestic maintenance, repair and overhaul (MRO) was reduced to 5 per cent. This will give a boost to both civil and military MRO activities in India.

The Prime Minister has also set an ambitious target of $5 billion defence exports by 2025. Indian Embassies have been empowered to encourage defence exports. India's signature exhibitions Aero India and Def Expo as well as Defence Minister's conclave have become regular features and gained visibility. Defence industrial corridors in Uttar Pradesh and Tamil Nadu will provide special incentives to companies involved in defence manufacturing.

The conceptual framework of his clarion call for Aatmanirbhar Bharat brought about a transformational change in the mindset of the entire security community of the nation. Most with conviction, and few with compulsion, have started internalizing the reality that we have to rely on what is available indigenously. A positive indigenization list has been promulgated to encourage domestic manufacturing. His direction to prepare a list of defence procurement items that will be on the negative list for imports was not an easy decision to implement. Today, there are two hundred such items and more are in the pipeline to follow.

He wanted self-reliance to transcend from the drawing board to the battle field. It encompassed all activities from conceptualization, indigenous technology development, design and development capabilities and validation of prototypes to production—all to be executed within the country.

Expensive and complex weapon systems are not only costly to buy, but also expensive to maintain. It eats into the defence budget, sparing little money to develop, operate and maintain new platforms. It has a cascading effect on training standards and escalates the maintenance costs of equipment. The end effect is that the nation has lesser money to strengthen its defence forces.

When Aatmanirbhar Bharat model fructifies, our services will be able to procure the best and critical equipment and systems from indigenous sources.

CONSCIOUS ORDNANCE FACTORY REFORM

In early 2015, the Prime Minister was briefed about the unsatisfactory functioning of ordnance factories—they were producing sub-optimal defence equipment based on obsolete technologies at exorbitant costs. Transforming the regimen of defence ordnance factories, with a two centuries old legacy work culture, was no easy task. The Prime Minister responded to the challenge with alacrity and clarity. He stated—it has to be changed and I will change it. However, he insisted in protecting the interests of all workers. It was the result of his direct involvement in the entire process, including enduring with a series of long presentations to work out various options that could maximize national needs, and at the same time protect the interests of the work force. Eventually, he succeeded in corporatizing all forty-one ordnance factories of the country.

THINKING LONG-TERM, BRINGING A FRESH PERSPECTIVE

Prime Minister Modi has a penchant for fresh thinking and coming out with new and ingenious solutions to vexed problems. Rapid technological development, particularly in the defence and security spheres, is one of his focus areas. In his first address to DRDO scientists in August 2014, he wanted young scientists to be given an opportunity to come up and experiment with innovative ideas. He directed that some of the DRDO labs may be placed under select eminent young scientists below the age of thirty-five years. By 2020, out of DRDO's fifty-two labs across the country, five were designated Young Scientists Laboratories with full decisional autonomy to develop next-generation equipment.

Similarly, during the DGPs' conference in 2020, he announced the constitution of a High-Power Police Technology Mission under the chairmanship of a minister.

The Prime Minister's other striking characteristic has been his ability to approach national security matters from a long-term strategic perspective. He has an uncanny futuristic sense, and observes risks and opportunities that are often missed even by experts.

We often get inundated by problems of immediate nature in our decision-making, and fail to assess or cater for long-term implications and interests of the nation. Decades back, we commenced manufacturing defence items in India with Soviet collaboration, and later, Russian. In addition to making payments of other items, we had followed the practice of paying 'royalties' for each item produced in India. Even after disbursing the transfer of technology costs and indigenously manufacturing all items—the practice of royalty payments continued—as it constituted a part of the original contract. Over the years, we all had started believing it to be too sacrosanct to be challenged.

The Prime Minister was furious—that even for domestically manufactured T-72 tanks, royalty amount was being paid to the Russian original equipment manufacturer. He was astonished that the royalty clause had no time or other limits. He wanted all of us to not only discontinue the practice in future, but also work towards getting the old contracts reviewed. When we failed to achieve much success, he took it up most strongly with President Putin. With his persuasive arguments and articulation skills, he was able to impress the irrationality of the practice upon President Putin. He emphasized on the fact that when we take decisions, sign agreements or enter into contractual obligations, we must look at its long-term consequences.

The royalties that we paid for decades was the slip of negotiators of the time, who could not evaluate its long-term consequences. For achieving long-term gains, the Prime Minister was willing to bear short-term pains—pressures notwithstanding. His insistence on bringing out a list of banned items for defence imports (now called positive list) is part of this approach. He realizes that in the long run, not only will the country achieve the capability of producing these items—but it will also make India less vulnerable to the whims of the original manufacturers and countries selling those armaments.

TECH GETS A PUSH

The Prime Minister's unconventional approach to finding technological solutions for national security problems reflects a deep understanding of how the global mechanisms of industrial production have changed. Technology in a globalized world invariably appears first in the private sector. Therefore, the PM has encouraged harnessing the energies of a larger ecosystem that exists outside the public sector. The 'Bhoomi' hackathon initiative conducted by the Border Security Force (BSF) helped find solutions in tunnel detection and anti-drone systems. The Baba Mehar Singh competition of the Indian Air Force was organized to create an ecosystem in unmanned systems and swarm drones. Defence India Start-up Challenge 5.0 has identified thirty-five areas including underwater domain awareness, situation awareness, artificial intelligence, augmented reality and unmanned systems as focus areas. This is a like a silent revolution. It will not only strengthen security but also ensure that the expertise available outside government can be harnessed towards national security objectives, especially in the technology sector.

Strategy formulation and articulation have received a boost with the drafting of the National Cyber Security Strategy. Several structures in the cyber domain have been created including the Cyber & Information Security (CIS) Division and Indian Cybercrime Coordination Centre (IC4) Scheme in the Ministry of Home Affairs. In addition, the National Cyber Coordination Centre (NCCC) under the Ministry of Electronics and IT will enhance situational awareness of web traffic to identify threats in a proactive manner. The Cyber Diplomacy Division under the Ministry of External Affairs (MEA) deals with external engagements with partners and multilateral agencies. The National Cyber Security Coordinator in the NSCS ensures synergy across policy formulation and capacity-building dimensions. New policies have also been put in place to ensure that only trusted telecom products are connected to our networks.

STRENGTHENING INDIA'S MARITIME RELATIONS

Policy articulation in the maritime sphere has been a priority for the Prime Minister. His awareness of India's rich maritime history and his administrative experience in Gujarat in dealing with coastal security issues reflect in the articulation of his maritime vision. PM Modi laid out his vision of Security and Growth for All in the Region (SAGAR) during his Indian Ocean Yatra to Mauritius and Seychelles in 2015. This set the stage for formulating approaches to maritime security in the Indian Ocean Region. He elaborated on this vision at the Shangri La dialogue in Singapore in 2018, where he articulated India's Indo-Pacific vision.

In line with the Prime Minister's vision, arrangements were concluded with Seychelles, Mauritius, Oman, France (Reunion Islands), Iran (Chabahar) to use ports. The PM has prioritized engagement with Russia's Far East, upgraded India's 'Look East Policy' to 'Act East' without neglecting 'Look West'. India has concluded foundational agreements with the US and logistics exchange agreements with Russia, Japan, Australia, Singapore, the US and others as part of efforts to consolidate inter-operability. Several countries have joined India's International Fusion Centre (IOR) to enhance maritime domain awareness. India has also provided maritime assistance in crisis situations to neighbours including Sri Lanka and Mauritius. India's Arctic policy was received well by international partners and commentators. India is also playing a more active role in the 'International Arctic Forum', the Arctic Council and engaging with Arctic states.

The recently concluded UNSC meeting on maritime security is important for two reasons. It was the first time that an Indian Prime Minister presided over a meeting of the UNSC. The meeting also adopted the first-ever outcome document on maritime security. This is a reflection of a new and confident India, which boldly assumes greater international responsibilities. The PM has not hesitated to upgrade the quadrilateral or QUAD from working-level to ministerial-level and now summit-level. At the same time, India remains an important partner in the Shanghai Cooperation Organization (SCO) and BRICS—an alliance comprising Brazil, Russia, India, China, and South Africa. While engagements under the QUAD focus on maritime security, vaccines and supply chains, the SCO addresses threats such as radicalization, terrorism and extreme faith-based fundamentalism.

While developing new partnerships, India's traditional partners have not been neglected. The ten guiding principles for India-Africa relations reflect India's continued solidarity with Africa. Relations with the Association of Southeast Asian Nations (ASEAN) have grown from strength to strength. All ASEAN leaders jointly attended India's Republic Day as Chief Guests. The IBSA Summit was held in September 2021. The first meeting of IBSA NSAs was also held in August 2021. The Raisina Dialogue conducted by the MEA has become an annual feature. In this dialogue, the MEA ensures that issues of importance in national security are discussed at the highest levels. Such multidimensional engagement reflects India's growing confidence to engage with diverse partners with seemingly contradictory approaches. This has diversified India's options to pursue its national interests in an increasingly complex and constantly evolving world order.

CONCLUSION

The world order is made by victors—in the current case by the victors of World War II. The UN and the Bretton Woods financial systems that govern today's global order emerged out of the post war geo-political realities. But, the lack of consensus soon became apparent, when another victor challenged it for decades. Then followed a period of stability for two decades or so, when another of those victors has now begun to challenge the world order. Its manifestation is seen all around us.

Whether the world order continues in the shape and form, as we have known it, depends on the collective action by like-minded countries. India has every reason to remain invested in the current world order, which despite many conflicts, has not resulted in total wars. In today's world order, India is seen as a factor of stability and agent for global good. Prime Minister Modi's long-term strategic vision is guiding all our actions today, so that not only does India secure itself against future challenges, but also cements its rightful place in the comity of nations.

India is expected to be the third-largest economy in the world by 2030. However, it needs to catch up in terms of national power. The quality of its institutions, its ability to guarantee the rule of law and its skilled manpower will be key enablers of the transformation process. The

Prime Minister's vision is to transform India into a leading power while preserving its core values, rich culture and constitutional systems. In the rise of India lies hope for the world in democracy, pluralism and inclusive systems. Anything that erodes India's national will has to be avoided. The power of false narratives can be debilitating for the nation. We need to take hard decisions. For this, we need decisive leadership. Local and sectoral interests taking precedence over national interests is a recipe for disaster. Credible deterrence through strong and effective national security policies will provide stability and act as a steel cover for the nation.

The Prime Minister conducts himself strategically. His emphasis is on anticipating changes in the world order to best formulate our strategy. His vision is to re-establish India's prominence in the world order and utilize new geo-political alignments to suit India's interests. He has given a clear mandate for proactive reforms in structures and processes, and applying Indian concepts to thinking and strategy. Taking a leaf from his experiences as a Chief Minister and the importance of last-mile delivery, he wants the tip of the spear to be made powerful—and future ready.

Prime Minister Modi has enunciated his vision. He has shown political will to execute policies to achieve the goals envisioned and set by him. It is for future generations to take forward the strong foundations laid by Prime Minister Modi.

THE EMERGENCE OF A GLOBAL PHENOMENON

MANOJ LADWA, BHARAT BARAI

Prime Minister Narendra Modi's position as a global phenomenon of our age is undoubted. His international diplomacy has won many friends and secured precious relationships. He has often acted in ways that are different from the traditional means. But what may appear at times to be unconventional methods of engagement and diplomacy with the international community have also enabled an unparalleled rise in India's reputation as a predictable and dependable partner. Modi's India is a partner for the world's economic hopes, political ambitions and social and environmental concerns. It has also led to a new-found confidence within India as an inevitable superpower, most importantly amongst aspirational Indians at home and abroad.

So what drives Modi, and what is behind the tapestry of this new global India story?

MODI'S LIVING BRIDGE

The genesis of Modi's experiments with global engagement began even before he became the Chief Minister of Gujarat. In the early 1990s, when India had just started breaking out of the shackles of the insular command economy that Nehruvian Socialism had caged it for the preceding decades, Modi was assiduously building relations with people of Indian origin in countries such as the United States and the United Kingdom.

One such person he had reached out to was Dr Bharat Barai, a renowned oncologist. He first met Modi in 1993, when Modi travelled to the United States to participate in the one hundredth anniversary of the World Parliament of Religions and the commemoration of the historic speech of Swami Vivekananda, a reformist Hindu monk.

Dr Barai recalls, 'Narendra bhai came with a small 22-inch suitcase. I remember him talking to my wife, Dr Panna Barai. He asked her, "Pannaben, I know you do laundry in the US over the weekend, but I have only two pairs of clothes, and so, can I do my laundry daily?" He was a simple man with simple needs and means.'

But it was not just Modi's simplicity that struck a chord with those he met during the early years. As Dr Barai further recalls, 'We had the honour to host this young, dynamic political party worker who had no government position. I was so astonished and impressed by his in-depth analysis, knowledge, dedication and his vision for India—its problems and possible solutions. I could see his wet eyes while discussing India, during our *chai pe charcha*.'

This was at a time when the term 'NRI' (Non-Resident Indian) was regarded by India's political establishment as a dirty phrase, with many Indian politicians describing NRIs as 'Not Required in India'. Those who had left India for better opportunities overseas were labelled as worthless do-gooders or even worse, as traitors, and their offers to support India's growth through fresh ideas, capital and technology gained from their experiences in the West were shunned as unwanted and insincere.

I recall, as late as 2013, a television debate on *Times Now*, in which (to my utter astonishment), a fellow guest and Congress party MP, said that Modi was a 'desperate individual talking to NRIs… which is not going to lead him anywhere.'

But Modi's instinct was often countercultural. He saw the diaspora as an untapped advantage for India that needed to be harnessed and not seen as a bunch of deserters—just as many in the political establishment of the time had painted them. I recall speaking to him much later when he became the Prime Minister, where he described the thirty million Indian diaspora as an 'untapped brain bank' rather than the 'brain drain' that others had described.

Modi strategically redefined this engagement. He leveraged the early years of the Pravasi Bhartiya Divas by ensuring the timing of the Vibrant Gujarat Summit (a now premier bi-annual gathering conceived by Modi for

Indian and global business leaders to woo trade, investment and technology opportunities to and from the state) was aligned so that international attendees could readily make a visit to Gujarat as part of their trip. This planted seeds amongst the diaspora by giving them a first-hand view of the Modi governance model. His proactive approach turned suspicions of the past into a supercharged partnership for India's global outreach, where under Modi's rule, every Indian, wherever in the world, could feel that he or she could count on India, and count for India.

Dr Barai reflects on this period of Modi's increasing international engagement, 'Starting in 2005, every two years, we used to celebrate Gujarat Day with a live video-cast by Chief Minister Narendra Modi to thousands of Gujarati diaspora in various US cities. Then, in 2009, there were requests from non-Gujarati Indians to hear him and so, I requested Narendra bhai speak in Hindi so that others could also understand. And in 2013, when he was on the verge on making a bid to become India's Prime Minister, the live event was simultaneously video-cast in twenty US cities, with the participation of thousands of Indian Americans.'

In London in 2015, Modi eloquently captured the power of the diaspora by coining for them the phrase, 'living bridge'—a phrase which has now been immortalized by both governments in the *2030 Roadmap for India-UK Future Relations*. This idea, summed up in two words, over two decades of Modi's consistent, committed and open engagement with probably India's most ardent constituency of natural ambassadors: global Indians.

A NEW SYMPHONY IN PLAY

One of the iconic moments of Modi's first term as Prime Minister was the frenzied reception he received on 28 September 2014 at the legendary Madison Square Garden in the heart of New York City, US. During the reception, Modi shared the stage with dozens of elected US officials, and addressed a roaring crowd of more than 20,000 people of Indian origin, from all across America. I remember at the time, the earlier sceptical staff of Madison Square Garden remarking that the crowd's volume rivalled the venue's most storied performances.

Modi intuitively understood what would unfold. He recognized the hunger of the diaspora to engage with the new aspirations that his election represented. He knew that his promise of a new India would resonate with those who had left India to seek dignity and potential.

The historic reception in New York made Modi a global political icon overnight. Receiving Modi at the US State Department in Washington two days later, Secretary John Kerry aptly remarked, 'We're never going to be able to top your rock star reception at Madison Square Garden … None of us have been able to turn on a television or pick up a newspaper without seeing the celebrity coverage that the Prime Minister has received. And with it, for all of us, there's a sense of shared excitement and a sense of shared possibility.'

The irony could not have been so stark. *The Washington Post* headline on 28 September 2014 was: 'India's Modi was once denied US entry, Sunday, he was the star at Madison Square Garden.' Here was a man who had been systematically vilified by the international media for over a decade. He was now filling every seat in iconic venues reserved for big sporting and music shows, being enthusiastically feted by US politicians from across the political divide and, later in 2016, given the honour of a rare address to a joint session of the US Congress. Much to Modi's credit, and testimony to the man he is, with an admirable stoicism, not once since he became Prime Minister, has Modi referred to or expressed even a hint of a grudge.

In his historic address to the US Congress on 8 June 2016, he rather poetically drew a line on the past by saying, 'The orchestra has sufficiently tuned their instruments; the baton has given the signal. And there is a new symphony in play.'

Madison Square Garden was a first. Never before had a democratically elected foreign leader attracted such a huge reception on US soil. I emphasize *democratically* elected as the Pope and Nelson Mandela are probably the only two other world leaders in recent living memory who have received stadium capacity welcomes in foreign lands.

IN PURSUIT OF HEARTS AND MINDS

Huge crowds now greet him wherever he travels in the world. The global rise of India under Modi has helped Indians everywhere ealizes that they have a role to play in India's progress. For instance, a few days before the 60,000-plus reception he received at the Wembley Stadium on 13 November 2015, I, along with the BJP's head of foreign affairs, Vijay Chauthaiwale, went to 10 Downing Street to formally invite the then Prime Minister, David Cameron. Cameron was visibly fascinated by the scale of the audience and preparations for Modi's visit. He self-deprecatingly quipped that he would struggle to fill a room of six hundred people at the local town hall.

On the morning of 14th November, 2015, Modi met with the then Leader of UK's Opposition and a long-time detractor, Labour's Jeremy Corbyn. A few weeks earlier, Corbyn's team-led shadow Foreign Secretary Hilary Benn had sent out feelers on whether Modi would meet Corbyn. Protocol did not demand that he meet the Leader of the Opposition, nor was it regarded as customary. Given the history of Corbyn, the Labour team, I remember, was rather sheepish. Modi, by contrast, welcomed the meeting without any hesitation. This only underlined his reputation of wanting to build a wide spectrum of political relationships, not wishing to be caged into Western dictums of right wing and left wing.

Modi's formidable communication skills on the global stage are not limited to the diaspora, or expressed just through his mesmerizing oratory. He is as conscious of the importance of visual messaging as he is about the spoken word. Known for his 'Modi-cut kurtas', traditionally woven Indian cottons (khadi) and for his passion to popularize Indian fashion globally, brand ambassador Modi has worn his Indianness literally on his sleeves wherever he has travelled.

One exception, however, was in Johannesburg in 2016, where much to the surprise and pleasure of South Africans, when addressing the Indian community, Modi donned a 'Mandela' shirt. In doing so, he captured the moment, and the hearts and minds of his hosts.

He was, on the one hand, addressing his Indian community, but through them, also talking to a much wider audience. By wrapping himself in the Mandela shirt that evening in Johannesburg, he was sending a message to the whole of South Africa and indeed, to the world, that he held the values of Nelson Mandela, and those who fought for democracy and freedom and took on the abhorrent apartheid regime, close to his heart.

People often ask me how Modi manages to fill huge stadiums, mostly out of fascination but, occasionally, with suspicion. This is where the depth and breadth of Modi's fabled community connect has transcended Gujarat and the shores of India. A Modi visit brings together communities to make such events possible, through what is possibly the most formidable global network of grassroots volunteers and community organizations. For instance, over seven hundred diverse organizations across the US mobilized their communities to make Madison Square Garden possible, and close to five hundred big and small British Indian community organizations from diverse regional, religious and cultural backgrounds came together to welcome Modi to the UK.

These mammoth outreach programmes have not appeared overnight. Modi has, over the decades, built relationships from the base upwards, where he has kept in regular touch, maintained personal rapport and enthused a genuine sense of pride and a 'can do' attitude amongst the very people who, only a few years ago were regarded as 'Not Required in India' by the Indian political elite.

Barry Gardiner, the veteran UK Member of Parliament for Brent North, whom I had introduced to Modi in 1999 over an aubergine curry at Kundan restaurant in Westminster, was in the audience at the Wembley Conference Centre in 2003, when Modi was Chief Minister. That evening, Modi spoke in a mix of Hindi and Gujarati. I later asked Barry if he had understood anything what Modi was saying. He replied, 'I understand the language of political communication. Narendra is a master.'

Modi could have easily played to the gallery that day on 18 August 2003. But instead, like he has done throughout his elected political life, he focused his entire hour-long speech, without an autocue or notes, on Gujarat's development and how the Gujarati diaspora could contribute to his state's progress.

Earlier in the morning, at the Taj Hotel in Buckingham Gate, soon after he had landed, the very first meeting of his visit was with a delegation of Indian Muslims, organized by Zafar Sareshwala. Modi has, despite consistent attempts to paint him otherwise, always been open to frank and honest dialogues.

Lord Meghnad Desai, eminent economist and one of Gujarat's most famous sons, had once proclaimed that he would never step foot in Gujarat so long as Modi was in power. But in 2010, and much to his credit,

Lord Desai met Modi for the first time at the latter's official residence in Gandhinagar. I sat outside, and what was supposed to be a fifteen-minute courtesy meeting, turned into an almost hour-long conversation. Lord Desai, came out with a beaming grin, and said to me that they had discussed 'diabetes'. I was left rather baffled given their history, but the two have remained friends ever since.

Similarly, the late Lord Gulam Noon, known as the UK's Curry King, had in the early years been a major critic of Modi. But after meeting him in Gandhinagar in 2009, Noon went on to become one of Modi's biggest admirers. There are countless such examples.

Over the years, Modi has nurtured the most potent of skills—an ability to disarm and seek common cause with even the most ardent critics. He attracts respect and intrigue in almost equal measure. His formula of stoicism in adversity, political astuteness in building relations with critics, and instinct to seize the moment of opportunity, often in the most dramatic of ways, have made him a standout global leader of our generation.

RADIATE TO OTHERS

Many would regard Modi's ability to fill stadium after stadium around the world and his receiving rock-star-like adulation as the pinnacle of political glory. What more would a politician desire than the acclaim of millions? But by any account, Modi is no ordinary politician. And he is certainly not a man who is swayed from the mission he sets himself by the frills of global fame.

At the core of this rests his own desire to serve Mother India and to connect with others on that journey. I believe the ideological underpinning of this goes back to his days as a humble young Swayamsevak (volunteer) of the Rashtriya Swayamsevak Sangh (RSS) attending the daily shakha (gathering) where the last command at the end of each session is '*Sangha Vikeer*', a call to connect with and 'radiate' to others the wisdom and values of patriotism and selfless service that are imbibed through these daily gatherings.

There are numerous examples of Modi's ability to turn what others would view as local or domestic Indian issues into global campaigns that join people from all over the world. For instance, as Chief Minister he ensured that the celebration of fifty years of Gujarat's statehood (Swarnim Gujarat) became a drive to connect Gujaratis across India and beyond to the state's numerous development programmes that he had initiated.

Similarly, Modi could have simply allowed the regeneration of the river Ganga to remain essentially a state-driven urban development and conservation scheme, albeit a complex and mammoth one. Instead, in true Modi style, from coining the catchy phrase 'Namami Gange', to using the stage at Madison Square Garden to encourage global Indians to contribute with money and know-how to the mission of cleaning their Mother Ganga, he brought belief and action to a mass-project mode.

Modi's mission to win hearts and minds for the service of his nation does not start or stop with big schemes and big audiences. In the summer of 2000, I recall travelling with Modi on the Piccadilly Line underground into Central London from my humble flat in Hounslow, to the house of an Indian businessman in the plush Mayfair. After tea and pleasantries, Modi leaned over and looked deep into the eyes of our host, and rather dramatically, he asked, 'Will you do something for me?' For most, a politician asking such a question to a wealthy businessman could only mean that a personal favour was being sought.

Instead, Modi explained that the businessman's father had contributed significantly to social causes in India and the world over, and that his son should ensure that a biography is written to capture all those good deeds as an inspiration to others. There are countless such incidents where Modi has combined his phenomenal memory, energy, ideas and that human touch to mobilize Indians around the world for social, economic and cultural causes.

If one looks closer at Modi's approach in developing people-to-people connections, one starts to see a pattern emerging. He has, time and again, demonstrated his ability to capture the public mood, address public grievances, operationalize (often at scale) ideas and institutionalize these within the existing governance framework. Examples of these include how Indian embassies around the world are mandated to engage with diaspora organizations in a manner and depth never witnessed before—through regular outreach programmes, celebration of Indian festivals and important national days, and to actively seek inputs on governance and policy matters. Similarly, significant work has been done to streamline and make visa and OCI card processing as automated as possible, reducing arbitrary human intervention.

PROJECTING BRAND INDIA

Despite inheriting a deeply convention-driven and conservative diplomatic service, Modi has sought to practise foreign affairs and economic diplomacy differently throughout his premiership. From the famous 'Modi hug', to hosting world leaders at interesting places outside the capital city of New Delhi, and unscripted walks and talks with counterparts, Modi certainly leaves his mark on every world leader he meets. Intuitively, he gets it that all diplomacy is ultimately personal.

When Modi took office in 2014, it was rare for incumbent Prime Ministers to venture with visiting world leaders outside the confines of Lutyens' Delhi. Perhaps they were shy, or even embarrassed by the India they ruled. In contrast, Modi uses every opportunity to showcase his beloved India, the history, cultural diversity and above all, the potential of its people to the world.

From images of Japanese Prime Minister Shinzo Abe performing the sacred aarti in Kashi on the banks of the river Ganga to Australian Prime Minister Malcolm Turnbull sitting and chatting causally with Modi on steps of the iconic Akshardham temple, and China's President Xi Jinping and Modi spinning cotton in traditional style at Mahatma Gandhi's ashram in Ahmedabad—all carried a subtle but profound message. That in Modi's India, there is no need to hide or shy away from your rich Indian identity. You may not have the resources today to travel the world, but Modi will bring the world to your doorstep; it's now up to you to make the most of that opportunity.

Such diplomatic and economic outreach initiatives have their origins in Gujarat to the period when Modi was Chief Minister. Gujarat is a land of festivals. Two of its most popular festivals are Navraatri, a festival preceding Diwali that features nine nights of traditional dance called Garba. The other is Uttarayan, also known as Makar Sankranti, which is celebrated with the flying of kites. Modi saw the potential of both to project Gujarat's soft power to the world, and in doing so, drive tourism and economic outcomes. He branded Garba as the world's largest dance festival—which it is—and invited dance troupes and the Indian diaspora to travel and join in the celebrations. Today, the Garba festival and Gujarat are synonymous.

Likewise, Modi branded Uttarayan as an International Kite Festival, inviting avid kite flyers and teams from around the world to the state. Little known at the time, but Modi had another agenda. The manufacturing of kites in India, and especially in Gujarat, is dominated by the minority Muslim community. In one fell swoop, by making the festival global, Modi resurrected a languishing industry, boosting demand and bringing in new technologies. By conservative estimates, the turnover of the kite industry in Gujarat shot up by thirty times during Modi's tenure as Chief Minister. Modi's signalling has always been through well-calibrated actions and not glib words.

Modi continued his formula of cultural diplomacy after becoming Prime Minister. The entire world knows that Modi is an avid yoga practitioner, extolling its virtues wherever he goes. In fact, on a visit to a country, Modi's host asked if he could join Modi for a session one morning.

And so, when in 2014, on his first-ever visit to the United Nations as Prime Minister, Modi suggested that the UN declare an International Day of Yoga, many back in India were completely surprised. The sniggering Indian 'Left liberal' elite branded it as yet another demonstration of Modi's Hindutva agenda, out of touch on the world stage. But Modi's motion received the largest number of votes, including from Christian and Islamic states. Modi had smartly reclaimed the ancient science of yoga by ensuring that its Indian origins were recognized and respected. He institutionalized a permanent channel for soft power diplomacy that disarmed his detractors. Yoga became part of the global dialogue on health and well-being.

A related pursuit for Modi has been the international propagation of the ancient Indian health science of Ayurveda. In 2018, with the support and encouragement of His Royal Highness, the Prince of Wales, Prince Charles, the two jointly inaugurated an Ayurvedic Centre of Excellence (ACE) at London's Science Museum. ACE's vision includes the study of ayurvedic practices and the exploration of the possibility of its integration as a recognized therapy and system of medicine within the UK's National Health Service. In doing so, Modi has opened up the potential for the globalization of India's already multi-billion-dollar Ayurvedic health industry.

Modi has proven time and again, through years of experiment and audacious implementation that culture and commerce go hand in hand. And that these can help build long-term successful partnerships anchored on mutual trust and respect.

Perhaps one of the most striking examples of Modi's formula of projecting brand India through building mutual trust and respect was reflected through the generous offer by the UAE for permitting the building of a grand traditional Hindu temple in the capital, Abu Dhabi. It would have been considered unthinkable, even impossible only a few years earlier. Modi, through his personal rapport with the Crown Prince, Mohamed bin Zayed Al Nahyan, ensured that the cultural and religious sentiments of the millions of Hindus living in the Emirates are respected and, indeed, celebrated. Bramavihari Swami, the energetic Leicester-born monk of the BAPS Swaminarayan organization coordinating this initiative, told me during my visit in September 2020 that Modi and the Crown Prince referred to each other as brothers.

In the first term of his premiership, Modi bet big on the Middle East, despite knowing full well that his opponents back home had done everything possible to malign him in the Islamic world. Instead, through his clarity of purpose, Modi has won the highest accolades and awards in both Sunni- and Shia-dominated countries, opening up a flood of investment commitments and cooperation pacts from the region into India unlike ever before.

Equally striking has been Modi's ability to deepen India's relations with Israel on all fronts. Long before the Abraham Accords, Modi had de-hyphenated the Arab-Israeli conflict from India's dealings with the region and its peoples. And without sacrificing India's principled support for a just solution to the problems of the Palestinian people. In cricket terms, the so-called foreign affairs novice has judged each ball on its merits and in that process, played a blinder of an innings on probably the most complex geo-political pitch.

ADDRESSING GLOBAL CHALLENGES

It is frequently said these days that if you can solve a problem for a billion people, you can solve them for the world. So many of Modi's achievements on the domestic front are abundantly exportable and universally scalable. For instance, soon after assuming office in August 2014, Modi embarked on the world's biggest financial inclusion programme. For decades, the poorest in India were regarded as un-bankable, leading to mass corruption in the deployment of welfare programmes, crippling the economy and creating disharmony and despondency across swathes of rural and urban poor India. Modi's Jan Dhan Yojana led to the opening of a staggering 318 million bank accounts within four years. This single-minded drive to 'bank the un-bankable', coupled with the roll out of a national identity scheme, Aadhaar Card, and to push mobile-enabled public services through Modi's Digital India programme, has been nothing short of a revolution in poverty alleviation.

Most recently, during the COVID-19 pandemic, whilst many countries including some of the more developed in the world, struggled to ensure state benefits reached citizens without bank accounts, Modi's financial inclusion and mass digitization programme ensured state benefits reached the needy in India much more efficiently than ever before.

Modi's pet mantra when he was Chief Minister of Gujarat was that he was solving the problems of his sixty million fellow Gujaratis through the application of 'Skill, Scale and Speed'. Today, his canvas is 1.5 billion people. Time and again he invokes this mantra, and in doing so he is offering solutions for many of the big global challenges of our time.

Whilst on a trade mission to Uganda in November 2008, to promote an upcoming Vibrant Gujarat Summit, I recall having a deep conversation with Chief Minister Modi about an award-winning documentary film I had recently seen called *An Inconvenient Truth*, the story of former US President Al Gore's campaign to educate people about global warming. Modi was curious to know the details and expressed surprise that there was little discussion within India's political leadership on what he quickly realized was a vital global issue.

Grasping the importance and urgency to act on climate change, within a matter of months, Modi had announced in 2009, the establishment of what was Asia's first Climate Change Department. He also started setting stringent targets in the state and working with business and communities to mitigate the state's carbon footprint. He brought in policies that encouraged the adoption of various green initiatives, including those involving solar and wind and spoke in impassioned terms about the need for 'green growth economics.'

Modi has since, as Prime Minister, been at the forefront of the country's and now the world's drive to address climate change, including conceiving the UN-backed International Solar Alliance.

The most recent example of Modi's ability to think big and implement fast has been the drive to vaccinate India's population against COVID-19. Within a matter of months from ground zero and through immense scepticism, India is (as of September 2020) vaccinating over ten million people every day—that is the population of Australia, as Modi reminded me when we last met. Again this, like the implementation of the world's largest uniform taxation system (GST), has been enabled by Modi's hallmark of clear and unambiguous decision-making, support for and deployment of effective technological solutions and by inspiring a movement of national service amongst citizens and public servants alike.

Therefore, Modi, by relentlessly addressing India's Sustainable Development Goals (SDG) issues, he is in effect solving much the world's SDG issues too, since so much of the global SDG gap is in India.

Earlier in the pandemic, whilst other powers were dithering over domestic pressures, Modi made a commitment to distribute vaccines under his Vaccine Maitri programme to over a hundred countries around the world, including some of the poorest nations as a gift from the people of India. He saw the bigger picture and long-term interests of India—at precisely the time where other world leaders were at their most insular and protectionist phase. Modi's signalling was clear domestically, that the post-COVID-19 world will judge and thank India for standing up in this time of need, and that this will open-up further opportunities for India's aspirational young.

PHENOMENON MARCHES ON

Modi has cleaned the lens through which the world now views India. He has given focus to India's domestic priorities and aligned the world, not through muscular showmanship, but by connecting hearts and minds to the possibility that India can offer the world. He has in many ways single-handedly changed the rules of engagement.

Modi has aimed high, and by raising the profile of India, solving historically intractable problems and by relentlessly improving Indian governance, he has given agency to Indians globally to hold their heads up high, too.

With twenty years of elected public service behind him, Modi's record speaks for itself. Whether he will be regarded as India's greatest ever Prime Minister, and in turn, as one of the world's greatest ever leaders, are questions that will be answered at a time when history is ready for him. And there is still some way to go for that. For now, the man, the mission and the phenomenon that is Modi, marches on.

FOREIGN POLICY: VISION AND ACHIEVEMENTS

DR S. JAISHANKAR

As he took over as Prime Minister on 26 May, 2014, Narendra Modi surprised India's foreign policy establishment by making a bold move in that domain. He invited neighbouring leaders to the swearing-in ceremony of his Council of Ministers in New Delhi. This unusual decision, leave alone the enthusiastic response, was not even contemplated by most observers. There was even more surprise that this initiative should come from someone who many thought of as a novice in international relations. Over the next few years, the world was to discover that he was, in fact, a leader who had developed his policy insights and ideas over many years. Not just that, he also had his unique way of messaging, implementation and follow-up. Since then, we have all become a little more familiar with the strategy and approach of Narendra Modi. Only the very partisan would dispute that their cumulative impact has significantly enhanced India's global stature.

It is, therefore, worth reflecting on the habits and worldview of a Prime Minister who has put such a strong personal imprint on foreign policy. Along with his legendary energy level, what is striking about Narendra Modi is his enormous curiosity about the world. His zest to absorb and process information is matched only by the ability to deploy it effectively. For us, it may be a data point; for him, it is a way of connecting and influencing. This may be an innate trait of a politician, but he has taken it to an altogether different level. The goal is obviously to arrive at the best possible understanding of what awaits him and to shape it to advantage. It could be the intricacies of American politics before meeting President Obama, Chinese history as he was going to Xian, or perhaps the post-

Soviet era to get a good feel for President Putin. He would not only soak in what was being explained but constantly push us to do better. The interest may pertain to happenings, subjects and domains; it could as easily be about people and their interplay. There is also a sense of self-discipline in the exercise. He wants to be clear about the red lines before engaging. For the PM himself, sources of information are broad and diverse, ranging from the spoken and written word to the officialdom, political world, media or networking. The idea is to get into the mind of the other party. Interacting with him as Foreign Secretary, I noted that he was never hesitant to ask and always patient in listening. What has now become an SOP (standard operating procedure) for the Delhi bureaucracy was initially a novel experience for all of us. Anyone engaging with him at any level clearly had to prepare thoroughly to hold their own.

A clinical analysis of a period that I know well brings out how much the Prime Minister has shaped its contours. But the experience of participating in policymaking has also been a process of discovery about him. There are clearly learnings and judgments that Narendra Modi brings to bear from his chief ministership days. His extensive travels within India and around the world in the period before joining the government have given him a good feel for social forces and political sensitivities. I had anticipated some of that but was still sometimes taken aback at the highly-informed references he would make to countries and persons in our conversations. During his 2014 visit to the US, while discussing the instincts of Americans, I spoke of travelling across that country in my younger days, only to discover that he had been to more states than me. And as he jokingly told me, not by car or air but on a Greyhound bus! Similarly, his long-standing acquaintances in diaspora societies suggest an early interest in foreign affairs. It could be Mauritius, Guyana or Suriname; he seemed to know so many people. His sojourns in Nepal were similarly a revelation, be it insights or factoids about that society. For someone schooled in orthodox diplomacy, it dawned on me that he had approached the same landscape from a more socio-political and grounded perspective.

It is said that travel broadens the mind and certainly in his case, it appears an important contribution to PM's global awareness. This is because he is autodidactic by nature with a perpetual desire to comprehend the world better.

That PM Modi has little appetite for conventional sightseeing is well known. What I discovered accompanying him was how strongly the experiences abroad were driven by a goal of identifying and absorbing best practices. The railway station we went to in Berlin fed into his modernization plans at home. The bullet train in Japan actually ended up as a project. The convention centres where we spent time, each of them had a lesson to offer as we went about building our own. A cleaned up river in Seoul further strengthened our resolve on rejuvenating the Ganga. The public housing in Singapore was an input into our affordable housing scheme. As a student of history, the Prime Minister reminded me of the Meiji era reformers in Japan who contemplated the world through the lens of changes at home.

One of the shifts that PM Modi brought into Indian foreign policy is its focus on leveraging external relationships for domestic development. After all, the Asian economies that developed rapidly in the era of globalization were those that had accorded precisely this primacy to economic growth. This, of course, was a far cry from the earlier days of ideological hubris and looking down on business. But to understand this facet of Prime Minister Modi, it is necessary to go back to Chief Minister Modi. By initiating the Vibrant Gujarat Global Summits, he created a platform to encourage flow of resources, technology and best practices. Visits and interactions that were at its core were clearly an invaluable experience for him. Whether it was partners like Japan, Canada, Denmark, South Korea or Kenya, or sectors like automobiles, railways, pharmaceuticals, renewables and chemicals, they demonstrated that the world would respond to right policies. Interestingly, many of the relationships formed in this period helped to give a head start as new directions were set in his prime ministership. His conviction that India must grow with the world would constantly lead him to advise his Cabinet colleagues to be connected and open-minded. The practice of global personalities, starting with Singapore Deputy Prime Minister Tharman Shanmugaratnam, delivering the NITI Lectures to policymakers is very much in that vein.

The Vibrant Gujarat gathering of entrepreneurs and investors certainly helped to make Gujarat think internationally. There were not many other events in the country that could be put in the same class. Pulling off this achievement regularly clearly infused confidence in the ability to think bigger. This ambition kicked in strongly once Prime Minister Modi raised his global profile after assuming office. In the years that followed, India's engagement with the world reflected the vision that he had for his nation. India had done two collective summits till then with Africa; the third one, held in 2015 under the vision of PM Modi was of a different order with forty-one leaders present from that continent. Before 2014, the country had invited individual ASEAN heads for the Republic Day; the celebrations held in 2018 saw all ten ASEAN heads of state attending. Meetings with the European Union had taken place before; the 2021 engagement involved all twenty-seven EU leaders for the first time. Whether it was the Nordic States, Central Asia or the Pacific Islands, the collective engagement carried its own message. This was a Prime Minister who, by the dint of his earlier experience, has made the country think 'scale' in a range of domains.

There are other examples of the influence of the Gujarat period on Modi's prime ministership. As a Chief Minister, he was an enthusiastic proponent of renewable energy well before this became mainstream thinking. His experiments with solar panels on canals also attracted international attention. Tellingly, he authored a book called *Convenient Action* in response to the perception of climate change being an inconvenient truth. And being Modi, he also established a department within the state government on climate change as far back as 2009. If we fast-forward to COP-21 in Paris, it is no accident that he was now a prime mover to establish the International Solar Alliance. Similarly, his state-level experience on disaster recovery led him to propose another global initiative: the Coalition for Disaster Resilient Infrastructure. It was revealing that global issues that he took up as PM—especially terrorism, climate change or disasters—were confronted squarely by Chief Minister Modi during his terms in office. The long stint heading the state also gave his foreign policy thinking a greater federal perspective.

From the very start, PM Modi was insistent that visiting foreign leaders should be exposed to an India beyond its capital. Through these experiences, he felt that the full Indian narrative would be much better understood across the world. And sure enough, Amritsar saw a 'Heart of Asia' Conference, Goa a BRICS Summit, Kashi and Ahmedabad visits by Shinzo Abe, Bengaluru and Chandigarh by Angela Merkel and François Hollande respectively, and

Mamallapuram by Xi Jinping. He was also keen that the federal nature of our polity be factored into policymaking, leading to the establishment of a States Division within MEA. Partnerships, events and visits organized with state government collaboration rapidly became the norm. And their cumulative result broadened the message of Indian diplomacy.

The perseverance that has driven the transformation of Gujarat in the past two decades is now also in evidence when it comes to India's projects abroad. The Pragati model of project review instituted at the national level has led the Foreign Ministry to follow similar practices for its own endeavours abroad. As a result, long-pending projects like the Terai roads in Nepal, housing and hospitals in Sri Lanka, rail connectivity and power transmission in Bangladesh or the Salma dam and public buildings in Afghanistan were finally completed. And the new ones undertaken have been executed at a much faster pace, denoting the improvement in the manner of delivery. Whether it is the Metro or Supreme Court in Mauritius, post-earthquake rebuilding of houses in Nepal or the ambulance service in Sri Lanka, India's reputation as a development partner has undergone a sea change.

Among the Prime Minister's many attributes, one that stands out is his deep sense of nationalism. This is, of course, intrinsic to his political beliefs and one very much in evidence even when he was Chief Minister. When I first met him as Ambassador in China in 2011, unlike many other Chief Ministers, he specifically sought a political briefing. I recall his emphasizing that on issues of terrorism and sovereignty, we needed to make sure that we spoke with one voice abroad; especially in China. This, incidentally, was also my first exposure to his method of working. Among the takeaways was insistence that I should not hesitate to indicate clearly what he should say, and equally, what he should not say. His letter on return to India went beyond the normal appreciation that visitors express for hospitality, etc. What was different was a pointed mention of my successful upholding of the interests of our country in China. As Prime Minister, it was only to be expected that he would be confronted with national security challenges, on a recurring basis and on occasion, as a crisis. When it came to terrorism, especially of a cross-border nature, he has been crystal clear that he would never allow it to be normalized. This determination has shaped our Pakistan policy since 2014.

My own recollection in this regard goes back to the SAARC Yatra that I was undertaking soon after becoming Foreign Secretary in 2015. In his parting instructions, the PM told me that he had great confidence in my experience and judgement, but there is one thing I should keep in mind when I arrive at Islamabad. He was different from his predecessors and would neither overlook nor tolerate terrorism. There should never be any ambiguity on this score. Insofar as China is concerned, Prime Minister Modi is a firm believer that our relationship should be based on mutual respect and mutual sensitivity. He recognizes that we are two unique civilizations whose near-parallel rise poses its own challenges. In all the meetings with Chinese counterparts that I have been present, he has never held back from voicing our interests and concerns. Like his predecessors, he too has had to tackle the boundary dispute. While he has displayed the requisite patience, this has been accompanied by a steely resolve not to allow the LAC to be changed unilaterally.

As Foreign Secretary and thereafter as External Affairs Minister, I have been associated with the neutralization of insurgent camps on the Myanmar border in 2015, the surgical strike at Uri in 2016, the face-off at Doklam in 2017 and the robust response at the border in Ladakh since 2020. On each of these occasions, a decision-making style honed by a strong understanding of ground complexity has been very much in evidence. Goals have been set clearly after due deliberation and those charged with the responsibility of execution have been given the requisite space. This is true as much of the diplomatic side as the security one. But the Prime Minister's approach is not one of just reacting to the moment. For the first time, there is a serious and comprehensive effort to create an effective border infrastructure. What remained on the drawing board for years or was work in progress now started to become reality. Changes introduced included adoption of new technologies and equipment, a better mode of execution, a greater delegation of powers and faster clearances. The budget itself has more than doubled since 2014. The roads completed also almost doubled in the 2014–21 period in comparison to 2008–14. For the same periods, the bridges completed in fact virtually tripled, while tunnel construction took a quantum jump. Of course, making up for the past in this sphere is particularly challenging, especially vis-à-vis a neighbour who has outstripped us so much since 1988. Yet, the gaps have started to narrow in some critical sectors and operational deployments have become more feasible. The leadership and willpower was equally in evidence when it came to the deployment of forces in challenging conditions on the China border. The effective response of our armed forces in 2020 is a story in itself.

The Modi era may have started on the foreign policy front with a gathering of the neighbourhood. But from this gesture, we rapidly developed what came to be known as the 'Neighbourhood First' policy. This encouraged a transformation of South Asia by settling a land and maritime boundary, building stronger connectivity, expanding societal contacts and nurturing close leadership bonds. In each case, the Prime Minister led from the front by visiting all neighbours, many after a gap of decades. At the same time, he pushed on the policy and implementation side for better delivery on more ambitious development projects. During the COVID-19 period, India not only went the extra mile in terms of vaccines, supplies and logistics, but also followed that up with generous financial support, Sri Lanka being the most notable case. An approach to embrace neighbours closely may have been the most dramatic of his early moves. But it was just one illustration of a larger review and repositioning under PM Modi's stewardship. This includes a conscious 'all of the government' approach, seeking to overcome departmental silos that have long dominated policy processes. A more rigorous budgeting process and regular monitoring of projects abroad have contributed to enhanced performance.

Under Narendra Modi, we have witnessed the unfolding of a different approach to world affairs. It revolves around changing the thinking of the world about India. Entrenched prejudices and vested interests may be deep; but they are being contested vigorously through policies and actions. An important aspect is to ensure that our capabilities and contribution receive greater recognition. The 'Make in India' and 'Start-up India' campaigns, followed by the production-linked incentive (PLI) initiative, have increased our economic relevance. The world regards us now as much more than a market. Improving India's standing in the 'Ease of Doing Business' index has also made a discernible difference. Even the challenges of the COVID-19 pandemic have not deflected focus from this approach. That the vulnerable were supported through the pandemic by a massive food and financial support programme said something for our governance. By responding to the medical and vaccine requirements of the world, our reputation as the 'pharmacy of the world' was also established. Nor is it lost on others that some vaccines have been invented in India. An earlier image of an IT power has been consolidated through digital governance and delivery on a mega scale. The greening of India's energy mix is another notable achievement that has elicited global appreciation. The overall messaging is of an India determinedly proceeding on a path of modernization, addressing challenges that may arise, but embracing bold and progressive solutions to its future.

PM Modi has undoubtedly brought into foreign policy a greater focus on economic objectives. He interacts regularly with entrepreneurs and innovators across the globe so that India stays abreast with latest developments. He also actively woos them to set up operations in India, realizing that this can contribute to employment expansion and deep strengths. As I can testify from numerous sittings, his business meetings are real problem-solving exercises with rigorous follow-up. And when the leader personally makes such a big effort, his message resonates. India stands to benefit enormously from international collaboration, whether it is in clean technologies, efficient logistics or modern manufacturing. Increased FDI flows are one parameter of our performance; the expansion of trade is another. For the first time, trade targets have been set country-wise and the PM himself participates in the exercise of motivating our representatives abroad. At the end of the day, we are seeing a foreign policy aimed at increasing employment, developing national capabilities and enhancing the quality of life of our people.

In a competitive and diverse world, it is obviously necessary to navigate multiple interests in the most effective manner. This can either be done with trepidation and timidity, or practised with confidence and skill. On his part, Prime Minister Modi perceives opportunities more readily than others and is confident about exploiting them. For example, the two back-to-back trilaterals in Buenos Aires in 2018 told their own tale. One was with Shinzo Abe and Donald Trump and the second with Vladimir Putin and Xi Jinping. Even at other levels, past challenges of hesitancy have needed to be overcome. Regional dichotomies are one such example, be it Israel and Palestine, Iran and the Gulf or Japan and Korea. These have been addressed with dexterity and self-assurance. Significantly, Prime Minister undertook separate bilateral visits to Israel and Palestine, without succumbing to hyphenation. The Israel visit was, of course, also about transcending our vote-bank politics. Interestingly, the Prime Minister transited Arab airspace *en route* to Israel and was escorted by Israeli helicopters when arriving at Ramallah. Closer home, a similar mindset was set aside by the PM going to Colombo, Anuradhapura and Jaffna on the same visit. At the highest level, this ability to manage competing powers is essential to success in a multipolar world. Those who have followed Indian diplomacy under Narendra Modi would agree that his willingness to go beyond precedents has helped infuse a new determination to do so. *Sabka Saath, Sabka Vikas, Sabka Vishwas*, has also been a foreign policy maxim.

The diplomatic achievements of recent years only underline how much more can be done by greater assurance and stronger leadership. We have connected better with the societies of the subcontinent, broadened linkages with Southeast Asia, reached out to Gulf nations, partnered Central Asia, deepened our Africa footprint, and engaged distant geographies from Latin America to the Pacific Islands. At the peak of world politics, India is dealing effectively with all the major power centres simultaneously. Our multilateral activities have been energetic, especially at the United Nations. The record of electoral wins in international organizations has improved, including an important one in the International Court of Justice. And we have been leading the plurilateral trend of nations coming together for issue-based cooperation. India has advanced its Indo-Pacific vision and taken forward the Quad platform. At the same time, it has joined the Shanghai Cooperation Organization of Eurasian nations. Similarly, collective initiatives on solar energy and disaster resilience have been paralleled by national actions on vaccine and other medical supplies. Obtaining the membership of the Missile Technology Control Regime, the Australia Group on chemicals and the Wassenaar Arrangement on conventional arms have also been milestones.

Shaping the global agenda more effectively is part of the natural progression for a rising power. Prime Minister Modi undertook this mission with his characteristic passion and energy, making his presence felt at international platforms. Be it the G-20 meetings, Quad summit, SCO gatherings or the UN General Assembly, the impact of that is visible. The public intuitively appreciates this, whether they see pictures of leaders huddling or hear how India is spoken about. The presence of India at global events is also marked by the relevance of its initiatives and the diligence of its preparations. At the United Nations and SCO, the PM made fighting terrorism a global priority and overcame the challenge of this being perceived as India's particular quest. At the G-20, be it Brisbane or Rome, he shone the spotlight on black money and tax evasion. In regional forums like East Asia Summit, BIMSTEC and India-Africa Forum, he gave the much-needed attention to building adequate and viable connectivity. At Paris and Glasgow, he not only led climate action side-by-side with climate justice but also established the International Solar Alliance. The Vaccine Maitri programme stood out at a time in the world when most nations were watching out only for themselves. While doing all this, PM Modi has been able to harmonize national interest with that of the world at large. He has repeatedly underlined that this is very much in tune with Vasudhaiva Kutumbakam (the world is a family). In that sense, he has overcome a contradiction that has plagued many of his peers. In fact, in 2018, no one less than former Singapore PM Goh Chok Tong publicly recognized Narendra Modi's ability to engage multiple centres of the world and articulate a common vision.

Prime Minister Modi also has a strong conviction that communities should stand by each other. The roots of this belief probably lie in his own life experiences. When it comes to humanitarian and disaster situations, man-made or natural, he has stepped forward and often led the response. Since 2014, India has deservedly developed the reputation of a 'first responder' in the region. We have seen Op Neer that took drinking water to Maldives in 2014, Op Rahat that rescued those trapped in the Yemen civil war in 2015, Op Maitri the same year that went to the aid of Nepal during its earthquake, Op Insaniyat in Bangladesh for Rohingya relief in 2017, Op Samudra Maitri in Indonesia during the 2018 tsunami, Op Vanilla during the 2020 cyclone in Madagascar and Op Sagar that unfolded in the Indian Ocean providing pandemic-related assistance. Nepal 2015 is etched particularly strongly in my memory as the PM tracked our relief efforts continuously till the first Indian plane touched down in Kathmandu. And then, true to form, he did not let up on the follow-up!

It is also to be expected that a Modi foreign policy would accord greater primacy to the projection abroad of India's heritage, culture and tradition. These may be expressions of a larger cultural rebalancing that is underway in the world. But they were also reflective of the broadening of Indian democracy and the cultural authenticity that the Prime Minister himself embodies. In keeping with India's greater political and economic weight, there was a natural desire to encourage a global appreciation of the Indian civilization. The initiative at the UN to recognize and observe an International Day of Yoga was among the early moves of the Prime Minister. This was followed by a strong focus on familiarizing the world more with the benefits of Ayurveda. Reclaiming India's Buddhist traditions was another endeavour, advanced through conclaves, pilgrimage and heritage conservation. In parallel, there was a stronger push to secure recognition of world heritage sites in India by the UNESCO. Culture itself became an intrinsic element of policy, especially in regard to our immediate neighbourhood. The Ramayana circuit was a notable example of developing a shared heritage. The policy emphasis is, however, not only on a projection of soft power. It is also in ensuring respect for a civilization that has been preyed upon in the past. The return of Indian antiquities from the US, Canada or Australia is a big step in that direction. When it came to the political debates of the day too, drawing on our history and sociology reinforces our democratic credentials. By now, these activities have sharpened the perception of India as a civilizational state on the rise again. That messaging has also been relevant to the welfare of the diaspora. Their right to practise their faith has been a long-standing issue in many geographies. The building of a temple in Abu Dhabi has been a milestone in that regard. Other examples have included support for the Sikh community abroad to carry articles of faith. Or getting the Haj quota for Indian Muslims increased. Commemorating the anniversaries of those who have shaped India's destiny—from Mahatma Gandhi and Guru Gobind Singh to Swami Vivekananda and Dr B.R. Ambedkar—across the world has also globalized our outreach. Even the manner by which Azadi Ka Amrit Mahotsav is being celebrated speaks of a different level of confidence and ambition.

Gujarat is among the states with a tradition of going beyond our shores. Consequently, it puts a premium on the welfare of Non-Resident Indians (NRIs) and Persons of Indian Origin (PIOs). It was not surprising that Prime Minister Modi elevated this concern in his foreign policy. In fact, the

Cabinet Resolution of 1 January 2015 establishing the NITI Aayog refers to the diaspora as a geo-economic and geo-political strength. And like so much else, this was with as much an eye for the future as an acknowledgment of the past. Prime Minister Modi obviously envisages the world as a global workplace, not just as a marketplace. This means new initiatives to care for those working abroad, especially in the Gulf. He signalled his personal commitment in that regard by visiting labour camps in the UAE and Qatar. His support for expanding the usage of the Indian Community Welfare Fund made a huge difference during the pandemic. The work prospects of students who went abroad have also been in greater focus. He has taken this up with his counterparts in France, the UK, Germany and Australia. On the same note, work opportunities for Indians abroad have been expanded with skill and mobility agreements signed with Japan and Portugal. And in times of trouble, whether an individual situation or a collective crisis, there have been purposeful responses from his government. From Libya and Yemen to Iran, Iraq and Afghanistan, strenuous efforts have been made to help those in distress. They could be seamen or missionaries, workers or professionals; Indians were no longer left to fend for themselves.

The welfare of Indians and Indian-origin persons abroad has naturally become a significant preoccupation in a globalized era. They too have greater expectations of a rising India. Apart from the emotional bonding, we know that the success of one is to the benefit of the other. So, it is appropriate that Prime Minister Modi should infuse into the domain of diaspora policy a sense of care and attention. He has pushed the Indian system to deal with the problems of NRIs and PIOs more sympathetically. Their requirements, big and small, have merited his consideration and the results are there for all to see. The attitude of our Embassies abroad has changed, just as the response of offices in India. Getting passports has got easier and corruption-free. And using post offices to that end has been a smart move. It is also a case study of 'maximum governance, minimum government'. So too have other bureaucratic processes like attestation of documents. Situations of difficulty have merited particular focus. The online MADAD portal, in fact, has been second only in impact to the faster delivery of passports. But what has made a real difference is how grounded the policy reform has been, surely the imprint of a mind that has grappled with governance challenges over years. The more liberal usage of the Indian Community Welfare Fund has been a lifesaver for those struggling to find shelter, get legal defence or even bring back mortal remains from abroad. During the COVID-19 period, its utility was particularly visible in terms of housing, feeding and transporting Indian citizens in need.

Since 2014, there were numerous dedicated operations to rescue Indians in distress: Op Sankat Mochan in Sudan 2016, Op Nistar in Yemen in 2018, and most recently, Op Devi Shakti in Afghanistan. The Vande Bharat Mission that repatriated seven million Indians during the pandemic is, of course, the most gigantic of these endeavours. The movement of people was a formidable challenge in itself; addressing their health, stay and logistics was equally effectively undertaken. There are few better examples of the Prime Minister's maxim that policies are all about people.

When we first met in China in 2011, the Embassy was working on the release from detention of some diamond traders from Gujarat in Shenzhen. It was not unusual for state authorities in India to take up such cases with Embassies. But in this case, the Chief Minister himself took it up in the strongest terms with Chinese interlocutors. When the freedom of twelve detainees was secured the following month, we were recipients not of a routine acknowledgement but a personalized thanks. As I think back on it, the significance of this episode lies in the sense of responsibility for Indians who are stuck abroad. The same single-mindedness has been visible in the Vande Bharat Mission during the outbreak of COVID-19 or the times when Indians were stranded in Afghanistan, Yemen, Iraq or Sudan. Obviously, anything to do with India and Indians is personal and deeply felt. And when we juxtapose this against Neighbourhood First, that is the reason why our flights also have seats for the citizens of our neighbours.

The evolution of our diaspora policy bears similar hallmarks of core beliefs and strong care. It is now widely accepted that the Madison Square Garden event on 28 September 2014 was a watershed in that domain. Prime Minister Modi had been invited to come to the US by President Obama during the congratulatory phone call. My first call on him thereafter as the Ambassador in the US naturally focused on a possible visit. The PM brought up the subject of the diaspora, which he described as a great strength of the nation. They needed to discover their own voice and we needed to consolidate their role as a bridge.

The instructions for the MSG event flowed from this belief. It must be organized in a manner that its sound would reverberate not just in the US and India, but across the world. That it certainly did, for most part because the intensity of the PM's connect to the audience was so manifest. Thus began a unique experiment in popular diplomacy that has been the envy of many other leaders and countries. Equally, it has boosted the pride of the diaspora wherever he spoke.

It is a truism that countries have permanent interests and that international relations are based on this foundation. But interests are rarely secured by themselves; indeed, that is why we need diplomacy. Relationships are required to make the most of convergences and intersections. And those, in turn, are best advanced by personal chemistry and an effective ability to communicate and persuade. During his tenure, Prime Minister Modi has strenuously sought to make up for previous indifference and neglect. And he has done so in a purposeful manner rather than as a bureaucratic ritual. His visits may be famous for their gruelling schedule and single-minded focus. But what it has done is to put India much more seriously on the global map. With the leaders of powers like the US, Russia, France, China, Japan, Germany or the UK, he has established a regular direct dialogue. Bilateral visits to the immediate neighbourhood made up for long gaps even with critical partners like Nepal and Sri Lanka. Even in the extended region, a nation like the UAE that hosts millions of NRIs had not seen an Indian Prime Minister since Indira Gandhi in 1981. But now, the leaders themselves led a radical transformation in these ties. To a considerable degree, this story of under-engagement prevailed across other geographies. It could be a Quad partner like Australia, some of the Central Asian states, significant members of the European Union, long-standing friends in Africa, or even some members of the G-20. Quite understandably, renewed contacts that resulted from leadership energy got the attention of the world.

Diplomacy being what it is, personal interest is bound to evoke a positive response. Many global leaders made gestures in terms of protocol and venues. Angela Merkel welcomed PM at her country retreat Schloss Meseberg, Shinzo Abe at his personal residence at Yamanashi, David Cameron at Chequers or Vladimir Putin on board his presidential yacht at Sochi. President Biden, who as Vice President, had hosted the PM in the State Department, undertook a full bilateral engagement in the midst of the Quad Summit. Some nations conferred their highest awards, notably Saudi Arabia, UAE, Palestine, Russia, Maldives, Bahrain, the US and Bhutan. Even something as routine as the exchange of gifts came to have a new meaning. PM Modi would take personal interest in their selection, usually making a statement of our heritage or providing a reminder of history. Some of them have stuck in my mind even after these many years. As the Republic Day guest in 2015, President Obama was given a copy of the American telegram read out to the Constituent Assembly in December 1946. President Putin was presented a Kalaripayuttu set given his interest in martial arts. President Macron got a replica of a Pala dynasty Surya at the founding conference of the International Solar Alliance. Tajik President Rahmon received a painting of the tomb of the poet Abdul Qadir Bedil, who is revered in his country. The one which made the greatest impression was the Australian John Lang's legal memorial of June 1854 on behalf of Rani Laxmi Bai of Jhansi in her fight against the East India Company. This was presented to Prime Minister Tony Abbott.

The point to note is that these courtesies and sentiments are not without meaning. They do create the comfort for serious diplomacy to deliver on matters of greater importance. In concrete ways, the personal ties PM has forged have directly advanced the interests of our nation and people. It could be the Saudi King responding to his request for a ceasefire in Yemen to allowing evacuation of Indians. Or indeed, the increase in the Haj quota for Indian Muslims and the construction of the Hindu temple in Abu Dhabi. Some like Qatar responded to his personal appeal on a significant proposal to reduce energy costs. Conversations with his Russian counterpart facilitated the expansion of our hydrocarbon investments in that country. And with more than one partner, there has been an exceptional response to urgent security needs. Truth be told, a vigorous and interactive leader makes all the difference.

There is no gainsaying the fact that Prime Minister Modi looms large on the world stage. Definitely, his policies and initiatives have had their impact. But there is also a personal respect that influences the attitude of others. Peers perceive him as quintessentially Indian, and respond accordingly. His language, metaphors, appearance, mannerisms and habits—they define a persona that the world has come to recognize. I recall how fascinated American leaders were about his fasting habits during the 2014 visit. Or the interest that Europeans showed in his yoga routine. A large element of this is also the manner in which the Prime Minister carries himself. Not just that, he is equally enthusiastic about sharing India's traditions and customs with his interlocutors. His own intuitive feel for diplomacy has also led him to find connects between foreign countries and their leaders with India.

Shaping the narrative is always a challenge in the quest for change. Departures from the past are ready targets for criticism in the name of political correctness. Prime Minister Modi has faced more than his fair share of such attacks. They could be on his efforts to remedy historical wrongs, disregard vote-bank politics and consolidate national unity. Or at the other extreme, the fact that he chose to elevate mundane issues like toilet shortages and firewood usage to the level of national debate. In a globalized world, it was also inevitable that these conversations would spill beyond our borders. Having weathered many storms during his chief ministership, he is obviously dealing with them with his characteristic confidence. But these discussions also drive home the need for India to have an adequate say in the global discourse. With this realization, Prime Minister Modi encouraged the proliferation of international platforms in India on a range of issues. Some of them, especially the Raisina Dialogue, have made their mark even in this short period.

In pursuit of his goal to make India a leading power one day, Prime Minister Modi has been as demanding of the Indian system as he has been unsparing of himself. His visits abroad are legendary for their punishing schedule; a five-day trip to Afghanistan, Qatar, Switzerland, the US and Mexico would probably rank among the toughest at that level. In his era, Indian diplomacy has learnt to be more responsive, effective, practical and ambitious. And this has happened due to the exhortative and motivational efforts coming from the very top. If our profile is higher, responsibilities greater, delivery better and capabilities more recognized, much of the difference is due to leadership.

Twenty years in the government have enabled Narendra Modi to comprehensively reshape our foreign policy. It is today much more integral to a larger agenda of national development. There is a strong emphasis on delivery and an even clearer commitment to the ease of living of our citizens. It has national interest at its core, but in a manner that is harmonized with global good. In short, it is the world outlook of a New India.

REFLECTIONS

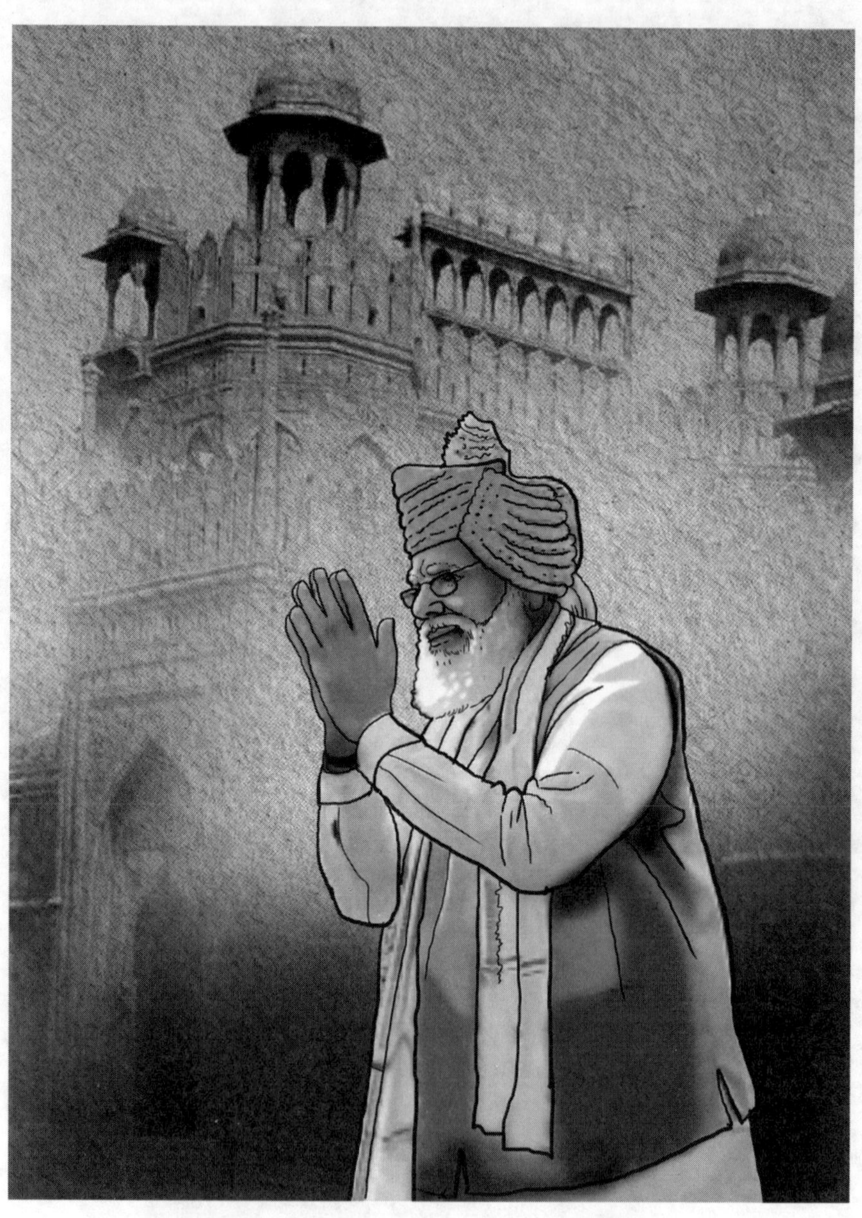

I would like to congratulate our honourable Prime Minister, Narendra Modi, for completing twenty years in office, first as the Chief Minister of Gujarat, and then as the Prime Minister of India.

I feel that PM Modi's most remarkable quality is the tenacity and single-mindedness with which he endeavours to achieve anything that he sets his mind to.

He is one of the most remarkable communicators that Indian politics has ever seen. His ability to connect with people, reach out to citizens and make a place in their hearts is unparalleled.

In my few interactions with him I found him full of grace and dignity. He is one of the few politicians I know who fully understands the potential of soft power and its importance in foreign relations.

I hope and pray that he succeeds in bringing happiness and joy in every Indian's life.

Aamir Khan, award-winning Indian actor

The Prime Minister with a smile!

If there is one person in public life who decidedly shatters all your pre-conceived notions when you meet him in person, it has to be Modi ji. I first met him in 2012, when he was the Chief Minister of Gujarat.

He met me with a smile—not a formal one, but a warm smile that was as much in his eyes as it was on his face. He started the conversation by telling me jokes, one after another. I remember all my anxiety just melted away. I had been told that I had ten minutes with him; our meeting lasted for forty-seven minutes, forty of which must have gone into both of us laughing.

When he became the Prime Minister two years later, one of my initial thoughts was: finally we have a PM with a sense of humour!

Seven years later, when I got a rare opportunity to interview him on television, I impulsively asked him to tell a joke, and later, showed him some funny memes on him that were doing the rounds on social media. A lot of people wondered why I did that. They just didn't know that this was my chance to let everyone know that here is a world leader who isn't just about being serious and uptight. He is as real as they get, with the most amazing sense of humour—be it directed at others or at himself.

I can go on and on about Shri Narendra Modi but I would just like to recall a special moment at an event in 2016 when, like a truly caring family elder, he lovingly pulled the cheeks of my son Aarav, and smilingly told him 'Theek se rehna. Mummy-Papa ka naam roshan karna.' My son later said, 'He's so cool!'.

'Well, he is the Prime Minister with a smile,' I replied.

Akshay Kumar, award-winning Indian actor

As Prime Minister Narendra Modi reaches the milestone of twenty years of captaincy of an elected government, there is no doubt that he remains one of the most popular leaders of a major democracy.

Yet, the world of politics is today more tumultuous than ever, and on this milestone, there will inevitably be high-decibel debates around policy outcomes. However, I hope that will not mean an absence of reflection on him as an individual.

Narendra Modi, while leading over a billion people and enthusiastically engaging with them through several channels, is actually an intensely private individual.

In the few personal interactions I have had with him over the years, I have always come away with unexpected inputs on how to take control of my own mind; how to make it quiet and capable of facing myriad external challenges. I always came away thinking: *that's not what I went to his office to discuss ... how did that conversation come about?*

Most memorably, I remember once referring to a particularly controversial debate that was raging in Parliament and casually commenting on how unflappable he appeared. He looked at me with unusual concentration, and said, 'I live in the moment. If I am talking to you, no matter how inconsequential the conversation may seem, I will give you my full attention. The problems of the world won't be solved by being distracted and trying to address everything at once.'

There was one other thing about him that I learned from my occasional personal interactions. He is a man on a mission to make India a benevolent, yet a powerfully influential force in the world. He has dedicated his life to making that a reality.

This combination of mission-orientation, self-belief and a mind-boggling capacity for continuous hard work makes him stand out on the world stage.

Anand Mahindra, Chairman of the Mahindra Group

Prime Minister Narendra Modi has changed the trajectory of the US-India relationship, placing it on a steady, upward path. He reminded us of the great potential of the world's largest democratic powers working together for the good of our people, but also for the betterment of the world. This is a turbulent time in our collective histories, with real challenges confronting our populations. He provided strategic clarity at a time when it was most needed, and he did so with a generosity of spirit and a focus on our shared values.

The Prime Minister brings a studied, steady and incisive approach to navigating the issues before us. He has been accessible, approachable and one who listens carefully and looks for solutions rather than getting bogged down with problems. We are grateful for his partnership, and for his twenty years of distinguished public service. Thank you, Prime Minister Modi, for deepening the bonds between our two great nations. May our work together across a range of areas grow only stronger in the years ahead.

Ajay Banga, former president and CEO of Mastercard Inc

Many congratulations to Prime Minister Modi on twenty years of public service. Each time I visit India, I am impressed by the rapid pace of digital transformation across the country. It's incredible to see the Digital India footprint and billion-scale platforms that India is enabling, all of which is helping make Indian small businesses more productive, enterprises more competitive, non-profits more effective, the public sector more efficient and improving health and education outcomes. It's why we, at Microsoft, continue to invest in India, and why it's so important for government leaders to prioritize digital infrastructure as a core part of their agenda in order to ensure that citizens and organizations across the country can benefit.

Satya Nadella, Chairman and CEO of Microsoft

I have had the pleasure and honour of observing, engaging and advising Prime Minister Narendra Modi on his strategy of a Digital India. In the last twenty years of his public service, he has embarked on a transformational journey—first, for the state of Gujarat, and now, for India as a whole. His vision, communication and execution has been methodological and relentless. He inspires hope and implements a vision for the future. In my experience of engaging with a wide array of global leaders over the last forty years, Prime Minister Modi is undoubtedly one of the very top leaders I've ever met—and I've met them all. I have always believed in India as the key emerging nation in Asia and the most strategic partnership for the United States. Prime Minister Modi's leadership has dramatically accelerated India's role as an inclusive economic and job creation engine, first as a nation, and also on the global stage.

John Chambers, former executive chairman and CEO of Cisco Systems

NOTES ON THE CONTRIBUTORS

Dr Ajay Mathur is the Director General of the International Solar Alliance (ISA). ISA was created by PM Narendra Modi of India and President François Hollande of France at the Paris Climate Negotiations in 2015. Dr Mathur was earlier in the Bureau of Energy Efficiency and TERI as its Director General.

Ajit Doval is the National Security Advisor of India since 2014. He previously served as Director of Intelligence Bureau from 2004–05 and later became the founding director of leading think tank, the Vivekananda International Foundation, New Delhi. He is a recipient of the President's Police Medal and the Kirti Chakra.

Amish Tripathi is the international bestselling award-winning author of the Shiva Trilogy, Ram Chandra Series, *Legend of Suheldev*, *Immortal India* and *Dharma*. A columnist in many leading papers, Amish is presently serving as the Director of the Nehru Centre, London. Amish holds a management degree from the Indian Institute of Management, Calcutta.

Amit Shah is Minister for Home Affairs, and Cooperation in the Government of India. Between 2014 and 2020, he was president of the BJP. Shah has been a political associate of Narendra Modi for the past four decades. Working intimately with Modi has allowed him an insight that is impossible to match.

Anupam Kher is an award-winning international actor. He is a recipient of the IIFA Award for Outstanding Achievement in Indian Cinema, was nominated for the British Academy Film Awards (BAFTA) and has received eight consecutive Filmfare Awards. In 2016, Kher was bestowed the Padma Bhushan, the third highest civilian award in India.

Arvind Panagariya is Professor of Economics and Jagdish Bhagwati Professor of Indian Political Economy in the School of International and Public Affairs at Columbia University. From 2015 to 2017, he served as the first Vice Chairman of the NITI Aayog. He has been bestowed the Padma Bhushan, the third highest civilian award in India.

Ashok Gulati is currently Infosys Chair Professor for Agriculture at ICRIER; formerly Chairman of CACP, and Director at IFPRI. He was the youngest member in the Economic Advisory Council of the PM Atal Bihari Vajpayee. He has been on the Board of Directors of RBI, Nabard, NCDEX, etc., and honoured with the Padma Shri.

Dr Bharat H. Barai is medical director of the Cancer Institute, Methodist Hospitals, USA. The life story of Dr Bharat Barai and his wife, as successful immigrants to USA, is featured in the United States National Museum of Immigration (Recent Immigration Section) on the Ellis Island in New York.

Dr Devi Shetty is the Founder-Chairman of Narayana Health. A renowned cardiac surgeon, he was the past Governor of the Medical Council of India and current Chairman of the Board of Governors at IIM Bangalore. A strong advocate of technology applications in healthcare, Dr Shetty has a US Patent registered as an inventor.

Manoj Ladwa is the Chairman and Chief Executive of London head-quartered India Inc. Group, publishers of *India Global Business* and *iGlobal News*, and is the founder of India Global Forum. An accomplished media commentator and writer and columnist, Manoj is a visiting professor in media and communications at Birmingham City University.

Nandan Nilekani is Chairman and Co-Founder of Infosys. He was the Founding Chairman of the Unique Identification Authority of India (UIDAI-Aadhaar). He was awarded the Padma Bhushan in 2006 and the 22nd Nikkei Asia Prize for Economic & Business Innovation in 2017. Nandan Nilekani is the author of three books.

Nripendra Misra was Principal Secretary to Prime Minister Narendra Modi from 2014-19. He is currently the Chairperson of the Construction Committee of Shri Ram Janmbhoomi Mandir Trust. He has been conferred the Padma Bhushan by Government of India and "The Order of the Rising Sun, Gold and Silver Star" by the Japanese government.

Pradeep Gupta is a renowned Indian psephologist and founder of Axis My India Ltd. He is an alumnus of the OPM programme of the Harvard Business School. Axis My India has accurately predicted the last 48 of the 52 elections and is now a part of the Harvard Business School case study and curriculum.

P.V. Sindhu is India's premier badminton player who has won two Olympic medals; bronze, silver and gold medals at the World Championships; gold medal at World Tour Finals; silver medal at Asian Games and a gold medal at the Commonwealth Games. Sindhu has been awarded the Dhyan Chand Khel Ratna Award and the Padma Bhushan.

Sadhguru, a Yogi, mystic and visionary, is one of the most influential people of our times. Over the past four decades, Sadhguru has offered the technologies of well-being to millions of people and has established Isha Foundation, which is supported by over 11 million volunteers in 300 cities worldwide. Sadhguru has been conferred the Padma Vibhushan.

Dr Shamika Ravi is Vice President of Economic Policy at the Observer Research Foundation and is a Visiting Professor of Economics at BITS School of Management. She is a former member of the Economic Advisory Council to the Prime Minister of India. Dr Ravi holds a PhD in economics from New York University.

Shobana Kamineni is a member of the founding family who run the Apollo Hospitals Group. In 2017, she became the first woman president of the Confederation of Indian Industry. She is a board member of the World Economic Forum's (WEF) EDISON Alliance and is the Co-Chair of WEF's Health and Healthcare Industry Governors Community.

Sudha Murty was until recently the chairperson of Infosys Foundation. A prolific writer, Murty has 40 books to her credit and has sold over 3 million copies. She is recipient of the R.K. Narayan Award, the Padma Shri, the Attimabbe Award, the Lifetime Achievement by Crossword Book and the Lal Bahadur Shastri National Award.

Surjit Bhalla is Executive Director, IMF, for India, Bangladesh, Bhutan and Sri Lanka. A former part-time member of Prime Minister Narendra Modi's Economic Advisory Council, Surjit holds a PhD in economics from Princeton University, a master's in public and international affairs from Woodrow Wilson School, Princeton University, and a BSEE degree from Purdue University.

Dr S. Jaishankar is the External Affairs Minister of India. He was a career diplomat for forty-one years, holding the positions of Foreign Secretary to Government of India and Ambassador to the USA, China, Singapore and the Czech Republic. He is also the author of *The India Way: Strategies for an Uncertain World*.

Uday Kotak is Founder and CEO of Kotak Mahindra Bank. He was President of the Confederation of Indian Industry in 2020-21. Uday is Co-Chairman of Indo-UK Financial Partnership (IUKFP) and serves on International Advisory Panel of Monetary Authority of Singapore, as well as the International Advisory Board of the Government of Singapore Investment Corporation.

Dr V. Anantha Nageswaran is the Chief Economic Advisor to the Ministry of Finance, Government of India. He holds a doctoral degree from the University of Massachusetts in Amherst for his work on exchange rate behaviour. In 1985, he received a post-graduate diploma in management from the Indian Institute of Management, Ahmedabad.

The Oaths of Narendra Modi as Chief Minister of Gujarat

7 October 2001: The first oath for any public office.

22 December 2002: Sworn in as Chief Minister for a full term after a resounding win in the 2002 assembly elections.

25 December 2007: Sworn in for a third time after another emphatic win in the 2007 assembly elections.

26 December 2012: Fourth and final oath as Chief Minister after another resounding win.

A unique Yatra in the annals of Indian polity: Chief Minister Modi leading the 'Samvidhaan Gaurav Yatra' in 2010 with a giant replica of the Constitution mounted on the back of an elephant to celebrate the 60th anniversary of its adoption.

કૃષિ વિભાગ - ગુજરાત સરકાર
કૃષિ મહોત્સવ
૨૦૦૫
SHINGALA
ઈ-ધરા કેન્દ્ર

Krishi Mahotsav was a pathbreaking initiative that Modi conceptualized to bring all agricultural stakeholders on one platform along with the farmers. Held every year, this month-long interaction was the fulcrum that ignited Gujarat's agricultural miracle. Seen here is Modi addressing the Mahotsav in 2004.

Vibrant Gujarat, an innovative biennial business leaders' summit, was conceptualized by Modi for promoting investment and ease of doing business. It has since evolved into a model that has been replicated by many other states. Seen here is Modi addressing the summit in 2013.

Girl child education was one of the big successes of Modi's tenure as Chief Minister. Each year, the Gujarat government conducted a three-day intensive exercise to encourage girls to enroll in schools. Here Modi is seen escorting two young girls to their very first day of school, as part of Shala Praveshotsav.

Modi inspecting the proposed design for the Sabarmati Riverfront. Thanks to the completion of this project, the once dying river now flows majestically through the city of Ahmedabad and has become a major tourist attraction.

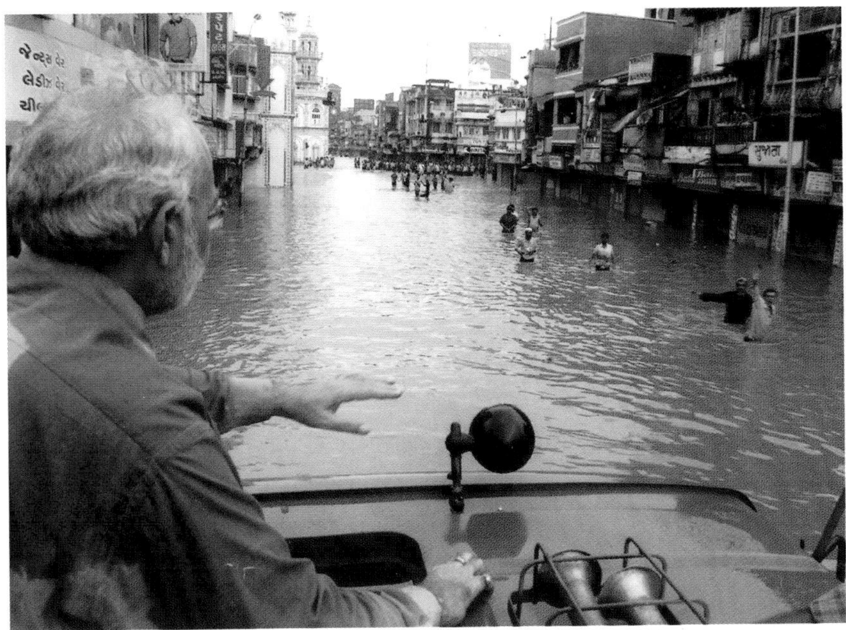

In 2006 when floods raged in the city of Surat in Gujarat, Modi was immediately on the ground leading rescue and relief efforts.

Modi receiving the India Today 2010 award for the 'Best State in Agriculture' from the then Vice President of India Hamid Ansari.

The Modi phenomenon that gripped India: Nomination rally in Varanasi for BJP's PM candidate Narendra Modi on 24 April 2014.

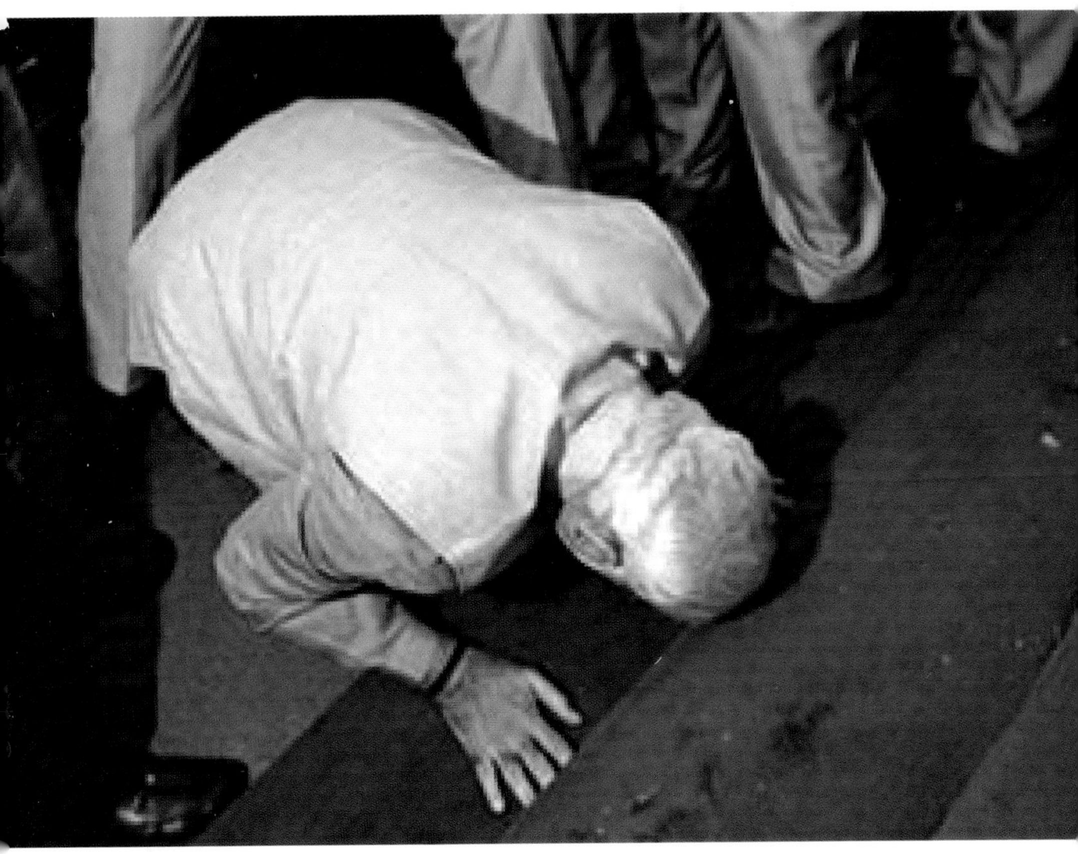

Modi bowing on the steps leading to the Indian Parliament—the Temple of Democracy—as he stepped into it for the first time.

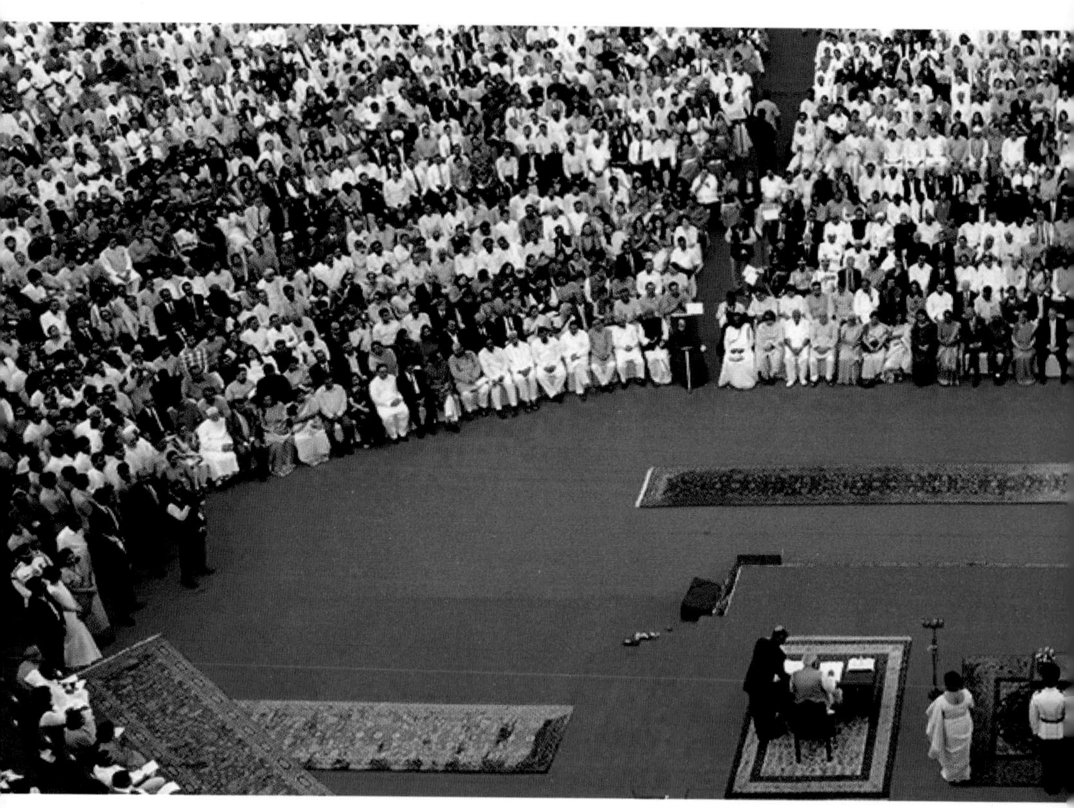

26 May 2014: The grand oath-taking ceremony of Modi as the Prime Minister of India. Unlike the past, the event was thrown open to the common people. In a historic first, leaders of the SAARC countries also attended this historic event.

Narendra Modi being sworn in for his first term as Prime Minister of India in May 2014.

Women voters, across geography, demography, class and religion have formed the strongest base of Modi's supporters. They also attend his rallies in large numbers and are among the most vocal.

'Modi Hai Toh Mumkin Hai' (If Modi is there then everything is possible) was a slogan that emerged organically from the ground in the run up to the 2019 general elections. It became so popular and ubiquitous that BJP ultimately embraced it as one of the official campaign themes.

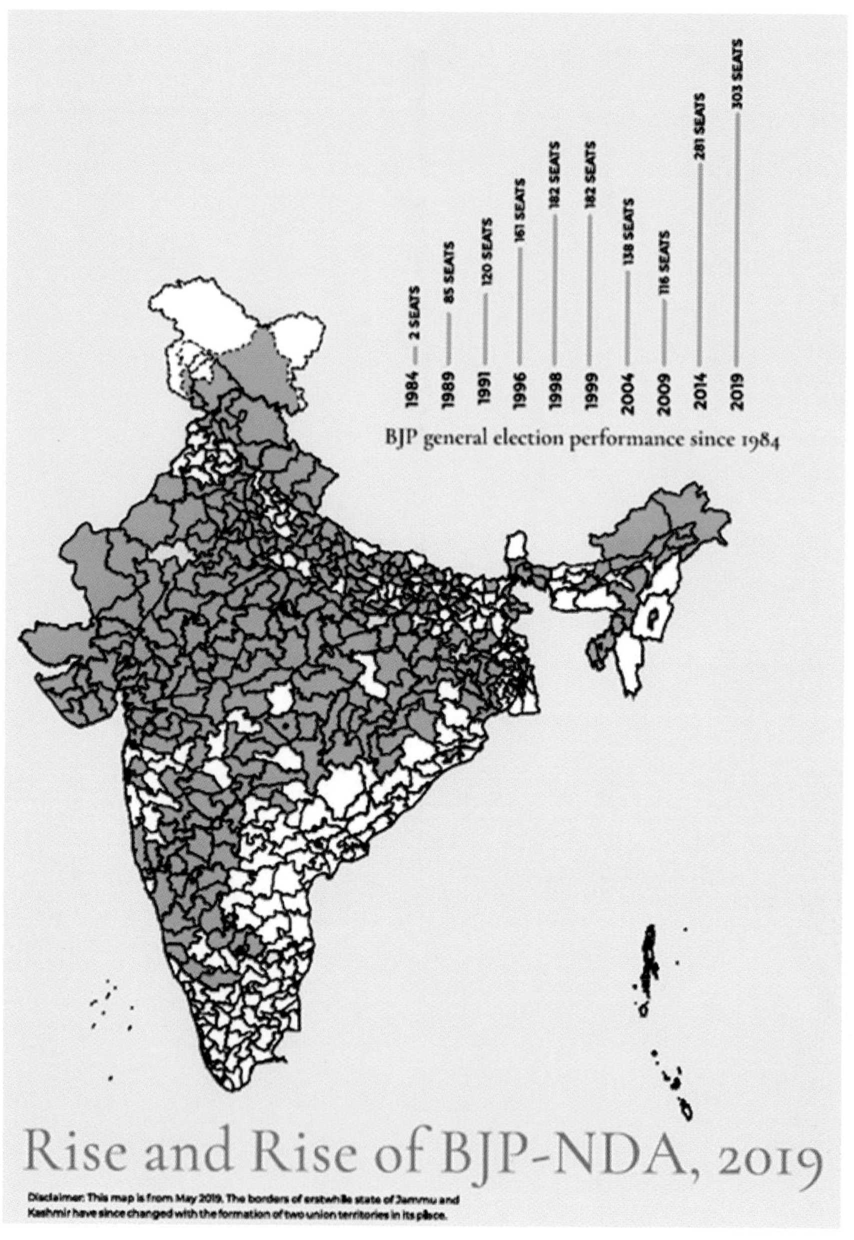

The Modi impact on the rise of BJP as the natural party of governance can be seen in this graph of Lok Sabha seats won by BJP in the 2019 elections. BJP by itself registered wins across every region of the country and along with its alliance partners won close to two-third majority.

Modi bowing to the Constitution in the Central Hall of Parliament before assuming the office as Prime Minister for the second term in 2019.

On 30 May 2019, Narendra Modi took oath of office for his second term as the Prime Minister of India.

Paying tribute to Mahatma Gandhi at the Sabarmati Ashram in Ahmedabad, Gujarat.

Over 1.5 crore (15 million) bank accounts were opened on the launch day of what would become the world's largest financial inclusion programme. Pradhan Mantri Jan Dhan Yojana has since become the bedrock of Modi's last-mile delivery of welfare schemes. Launched on 28 August 2014, the scheme has since empowered over 442 million account holders.

The Big Tech: Prime Minister Narendra Modi with (first from left) John T. Chambers, Executive Chairman of Cisco; (second from left) Microsoft CEO Satya Nadella; (second from right) Paul E. Jacobs, Executive Chairman of Qualcomm; and (first from right) Google CEO Sundar Pichai at the Digital India event in San Jose, USA on 26 September 2016.

Make-in-India, For India: Vande Bharat trains are synonymous with Modi's 'Make in India' initiative, and have now been scaled to 400 trains. Vande Bharat Express, India's first semi-high-speed train, was flagged off by Modi on 15 February 2019 from the New Delhi railway station.

Modi at a MyGov Townhall in August 2016. The government's unique participative governance and citizen engagement platform, MyGov, was launched on 26 July 2014 as part of the 'Jan Bhagidari' vision championed by Modi.

The National War Memorial, built 60 years after it was first proposed, commemorates India's fallen heroes. Modi inaugurated the memorial on 25 February 2019.

A rockstar reception: PM Narendra Modi after his address to a joint session of the US Congress on Capitol Hill on 9 June 2016.

The QUAD in person: (Left to right) Japanese Prime Minister Suga Yoshihide, Prime Minister Narendra Modi, US President Joe Biden, Australian Prime Minister Scott Morrison at the White House balcony on 27 September 2021.

(Left to right) Australian Prime Minister Scott Morrison, World Bank President David Malpass and UN Chief António Guterres during an informal interaction with Prime Minister Modi on the sidelines of the G20 Summit on 30 October 2021.

Showcasing the vibrant culture of India has been a consistent practice that Modi has followed during visits by foreign dignitaries. Seen here with French President Emmanuel Macron along Kashi's Ganga Ghats during the latter's visit to India on 12 March 2018.

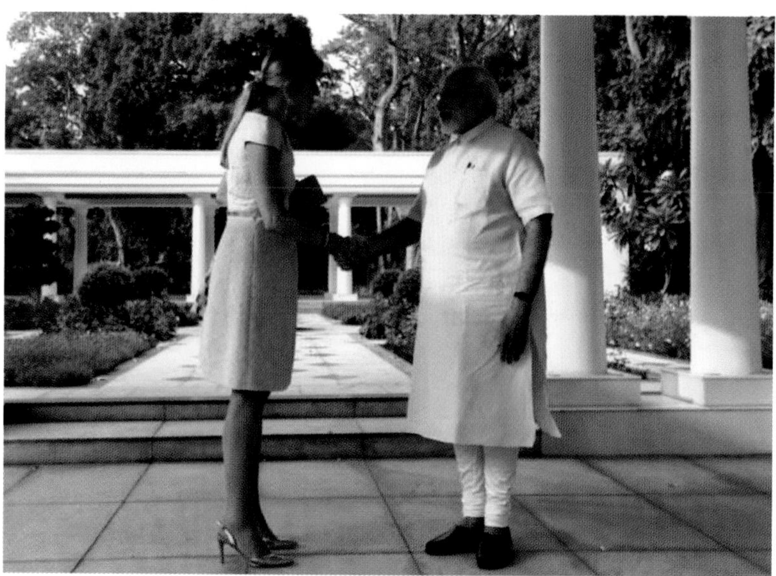

Welcoming Her Majesty, Queen Maxima of The Netherlands, at his official residence on 29 May 2018.

Then Prime Minister of Australia, Malcolm Turnbull, at the Swaminarayan Akshardham Temple in Delhi along with Modi.

In 2014, Modi became the first Indian prime minister to visit Australia in 28 years. A packed Allphones Arena in Sydney, Australia, welcomed him with a rollicking reception.

Bringing a piece of India to Indians abroad: Indian expatriates in Colombo, Sri Lanka, welcoming Modi with loud 'Modi Modi' chants during his visit on 9 June, 2019.

He's Looking at You: Modi is seen here greeting a child from among the diaspora on his visit to Bangladesh in March 2021. The Prime Minister enjoys a special bond with youngsters that transcends boundaries.

An ode to Nari Shakti: 103-year-old athlete Mann Kaur blessing Prime Minister Narendra Modi during a special Women's Day interaction with Nari Shakti awardees in Delhi on 8 March 2020.

Breakfast with champions: Modi hosting a breakfast at his official residence in honour of the Indian contingent returning from the Tokyo 2020 Olympics. This was India's best ever Olympics medals tally with 7 medals.

Respecting wealth creators has been a consistent theme for Modi government. Seen here standing alongside India's leading industrialists and wealth creators.

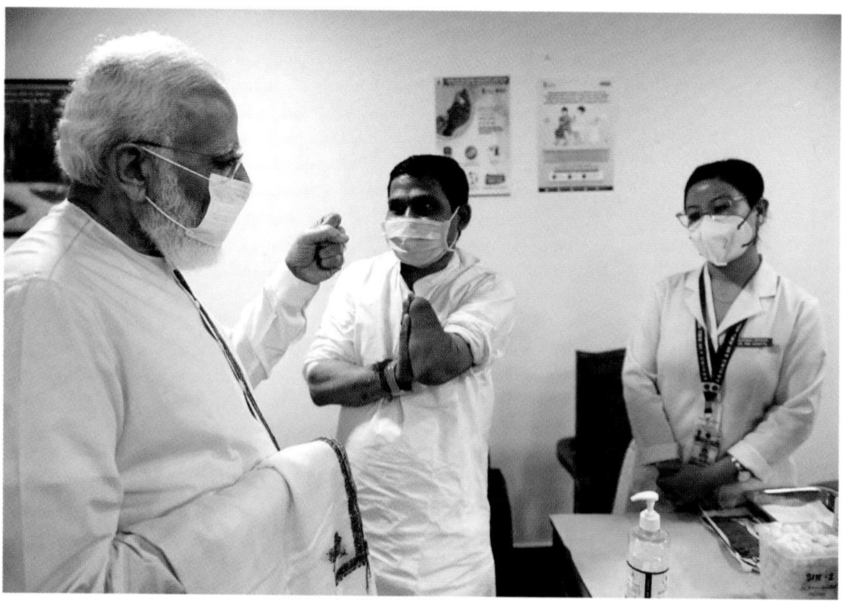

A Billion Delivered: Modi greeting the man who received India's billionth COVID-19 jab at the Ram Manohar Lohia Hospital in New Delhi on 21 October 2021. He also paid his respects to the frontline workers who helped achieve this momentous landmark.

Taking a closer look at the finer details of the Aatmanirbhar Bharat vision before its launch.

Bowed in reverence to a life-long Sanyasi: Modi paying his respects to the Ram temple trust chairperson, Mahant Nritya Gopal Das.

The moment millions had been waiting for over half a millennium: On 5 August 2020, Narendra Modi laid the foundation stone for the construction of the Ram Mandir in Ayodhya, followed by the Bhoomi Pujan ceremony.

Modi offering prayers to *Ram Lalla Virajman* on 5 August 2020, the historic date when the foundation stone was laid for the Ram temple in Ayodhya.

Cultural renaissance in the world's oldest city: Modi speaking at the inauguration of the first phase of the Kashi Vishwanath Dham Corridor project on 13 December 2021.

PM Modi sharing a meal with hundreds of workers who constructed the Kashi-Vishwanath corridor to express his gratitude for their sweat, blood, and tears. Prior to the project's inauguration, Modi showered them with flowers.

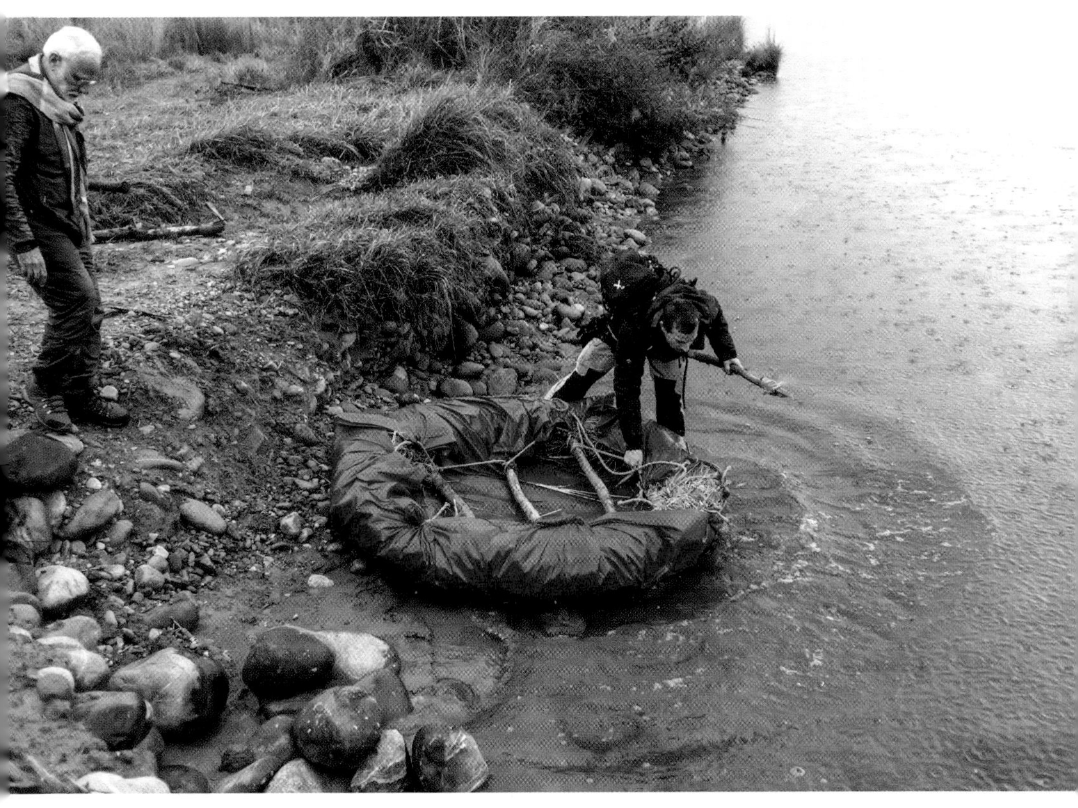

The adventurous streak: Embarking on a small dinghy along with Bear Grylls for a *'Man vs Wild'* conversation.

Meetings that extend late into the night are not a rare occurrence but a part of Modi's daily routine. In this photograph, PM is sitting through one such meeting.

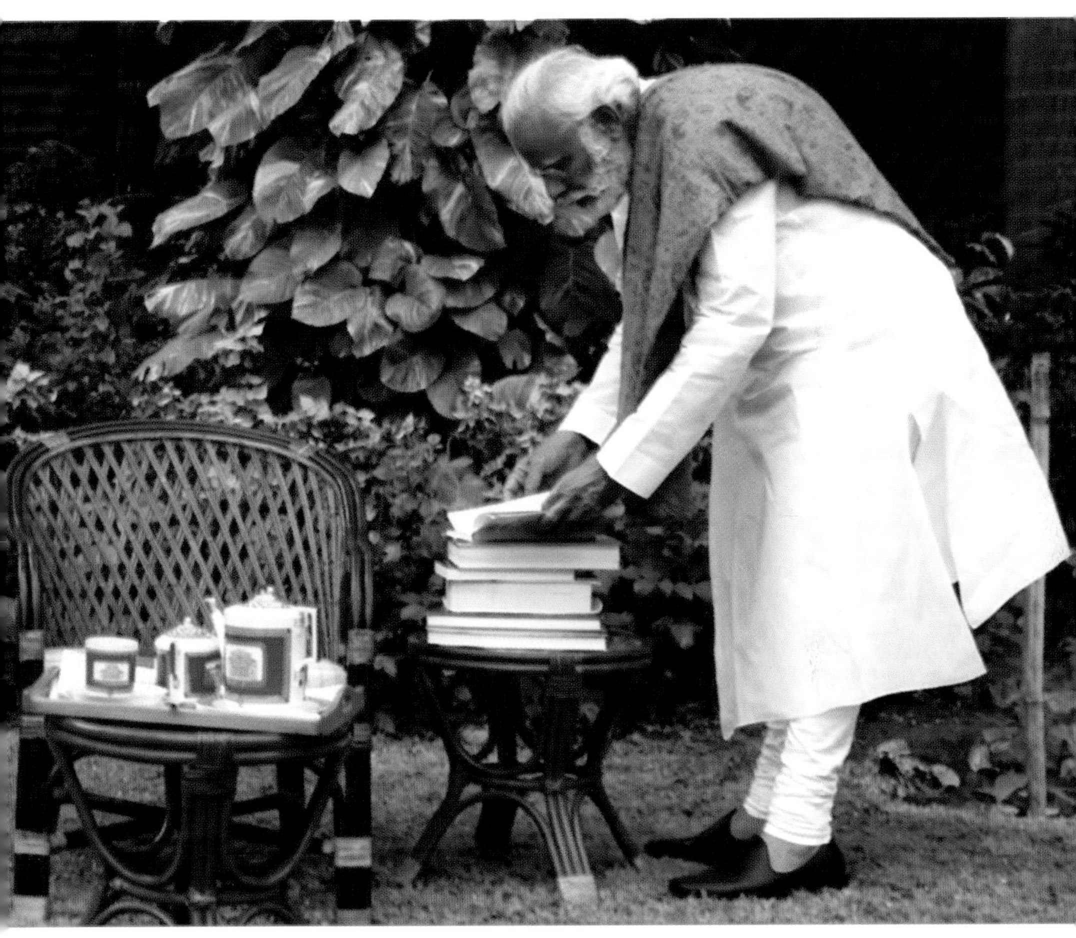

A voracious reader: Modi's experiential learning is just as matched by his keen habit of reading. His passion for reading has been life-long. At his residence, he is seen picking up a book.

With the ubiquitous chai and a stack of files, the day begins: Modi during a morning tea break at Port Blair in the Andaman and Nicobar Islands on 30 December 2018.

Leaving his footprints in the sands of time: Prime Minister Narendra Modi in a contemplative mood while walking on the beaches of Mamallapuram, Tamil Nadu.

The builder of New India: Modi speaking at a function on 16 October 2019.

NOTES

Why Modi is the Undisputed Youth Icon

1. https://www.business-standard.com/article/technology/digital-payments-google-wants-us-fed-to-replicate-india-s-upi-model-119121401013_1.html
2. https://pib.gov.in/PressReleseDetail.aspx?PRID=1665779
3. https://www.narendramodi.in/vikasyatra/articledetail/empowering-youth-with-opportunities/encouraging-sports-and-fitness-in-india-549945
4. https://www.indiatoday.in/india/story/breaking-news-india-today-februa ry-6-2013-153353-2013-02-06

New Grammar of Women Empowerment

1. https://economictimes.indiatimes.com/news/politics-and-nation/female-foeticide-a-matter-of-shame-pm-narendra-modi/articleshow/44783356.cms?from=mdr;https://economictimes.indiatimes.com/news/politics-and-nation/female-foeticide-a-matter-of-shame-pm-narendra-modi/articleshow/44783356.cms?from=mdr; https://www.narendramodi.in/gujarat-ensuring-a-golden-future-with-eyes-on-girl-child-education-4010
2. https://www.ndtv.com/elections-news/narendra-modis-parting-gift-rs-21-lakh-for-educating-gujarat-staffs-daughters-563633
3. https://indianexpress.com/article/opinion/columns/beti-bachao-beti-padhao-girl-child-education-women-empowerment-6297784/
4. https://time.com/5614642/india-girls-education/
5. https://www.asercentre.org/p/51.html?p=61, https://byjus.com/free-ias-prep/aser-annual-status-education-report/
6. https://pmjdy.gov.in/account
7. http://glpc.co.in/showpage.aspx?contentid=136
8. http://glpc.co.in/downloads/glpc_5th_jan_low_res.pdf
9. https://pib.gov.in/PressReleaseIframePage.aspx?PRID=1604929
10. https://pib.gov.in/PressReleaseIframePage.aspx?PRID=1709989
11. https://www.dnaindia.com/india/report-pm-narendra-modi-interacts-with-over-100-mudra-beneficiaries-2603832
12. https://pib.gov.in/PressReleaseIframePage.aspx?PRID=1604929
13. https://pib.gov.in/Pressreleaseshare.aspx?PRID=1703083
14. https://pib.gov.in/PressReleaseIframePage.aspx?PRID=1702495
15. https://archive.pib.gov.in/archive2/erelease.aspx

16. https://www.firstpost.com/india/amendment-to-maternity-benefits-act-is-a-case-of-good-intentions-backfiring-ends-up-disincentivising-hiring-of-women-4636421.html
17. https://www.ndtv.com/video/business/news/shobana-kamineni-on-becoming-first-woman-president-of-industry-body-cii-456677
18. https://www.facebook.com/IndiaToday/videos/640965223960723/
19. https://www.hindustantimes.com/india-news/two-women-army-officers-selected-to-train-as-combat-pilots-101623180458434.html
20. https://www.indiatoday.in/india/story/pm-modi-75th-independence-day-speech-highlights-1840974-2021-08-15
21. https://www.news18.com/news/india/chandrayaan-2-meet-the-rocket-women-behind-indias-second-lunar-mission-2228905.html

Success of People-centric Approach

1. https://ejalshakti.gov.in/jjmreport/JJMIndia.aspx
2. Climate Change Performance Index (CCPI), Germanwatch, https://newclimate.org/2020/12/07/the-climate-change-performance-index-2021/.

Modi, the Bhagirath Prayaasi

1. https://bangkok.unesco.org/sites/default/files/assets/article/Asia-Pacific%20Heritage%20Awards/files/2004-winners.pdf
2. http://pibmumbai.gov.in/scripts/detail.asp?releaseId=E2015PR1331
3. https://indianrailways.gov.in/railwayboard/view_section.jsp?lang=0&id=0,1,304,366,535,1419#%22ME%22
4. https://economictimes.indiatimes.com/news/politics-and-nation/pm-modi-cautions-international-community-on-growing-arc-of-violence/articleshow/58639769.cms
5. https://economictimes.indiatimes.com/news/politics-and-nation/dr-ambedkar-international-centre-to-be-developed/articleshow/66645964.cms
6. https://pib.gov.in/Pressreleaseshare.aspx?PRID=1579772
7. https://www.deccanherald.com/content/660426/modi-recites-gomateshwara-stuti-explains.html
8. http://www.iuu.net.in/about-iuu/
9. https://pib.gov.in/newsite/PrintRelease.aspx?relid=159550
10. https://minorityaffairs.gov.in/en/gallery/today-offered-chadar-behalf-pm-shri-narendra-modi-dargah-sufi-saint-hazrat-khwaja-13
11. https://www.firstpost.com/india/pm-modi-sends-chaadar-to-ajmer-dargah-hails-sufi-saint-as-symbol-of-indian-tradition-3350896.html
12. https://www.narendramodi.in/delegation-of-sufi-scholars-calls-on-pm-282794
13. https://www.thehindu.com/news/national/prime-minister-narendra-modi-at-world-sufi-forum/article8366628.ece
14. https://www.thehindu.com/news/national/other-states/at-saifee-mosque-

narendra-modi-speaks-about-vasudhaiva-kutumbakam/article24944033.ece

15. https://www.indiatoday.in/fyi/story/shinzo-abe-japan-prime-minister-narendra-modi-india-visit-sidi-saiyyed-mosque-1042980-2017-09-12
16. https://www.narendramodi.in/mobile/pm-modi-s-gift-to-iranian-president-dr-hassan-rouhani
17. https://pib.gov.in/newsite/PrintRelease.aspx?relid=186549
18. https://www.indiatoday.in/india/story/india-gifts-17th-century-relics-st-queen-ketevan-georgia-1826306-2021-07-10
19. https://www.indiatoday.in/india/story/pm-narendra-modi-sri-lanka-visit-st-anthony-s-church-1545331-2019-06-09
20. https://www.bbc.com/news/world-asia-india-28173993
21. https://www.bbc.com/news/world-asia-india-31582002
22. https://indianexpress.com/article/india/kerala-christian-priest-father-tom-uzhunnalil-kidnapped-in-yemen-rescued-with-omans-help-4840018/
23. https://www.news18.com/news/opinion/opinion-transformation-of-unesco-heritage-site-dholavira-when-modi-was-gujarat-cm-is-worth-emulating-4103360.html
24. https://www.financialexpress.com/lifestyle/travel-tourism/kutch-rann-utsav-how-then-gujarat-cm-modi-turned-a-tragedy-into-opportnity-for-the-desert-region/1867234/
25. https://www.indiatvnews.com/news/india/modi-inaugurates-garba-festival-in-gujarat-28871.html
26. https://www.narendramodi.in/cm-lays-stone-for-renovating-shamlaji-temple-complex-at-a-cost-of-rs-70-cr-4690
27. https://pib.gov.in/PressReleaseIframePage.aspx?PRID=1606638
28. https://embindpp.gov.in/gallery?id=enrle
29. https://mea.gov.in/rajya-sabha.htm?dtl/31676/QUESTION+NO3695 +RELATIONSHIP +WITH+BUDDHIST+COUNTRIES
30. https://economictimes.indiatimes.com/news/politics-and-nation/india-extends-15-million-grant-for-promotion-of-buddhist-ties-with-sri-lanka/articleshow/78334018.cms
31. https://indiaculture.nic.in/about-us/autonomus-bodies/buddhist-institutes
32. https://pib.gov.in/PressReleseDetailm.aspx?PRID=1592009
33. https://www.indiatoday.in/india/story/narendra-modi-tony-abbott-rani-lakshmibai-petition-canberra-australian-parliament-227592-2014-11-18
34. https://timesofindia.indiatimes.com/india/pm-modi-gifts-200-cows-to-villagers-in-rwanda/articleshow/65117263.cms
35. https://indianexpress.com/article/explained/narendra-modi-cheraman-juma-masjid-replica-saudi-king-gift/
36. https://www.narendramodi.in/mobile/pm-modi-s-gift-to-iranian-president-dr-hassan-rouhani-

37. https://www.dnaindia.com/india/report-chancellor-merkel-gifts-pm-modi-first-edition-print-of-max-mueller-book-2077571
38. https://www.hindustantimes.com/india/obama-s-gift-to-modi-a-rare-book-with-the-vivekananda-touch/story-ARAFDVQvG9q5r1lqFPLdgO.html
39. https://www.hindustantimes.com/india-news/queen-elizabeth-gave-pm-modi-her-wedding-gift-from-gandhi/story-SE650Jz7dFJLsHuZTteT2L.html
40. https://www.indiatoday.in/india/story/vadnagar-narendra-modi-gujarat-hiuen-tsang-xi-jinping-xian-1060300-2017-10-08
41. https://www.indiatvnews.com/news/world/from-modi-s-vadnagar-to-jinping-s-shaanxi-the-huien-tsang-connection-24517.html
42. https://edition.cnn.com/2016/06/07/us/stolen-artefacts-returned-india/index.html (200)
43. https://pib.gov.in/PressReleasePage.aspx?PRID=1742760 (44)
44. https://archive.pib.gov.in/newsite/PrintRelease.aspx?relid=162199

Democracy, Delivery and The Politics of Hope

1. Party–wise and state–wise seats won and votes polled during Lok Sabha Election 2009 (Election Commission of India)
2. Party–wise and state–wise seats won and votes polled during Lok Sabha Election 2014 (Election Commission of India)
3. Party–wise and state–wise seats won and votes polled during Lok Sabha Election 1996 (Election Commission of India)
4. Key Highlights: Lok Sabha Election 2009, Election Commission of India.
5. Key Highlights: Lok Sabha Election 2014, Election Commission of India.
6. Key Highlights: Lok Sabha Election 2009, Election Commission of India.
7. https://www.india.gov.in/spotlight/pradhan-mantri-garib-kalyan-package-pmgkp

Changing Elections and Electioneering Forever

1. Uday Mahurkar, *Centrestage: Inside the Narendra Modi Model of Governance* (Random House India: 2014)
2. https://panchayat.gujarat.gov.in/en/samras-gram-yojna
3. Kishor Makwana. 2015. *Modi Common Man's PM.* Prabhat Prakashan.
4. https://www.narendramodi.in/largest-mass-outreach-campaign-in-electoral-history-of-a-democracy-3136
5. https://www.narendramodi.in/extensive-innovating-and-satisfying-the-story-of-2014-campaign-2-3121
6. Shashi Shekhar. 2014. *The Story of Mission 272+*
7. https://www.narendramodi.in/extensive-innovating-and-satisfying-the-story-of-2014-campaign-2-3121.
8. https://www.narendramodi.in/largest-mass-outreach-campaign-in-electoral-history-of-a-democracy-3136

9. https://www.narendramodi.in/largest-mass-outreach-campaign-in-electoral-history-of-a-democracy-3136

Thinking Big and Executing in Scale

1. http://timesofindia.indiatimes.com/articleshow/14682320.cms
2. https://economictimes.indiatimes.com/news/politics-and-nation/the-transformation-of-sabarmati-from-a-parched-river bed-with-puddles-of-industrial-effluents-to-a-bustling-swanky-riverfront/articleshow/45998310.cms)
3. http://swaminomics.org/agriculture-secret-of-modis-success/ accessed on 7 September 2021
4. https://www.livemint.com/opinion/columns/steps-to-sustain-the-big-success-that-our-dbt-mission-has-been-11627919754109.html
5. https://pib.gov.in/PressReleseDetailm.aspx?PRID=1749749 (accessed on 28 August 2021)
6. Yakshup Chopra, Nagpurnanand Prabhala and Prasanna L. Tantri (2018): 'Bank Accounts for the Unbanked: evidence from a big bang experiment', Robert H. Smith School Research Paper No. RHS 2919091 https://papers.ssrn.com/sol3/papers.cfm?abstract_id=2919091 (accessed on 30 August 2021)
7. See https://nasscom.in/knowledge-center/publications/digital-india-digital-public-goods-platformisation-play (accessed on 29 August 2021)
8. https://indianexpress.com/article/opinion/columns/demonetisation-india-economic-slowdown-gdp-data-COVID-19-impact-7014835/
9. https://economictimes.indiatimes.com/news/economy/policy/how-an-in-house-e-commerce-platform-has-revolutionised-government-procurement/articleshow/70310110.cms
10. https://www.financialexpress.com/industry/sme/msme-eodb-gem-amazon-of-govt-procurement-sees-over-5x-increase-in-msme-seller-base-in-12-months-amid-COVID-19/2285112/ (accessed on 7 September 2021)
11. https://www.business-standard.com/article/opinion/tranformational-tax-reform-120063002277_1.html
12. https://www.bloombergquint.com/business/four-years-on-did-rbis-ibc-gamble-with-40-large-defaulters-work
13. https://pib.gov.in/Pressreleaseshare.aspx?PRID=1748297 (23 August 2021; accessed on 28 August 2021)
14. https://www.business-standard.com/article/companies/mobile-export-hub-india-may-pip-china-vietnam-120100701643_1.html
15. https://swarajyamag.com/economy/why-it-may-be-the-wrong-time-to-give-up-hope-on-india
16. https://www.livemint.com/opinion/online-views/opinion-the-challenge-of-overcoming-an-extended-crisis-in-our-economy-11593704561035.html
17. https://www.worldometers.info/coronavirus/ (accessed on 22 December 2021)

18. https://dashboard.cowin.gov.in/
19. https://dashboard.cowin.gov.in/
20. http://swachhbharaturban.gov.in/Home.aspx
21. Lance Price, *'The Modi Effect—Inside Narendra Modi's campaign to transform India'* (Hodder & Stoughton, 2016)
22. https://indianexpress.com/article/opinion/columns/economic-package-agriculture-relief-fund-farmers-nirmala-sitharaman-ashok-gulati-6414759/
23. https://indianexpress.com/article/explained/rs-150000-crore-plus-the-govt-stimulus-for-rural-areas-post-lockdown-6474873/)
24. See footnote 15 for details
25. 'Labour Reforms: a historical change', Credit Suisse (India), 28 September 2020

Towards a Prosperous India

1. I had returned to India to take the position after spending forty years in the United States.
2. During the second UPA term, reforms had come to a standstill, fiscal deficit had ballooned and the rupee had become highly overvalued in real terms. The last two years of the government's tenure also saw the decision-making process entirely paralyzed with large infrastructure projects stuck due to lack of environmental or other clearances. Growth fell to below 6 per cent and inflation reached near-double-digit levels during these two years. Citing alarming macroeconomic indicators, an August 2013 story in *The Economist* had concluded, 'It is widely agreed the country is in its worst economic bind since 1991.' In a similar vein, a 2012 Standard and Poor report rhetorically asked in its title, 'Will India Be the First BRIC Fallen Angel?'
3. For instance, full effect of the reforms enacted by Prime Minister Narasimha Rao and Atal Bihari Vajpayee during the 1990s and early 2000s was not realized until the decade beginning in 2003–04.

Micro-revolutions that improved the lives of ordinary citizens

1. Telecom Regulatory Authority of India. *Telecom Regulatory Authority of India* https://www.trai.gov.in/sites/default/files/PR_No.04of2022_2.pdf.
2. Press Information Bureau – Direct Benefit Transfer https://static.pib.gov.in/WriteReadData/specificdocs/documents/2022/jan/doc2022153101.pdf 3. Muralidharan, K., Niehaus, P. & Sukhtankar, S. *Identity Verification Standards in Welfare Programs: Experimental Evidence from India.* https://www.nber.org/papers/w26744 (2020) doi:10.3386/w26744.
4. Muralidharan, K., Niehaus, P., Sukhtankar, S. & Weaver, J. *Improving Last-Mile Service Delivery using Phone-Based Monitoring.* https://www.nber.org/papers/w25298 (2018) doi:10.3386/w25298.
5. Sanitation. https://www.who.int/news-room/fact-sheets/detail/sanitation.
6. Curtis, V. Explaining the outcomes of the 'Clean India' campaign: institutional

behaviour and sanitation transformation in India. *B.M.J. Glob. Health* 4, e001892 (2019).

7. Swachh Bharat Mission-Gramin. https://sbm.gov.in/sbmreport/home.aspx.
8. Dandabathula, G., Bhardwaj, P., Burra, M., Rao, P. V. V. P. & Rao, S. S. Impact assessment of India's Swachh Bharat Mission – Clean India Campaign on acute diarrheal disease outbreaks: Yes, there is a positive change. *J. Fam. Med. Prim. Care* 8, 1202–1208 (2019).
9. Mahajan, K. & Sekhri, S. Access to Toilets and Violence Against Women. 36.
10. World Economic Outlook Update, July 2021: Fault Lines Widen in the Global Recovery. https://www.imf.org/en/Publications/WEO/Issues/2021/07/27/world-economic-outlook-update-july-2021.
11. NCAER releases findings of the Delhi N.C.R. Coronavirus Telephone Survey. https://www.ncaer.org/news_details.php?nID=328.
12. Kapoor, M. & Ravi, S. Poverty, Pandemic and Elections: Analysis of Bihar Assembly Elections 2020. *Indian J. Hum. Dev.* 15, 49–61 (2021).
13. Ravi, S. The role of technology and cash transfers in Indian elections during the pandemic. *Brookings* https://www.brookings.edu/blog/techtank/2021/03/23/the-role-of-technology-and-cash-transfers-in-indian-elections-during-the-pandemic/ (2021).
14. United Nations. *U.N. General Assembly resolution on women's political participation* https://www.un.org/ga/search/view_doc.asp?symbol=A/RES/66/130 (2011).
15. The Global Gender Gap Report. *World Economic Forum* https://www.weforum.org/reports/the-global-gender-gap-report-2017/ (2017).
16. Chattopadhyay, R. & Duflo, E. Women as Policy Makers: Evidence from a Randomized Policy Experiment in India. *Econometrica* 72, 1409–1443 (2004).
17. Clots-Figueras, I. Are Female Leaders Good for Education? Evidence from India. *Am. Econ. J. Appl. Econ.* 4, 212–244 (2012).
18. Bhalotra, S. & Clots-Figueras, I. Health and the Political Agency of Women. *Am. Econ. J. Econ. Policy* 6, 164–197 (2014).
19. Bhalotra, S., Clots-Figueras, I. & Iyer, L. Pathbreakers? Women's Electoral Success and Future Political Participation. *Econ. J.* 128, 1844–1878 (2018).
20. Iyer, L. & Mani, A. The road not taken: Gender gaps along paths to political power. *World Dev.* 119, 68–80 (2019).
21. Kapoor, M. & Ravi, S. Women Voters in Indian Democracy: A Silent Revolution. *Econ. Polit. Wkly.* 49, 63–67 (2014).
22. Roy, P. & Sopariwala, D. R. The Verdict. *Penguin Random House India* https://penguin.co.in/book/the-verdict/ (2019).
23. Rai, P. Electoral Participation of Women in India: Key Determinants and Barriers. *Econ. Polit. Wkly.* 46, 47–55 (2011).
24. PRS India. *PRSIndia* https://www.prsindia.org/.
25. What we do. *PRSIndia* https://www.prsindia.org/aboutus/what-we-do (2020).

26. *The Making of Miracles in Indian States: Andhra Pradesh, Bihar, and Gujarat.* (Oxford University Press, 2015). doi:10.1093/acprof:oso/9780190236625.001.0001.
27. Indicator Metadata Registry Details. https://www.who.int/data/gho/indicator-metadata-registry/imr-details/67.
28. United Nations Sustainable Development Goal 3. Health. *United Nations Sustainable Development* https://www.un.org/sustainabledevelopment/health/.
29. Hug, L., Alexander, M., You, D. & Alkema, L. National, regional, and global levels and trends in neonatal mortality between 1990 and 2017, with scenario-based projections to 2030: a systematic analysis. *Lancet Glob. Health* **7**, e710–e720 (2019

Modi: The Man India Trusts in a Crisis

1. https://www.bbc.com/news/world-south-asia-12309791
2. Pramod K. Mishra. 2004. The Kutch Earthquake 2002: Recollections, Lessons and Insights. National Institute of Disaster Management. Available: https://nidm.gov.in/PDF/pubs/KUTCH%202001.pdf
3. Pramod K. Mishra. 2004. The Kutch Earthquake 2002: Recollections, Lessons and Insights. National Institute of Disaster Management. Available: https://nidm.gov.in/PDF/pubs/KUTCH%202001.pdf
4. https://www.indiatoday.in/magazine/indiascope/story/20020121-gujarat-from-epicentre-of-quake-to-epicentre-of-development-750507-2002-01-21
5. Pramod K. Mishra. 2004. The Kutch Earthquake 2002: Recollections, Lessons and Insights. National Institute of Disaster Management. Available: https://nidm.gov.in/PDF/pubs/KUTCH%202001.pdf
6. https://timesofindia.indiatimes.com/city/ahmedabad/kutch-once-a-tax-haven-now-an-investment-hub/articleshow/56786939.cms
7. http://www.gsdma.org/Content/gujarat-state-disaster-management-act-2003-4239
8. https://economictimes.indiatimes.com/news/politics-and-nation/how-india-got-back-46-nurses-from-isis-in-2014/classified-negotiations/slideshow/62220976.cms
9. https://www.thehindu.com/news/national/catholic-priest-prem-kumar-freed-from-taliban-captors/article6922145.ece
10. https://www.firstpost.com/india/father-tom-reaches-india-after-18-months-in-islamic-state-captivity-meets-narendra-modi-4089517.html
11. https://economictimes.indiatimes.com/news/politics-and-nation/narendra-modis-call-to-saudi-king-helped-indias-operation-rahat-in-yemen-sushma-swaraj/articleshow/62405284.cms?from=mdr
12. https://www.business-standard.com/podcast/current-affairs/seven-major-evacuation-operations-conducted-in-india-s-history-120050601535_1.html; https://www.thehindu.com/specials/the-great-yemen-escape-operation-rahat-by-numbers/article7089422.ece

13. https://www.hindustantimes.com/india-news/operation-devi-shakti-india-evacuates-more-than-800-people-from-afghanistan-101629794300934.html
14. https://pib.gov.in/PressReleaseIframePage.aspx?PRID=1542250
15. https://twitter.com/PMOIndia/status/719024390885650432
16. https://pib.gov.in/PressReleasePage.aspx?PRID=1608345
17. https://pib.gov.in/PressReleseDetail.aspx?PRID=1623391
18. https://indianexpress.com/article/opinion/columns/political-gain-COVID-19-pandemic-election-healthcare-crisis-7297316/

Agriculture: Good, but can be Better

1. Fan, Shenggen, Ashok Gulati and Sukhdeo Thorat (2007): *Investment, subsidies, and pro-poor growth in rural India*, IFPRI Discussion paper 716, New Delhi.
2. Dholakia, H. and Samar Datta (2010): *High growth trajectory and structural changes in Gujarat agriculture*, MacMillan Publishers India Ltd.
3. Government of India (2001, 2011): *Census of India*, Registrar General of India, Ministry of Home Affairs, Government of India.
4. Government of India (various issues): *Statewise and itemwise estimates of Value of Output from Agriculture and allied activities*, Central Statistical Office, Ministry of Statistics and Programme Implementation (MOSPI).
5. Gulati, Ashok, Tushaar Shah, and Ganga Shreedhar (2009): *Agricultural performance in Gujarat since 2000: Can it be a divadandi (lighthouse) for other states?*, Report by International Water Management Institute (IWMI) and International Food Policy Research Institute (IFPRI).
6. Gulati, Ashok, Ranjana Roy and Siraj Hussain (2021): '*Performance of Agriculture in Gujarat*' in Revitalizing Indian Agriculture and Boosting Farmer Incomes, edited by Ashok Gulati, Ranjana Roy and Shweta Saini, Springer, 2021.
7. Shah, Tushaar, Ashok Gulati, Ganga Shreedhar, and R.C. Jain (2009): *Secret of Gujarat's agrarian miracle after 2000*, Economic and Political Weekly, 45-55.

Leading from the Front

1. https://web.archive.org/web/20211231224224/https://www.mohfw.gov.in/
2. As on December 8, 2021. Accessed from: https://ourworldindata.org/COVID-19-cases
3. https://www.thehindu.com/news/national/indias-first-coronavirus-infection-confirmed-in-kerala/article30691004.ece
4. https://time.com/5791661/who-coronavirus-pandemic-declaration/
5. https://pib.gov.in/PressReleseDetail.aspx?PRID=1607995
6. https://twitter.com/narendramodi/status/1235083359501430789?s=20
7. https://indianexpress.com/article/explained/coronavirus-india-lockdown-vs-global-lockdown-COVID-19-deaths-cases-cure-6399181/
8. https://pib.gov.in/PressReleaseIframePage.aspx?PRID=1607248
9. https://www.hindustantimes.com/india-news/after-lockdown-plan-to-unlock-

india-in-phases/story-vsK1wGQ7moLTMjlKkUelHP.html
10. https://pib.gov.in/PressReleseDetail.aspx?PRID=1607995
11. https://www.thehindu.com/news/national/52-labs-made-functional-across-india-for-coronavirus-testing/article31008011.ece
12. https://pib.gov.in/PressReleasePage.aspx?PRID=1787361
13. https://pib.gov.in/PressReleseDetail.aspx?PRID=1777643
14. https://theprint.in/health/how-india-increased-its-COVID-19-testing-capacity-from-52-labs-to-over-1300-in-4-months/471262/
15. https://www.indiatoday.in/india-today-insight/story/how-india-became-a-ppe-manufacturing-hub-1771584-2021-02-21
16. https://cddep.org/wp-content/uploads/2020/04/State-wise-estimates-of-current-beds-and-ventilators_20Apr2020.pdf
17. https://pib.gov.in/PressReleasePage.aspx?PRID=1633516
18. https://www.business-standard.com/article/current-affairs/bel-makes-30-000-ventilators-in-record-time-to-help-govt-in-COVID-19-fight-120081401780_1.html
19. https://indianexpress.com/article/opinion/columns/india-COVID-19-situation-second-wave-oxygen-vaccine-shortage-pm-modi-7308610/
20. https://pib.gov.in/PressReleasePage.aspx?PRID=1721032
21. https://economictimes.indiatimes.com/news/defence/indian-air-force-airlifts-twelve-empty-cryogenic-oxygen-containers-from-bangkok-singapore-dubai/articleshow/82310477.cms?from=mdr
22. https://www.hindustantimes.com/india-news/world-s-largest-COVID-19-care-facility-with-10-000-beds-inaugurated-in-delhi/story-JS0yy17MTSVheVwgrukkPN.html
23. https://www.hindustantimes.com/india-news/as-COVID-19-cases-surge-itbp-to-reopen-sardar-patel-care-centre-in-delhi-101619100012448.html
24. https://pib.gov.in/PressReleaseIframePage.aspx?PRID=1713069
25. https://hal-india.co.in/Common/Uploads/pdfs/RM%20write%20up%20on%20COVID-19.pdf
26. https://hal-india.co.in/Common/Uploads/pdfs/RM%20write%20up%20on%20COVID-19.pdf
27. https://pib.gov.in/PressReleasePage.aspx?PRID=1714683
28. https://ourworldindata.org/COVID-19-vaccinations
29. https://www.thehindu.com/coronavirus/
30. https://twitter.com/mygovindia/status/1467726844698845184?s=20
31. https://twitter.com/mygovindia/status/1467436053451526145?s=20
32. https://twitter.com/mygovindia/status/1451105386262450176/photo/1
33. https://www.who.int/india/news/feature-stories/detail/india-deploys-drones-to-deliver-COVID-19-vaccines#:~:text=India%20is%20using%20indigenously%20developed,and%20Andamans%20and%20Nicobar%20Islands.

34. https://pib.gov.in/PressReleasePage.aspx?PRID=1772536
35. https://twitter.com/mygovindia/status/1467436312084897792?s=20
36. https://www.thehindu.com/opinion/op-ed/a-paradigm-shift-in-vaccination/article34824529.ece
37. https://pib.gov.in/PressReleaseIframePage.aspx?PRID=1676998
38. https://pib.gov.in/PressReleasePage.aspx?PRID=1676814
39. https://www.thehindu.com/news/national/pm-modi-has-virtual-conference-with-COVID-19-vaccine-companies/article33211511.ece
40. https://pib.gov.in/PressReleaseIframePage.aspx?PRID=1676998
41. https://www.hindustantimes.com/india-news/monthly-output-of-25mn-doses-to-continue-till-aug-bharat-biotech-101624387840098.html
42. https://www.businesstoday.in/coronavirus/story/hester-biosciences-to-produce-bharat-biotech-covaxin-297241-2021-05-28
43. https://pib.gov.in/PressReleasePage.aspx?PRID=1715649
44. https://pib.gov.in/PressReleasePage.aspx?PRID=1723933
45. https://pib.gov.in/PressReleseDetail.aspx?PRID=1777643; https://mea.gov.in/vaccine-supply.htm
46. https://pib.gov.in/PressReleasePage.aspx?PRID=1778831
47. https://pib.gov.in/PressReleseDetail.aspx?PRID=1740268
48. http://164.100.24.220/loksabhaquestions/annex/174/AU1090.pdf
49. https://pib.gov.in/PressReleasePage.aspx?PRID=1583290
50. http://pmssy-mohfw.nic.in/
51. https://pib.gov.in/PressReleasePage.aspx?PRID=1780145
52. https://pib.gov.in/PressReleseDetail.aspx?PRID=1777643
53. https://pib.gov.in/PressReleasePage.aspx?PRID=1780152
54. https://pib.gov.in/PressReleaseIframePage.aspx?PRID=1607248

INDEX